Life Styles

LIFE STYLES
Diversity in American Society

SECOND EDITION

Edited by

Saul D. Feldman
Case Western Reserve University

Gerald W. Thielbar
University of Wisconsin

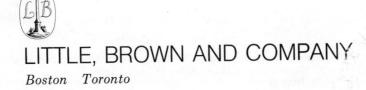

LITTLE, BROWN AND COMPANY
Boston   Toronto

FIRST PRINTING

Published simultaneously in Canada by
Little, Brown & Company (Canada) Limited

PRINTED IN THE UNITED STATES OF AMERICA

Cover photographs: Top left — Cary Wolinsky, Stock Boston; top center — Tim Carlson, Stock Boston; top right — Julie O'Neil, Stock Boston; bottom — Cary Wolinsky, Stock Boston

This book is dedicated

to the memory of

Gioachino Rossini (1792–1868)

Acknowledgments

We would like to acknowledge the contributions of those who assisted in the creation of this book. Ed Mason, Lloyd Rogler, and Abdul Singh suggested inclusion of some of the key material. Bob Davis and Hildegarde Dorrer provided us with helpful editorial comments. H. A. Bouraoui and Charles Choy Wong contributed original papers. Technical assistance was provided by Caryl Goodman. Mary Tondorf and Mary Woodcock were of invaluable assistance at Little, Brown. Kathleen Anderson and Kathryn Reichow cheerfully typed several drafts of our manuscript. Air traffic controllers at O'Hare let us get between Cleveland and Madison with no delays. Many users of the first edition gave us many helpful suggestions for revisions.

Saul D. Feldman
Gerald W. Thielbar

Contents

CULTURE AND SOCIETY: IS THERE AN AMERICAN LIFE STYLE?

This book — about beauty queens, rich people, homosexuals, tramps, Navaho Indians, people from New Jersey, and other assorted Americans — examines the great diversity of life styles within American society. The term "life style" was coined by the German sociologist Max Weber, who also contributed the word "charisma" to the sociological vocabulary.* Such terms, once they have been popularized, mean different things to different people. Thus we want to make clear our use of the term "life style."

1. Life style is a group phenomenon. *A person's life style is not a unique or individual pattern of behavior; it is influenced by participation in various social groups and by relationships with significant others. We can predict a person's life style with reasonable accuracy from certain social and demographic characteristics. For example, the life style of a teenager is different from that of a sexagenarian. The life*

---

* The term "life style" was also used independently by Alfred Adler. See Heinz Ansbacher and Rowena Ansbacher (eds.), *The Individual Psychology of Alfred Adler,* (New York: *Basic Books,* 1956), pp. 172–203. We thank Robert C. Davis for bringing this to our attention.

style of a hairdresser differs from that of a college professor. And the life style of a man who is concerned with his reputation in the community is different from that of a man who has rejected the values of society. Therefore, to identify a life style is to designate the existence of a group, and thus the study of life styles is of major interest to sociologists.

2. Life style pervades many aspects of life. *Knowing how an individual behaves in one area of life may allow us to predict how he or she will act in other areas. For example, people who prefer oil and vinegar on salads are more likely to attend a ballet than are those who prefer commercial French dressing. People whose self-rated political leanings are left or liberal will more likely attend an art film than those whose politics are conservative or middle-of-the-road. A journalist has noted, "When people tell me what they think about disarmament, I have a pretty good idea of what they are likely to think about school integration."* *

3. Life style implies a central life interest. *In American society, various things may be of central interest to a person: work, ethnic heritage, politics, lineage, children, avocational pursuits, and others. A distinct life style is evident when a single activity or interest pervades a person's other interests and unrelated activities — a drug addict is an extreme example. Avid baseball fans, television enthusiasts, and "professional" San Franciscans also provide examples of life styles based on a central life interest. Some people are interested in astrology; if this interest is central, it too may color their lives. They may wear signs of the zodiac, prefer to interact with and marry only those of certain birth signs, and make crucial decisions according to the position of the planets. Central life interests are not always a matter of choice. A black person may prefer to order his or her life around occupation rather than race, but may be defined by others according to race rather than occupation. Thus the situation demands that race become a central life interest for that individual.*†

4. Life styles differ according to sociologically relevant variables. *The first writings about life styles‡ took the view that different ways of life within a society varied by social class. Karl Marx§ felt that the sole determinant of a person's life style is his position in a system of pro-*

---

* Calvin Trillin, "G. T. Miller's Plan," *The New Yorker,* 46 (August 29, 1970), p. 54.

† See e.g., Everett C. Hughes, "Dilemmas and Contradictions of Status," *American Journal of Sociology,* 50, pp. 353–359.

‡ Max Weber, "Class, Status, and Party," in Hans H. Gerth and C. Wright Mills (eds., and trans.) *From Max Weber* (New York: Oxford University Press, 1946), pp. 180–195; Thorstein Veblen, *Theory of the Leisure Class* (New York: Macmillan, 1899).

§ Karl Marx, *Capital* (New York: Modern Library, 1906).

duction. *People who control the means of production also control the means of consumption. Thus, according to Marx, life style is an economic matter. Max Weber observed that all people at a given economic level need not share a common life style, but those with a similar degree of prestige generally do. "Status honor is normally expressed by the fact that above all else a specific style of life can be expected from all those who wish to belong to the circle."* In the United States, there is not a single circle, but many circles. Life styles in America vary according to age, sex, ethnicity, religion, region, and more.*

5. American life styles are a reflection of American culture and society. *Each part of this book shows how diverse this nation is, and the United States thus could be viewed as a conglomeration of more than 200,000,000 people who have little in common. Another view would be that this nation is polarized along ethnic, religious, age, sex, or economic lines; while a third view might regard all citizens of this nation simply as Americans, sharing a more or less similar life style.*

To the world outside the United States our diversity may be a parochial issue of interest only to Americans, who make up less than six percent of the world's population. Many American blacks, proud of their race and acutely conscious of life-style differences between blacks and whites, are surprised to discover when they visit Africa that they are not viewed as fellow blacks but simply as Americans. To a New Yorker, there may seem to be a crucial distinction between Brooklynites and Manhattanites, or to a Minnesotan, between Minneapolitans and St. Paulites. But a European sees little or no difference between a New Yorker and a Midwesterner — they are all Americans. From the perspective of the outsider, there is a recognizable American character type based on what is believed to be common life style.

The common experience of Americans includes the products and the mass media that they consume and the manner in which these are presented to them for consumption. With the rise of mass marketing (especially franchising), an American can have tacos in Duluth, chow mein in Dallas, and Coney Island hot dogs in San Diego. The franchised taco is the same in Albuquerque and Duluth; thus food becomes uniformly bland. Diversity in packaging creates the myth of great diversity in America, while the contents of these packages indicate its great uniformity.†

---

* Weber, *op. cit.*, p. 187.

† Adrian Delfino, writing for United Airlines' *Mainliner,* has commented on the Hawaiian luau encountered by tourists on the manicured lawns of some Hawaiian hotels: "While the color is all there and the aroma is all there, the native foods have been intentionally debased to spare the digestive tracts of the uninitiated." Adrian G. Delfino, "Culinary Traditions of Hawaii," *Mainliner,* 14 (September 1970), p. 26.

The theme in American mass merchandising is uniformity, quantity, and mediocrity. Some say that these traits typify the American character and American values. The mass market is not a recent development in the United States; neither is criticism of it. Speculation about the effects of mass marketing on American society has been a popular theme of journalists, social critics, and social scientists.*

Calvin Trillin, a freelance writer who writes regularly for The New Yorker *on the current American scene, describes buying and selling in a suburban county outside Philadelphia. In Lower Bucks County, there is a lot of what may best be described as "typically American."*

Trillin's description of commerce in suburban Philadelphia could as easily have been written about Los Angeles County in California or Cook County in Illinois. Three-scoop ice-cream cones, discount stores, and "the world's largest" car dealers are a familiar part of American life.

* See e.g., David Riesman and Howard Roseborough, "Careers and Consumer Behavior," in Lincoln H. Clark (ed.), *Consumer Behavior, Vol. II: The Life Cycle and Consumer Behavior* (New York: New York Univ. Press, 1955), pp. 1–8; Don Martindale, "Manipulation of Taste and Values," in *American Society* (Princeton, New Jersey: L. Van Nostrand, 1960), pp. 18–40.

Lower Bucks County, Pa. . . . Buying and Selling Along Route 1

Calvin Trillin

I WAS A PIG AT GREENWOOD DAIRIES

An ice-cream cone at the Greenwood Dairies has half a pound of ice cream on it — making it so topheavy that it is ordinarily presented to the customer

upside down, resting on a piece of waxed paper. That's the single-dip cone. The double-dip cone has an even pound, or about a quart of ice cream — the same amount that Greenwood serves in a locally famous sundae called a Pig's Dinner. A Pig's Dinner has four scoops of ice cream resting on a bed of sliced bananas, covered with a choice of topping, and served in an eight-inch plastic trough. The customer also gets a yellow button that says "I Was a Pig at Greenwood Dairies." The buttons are a particularly popular item.

In the thirties, when Paul Sauerbry, a former 4-H champion from Oelwein, Iowa, came to Lower Bucks County, the area between Philadelphia and Trenton, it was almost as rural as Iowa — despite the impression Sauerbry had received at a Washington 4-H convention that "lots more was going on in the East than in Iowa, and where things are going on there must be money." Sauerbry bought Greenwood Dairies, a small, two-route milk business, and moved it to Route 1, then the main route up the East Coast and the only direct road between Philadelphia and New York. There was plenty of milk available from farmers right across the highway — at least until the early fifties, when all of that farmland became Levittown, Pennsylvania, a community of seventeen thousand houses. Even before Levittown, Sauerbry had steadily expanded his operation. He now has a fleet of green-and-white trucks that deliver ten to twelve thousand quarts of milk a day. The store that he began in the early forties to sell his own ice cream now looks more like a restaurant than a store and does a few hundred thousand dollars' worth of business a year in bulk ice cream, ice-cream cones, Pig's Dinners, light lunches, a small line of groceries, souvenirs, and stuffed animals.

Sauerbry still thinks of himself as a dairyman. The store has a modest sign, decorated with a sundae not much larger than the ones served inside. The store accounts for less than a third of Greenwood's annual sales — although, as the *Milk Plant Monthly* has pointed out in an admiring article on Sauerbry, it brings in not only money but prospective customers for milk delivery. Sauerbry and his son, who also works in the business, are proud that their ice cream is made of freshly condensed milk rather than dried milk, that the mint chocolate chip has the same kind of authentic chocolate found in a chocolate bar, and that the vanilla is made with real vanilla beans. But they real-

ize that the size of the portions is what brings many people into the store.

Sauerbry is also aware that a lot of people can't finish the portions, causing a certain amount of waste. The trash bin in front of the dairy always contains a number of half-eaten half-pound ice-cream cones. Sauerbry has thought of cutting down portions rather than steadily raising prices; in fact, the Pig's Dinner used to have five scoops of ice cream rather than four.

But he doesn't think his customers will stand for further reductions. The most common complaint at Greenwood is not that the helpings are too big but that the customer did not receive his fair share. Sometimes people return a sundae complaining of niggardliness, and the Sauerbrys have to put the sundae on the scale to demonstrate that it does indeed weigh a pound. The Sauerbrys do not seem to be the kind of people who might spend a lot of time musing on why a dairy that makes its vanilla from real vanilla beans finds it necessary to sell it by serving more than most people can eat — and throwing in a pig button. "When we started dipping cones, in them days there were quite a few dairy stores," Sauerbry says. "We all gave big portions." If the younger Sauerbry is asked why Greenwood Dairies customers are so fond of large portions, he just shrugs and says, "Everybody wants quantity."

WORKING OUT A DEAL

The merchandising method of Reedman's, the world's largest car dealer, seems to be based on the theory that a lot of Americans have bought so many new cars that they consider themselves experts at the art. Respecting the fact that a man of experience will have gone beyond loyalty to any one make of car, Reedman salesmen are equally helpful about selling him a new Chevrolet or a new Plymouth or a new almost anything else; Reedman's has fourteen new-car franchises. Reedman salesmen will reassure a customer that the small Plymouth station wagon and the small Dodge station wagon, both of which Reedman's handles, are virtually the same car — the slight difference in headlights and the different names being merely a way to make one car do for two different dealers. Good hard shoptalk is expected among experts. Included in the Reedman display of the Plymouth Duster and the American Motors' Hornet is the competing car not handled by Reedman's, the Ford Maverick — its roof decorated with a sign drawing attention to the relative puniness of its wheelbase, its trunk open to reveal a sign that says "The Exposed Gas Tank Is in the Trunk Floor." Since the customer will be sophisticated enough to know precisely what he wants in a car — whether, for example, he can do without air-conditioning but must have vinyl bucket seats — Reedman's has an inventory of some five thousand cars, and a computer that will instantly find out if a particular model is available and will then type out a precise description of it before the customer's eyes. An enormous selection being a great advantage in dealing with expert car purchasers, some people in the trade say that Reedman's sells so many cars because it has so many to sell — a merchandising adaptation of Mies van der Rohe's "Less is More" dictum that comes out "More is More."

The Reedman newspaper advertisement invites customers to a hundred-and-fifty-acre, one-stop car center that has a ten-million-dollar selection of cars — and then, adding the note of exclusivity that is considered necessary in advertising even the world's largest, it says, "Private Sale Now Going On." The premises on which the private sale is held look like the average citizen's vision of the supply depot at Cam Ranh Bay. Behind a series of showrooms on Route 1, just down the road from the Greenwood Dairies, the five thousand cars are lined up on acres and acres of asphalt — the neat rows interrupted by occasional watchtowers and the entire area surrounded by a heavy, iron, electronically monitored fence. On a busy Saturday, attendants direct streams of traffic in and out of the customers' parking lot. Hostesses with the dress and manner of airline stewardesses circulate in the showrooms offering to call a salesman for anybody who feels the need of one. Muzak, which reaches the most remote line of hardtops, is interrupted every two or three bars by calls for salesmen.

The opportunity to perfect a veteran car buyer's style is so great at Reedman's — the opportunity to shrug off a computer's offer of a Dodge Coronet with fourteen extras, to exchange jargon about engines and wheelbases, to take a new model for a few spins around the Reedman test track and make some observations to the family about how she handles on the curves — that some people seem to make Saturday at Reedman's a kind of outing. A lot of them, of course, find themselves buying a car, with vinyl bucket seats *and* air-conditioning. The route back to the customers' parking lot leads through a small building where the customer is greeted by a man even more helpful than the hostesses. "How'd you make out, sir?" the man asks. "What kind of car were you looking at? What was your trade-in? Who was your salesman? Of course you want to think about it, but why wait?" There is no reason for an experienced car buyer to concern himself with the fact that his most recent experience was so recent that he has yet to pay for the car he has; the first sign on the Reedman lot begins, "If you still have payments on your present car, truck, etc., we will pay off the balance and work out a deal."

Although selling at Reedman's is based on working out a deal rather than on glamour or showmanship, a car dealer cannot afford to create an atmosphere of pure, unglamorous functionalism. If anyone is going to be totally practical, why should he spend his money on an overlarge, gas-eating, nonfunctional, instantly depreciating new car? Although the Chevrolet section of the Reedman showrooms is crowded with as many models as can be crammed in, the décor includes huge crystal chandeliers and wallpaper of raised-velvet fleur-de-lis patterns on ersatz gold leaf. On one wall of the showroom, a picture display of Reedman service facilities describes one of the three waiting rooms available for service customers as having "fifteen stereophonic speakers mounted in the acoustical ceiling," as well as "embossed vinyl covered walls, plus carpeting, velvet draperies, a crystal chandelier and living-room type furniture." Any car buyer of experience recognizes that as a description of something that, with the addition of some heavy-duty whitewall tires, could provide great transportation until next year's models come out.

DON'T SIT DOWN

Only a few small, arrow-shaped signs lead customers a mile or so off Route 1, near Reedman's, to the farm outlet of Styer's Orchards. Styer's advertises in a local shopping paper, but Walter Styer believes that, basically, satisfied customers bring business and dissatisfied customers keep it away. "It's important never to have anybody griping on you," he says. Styer's will usually replace a jug of spoiled apple cider even if the customer himself let it spoil by leaving it unrefrigerated — as if it contained preservatives, like the processed cider that Styer cannot mention without a slight grimace. Walter Styer is a small, almost bald man in his seventies. His family came to Lower Bucks County in 1910 to start a tree-nursery business, which gradually changed into a fruit business. In the forties, people in the area used to come down the narrow lane to the Styers' farmhouse to buy apples, and eventually the Styers started using the barn as a store and the neighbors started coming in to help with the selling. After the building of Levittown and the opening of a United States Steel plant in Fairless Hills, the Styers finally opened a store out on the road. Styer says the business has now grown to the point of having an overhead of three hundred and fifty thousand dollars a year.

Styer believes in salesmanship. "I used to sell at the Farmer's Market in Trenton, and we almost took over that market," he has said. "It got so the other farmers didn't like us. For one thing, I never sat down. I was always ready to help the customer. Some of the farmers would turn over a box and sit down and just stare at people, but I would always get people talking — ask them what kind of apples they liked, or something like that. Once, I was selling strawberries at fifteen cents a box, and next to me a fellow was selling the identical strawberries at two boxes for a quarter. Pretty soon, I sold all my strawberries, and he hadn't sold any. And he asked me why. I looked at his strawberries and I said, 'First of all, look how you've got them arranged. The stems are sticking up. People don't eat stems. Rearrange them with the stems down. Then you ought to get paid for your time for doing that, so charge fifteen cents a box like I did.' Then I stayed to watch, and I told him, 'Don't sit down.' Pretty soon, he sold all his strawberries."

The Styers are not in the position of having to think up sales pitches to justify changes made in this year's model by somebody they don't even know. Almost everything sold at the farm outlet is from their own farm. A lot of the salesmanship is merely a matter of presenting well what they are confident is good merchandise. The store is immaculate. All of the apples are washed and displayed in neat rows of clean half-bushel baskets. There is always a bin of free apples near the door. The apple pies and pumpkin pies are baked in stainless-steel ovens before the customers' eyes. The walls are decorated with Indian corn. There are a few standard signs for Pennsylvania apples ("Nature's Toothbrush"), but most of the signs are done in crayon — giving them a nice, neat homemade look, as if

they had been commissioned to the best drawer in the sixth grade.

Styer is proud of the store, although he laments the failure of most of the clerks to lead customers into conversation. "You *got* to be a salesman," he says. When Styer greeted an out-of-town visitor at the farmhouse recently, he had just returned from a business meeting (the family has other interests in Lower Bucks County, including some of the real estate on Route 1), and he looked like a banker who had been home only long enough to take his jacket off. Before taking his visitor to see the store, he excused himself for a few minutes and returned wearing an old pair of corduroy pants and a dark cardigan sweater very much like one Paul Sauerbry wears around the dairy. "That's a farm outlet, and people don't want to see a business executive out there," he said. "You got to look the part."

Mostly Sell

The Two Guys Discount Department Store in the Levittown Country Club Shopping Center, across Route 1 from Reedman's, is small by the standards of Two Guys stores but large by the standards of, say, football fields. It is a hundred and five thousand square feet, and, like all Two Guys stores, it is what people in the Two Guys chain call "mostly sell" — that is, most of its space is space in which customers actually buy merchandise. In a Two Guys store, the stockrooms and the sales space are virtually identical; one step in the supply process is saved by having customers help themselves from merchandise that is brought in by Two

Guys trucks from a central warehouse and stored right on the selling floor. The Two Guys store in Levittown has a kind of warehouse look — one huge room containing massive stacks of every type of merchandise, with the merchandise on the lower part of some stacks still in packing cartons. In the toy department, the customer sees not just one or two Talk 'n' Do Choo-Choos but twenty Talk 'n' Do Choo-Choos. In the hardware department, a dozen or so examples of each type of hammer extend from racks on the wall. The art department has three-dimensional "Last Supper's" fifteen deep. In Boutique Shoes, one shelf includes thirty-five identical pairs of black pumps.

Displaying merchandise in mass contributes to the efficiency of the Two Guys central-warehouse operation, and it also makes people buy more. Since the advent of the supermarket, retailers have known that seeing, say, twenty cartons of avocado-colored Tahiti tumblers in a mass creates an impulse to buy some avocado-colored Tahiti tumblers. A lot of shoppers who might pass up a display demonstrating the virtues of a hair dryer find a six-foot stack of hair dryers irresistible. Two Guys had even discovered that if all the red coats are hung together rather than scattered among the other coats on the rack, they sell faster. More is More.

COME FLY WITH US

Jim Flannery's Constellation Lounge is a Constellation. It originally belonged to Cubana Airlines. Flannery bought it two years ago from an air-line based in Delaware and had it placed over his restaurant, on Route 1, not far down the road from Two Guys. Motorists approaching from the south come around a curve just before Flannery's and find the Constellation suddenly in front of them — coming in low over the Esso station, as if some desperate T.W.A. pilot who had been on a holding pattern over La Guardia since before the jets came in finally decided to land on Route 1.

Except for having a Constellation on top of it, Jim Flannery's looks like a lot of suburban restaurants — a windowless building with the owner's name written on the side in plastic script. It has leatherette booths as well as tables, a menu specializing in steaks and seafood, a bar, and a piano player who was once with Arthur Godfrey. The walls are lined with the paintings of local artists — many of the local artists in this case being Levittown housewives who specialize in still-lifes and matadors and sad-faced clowns. The Constellation provides a second bar, entered from the main restaurant by a stairway decorated with a mural called "A History of Flight."

Flannery says that a lot of men whose wives have been reluctant to take their first flight bring them to the Constellation Lounge as a kind of transition step. The waitresses have found that the reaction of most people to being in a lounge that is also an airplane is to make a joke about hijacking. As part of his effort to give a feeling of actual flight, Flannery covered the windows with color transparencies of aerial views of places like Miami and New York, and some customers complain about not being able to see the actual view out the window — although the actual view happens to be a section of Route 1 lined with four or five filling stations, a furniture store, a Kiddie City discount toy store, a used-car lot, and an enterprise called the Skyline Diner and Carwash. Flannery, who considers the Constellation a "functional sign," serves drinks in the kind of throwaway glasses used in airplanes and uses "Come Fly with Us" as his motto for billboards and radio ads and napkins. He gives away souvenir pins and tie clasps that are in the shape of Constellations but do not mention the name of the restaurant. "It's subtle," he says. "Very subtle."

On a week night recently, the downstairs bar was crowded — a jolly group was singing "Happy Birthday" to somebody named Arthur — but there were few diners, and the Constellation Lounge looked like a ghost ship. Flannery said business had been slow all week. He thought it might have had something to do with the President's asking people not to spend so much. "Have you seen those TV ads they're running where the guy keeps buying things and pretty soon he turns into a pig?" he asked a guest. Flannery shook his head in wonderment over the ways of government, and said, "A few years ago they were encouraging people to buy."

We think of mass merchandising as limited to consumer commodities such as cars, televisions, and canned soup; yet, mass marketing pervades all aspects of the American ethos, Presidential candidates,* religion, sex, and colleges and universities† are often sold in a manner which many think should be reserved only for standard consumer products.

Classical music, literature, and art are relatively unfamiliar to many Americans. These may become marketable commodities — often in a watered-down fashion. Classical music may thus be sold as "Fifty Great Moments in Music," literature as condensed books, and original art as anything hand painted on canvas. What is marketed in these cases may be the illusion that a purchaser is a participant in high culture. As Thomas Albright points out in his discussion of the art world, there is often little correspondence between the marketed illusion and fine art.

* See Joe McGinnis, *The Selling of the President 1968.* (New York: Trident, 1968).

† In an era of dwindling enrollments, many colleges and universities are hiring commercial firms to sell their schools to potential students through brochures and advertisements on television and radio and in magazine and newspapers. See, Larry Van Dyne, "Quests for Students Leads Many Colleges to Adopt Sales Techniques Once Shunned on Campuses," *The Chronicle of Higher Education* (May 13, 1974), pp. 1, 7–9.

On the other hand, Americans are also buying records of complete operas, joining book clubs devoted to specialized topics such as history or urban problems, and are becoming members of local art museums and galleries. These items too are often mass merchandised. In a society based on free enterprise everything may be marketed. This may be one of the important aspects of American life styles. Americans may be aware of the pervasiveness of mass marketing, but do they know what they are buying?

Galleries of Commodities— and Customers

Thomas Albright

As readers sometimes point out, there is an entire circuit of local art galleries that is omitted from our regular itinerary of viewing and reviewing.

These galleries are overlooked because they are the art world's counterpart of TV situation comedies, mood music LPs, or the more strictly commercial segment of the local night spot circuit. There is a range among them, comparable to the range between, say, the Venetian Room and Tenderloin topless. But the principle is the same: Pack the rubes in and give them what they're supposed to want, meaning anything they'll buy.

From the *San Francisco Chronicle* (December 31, 1972). © Chronicle Publishing Co., 1972.

There's no real sense in reviewing spots like these; their "exhibitions" are either unchanging or interchangeable; ditto, the work of the individual exhibitors. To be fair, these places almost never ask to be reviewed; although they call themselves galleries, and peddle objects that often bear coincidental resemblance to paintings or sculpture, they are really dealing in commodities rather than art; they need money, advertising and customers rather than prestige, opinions or critics.

Nonetheless, in a fit of dauntless perversity, I made it around to several of these downtown "art" shops the other day. Bad, or dubious, taste is certainly the only real "universal" or "eternal" verity to be found in art; it is virtually the same everywhere, and it hardly ever changes. So, in the interest of keeping readers informed of such transcendent matters, herewith, gratis and gratuitously, is the Chronicle's first, and probably last, report from schlockland.

The king of topless-bottomless art in San Francisco is, of course, Ed Cory, who runs two shops, one on Geary street for the downtown hotel tourists, the other for the Fisherman's Wharf trade. Cory used to be a food broker. His Geary street premise looks more like a posh automobile dealership, with its army of slick sales people and warrens of private sales rooms. In the merchandising, however, the supermarket principle strictly prevails.

SOMETHING FOR EVERYBODY

Like a supermarket, the display space is crammed with a something for everybody (well not quite everybody) grab-bag of cliche ideas packaged in easily marketable styles — or, to resume the night spot analogy, with a chorus line of interchangeably appealing hoofers differing only in minor details of physiognomy and cosmetics. Artist wanted, no experience necessary. The common denominator at Cory's, as in these other art stores, is that the "art" has all clearly been generated by sales, maybe even by market research, rather than the other way around.

Of course, even a topless club has waitresses and stars, and Cory's featured performers include a bevy of high-priced names with over-inflated reputations (as visual artists, at least), like Dali, Bufano, John Lennon and Henry Miller. His Carol Doda, however, is a hack named Pat Cucaro whom Cory propelled to stardom four years ago on sheer promotion alone, most of it deriving from a bounced check for $50,000 written by a certified mental patient for one of Cucaro's paintings; the "price" "established" a West Coast "record." The list of public collections housing Cucaro's works now includes many of the 10th rate museums in the country. Unlike most such painters, Cucaro has not one, but

half a dozen formulas, although his opus may conveniently be divided into paintings that apparently took two hours to dash off, and those which may have taken all of three.

The premises, by the way, are protected by See-All Theft Controls.

The Cory formula extends to a number of other downtown sales rooms, such as the Galerie de Tours, where the atmosphere is more low key and the sprinkling of "names" is more likely to include a few School of Paris ballerinas like Dufy, and the Gilbert, where the loss-leaders include prints and multiples by such big name contemporaries as Vasarely and Jim Dine.

There is Arts International, where the merchandise is limited to schlock by unknown artists only — gallery of "discoveries," it's called; it is a franchise operation, Kentucky Fried painting. Likewise, the Sutter Artists Guild, which specializes in murky seascapes, except here many of the unknown artists have already been discovered by anonymous "museum critics" whose accolades hang beside the paintings. A. Trebor, on the other hand, also has a painter of star billing. I won't mention his name, but he does Emmet Kelly-style clowns. He makes Norman Rockwell seem as profound as Rembrandt.

At the Venetian Room end of the scale, there is the Conacher Gallery on Maiden Lane. The specialty here is flawless craftsmanship, applied with taste and even style to themes of picturesque banality: Landscape, seascape, townscape, trompe l'oeil still lifes of sweating fruit. The artists here are the Tony Bennetts of artkitsch.

Some of Conacher's artists are

"name" personages booked out of big Hollywood studios, and a recent show featured Peter Ellenshaw, who won an Oscar for his work on Mary Poppins. His paintings are mostly landscapes of Ireland, greener than green, bluer than blue, with little roads and paths to guide you through the fields, the paint roughed up here and there to suggest rugged stone walls or sun-flecked grass. Not roughed up much, mind you, but just enough to demonstrate that these are really "original" oils, not Redemption Center reproductions, which they resemble in every other respect.

Whether this touch is enough to justify the difference between a few books of trading stamps and $4,800 — the average price of Ellenshaw's paintings, although you can pay as little as $2,450 or as much as $8,500 — is for the customer to decide. Judging by the number of red stars up the day I was there, enough people feel it does.

A different shtick is exemplified by a pair of downtown shops that specialize in a brand of conversation-piece "surrealism": "I realize it's not very *pretty*, but it is *original*, and *look* how well it's done!"

Fred Fredden Goldberg, who shows in his own gallery on Tillman Place, paints cracked eggs, human puppets and similarly daring surrealist themes. He does so with a sober, dullish realism that could have been transplanted directly from the German academies of 75 years ago.

Cosmic Ideas

The Frank Gallery specializes in the work of a painter named Lee Mulleian, who does crucifixions, Aladdin's lamps and Doors Opening to Eternity in a slickly varnished, fluorescent, meller-dramatic style that suggests an aborted attempt to cross-breed El Greco with Salvador Dali. Cosmic ideas like these inevitably require cosmic scale, so Mulleian's paintings are huge, sometimes reaching 10 or 15 feet high or awfulness to the 15th power.

Of course, such things were daring and audacious once, when they were originated half a century ago; presumably, some people still find them so, for they have no other apparent virtues. The analogy here is to those "jazz" clubs which attract middle-class white Americans from the suburbs for the reckless and vaguely sinister adventure of hearing Dixieland performed by middle-class white musicians — blacks welcome, of course, but you just never see many around.

Last, but not least, is the posh new gallery on Sutter street in which Nong, the Korean painter, displays his and other work. Nong's paintings usually center on simple, stylized images — a cat, an Oriental vase — in closely harmonized colors and elegantly worked, abstract-expressionist derived textures and surfaces. They are triumphs of taste, refinement, craft and decoration, much like the piano stylings that ripple on forever in the background at top-of-the-roof cocktail lounges. Once in a while, when there are no requests from the crowd, there are even flashes of real, hard-driving artistry in Nong's paintings.

A Tough Job

Paintings like these shade almost imperceptibly into the kind of art displayed in galleries that we do view and review on our regular rounds.

Can one really define a difference between such facsimiles of art and the real thing? Although popular, schlock is too flaccid and artsy to be pop; bad as it is, it is usually not bad enough to be good, or camp. It is not identical with earnest amateurism or Sunday painting, although such work usually follows a schlock esthetic. Neither is it synonymous with conservative or traditional styles, and in fact one of a critic's toughest jobs is trying to isolate and identify the coat-tail schlock that has attached itself to various modern, contemporary and avant-garde movements.

For all the aesthetic theorizing beginning with Plato and Aristotle, art remains a mysterious thing, succinctly defined in the laconic words of two 20th century American philosophers, Duke Ellington and Fats Waller: "It don't mean a thing if it ain't got that swing" and "If you gotta ask what it is you'll never know." In general, though, art is not merely "original" but is truly unique, a creation that brings into being a form or expression that hasn't existed before, or that interprets. familiar things and ideas in new, or distinctly personal, ways.

Great works of art can totally alter one's perception of the world — try looking at people on the street after seeing a Rembrandt portrait or a Robert Frank photograph, or at a debris-strewn vacant lot after seeing a William Wiley watercolor. But even the most humble of art works is an honest attempt at communicating one person's view. Like any form of real human communication, it requires that you go half way — or more — to meet

it. So art is often challenging to the viewer, but the artist is also constantly challenging himself.

In schlock, however, the challenge has all been eliminated, the "communication" is strictly one-sided, and the messages are always the same. Like a can-opener "chef," the "artist" dips into his supply of pre-cooked, ready-to-serve ideas and styles, mixes them up a little and, presto, an "original," hot off the assembly line.

Far from altering anyone's perception of anything, the idea is to turn out soporifics that reaffirm all the old cliches and pander to all the stereotyped sentiments. Schlock rarely raises questions, and if it does, it answers every one — twice. All the seeing and thinking and responding are already done for you, all part of the package, and the only trace of effort to be found is in the labor that went into making the wrapper.

At best, the result is innocuous, well-crafted wall decoration. At worst, it is a counterfeit of art and life as well. Prosecutors in pornography trials frequently try to build their cases by questioning the quality of the artistry involved: I've never heard any objection raised to this line of arguing, but if bad art is a criminal offense, look forward to the biggest mass arrests in history.

It's a free enterprise society, though, so there's a place for everything. There's nothing really wrong with wall decoration or cocktail music, if you're willing to pay the cover. And if you operate a motel, it isn't bad for business to appoint every room with cheap paintings, or to have a few topless-bottomless dancers around.

The portraits presented by Trillin and Albright may be an accurate view of the American as consumer; but American life styles are more than just consumption patterns. There is something uniquely American not only in our economic system but in our family patterns, our religious networks, in our educational and in our political systems. Every society has an economic system and a family, religious, educational, and political structure. These five spheres of life are important for the functioning of any society, and the networks, beliefs, and practices around these five spheres are known as institutions. No matter how much a person focuses his or her life style in one of these institutions, he or she is affected by all of them.

American society, like all societies, has a delimited territory, a sense of common identity among its people, continuity beyond one generation, autonomy (at least to some extent, although all societies are interdependent), and, most important, a common culture. Culture, which may be defined as the sum total of a society's ideas, beliefs, values, and material possessions, is what creates a unique national life style. No other society exhibits the same configuration of family patterns, economic practices, etc. as is found in the United States. Simply stated, America's life styles are unique because no other nation has its patterns of society and culture. The forces that bring about any nation's unique life styles may be varied. For example, America's geography, migration patterns and its history have profoundly affected current life styles.

The United States prides itself on its diversity of ethnicity, race, religion, and cultural backgrounds. This great diversity forces a high degree of generality when we attempt to articulate what it is that we all share as members of a society with a common culture. Some nations are united by a national religion; for example, Brazil's dominant religion is Roman Catholicism, England's state church is Anglican, and Israel's official religion is Judaism. Religion may be a uniting force helping to foster a common identity among a nation's people. The United States, even more than other nations, may need such a unifying belief system to overcome problems of diversity.

Out of American religious diversity has come an American "civil religion" based on the assumption that all Americans should believe in God, a higher law, and the sacredness of the nation. Presidents and presidential candidates must appear publicly as devout followers of this national religion. Richard Nixon expressed the enduring creed of civil religion in his second inaugural address, when he said, "We shall answer to God, to history, and to our conscience for the way in which we use these years."

Civil Religion in America

Robert N. Bellah

While some have argued that Christianity is the national faith, and others that church and synagogue celebrate only the generalized religion of "the American Way of Life," few have realized that there actually exists alongside of and rather clearly differentiated from the churches an elaborate and well-institutionalized civil religion in America. This article argues not only that there is such a thing, but also that this religion — or perhaps better, this religious dimension — has its own seriousness and integrity and requires the same care in understanding that any other religion does.[1]

Reprinted by permission of *Daedalus;* Journal of the American Academy of Arts and Sciences, Boston, Massachusetts (Winter 1967); *Religion in America.*

[1] Why something so obvious should have escaped serious analytical attention is in itself an interesting problem. Part of the reason is probably the controversial nature of the subject. From the earliest years of the nineteenth century, conservative religious and political groups have argued that Christianity is, in fact, the national religion. Some of them have from time to time and as recently as the 1950's proposed constitutional amendments that would explicitly recognize the sovereignty of Christ. In defending the doctrine of separation of church and state, opponents of such groups have denied that the national polity has, intrinsically,

THE KENNEDY INAUGURAL

Kennedy's inaugural address of 20 January 1961 serves as an example and a clue with which to introduce this complex subject. That address began:

> *We observe today not a victory of party but a celebration of freedom — symbolizing an end as well as a beginning — signifying renewal as well as change. For I have sworn before you and Almighty God the same solemn oath our forebears prescribed nearly a century and three quarters ago.*

> *The world is very different now. For man holds in his mortal hands the power to abolish all forms of human poverty and to abolish all forms of human life. And yet the same revolutionary beliefs for which our forebears fought are still at issue around the globe — the belief that the rights of man come not from the generosity of the state but from the hand of God.*

And it concluded:

> *Finally, whether you are citizens of America or of the world, ask of us the*

anything to do with religion at all. The moderates on this issue have insisted that the American state has taken a permissive and indeed supportive attitude toward religious groups (tax exemption, et cetera), thus favoring religion but still missing the positive institutionalization with which I am concerned. But part of the reason this issue has been left in obscurity is certainly due to the peculiarly Western concept of "religion" as denoting a single type of collectivity of which an individual can be a member of one and only one at a time. The Durkheimian notion that every group has a religious dimension, which would be seen as obvious in southern or eastern Asia, is foreign to us. This obscures the recognition of such dimensions in our society.

same high standards of strength and sacrifice that we shall ask of you. With a good conscience our only sure reward, with history the final judge of our deeds, let us go forth to lead the land we love, asking His blessing and His help, but knowing that here on earth God's work must truly be our own.

These are the three places in this brief address in which Kennedy mentioned the name of God. If we could understand why he mentioned God, the way in which he did it, and what he meant to say in those three references, we would understand much about American civil religion. But this is not a simple or obvious task, and American students of religion would probably differ widely in their interpretation of these passages.

Let us consider first the placing of the three references. They occur in the two opening paragraphs and in the closing paragraph, thus providing a sort of frame for the more concrete remarks that form the middle part of the speech. Looking beyond this particular speech, we would find that similar references to God are almost invariably to be found in the pronouncements of American presidents on solemn occasions, though usually not in the working messages that the president sends to Congress on various concrete issues. How, then, are we to interpret this placing of references to God?

It might be argued that the passages quoted reveal the essentially irrelevant role of religion in the very secular society that is America. The placing of the references in this speech as well as in public life generally indicates that religion has "only a ceremonial sig-

nificance"; it gets only a sentimental nod which serves largely to placate the more unenlightened members of the community, before a discussion of the really serious business with which religion has nothing whatever to do. A cynical observer might even say that an American president has to mention God or risk losing votes. A semblance of piety is merely one of the unwritten qualifications for the office, a bit more traditional than but not essentially different from the present-day requirement of a pleasing television personality.

But we know enough about the function of ceremonial and ritual in various societies to make us suspicious of dismissing something as unimportant because it is "only a ritual." What people say on solemn occasions need not be taken at face value, but it is often indicative of deep-seated values and commitments that are not made explicit in the course of everyday life. Following this line of argument, it is worth considering whether the very special placing of the references to God in Kennedy's address may not reveal something rather important and serious about religion in American life.

It might be countered that the very way in which Kennedy made his references reveals the essentially vestigial place of religion today. He did not refer to any religion in particular. He did not refer to Jesus Christ, or to Moses, or to the Christian church; certainly he did not refer to the Catholic Church. In fact, his only reference was to the concept of God, a word which almost all Americans can accept but which means so many different things to so many different people that it is almost an empty sign. Is this not just another indication that in America religion is considered vaguely to be a good thing, but that people care so little about it that it has lost any content whatever? Isn't Eisenhower reported to have said, "Our government makes no sense unless it is founded in a deeply felt religious faith — and I don't care what it is," [2] and isn't that a complete negation of any real religion?

These questions are worth pursuing because they raise the issue of how civil religion relates to the political society, on the one hand, and to private religious organization, on the other. President Kennedy was a Christian, more specifically a Catholic Christian. Thus, his general references to God do not mean that he lacked a specific religious commitment. But why, then, did he not include some remark to the effect that Christ is the Lord of the world or some indication of respect for the Catholic Church? He did not because these are matters of his own private religious belief and of his relation to his own particular church; they are not matters relevant in any direct way to the conduct of his public office. Others with different religious views and commitments to different churches or denominations are equally qualified participants in the political process. The principle of separation of church and state guarantees the freedom of religious belief and association, but at the same time clearly segregates the religious sphere, which

is considered to be essentially private, from the political one.

Considering the separation of church and state, how is a president justified in using the word *God* at all? The answer is that the separation of church and state has not denied the political realm a religious dimension. Although matters of personal religious belief, worship, and association are considered to be strictly private affairs, there are, at the same time, certain common elements of religious orientation that the great majority of Americans share. These have played a crucial role in the development of American institutions and still provide a religious dimension for the whole fabric of American life, including the political sphere. This public religious dimension is expressed in a set of beliefs, symbols, and rituals that I am calling the American civil religion. The inauguration of a president is an important ceremonial event in this religion. It reaffirms, among other things, the religious legitimation of the highest political authority.

Let us look more closely at what Kennedy actually said. First he said, "I have sworn before you and Almighty God the same solemn oath our forebears prescribed nearly a century and three quarters ago." The oath is the oath of office, including the acceptance of the obligation to uphold the Constitution. He swears it before the people (you) and God. Beyond the Constitution, then, the president's obligation extends not only to the people but to God. In American political theory, sovereignty rests, of course, with the people, but implicitly, and often explicitly, the ultimate sovereignty has been attributed to God. This is the

[2] Quoted in Will Herberg, *Protestant-Catholic-Jew* (New York, 1955), p. 97.

meaning of the motto, "In God we trust," as well as the inclusion of the phrase "under God" in the pledge to the flag. What difference does it make that sovereignty belongs to God? Though the will of the people as expressed in majority vote is carefully institutionalized as the operative source of political authority, it is deprived of an ultimate significance. The will of the people is not itself the criterion of right and wrong. There is a higher criterion in terms of which this will can be judged; it is possible that the people may be wrong. The president's obligation extends to the higher criterion.

When Kennedy says that "the rights of man come not from the generosity of the state but from the hand of God," he is stressing this point again. It does not matter whether the state is the expression of the will of an autocratic monarch or of the "people"; the rights of man are more basic than any political structure and provide a point of revolutionary leverage from which any state structure may be radically altered. That is the basis for his reassertion of the revolutionary significance of America.

But the religious dimension in political life as recognized by Kennedy not only provides a grounding for the rights of man which makes any form of political absolutism illegitimate, it also provides a transcendent goal for the political process. This is implied in his final words that "here on earth God's work must truly be our own." What he means here is, I think, more clearly spelled out in a previous paragraph, the wording of which, incidentally, has a distinctly Biblical ring:

Now the trumpet summons us again — not as a call to bear arms, though arms we need — not as a call to battle, though embattled we are — but a call to bear the burden of a long twilight struggle, year in and year out, "rejoicing in hope, patient in tribulation" — a struggle against the common enemies of man: tyranny, poverty, disease and war itself.

The whole address can be understood as only the most recent statement of a theme that lies very deep in the American tradition, namely the obligation, both collective and individual, to carry out God's will on earth. This was the motivating spirit of those who founded America, and it has been present in every generation since. Just below the surface throughout Kennedy's inaugural address, it becomes explicit in the closing statement that God's work must be our own. That this very activist and non-contemplative conception of the fundamental religious obligation, which has been historically associated with the Protestant position, should be enunciated so clearly in the first major statement of the first Catholic president seems to underline how deeply established it is in the American outlook. Let us now consider the form and history of the civil religious tradition in which Kennedy was speaking.

The Idea of a Civil Religion

The phrase *civil religion* is, of course, Rousseau's. In Chapter 8, Book 4, of *The Social Contract*, he outlines the simple dogmas of the civil religion: the existence of God, the life to come, the reward of virtue and the punishment of vice, and the exclusion of religious intolerance. All other religious opinions are outside the cognizance of the state and may be freely held by citizens. While the phrase *civil religion* was not used, to the best of my knowledge, by the founding fathers, and I am certainly not arguing for the particular influence of Rousseau, it is clear that similar ideas, as part of the cultural climate of the late-eighteenth century, were to be found among the Americans. For example, Franklin writes in his autobiography,

> *I never was without some religious principles. I never doubted, for instance, the existence of the Deity; that he made the world and govern'd it by his Providence; that the most acceptable service of God was the doing of good to men; that our souls are immortal; and that all crime will be punished, and virtue rewarded either here or hereafter. These I esteemed the essentials of every religion; and, being to be found in all the religions we had in our country, I respected them all, tho' with different degrees of respect, as I found them more or less mix'd with other articles, which, without any tendency to inspire, promote or confirm morality, serv'd principally to divide us, and make us unfriendly to one another.*

It is easy to dispose of this sort of position as essentially utilitarian in relation to religion. In Washington's Farewell Address (though the words may be Hamilton's) the utilitarian aspect is quite explicit:

> *Of all the dispositions and habits which lead to political prosperity, Religion and Morality are indispensable supports. In vain would that man*

> *claim the tribute of Patriotism, who should labour to subvert these great Pillars of human happiness, these firmest props of the duties of men and citizens. The mere politician, equally with the pious man ought to respect and cherish them. A volume could not trace all their connections with private and public felicity. Let it simply be asked where is the security for property, for reputation, for life, if the sense of religious obligation desert the oaths, which are the instruments of investigation in Courts of Justice? And let us with caution indulge the supposition, that morality can be maintained without religion. Whatever may be conceded to the influence of refined education on minds of peculiar structure, reason and experience both forbid us to expect that National morality can prevail in exclusion of religious principle.*

But there is every reason to believe that religion, particularly the idea of God, played a constitutive role in the thought of the early American statesmen.

Kennedy's inaugural pointed to the religious aspect of the Declaration of Independence, and it might be well to look at that document a bit more closely. There are four references to God. The first speaks of the "Laws of Nature and of Nature's God" which entitle any people to be independent. The second is the famous statement that all men "are endowed by their Creator with certain inalienable Rights." Here Jefferson is locating the fundamental legitimacy of the new nation in a conception of "higher law" that is itself based on both classical natural law and Biblical religion. The third is an appeal to "the Supreme

Judge of the world for the rectitude of our intentions," and the last indicates "a firm reliance on the protection of divine Providence." In these last two references, a Biblical God of history who stands in judgment over the world is indicated.

The intimate relation of these religious notions with the self-conception of the new republic is indicated by the frequency of their appearance in early official documents. For example, we find in Washington's first inaugural address of 30 April 1789:

> *It would be peculiarly improper to omit in this first official act my fervent supplications to that Almighty Being who rules over the universe, who presides in the councils of nations, and whose providential aids can supply every defect, that His benediction may consecrate to the liberties and happiness of the people of the United States a Government instituted by themselves for these essential purposes, and may enable every instrument employed in its administration to execute with success the functions allotted to his charge.*
>
> *No people can be bound to acknowledge and adore the Invisible Hand which conducts the affairs of man more than those of the United States. Every step by which we have advanced to the character of an independent nation seems to have been distinguished by some token of providential agency....*
>
> *The propitious smiles of Heaven can never be expected on a nation that disregards the eternal rules of order and right which Heaven itself has ordained.... The preservation of the sacred fire of liberty and the destiny of the republican model of government are justly considered, perhaps, as*

deeply, as finally, staked on the experiment intrusted to the hands of the American people.

Nor did these religious sentiments remain merely the personal expression of the president. At the request of both Houses of Congress, Washington proclaimed on October 3 of that same first year as president that November 26 should be "a day of public thanksgiving and prayer," the first Thanksgiving Day under the Constitution.

The words and acts of the founding fathers, especially the first few presidents, shaped the form and tone of the civil religion as it has been maintained ever since. Though much is selectively derived from Christianity, this religion is clearly not itself Christianity. For one thing, neither Washington nor Adams nor Jefferson mentions Christ in his inaugural address; nor do any of the subsequent presidents, although not one of them fails to mention God.[3] The

---

[3] God is mentioned or referred to in all inaugural addresses but Washington's second, which is a very brief (two paragraphs) and perfunctory acknowledgement. It is not without interest that the actual word *God* does not appear until Monroe's second inaugural, 5 March 1821. In his first inaugural, Washington refers to God as "that Almighty Being who rules the universe," "Great Author of every public and private good," "Invisible Hand," and "benign Parent of the Human Race." John Adams refers to God as "Providence," "Being who is supreme over all," "Patron of Order," "Fountain of Justice," and "Protector in all ages of the world of virtuous liberty." Jefferson speaks of "that Infinite Power which rules the destinies of the universe," and "that Being in whose hands we are." Madison speaks of "that Almighty Being whose power regulates the destiny of nations," and "Heaven." Monroe uses "Providence" and

God of the civil religion is not only rather "unitarian," he is also on the austere side, much more related to order, law, and right than to salvation and love. Even though he is somewhat deist in cast, he is by no means simply a watchmaker God. He is actively interested and involved in history, with a special concern for America. Here the analogy has much less to do with natural law than with ancient Israel; the equation of America with Israel in the idea of the "American Israel" is not infrequent.[4] What was implicit in the words of Washington already quoted becomes explicit in Jefferson's second inaugural when he said: "I shall need, too, the favor of that Being in whose hands we are, who led our fathers, as Israel of old, from their native land and planted them in a country flowing with all the necessaries and comforts of life." Europe is Egypt; America, the promised land. God has led his people to establish a new sort of social order that shall be a light unto all the nations.[5]

This theme, too, has been a continuous one in the civil religion. We have already alluded to it in the case of the Kennedy inaugural. We find it again in President Johnson's inaugural address:

> *They came here — the exile and the stranger, brave but frightened — to find a place where a man could be his own man. They made a covenant with this land. Conceived in justice, written in liberty, bound in union, it was meant one day to inspire the hopes of all mankind; and it binds us still. If we keep its terms, we shall flourish.*

What we have, then, from the earliest years of the republic is a collection of beliefs, symbols, and rituals with respect to sacred things and institutionalized in a collectivity. This religion — there seems no other word for it — while not antithetical to and indeed

---

"the Almighty" in his first inaugural and finally "Almighty God" in his second. See, *Inaugural Addresses of the Presidents of the United States from George Washington 1789 to Harry S Truman 1949,* 82d Congress, 2d Session, House Document No. 540, 1952.

[4] For example, Abiel Abbot, pastor of the First Church in Haverhill, Massachusetts, delivered a Thanksgiving sermon in 1799, *Traits of Resemblance in the People of the United States of America to Ancient Israel,* in which he said, "It has been often remarked that the people of the United States come nearer to a parallel with Ancient Israel, than any other nation upon the globe. Hence OUR AMERICAN ISRAEL is a term frequently used; and common consent allows it apt and proper." Cited in Hans Kohn, *The Idea of Nationalism* (New York, 1961), p. 665.

[5] That the Mosaic analogy was present in the minds of leaders at the very moment of the birth of the republic is indicated in the designs proposed by Franklin and Jefferson for a seal of the United States of America. Together with Adams, they formed a committee of three delegated by the Continental Congress on July 4, 1776, to draw up the new device. "Franklin proposed as the device Moses lifting up his wand and dividing the Red Sea while Pharaoh was overwhelmed by its waters, with the motto 'Rebellion to tyrants is obedience to God.' Jefferson proposed the children of Israel in the wilderness 'led by a cloud by day and a pillar of fire at night.'" Anson Phelps Stokes, *Church and State in the United States,* Vol. 1 (New York, 1950), pp. 467–68.

sharing much in common with Christianity, was neither sectarian nor in any specific sense Christian. At a time when the society was overwhelmingly Christian, it seems unlikely that this lack of Christian reference was meant to spare the feelings of the tiny non-Christian minority. Rather, the civil religion expressed what those who set the precedents felt was appropriate under the circumstances. It reflected their private as well as public views. Nor was the civil religion simply "religion in general." While generality was undoubtedly seen as a virtue by some, as in the quotation from Franklin above, the civil religion was specific enough when it came to the topic of America. Precisely because of this specificity, the civil religion was saved from empty formalism and served as a genuine vehicle of national religious self-understanding.

But the civil religion was not, in the minds of Franklin, Washington, Jefferson, or other leaders, with the exception of a few radicals like Tom Paine, ever felt to be a substitute for Christianity. There was an implicit but quite clear division of function between the civil religion and Christianity. Under the doctrine of religious liberty, an exceptionally wide sphere of personal piety and voluntary social action was left to the churches. But the churches were neither to control the state nor to be controlled by it. The national magistrate, whatever his private religious views, operates under the rubrics of the civil religion as long as he is in his official capacity, as we have already seen in the case of Kennedy. This accommodation was undoubtedly the product of a particular historical moment and of a cultural background dominated by Protestantism of several varieties and by the Enlightenment, but it has survived despite subsequent changes in the cultural and religious climate.

CIVIL WAR AND CIVIL RELIGION

Until the Civil War, the American civil religion focused above all on the event of the Revolution, which was seen as the final act of the Exodus from the old lands across the waters. The Declaration of Independence and the Constitution were the sacred scriptures and Washington the divinely appointed Moses who led his people out of the hands of tyranny. The Civil War, which Sidney Mead calls "the center of American history," [6] was the second great event that involved the national self-understanding so deeply as to require expression in the civil religion. In 1835, de Tocqueville wrote that the American republic had never really been tried, that victory in the Revolutionary War was more the result of British preoccupation elsewhere and the presence of a powerful ally than of any great military success of the Americans. But in 1861 the time of testing had indeed come. Not only did the Civil War have the tragic intensity of fratricidal strife, but it was one of the bloodiest wars of the nineteenth century; the loss of life was far greater than any previously suffered by Americans.

[6] Sidney Mead, *The Lively Experiment* (New York, 1963), p. 12.

The Civil War raised the deepest questions of national meaning. The man who not only formulated but in his own person embodied its meaning for Americans was Abraham Lincoln. For him the issue was not in the first instance slavery but "whether that nation, or any nation so conceived, and so dedicated, can long endure." He had said in Independence Hall in Philadelphia on 22 February 1861:

All the political sentiments I entertain have been drawn, so far as I have been able to draw them, from the sentiments which originated in and were given to the world from this Hall. I have never had a feeling, politically, that did not spring from the sentiments embodied in the Declaration of Independence.[7]

The phrases of Jefferson constantly echo in Lincoln's speeches. His task was, first of all, to save the Union — not for America alone but for the meaning of America to the whole world so unforgettably etched in the last phrase of the Gettysburg Address.

But inevitably the issue of slavery as the deeper cause of the conflict had to be faced. In the second inaugural, Lincoln related slavery and the war in an ultimate perspective:

If we shall suppose that American slavery is one of those offenses which, in the providence of God, must needs come, but which, having continued through His appointed time, He now wills to remove, and that He gives to both North and South this terrible war

[7] Quoted by Arthur Lehman Goodhart in Allan Nevins (ed.), *Lincoln and the Gettysburg Address* (Urbana, Ill., 1964), p. 39.

as the woe due to those by whom the offense came, shall we discern therein any departure from those divine attributes which the believers in a living God always ascribe to Him? Fondly do we hope, fervently do we pray, that this mighty scourge of war may speedily pass away. Yet, if God wills that it continue until all the wealth piled by the bondsman's two hundred and fifty years of unrequited toil shall be sunk, and until every drop of blood drawn with the lash shall be paid by another drawn with the sword, as was said three thousand years ago, so still it must be said "the judgements of the Lord are true and righteous altogether."

But he closes on a note if not of redemption then of reconciliation — "With malice toward none, with charity for all."

With the Civil War, a new theme of death, sacrifice, and rebirth enters the civil religion. It is symbolized in the life and death of Lincoln. Nowhere is it stated more vividly than in the Gettysburg Address, itself part of the Lincolnian "New Testament" among the civil scriptures. Robert Lowell has recently pointed out the "insistent use of birth images" in this speech explicitly devoted to "these honored dead": "brought forth," "conceived," "created," "a new birth of freedom." He goes on to say:

The Gettysburg Address is a symbolic and sacramental act. Its verbal quality is resonance combined with a logical, matter of fact, prosaic brevity. . . . In his words, Lincoln symbolically died, just as the Union soldiers really died — and as he himself was soon really to die. By his words, he gave the field of battle a symbolic significance that it had lacked. For us and our country, he left Jefferson's ideals of freedom and equality joined to the Christian sacrificial act of death and rebirth. I believe this is a meaning that goes beyond sect or religion and beyond peace and war, and is now part of our lives as a challenge, obstacle and hope.[8]

Lowell is certainly right in pointing out the Christian quality of the symbolism here, but he is also right in quickly disavowing any sectarian implication. The earlier symbolism of the civil religion had been Hebraic without being in any specific sense Jewish. The Gettysburg symbolism ("... those who here gave their lives, that that nation might live") is Christian without having anything to do with the Christian church.

The symbolic equation of Lincoln with Jesus was made relatively early. Herndon, who had been Lincoln's law partner, wrote:

For fifty years God rolled Abraham Lincoln through his fiery furnace. He did it to try Abraham and to purify him for his purposes. This made Mr. Lincoln humble, tender, forbearing, sympathetic to suffering, kind, sensitive, tolerant; broadening, deepening and widening his whole nature; making him the noblest and loveliest character since Jesus Christ. ... I believe that Lincoln was God's chosen one.[9]

With the Christian archetype in the background, Lincoln, "our martyred president," was linked to the war dead, those who "gave the last full measure of devotion." The theme of sacrifice was indelibly written into the civil religion.

The new symbolism soon found both physical and ritualistic expression. The great number of the war dead required the establishment of a number of national cemeteries. Of these, the Gettysburg National Cemetery, which Lincoln's famous address served to dedicate, has been overshadowed only by the Arlington National Cemetery. Begun somewhat vindictively on the Lee estate across the river from Washington, partly with the end that the Lee family could never reclaim it,[10] it has subsequently become the most hallowed monument of the civil religion. Not only was a section set aside for the Confederate dead, but it has received the dead of each succeeding American war. It is the site of the one important new symbol to come out of World War I, the Tomb of the Unknown Soldier; more recently it has become the site of the tomb of another martyred president and its symbolic eternal flame.

Memorial Day, which grew out of the Civil War, gave ritual expression to the themes we have been discussing. As Lloyd Warner has so brilliantly analyzed it, the Memorial Day observance, especially in the towns and smaller cities of America, is a major event for the whole community involving a rededication to the martyred dead, to the spirit of sacrifice, and to

[8] Ibid., "On the Gettysburg Address," pp. 88–89.

[9] Quoted in Sherwood Eddy, *The Kingdom of God and the American Dream* (New York, 1941), p. 162.

[10] Karl Decker and Angus McSween, *Historic Arlington* (Washington, D.C., 1892), pp. 60–67.

the American vision.[11] Just as Thanks-giving Day, which incidentally was se-curely institutionalized as an annual national holiday only under the presi-dency of Lincoln, serves to integrate the family into the civil religion, so Memorial Day has acted to integrate the local community into the national cult. Together with the less overtly religious Fourth of July and the more minor celebrations of Veterans Day and the birthdays of Washington and Lincoln, these two holidays provide an annual ritual calendar for the civil re-ligion. The public-school system serves as a particularly important context for the cultic celebration of the civil rituals.

The Civil Religion Today

In reifying and giving a name to something that, though pervasive enough when you look at it, has gone on only semiconsciously, there is risk of severely distorting the data. But the reification and the naming have al-ready begun. The religious critics of "religion in general," or of the "reli-gion of the 'American Way of Life,'" or of "American Shinto" have really been talking about the civil religion. As usual in religious polemic, they take as criteria the best in their own reli-gious tradition and as typical the worst in the tradition of the civil religion. Against these critics, I would argue that the civil religion at its best is a genuine apprehension of universal and transcendent religious reality as seen in or, one could almost say, as revealed through the experience of the Amer-ican people. Like all religions, it has suffered various deformations and de-monic distortions. At its best, it has neither been so general that it has lacked incisive relevance to the Amer-ican scene nor so particular that it has placed American society above univer-sal human values. I am not at all con-vinced that the leaders of the churches have consistently represented a higher level of religious insight than the spokesmen of the civil religion. Rein-hold Niebuhr has this to say of Lin-coln, who never joined a church and who certainly represents civil religion at its best:

---

[11] How extensive the activity associated with Memorial Day can be is indicated by Warner: "The sacred symbolic behavior of Memorial Day, in which scores of the town's organizations are involved, is ordinarily di-vided into four periods. During the year separate rituals are held by many of the associations for their dead, and many of these activities are connected with later Memorial Day events. In the second phase, preparations are made during the last three or four weeks for the ceremony itself, and some of the associations perform public rit-uals. The third phase consists of scores of rituals held in all the cemeteries, churches, and halls of the associations. These rituals consist of speeches and highly ritualized be-havior. They last for two days and are cli-maxed by the fourth and last phase, in which all the separate celebrants gather in the center of the business district on the afternoon of Memorial Day. The separate organizations, with their members in uni-form or with fitting insignia, march through the town, visit the shrines and monuments of the hero dead, and, finally, enter the cemetery. Here dozens of ceremonies are held, most of them highly symbolic and for-malized." During these various ceremonies Lincoln is continually referred to and the Gettysburg Address recited many times. W. Lloyd Warner, *American Life* (Chicago, 1962), pp. 8–9.

An analysis of the religion of Abraham Lincoln in the context of the traditional religion of his time and place and of its polemical use on the slavery issue, which corrupted religious life in the days before and during the Civil War, must lead to the conclusion that Lincoln's religious convictions were superior in depth and purity to those, not only of the political leaders of his day, but of the religious leaders of the era.[12]

Perhaps the real animus of the religious critics has been not so much against the civil religion in itself but against its pervasive and dominating influence within the sphere of church religion. As S. M. Lipset has recently shown, American religion at least since the early-nineteenth century has been predominantly activist, moralistic, and social rather than contemplative, theological, or innerly spiritual.[13] De Tocqueville spoke of American church religion as "a political institution which powerfully contributes to the mainte-

nance of a democratic republic among the Americans"[14] by supplying a strong moral consensus amidst continuous political change. Henry Bargy in 1902 spoke of American church religion as "la poésie du civisme." [15]

It is certainly true that the relation between religion and politics in America has been singularly smooth. This is in large part due to the dominant tradition. As de Tocqueville wrote:

The greatest part of British America was peopled by men who, after having shaken off the authority of the Pope, acknowledged no other religious supremacy: they brought with them into the New World a form of Christianity which I cannot better describe than by styling it a democratic and republican religion.[16]

The churches opposed neither the Revolution nor the establishment of democratic institutions. Even when some of them opposed the full institutionalization of religious liberty, they accepted the final outcome with good grace and without nostalgia for an *ancien régime*. The American civil religion

---

[12] Reinhold Niebuhr, "The Religion of Abraham Lincoln," in Nevins (ed.), op. cit., p. 72. William J. Wolfe of the Episcopal Theological School in Cambridge, Massachusetts, has written: "Lincoln is one of the greatest theologians of America — not in the technical meaning of producing a system of doctrine, certainly not as the defender of some one denomination, but in the sense of seeing the hand of God intimately in the affairs of nations. Just so the prophets of Israel criticized the events of their day from the perspective of the God who is concerned for history and who reveals His will within it. Lincoln now stands among God's latter-day prophets." *The Religion of Abraham Lincoln* (New York, 1963), p. 24.

[13] Seymour Martin Lipset, "Religion and American Values," Chapter 4, *The First New Nation* (New York, 1964).

[14] Alexis de Tocqueville, *Democracy in America,* Vol. 1 (New York, 1954), p. 310.

[15] Henry Bargy, *La Religion dans la Société aux États-Unis* (Paris, 1902), p. 31.

[16] De Tocqueville, op. cit., p. 311. Later he says, "In the United States even the religion of most of the citizens is republican, since it submits the truths of the other world to private judgment, as in politics the care of their temporal interests is abandoned to the good sense of the people. Thus every man is allowed freely to take that road which he thinks will lead him to heaven, just as the law permits every citizen to have the right of choosing his own government" (p. 436).

was never anticlerical or militantly secular. On the contrary, it borrowed selectively from the religious tradition in such a way that the average American saw no conflict between the two. In this way, the civil religion was able to build up without any bitter struggle with the church powerful symbols of national solidarity and to mobilize deep levels of personal motivation for the attainment of national goals.

Such an achievement is by no means to be taken for granted. It would seem that the problem of a civil religion is quite general in modern societies and that the way it is solved or not solved will have repercussions in many spheres. One needs only to think of France to see how differently things can go. The French Revolution was anticlerical to the core and attempted to set up an anti-Christian civil religion. Throughout modern French history, the chasm between traditional Catholic symbols and the symbolism of 1789 has been immense.

American civil religion is still very much alive. Just three years ago we participated in a vivid re-enactment of the sacrifice theme in connection with the funeral of our assassinated president. The American Israel theme is clearly behind both Kennedy's New Frontier and Johnson's Great Society. Let me give just one recent illustration of how the civil religion serves to mobilize support for the attainment of national goals. On 15 March 1965 President Johnson went before Congress to ask for a strong voting-rights bill. Early in the speech he said:

Rarely are we met with the challenge, not to our growth or abundance, or our

welfare or our security — but rather to the values and the purposes and the meaning of our beloved nation.

The issues of equal rights for American Negroes is such an issue. And should we defeat every enemy, and should we double our wealth and conquer the stars and still be unequal to this issue, then we will have failed as a people and as a nation.

For with a country as with a person, "What is a man profited, if he shall gain the whole world, and lose his own soul?"

And in conclusion he said:

Above the pyramid on the great seal of the United States it says in Latin, "God has favored our undertaking."

God will not favor everything that we do. It is rather our duty to divine his will. I cannot help but believe that He truly understands and that He really favors the undertaking that we begin here tonight.[17]

The civil religion has not always been invoked in favor of worthy causes. On the domestic scene, an American-Legion type of ideology that fuses God, country, and flag has been used to attack nonconformist and liberal ideas and groups of all kinds. Still, it has been difficult to use the words of Jefferson and Lincoln to support special interests and undermine personal freedom. The defenders of slavery before the Civil War came to reject the thinking of the Declaration of Independence. Some of the most consistent of them turned against not only Jeffersonian democracy but Reformation religion; they dreamed of a South

[17] U. S., *Congressional Record,* House, 15 March 1965, pp. 4924, 4926.

dominated by medieval chivalry and divine-right monarchy.[18] For all the overt religiosity of the radical right today, their relation to the civil religious consensus is tenuous, as when the John Birch Society attacks the central American symbol of Democracy itself.

With respect to America's role in the world, the dangers of distortion are greater and the built-in safeguards of the tradition weaker. The theme of the American Israel was used, almost from the beginning, as a justification for the shameful treatment of the Indians so characteristic of our history. It can be overtly or implicitly linked to the idea of manifest destiny which has been used to legitimate several adventures in imperialism since the early-nineteenth century. Never has the danger been greater than today. The issue is not so much one of imperial expansion, of which we are accused, as of the tendency to assimilate all governments or parties in the world which support our immediate policies or call upon our help by invoking the notion of free institutions and democratic values. Those nations that are for the moment "on our side" become "the free world." A repressive and unstable military dictatorship in South Viet-Nam becomes "the free people of South Viet-Nam and their government." It is then part of the role of America as the New Jerusalem and "the last hope of earth" to defend such governments with treasure and eventually with blood. When our soldiers are actually

dying, it becomes possible to consecrate the struggle further by invoking the great theme of sacrifice. For the majority of the American people who are unable to judge whether the people in South Viet-Nam (or wherever) are "free like us," such arguments are convincing. Fortunately President Johnson has been less ready to assert that "God has favored our undertaking" in the case of Viet-Nam than with respect to civil rights. But others are not so hesitant. The civil religion has exercised long-term pressure for the humane solution of our greatest domestic problem, the treatment of the Negro American. It remains to be seen how relevant it can become for our role in the world at large, and whether we can effectually stand for "the revolutionary beliefs for which our forebears fought," in John F. Kennedy's words.

The civil religion is obviously involved in the most pressing moral and political issues of the day. But it is also caught in another kind of crisis, theoretical and theological, of which it is at the moment largely unaware. "God" has clearly been a central symbol in the civil religion from the beginning and remains so today. This symbol is just as central to the civil religion as it is to Judaism or Christianity. In the late-eighteenth century this posed no problem; even Tom Paine, contrary to his detractors, was not an atheist. From left to right and regardless of church or sect, all could accept the idea of God. But today, as even *Time* has recognized, the meaning of the word *God* is by no means so clear or so obvious. There is no formal creed in the civil religion. We have had a Catholic president; it is conceivable that we

---

[18] See Louis Hartz, "The Feudal Dream of the South," Part 4, *The Liberal Tradition in America* (New York, 1955).

could have a Jewish one. But could we have an agnostic president? Could a man with conscientious scruples about using the word *God* the way Kennedy and Johnson have used it be elected chief magistrate of our country? If the whole God symbolism requires reformulation, there will be obvious consequences for the civil religion, consequences perhaps of liberal alienation and of fundamentalist ossification that have not so far been prominent in this realm. The civil religion has been a point of articulation between the profoundest commitments of the Western religious and philosophical tradition and the common beliefs of ordinary Americans. It is not too soon to consider how the deepening theological crisis may affect the future of this articulation.

The Third Time of Trial

In conclusion it may be worthwhile to relate the civil religion to the most serious situation that we as Americans now face, what I call the third time of trial. The first time of trial had to do with the question of independence, whether we should or could run our own affairs in our own way. The second time of trial was over the issue of slavery, which in turn was only the most salient aspect of the more general problem of the full institutionalization of democracy within our country. This second problem we are still far from solving though we have some notable successes to our credit. But we have been overtaken by a third great problem which has led to a third great crisis, in the midst of which we stand. This is the problem of responsible ac-

tion in a revolutionary world, a world seeking to attain many of the things, material and spiritual, that we have already attained. Americans have from the beginning, been aware of the responsibility and the significance our republican experiment has for the whole world. The first internal political polarization in the new nation had to do with our attitude toward the French Revolution. But we were small and weak then, and "foreign entanglements" seemed to threaten our very survival. During the last century, our relevance for the world was not forgotten, but our role was seen as purely exemplary. Our democratic republic rebuked tyranny by merely existing. Just after World War I we were on the brink of taking a different role in the world, but once again we turned our back.

Since World War II the old pattern has become impossible. Every president since Roosevelt has been groping toward a new pattern of action in the world, one that would be consonant with our power and our responsibilities. For Truman and for the period dominated by John Foster Dulles that pattern was seen to be the great Manichaean confrontation of East and West, the confrontation of democracy and "the false philosophy of Communism" that provided the structure of Truman's inaugural address. But with the last years of Eisenhower and with the successive two presidents, the pattern began to shift. The great problems came to be seen as caused not solely by the evil intent of any one group of men, but as stemming from much more complex and multiple sources. For Kennedy, it was not so much a struggle against particular men as against "the common enemies of man: tyranny, poverty, disease and war itself."

But in the midst of this trend toward a less primitive conception of ourselves and our world, we have somehow, without anyone really intending it, stumbled into a military confrontation where we have come to feel that our honor is at stake. We have in a moment of uncertainty been tempted to rely on our overwhelming physical power rather than on our intelligence, and we have, in part, succumbed to this temptation. Bewildered and unnerved when our terrible power fails to bring immediate success, we are at the edge of a chasm the depth of which no man knows.

I cannot help but think of Robinson Jeffers, whose poetry seems more apt now than when it was written, when he said:

Unhappy country, what wings you have! . . .
Weep (it is frequent in human affairs),
weep for the terrible magnificence
of the means,
The ridiculous incompetence of the reasons, the bloody and shabby
Pathos of the result.

But as so often before in similar times, we have a man of prophetic stature, without the bitterness or misanthropy of Jeffers, who, as Lincoln before him, calls this nation to its judgment:

When a nation is very powerful but lacking in self-confidence, it is likely to behave in a manner that is dangerous both to itself and to others.
Gradually but unmistakably, America is succumbing to that arrogance of

power which has afflicted, weakened and in some cases destroyed great nations in the past.

If the war goes on and expands, if that fatal process continues to accelerate until America becomes what it is not now and never has been, a seeker after unlimited power and empire, then Vietnam will have had a mighty and tragic fallout indeed.

I do not believe that will happen. I am very apprehensive but I still remain hopeful, and even confident, that America, with its humane and democratic traditions, will find the wisdom to match its power.[19]

Without an awareness that our nation stands under higher judgment, the tradition of the civil religion would be dangerous indeed. Fortunately, the prophetic voices have never been lacking. Our present situation brings to mind the Mexican-American war that Lincoln, among so many others, opposed. The spirit of civil disobedience that is alive today in the civil rights movement and the opposition to the Viet-Nam war was already clearly outlined by Henry David Thoreau when he wrote, "If the law is of such a nature that it requires you to be an agent of injustice to another, then I say, break the law." Thoreau's words, "I would remind my countrymen that they are men first, and Americans at a late and convenient hour," [20] provide an essential standard for any adequate

[19] Speech of Senator J. William Fulbright of 28 April 1966, as reported in *The New York Times*, 29 April 1966.
[20] Quoted in Yehoshua Arieli, *Individualism and Nationalism in American Ideology* (Cambridge, Mass., 1964), p. 274.

thought and action in our third time of trial. As Americans, we have been well favored in the world, but it is as men that we will be judged.

Out of the first and second times of trial have come, as we have seen, the major symbols of the American civil religion. There seems little doubt that a successful negotiation of this third time of trial — the attainment of some kind of viable and coherent world order — would precipitate a major new set of symbolic forms. So far the flickering flame of the United Nations burns too low to be the focus of a cult, but the emergence of a genuine transnational sovereignty would certainly change this. It would necessitate the incorporation of vital international symbolism into our civil religion, or, perhaps a better way of putting it, it would result in American civil religion becoming simply one part of a new civil religion of the world. It is useless to speculate on the form such a civil religion might take, though it obviously would draw on religious traditions beyond the sphere of Biblical religion alone. Fortunately, since the American civil religion is not the worship of the American nation but an understanding of the American experience in the light of ultimate and universal reality, the reorganization entailed by such a new situation need not disrupt the American civil religion's continuity. A world civil religion could be accepted as a ful-

fillment and not a denial of American civil religion. Indeed, such an outcome has been the eschatological hope of American civil religion from the beginning. To deny such an outcome would be to deny the meaning of America itself.

Behind the civil religion at every point lie Biblical archetypes: Exodus, Chosen People, Promised Land, New Jerusalem, Sacrificial Death and Rebirth. But it is also genuinely American and genuinely new. It has its own prophets and its own martyrs, its own sacred events and sacred places, its own solemn rituals and symbols. It is concerned that America be a society as perfectly in accord with the will of God as men can make it, and a light to all the nations.

It has often been used and is being used today as a cloak for petty interests and ugly passions. It is in need — as is any living faith — of continual reformation, of being measured by universal standards. But it is not evident that it is incapable of growth and new insight.

It does not make any decision for us. It does not remove us from moral ambiguity, from being, in Lincoln's fine phrase, an "almost chosen people." But it is a heritage of moral and religious experience from which we still have much to learn as we formulate the decisions that lie ahead.

Even civil religion has its heretics. H. L. Mencken, an iconoclastic Baltimore journalist, was very aware of our civil religion when he wrote the following* in the early 1920s:

Yet here I stand, unshaken and undespairing, a loyal and devoted Americano, even a chauvinist, paying taxes without complaint, obeying all laws that are physiologically obeyable, accepting all the searching duties and responsibilities of citizenship unprotestingly, investing the sparse usufructs of my miserable toil in the obligations of the nation, avoiding all commerce with men sworn to overthrow the government, contributing my mite toward the glory of the national arts and sciences, enriching and embellishing the native language, spurning all lures (and even all invitations) to get out and stay out — here am I, a bachelor of easy means, forty-two years old, unhampered by debts or issue, able to go wherever I please and to stay as long as I please — here am I, contentedly and even smugly basking beneath the Stars and Stripes, a better citizen, I daresay, and certainly a less murmurous and exigent one, than thousands who put the Hon. Warren Gamaliel Harding beside Friedrich Barbarossa and Charlemagne, and hold the Supreme Court to be directly inspired by the Holy Spirit, and belong ardently to every Rotary Club, Ku Klux Klan, and Anti-Saloon League, and choke with emotion when the band plays "The Star-Spangled Banner," and believe with the faith of little children that one of Our Boys, taken at random could dispose in a fair fight of ten Englishmen, twenty Germans, thirty Frogs, forty Wops, fifty Japs or a hundred Bolsheviki.

Territorially, the United States is one of the largest nations in the world. Starting from 13 eastern states, the American people moved westward. The United States became known as a nation with "pioneer spirit." We today still glorify our past heritage and many believe that it was this pioneer heritage that shaped our nation.† Since the United States was so large, immigration was encouraged, and new immigrants were supposedly infused with this pioneer spirit. On the other hand, there were those who believed that the immigrants who came to the United States lacked the ability to make it in their own countries and were equally incompetent in settling our frontier.‡

The settling of the West is frequently seen as a violent period in our history. It was popularly believed that with the closing of the frontier, violence as an American ethos disappeared except among the "lower classes." Yet violence is still a part of the American scene. Our mass

---

* H. L. Mencken, "On Being an American," from H. L. Mencken, *Prejudices: Third Series* (New York, Alfred Knopf, 1922), pp. 11–12.

† See Don Martindale, "The American People," in Don Martindale, *Community, Character, and Civilization* (New York: Free Press, 1963), pp. 291–360.

‡ See Mencken, loc. cit.

media are dominated by violence.* The Viet Nam War was regularly televised, and just as many movies have obligatory sex scenes, they may also have obligatory scenes showing brutal beatings or murders. Like soap or art, violence also may be mass marketed. In the article that follows, Rodney Stark and James McEvoy demonstrate that violence may be an integral part of the dominant American life style.

* See Otto Larsen (ed.), *Violence and the Mass Media* (New York: Harper and Row, 1968) and George Gerbner, Michael Eleey, and Nancy Tedesco, *The Violence Index* (Philadelphia: Annenberg School of Communications, 1972).

Middle-Class Violence

Rodney Stark and
James McEvoy III

True or false?

Wife-slapping and marital violence occur most commonly among the poor, the uneducated and the blacks.

Middle-class Americans are more likely than working-class persons to vent their rage in symbolic and non-physical ways.

The use of guns and knives to settle disputes tends to be concentrated in violent subcultures: among slum-dwellers, Southerners and ghettos.

From *Psychology Today* (November 1970). This article is based on *Mass Media and Violence, A Staff Report to the National Commission on the Causes and Prevention of Violence*, Robert K. Baker and Sandra J. Ball (Rokeach). U.S. Government Printing Office, Washington, 1969.

Americans are becoming more permissive in rearing their children; spanking is less common than it used to be.

Many Americans would take up arms against a tyrannical government.

Men who have had experience in war are more likely to condone the use of force to settle social ills.

Are Americans a violent people? Blacks and whites, conservatives and liberals, young and old, Europeans and Americans alike seem agreed that the answer is yes. To be sure, there is disagreement on the kinds of violence that predominate. Conservatives are alarmed by rising crime rates, mass disorder coming from protest — black, student and antiwar — and recent episodes of bombing and arson attributed to the New Left. Liberals and radicals are primarily upset about institutional violence aimed at the poor and non-white; police and hard-hat violence directed toward students, demonstrators and dissenters; and the military violence we inflict abroad.

To discover whether the impression of America-the-violent is justified, we analyzed a survey conducted for the National Commission on the Causes and Prevention of Violence by Louis Harris and Associates. The poll was conducted in October 1968, and consisted of 1,176 interviews with a representative national sample of adult Americans. The study was designed by a number of social scientists, including the junior author, and was supervised by Dr. Sandra J. Ball (Rokeach). We wished to determine (1) the extent to which Americans have been the victims of violence or have acted violently themselves; (2) American willingness to engage in political violence and vigilantism; and (3) attitudes toward police brutality, political assassination and military force.

INTERPERSONAL VIOLENCE

How aggressive are we toward each other? [See Table 1.] Almost 13 per cent of all Americans have, as adults, been slapped or kicked by other persons; 18 per cent recall that they have slapped or kicked someone else. (There is apparently a tendency to recall aggression more than victimization, or else there were a few scapegoats among the respondents.) About one in eight of us has, as an adult, punched or beaten another person or has been punched; among men this figure becomes one in five.

Overall, one fifth of all Americans approve of slapping one's spouse on appropriate occasions. Surprisingly, approval of this practice *increases* with income and education: among those with eight years of schooling or less, 16 per cent approve of a husband's slapping his wife, but the comparable figure is 25 per cent among the college-educated.

A substantial number of us have, as adults, been threatened with knives or actually been cut: one out of every 12. Some of us have been threatened by guns or been shot at: about one out of every 17. (The figures exclude encounters in military combat.) Furthermore, one adult out of 17 admits to having used a gun or knife to defend himself.

Weapons are used in all areas of the country, at all income and educational levels. Blacks are slightly more likely to have confronted or used such weapons, but differences are not large enough to justify much attention, let alone hysteria (whether by racists or revolutionaries).

Firearms are about as common as coffeepots in our society. Forty-one per cent of all American adults admit that they own at least one gun, and many own several. Blacks are much less likely than whites to own guns, and women are less likely than men (32 per cent of the females compared to half of the males). Regionally, Easterners own fewer guns than persons in other parts of the country and members of higher-income groups are more likely to own guns than the poor. Age and level of education apparently make little difference in patterns of gun ownership.

These data seriously challenge some of our myths about violence.

1. Blacks do not constitute an especially violent subculture. They are somewhat more likely to have engaged in and been victims of physical assault, but the differences between blacks and whites are not important.

2. The South does not appear to be more violent than any other part of the country. To be sure, official statistics on murder and assault rates show the South to be our most violent region; perhaps then our findings reflect a cultural denial of violence in order to maintain our image of Southern gentility. Alternatively, it may be that the South's surface pattern of gentility suppresses many violent urges — so that there is less violence generally, but when it erupts it does so with greater passion and more deadly results.

3. The poor and less educated are not more likely than the middle class to resort to physical forms of aggression. We have assumed that middle-class persons vent their hostilities through more sedate channels; i.e., they are supposed to be more verbally violent. Actually, physical violence is reported as equally common among all income groups and education levels. This finding is also true for *frequency* of physical violence. The middle class is not only as likely as others ever to have engaged in physical aggression, but have done so as often. If anything, the middle class is more prone toward physical assault (punching, beating, slapping) than the poor.

This finding directly contradicts police statistics that suggest that the poor commit more acts of assault, get embroiled in more violent family arguments and otherwise act out their aggressions more frequently than the members of higher social strata. We suggest that altercations among the poor are simply more likely to become police matters. Middle-class persons have recourse to friends and professional counselors to help settle their disputes; they report more effective intervention by third parties (not the police). Further, lower-class people are denied privacy for their quarrels: neighborhood bars, sidewalks, and crowded, thin-walled apartments afford little isolation. The privacy of the middle-class life-style preserves an illusion of greater domestic tranquility; but it is, apparently, only an illusion.

4. Of all the results, only the data for women support our common-sense impressions. Women are less likely to have committed acts of violence, to have been victims of aggression, or to approve of violence.

CHILDHOOD VIOLENCE

Our data [Table 2] challenge the complaints now in vogue that our permissive child-rearing practices have increased over the last generation. More than nine out of 10 adults say that they were spanked at least sometimes as children, a third were spanked frequently. This self-report does not change with age: younger persons are just as likely to have been spanked as older ones. Although there are no sex differences on this question, there are race and regional variations. More black persons than white ones and more Southerners than residents of other sections report having been spanked frequently.

Almost eight in 10 men have spanked a child, and nine in 10 women (mothers, apparently, do most of the spanking). There are, interestingly, no meaningful racial, regional, educational, income or age differences.

TABLE 1 PHYSICAL VIOLENCE[a]

Percentage who:

	Race		Sex		Region				Income			Education				Age				National average
	Black	White	Male	Female	East	Midwest	South	West	$5,000 or less	$5,000 to $9,999	$10,000 or more	8th grade or less	Some high school	High-school graduate	College	30 and under	31 through 50	51 through 65	65+	
1. Have been slapped or kicked by another person:	18	13	13	12	15	15	9	17	12	16	14	11	15	12	17	16	14	15	6	13
2. Have slapped or kicked another person:	22	18	22	13	17	19	14	23	14	19	20	15	20	16	20	18	21	17	10	18
3. Have been punched or beaten by another person:	17	12	19	4	16	10	8	9	11	13	13	14	9	13	12	10	15	10	5	12
4. Have punched or beaten another person:	20	13	21	4	15	12	7	20	7	16	15	9	19	11	13	15	14	10	4	13
5. Could approve of a husband's slapping his wife's face:	25	20	25	16	22	18	16	26	14	22	23	16	23	17	25	26	23	15	11	20
6. Could approve of a wife's slapping her husband's face:	27	22	26	19	24	21	18	25	18	24	24	19	22	18	28	33	20	18	13	22
7. Have been threatened with, or actually cut with, a knife:	11	8	12	3	8	5	10	11	9	8	8	7	10	6	9	11	7	7	7	8
8. Have been threatened with a gun or shot at:	9	6	10	2	6	4	7	9	6	7	7	7	6	7	5	9	5	8	4	6
9. Have had to defend themselves with a knife or a gun:	14	4	10	2	10	3	5	5	5	5	8	4	7	5	6	9	6	4	2	6
10. Own firearms:	27	43	50	32	24	45	50	46	34	41	47	40	39	41	43	38	47	40	36	41

[a] (Childhood incidents and experiences in military combat have been eliminated.)

TABLE 2 CHILDHOOD VIOLENCE

Percentage who:

	Race		Sex		Region				Income			Education				Age				National average
	Black	White	Male	Female	East	Midwest	South	West	$5,000 or less	$5,000 to $9,999	$10,000 or more	8th grade or less	Some high school	High-school graduate	College	30 and under	31 through 50	51 through 65	65+	
1. Were spanked as children:																				
Frequently	43	30	33	31	27	26	42	33	38	35	23	42	41	29	22	32	29	38	34	32
Sometimes	54	63	62	61	65	65	53	63	54	61	69	49	54	65	71	64	67	53	53	61
2. Have ever spanked a child:	84	84	78	90	79	85	88	84	81	85	87	82	86	89	80	79	94	81	73	84
3. Agree that "What young people need most of all is strong discipline by their parents":	88	86	84	89	82	87	91	85	87	89	82	90	92	89	77	81	87	88	92	86
4. Could approve of a public schoolteacher's hitting a student:	55	49	53	46	46	52	50	51	48	47	54	50	46	48	53	44	53	48	48	49
5. Could approve of a parent's beating his or her child:	23	6	11	7	17	4	8	4	8	9	8	10	11	8	7	12	7	9	5	8
6. Agree that "When a boy is growing up, it is very important for him to have a few fistfights":	75	69	68	71	69	74	65	73	72	72	65	70	77	73	62	71	66	72	70	70

DISCIPLINE

A great majority of the public — 86 per cent — agree that "what young people need most is strong discipline by their parents." Agreement declines among the college-educated and those under 30, but the decline is slight. Apparently American parents have not become particularly permissive, Spiro Agnew's views to the contrary notwithstanding.

Half of all American adults approve of schoolteachers' striking students, given proper cause. Among those who approve, 28 per cent would accept "being noisy in class" as sufficient reason, 67 per cent would approve if the student had destroyed school property, and 84 per cent if the student had hit someone. Age does not influence opinion here, again contradicting our impression that we have become less willing to use physical force to discipline children.

For the overwhelming majority of us, however, spanking a child is one thing and beating is something else. Eight per cent can imagine situations in which they would approve of a parent's beating his child. Some groups are substantially above this figure: 23 per cent of the blacks, 17 per cent of the Easterners, and 12 per cent of those under 30 approve of child-beating under some conditions. Midwesterners and Westerners are below the norm of four per cent.

FISTFIGHTS

We are likely to punish our children by physical means, and the vast majority (seven in 10) believe that it is good for growing boys to have a few fistfights. This approval reflects and inculcates a concept of masculinity that emphasizes physical aggressiveness.

We asked questions on five kinds of violence committed in the name of institutions or ideologies: vigilantism; direct action against government repression; police use of force; political assassination; and military violence.

VIGILANTISM

In his report to the Violence Commission, Richard Maxwell Brown defined the vigilante tradition as "extralegal movements which take the law into their own hands." Brown identified a vigilante movement in the United States as early as 1767 and noted that from then "until about 1900, vigilante activity was an almost constant factor in American life." In early America this was a response to a lack of effective law and order, especially in the frontier regions. In the last half-dozen years there has been a resurgence of vigilante activity all along the political continuum, from the Klan to the Weathermen. Of the many causes of this phenomenon, a prominent one is renewed lack of faith in law enforcement and legal institutions.

Disenchantment with modern legal institutions is widespread today. Half of the respondents agree that "justice may have been a little rough-and-ready in the days of the Old West, but things worked better than they do now with all the legal red tape" [Table 3]. Blacks are less likely than whites to prefer rough-and-ready justice, but sex and region have little influence on this opinion.

Social class matters considerably, however. According to Brown, traditional vigilantism was a middle-class affair, an effort of "upright" citizens to secure order and safety. Today lack of faith in law and order is felt more by the less educated and by lower-income groups. About two thirds of those with high-school education or less agreed with the statement, but only one third of college graduates did.

We then asked for a more focused opinion of vigilantism: "Groups have the right to train their members in marksmanship and underground warfare tactics in order to help put down any conspiracies that might occur in the country." Overall, one fourth of the respondents agreed with this statement. Approval was most widespread among the less educated and poor; Southerners were most likely to agree (34 per cent) and Westerners least likely (17 per cent).

Blacks were also more willing to endorse this statement than whites (41 per cent to 24 per cent), which may reflect increasing black concern with self-defense. Recall, however, that blacks are only half as likely as whites to own firearms.

Interestingly military veterans are less willing to support vigilantism t. an are those who have never served in the armed forces: 17 per cent of the veterans approve, compared to 29 per cent of the nonveterans. In fact we found veterans consistently more reluctant to support social violence of all types.

One American in 10 justifies private gun ownership as a counter to governmental power: "One of the best reasons for people to have guns is to make sure that the government doesn't get too much power." This seems to us to be a fairly low percentage, considering the energy with which this argument was promulgated during conflicts over gun legislation.

Ten per cent of Americans say that they would take part in physical assault or armed action against a group of antiwar demonstrators who deliberately blocked rush-hour traffic. This willingness to attack is fairly evenly distributed among all regional, income, education and age groupings.

We then set up for our respondents three hypothetical situations involving repression and violence by the government. For each of these, we asked whether they would participate in nonviolent civil disobedience (e.g., sit-ins) or attempt physical assault or armed action as a response [Table 4].

1. "Imagine that Congress has just passed a law prohibiting anyone from saying anything against the government." Seventeen per cent would engage in nonviolent dissent, while nine per cent would be willing to use violence. Black persons are more likely to try civil disobedience, but are not more willing to turn to force. Westerners, the more well-to-do, and the better-educated surpass the norm in their willingness to use violence to preserve the freedom of speech.

2. "Imagine that the government has just arrested and imprisoned many of the Negroes in your community even though there had been no trou-

TABLE 3 VIGILANTISM

Percentage who agree that:

	Race		Sex		Region				Income			Education				Age				National average
	Black	White	Male	Female	East	Midwest	South	West	$3,000 or less	$3,000 to $9,999	$10,000 or more	8th grade or less	Some high school	High-school graduate	College	30 and under	31 through 50	51 through 65	65 +	
1. "Justice may have been a little rough-and-ready in the days of the Old West, but things worked better than they do now with all the legal red tape":	45	51	51	49	47	53	51	51	56	52	44	63	62	50	34	47	45	49	68	50
2. "Groups have the right to train their members in marksmanship and underground-warfare tactics in order to help put down any conspiracies that might occur in the country":	41	24	22	27	24	24	34	17	37	24	18	37	38	22	13	25	25	26	28	26
3. "One of the best reasons for people to have guns is to make sure that the government doesn't get too much power":	6	11	12	8	8	9	11	13	15	7	7	16	8	10	7	8	8	11	17	10
4. They would "participate in a physical assault or armed action" against "a group of people who are deliberately blocking rush-hour traffic to protest the war in Vietnam":	8	10	12	6	11	9	9	11	7	10	12	8	12	9	10	10	13	6	5	10

TABLE 4 DIRECT ACTION AGAINST REPRESSION[a]

	Race		Sex		Region				Income			Education				Age				National average
	Black	White	Male	Female	East	Midwest	South	West	$3,000 or less	$3,000 to $9,999	$10,000 or more	8th grade or less	Some high school	High-school graduate	College	30 and under	31 through 50	51 through 65	65 +	
1. "Imagine that Congress has just passed a law prohibiting anyone from saying anything against the government."																				
Percentage who would take up civil disobedience:	31	14	20	14	22	13	13	21	14	16	21	12	17	12	25	23	19	13	8	17
Percentage who would turn to assault or armed action:	10	9	12	5	8	8	6	14	7	7	11	5	6	7	15	14	9	5	3	9
2. "Imagine that the government has just arrested and imprisoned many of the Negroes in your community even though there had been no trouble."																				
Civil disobedience:	43	13	20	17	26	15	13	19	17	18	19	14	18	15	25	23	19	14	13	18
Assault or armed action:	24	7	13	7	15	7	6	10	11	9	9	7	10	8	11	13	11	5	7	9
3. "Imagine that in order to keep control of the country, the government starts arresting and shooting large numbers of innocent people including members of your family."																				
Civil disobedience:	50	34	37	36	42	34	33	37	34	36	39	31	36	34	43	45	39	30	23	37
Assault or armed action:	41	49	53	41	44	49	49	49	39	48	57	30	43	51	59	60	52	37	30	48

[a] Percentages exclude persons who favor such government action (four percent approved of #1, and one percent approved of #2 and #3).

ble." The overwhelming majority of white Americans would apparently be "good Germans" if the government turned to massive racial repression; only 18 percent would protest non-violently and nine per cent would turn to violence. Blacks, understandably, would be more willing to act; but even so, activists are a minority: 43 per cent would use civil disobedience and one fourth would attempt counter-violence. This may reflect a pragmatic judgment that if such things came to pass, blacks would be wiped out if they rebelled.

3. "Imagine that in order to keep control of the country the government starts arresting and shooting large numbers of people, including members of your own family." Thirty-seven per cent would turn to nonviolent protest in such an extreme event, and almost half say they would fight.

The willingness to protest — in whatever form — is strongly related to income and education. For example, only 30 per cent of those with eight years of schooling would rebel violently against a totalitarian government, but 59 per cent of the college-educated would do so, a finding that parallels every known study showing greater support for civil liberties among the well-educated.

POLICE VIOLENCE

Americans are generally opposed to the illegitimate use of force by police, but at the same time they find it difficult to recognize the possibility of police brutality. For example, only 20 per cent would condone a policeman's

striking an adult male because he had said obscene words to the officer; but not many more than that (28 per cent) accept the view that "the police frequently use more force than they need to."

ASSASSINATION

Until the 1960s Americans regarded assassination as a foreign phenomenon. No president had been killed for decades and the killing of lesser political leaders was infrequent. Since then John F. Kennedy, Medgar Evers, Malcolm X, Martin Luther King, and Robert F. Kennedy have all been murdered. Some explanations for this have concentrated on the psychology of assassins and how they can be anticipated or foiled. Other analyses have pointed to the social climate of hatred and the propensity for violence in this country. Is there social support for this ultimate, tragic expression of political discontent?

One American out of 11 agrees that "sometimes I have felt that the best thing for our country might be the death of some of our political leaders" [Table 5]. This opinion is fairly evenly distributed through all sectors of the public; income and education make little difference. Similarly, two out of 10 agree that "some politicians who have their lives threatened probably deserve it." We feel that the extent of agreement to these two questions indicates that a substantial minority of Americans, far from being horrified by political assassination, tacitly condone it. In fact, many Americans seem resigned to assassination as a fact of our political life. A majority — 55 per cent — agree

TABLE 5   POLITICAL ASSASSINATION

Percentage who agree that:

	Race		Sex		Region				Income			Education				Age				National average
	Black	White	Male	Female	East	Midwest	South	West	$3,000 or less	$3,000 to $9,999	$10,000 or more	8th grade or less	Some high school	High-school graduate	College	30 and under	31 through 50	51 through 65	65+	
1. "Sometimes I have felt that the best thing for our country might be the death of some of our political leaders":	12	9	10	8	10	4	13	8	10	9	6	12	10	8	7	10	8	10	9	9
2. "Some politicians who have had their lives threatened probably deserve it":	25	17	18	19	18	20	20	12	23	20	12	28	21	17	10	20	16	15	24	19
3. "Politicians who try to change things too fast have to expect that their lives may be threatened":	60	55	53	57	48	52	67	58	62	53	51	66	59	53	46	53	49	61	62	55

TABLE 6   MILITARY VIOLENCE

Percentage who agree that:

	Race		Sex		Region				Income			Education				Age				National average
	Black	White	Male	Female	East	Midwest	South	West	$3,000 or less	$3,000 to $9,999	$10,000 or more	8th grade or less	Some high school	High-school graduate	College	30 and under	31 through 50	51 through 65	65+	
1. "Our government is too ready to use military force in dealing with other countries":	44	38	34	44	44	43	34	32	43	40	33	42	48	37	34	40	36	43	40	39
2. "Human nature being what it is, there must always be war and conflict":	65	57	57	59	51	58	63	62	63	59	52	63	66	56	52	54	59	52	77	58
3. "In dealing with other countries in the world, we are frequently justified in using military force":	60	62	62	63	57	54	70	56	66	64	58	66	70	63	55	61	64	60	61	62
4. "It is unfortunate that many civilians are killed by bombing in a war, but this cannot be avoided":	68	72	75	70	63	76	79	73	72	70	76	69	73	75	73	71	74	71	73	72

that "politicians who try to change things too fast have to expect that their lives may be threatened." Only among Easterners, those with college training and the 31 to 50 age group, does the proportion fall (barely) below half. Again, men with military service are less likely to concur with any of the three items.

MILITARY VIOLENCE

A majority of Americans are fatalistic about war: 58 per cent agree that "human nature being what it is, there must always be war and conflict" [Table 6]. Nearly two thirds justify war as a legitimate instrument of political policy: "In dealing with other countries in the world, we are frequently justified in using military force." And nearly three fourths agree that "It is unfortunate that many civilians are killed in a war, but this cannot be avoided."

At the same time, a substantial minority is disenchanted with the U.S. policy: almost four out of 10 agree that "Our government is too ready to use military force in dealing with other countries." Women are more likely than men to believe this (44 per cent to 34 per cent), and blacks more than whites (44 per cent to 38 per cent). Surprisingly, approval of our government's policy increases modestly with education: among those with an eighth-grade education or less, 42 per cent agree with the statement compared to only 34 per cent of the college-educated.

Now we may legitimately ask: are we a violent people?

More than two in five adults in our country are gun owners, and one out of 17 of us has been victimized by one of those guns.

We believe it is good for little boys to have some fistfights during childhood; and one out of five American males keeps it up after becoming an adult.

The willingness to use corporal punishment on children and each other is common to all classes, ages, regions and races, although we persist in acknowledging only lower-class violence.

We are suspicious of due process and civil liberties; one in four of us upholds vigilante preparations to resist "conspiracies," and one in 10 would join in armed assault on antiwar protesters. (Yet only one in 11 would fight to defend freedom of speech and only one in 14 whites would fight to defend blacks from unlawful and unjustified mass imprisonment.)

The majority expect death threats for politicians who "try to change things too fast"; one in five thinks that those politicians who have their lives threatened probably deserve it; and one out of 11 has favorably contemplated the death of some of our political figures.

While we systematically destroy societies and people in Southeast Asia, we deny that we employ our might unreasonably, we dismiss the civilian casualties as unavoidable and we regard war as inevitable.

Are Americans a violent people?

Drive into almost any medium-sized town in the United States and you will invariably find the McDonald's golden arches, Colonel Sanders' Fried Chicken and a Holiday Inn. However, you now find the same establishments (or not so subtle imitations) throughout the world. American styles of life may be decried throughout the world but no other life style is as emulated. Supermarkets and drive-ins are found throughout the world. American television shows predominate (with or without subtitles) in all continents and in the Paris flea market one of the most sought after commodities is a well worn pair of American blue jeans.

Familiarity with only selected aspects of American life styles often results in stereotypical images of Americans. A study of Canadian university students found that they stereotyped Americans as "aggressive, outspoken, and manipulative, money-status-power hungry. . . . [The American] wants to take over the whole world and cram the 'American way' of government, industry, and social life down the throats of unwilling victims." *

These same students stereotyped the Canadian as "ultraconservative, uncertain, inhibited, and passive. He is reserved, self-conscious, intellectual, aloof, critical, and dull. Although money and achievement oriented, he is cautious and not inclined toward risk taking." †

Although these conceptions are overgeneralized, they are based on real elements of American (and Canadian) life styles and a recognition that the way Americans live has an extensive influence outside their national boundaries. Over 90 percent of all Canadians live within 200 miles of the United States border and are engulfed by American life styles. Europe may be influenced by American life styles, but Canada is dominated by them. Until recently, there has been a strong sense of Canadian inferiority and a lack of Canadian identity. (In addition to the influence of the United States, there has also been traditional British influence.)

Canadian nationalism is becoming a real force, but unlike United States nationalism, it is a movement of the political left. By legislation, colleges and universities in Ontario are limiting the number of Americans on their faculties. Sociology courses in Canada are no longer mirror images of courses taught in the United States but now contain "Canadian content." A certain percentage of popular music heard over Canadian radio stations must be written and performed by Canadians. Thus we are seeing an effort to create a distinct Canadian life style. Although

---

* A. H. Diemer and M. L. Dietz, "Canadian University Students' Stereotypes of Canadians and Americans." *McGill Journal of Education.* 5 (Spring 1970). p. 3.
  † *Ibid.*

one can legislate against certain types of American dominance, one cannot by legislation create a Canadian life style. American radio and television remain very much a part of Canadian life, and American styles of life will continue to diffuse into Canada. On the other hand, very little of the Canadian life style becomes diffused into the United States, and that small part may lose much of its Canadian character. For years, the National Hockey League was relatively small with about an equal number of teams in Canada and the United States. When this league expanded, most of the new teams were in the United States; this sport has thus lost some of its Canadian character (even though most players are still Canadian).

The following article by a Canadian professor of French Literature explores some aspects of the love-hate relationship with American life styles that many Canadians experience.

"Living Next Door to an Elephant:" Canadian Reactions to the American Ethos

H. A. Bouraoui

A member of one culture is in a privileged position when he examines another because he is capable of objectivity that comes with distance from his subject. But his view may also be distorted by his own cultural interferences and self-interest — after all, we are, each of us, at the center of our own world vision, even though the world at large may insistently demonstrate its total indifference to our existence.

This article was prepared especially for this book.

Nowhere is this generalization more true than in the love-hate relationship between the United States and Canada, both despite and because of the often-repeated fact that between them lies the longest undefended border in the world.

A chance remark made by Prime Minister Pierre Elliott Trudeau during the financial crisis of 1971 when Canada was still reeling from President Nixon's imposition of trade restrictions and a surcharge on imported goods accurately delimits the Canadian awe of the United States, tinged at times with distrust. He commented that Canadians must realize that living just across the border from the United States is like living next door to an elephant: the elephant is displaying no personal animus, but if it just happens to roll over, its neighbor may inadvertently be crushed. Concomitant with the Trudeau analogy, of course, is the assumption that the unfortunate neighbor is a hapless mouse, a literally accurate image if he was thinking of a sparsely settled nation of 20,000,000 living next to the world's richest nation, with a population of 220,000,000. But his figure of speech also betrays the omnipresent Canadian inferiority complex whose anxieties at having a "branch-plant economy" are exacerbated by the well-documented fear that it also has a "branch-plant" cultural identity. It is difficult for Americans, coping with the catastrophic effects at home and abroad, war in the wrong place at the wrong time, and with the consequent neglect, "benign" or otherwise, of civil rights, women's rights, the poor, education, to become very excited about the Canadian "identity crisis." But this crisis is a very real part of the reassessment of values and priorities in North America at large. One cannot resist the suspicion, also, that the witty and politically aware Trudeau may have chosen the "elephant" simile deliberately to suggest the increased perils of, not a peaceful, but a productive coexistence with a conservative Republican administration.

When we refer to "Canadian culture," we should realize that we are speaking of a useful, but largely fictitious construct. It has been said that Canada is really not one nation, but five, roughly divided up regionally from east to west. Thus, when we discuss Canadian reactions to the United States, we are mythologizing, because there is no single response but a whole spectrum of attitudes which become clearer as we move from coast to coast. For the most part, these attitudes are tied in with economic and geographical factors, because of the common element of self-interest.

The Maritime provinces have a bond with northern New England, whose fishing, hunting, and tourist resources they share, and who live off the produce of land and sea, like their neighbors. On the opposite coast, British Columbia, similarly, leans towards the U.S. West Coast in its life style, values, and economy, rather than towards the Toronto-Ottawa hub. The Prairie Provinces, as one might expect, produce the meat and grain for their nation, much like their neighbors across the border in North Dakota, Montana, and Wyoming.

As an inhabitant of Ontario, the richest province, and as a member myself of a francophone culture, most of my illustrations of Canadian attitudes towards the United States are drawn from the peculiar triangle — almost in the sexual sense — of Ontario, the United States, and Québec. Québec, as a "have-not" province, harbors the deepest resentment and distrust of Ontario, and looks to the United States to restore the balance of power. In fact, many radical Québec separatists would, if offered the choice, probably prefer to be annexed by the United States than to remain, as they conceive it, under the yoke of "les Anglais" — the English Canadians.

The federal government's official policy of bilingualism and biculturalism has apparently served only to widen the gap between French and English Canada, which tends to feel that it is too much to expect two-thirds of the country to become readily conversant with the native tongue of only one-third of the population. In point of fact, French Canadians come closer to achieving the expressed ideal, although they will often chauvinistically pretend that they do not speak or understand English. By achieving fluency in Enlish they may be making a virtue of necessity, since they have little choice in a British Commonwealth nation. English-speaking Canadians often seem to feel, on the other hand, that the promotion of bilingualism and biculturalism is tantamount to granting special privileges to French Canada.

In view of the fact that a New Yorker or Midwesterner traveling in Ontario would have a little difficulty, linguistically and culturally, discerning just when he has crossed the border, and that it has probably never occurred to him to distinguish between his Canadian friends living in the States and Americans, it is perhaps paradoxical that Ontario should be the focus and source of most anti-American sentiment in Canada. On further consideration, however, the reason for the resentment is apparent: it is the very blurring of the Canadian identity with that of their neighbors to the south which they find disturbing. While Americans, by and large, intend no harm — in fact, if they thought about it, would probably consider it a compliment to treat their neighbors as themselves — Canadians have become increasingly sensitive in recent years to American domination of the media, of literature, education, and international politics.

Québec, in contrast to Ontario, is experiencing no "identity crisis," whatever else. Possessing a separate language and culture as well as a distinctive religion, the Québecois are sure enough of who they are to experience little fear of an American "takeover." On the economic level, they welcome any investment from whatever source.

Not surprisingly in this context, when we speak of Canadian films, music, literature, we are in most instances looking at *French* Canada which has produced a rich, albeit in some ways provincial utterance. Far too often English Canada, in the arts, produces only laments on American domination. As Robert Barlow, a free-lance Toronto writer, editorialized in the Toronto *Star:*

> *It seems fashionable these days to be anti-American. Our writers and poets warn us about the horrors advancing from the south: solemn professors tell us it may already be too late; students in the campuses around the land protest against the hiring of Americans and complain as if everything were American-controlled, including their own wills.*
>
> *But all this is nothing more than cant. It's shallow and provincial, and as long as our writers keep talking about unfortunate Canada and the American threat, we're going to continue having a second-rate literature because we overlook our own qualities in attacking the faults of the United States.*[1]

Although we are talking principally about the reactions of two major clearly differentiated cultures, English and French Canadian, this division is an oversimplification. The "English" Canadian — the immigrant from the British Isles or the descendant of immigrants — is himself becoming as minuscule a part of the population as he already is in the United States. There is, to be sure, clearly in evidence a

---

[1] Robert Barlow, "U.S. has nothing to be ashamed of and neither do we," The Toronto *Star,* February 1, 1973, p. 6.

British tradition in the Parliament, the bewigged lawyers, the Honors Degrees in university. Canadians never forget that much of the founding population of their country was composed of United Empire Loyalists in full flight from the south during the American Revolution, and this has engendered in some Canadians a suspicion that they are historically really "Beautiful Losers," to borrow the title of Leonard Cohen's novel, fleeing from radical experimentation to the protecting wing of the British Empire. There still persists a certain tension between the British heritage and the American linguistic and cultural influence whose proximity makes it more powerful even though the legal-governmental ties are absent.

Modern Canada is, however, not so much a bilingual, bicultural as a multilingual, multi-cultural country. Prime Minister Trudeau has referred to it as a "cultural mosaic," in which important aspects of different ethnic groups should be preserved. The "mosaic" is obviously opposed to the "melting pot" concept of assimilation and cultural homogeneity which governs American society and which many Canadians feel has proven to be a failure in practice. But the "mosaic" ideal in practice also has its shortcomings: it tends to degenerate into the "cuteness" and quaintness of, for instance, the Kitchener "Oktoberfest."

The second largest ethnic grouping in metropolitan Toronto is Italian, and the Italians have done much to lend some Mediterranean warmth, color, and verve to a gray city which used to be known as "Toronto the Good," city of churches and the Puritan ethic.

Other sizable immigrant groups include Israelis and Central European Jews, Ukrainians, Germans, Greeks, and Yugoslavs, who are not "English" Canadians, though for the most part they do tend to become anglophone rather than francophone, largely because of employment opportunities. Many of these groups have relatives in the States, and take no particular interest in the U.S.-Canadian conflict.

It is also important to remember that there is a tremendous cleavage between reactions to the American ethos on the part of the media, the wealthy industrialists and businessmen, university professors, writers and intellectuals — the upper middle class generally — and the average working man, the hypothetical "man in the street." Broadly speaking, the anti-Americanism there is probably receives an inordinate amount of publicity for its extent, because it stems from the upper middle classes and the most articulate Canadians. The working man, on the other hand, is inclined to consider good relations with the United States as, if not a moral, at least a financial imperative, since his firm invariably does most of its business across the border, and may in many instances be an American subsidiary. It is important to remember also that some anti-American sentiment elsewhere in Canada is promulgated by the principal voice of Ontario, the Toronto *Star*, with the largest circulation in Canada, which is much given to inveighing against the American "threat."

For the most part, in dealing with Anglophone Canadian reactions to America, we cannot speak of "cultural shocks," but rather of cultural "glissements" — of subtle nuances and shadings which an American would probably have to live in Canada to discover. For instance, an Ontario accent is virtually identical with the speech pattern of western New York and the American Midwest and infinitely closer to "General American" than a Bronx or a Texas or a Georgia accent. The one difference I can detect is the faintly Scottish echo in words containing the syllable "-out." The initiated also know to spell "programme" and "colour" in the English manner, but with American textbooks dominating the market and "Sesame Street" children's television, this is scarcely a sure indication of a native-born Canadian.

Major cultural themes in which Canadians betray an overriding fear of American influence fall into one of three categories: politics, if loosely enough defined to include economics, education, and the arts. These three concerns in the broadly based symbiotic American-Canadian relationship are funneled through the various media and modes of articulation from which we can disengage meaningful and comprehensible patterns. The confrontation of American value systems with Canadian interpretations, by exploiting different techniques of cultural criticism, can offer fresh insights on both cultures.

The political relationship between Canada and the United States has undergone drastic changes in recent years since the Vietnam War has served as a catalyst. Perhaps the Canadian revulsion at the war and alarm at the consequent U.S. economic and trade crisis, however, only brought to the surface and crystallized both the Canadian resentment of American high-handedness and the Canadian inferiority complex. In psychological terms, Canada manifests on the political level a kind of national paranoid schizophrenia in relation to the United States. Canadians are paranoid in assuming that Nixon's repressive trade restraints were aimed at "getting them" in particular, rather than the more obvious targets of West Germany and Japan. The news media not so subtly reflected this view by publishing photographs of Nixon and John Connolly, then Treasury Secretary, "talking tough" about trade. It was obvious that the photographer had selected the least flattering, most grotesque shots, in which every facial line and shadow revealed ruthlessness and insensitivity. Similarly, in political cartoons Nixon and Connolly were almost always lampooned.

During the 1972 Presidential campaign, both Canadian television and newspapers promptly espoused the cause of Senator George McGovern — not, so far as one could tell, because of his stand on the war, but principally because he was judged sympathetic to Canada as a North Dakotan who had lived there for a time and who felt, as a border state senator, that Nixon's financial policies were disastrous for Canadians. In fact, from whatever film we saw on the networks or from newspaper reports, Canadian reporters on the Washington beat invariably questioned the Senator only on their own financial and identity problems, rarely touching even on the question of draft resisters who had fled to their country.

The Canadian persecution complex is balanced by a tremendous drive to be admired and respected by their neighbors (even when this drive comes into conflict with some of their own denunciations of American policies or of the "American Dream" in general). Some aspects of this split personality are thoroughly human, likable, and understandable. They are never quite sure whether to be relieved that they do not share the American "guilt," or to feel impotent because they are so often disregarded as a world power. Recently, the NBC News ran a feature on how the United States, in abandoning the draft, was using the Canadian Volunteer Army as a model for its own. They praised the Canadian attitude towards the honor and respectability of a military career. Just a few days later, the Canadian CTV network picked up the NBC film clip, and the Canadian anchorman was visibly moved that the Americans were looking to Canada for help. Similarly, the Canadians take enormous pride in the fact that Toronto-born and -educated CBS newsman Morley Safer "was one of the first television journalists to blow the whistle on American terrorism in Viet Nam." [2] They would like desperately to believe that their Parliamentary condemnation of President Nixon's final saturation bombing of North Vietnam had some effect on the subsequent resumption of the Paris peace talks.

Canadians display a remarkable objectivity, detachment, and balanced judgment concerning the war and its aftermath. No Canadian viewer could have failed to remark that, when President Nixon announced the ceasefire finally on the evening of January 23, the CBS network cut away briefly from the Entertainer of the Year awards and then promptly returned to Liza Minnelli, Joel Grey, Ed Sullivan, and Tanya the Elephant. The Canadian CBC and CTV, on the other hand, preempted the rest of their prime-time programming in favor of lengthy news specials on the background of the war. Since that night, the Canadian news media have consistently presented a proud picture of Canada's subsequent peacekeeping role, replete with jokes from the soldiers hoping that their green berets will not be mistaken for American ones by the Viet Cong and North Vietnamese.

The Canadian view of the United States is, however, also schizophrenic in a more ominous sense. The attitude towards the American presence in Canada is ambivalent. At times it feeds the Canadian sense of their own moral superiority, but at times it feeds their fear of a takeover. Thus, the draft resisters are consistently welcomed, and Canada pats itself on the back when, after the ceasefire, many still affirm their desire to stay and become citizens. As the *Star* headline reads, "War Resisters: We Still Don't Want to Go Back." [3] Less welcoming, however, is the attitude towards other American immigrants, whether refugees from urban violence, the war, or disenchanted liberals of various stripes. These are frequently regarded as mere economic opportunists, and the "Yankee Go Home" attitude is much in evidence.

---

[2] Stan Fischler, "Veteran TV newsman says Viet Nam peace brings no one honor," The Toronto *Star,* January 27, 1973, p. 20.

[3] The Toronto *Star,* January 27, 1973, p. 21.

In 1971, for the first time, U.S.-born immigrants displaced British as the most numerous group. Even more remarkably, the 24,424 American immigrants to Canada was almost double the number of Canadian immigrants to the United States (13,128). In contrast to these figures, in the early 1960's there were more than three times as many Canadian immigrants to the United States as the reverse.

Canadians are pleased that Americans are increasingly coming to accept the judgment stated by then energies minister Joe Greene in Denver in 1970, that the American Dream "in some ways has turned into a nightmare":

> *Viet Nam and Cambodia, disorder in the streets and on the campus, the disaffection of the poor, the colored people and youth, indicate to many of our people, particularly our young, that we should not seek to make the American dream ours.*[4]

Yet Americans who move to Canada to escape these very evils are frequently greeted with distrust or open hostility. Canadians like to feel that Americans display "a predilection for violence" whereas they themselves demonstrate "a preference for settling disputes by law or compromise."[5] They attribute this to "the historical fact that the U.S. frontiers were opened up by violence while law and order was established in Canada, mostly by the Mounted Police, before or as the pioneers moved into the lonely lands."[6]

One occasionally detects in Canada, however, a certain tendency to smug self-righteousness which fails to take cognizance of the fact that Canada is still a very young, undersettled, growing country, and that it is even now beginning to experience growing pains with an increase in the rate of violent crime in its cities, and all the other problems of urban sprawl. Canadians, too, are competing to see which bank can build the highest skyscraper, and are studying how to exclude certain kinds of immigration that might take jobs from Canadians. My overall impression, however, is that they are conscious of the pitfalls of increasing population and crowded cities, largely because of the dismal American experience, and that they are at least planning to combat these dangers.

Trudeau's apparently tactless statement in Moscow that "the overpowering presence of the United States poses dangers to Canada's national identity from a cultural, economic and perhaps even military point of view" touched off controversy in both countries and leant open encouragement to the paranoia of some Canadian nationalists.[7] Many Canadians simplistically hold *all* Americans responsible for the war, despite the presence in their midst of so many of the disenchanted. The *Star*, for instance, reports the naive response of one Saskatchewan couple who used to do much of their holiday shopping across the border in Great Falls, Montana. But now, as the husband remarked, "I didn't want to spend even our little bit of money in the United States. I didn't want to help down

---

[4] Jack Cahill, "Legacy of war: Many Canadians distrust the U.S.," The Toronto *Star*, January 27, 1973, p. 4.

[5] Ibid.

[6] Ibid.

[7] Ibid.

there in any way." [8] Needless to say, he hasn't thought of the possibility that a high proportion of the goods he buys in Saskatchewan are U.S. imports, and that he is helping, like it or not — like many U.S. citizens — whether he buys in the States or not.

The increasing distrust of Americans has been manifested especially on the level of post-secondary education. Because almost all universities are provincially funded, now that serious unemployment among Ph.D.'s is rampant on both sides of the border, the "Yankee Professors," which one cartoon depicts coming over in a boatload, are to be blamed, even though the universities are hiring hardly anyone, least of all Americans, at present, and although those already in Canada came up at a time when the universities were expanding rapidly and there weren't enough Canadians to staff them. Now there are demands that Americans who have been teaching in Canada for years become citizens or lose their positions. As one American teaching in Canada warned, this attitude may have unfortunate repercussions when the employment situation improves marginally in the United States but worsens in Canada, so that Canadians are once again forced to look across the border themselves for positions.

It is startling to find just pages away from a lucid analysis of the American mistakes in the war a lead editorial denouncing York University for appointing an American (Chairman of the Philosophy Department) as Acting President in the wake of the President's resignation. The editorial is

headlined "York Presidency: Relic of the Colonial Campus," and is full of the most loaded or misinformed statements in an effort to manipulate the Canadian taxpayer.[9] It begins with the rhetorical, self-pitying question, "Is Canadian higher education so weak in administrative talent that York University can find only American citizens to qualify for its presidency?" This ignores the fact that, considering the power struggle which triggered the President's resignation, they were lucky to find someone capable and willing to step in and set the house in order, and that it is not the Presidency in any case which is in question, but the *Acting* Presidency. Secondly, the editorial taunts taxpayers with the fact that "Canada . . . still maintains an income tax holiday for foreign teachers who go home after two years — a direct legacy from the days when Britain thought its scholars should be coaxed abroad to enlighten the colonies." This statement blithely ignores the fact that the tax "holiday" is a reciprocal treaty arrangement with countries which give visiting *Canadian* teachers the same break. And the writer slips in a hidden and totally unfair analogy between British Colonialism of the nineteenth century and the until-recent North American tendency to treat U.S. and Canadian degrees as reciprocal and the North American continent as a single free market on the intellectual level.

Canadians are delighted, on the other hand, when American intellectuals seek to deepen their knowledge of Canadian affairs. After being understandably offended by President

[8] Ibid., p. 1.

[9] The Toronto *Star,* January 25, 1973, p. 6.

Nixon's *gaffe* in referring to Japan, rather than Canada, as the largest U.S. trading partner, they have been compensated by witnessing the growth of a new U.S. clique, "the Canada-watchers." As the *Star*'s Ottawa editor, Peter Desbarats, put it, "the American 'elephant' is no longer as dumb or as uninformed about Canada as many Canadians continue to imagine." [10] But he shrewdly warns Canadians that knowledge is not necessarily to be equated with sympathy, and that, "On the contrary, the most benevolent attitudes toward Canada are found today among the many Americans who still know nothing about Canada. . . ."

A few years ago a Canadian TV network presented "Countdown Canada," a nightmare image of the future in which Canada is literally annexed by its nextdoor neighbor, thus bearing out Walt Whitman's alarming prophecy in *Democratic Vistas*. Even if such aspirations are the last thing from the minds of most Americans, Canadians do fear the danger of America's often arrogant assertions that it has a *right* to their natural resources, especially during the current energy crisis. But they also hope to use their resources as a trump card during the upcoming trade negotiations.

In many ways Canadians worry about their inability to compete equally with the United States even in in the field of sports, where the media lavish tremendous attention on the outstanding people they do have. The most striking example of their near-

hysteria was the reaction to the hockey victory of Team Canada over Russia, after the Olympic débâcle in which the U.S. and Russia walked off with all the honors. They saw the victory as a vindication of the national ego, as one area in which they are really first. The team were made national heroes, and for one feverish week all one heard were choruses of "O Canada" sung by team and sports fans with tears streaming down their faces. As one man commented, "It makes me proud to be a Canadian." In the euphoria that followed, only a few poets and intellectuals like Irving Layton wondered aloud whether a hockey victory was really the best reason one could come up with for national pride. Ironically, too, most members of Team Canada were drawn from U.S. teams because Canada cannot really afford to support many players.

Also on the lighter side, a recent Canadian university conference was concerned with the journalistic failure of Canadian "pop art" in the form of comic strips. "Superman," for instance, was originally Canadian: "Metropolis" was modelled on Toronto, and the "Daily Planet" on the "Toronto Star" — but again, the market was substantial only in the United States and the original identification with Canada has been long forgotten. As one American artist commented, "There's no use setting up a new comic industry in Canada. Comics are dying. What's a promoter supposed to say? 'Let's go set up a dying industry in Canada'?" [11]

[10] Peter Desbarats, "Canada-watchers: A new U.S. clique," The Toronto *Star,* November 30, 1972, p. 9.

[11] Warren Clements, "Cosmicon II," *Excalibur,* February 1, 1973, p. 11.

Canadians show a marked ambivalence towards national celebrities who emigrated to the United States in search of fame and fortune, and they vacillate accordingly between boastfulness and a sense of betrayal and loss. Canadian consuls in the United States can even supply lists of Canadian-born stars now living and working mainly in the States: Raymond Burr, Christopher Plummer, William Shatner, Lorne Greene, John Vernon, Arthur Hill, etc. The truth is that most American audiences are unaware of their Canadian origins, unless there was some clear connection with the Stratford Festival, and that these actors are invariably cast as Americans. Canadian TV listings and reviews of American shows and films, however, always inform us that "Canadian actor ——— appears in such and such a role." One journalist tried to envision the reaction of the American Consul on University Avenue, Toronto, if one were to ask him for a list of famous Americans who have immigrated to Canada (it would probably start and end with Henry Morgan).

In reacting to America, it is important to remember that Canadians are in large measure reacting against the American failure to be interested in them — or, at any rate, to be interested in them as *Canadians*. Broadcaster Pierre Berton made a point recently of asking a number of American celebrities about their mental image of Canada, and time and again was fed back the stereotype: mountains, snow, clean air, a slower pace, the Mounties, "Canadian Sunset," Calgary Stampede, "Rose Marie" and all. Berton commented that Americans see Canada only through rose-colored glasses, as a vacation-land or playground; but watching the program, I had rather mixed feelings, since I was at least as much impressed by the typically Canadian Berton's prickliness on the subject and obsession with asking the question, as with the Americans' characteristic Utopianism based on ignorance. Indeed, I was forcibly struck by how really *North American* Berton's concern with a national image was, rather than, for instance, English. The concern is rather touching, since both Americans and Canadians are open-minded, if rather insecure, in caring intensely what others think of them. Actor Arthur Hill perceptively remarks that the Americans' image of Canada is, if anything, complimentary, for they see Canada as a new, unspoiled frontier, as their own was in the early nineteenth century. He further comments that American film and television makers frequently cast him as an American of one hundred or more years ago, because something in his craggy, open Canadian face seems to remind Americans of their own more innocent past.

Except for the news shows, one would be hard put to define the image the Canadian television industry presents of America, partly because it is difficult to define just what is distinctively Canadian about Anglo-Canadian television. All major Canadian cities are clustered along the relatively temperate U.S. border, but one result of this is that in the Toronto viewing area, for instance, outside of educational television, there are two channels emanating from Toronto — the government-controlled CBC and the independent CTV — one from Hamilton, but four from Buffalo. The four Buffalo channels receive a disproportionate share of the viewing public, which is consequently also largely conditioned in its consumer needs by American advertising. Moreover, both the CBC and CTV subsist mainly on American programs which they steal a march on by running a week or so earlier than the U.S. networks. Commercially profitable as this practice may be, it does little to promote an awareness of a separate Canadian cultural identity.

The Canadian film industry, similarly, provides only the most oblique commentary on U.S.-Canadian relations. The most successful films, both artistically and financially, are deliberately provincial and as often as not French Canadian. One thinks, for instance of Claude Jutra's *Mon Oncle Antoine* (which American critics recently voted the best foreign film which received insufficient attention), *La Vraie Nature de Bernadette*, and Paul Almond's films starring his wife, Geneviève Bujold. One notable exception to the French Canadian dominance is Gordon Pinsent's *The Rowdyman*, which is apparently doing better business in Boston than it did in Toronto. But again, *The Rowdyman* is a provincial film, set in Pinsent's home, Newfoundland, and as we have indicated earlier, it is not surprising that New Englanders should appreciate a Maritime mentality. None of these films shows the slightest concern with U.S.-Canadian relations, but rather with the generation gap in Québec, the tension between the urban and rural ways of life, and the whole question of

identity and responsibility in a limited setting — good Faulknerian themes, all! One suspects that most of English-speaking Canada, especially Ontario, cannot generate successful films out of a culture that is not clearly distinguishable from that of its wealthier neighbors to the south.

French Canada, under the impetus of a general French tradition seen from a provincial setting, has produced many noted authors — Anne Hébert, Marie-Claire Blais, Régean Ducharme, Jacques Godbout, the poets Gaston Miron, Jean-Guy Pilon, Robert Charleboie — whose works are recognized and appreciated in France and Europe generally as well as in Canada. Québec chansonniers like Gilles Vigneault and Pauline Julien also use their art as a protest against the Anglo-Canadian political dominance. But nothing from French Canada indicates a preoccupation with the American presence.

Anglo-Canadians, however, offer strong resistance to the view that they are poor stepchildren grafted onto the American Dream. Their literature tends to expend most of its energy on invective directed against the surrogate American culture which they feel has been imposed on them. Recent characteristic expressions of the Canadian fear that it has sold its birthright to the American giant are the poet Margaret Atwood's novel, *Surfacing*, which views the Americans as monsters creeping up from the south, and her book of literary essays, *Survival*, whose title indicates what she takes to be the key theme in Canadian literature: the attempt to merely survive in the face of the overwhelming American cultural dominance. This key motif she contrasts to the central symbol in American literature, the Frontier, and in English, the Island.[12]

The Americans, she feels, tend to stress victory and the American Dream, whereas Canadians identify with the suffering victims. One of her opening epigraphs, from Germaine Warkentin, sets the tone for the book: "No other country cares enough about us to give us back an image of ourselves that we can even resent." Conversely, she must care deeply about America because she has no difficulty in conjuring up an image that Americans are bound to resent. What she tends to forget is that the greatest American writers were themselves critical of the American undercurrent of violence, anti-intellectualism, and imperialism long before Canadians began to be concerned, so that she reads their works as a surface affirmation of an American ethos which, in many cases, they were repudiating. She misses the point, for instance, that Hemingway was a conservationist who felt that Africa was the last unspoiled continent, and identifies him instead with the simple-minded American hunters who cross the border to take pot shots at deer, elk, and bears, without regard to the preservation of the species. The Hemingway hunting ritual, in fact, demands a close partnership with nature: the desire to "tame" and shape her is more French than American or Canadian. Atwood believes that American

"animal stories" focus on the hunter, whereas Canadian ones are "about animals being killed, as felt emotionally from inside the fur and feathers" (p. 74). Thus Americans "are the killers, Canadians are the killed" (p. 77). The American hero is, moreover, strongly individualistic, even to the point of alienation (p. 174), whereas Canada, which sees itself as "a collective victim" (p. 36), can conceive of only "collective heroes" (p. 172).

She depicts various aspects of the American frontier mythos: the extinction of the "good Indians" (Cooper's *Last of the Mohicans*); the family, which is "a skin you shed" whereas in Canada "it's a trap in which you're caught" (p. 131); the immigrant's "leap into the melting pot" in contrast to the Canadian "mosaic" (p. 149). But she fails to consider that Natty Bumppo is as extinct as Chingachgook; that Thomas Wolfe's *You Can't Go Home Again* and Fitzgerald's *The Great Gatsby* have heroes who never escape their obsession with a dead past; and that Cather depicts poignantly the serious cultural loss suffered by her assimilated immigrants. In other words, American writers themselves were the first to perceive the dark side of the American Dream, the Melvillean "power of blackness."

Atwood writes that "If the central European experience is sex and the central mystery 'what goes on in the bedroom,' and if the central American experience is killing and the central mystery is 'what goes on in the forest' (or in the slum streets), surely the central Canadian experience is death and the central mystery is "what goes

---

[12] Margaret Atwood, *Survival* (Toronto: House of Anansi, 1972), p. 32. All subsequent references to this edition will appear in the text.

on in the coffin' " (p. 222). In reacting to the American literary image, however, Atwood is revealing as much of Canada as of America, for the preoccupation with killing is only a small part of the preoccupation with death shared by North American writers, starting with Brockden Brown and Poe. American writers, like Canadian, have as often as not elected to side with the victim — and I am thinking not only of the "Jewish novel" of Bellow and Malamud or the "black novel" of Ellison and Baldwin, but also of Hemingway, Fitzgerald, Faulkner.

Atwood speculates that a Canadian would have told *Moby Dick* from the point of view of the whale (p. 74). Actually, of course, Ahab is the "loser," not the whale, and Melville does attempt, insofar as possible, to present the whale's "side of the story." I suspect, in fact, that if a Canadian were to write a new *Moby Dick*, he would identify with Ahab and see the monstrous whale, "the monomaniac incarnation of all those malicious agencies which some deep men feel eating in them," as a symbol for the encroaching Americans! [13] Trudeau's choice of an elephant symbol for the United States, incidentally, supports this view.

Margaret Atwood's theory is more than a bit apologetic and defensive, especially after D. H. Lawrence and others have said many of the same things about *American* literature, as being an escape from the relative freedom of Europe, an evasion. One also wonders how she can support this

theory of the American consciousness in Hawthorne, Melville, James, who were concerned about the supposed cultural inferiority of America to the long European tradition. But her analysis, which has been on the bestseller list for many weeks now, is symptomatic of current Canadian popular opinions of the United States.

On further consideration, one begins to suspect that if Americans see their idealized past in contemporary Canada, Canadians might — and should — foresee their possible futures in America and learn to avoid making the same mistakes. The sociologist Edgar Friedenburg claims that Canada lacks a tragic sense[14] — but so, a little more than a century ago, did the United States, when Hawthorne complained of "the difficulty of writing a romance about a country where there is no shadow, no antiquity, no picturesque and gloomy wrong, nor anything but a commonplace prosperity, in broad and simple daylight, as is happily the case with my dear native land." [15] America was soon enough to develop a tragic sense, first with the Civil War and now in our time with the Vietnam War. French Canadians have a similar sense of alienation, loss of innocence, if not a tragic sense. The country as a whole came close to experiencing tragedy in the crisis of October 1970. Hopefully Canadians may learn vicariously from

[13] Herman Melville, *Moby Dick* (New York: Modern Library, 1950), p. 183.

[14] Quoted by Rob Barlow, "Education expert calls Canadians leftover bits," *Excalibur,* February 1, 1973, p. 4.
[15] Nathaniel Hawthorne, "Author's Preface" to *The Marble Faun* (New York: Pocket Library, 1958), p. xi.

American errors without having to commit them themselves. They may then achieve a firm enough self-confidence to produce an indigenous and ambitious art without succumbing to self-pity and despair. Then they may learn to judge themselves as objectively as — at least in those matters where their own self-interest does not interfere — they now judge Americans.

THE IMPACT OF SOCIAL CATEGORIES AND GROUPS: LIFE STYLE VARIATIONS

The belief that Americans share a common life style has led some to say that there is a distinct American national character.* In Part 1, the theme of the American life style was developed through examination of that which all Americans share. In this unit, we shall look for differences rather than similarities.

A paradox appears in that the United States is characterized at the same time by both uniformity and diversity. Diversity of life styles generally has been inferred from the investigation of many aspects of everyday life,† however, behavior patterns are often studied without

---

* David Riesman, "Some Questions About the Study of American Character in the Twentieth Century," *The Annals* 370 (March 1967):36–47.

† For examples of the study of every day life, see Erving Goffman, *Presentation of Self in Everyday Life* (Garden City, N.Y.: Doubleday, 1958); *Interaction Ritual: Essays in Face-to-Face Behavior* (Chicago: Aldine, 1967); Harold Garfinkel, *Studies in Ethnomethodology* (Englewood Cliffs, N.J.: Prentice-Hall, 1967); and Alfred Schutz, *Collected Papers, I: The Problem of Social Reality* (The Hague: Martinus, Nijhoff, 1962).

regard to how they are related to life style. For example, the survey researcher might investigate the relationship between political party preference and religion without trying to ascertain the central life interests of individuals. Or observational studies might be conducted of a situation — for example, life within schools, hospitals, or prisons — ignoring the relationship of behavior to influences outside the particular setting.*

Descriptive studies may show that both executives and skilled workers engage in some of the same leisure activities, but further investigation may reveal that this same behavior reflects two distinct life styles. Recreation for an executive may mean a temporary escape from work (so that he can function better when he returns to the office) or may serve as an informal setting for business contacts. For a skilled worker, recreation may serve as a family-centered activity. Thus leisure activities for executives may be integrated with their central life interest of career, while for skilled workers a reflection of their central life interest of family.†

To identify life styles, it is not enough to study minute facets of everyday life — e.g., card playing or telephoning.‡ Patterns of leisure and communication, superstition, death and mourning, marriage ceremonies, and routine aspects of family life are all aspects of daily activity, but to understand them, one should study these activities as part of a larger social context. Anthropologists, more than other social scientists, study a variety of aspects of daily life attempting to uncover a theme that explains how these many mundane activities are interrelated.§

The description and analysis of life styles is not limited to social and behavioral scientists and indeed some of the selections in this book were

* For a discussion of some negative consequences of such narrow focus, see Virginia Olesen and Elvi Whittaker, *The Silent Dialogue* (San Francisco: Jossey-Bass, 1968) pp. 2–13.

† See e.g., "The Working Man: Do Marketing Men Know Him?," *Printer's Ink.* 277 (December 1, 1961), pp. 48–49.

‡ Irving Crespi, "The Social Significance of Card Playing as a Leisure Time Activity," *American Sociological Review,* 21 (1956) pp., 717–721; Donald W. Ball, "Toward a Sociology of Telephones and Telephoners," in Marcello Truzzi (ed.), *Sociology and Everyday Life* (Englewood Cliffs, N.J.: Prentice-Hall, 1967) pp. 59–75.

§ See e.g., Elman R. Service, *Profiles in Ethnology* (New York: Harper, 1963; H. G. Barnett, *Becoming a Palauan* (New York: Holt, 1960); C. W. M. Hart and Arnold R. Pilling, *The Tiwi of North Australia* (New York: Holt, 1960); Roger C. Owen, James Deetz, and Anthony Fisher, *The North American Indians: A Source Book* (New York: Macmillan, 1967).

written by journalists; however, none of the articles in this book are mere descriptions. Life styles occur within some social context or social situation; hence, as sociologists we want to know the effect of social variables upon life styles. Variables that have a significant effect on American life styles include age, sex, marital status, occupation, education, race and ethnicity, and geographic region.

Social scientists are often interested in how life styles are affected by group membership or by being in a particular social category. A social category is a way of describing individuals' social characteristics such as age, race or sex. Individuals are also characterized by their membership in certain groups. Groups are identifiable collectivities of people (two or more) who interact with each other or who take each other into account.

Not all social categories or group memberships are equally important in delineating life styles; consequently one of the goals of social science is to learn which factors are important and why. The importance of a given variable may differ from person to person. For example, two individuals may join a group such as a Chinese cooking class. The first individual may learn a few culinary skills and that would be all. The same class for the other individual may assume a great deal of importance. An individual might wish to learn more about Chinese culture, might start thinking of becoming a Chinese cook, and begin to develop a life style around things oriental.

Although many variables may be required for explaining a particular person's life style, broad generalizations are possible. For example, on the whole, rich people are happier than poor people,* divorced women are better graduate students than married women,† and blacks are less likely to participate in politics than whites.‡ Knowledge about relationships among variables allows us to make predictions about people's behavior, and nobody is more aware of this than political strategists.

Voting and life styles of voters are bound together. Today, politics are more issue-oriented than in the past. Candidates are more aware than ever that social science can pinpoint what the issues are and who is concerned about them.

---

* *Society Today: Second Edition* (Del Mar, Calif., C.R.M. Books, 1973), p. 197.

† Saul D. Feldman, *Escape from the Doll's House: Women in Graduate and Professional School Education* (New York: McGraw-Hill, 1974), pp. 103–136.

‡ Lester W. Milbrath, *Political Participation: How and Why Do People Get Involved in Politics* (Chicago: Rand McNally, 1965), pp. 110–141.

Where Are the Voters?

Jerry Friedheim

We now know something about how many potential voters there are in the United States and something about where they live. We also are aware that those potential voters have two choices to make as election year rolls around. They must decide not just how to vote, but whether to vote at all.

It is up to us now to identify some general ground rules by which we may find voters and nonvoters, because our history's dramatic electoral turns have been typified not only by the shifting of partisan support between the two major parties but also by changes in the level of voter turnout. Luckily for us, the body politic has been observed and probed for years by politicians with an ear to the ground; and by social-political scientists with sharp pencils and lots of patience; and more recently by Census Bureaucrats with a spare computer or two.

While the significance is weighty, indeed, we can state the facts rather simply. Past experience proves to us that the nation's electorate consists disproportionately of the better-skilled, better-housed, better-educated, better-incomed, better-fed, better-employed and better-informed Americans. In fact, we

From Jerry Friedheim, *Where Are the Voters?* (Washington: National Press, 1968), pp. 27–45. Reprinted by permission.

can state with authority that the average American voter in 1968 will be a suburbanite, white, Anglo-Saxon-stock, Protestant, 44 or 45 years old. And, we expect this characterization to change by 1972 only with the creeping of the age into the earlier forties.

Here is another way of looking at it:

TABLE 1

Those who vote more	Those who vote less
Men	Women
Whites	Nonwhites
Suburbanites	Urbanites
College-trained	Grade-school educated
Middle-incomed	Poor
White-collar workers	Farm workers
Northerners	Southerners
Westerners	Rural residents
Employed	Unemployed
Non-movers	Migrants
Concerned	Disinterested
Partisans	Independents
Middle-aged	Young and old
Republicans	Democrats

Admittedly, those are rather rough categories, but we will classify and subclassify them further as we go along (if we do not run out of percentage points).

Lots of practical political events affect voter turnout in the same way as an individual's personal characteristics do. We know that the turnout rate of persons strongly interested in a campaign runs nearly one-third higher than among those not interested. It is practically a law of human nature that concern over the closeness of an election redoubles a citizen's determination to get to the polls and to do his part to dispell doubt over the outcome. Also, we observe that in close elections the parties work harder to excite their own partisans.

Those partisans, themselves, are more likely to vote than nonpartisans because of their individual commitments to "the cause." Thus, politicians long have championed the value of getting even a $1 contribution or even one day's volunteer work from a citizen, knowing such actions — however limited — will help ensure the involvement and eventual polling of that person's vote.

> Precinct Workers' Note: *If somebody tells you he wants to work, find something for him to do and you will be able to quit worrying about getting that vote out election day.*

There can be no doubt that throughout the history of Western democracies a high value has been placed by social groups on the privilege of the vote franchise — at least until the privilege has been won. Once suffrage has been gained by a group it is in a more powerful position to protect and promote its causes, but it first must gain, without the ballot, enough power of some sort to win the right to vote. That is a formidable task, but American history is evidence that it can be accomplished.

We regard as rather commonplace nowadays the concept and principle of universal suffrage, but it did not emerge in full growth with the instant birth of democratic governments. At first, only a small part of the populace was allowed to vote by "popular" governments. In Western democracies the vote has been gradually and methodically extended to additional groups in studied response to the growing demands of those groups for an end of their political subordination and a beginning of their participation in the management of public affairs.

The first great suffrage battle in the United States was the breaking down of property and taxpaying restrictions on manhood suffrage. Such restrictions were widespread until Jacksonian Democracy began to flourish, propelled by the Frontier and the Old Frontiersmen. As an example, Virginia provided in 1736 that a man must hold 100 acres (or 25 acres with a house) in order to vote in the Old Dominion. In New England the concurrent restrictions were more often in terms of the monetary value of real estate rather than its physical acreage or squarefootage.

After our Revolution (we sometimes forget that we are a revolutionary government), the general social pattern was toward elimination of property restrictions on voting and substitution therefore of taxpaying restrictions. (Even today in bond-issue elections most American communities permit only taxpayers to vote since only taxpayers will be paying off the bonds.) But out in the early American West — in Kentucky and Ohio and Missouri — there was a growing body of impatient and determined men who owned little or no land and paid little or no taxes and yet held to the neo-revolutionary idea that all men were entitled to participate in government. Not that they wanted too much government. What they wanted was virtually unrestricted suffrage for men.

These Frontiersmen managed to find a lot to poke fun at in the complexities of property-regulated voting. One of the most effective of their concatenations on the subject was this wonderful ridicule attributed variously but unusually to patriot-philosopher Thomas Paine:

> *You require that a man shall have 60 dollars worth of property or he shall not vote. Here is a man today who owns a jackass, and the jackass is worth 60 dollars. Today the man is a voter, and he goes to the polls with his jackass and deposits his vote. Tomorrow the jackass dies. The man then goes to vote without his jackass and he cannot vote at all. Now tell me, which was the voter? The man or the jackass?*

From the jackass period of voter restrictions our United States has moved progressively to enlarge the electorate with the 14th amendment providing Negro suffrage and the 19th amendment womanhood suffrage — about both of which we will have more to say later on. As a general rule we still constitutionally recognize that the setting of voting regulations and restrictions is a matter reserved for exercise by state governments, but there are now some federal preemptions in the field.

The Equal-Protection Clause of the 14th Amendment is construed to prevent state discrimination on racial or other grounds in the field of voting. And, the 1965 Voting Rights Act invalidated some voter restrictions in states of the Deep South, but nowhere else even though some more thoughtful politicians suggested that all Americans in all states were entitled to equal protection under that law. Poll taxes have been declared unconstitutional after a long series of court cases, and

the suffrage restrictions still retained by states normally include citizenship, literacy and exclusion of the insane and various inmates.

With the assimilation of women, Negroes and Southerners into the American electorate we have arrived and are arriving still at conditions which dictate the placing of main political campaign emphasis on turning out your side's vote, rather than changing the other side's mind. In a very real sense, modern presidential campaigns are over before they begin. Voter decisions are influenced by and made over many months prior to the election, and the candidate who strikes "furstest with the mostest" can build a virtually unassailable base of strength. The only election-day problem remaining for such a candidate is turning out his vote.

In today's presidential elections the candidates are not looking for a mandate, but for a victory. It does not matter to them where their votes come from so long as they come. Richard Nixon is still wondering where those 12,000 or so voters were that could have tipped five states (Illinois, Missouri, New Mexico, Hawaii and Nevada) and made him 1960's winner.

The significance of relatively small percentage shifts in voter turnout cannot be overestimated. As our electorate grows and grows into the hundreds of millions a shift of a single or even fractional percentage point means a national variation up or down of a million or more votes. It is no secret to politicians that the factor of turnout may govern election outcome. Harry Truman's 1948 election was based in considerable part on the higher degree of turnout among lower-income citizens than had occurred in 1944, coupled with a corresponding decrease in the number of 1948 upper-income voters. On the state and local level many a Republican in a Democratic environment (and Democrat in a Republican environment) has been known to court a low turnout. Party divisions in many states may be altered solely by a change in the turnout of only one specific voter group. This is one reason many states choose to elect their governor in non-presidential years, "protecting" the state against the violent, high-turnout winds of change that sometimes blow in presidential years.

And, most elemental of all, ... those elements of the population with lowest normal participation — from which any appreciable increase in turnout must come — consist in larger measure of Democrats than Republicans.

Recent history tells us that in the 1952 presidential election 62.7 percent of the potential American electorate voted; in 1956 the percentage was 60.4; in 1960 it jumped to 63.3; and in 1964 it was 62.0. We have observed that races between two *non-presidents* excite the populace more than re-runs by incumbent presidents, and we see a number of other pressures gradually

inflating our turnout rates. So, we can guesstimate that 1968 will attract a national turnout of perhaps 64 percent.

For 1968 the candidates face the prospect of an American population of about 202 million, fielding a voter-age group of some 120 million persons. At the expected 64 percent turnout rate that means the 1968 winner must be prepared to convince at least 38 million or so Americans he is the best man. (Both Kennedy and Nixon got 34 million 1960 votes; Lyndon Johnson polled 43 million in 1964, a plurality of 16 million.)

The 1960 presidential vote total of 68,883,341 for Nixon and Kennedy was an all-time high mark. And 1964's figure of 70,641,128 was another record even though in percentage relatively less than 1960. In 1960 every state except Montana and Nevada increased its turnout over 1956; in 1964 only 14 states upped their turnout relative to four years earlier — Alabama, Arizona, Georgia, Louisiana, Mississippi, South Carolina (Goldwater carried them all), Alaska and Hawaii (the newest states), Arkansas, Florida, New Mexico, Tennessee, Texas and Virginia (all in the South or Southwest).

Table 2 is a Twentieth Century tally sheet on presidential voter turnouts. Remember that the infusion of women into the eligible electorate brought on

TABLE 2   PRESIDENTIAL YEAR VOTING PARTICIPATION PERCENTAGES

1900	74%	1924	49%	1948	53%
1904	66	1928	57	1952	63
1908	66	1932	58	1956	60
1912	60	1936	61	1960	63
1916	63	1940	62	1964	62
1920	49	1944	55	1968	64 (est.)

lower participation percentages after 1919, and that 1944 and 1948 reflect World War II and its aftermath.

Another useful way of considering turnout percentages for our last presidential election year is to rank the states as Table 3 does. We see Utah leading the 1964 turnout list with 76.9 percent. And, there is West Virginia near the top of the list along with Wyoming and Iowa in a reversal of their population-growth rankings of recent years. It is interesting that 33 states provided 1964 voter turnouts higher than the national average, an average weighted heavily down by the

only-one-third turnouts still plaguing South Carolina, Alabama, Mississippi and the first-time-voting District of Columbia. Of the big states Illinois does best with 74.0 percent; California (64.7) and New York (63.2) rank 30th and 32nd respectively; and Texas lags in 45th place with only a 44.4 turnout.

Americans who conscientiously get out and vote tend to worry quite a bit about their state's percentage and the national percentage. They read stories and teleview via satellite about foreign countries where nearly 100 percent of the citizens vote. Of course in such

TABLE 3   PRESIDENTIAL VOTE TURNOUT — 1964 (PERCENTAGE OF POTENTIAL VOTE)

1. Utah	76.9		28. Maine	65.6
2. Minnesota	76.8		29. Kansas	64.8
3. Idaho	75.8		30. California	64.7
4. West Virginia	75.2		31. New Mexico	63.9
5. Illinois	74.0		32. New York	63.2
Indiana	74.0		33. Oklahoma	62.5
7. Wyoming	73.2			
8. South Dakota	72.6		**UNITED STATES**	**62.0**
9. Iowa	72.3			
New Hampshire	72.3		34. Maryland	56.0
11. North Dakota	72.2		35. Nevada	55.5
12. Connecticut	71.8		36. Arizona	54.7
13. Washington	71.5		37. Kentucky	52.9
14. Massachusetts	71.3		38. Florida	52.7
15. Delaware	71.1		39. Hawaii	52.5
16. Wisconsin	70.8		40. North Carolina	51.8
17. Montana	69.8		41. Tennessee	51.1
18. Oregon	69.6		42. Arkansas	49.9
19. Michigan	68.9		43. Alaska	48.7
20. Rhode Island	68.7		44. Louisiana	47.3
21. New Jersey	68.6		45. Texas	44.4
22. Pennsylvania	68.1		46. Georgia	43.2
23. Colorado	68.0		47. Virginia	41.0
Vermont	68.0		48. D.C.	38.4
25. Missouri	67.4		49. South Carolina	38.0
26. Nebraska	66.6		50. Alabama	36.0
Ohio	66.6		51. Mississippi	32.9

SOURCE — Republican National Committee

nations as Belgium, Brazil, Chile, Ecuador, Italy, the Netherlands and Peru voting is a compulsory thing; made so by law, fines, custom or a combination of all three. And, voter eligibility varies widely over the world in terms of literacy, property and residence.

Even so, in 1965 Canadians turned out 75 percent in their election; Frenchmen trooped to the polls at an 85 percent rate to vote for president; and little Austria managed a presidential turnout of fully 95 percent. Other nations in which voter turnout is normally in the eighty percents include Denmark, Finland, Norway, Sweden, West Germany, Israel, Japan, South Korea, New Zealand and even Venezuela.

Why, then, is the U.S. vote turnout record so low?

First: Our Constitution, laws and election traditions place an unusual number of roadblocks before voters, not the least of which in a moving society is residence requirements. (In an attempt to alleviate this particular problem some states now allow presidential ballots from persons two-weeks on the scene who swear they haven't and won't vote elsewhere or by absentee ballot.)

Second: Non-partisan politics in some localities and two-party politics nationally give some potential voters a Tweedledee-Tweedledum complex in which, seeing no choice, they choose not to choose.

Third: Our American system is so undeniably stable compared to the world's other governments that our free citizens know things will not go completely to pot if they miss one elec-

tion. They can be certain there will be another election in two years; another presidential one in four years. They have less need to get excited about a current election than do citizens of more volatile, revolutionary, coup-minded societies.

Worries about U.S. "low" turnouts are fun for the high school civics class, but not really worth the bother. There is as yet no convincing evidence that American government or politics would be drastically different (not to mention better) if 80 or 90 percent suddenly voted. The argument of civics teachers might, for our nation's good, better be in favor of steady increases in the size of the informed citizenry, rather than for sudden, vast turnouts. Inform an American and he will turn out to vote soon and of his own accord. Besides, there is a place in American governmental society for the person who wishes to withdraw from the electorate. Such withdrawal can be just as important and effective an individual act as voting, and no American should be denied the right to throw up his hands and go fishing. Fishermen have been known to decide elections in several of our states while patiently tending their lines awaiting a bigger political catch another day.

Just a word is in order here about the American *nonvoter*. Although it is the preference of *voters* which is registered at the polls and statistically compiled, reported, culled, sorted, analyzed and pontificated about; the *nonvoters* also are influential in determining the actual election outcome.

Aside from the fact that we know nonvoters are Democratic-leaning by a five to one margin, it is also true that they are shifters in partisanship and when asked after an election how they voted normally choose the winner no matter what his party. They ride psychological bandwagons after the fact. The nonvoter has lower involvement and emotional investment in elections and thus is less stable, more swayable and seldom so moved that he will move to vote. When he has an opinion it is likely more radical than the voter's opinions.

Nonvoters often are underdog-types who self-consciously but flatly reject the sidewalk-paint slogan, "If you don't vote, don't gripe." They are gripers about public policy who more likely than not simply can't bring themselves to vote for any of the candidates all of whom they regard (if they regard at all) as incompetents who will endanger the nation's (their) safety and security.

Precinct Workers' Note: *Don't waste doorbell-ringing time in long, issue arguments with known or admitted habitual nonvoters.*

We might also venture to point out the obvious but sometimes unpolitic view that any *sudden* 1960's jump of the electorate to say 80 percent could only bring to the polls in greater proportions those who don't vote today — the very young, very old, less informed, less educated, more mercurial citizens (in the idom of the day "extremists"). In that case, the electorate's *quality* would decline; so would the level of campaigns; and things being how they are Democrats would win virtually everything in sight. In such sudden circumstances (now calm down Democrats) the American two-party system would likely be replaced by a benevolent one-party dictatorship able to perpetuate itself in power, eliminate dissension even in its own ranks, and end American government as we know it.

Far better that we await an 80 percent turnout when it also means 80 percent educated, informed and active in understanding American life and helping make America work. Besides, any American who did not vote in an election like we had in 1960 is unlikely to vote in any election ever; he is so far out of it that he would even ignore a compulsory-vote law and only force could get him to the ballot box regularly.

Putting force aside, it could be gently suggested right here that despite all the philosophy on the presidency we remember there are also non-presidential-year elections. In fact, when voter turnout percentages are charted showing the peak turnouts in presidential years and the droops in non-presidential-year turnouts, the result is a sawtoothed graph that rivals a shark's lower plate.

Our most recent non-presidential elections, 1962 and 1966, both brought to the polls only 49 percent of the potential electorate. The hard-fought 1967 city elections attracted a surprisingly large turnout averaging nearly 70 percent.

A total of 53.5 million voted in 1962 with the state turnouts running from 68 percent in Idaho to 14 percent in Mississippi. In 1966 some 56.8 million Americans balloted in state turnouts ranging between the 65 percent of Idaho and Montana and the 25 percent of Texas. California totaled up the most votes in each year as she firmly established her first-place national rank.

The 1962 figures showed that the South was making increasingly large contributions to the national vote count with the turnout up over 1958 in 10 of the 11 Southern states (Virginia slipped a bit). In 1966 10 Southern states again gained over their turnout four years previous (Texas slipped). Still, of the 25 states that increased turnout in 1966 the gains of particular note were those of Alabama, Georgia, Tennessee, Arkansas and Mississippi all of which gained more than 17 percent.

These Southern gains reflect increased Negro voting in the South and increased Republican efforts in general elections as two-party philosophy begins to osmose slowly into the region's habits.

THE SPECIFICS OF 1964

At this stage of the game and knowing the things we now know about what makes voters out of just plain people, it is in order for us to take a brief, more specific look at what happened in the elections of 1964 and 1966.

It is possible for us to do this with some confidence because beginning in 1964 the Census Bureau of the United States Department of Commerce began for the first time extensive special questioning, tabulation and publication of nationwide statistics on voting participation. Why the Census Bureau decided to do this is not immediately obvious since federal, taxpayer-supported bureaus seldom openly admit that they

think about practical politics — although of course they all do.

A combination of events probably pushed the Census Bureau into a decision to enter the field of turnout statistics. For one thing the men who staffed the New Frontier administration started by John F. Kennedy in 1961 were men who not only understood the value of voter statistics, but men who had used those statistics more and better than anybody before in American political history. For all their success with finding voters, they also realized that even the best of past turnout studies had necessarily been based on small, usually-localized samples of voters and had been nothing like as extensive as the Census Bureau could undertake. So, when their administration took the Census Bureau, they also took the opportunity to make election turnout statistics a regular part of the Bureau's service to American public and politician.

These New Frontiersmen immediately ran into difficulties in obtaining *valid* statistics. Census Bureau interviewers asked Americans two weeks after the election of 1964 whether they and their families had voted. Fully 69 percent said they had. But, obviously, that figure does not square with the 62 percent of eligible voters reflected by the presidential vote totals which we already have considered in this chapter.

The Census Bureau, counting question-answers not votes, simply ran into the grand old American tradition of over-reporting voting participation. Many Americans were reluctant to report that they had lapsed in their civic duty to vote. Others said family members had voted when, in fact, they did not know for sure whether they had or not. And, there always are some who think they voted and report they voted but never know that through carelessness they somehow mismarked or otherwise invalidated their ballots so that election judges had to throw them out. In addition (and there is evidence this was abnormally widespread in 1964), there are some citizens who vote but because they just don't care or just can't stand either candidate do not mark their ballot for president, only for lesser offices.

A number of studies have been made in an effort to determine how widespread these several voter variations are, and percentage estimates of over-reporting of voting range generally from 5 to 10 percent. It appears 7 percent would be a good compromise figure for the over-reporting. A 7 percent reduction in the reported 69 percent national voter total would make it coincide precisely with the 62 percent obtained from the vote count. By reducing the reported Census Bureau turnout figures by 7 percent across the board, we can arrive at some realistic figures, and without a doubt we can obtain reflections of real differences in the voting behavior of various groups of Americans. So here goes.

In the 1964 presidential election 62 percent of Americans voted for chief executive. These figures are based on the potential voters over 21 in every state except Georgia and Kentucky where 18-year-olds vote, Alaska where 19-year-olds vote, and Hawaii where 20-year-olds vote.

It is immediately obvious from the 1964 Census Bureau figures that sub-

stantial differences occur by *age* in voter participation. Persons less than 25 years old had the lowest voter participation rate — about 45 percent. About two-thirds of the population aged 25 to 44 voted; and nearly three-fourths of those from 45 to 64. At age 75 and over, however, the proportion voting dropped to the vicinity of 60 percent.

A smaller proportion of women than men voted in 1964; 60 percent to the men's 65 percent. (But, because there are more women in America than men, in 1964 nearly two million more women, in absolute numbers, voted than did men.) The difference in the proportion of voters among men and women increased with age. At the younger adult levels men held an advantage of two percentage points; from ages 65 to 74 men voted 11 percent more often; and over 75 years of age men voted 15 percent more often than women.

In 1964 the proportion of voters was considerably higher for the white population than for the Negro population. The figures were about 65 percent of whites and 52 percent of Negroes. The difference between the proportions of men and women voters was greater among whites than among nonwhites. Among whites the lowest proportion of voters was found in the age group under 25; among nonwhites the lowest proportion was shared by *both* the youngest and the oldest voters.

Among the regions of our country the South had, in 1964, the lowest proportion of voters — 50 percent. In the North Central region 69 percent voted; 67 percent in the Northeast; and 65 percent in the West.

Although the participation of the nonwhite population generally was lower than that of whites for the United States as a whole, it was higher in the North Central region where 73 percent of nonwhites and 67 percent of whites voted. Here are the figures:

TABLE 4   TOTAL TURNOUT PERCENTAGE IN 1964 BY REGION AND RACE

	Total	Nonwhite
Northeast	67	62
North Central	69	73
South	50	37
West	65	57

Metropolitan area residents showed a greater proportion of voting participation in 1964 than did nonmetropolitan residents — 64 percent to 60 percent; and the metropolitan-nonmetropolitan difference was even sharper among nonwhites, running 58 percent to 34 percent. The percentage of voters in central cities was just slightly lower than the rate in the suburbs — 62 percent to 65 percent. Central city nonwhites however, voted at a 58 percent rate compared to only 54 percent for suburban nonwhites.

With regard to education level in 1964, findings showed some 73 percent of those with a year or more of college voted, compared to only 44 percent of those with less than an eighth-grade education. Among both white and nonwhite persons the better-educated voted more with the differences tending to equalize between the races and the sexes as education levels improved. Among nonwhites 75 percent of the college graduates voted compared to only 36 percent of the grade-school educated.

Unemployed men of voting age balloted in 1964 to a significantly lesser extent than employed men — 50 to 67 percent. Those who had been unemployed longest had a *higher* voting rate than those unemployed for a shorter period, probably because those in the recently unemployed group included a number of movers in search of a job and disenfranchised by new residence requirements.

White-collar workers were confirmed in 1964 as more likely to vote. Seventy-seven percent of them went to the polls compared to 67 percent of service workers and 60 percent of farm workers. At the peak voting age of 45 the substantial totals of 82 percent of white-collar men and 79 percent of white-collar women voted.

Persons from high-income families voted more, too. In 1964 less than 45 percent of eligible voters in families earning under $2,000 a year voted; but 77 percent voted from families earning more than $10,000 a year. Among nonwhite families the corresponding percentages were 32 and 75. At each income level the rate for men over age 45 was greater than for men under that age. Men over 45 with family incomes of more than $10,000 reached the peak of 85 percent presidential voters, probably a near saturation level. Inside each income group those persons with higher education levels had substantially higher voting rates. About 56 percent of all persons with incomes between $3,000 and $5,000 voted, but *within* this income group the proportion of voting was 69 percent for those with some college compared to 51 percent for grade-school-only graduates.

Among farm workers, 75 percent of high-school graduates voted compared with only a 57 percent participation rate among farm workers as a whole. Nonwhite persons in farm occupations voted less than 30 percent, making them the population group which participated least in the 1964 election.

In families in which the head of the household voted, other family members of voting age were more likely to vote. In 60 percent of husband-wife families both voted, and they differed in their votes less than 10 percent of the time. In about 35 percent of those families including husband, wife and *other* relatives everybody voted; in less than 10 percent of such families did nobody vote. And, all of these relationships varied expectedly depending on income, occupation and education of the head of household. White-collar, husband-wife families voted fully in 71 percent of the cases.

Thus, all of the specific Census Bureau findings for 1964's election support the observed turnout-trends discovered by practical politicians and probing political scientists in previous years.

And, though non-presidential-year percentages are less, the Census Bureau found the same sort of turnout relations in its studies of the 1966 election. An estimated 50 percent of Americans voted in 1966 with their participation varying by sex, race, and region. In the North and the West 56 percent voted; while in the South slightly less than 40 percent went to the polls. The proportion of voters remained considerably higher for whites than for Negroes. In the North and West 58 percent of whites and 47 percent of Negroes voted; in the South the figures were 40 and 28 respectively.

Thus, as a rough rule-of-thumb, Americans still can be expected to turn out for presidential elections at a rate 12 to 15 percent more often than they will bother themselves to vote in a non-presidential year.

Precinct Workers' Note: *While there is little likelihood you ever will have as precise a statistical breakdown of your precinct voters as the Census Bureau can develop, the general rules do prevail and you are shirking your responsibility if your campaign and election-day plans do not take seriously into account which of your voters will automatically vote and which you must, in effect, harass to the polls. But, resist the temptation to devote a lot of effort to low-turnout groups just because they are low-turnout groups. Remember that as a practical politician you hunt first where your ducks are and only when those ducks are in line do you concentrate elsewhere.*

Summing up the new social science approach to politics, political analysts Richard Scammon and Benjamin Wattenberg wrote that "Demography is destiny."* Just as all people are not equally attracted to the same brand of soap, not all people are attracted to the same political candidates. Advertisers and politicians now speak of demographics — what are the social characteristics of potential customers for their products? The more one knows about a potential customer's life style in addition to demographic data, the more effective the sales campaign can be.

Knowledge about group membership and social categories may also aid us in knowing about people's aspirations. Knowledge of a person's aspirations may allow researchers to predict political preferences and buying patterns with greater accuracy than knowledge of group memberships alone. For example, people who aspire to greater social status may not behave as others in their social milieu. Their desired life style affects their present behavior and may be geared toward life style change. Lynn Buller describes in the following article how encyclopedia sales are geared toward life style change. Purchasers of encyclopedias may believe that the knowledge acquired from such volumes will permit them or their children to master a new life style; or, the buyer may believe that simply the possession and display of an elaborately bound set of encyclopedias is worth their cost in expressing desires for upward mobility (or may aid in fostering a belief that the process of upward mobility has already begun). Encyclopedia sellers, like politicians, look to social categories and group membership in identifying buyers. Lynn Buller describes how salesmen become proficient in identifying certain combinations of variables that with high probability predict aspiration for upward social mobility. Once this aspiration is confirmed the salesperson can pitch his product to fit the life style aspiration projected by the prospective customer.

* Richard Scammon and Benjamin Wattenberg, *The Real Majority* (New York: Coward-McCann, 1970).

The Encyclopedia Game

Lynn M. Buller

Many people want to make a fast buck, and college students are no exception. They aspire to the high standard of living that comes to those with college degrees. Moreover, their few marketable skills and need for seasonal employment may heighten their receptivity to schemes that promise fast money. During the month of May, when college students most tenaciously seek summer jobs, the classified sections of newspapers are filled with provocative want-ads offering quick and easy money in the promotional field. Encyclopedia companies advertise positions for "advertising representatives" which promise time for boating and water-skiing, travel within a five-state area, and a salary of $150 or more per week. With this kind of appeal and few available alternatives, it is not difficult to explain why each summer hordes of students across the country turn to selling encyclopedias. It was such an advertisement that resulted in my spending an entire summer participating in what turned out to be a complex manipulative racket and a fascinating subculture.

From Saul D. Feldman and Gerald W. Thielbar (eds.), *Life Styles: Diversity in American Society,* pp. 60–72. Reprinted by permission of Little, Brown and Company (Inc.).

RECRUITMENT, INDOCTRINATION, PERSONNEL

Upon answering by telephone a provocative advertisement much like the one described above, I was told the employment supervisor was not in but that his "assistant," to whom I was speaking, would help me. He "just happened" to have an appointment available Saturday at one o'clock, and asked if I could come in then for a personal interview. When I asked the nature of the job, he explained that it would take several hours to explain the job and that he had seven other phones to answer. I had already been conned.

On Saturday, there were twenty other people at my "personal interview," and I later discovered the office had only two telephone lines. The absent "employment supervisor" did not exist, which made it possible for any employee answering the phone to set up job interviews.

A man resembling W. C. Fields — fifty-five-ish, complete with dime-store socks and cheap initial cufflinks — whisked into the room, the inevitable cigarette dangling from his busy mouth. He told us we were permitted to leave during the presentation if we objected to any part of the program or felt we wouldn't like the job; all he asked was that we display enough courtesy to stay until one of the three breaks he would give us. First we saw a film featuring a gentleman wearing a maroon smoking jacket seated in his private library, his soft hand resting fondly upon a leather globe. The musty aura of Classic Education pervaded the room. We were shown scholarship winners from previous summers receiving their thousand-dollar checks, and travelogue stills of the foreign city where all the successful salesmen would vacation late that summer.

Then the salary was explained to us. We were to receive a base salary of $115 for three weeks, which would be increased to $154 the fourth week. For this amount we were required to "place" two sets of encyclopedias each week with families who promised to "value and appreciate" the books, although we were allowed two fruitless weeks without being fired. For each ten sets above our quota of two per week we were to receive a $500 bonus. Fantastic, we thought.

Following the movie and the salary talk we were given the opportunity to leave, with Oil Can Harry standing in front of the class, daring us to scrape our folding chairs and crawl over six pairs of feet in the quivering silence. His beady eyes accused us, one by one, of disbelief.

No one left, and our mesmerizer demonstrated the material we would be offering in the "promotional combination offer," complete with commitment questions which were directed at us. He was, in fact, trying to convince us to accept the books. We agreed that the material was truly beautiful and would "place" itself. He said all we had to do was show the material to three interested couples each night and one of them would surely accept the books. It sounded like a whiz. Leading us to anticipate giving three demonstrations nightly made us think we'd be chatting with lots of interested, supportive people and knocking on comparatively few doors.

This was far from the truth. (A corporation higher-up confirmed later in an interview that prospective employees are purposely led to believe that they will place more sets than it is likely they will.) He didn't tell us that there would be nights when everyone in a salesman's territory with school-age children was attending high school graduation, or nights when the wind came up and the rain came down hard, and the field manager sat out the storm in a local bar, not deigning to rescue his rain-soaked crew a minute before the appointed hour. Or that we'd be dodging police all summer and, even more difficult, trying to keep frustration and depression, those white-eyed dogs, from constantly nipping at our heels. Although I didn't believe the job would be as easy as it sounded, I liked the idea of being an advertising representative for a large corporation and living in my own apartment for the summer, instead of going back home to fry hamburgers.

After the pitch we were called into the district manager's office in pairs and asked if we wanted the job. I didn't know whether I'd like it or not, but for $154 a week it seemed an irrelevant point. The girl in the office with me, however, insisted that she couldn't assess something until she'd tried it. I never saw her again. I remember the Weasel asking me some closing question akin to "Do you take this company as your personal Savior and promise to uphold it with your prayers, your presence, your gifts, and your future," and I remember the guilty twinge of my mouth as I answered yes. He looked like a congenital con-man to me, but if he was capable of asking silly questions like that, maybe he was stupider than I thought. There was a chance I could beat him at his own game. I got the job.

Later that week, at the end of the training period (unpaid), we were given a test in which we were asked the names of several corporation higher-ups, five reasons why we believed in the company, and whether, "given the choice," we would rather be paid the salary or a straight commission of $83 each for the first ten placements, $92 for each order thereafter, and a free set of encyclopedias as soon as we'd sold twenty sets. Though the employees could nominally choose between the pay plans, I knew of no one who was on the salary plan more than two weeks, either because he quit before that time or because he changed pay plans. The test was a means by which the field managers selected their crews. Anyone who had designated the salary plan was not cheerfully chosen by the field managers, for they had no motivational whip to use on the salary boys.

A small but irritating part of our salaries went to pay for the savings banks we gave to our "placement families" in which to daily save their dimes. Another small portion went into a bail fund to aid salesmen run afoul of local Green River ordinances (prohibiting unlicensed solicitors). The field managers (staff sergeants for one to five advertising representatives) were given no car expense, although they did get a substantial override (kickback) on any orders written out of their cars. In fact, everyone up the management line of the sales division received a percentage of the profit. No employees were salaried; conse-

quently, everyone in management rode the salesmen ("advertising representatives") for orders, and rode them all the time. The salesmen paid for their own motel and food expenses while traveling and for demonstration materials, and had no money deducted for taxes or Social Security.

After I'd worked with the company some time, I realized that almost anyone was hired. It was also practically impossible to be fired (mainly because for tax purposes we were considered individual contractors). One man, I heard, was welcomed back "like a long-lost brother" after serving five years in the pen for grand larceny. One girl was said to be an ex-call girl; at any rate, she was a cocktail waitress on weekends. Two seminary students were also hired, plus an honors graduate with a fellowship in psychology at a top university.

SALESMEN

According to my observations, the typical experienced bookman has been married twice, has three children, and is occupationally unskilled, although his intelligence is well into the second standard deviation. As a youth, he had high aspirations which were deflected by circumstance or frustration; he aspires to professional status. Most often he grew up on a farm; converted to city-dwelling, he regards small-town residents as cornball and sometimes feels revengeful toward farmers. His style is flamboyant and unsophisticated; his sexual attitudes are adolescent.

Even though nearly all the men in my office had frequent extra-, post-, or pre-marital sexual relations, they talked about their conquests in the same way ninth-graders are said to brag in the locker room. Any virgin was "open game"; and other salesmen heard about every aspect of the hunt. Some salesmen always had a girlfriend. One female seemed to fulfill their need about as well as another, and they followed a sequential pattern of courtship-monogamy. Other men tried to manipulate several salesgirls at once. One in particular was such a lady-killer that he talked the psychology graduate out of her fellowship so she could follow him to sell books and live with him in Sioux Falls, South Dakota. Meanwhile he courted the cocktail waitress, and later spontaneously married her. Several months later his wife departed with his car and color television. Lately, I hear, he's been dodging authorities regarding a charge of statutory rape. This man is 23 years old; he was the president of his high school graduating class, and has experienced two unsuccessful marriages. He is an extreme case. Another extreme case is a man who carried his pajamas, a clock-radio, and a fifth of whiskey in his briefcase to be prepared for any available sexual conquest.

Not all the men were disloyal to their wives — several were very happily married. But when one considers that all were away from their families at least twelve hours a day, from noon to midnight, and that most of their wives worked from eight to five, it's easily understandable that their marriages were characteristically less-than-ideal.

Of course, the female employees were hardly prudish. Several of them had strange habits too. One girl hitch-hiked home seven miles through a woods each night after work. She'd been "raped" twice since Christmas. Strangely enough, although she claimed to hate men because of their disloyal and lustful natures, she seduced any available male. After she climbed into bed with me one morning, however, we decided she was most likely a lesbian.

It was not unusual for a crew of males and females to share one motel room, either. This probably was quite a wholesome arrangement, considering the potential audience. But it was hardly the thing to write home to mother.

The book business attracts men of similar life style. Most of the salesmen with my company drove big, bright-colored cars with factory air-conditioning: Pontiac convertibles, Chryslers, Buicks. One salesman drove a Jaguar and sold realty on the side. Their clothes were frequently flashy, but never cheap. They treated themselves to three-dollar lunches and good clothes because the money came in easily, if they worked. (Not working was referred to as "leaking off.") The fact that they were paid commissions instead of a salary encouraged free spending. Purchases were priced in order-units: a salesman considered that his rent was two orders a month, food another one, a new coat was one order, and a pinky ring cost a half.

Alan Lippett[1] writes that diamond pinky rings signified success among the salesmen with whom he worked. In my

[1] Alan Lippett, "There's One Born Every Minute," *Seattle Magazine,* 5 (June, 1968), pp. 25–30.

company, no one wore pinky rings. My cohorts apparently aspired to conspicuous consumption of higher class indication than did the other company's salesmen. This statement is supported by my observations within Alan's former company, where I noticed that salesmen drove late-model Fords and Chevrolets and Ramblers with home-installed stereo systems, although they too, frequented the best restaurants and bars. I think they were less likely to know they were selling books, although my company did a pretty good job of keeping the truth from us. Maybe they were just dumber.

In my company, sales representatives and field managers (called "F.M.s") were very chummy. We called each other by first names from the start. We knew each other's past and present states of mind and affairs, as well as the number of orders each had written for the week. The other company's representatives seemed reluctant to divulge the circumstances of their private lives to each other, and offered no references to their business success or unsuccess. There was apparently less sexual fraternization than in my company, too. Of course, I observed them during the winter when there were fewer opportunities for the kind of hanky-panky which went on within my company while we were traveling in the summer.

Motel owners were not always enthusiastic about letting rooms to encyclopedia salesmen, because of their reputation for sneaking off without paying. I never knew salesmen who did this. I did know of a young crew who had a water fight in their cabin one night and sopped the furnishings so thoroughly they couldn't sleep there.

They left the motel, after paying, by telling the proprietor that one fellow's father had got his leg caught in a corn-picker and they had to rush to another city to see him. That the informing telephone call would have had to come across the motel switchboard, if the family even knew where their son was staying, must never have occurred to the innkeeper.

One salesman's many subpoenas on charges of damage to motels and hotels became a joke among the salesmen. Whenever this salesman came off a road trip, his friends would go over to his house to have a few beers, see the subpoenas he'd accumulated, and hear the story behind each one. This particular salesman was a legend in his own time. One night, the story goes, he and a buddy bought a watermelon. Because they didn't have a knife in their hotel room, the big brute smashed the melon down upon the sink to break it open. He also broke the lavatory off the wall and was accordingly sued for several thousand dollars after twelve inches of water filled the whole motel. On a bet, this same fellow cut a square of deer meat from an animal they'd struck with a car and ate it raw, impaled on his jack knife, and chased it down with straight whiskey. He was also known to drink whiskey for breakfast — tumblersful.

REVELATIONS

It took me almost six weeks to figure out that I wasn't really an advertising representative for the company; I was a book peddler. The "Promotional Combination Offer" was a gimmick clean through. Although people allegedly got the books for writing the company a letter of endorsement, and paying only for the services which kept the set up-to-date, they actually paid for everything they received. Their letters of endorsement were used only, if ever, to parlay new promotional participants.

It was claimed by the management that the product was far superior to any other encyclopedia. This encyclopedia had "just been completely rewritten and, indeed, was not on regular sale yet." It was new in the sense that a new edition is printed each year, and it was actually true that the set had been completely rewritten, even though the new version had been on regular sale since 1962. The "new edition" ploy was helpful in several ways. Whenever a prospective buyer voiced a complaint against this brand of encyclopedia, the salesman could answer assuringly, "That was our *old* set." The completely revised edition was also the basis of the promotional pitch. Placement families were supposedly pretesting this new publication which was "not yet on the general market," and writing letters of endorsement to be used to persuade their neighbors to buy the encyclopedias when they were finally released "for general consumption." Actually, the promotional families are the most general market to which the product is released. Families can obtain the books only through direct sales methods. The sales pitches are informally synthesized by innovative salesmen and lower management personnel. Yet somehow, these bubble-gum and bobby-pin methods sell $450 million worth of books each year.[2]

[2] Eric Geller, "Selling Encyclopedias," *New Republic* (August 24, 1968), p. 10.

It was claimed that we were giving the people something they really needed, even if they were sometimes too stupid to realize their need. After all, it was not like we were peddling cyanide pellets disguised as diet pills. If purchasers used the books, they were sure to become better people. Representatives might even have looked upon themselves as missionaries bringing enlightenment to the backwoods. Pouring on the book pitch like cod-liver oil, confident that it was all "for their own good," employees could gloat in good conscience all the way to the bank.

Through talking with many people, especially those in small towns, we came to see ourselves as serving another positive social function — that of relieving people's boredom. Several times, I'm sure, people bought books from me because they were hopelessly bored, and I'd come from afar to entertain them for an hour. They were simply grateful.

The salespeople's true purpose was supposedly withheld from new employees; however, the varying levels of operational awareness within the district's personnel made it nearly impossible to keep the pose intact. Because my field manager confirmed that I wasn't giving books away, I was in a good position to watch other employees' reactions to what they thought they were doing for the company.

It is my theory that three classes of people were hired: "fishes," "sneakers," and "con-men." The fishes actually believe they are advertising representatives and they stay with the company not only for the money, but because they believe in education and in the product. (These people become very defensive of their jobs to outsiders and bristle at the mention of any other encyclopedia.) The sneakers figure the sales pitch isn't all on the up-and-up, but for the money they aren't going to bother with details. If they realized the extent of their deception, the sneakers probably would be forced by their disquieted consciences to quit. They need the rah-rah of product emotionalism to keep their minds from wandering where it might not be economically advisable. The con-men will do anything for the money offered. Even though the con-men don't always know precisely how they are misleading the public, they are fully aware that the public is being misled. Consequently, the fishes and the sneakers are protected from the truth by the con-men, who build up fine rationalizations to keep everyone enthusiastic and productive. Strangely enough, management is not composed primarily of con-men. It is easier for these people, too, to believe they are doing something worthwhile for mankind than to try to live with a conscience of conflict; some have become almost fish-like themselves.

Promotion in the encyclopedia game is quick and not difficult. If a representative has sold ten orders, holds the business attitudes of either the sneaker or the con-man, and owns a car, he'll soon become a field manager. When he's more senior than most employees (which may mean he's been with the company one year) and has won a sales contest or two, he's likely to be offered an office of his own within the district. This offer is largely a doggie bone tossed out to make eager young men come into the office two hours earlier, without salary, to train recruits, or to run from office to office within the district to help train recruits. The most strenuous aspect of the trainer's job is keeping curious neophytes from discovering what they'll really be doing. By and by someone who heads one of the offices will quit or go to another district or be proselytized by another company and the trainer will get an office of his own. Whoopee. He can now be at work by 9:30 every morning (which means at least a twelve-hour day) to interview, hire, train, and pick his own crews, a task which leaves him too tired to go out and write personal orders in the evening. Any money he earns will be in the form of commissions, overrides on the orders written by his crew, or trainer's fees on recruits he's trained, so it is imperative that his crew be in the field every evening, primed to write orders, and that he himself be knocking on numerous doors, lest he go broke on car, lunch, and bar expenses.

District managers, regional managers, and regional vice-presidents are all paid healthy percentages of the volume of business in their jurisdiction. It must be said that they work hard, goading their inferiors to better performance through sales contests, summer vacation contests, and short-term prize agreements. But their wages are almost ridiculously ample. Regional and district managers are paid in five figures; vice presidents get six, plus lots of time to parlay their earnings. Ironically, education is in no way the primary consideration for promotions within the encyclopedia business. Enthusiasm, endurance, and the ability to hold one's own are the main prerequisites of a management job. One regional vice-president was a dentist. He had no business training whatsoever — no knowledge of marketing, business law, or management. He is probably in the position he now holds because he is one of the few people in the business with a college degree, although he wouldn't have been considered for the job if he hadn't been phenomenally successful as a sales representative.

MOOCHES

In American society there exist people classified by encyclopedia salesmen as "mooches." Mooches can be generally defined as people who like to buy the product; they see the encyclopedia salesman as the bearer of a rare and desirable gift. Mooches are people whose incomes and occupational levels exceed their educational attainments; persons whose income is in the middle-middle range but whose education doesn't exceed high school, or may not even attain that level. Without education, mooches cannot have professional status, although they might make as much money as a professional; consequently, mooches try to assume professionalism by accruing what they think are indications of professional status. A conspicuously displayed set of encyclopedias tells the mooch's friends that he can afford to consume conspicuously, that he values a highly normative product over creature comforts, and that he provides for the long-range benefit of his protectorate. The mooch associates all these characteristics with professional persons. For him, then, encyclopedias function as easily interpreted professional-status indicators.

Mooches are vulnerable in two ways to a book pitch — because books themselves are status symbols, and because books are considered the tools of professionalism (if not for the parents, then for their children). Being uneducated, mooches cannot differentiate between being wise and being knowledgeable. Even if they memorized all twenty-four full-color volumes, they wouldn't have an Oxford education. But such is the dream mooches are made of.

It doesn't take a new salesman long to spot a mooch, because he's constantly schooled by his seniors to look for specific criteria and readily develops the intuitive knack of mooch-hunting. Mooches show status incongruity in all their material possessions, and are more easily described than defined. Tools in a station wagon typify the moochiness of an artisan, who brings home good money but has no professional status because he works with his hands. Brick houses are not moochy, as opposed to clapboard houses with paint peeling from the siding, because brick houses are too substantial. Someone who buys a small, well-built brick house will not easily be sold on the quick idealistic emotionalism of an encyclopedia pitch; he's too careful an investor.

A mooch is someone who: drives a red Mustang and lives in a small yellow frame house with hurricane fencing around it; leaves rained-on kids' books in the front yard; has all the neighborhood kids' trikes in his driveway plus a portable barbecue; buys a huge turquoise contemporary couch and burns a cigarette hole in it; lives in a maroon house in the midst of white houses; furnishes the living room with lots of big, gaudy ashtrays which match the drapes; buys a series of science books for his children but sits on a slip-covered couch; lives in a $15,000 stucco house in the midst of new $40,000 houses; has a swing set; drives a Cougar, Camaro, or other hot, flashy American car (foreign car owners are usually not moochy, being more economical and probably better educated); works as a mechanic and whose wife drives a bus for Head Start; has too much furniture in his living room, especially if it's formica-topped and includes a color TV set and console stereo; hangs plaster birds on his wall or has plastic flowers in the living room; has a shrine in his bedroom (these people will believe anything); or has a new rocking chair or a piano with sheet music standing on it. While novices are expected to knock on every door, experienced salesmen simply drive around "smelling out" mooches.

Selling Techniques

After three days of training and observing experienced salesmen for two evenings, we novices were dropped into the "field" to finagle on our own. Propagandized and at least half-believing, we were ready to sell encyclopedias for profit, for the good of mankind, or for both. We didn't knock on every door, though we were supposed to. The general age and status of people in a neighborhood proved to be the key to potential sales, and we sought this information in order to economize our effort. Spotting a house inhabited by an older couple we'd knock on the door, greet the woman, appearing as friendly and innocuous as possible, and

ask, "Say, is it the green house or the pink house next door that has the children in it?" and ramble on bewilderedly. We usually found out not only about the pink house, but about children's ages and husbands' employments all up and down the block. Another information-gathering tactic was to ask for a glass of water, or use of the bathroom. (It is surprising how many people will admit a stranger to their bathrooms; a family that will let you use their bathroom will tell you nearly anything you want to know.) By these means, we could meet potential customers with some preparation, and we learned which families in the neighborhood needed our services.

Many opening lines were used for getting inside the door. The tactic recommended by my company was composed of a friendly hello, an announcement of one's name as though it were well-known and ought to be recognized, and a request for the spouse of the salesperson's gender by saying, "Stopped out to see your wife (husband)." (Since many of the salesmen were pimple-faced eighteen-year-olds, their briefcases dropped conspicuously beside the front stoop, this tactic wasn't always successful.) The salesman explains that he's doing some work in the area and asks if he may step in and ask the people a couple of questions. Although it is forbidden for him to describe his work by using the words "survey," "market research," "advertising work," "promotional work," "school district," or any phrase which might indicate that the salesman is involved in one of the above types of work, it is intended for people to believe just that.

Once the salesman announces himself to the spouse of similar gender, he maneuvers the couple together and begins to deliver the spiel called "the Qualifier." This five-minute explanation of the promotional program is the most important tool of the trade. During the Qualifier, the salesman either wins or loses the people's interest and confidence, while taxing their emotions and reasoning to the point of submission. He can also assess the couple's interests, means of income, and special vulnerabilities, and utilize these assessments during the material demonstration. Most of the assessment is accomplished nonverbally by observing the family's material acquisitions, looking especially for signs of moochiness. Whenever possible he engages them in seemingly idle chatter.

After the Qualifier, the salesman brings his bottomless bag of educational goodies into the house and asks the couple to sit side by side facing him across the kitchen table or coffee table, where they can see his materials simultaneously. Saleswomen demonstrate the materials on a high table or on the living room floor from a kneeling position, in order to keep all eyes on the printed matter.

First, the size and binding of the set are displayed by means of a "stretcher," which is simply a foldable, two-dimensional replica of the book-backs with spacing between each volume, which makes the stretcher a third longer than the actual set of encyclopedias. The salesperson stresses that the lettering is stamped in "24-carat gold," sure mooch-bait. Then the couple is shown the Prospectus, a sample volume which contains nearly all the color pictures in the whole set, and generally highlights the encyclopedia. The "Pros" (rhymes with "loss") is broken down into sections which appeal to different age groups, including pre-schoolers, although the encyclopedia is written on at least junior-high reading level. Testimonials are numerous and flashy. The Pros of another company includes a full-page color picture of Pope Paul VI autographing their encyclopedia. Such audacity could only be tolerated by a true-blue mooch! Sports, hobbies, and practical skills are stressed, besides the academic appeal of this "particularly excellent recording of the sum knowledge of mankind."

During the demonstration of the Prospectus, the innovative salesman utilizes the earlier observations. If before entering the house he noticed a motorboat in the garage, he will show the couple a few boating pictures as he flips through the Pros; if they have an obvious interest in fine dogs, or their child has won a prize at a local science fair, he will pitch his demonstration to that particular interest. People often believe the salesman mentions their particular interest because it is part of his regular preplacement demonstration. This makes them feel their hobby is considered especially worthy of stress by the company and, transferring the impression, they feel important themselves. Of course, the salesman means for the couple to perceive his craftiness in this way. Hopefully it will make them feel so important that they readily believe their letter of endorsement will be an asset to the company, and consequently agree to "participate in the program." In other words, buy the books.

After signing the duplicate contract, in which the merchandise is described as a "combination offer" and the promotional program and required letter of endorsement are not mentioned, the couple has bought all 24 color volumes of the encyclopedia, 10 supplemental yearbooks, 100 reference service coupons (all of which they most certainly will not use), a dictionary, a bookcase, and 10 volumes of children's books, all at regular retail price. Their one-page, handwritten letter of endorsement received within ninety days of delivery will probably never be used. But the salesman's technique was effective because he kept "talking the letter" and making the people feel they were truly privileged to be one of a few chosen families in the area. The usual parting line was, "Well, John and Mary, it's been fun getting to know you, and I'm very glad to be able to accept you as one of our advertising families here in the area. I'd like to feel free, if I'm in the vicinity again sometime, to stop in for a cup of coffee with you. May I do that?" Of course, the couple assure the salesman that he is always welcome and the salesman is assured by their submission to his self-invitation that they won't suspiciously cancel the order.

INDIVIDUAL SALES TACTICS

Several guises are successful aids to book peddling. Some representatives use a hard-sell approach, misquoting any source which occurs to them to convince the victim-family that their children will be grammar school dropouts if their parents haven't the foresight or love to provide their children

with this complete home reference library. One often-used line goes like this: "You know, John and Mary, we all love our children" — this said by 18-year-old, single college students — "but there are so few things we can give them. One is our good name, and the other is a good education. If I died tomorrow and could leave my child $100,000, he could spend it and be poor within six months. But if I give him my good name and a better-than-average education, no one can take from him the potential to earn five times the money I could have left him." From there on, if the parents refuse to take the books, the salesman makes them feel they've cheated their child out of half a million bucks. This kind of salesman often has difficulty giving a pitch when an observer (potential salesman) accompanies him because, even though observers are strictly told not to say a word during the pitch, some novices burst out laughing when the diabolical haze becomes thick. The con-man types spontaneously make up religious affiliations, relatives, and common acquaintances to try to win the family's confidence. They are quite successful if they can find enough people to intimidate, so they seek out mooches, potential fascists, and people without enough courage to shove them out the door.

Sometimes the salesmen appear downright threatening. There is no doubt in my mind that encyclopedia contracts have been signed just to get the salesman out of the house and, hopefully, out of town. One bookman of my acquaintance is particularly successful in Montana and North Dakota, where he drives right out into a farmer's field, urges him off his tractor, slaps him on the back and offers the fellow a beer from the cooler in his trunk, then drives the man back to the farmhouse to talk with the wife about their views of education. This salesman looks like the original Hell's Angel, is usually half-soused, and doesn't brush his teeth for days. When he flails his timberlike arms in the air and yells, "Ah, you're stupid! Your wife's stupid! Ya want the kids ta be stupid? Sign the fucking card," they sign. For some odd reason his orders are verified the next morning, too.

Another approach, often used by students, is the innocent-little-girl approach. This type of saleswoman appears at the door looking like a runaway teenager needing directions or a glass of water, and is invited into nearly every home whose door she knocks upon. Once inside, she gives the Qualifier in an explanatory yet wide-eyed way, and if accosted with suspicion, jokes, "You know it can't be a trick — I couldn't sell anything if I tried." She never polishes her pitch but follows a routinized pattern, knocking on every door, looking sweet, showing the material, and collecting a reasonable check at the end of the week.

Wives often regret admitting college coeds into their living rooms to kneel on the floor in front of their husbands. For this reason it is expedient for female employees to wear wedding bands and explain that their husbands are in the business also, or serving in the armed services. Husbands are not usually hard to fool; wives, unthreatened by a young woman they think to be married, are reminded of their own early marriages and are usually quite

friendly, asking particulars which give them an excuse to relate their own wedding stories. Sometimes male and female representatives sell books together, posing as man and wife. Frequently this arrangement represents an actual mobile living arrangement, and works quite well if both salespeople are good actors and the age gap is not extreme.

An approach which is consistently successful when pitching married college students is the authoritative approach. This stance seems quite professional; it is very low-key, shows almost no enthusiasm for the product and, by so doing, assumes that the students are already aware of its great intrinsic value. College students are considerably more enthusiastic than most older couples about subscribing to the reference service, which purports to write term papers. This factor contributes to a low-key approach. One salesman pitches to no one but married college students and had developed the search for these couples into a technique which the FBI would be well-advised to emulate. He can spot an outside second-story staircase from a half-block away, and distinguish at the same distance if it's being rented to college students or pensioners. The authoritative approach complements the advertising representative pose advised by the company. Within the pitch it is emphasized that the representative has been asked to place the set only with families he or she deems worthy — reverse psychology at its money-making best.

Some salesmen stress the personal relationship between themselves and their customers while addressing the couple as they do all customers. This is the promiscuously personal approach. Foreign students have been particularly successful utilizing this technique. They appear friendly, casual, and informative, and people almost invariably invite them in to chat, if not to look at books. One foreign summer representative spent Thanksgiving at the home of a family to whom he'd sold a set of books, and hadn't previously known. They loved him! Several representatives worked on Sundays and holidays, and would walk right into the midst of a family's Fourth of July picnic to sell them the educational deal of a lifetime while patriotism, the Good Life, and the American Way were still primary in their minds.

The representative's manner of dress doesn't seem to affect his selling success, except that his dress should reinforce whatever poses he presents. One company's top salesman often went into the field dressed in shorts and a paint-spattered sweatshirt. He appeared at people's doors looking like the man next door wanting to borrow some paint to finish painting his boat, and often sold five sets of books over a weekend.

Although encyclopedias are almost always books of fine quality and an asset to any family receiving them, the shame of most encyclopedia companies is that they do not grant their customers the conscious privilege of buying books when, in fact, they are. They also do not allow their employees the knowledge that they are selling books when, in fact, they are. As long as the industry provides its customers with professional status indicators, and its employees with good wages and something to believe in, this colorful subculture will probably thrive among us, remindful evidence that the race goes not to the diligent, but to the crafty. And when it comes to crafty persuasion, encyclopedia salesmen could give the patent medicine hawkers of the Old West a sure run for the money.

According to Buller, the "mooch" is one who attains the symbols but not the substance of a desired life style. Even the most ambitious mooches, no matter how hard they hustle, may never realize their ambitions, as there are many obstacles to prevent attainment of a desired life style. One major barrier is that there is simply not room at the top for all. There is an opportunity structure in the United States which permits some upward social mobility, but all who desire to move up do not do so. Some people may have a remote desire to move upward but don't try because they believe that the opportunity structure will prevent them from doing so. Such individuals may be prevented from seeking a life style of upward mobility even before they start. Others may attempt to move up, but fail and then become convinced by their own experiences that upward mobility in the United States is difficult or impossible.

Belief in the American opportunity structure is basic to the American political creed; but as Rytina, Form, and Pease argue in the following article, belief in equality of opportunity for oneself and others varies according to membership group.

Income and Stratification Ideology: Beliefs about the American Opportunity Structure

Joan Huber Rytina, William H. Form, and John Pease

IDEOLOGY AND STRATIFICATION

Social stratification may be defined as the generational persistence of unequal distribution of valued rewards in a

From *American Journal of Sociology* (1970), pp. 703–716. Reprinted by permission of the American Journal of Sociology, University of Chicago Press.

This project was supported by grant no. 91-24-66-45 from the U.S. Department of Labor, Office of Manpower Policy, Evaluation and Research, pursuant to the provisions of the Manpower Development and Training Act of 1962. The authors are grateful for the department's support.

society. An ideology is a set of emotionally held beliefs and myths that account for social reality. The ideology of a stratification system explains and vindicates the distribution of rewards in an actual society or in a society believed to be possible,[1] and contains both normative and existential statements about the way things ought to be and the way things really are.[2] Thus, in American society a man who works hard ought to get ahead, does get ahead, and in getting ahead proves he has worked hard. By definition, then, a dominant stratification ideology justifies the distribution of power and rewards in the society. Transmitted by the communication and educational channels, this ideology becomes the "public ideology" which most social scientists study.

The integrative function of an ideology is high when all strata of the society support its tenets and concur in

[1] We do not follow Mannheim's distinction of ideology as a myth of an ongoing system and utopia as a myth of a system believed to be possible (Mannheim, 1954).

[2] For the elaboration of concepts of normative and existential elements in ideology, see Form and Rytina (1969).

its mode of application.[3] Ideologies lose this integrative character when people in various strata either reject the goals implicit in the ideology or believe that its tenets have little or no validity; that is, when they feel that the institutions of a society are failing to implement desired societal goals.

The major assumption of this study is that all strata in the United States generally accept the normative tenets of the American ideology of equality of opportunity, the description of how things ought to be. But we expected some reservation, especially among lower strata, in accepting the idea that American institutions are effective in implementing the opportunity norms. Probably most adults in literate societies tend to test their life situations against the existing ideology. Since the symmetry between normative and existential tenets of an ideology is generally higher for upper strata, they are less inclined to test the validity of its existential tenets. The reverse situation probably is true for lower strata. In closely integrated social systems, the differences among the strata may be small, especially if the stratification ideology is buttressed by religious beliefs, as in the Indian caste system. In such cases one may indeed speak of a "theodicy of stratification," or the need to justify the suffering resulting from

the inequality which God has ordained (Weber, 1946, pp. 275-277). In urban-secular societies, strata will probably vary in the degree that they test the validity of an ideology's existential tenets.

Most sociologists probably assume there is wide support for the normative aspects of the ideology of equal opportunity (Smelser, 1967, p. 8; Lipset, 1963, p. 101), but current unrest among some segments of American society indicates that belief in some aspects may be more problematical (Miller and Rein, 1966). Clearly, most studies have tested adherence to the ideology as it is expressed in general, ideal, or normative terms. It is relatively easy to obtain a consensus with regard to vague statements on how a system ought to and does operate.[4] Such statements, especially as presented in most public opinion studies, do not concretize the tenets of an ideology. The acid test of a system which offers money as its main reward, especially from the point of view of people in lower strata, is whether a person who is poor has the same opportunities as a person who has more money. The problem for this research was to devise a technique which permitted people to respond to both (*a*) general statements about how the American opportunity system operates and (*b*) specific statements of how the system operates for persons in different economic strata.

---

[3] The idea that an ideology plays a societal integrative function and the idea that an ideology serves to consolidate the power of an elite parallel two conceptions of the function of a stratification system: as a societal integrator (Parsons, 1953) and as a political formula of the elite (Mosca, 1966, p. 240).

[4] Ossowski (1963, pp. 110–113) has pointed out that on a high level of generality the normative structure of the American and Soviet stratification systems are very similar.

RESEARCH DESIGN

Two major hypotheses guided this research: (1) all income strata will tend to agree more with highly generalized statements than with situationally specific statements about the operation of the American opportunity system, but (2) lower strata will show less agreement than higher strata with both types of statements. This hypothesis was based on the proposition that for most people income is the most salient stratification variable.

The major areas of ideology explored were:

1. The existence of an open opportunity structure in the United States, the equality of chances for upward and downward occupational mobility, and the relative opportunity for mobility in the United States and in Europe. These areas focus on beliefs concerning the relative openness of the economic institution.

2. The relative accessibility of educational resources to all strata as the vehicle for mobility.

3. The impartial functioning of the political and legal systems.

4. Personal or social responsibility for economic status or rank. We hypothesized that those with higher incomes support tenets of personal responsibility for a person's economic status, while the poor place greater reliance on social structural explanations, which would follow from the belief that, for the poor, the economic, educational, political, and legal institutions fail to operate in accord with democratic norms of equality of opportunity.

Annual family income was used as the major independent variable in this study for two reasons:

First, one of our research aims was to discover how poor people perceive the structure of economic opportunity; for poor people, the most salient reward of the stratification system is probably income. If income is combined with incommensurate variables, such as occupation or education, the synthetic scale that results "will be concerned with social consciousness rather than objective position" (Ossowski, 1963, p. 56). However adapted to a particular environment, there is no a priori way of knowing whether the components of the scale have equal salience for all strata.[5] Annual family income, however, cannot be equated with class situation as Weber defined it (Weber, 1946, p. 181), nor is monetary income a completely adequate indicator of the economic position of a person (Miller and Rein, 1966, p. 433); nevertheless, although the income data obtained for this study are inexact,[6] they are sufficient to classify a respondent as rich, middle income, or poor.

The second reason for using income as the major variable is that we wanted to discover whether the rich support the tenets in the stratification ideology

[5] Ossowski (1963, p. 55) says that a synthetic scale is the result of the predilections of the evaluating individual because "in different social classes the particular criteria of class affiliation carry a different weight."

[6] For example, we obtained information only on the incomes of the household head and/or spouse, not for other dependents. Nor did we attempt to obtain information on income-in-kind.

differently than other strata. Because they are a small part of the population and, consequently, of samples, most studies include the rich in a stratum with persons whose income is only a few thousand dollars above median family income. Yet the opinions of the rich may have disproportionate influence because they contribute great financial support to political parties.[7] Such an assumption enables one to interpret the finding of McClosky et al. (1960, p. 416) that, on social welfare measures, Republican followers tend to have much the same opinions as Democratic followers, while Republican leaders are far more conservative. A reasonable assumption is that the leaders reflect the views of those who support them financially, namely, the rich.

Finally, our problem was to construct interview items which would elicit adherence to general and situational tenets in the ideology of opportunity. Because statements derived from the dominant ideology tend to sound like clichés, they probably represent "what everybody knows," and, consequently, most respondents would tend to agree with them. Such general statements are often not meaningfully nullifiable. For example, the statement, "Ambitious boys can generally get ahead,"

does not specify whether "getting ahead" means rising a few points on the NORC scale or crossing a major occupational boundary (e.g., from clerical to professional). In order to obtain a more meaningful response, we elaborated a technique developed by Prothro and Grigg (1960) and Westie (1965), who presented highly generalized normative statements followed by specific ones of application. An example of a general statement is, "Minorities should be free to criticize the majority," while a specific statement is, "If a person wants to make a speech against churches and religion in this city, he should be permitted to."

In using this technique, we first presented to respondents a highly generalized statement on opportunity derived from the dominant ideology; later in the interview we presented a statement similar in logical content but specifically linking opportunity and income. All statements were worded in "either-or" form because some investigators have suggested that lower-class people tend to agree with any positive statement regardless of substantive content (Campbell et al., 1960, pp. 510–515; Christie and Jahoda, 1954).

Respondents were heads of households or their spouses who, in December 1966–January 1967, lived in the area included in *Polk's City Directory* (1965) for Muskegon, Michigan, an industrial community whose Standard Metropolitan Statistical Area population in 1960 was 149,943. For the larger study of which this report is a part, a systematic sample (N = 186) was drawn. Because such samples typically include few respondents at income extremes, we drew supplementary sam-

---

[7] Heard (1962, pp. 46–48) says that "it has long been realized that the bulk of the income received by formally organized *national-level* campaign groups from individual contributors has arrived in sums of $500 or more.... Only people of means can make even a $100 contribution. Consequently, the forces of wealth dominate the political life of the nation."

ples of rich and poor.[8] The small number of rich in the systematic sample did not justify running statistical tests of significance for income strata. "Rich" was defined as annual family income of $25,000 or more which, in the 1959 Census, was the top 1 percent of the income distribution. "Poor" was defined in terms of a scale adjusted for the number of dependents; for example, a respondent was poor if his annual family income was less than $3,500 for four persons.

The analytic sample (N = 354) upon which this paper is based consisted of the systematic sample and the supplementary samples of rich and poor. By strata of income and race, the analytic sample included 37 poor Negroes, 70 poor whites, 48 middle-income Negroes, 152 middle-income whites, and 47 rich whites. The per capita income for the Negro poor was $671; for the white poor, $907; for middle-income Negroes, $1,591; for middle-income whites, $2,310; for rich whites, over $6,000. The sex division in each stratum was almost even. Education was associated with income: three-fifths of the respondents with 0–7 years of education were poor, and three-fifths of the college graduates were rich. We shall report Negro responses separately because there is ample evidence that Negro and white experiences with the opportunity structure differ greatly. All findings must be regarded with great caution because of the small sample.

FINDINGS

Background findings show that about three-fourths of the respondents in all income strata liked Muskegon as a place to live and work. Respondents were also asked to identify themselves as middle, lower, working, or upper class.[9] A little more than half identified with the working class, and a little less than half with the middle class. In a series of questions designed to tap interest in making money, Negroes and poor whites showed the highest interest, and larger proportions of them reported having fewer economic opportunities than "other people." These and other data point to the importance of money to lower-income strata and their feelings of economic deprivation. These feelings are also reflected in their attitudes toward economic opportunity.

*Beliefs in the Tenets of
Economic Opportunity*

Three tenets of the ideology of economic opportunity were explored: the importance of working hard for "getting ahead," the relevance of father's occupation to getting ahead, and whether occupational mobility is easier in the United States than in European countries. According to the main hypothesis, we expected more agreement with the general statements than with the specific statements, but we also expected respondents with higher in-

---

[8] Any definition of poverty is arbitrary. For definitions similar to the one used, see Keyserling (1964), Orshansky (1965), and Miller (1965).

[9] The question was adapted from Centers (1949). For a discussion of the consequences of using a forced choice or free choice question to ascertain class identification, see Gross (1949).

comes to show greater agreement to ideological tenets, however stated.

A general statement on economic opportunity was adopted from Campbell et al. (1954, p. 221):

> Some people say there's not much opportunity in America today — that the average man doesn't have much chance to really get ahead. Others say there's plenty of opportunity and anyone who works hard can go as far as he wants. How do you feel?

From this statement we derived an income-linked specification:

> Do you think that a boy whose father is poor and a boy whose father is rich have the same opportunity to make the same amount of money if they work equally hard, or do you think that the boy whose father is rich has a better chance of earning a lot more money?

In response to the general statement, over eight-tenths of the white respondents and less than six-tenths of the Negroes thought that America is a land of equal opportunity (see Table 1). But in response to the income-linked statement, almost three-fifths of the rich, a half of middle-income and poor whites, and less than one-fifth of the Negroes thought that rich and poor boys had equal opportunity (see Table 1).

Since sociologists commonly use occupation of father rather than family income as the base point for studies of occupational mobility, we decided to ask respondents about the relationship

TABLE 1   BELIEFS ON CHANCES TO GET AHEAD AND TO GO TO COLLEGE BY INCOME AND RACE (PERCENTAGES)

Income and race	Plenty of opportunity (general) (a)	Rich and poor have equal opportunity (income-linked) (b)	Equal opportunity for college (general) (c)	Poor as likely to be in college (income-linked) (d)
Poor:				
Negro	56	11	22	11
White	90	47	57	38
Middle:				
Negro	58	21	41	28
White	80	49	75	37
Rich:				
White	93	57	96	43
Total, analytic sample:				
%	78	42	64	34
(N)	(342)	(351)	(348)	(344)
Total, systematic sample:[a]				
%	76	41	69	38
(N)	(177)	(184)	(184)	(181)

[a] For race, col. $(a) - \chi^2 = 4.35$, df $= 1$, $p < .05$; col. $(b) - \chi^2 = 4.03$, df $= 1$, $p < .05$; col. $(c) - \chi^2 = 4.91$, df $= 1$, $p < .05$.

of father's occupation to mobility. Situational questions reflected significant mobility, that is, crossing a major occupational stratum boundary.

The first question pertained to upward occupational mobility:

Who do you think are more likely to become business executives and professional men: the sons of big business executives and professional men, or the sons of factory workers and small businessmen?

The second situational question pertained to downward occupational mobility:

Who do you think are more likely to become factory workers and small businessmen: the sons of factory workers and small businessmen, or the sons of big businessmen and professionals?

The questions must have appeared almost fatuous to the respondents, because nine-tenths or more of all income groups felt that occupational inheritance was more likely than upward or downward occupational mobility (see Table 2). Although none of the poor Negroes thought that sons of fathers in lower occupational strata had more chances for upward mobility than other sons, almost one-fifth of them thought that sons of executives had more chances for downward mobility than sons of fathers in lower strata. Perhaps there is some comfort in the thought that, if one's own sons are not likely to rise, the sons of men in prestigious occupations may fall. We may well ask, if the question used in the interview situation seemed fatuous, do similar

TABLE 2 BELIEFS CONCERNING GENERATIONAL MOBILITY AND OPPORTUNITY STRUCTURE IN AMERICA COMPARED WITH EUROPE, BY INCOME AND RACE (PERCENTAGE WHO AGREE)

Income and race	Blue-collar son more likely to become executive (a)	Executive son more likely to become blue-collar (b)	Opportunity better in America (c)
Poor:			
Negro	0	19	16
White	11	6	9
Middle:			
Negro	4	4	7
White	8	3	19
Rich:			
White	9	0	30
Total, analytic sample:			
%	7	5	16
(N)	(344)	(347)	(351)
Total, systematic sample:[a]			
%	6	2	15
(N)	(178)	(180)	(184)

[a] For middle income and poor, col. (c) $-\chi^2 = 4.95$, df $= 1$, $p < .05$.

general or normative statements of the ideology repeated in everyday life also appear fatuous? Surely people must test public ideologies against their daily life experiences.

Popular patriotic orators often proclaim that opportunity is greater in America than in European countries. Lipset and Rogoff have presented evidence casting doubt on the validity of such proclamations, but they nevertheless assumed that the belief was "traditional and universal" in the United States (Lipset and Rogoff, 1954; Lipset and Bendix, 1959). On the assumption that this belief is most supportive to the strata which have "made it," we predicted that the rich would be most likely to believe it and the poor least likely. Using situated class referents, we asked the respondents:

Do you believe that ambitious sons of lower-class fathers are able to rise into the middle class in most European countries like Germany, France, and England, or do you think that such ambitious boys can rise only in the United States?

Unfortunately, the statement used did not call for a judgment of relative mobility rates, although some respondents (mainly, 19 percent of the rich and 32 percent of college graduates) gave a free response, indicating that mobility was possible in Europe but easier in the United States. About one-sixth of the total sample responded that mobility was possible only in the United States, or that it was easier, but three-tenths of the rich and four-tenths of the college graduates endorsed the "myth" (see Table 2). The

responses obtained to this question cast some doubt on the universal acceptance of the idea that the United States has a more open opportunity structure than Europe.

In conclusion, the responses to the three statements on economic opportunity indicate considerable range and certainly no unanimity in support of the public ideology. Moreover, when family income and father's occupation are specifically mentioned in ideological statements, the degree of support for them is greatly reduced. Yet the rich consistently see greater equality of opportunity than the poor, except in the occupational structure, where the bulk of the respondents, rich and poor, white and Negro, see the general tendency of occupational inheritance. Even when the opportunity structure of the United States is compared with that of Europe, there is a general consensus that little or no difference exists.

Operation of Educational, Governmental, and Legal Institutions

A basic tenet of the ideology of opportunity is that educational resources needed for occupational mobility are equally available to all. Similarly, the government, the law, and the courts are supposedly blind to conditions of birth. General and situated questions involving education, government, and the law were devised to tap how different economic strata evaluated their functioning.

The general statement on education concerned the chance to go to college:

Do you feel that all young people of high ability have fairly equal opportunity to go to college, or do you feel that a large percentage of young people do not have much opportunity to go to college?

The income-specific corollary was:

Do you think that most young people in college come from families who can give them financial help or do you think that young people whose parents are poor are just as likely to be in college as anyone else?

The pattern of responses to the general question was similar to that dealing with economic opportunity, that is, greater support by the higher income strata and the whites. However, the range of responses among the strata was much greater, from one-fifth support by poor Negroes to total support among the rich (see Table 1). For the income-linked statement, there was a uniform decrease in support by all income groups, about one-half the proportions agreeing with the general statements. Responses to both types of statements show a much smaller degree of confidence in equal access to education in the United States than the literature suggests (Cremin, 1951; Coleman, 1968; Williams, 1967).

Education is primarily governmentally sponsored in the United States. Does this relative lack of confidence in the ability of the educational institution to function equitably hold for government itself? A basic tenet of democratic ideology is that the imperfections in the system are reparable — that the system is self-adjusting in response to inequities because voters are able to demand and generally get what they think the system should supply. The market analogy is clear. People who are trained to believe in political pluralism feel that all income strata

should have equal influence on the operations of government and other social institutions. To explore adherence to this tenet, we prepared the following general statement on the opportunity to obtain political equality through participation in the electoral process:

Some people think that voting is a vital part of the governmental process in this country, while others think it really doesn't make much difference who gets elected because the same people go on running things anyway. What do you think?

The income-linked specification:

Some people say that, regardless of who gets elected, people who are rich get their way most of the time, while others say that people who are poor have just as much influence in government as people who are rich. What do you think?

Almost nine-tenths of all the respondents thought that voting was vital, the rich most of all and the poor Negroes least of all (see Table 3). Agreement with the specific statement shifted dramatically downward, with only three-tenths supporting it. The lower the income strata, the less the belief that wealth played no role in influencing governmental policies. Poor whites were the exception, for their rate of support was the same as middle-income whites. Similar findings appeared for different educational levels. However, the range of differences among the educational strata was smaller than for the income strata, and this again points to the "softening effect" of the educational variable.

Equality before the law was the last institutional tenet of American ideology we examined. The general statement was:

> A number of people believe that in America everyone gets equal and fair treatment from the law, while others believe that the police and courts are basically unfair in the administration of justice. What do you think?

The income-linked corollary:

> Do you think that, if he breaks the law, a rich man is just as likely to end up in jail as a poor man, or do you think it's a lot easier for a rich man to stay out of jail?

A clear majority of the white respondents, irrespective of income, agreed to the general statement, but only a minority of the poor and middle-income Negroes agreed (see Table 3). In the income-linked corollary, the data clearly reveal that all income strata do not support the tenet of a fair legal system, for only one-fifth or less of the respondents in all strata felt that the courts operated equitably. When responses to the general and situated questions dealing with the legislative branch of government are compared with those dealing with the courts, there seems to be considerably less confidence in the operation of the judicial branch of government.

Why Are the Rich, Rich and the Poor, Poor?

What makes some people rich and others poor? The implications of this

TABLE 3   BELIEFS ABOUT LEGAL AND POLITICAL EQUALITY, BY INCOME AND RACE (PERCENTAGE WHO PERCEIVE EQUALITY)

Income and race	Voting influences government (a)	Rich and poor influence government equally (b)	Law and courts are fair (c)	Jail equally likely for rich or poor (d)
Poor:				
Negro	76	3	46	8
White	88	30	75	23
Middle:				
Negro	89	15	27	20
White	89	30	59	20
Rich:				
White	94	55	75	22
Total, analytic sample:				
%	88	29	58	20
(N)	(303)	(345)	(340)	(343)
Total, systematic sample:[a]				
%	91	35	60	21
(N)	(182)	(172)	(177)	(178)

[a] For middle income and poor, col. $(b)-\chi^2 = 4.34$, df $= 1$, $p < .05$; col. $(c)-\chi^2 = 4.41$, df $= 1$, $p = .05$. For race, col. $(c)-\chi^2 = 12.84$, df $= 1$, $p < .01$.

question are political. The traditional ideology is specific. Wealth is the result of hard work, ability, motivation, and other favorable personal attributes. Wealth is earned and deserved. Poverty is the result of laziness, stupidity, and other unfavorable personal attributes, and it too is earned and deserved. People in a society get what they deserve, and the social structure is just. Since justice prevails, changes in the social structure are rarely needed. In testing support for these beliefs, we expected that those who have the most of what there is to get would be most likely to define the system as just. We therefore expected that the higher the income, the greater the tendency to assign personal factors as causes of wealth or poverty; and the lower the income, the greater the tendency to assign social structural factors as causal.

Respondents were first asked two open-ended questions, why are rich people rich, and why are poor people poor? [10] The answers were coded as pointing to personal attributes, to social structure, or to a combination of these. Only the responses which were solely in terms of personal attributes are presented in the tables. The rich are much more convinced than others that wealth is a result of favorable personal attributes; 72 percent of the rich and 17 percent of the poor Negroes felt this way (see Table 4). As one rich white man said, "Inheritance is the ex-

ception today. If you have to generalize, it's the self-discipline to accumulate capital and later to use that capital effectively and intelligently to make income and wealth." An opposite point of view was held by a poor Negro: "The rich stole, beat, and took. The poor didn't start stealing in time, and what they stole, it didn't value nothing, and they were caught with that."

The rich are also much more convinced than the poor that poverty is the result of unfavorable personal attributes. Six-tenths of the rich and 17 percent of the poor Negroes supported this idea (see Table 4). The same general pattern of responses to the two questions was found when the data were analyzed by the educational level of the respondents. Support for the ideology increased directly with educational level, but the differences between educational extremes were smaller than for the top and bottom income strata.

The explanation for being on relief was similar. Only about 5 percent of the total sample thought that people were on relief during the Great Depression because of personal attributes. But four-fifths of the rich and three-fifths of the middle-income whites thought that relief status in the past six years was the result of personal characteristics, while less than half of those in other strata thought so (see Table 4). One rich man reported, "People on relief just don't want to work. I'm biased. I run a plant where we try to hire men and they just won't stay." Another rich man said, "It's an easy way to receive their allotments. It's just too easy. Like ADC and that kind of stuff. To me, it's just criminal." In contrast, a poor Negro woman re-

[10] A number of respondents wanted to know the definition of "rich." Very few raised questions about the definition of "poor." Respondents were told that "rich" and "poor" meant whatever they meant to the respondent in the context of the Muskegon area.

TABLE 4   PERSONAL ATTRIBUTES AS A CAUSE OF INCOME
BY INCOME AND RACE (IN PERCENTAGES)

Income and race	Wealth (a)	Poverty (b)	Being on relief last six years (c)	Poor don't work as hard (d)	Poor don't want to get ahead (e)
Poor:					
Negro	17	17	28	3	0
White	34	30	46	13	19
Middle:					
Negro	29	19	45	4	6
White	35	42	59	30	29
Rich:					
White	72	62	78	39	46
Total, analytic sample:					
%	37	36	54	21	23
(N)	(350)	(341)	(347)	(343)	(347)
Total, systematic sample:[a]					
%	31	40	57	25	25
(N)	(183)	(177)	(185)	(186)	(180)

NOTE — In the wealth column, the percentages represent those who saw favorable traits as a "cause" of wealth; in the poverty columns, unfavorable traits as a "cause" of poverty. The residual categories for the wealth column would include respondents who indicated both personal and structural responses as causal, and those who saw only structural factors as causal.

[a] For race, col. $(b) - \chi^2 = 10.29$, df $= 2$, $p < .01$; col. $(c) - \chi^2 = 9.63$, df $= 2$, $p < .01$; col. $(d) - \chi^2 = 4.85$, df $= 1$, $p < .05$; col. $(e) - \chi^2 = 7.6$, df $= 1$, $p < .01$.

ported, "I've been on for six years or more and it's because I can't make enough on a job to take care of my six kids."

Hard work and motivation to get ahead are also basic tenets in the ideology of opportunity. Respondents were first asked:

Naturally, everyone can think of exceptions, but on the whole, would you say that poor people work just as hard as rich people, or do you think that poor people generally don't work as hard as rich people?

Although only one-fifth of the total

sample felt that the poor do not work as hard, two-fifths of the rich but almost no Negro respondents thought so (see Table 4).

Respondents were then asked about the attitudes of poor people toward getting ahead:

Do you think that poor people want to get ahead just as much as everyone else or do you think that basically poor people don't care too much about getting ahead? Please try not to think of individual exceptions you know of, but rather in terms of the group in general.

About one-fourth of the respondents

thought that the poor did not want to get ahead, and the response variation was like that of the previous question (see Table 4).

Conclusions

Empirical studies of ideologies are only primitively developed in the social sciences, and we hope that this research provides some suggestions about how to proceed further in this study. Obviously, national studies are sorely needed in this area, for any community study necessarily has limited generalizability. However, our hypotheses seem to be verified in the community studied. There is far from universal acceptance of the tenets of the American ideology of opportunity, even when those tenets are enunciated in the most general and vague terms. There is even less acceptance of statements in which economic inequality is made the test for accepting a tenet on equality of opportunity. The shift downward in degree of support of a tenet from its general statement to concrete specification is not a surprising finding. This phenomenon has been observed in research whenever situations are specified (Centers, 1949; Prothro and Grigg, 1960; Jones, 1941). Our data confirm the hypothesis that the support of an ideology is strongest among those who profit most from the system which the ideology explains and defends, the rich in this case. In addition, the data reveal that people from various economic strata differ in their evaluation of the effectiveness of different institutions to implement the ideology of opportunity. Such differences are also found between Negroes and whites.

We may reasonably assume that ideologies are most firmly held when they are accepted as given and not concretely tested in life situations; yet scientific analysis of ideologies cannot proceed without ascertaining how firmly the public supports them when they are enunciated in both normative and existential terms. Apparently social scientists do not know what everyone else seems to know, that people test the validity of public ideologies concretely in everyday life. We are inclined to conclude from our data that there is less "false class-consciousness" than most social scientists assume. The best audience of an ideology is the audience which profits most from its repetition. Others may not really be listening, or not listening well.

It is important for social scientists to study how firmly various segments of the community adhere to various ideological tenets, for data from such studies should provide information needed to predict the formation and activation of social movements. Clearly, such data should be gathered periodically, so that historical trends in the degree of support for old ideologies and the emergence of new ideologies can be discerned. Participation in social movements occurs when large proportions of the people in certain strata believe that institutions are not functioning to meet societal norms. They then feel that the norms must be changed or support for them must be withdrawn. In both cases, the universality of collective representations is reduced. Our data show that some people are facing a second American dilemma by questioning how they can support the ideology of opportunity in the face of massive intergenerational poverty. The dilemma is being resolved differently by people who are located differently in the social structure. We have focused on the income variable in this study, but obviously other indicators of social location are important and need to be studied. Research on ideology must become the study of the layman's sociology of the society in which he lives. Only when sociologists have this picture clearly, can they elaborate a theory on the ideology of stratification.

REFERENCES

Campbell, Angus, Gerald Gurin, and Warren E. Miller. *The Voter Decides.* Evanston, Ill.: Row, Peterson, 1954.

Campbell, Angus, Phillip E. Converse, Warren E. Miller, and Donald E. Stokes. *The American Voter.* New York: Wiley, 1960.

Centers, Richard. *The Psychology of Social Classes.* Princeton, N.J.: Princeton Univ. Press, 1949.

Christie, Richard, and Marie Jahoda (eds.). *Studies in the Scope and Method of "The Authoritarian Personality."* Glencoe, Ill.: Free Press, 1954.

Coleman, James S. "The Concept of Equality of Educational Opportunity." *Harvard Educational Review,* 38 (Winter 1968): 7–22.

Cremin, Lawrence. *The American Common School: An Historical Conception.* Teachers' College Studies in Education. New York: Bureau of Publications, Columbia Univ., 1951.

Form, William H., and Joan Rytina. "Income and Ideological Beliefs on the Distribution of Power in the United States." *American Sociological Review,* 34 (February 1969): 19–31.

Gross, Llewellyn. "The Use of Class Concepts in Sociological Research," *American Journal of Sociology,* 54 (March 1949): 409–421.

Heard, Alexander. *The Costs of Democracy.* Garden City, N.Y.: Doubleday, 1962.

Jones, Alfred Winslow. *Life, Liberty and Property.* Philadelphia: Lippincott, 1941.

Keyserling, Leon H. *Progress or Poverty.* Washington, D.C.: Conference on Economic Progress, 1964.

Lipset, Seymour M. *The First New Nation.* New York: Basic Books, 1963.

Lipset, Seymour M., and Natalie Rogoff. "Class and Opportunity in Europe and the United States." *Commentary,* 18 (December, 1954): 562–568.

Lipset, Seymour M., and Reinhard Bendix. *Social Mobility in Industrial Society.* Berkeley: Univ. of California Press, 1959.

McClosky, Herbert, Paul J. Hoffman, and Rosemary O'Hara. "Issue Conflict and Consensus among Party Leaders and Followers." *American Political Science Review,* 54 (June 1960): 416.

Mannheim, Karl. *Ideology and Utopia: An Introduction to the Sociology of Knowledge.* New York: Harcourt, Brace, 1954.

Miller, Herman P. "Changes in the Number and Composition of the Poor." In *Poverty in America,* Margaret Gordon (ed.). San Francisco: Chandler, 1965.

Miller, S. M., and Martin Rein. "Poverty, Inequality and Policy." In *Social Problems: A Modern Approach,* Howard S. Becker (ed.). New York: Wiley, 1966.

Mosca, Gaetano. *The Ruling Class.* (Ed. Arthur Livingston, trans. Hannah D. Kahn.) New York: McGraw-Hill, 1966.

Orshansky, Mollie. "Counting the Poor: Another Look at the Poverty Profile." *Social Security Bulletin,* 28 (January, 1965): 3–29.

Ossowski, Stanislaw. *Class Structure in the Social Consciousness.* (Trans. Sheila Patterson.) New York: Free Press, 1963.

Parsons, Talcott. "A Revised Analytical Approach to the Theory of Social Stratification." In *Class, Status and Power: A Reader in Social Stratification,* Reinhard Bendix and Seymour M. Lipset (eds.). Glencoe, Ill.: Free Press, 1953.

Prothro, James W., and Charles M. Grigg. "Fundamental Principles of Democracy: Bases of Agreement and Disagreement." *Journal of Politics,* 22 (May 1960): 276–294.

Smelser, Neil J. (ed.). *Sociology.* New York: Wiley, 1967.

Weber, Max. *From Max Weber: Essays in Sociology.* (Ed. and trans. H. H. Gerth and C. Wright Mills.) New York: Oxford Univ. Press, 1946.

Westie, Frank. "The American Dilemma: An Empirical Test." *American Sociological Review,* 30 (August 1965): 527–538.

Williams, Robin M., Jr. *American Society.* New York: Knopf, 1967.

Horatio Alger was a turn-of-the-century American writer who produced many mythical stories about poor but honest men who struggled from a life of poverty to become rich and famous. His heroes all pulled themselves up by their bootstraps through hard work, perseverance, and a devout belief in the American free enterprise system. Many Americans today desire upward mobility and as Rytina et al. noted, many believe that the American opportunity structure will allow them to attain this mobility.

One important means of upward mobility is through educational attainment (in colleges and universities). Another way to attain this goal is to enter an occupation that offers opportunities for advancement with few barriers against those with little education. Some attain upward mobility through owning their own business. Small shopkeepers may become successful and own more and more or larger and larger stores. Truck drivers may save money to buy their own truck and become an independent trucker. What often happens is that a life style may develop around the means rather than around the goal. The occupation rather than social mobility may become the central life interest.

Most occupations have an important effect upon a person's life. All people who work are not equally enthusiastic or involved in their jobs; however, for many people, their occupation is a central life interest. Occupations regulate much of people's time and structure many of their social relations. For most people, occupations take up at least 7 hours a day for five days a week.

Jobs structure social worlds through daily routines and selective social interaction with people who share similar experiences. Work affects peo-

ple whether they like their jobs or not. Some people take work home with them, socialize with their fellow workers outside of the work setting, and "talk shop" whenever they can. Others focus their life style to help them forget what happens during the work day. The profound effect that a single social variable may have on life styles is illustrated in the following article by Studs Terkel, who describes the life style of independent truckers.

Frank Decker

Studs Terkel

He had been hauling steel "out of the Gary mills into Wisconsin. They call this a short haul, about 150 miles in radius." [1] He had been at it since 1949 when he was nineteen years old. "I figure about 25 hundred trips. Sounds monotonous, doesn't it?"

Most steel haulers are owner-operators of truck and trailer. "We changed over to diesel about fifteen years ago. Big powerful truck. You lease your equipment to the trucking companies. Their customers are the big steel cor-

porations. This is strictly a one-man operation."

Since the wildcat strike of 1967 he's been an organizer for the Fraternal Association of Steel Haulers (FASH). "Forty-six months trying to build an association, to give the haulers a voice and get 'em better working conditions. And a terrific fight with the Teamsters Union."

Casually, though at times with an air of incredulousness, he recounts a day in the life of a steel hauler.

I'll go into the steel mills after supper. Load through the evening hours, usually with a long waiting line, especially years ago before the Association started. We'd wait as high as twelve, fifteen hours to get loaded. The truck-

From *Working: People Talk About What They Do All Day Long and How They Feel About What They Do* by Studs Terkel. Copyright © 1972, 1974 by Studs Terkel. Reprinted by permission of Pantheon Books, a division of Random House.
[1] "The long hauler, if they give him a pickup to go over to Detroit from Chicago, he feels it's a waste of time, no trip at all. He wants to load New York. He'd leave Chicago, drop a drop in Cleveland and a drop in Pittsburgh, and peddle the rest of

it off in New York. Once a dispatcher told Jim — he's a little over fifty, been long haul for twenty-five years — 'We have a little box here, not a load, weighs thirty-five hundred pounds, do me a favor, pick it up.' Jim says, 'I don't have room for this box and it's goin' the other way. I'll pick it up next time I'm in New York.' He was heading for St. Louis. It takes a certain kind of individual that thinks in thousands of miles so casually, as you and I'll pick something up from my neighbor here next week."

ing companies didn't charge the corporations for any waiting time, demurrage — like they did on railroad cars.

We get a flat percentage no matter how much work we put in. It didn't cost the trucking company anything to have us wait out there, so they didn't charge the steel outfits anything. They abused us terribly over the years. We waited in the holding yard behind the steel mill. The longest I've ever waited was twenty-five hours.

You try to keep from going crazy from boredom. You become accustomed to this as time goes by — four hours, eight hours, twelve hours. It's part of the job to build patience. You sit in the cab of the truck. You walk a half mile down to a PX-type of affair, where you buy a wrapped sandwich in cellophane or a cup of coffee to go. You sit in the mill by the loader's desk and watch the cranes. You'll read magazines, you'll sleep four hours, you'll do anything to keep from going nuts. Years ago, there was no heat in the steel mills. You had to move around to keep from freezing. It's on the lakefront, you know.

Following the '67 wildcat strike, the trucking companies instituted a tariff that said four hours we give the steel mill for nothing, the fifth hour we begin to charge at $13.70 an hour. We get seventy-five percent of that or ten dollars. And when we deliver, they got four free hours at our point of delivery. So we start every day by giving away eight potential free hours. Besides your time, you have an investment ranging from fifteen to thirty thousand dollars in your truck and trailer that you're servicing them free. The average workingman, he figures to work eight hours

and come home. We have a sixteen-hour day.

If I were to go in the mill after supper, I'd expect to come out maybe midnight, two o'clock in the morning. The loading process itself is fifteen to thirty minutes. Once they come with the crane, they can load the steel on it in two or three lifts. Maybe forty-five to fifty thousand pounds.

We protect it with paper, tie it down with chains and binders, tarp it, sign our bills, move toward the gate. It takes you fifteen to twenty minutes to get to the front gate. I must weigh in empty and weigh out loaded. Sometimes, even though you're all loaded, tarped down, and everything, you get on the scale and you're off-weight. If you scale in at twenty-five thousand pounds empty and you come out weighing seventy-two thousand pounds, you're five hundred, six hundred pounds off the billed weight. You have to go back and find out who made a mistake. Let's say it's over the one percent they'll allow. They have to weigh everything again and find out that some hooker made a paper mistake. That's happened many times to haulers. Prior to '67, we never got paid a penny for it.

Years ago, we ran through city streets, alongside streetcars, buses, and what have you. It was a two-hour run from the mills of Gary to the North Side of Chicago. Some seventy-six traffic lights. Every one of them had to be individually timed and played differently. If you have to stop that truck and start it, it's not only aggravating and tiring, but you'd wear out the truck twice as fast as you would if you made those lights. It was a constant thing of playing these lights almost by instinct.

This is all changed with the expressways. It's just as if automation had entered the trucking business. Now you pull out of U.S. Steel in Gary and you don't have a light until you drop off at the expressway in the city of Milwaukee. It's a miracle compared to what it used to be. So much easier on yourself, on your equipment.

A stop at the Wisconsin state line, a place to eat. Big trucks stop there. Maybe meet a bunch that have been in the steel mill all night. Coffee-up, tell all the stories, about how badly you're treated in the steel mill, tell about the different drunks that try to get under your wheels. Then move towards your destination and make the delivery at seven o'clock in the morning. We're talking about thirteen hours already. My routine would be to drop two days like this and not come home. Halfway back from Milwaukee take a nap in the cab at a truck stop. You use the washroom, the facilities, you call your dispatcher in Gary, and pick up another load. Went home for a day of sleep, wash up, get rejuvenated, live like a human being for a day, come back to the mill after supper, and be off again. During the last ten years almost everybody bought a sleeper truck. It has facilities behind the seat. If you were to get a hotel room every night you were on the road, why, you'd be out of business shortly.

On weekends, if you're lucky enough to be home, you're greasing the truck and repairing it. It's like a seven-day week. There's nobody else to do the work. Years ago, the rate of truck repair was five dollars an hour. Today it's eleven, twelve dollars an hour. You do ninety percent of the work yourself, small repairs and adjustments.

I would make two round trips to Milwaukee and pass within four blocks of my house and never go home. You can't park a big truck in the neighborhood. If the police have anything to do with it, you can't even park on an arterial street more than an hour. It's a big joke with truckdrivers: We're gonna start carrying milk bottles with us. Everywhere we go now, there's signs: No Truck Parking. They want you to keep that thing moving. Don't stop around here. It's a nuisance; it takes up four spaces, which we need for our local people. You're an out-of-town guy, keep moving.

If I chose to park in the truck terminal, I'd have an eight-mile ride — and I don't think I'd be welcome. The owner-operator, we're an outcast, illegitimate, a gypsy, a fella that everybody looks down on. These are words we use. We compare ourselves to sailors: We sail out on the highways. The long-distance hauler is gone for a week, two weeks, picking up a load at one port, delivering it to another port.

You get lonely not talking to anybody for forty-eight hours. On the road, there's no womenfolks, unless there's a few waitresses, a couple of good old girls in the truck stop you might kid around with. They do talk about women, but they don't really have the time for women. There's a few available, waitresses in truck stops, and most of them have ten thousand guys complimenting them.

There's not much playing around that goes on. They talk of women like all guys do, but it's not a reality, it's dreaming. There's not these stories of conquest — there's the exceptional case of a Casanova — because they're moving too much. They're being deprived of their chance to play around. Maybe if they get more time, we'll even see that they have a little more of that. (Laughs.)

Truckers fantasize something tremendous. When they reach a coffee stop, they unload with all these ideas. I've seen fellas who build up such dreams when they come into a truck stop they start to pour it out, get about three minutes of animated description out of it, and all of a sudden come up short and realize it's all a bunch of damn foolishness they built up in their minds. It's still that they're daydreaming from the truck. He builds a thing in his mind and begins to believe it.

You sit in a truck, your only companionship is your own thoughts. Your truck radio, if you can play it loud enough to hear — you've got the roar of the engine, you've got a transmission with sixteen gears, you're very much occupied. You're fighting to maintain your speed every moment you're in the truck.

The minute you climb into that truck, the adrenaline starts pumping. If you want to have a thrill, there's no comparison, not even a jet plane, to climbing on a steel truck and going out there on the Dan Ryan Expressway. You'll swear you'll never be able to get out the other end of that thing without an accident. There's thousands of cars and thousands of trucks and you're shifting like a maniac and you're braking and accelerating and the object is to try to move with the traffic and try to keep from running over all those crazy fools who are trying to get under your wheels.

You have to be superalert all the time. Say I'm loaded to full capacity, seventy-three thousand pounds. That's equivalent to how many cars — at four thousand pounds a car? I cannot stop. I got terrific braking power. You have five axles, you'll have fourteen tires on the ground, you got eight sets of brakes. You have to anticipate situations a block ahead of you. You're not driving to match situations *immediately* in front of you. A good driver looks ahead two blocks, so he's not mousetrapped into a situation where he'll have to stop — because you can't stop like a car's gonna stop. You're committed. It's like an airplane crossing the ocean: they reach that point of no return. Your commitment's made a hundred, two hundred yards before you reach the intersection. It's really almost impossible.

You have to get all psyched up and keep your alertness all the time. There's a lot of stomach trouble in this business, tension. Fellas that can't eat anything. Alka-Seltzer and everything. There's a lot of hemorrhoid problems. And there's a lot of left shoulder bursitis, because of the window being open. And there's a loss of hearing because of the roar of the engine. The roar of the engine has a hypnotic effect. To give you an idea of the decibel sounds inside a cab, nowadays they're beginning to insulate 'em. It's so tremendous that if you play the radio loud enough to hear above the roar and you come to a tollgate and stop, you have to turn it down it's screaming so loud. You could break your eardrums. And the industrial noises in the background . . .

I'm sure his hearing's affected. There was a survey made of guys that transport cars. You've heard the loud metal noise, where the different parts of the gates comes together. They found these fellas have a great loss of hearing. It's one more occupational hazard. There has been different people I've worked with that I've seen come apart, couldn't handle it any more.

I'll tell you where we've had nervous breakdowns, when we got in this '67 thing, the wildcat. We've had four people associated with us in Gary have had nervous breakdowns. And at Pittsburgh, they've had several. The tension of this labor thing, forty-six weeks, is real strong. The tension's even greater for a guy with a family to support. . . .

There seemed an unusual amount of fellas having problems with their family, with the wife in particular. They're average guys with their wives going through the change and so forth. Really, that's an awful problem for the wife, because she has to raise the kids, she has to fight off the bill collectors on the phone. She can't even count on her husband to attend a graduation, a communion, any kind of social function. She's just lucky he's home Christmas and New Year's. He's usually so darn tired that he'd much rather be home sleeping than getting ready to go out Sunday night.

Sure, truckers eat a lot of pills. It's a lot more prevalent than I thought. I heard fellas say they get a better price on bennies if they buy them by the thousand. We know a lot of individuals we consider hopheads off on benzedrine. A couple of guys I know are on it, even though it's on the week-ends when they don't need to stay awake. It's become a habit.

The kids call 'em red devils. In trucking, they call it the Arkansas Turnaround — or whatever your destination is. A lot of 'em are dispensed by drugstores on prescription for weight control. So their wife gets the pills and the old man ends up usin' 'em to keep awake, because they're a benzedrine base. It'll be the little black ones or the little red ones . . .

They'd like to pick up the kids, hitchhikers, if it weren't for the prohibitions. I think the biggest transporters of hippies would be the owner-operators, because they want company. For years you didn't see a hitchhiker, but now with the hippie, with kids traveling across the country, every interchange has got a bunch of long-haired, packsacked kids hitchhiking from one end of the country to the other. It's a reborning. . . .

It's a strange thing about truckers, they're very conservative. They come from a rural background or they think of themselves as businessmen. But underneath the veneer they're really very democratic and softhearted and liberal. But they don't *realize* it. You tell 'em they're liberal and you're liable to get your head knocked off. But when you start talking about things, the war, kids, when you really get down to it, they're for everything that's liberal. But they want a conservative label on it. It's a strange paradox.

In the steel mill, the truckdriver is at the absolute bottom of the barrel. Everybody in that mill that is under union contract has some dignity, has some respect from management. If he's the fella that sweeps the floor, he has job status. The man in the crane, if there's no work for his crane, he doesn't have to do anything. If the fella that pushes the broom in Warehouse Four, if he's got everything groomed up, they can't tell him, "No, you go and do another job."

Now comes the steel hauler. Everybody in that mill's above somebody, from top management down. At the bottom of the ladder, there's the hooker on your truck. He wants to feel that he's better than somebody. He figures I'm better than this steel hauler. So you get constant animosity because he feels that the corporation looks down on this steel hauler, and he knows he can order him around, abuse him, make him wait. It's a status thing. There's a tremendous feeling.

The first couple of years when I got abused, I howled and I yelled and I did my dance: "You can't do this to me." After a few years, I developed a philosophy. When I scream, it gives them pleasure, they can put it to me. They're sadists. So the average steel hauler, no matter how abused he is, you always give them that smile and you leave it go over your head. You say to yourself: One day my time will come. If you don't take this philosophy, you'll go right out of your mind. You cause an incident, you're barred from the mill. It's such a competitive business that you dare not open your mouth because your company will be penalized freight — and you get it in the neck. You try to show 'em a cockiness like you could care less.

Over a number of years, your face becomes familiar. It breaks the ice. The loader considers you an old-timer, he has some identity with you. You

might find, on rare occasions, friendship. The loader is the foreman on the shift for truck loading. He has a desk in between all the piles of steel and he lays out the loads that are gonna be placed on the truck. If the hookers see the loader's giving you respect, they'll accept you.

The newer people get the most grief, do the screaming, and get the worst treatment. Younger fellas. The fella that comes into this business that's over forty takes his life's savings and buys a truck because somebody told him there's big money to be made and he wants to get in his own business. If you last the first five years, you last the worst hardships. Success means you survive. If you don't make a dime on your investment, but you're still in business after five years, we say he's a regular. Those first five years is your biggest nut to crack. You don't know the ropes, you don't know how to buy and service your truck reasonable, you make all the mistakes. Fifty percent turnover in our business every year. They drop out, lose their trucks. That's the only reward: In your mind, you feel you're in business.

There's been a change since the '67 wildcat. It spread across the country like wildfire. We're respected in a lot of places now because they know we stand up and fight for our rights. As much as it was a money problem, it was a problem of dignity.

Ninety percent of the fellas were Teamster Union members, but you'd never know it. Outside of the dues money they take out of your check, they did absolutely nothing. They did less than nothing. We know that a few telephone calls by high Teamster officials to steel mill officials could have changed our picture completely. If they would call up and say, 'Look, you're abusing our people and if you don't straighten it out we're gonna do something about it.' They could put one man down there at U.S. Steel, for instance, and say, 'I'm a Teamster official. We're asking you guys not to load in this mill until they treat you fairly.' In twenty-four hours we'd be getting loaded out there so fast we couldn't keep our hat on our head.

But they're establishment. They're interlocked with the steel mills and the trucking companies. They don't even know who their members are. Our guess is between twenty and thirty thousand steel haulers. Nobody can come up with the figures. A Teamster official was maybe a truckdriver twenty-five or thirty years ago. Fought the good fight, built the union, got high on the hog. So many years have passed that he doesn't even know what a truck looks like any more. He now golfs with his contemporaries from the trucking companies. He lolls about Miami Beach at the Hollywood Hotel that they own. To him, to have a deal with a truckdriver is beneath his station. It's awfully hard when you get to the union hall to talk to a Teamster official. They're usually 'busy.' That means they're down at the Palmer House, at the Steak Restaurant. It's a hangout for 'em.

Truckdrivers used to spend ninety percent of their time bitchin' about how they got screwed at the mill, how they got screwed by the state trooper. Troopers prey on truckdrivers for possible violations — mostly regarding weight and overload. It's extremely difficult to load a steel truck legally to capacity. If you're a thousand pounds over, it's no great violation but you

have to get around the scales. At regular pull-offs, they'll say: Trucks Must Cross Scales.

You pull in there and you find, lo and behold, you're five hundred or a thousand pounds over. You've got to pay a ticket, maybe twenty-five dollars, and you have to move it off. This is a great big piece of steel. You're supposed to unload it. You have to find some guy that's light and break the bands on the bundle and transfer sheets or bars over on the other truck. Occasionally it's something that can't be broke down, a continuous coil that weighs ten thousand pounds. You work some kind of angle to get out of there. You wish for the scale to close and you close your eyes and you go like hell to try to get out of the state. You have a feeling of running a blockade in the twenties with a load of booze. You have a feeling of trying to beat the police. Or you pay the cop off.

Most state troopers consider truckers to be outlaws, thieves, and overloaders. The companies and the union don't try to upgrade our image. They don't go to the police departments and say, "Stop abusing our members."

Everybody's preying on the trucker to shake him down. The Dan Ryan is unbelievable. They're working deals you couldn't believe, that nobody would care about, because they're out of state truckers. Who cares what happens to them? What would you think of a trucker coming up the Dan Ryan for the first time? He's coming from Pittsburgh with an overload. He approaches the South Side of the city and it says: All Trucks Must Use Local Lanes. But the signs aren't well enough marked and he's out in the

third lane and gets trapped. He can't
get over because of the other cars, he
goes right up the express lane. Well,
there's cops down there makin' their
living off these poor guys. They pull
him over and they say, "Hey buddy,
you're out where no trucks are supposed to be. We're gonna have to lock
you up." They go through their song
and dance about they're horrified
about how you've broken the law, endangering everybody. And they're
hinting around that maybe you want
to make a deal.

Maybe you don't want to make a
deal? Oh, you have to make bond and
appear in court, that's twenty-five dollars. If you've got an out-of-state
chauffeur's license, they'll take your
chauffeur's license. So if you're going
to come up with a ten, he'll hold court
right there and he'll tell you never
do it again. But if you're gonna be
hardheaded — I'm gonna fight this
thing — he'll say, "Okay, we're gonna
take you in the neighborhood out here
and we're gonna park your truck and
we're gonna take you over to the station in a squad car." I can't swear to
it, but there's a story goin' around that
these cops are working with the people
in the neighborhood. So you park your
car out on those streets. While you're
at the station making bond you come
back and there ain't much left to your
truck. The tires are gone, the cab's
been broken into, the radio's gone.
That's what happens to thousands of
truckdrivers.

The cops tell you, "You get back on
your truck any way you know how."
Because they don't want to be there
when you see your truck. You take a
cab over there and there you stand.

Now you call the copper, this official
paragon of law and order, and he tells
you, "How am I gonna find out who
wrecked your truck and stole everything off?" A truck tire costs a hundred
dollars. You're liable to come back
from the station, trying to fight your
ticket, to have four hundred-dollar bills
gone right off the trailer.

Why the devil do you do it, right?
There's this mystique about driving.
The trucker has a sense of power. He
has a sense of responsibility too. He
feels: I know everything about the
road. These people making mistakes
around me, I have to make allowances
for them. If the guy makes a mistake,
I shouldn't swear at him, I shouldn't
threaten him with my truck. You say,
"That slob can't drive. Look at that
dumb woman with her kids in there.
Look at that drunk." *You've* got status!

Every load is a challenge and when
you finally off-load it, you have a feeling of having completed a job — which
I don't think you get in a production
line. I pick up a load at the mill, going
to Hotpoint in Milwaukee. I take a
job and I go all through the process.
You have a feeling when you off-load
it — you see they're turning my steel
into ten thousand washing machines,
into a hundred farm implements. You
feel like your day's work is well done
when you're coming back. I used to
have problems in the morning, a lot
of heartburn, I couldn't eat. But once
I off-loaded, the pressure was off. I met
the deadline. Then I could eat anything.

The automobile, it's the biggest
thing in the country, it's what moti-
vates everybody. Even that model,
when they drape her across the hood

of that car.... In the truck stop, they're continually talking about how they backed into this particular place in one swing. The mere car drivers were absolutely in awe. When you're in that truck, you're not Frank Decker, factory worker. You're Frank Decker, truck owner and professional driver. Even if you can't make enough money to eat, it gives you something. . . .

There's a joke going around with the truckdrivers. "Did you hear the one about the hauler that inherited a million dollars?" "What did he do with it?" "He went out and bought a new Pete." [2] "Well, what did he do then?" "He kept running until his money ran out." Everybody knows in this business you can't make no money. Owning that big Pete, with the chrome stacks, the padded dashboard, and stereo radio, and shifting thirty-two gears and chromed wheels, that's heaven. And in the joke, he was using up the inheritance to keep the thing on the road.

You have to figure out reasons to keep from going crazy, games to try to beat yourself. After a number of years, you begin to be a better loader. They come with a thirty-thousand-pound coil. If you set it down on the truck three inches forward or backward of where it's supposed to be, you're misloaded. So there's a challenge every time you load. Everybody's proud of that. At the truck shop they'll flash a weight ticket: "Take a look at that." They've loaded a balanced load.

Now as we approach '67, I've about

[2] "That's a Peterbilt, the Cadillac of trucks. It's a great, big, long-nosed outfit. The tractor alone costs 30,000 dollars."

had it. I'm trucking seventeen years. There's nothing left to do. I never dreamt that our hopes of getting together some day was gonna come true. It was just a dream. I'll finish out the year, sell off my truck and trailer, and I'm gonna build a garage up at the Wisconsin-Illinois state line. I'm gonna service trucks in there. The guys needed a garage where they could get work done. The commercial garages — you got a bunch of amateurs working on your truck. To be an owner-operator, you gotta be a mechanic. I had a three-car garage when I was seventeen. So I was gonna build this garage. . . .

But I met an old-timer I'd seen around for years. This was at Inland Steel on a Thursday night. One of my last hauls — I thought. We sat for about six hours waiting to get loaded. He said to me, "Did you hear about the rumble going on down in Gary?" He showed me this one-page pamphlet: "If you're fed up with the Teamsters Union selling you out and all the sweetheart contracts and the years of abuses, go in front of your union hall Monday morning at ten o'clock. We're gonna have a protest."

Friday I talked to everybody. "We're finally gonna do something. We've been talkin' about it for years. . . ." I couldn't get anybody to talk to me. "Ah, hell, that's all you ever talk about."

Well, Monday morning I went out to Gary. There was twenty guys picketing. We didn't get much help through the day. We decided to go to the steel mills and intercept our people, who were coming in from all over the country with their trucks. You got the picture? Ninety percent of the guys didn't know where the union was at. For years, they paid dues as an extortion. They're hurting. Most of 'em are one paycheck away from the poorhouse. So we went there and tried to tell 'em, "Park your truck and come and picket." Well, it turned into something because the time was ripe. Everybody knew something had to happen.

We picketed for eight days on the mills. It built till we had five hundred, six hundred guys — most of 'em from out of town. Parked their trucks all over town. We hung on them gates. Sometimes we'd get down to two, three guys and we thought it was all over. But there's a new carload of guys come in from Iowa or from Detroit or from Fremont, Ohio, or something. They'd heard about this rumble that was going on and they come to help.

We picketed the steel mills and we talked to any steel haulers that come in, told them not to load, to join the picket line. Some of the haulers tried to run you down. You'd have to jump for your life. Other guys would come up and they wouldn't know what to do. They recognized a lot of faces. We met each other in truck stops for years. You know the guy — Tom, Dick, or Harry. But you never knew much more about him than just a service stop. We began to build relationships down here with these guys we'd seen for years, but we didn't know where they lived or anything else. They'll say, 'What kind of truck you drive again?' They recognize you by your truck, see?

So we're having meetings. The guys call from Detroit. They shut down Armco Steel or Great Lakes Steel. Then we heard they're picketing at Pittsburgh and finally they're picketing in Philadelphia. And then we heard

they blew up two trucks with dynamite in New Jersey. The Jersey crowd, they're always rough. It spread clear from here to the east coast. And it went on for nine weeks.

Steel mills got injunctions out against us. They took us into court and locked us up and everything else. The Teamsters helped the steel mills and the carriers to try to get us back to work. They come out in cars: a company official, a Teamster official, a marshal — pointing out who we were to serve papers on. They were working together.

Everybody's telling everybody: 'They'll go back to work. They're all broke. They can't last more than a couple of weeks.' But we hung on and we hung on, you know. (He swallows hard, takes a deep breath.) Some of the guys didn't go home at all. We raised money by going around asking truck stops and truck dealers and tire dealers to donate money and help us. A lot of 'em were dependent on us and knew we were poor payin' and knew that maybe if they helped us out we could start gettin' in better shape and start to pay our bills.

Truckdrivers are known as an awful lot of deadbeats. They live off credit and lay on everybody. Deprive their family, two legs ahead of the bill collectors, charge fuel at the new guy's station that's givin' credit to everybody and then, when they run up a big bill, they'll go by. All to keep that truck going. I don't think they're worse responsible than anybody else. But they get in a position like a businessman: you owe everybody and his brother and you start writin' paper and you try to survive. You get in deeper and deeper and deeper. . . .

So we formed an organization — the Fraternal Association of Steel Haulers, FASH. We organized like hell, leading up to the contract time again. We went on a nationwide strike because we didn't hardly scratch the door the first time. This time we asked the Teamsters Union to represent us, which they never did before. Fitzsimmons[3] promised in the agreement he'd set up a committee to meet with us. He sent us the very thieves that had locals where the steel haulers had members. These guys had vested interests to keep things the way it was. We met with 'em a couple of times and saw they weren't about to do nothin'.

> So we demanded Fitzsimmons meet with us — not that we thought he'd do anything. He's nothing but a dirty old man shuffling along and filling a hole for Hoffa. But we did feel we could get recognition if we'd meet with him. Nothing doing. He wouldn't even talk with us. He sent a big bully, that's Hoffa's right hand, the head of the goons, guy with a prison record as long as your arm. He started tellin' us all he's gonna do for the steel haulers. We said, 'You ain't doin' nothin' for us.' We told him we didn't have to listen to his baloney. He said, 'What do you want?' We told him we want the International to give us charters for steel locals. We want to have elections and we want to elect our own people. We want autonomy. And then we told him, 'We want you and your crooked pals to stay ten miles away from any of our halls.' He said he'd take the message back, and that's where it stands now.
>
> We'd become aware, checking our rates with the Interstate Commerce Commission and the Department of Labor, about their misuse of our pension fund. A nine-hundred-million-dollar pension fund that got about a billion finagled away. That's our pension. We don't have the freightside driver's feeling for good old Jimmy Hoffa. They don't care how much he steals. That ain't us. That's our pension money in that fund. He belongs in jail, a lot of 'em do.

In January '70, we went out on strike to reinforce our demands for recognition. We filed with 167 companies that employed steel haulers under Teamster contract. When the hearings began in Pittsburgh, there were thirty-seven lawyers from the carriers and Teamsters and two of our attorneys — one guy and another guy helping out. The hearings lasted sixteen days. It cost the Teamsters $250,000 for their legal costs. There was ten thousand pages of testimony. The National Labor Relations Board ruled against us. We think it was a politically inspired ruling. Nixon was playing footsie with Fitzsimmons.[4] We were fighting the mills, the union, the carriers, the President. Who else is there left?

I talked with a fella who sold trailers. He said, "You guys are nuts. You've taken on all these big people. You don't have a chance." But there's just one thing — we feel that we're a revolution. There's people's power here and truck power. And there's a lot of people in the Teamsters Union watchin' us. If they start to see that we don't get our heads busted, that

---

[3] Frank Fitzsimmons, president of the Teamsters Union.

[4] The conversation took place before Jimmy Hoffa was granted a pardon by President Nixon and long before the Teamsters Union came out in support of the Committee for the Re-election of the President.

we're tough enough to lead, they're gonna come out of the woodwork. *They* all want to know where their pension money went. What's wrong is that they're all scared.

We did extremely well till this last strike. We didn't make it in the strike. There were some defections in our ranks. They voted to go back to work. We were about gonna grab that brass ring when we dropped it. So there's been a lot of disillusionment on the part of a lot of guys. But we gained so much in these three years that a lot of guys are stickin'.

We're treated with quite a bit more respect, I'll tell ya, than we were before 1967. Sure, we're havin' problems. The Teamsters are trying to get the carriers to blackball us, trying to control the steel haulers. But they know they've lost us. We have membership stickers on the trucks. The sticker alone sometimes gets 'em loaded twice as fast. What they'll say, "You better load that guy, he belongs to that outfit and you don't load him you're gonna have to pay for it." We got a good reputation.

Our people are very cynical. They are always suspicious of leadership sellin' 'em out. They've seen the Teamsters. They gotta pay their dues whether they're workin' or not. So they turn on us. They're supercritical — every little thing. Between the day the strike started until March '68, I didn't pull a load of steel — that's eight months I didn't draw a penny. I been, since then, on a fifty-dollar-a-week salary, full-time for FASH, out of the Gary office. Had one guy tell me, "You only get fifty dollars a week, but that's how Hoffa started." Had another guy tell me, "I wouldn't have anybody

that dumb working for fifty dollars a week to represent me." The cynicism is unbelievable.

First thing they figure, These guys are after soft, cushy jobs. They're after Hoffa, they're after the same thing we've been taken advantage of. What you have to do is rebuild confidence. These people don't trust nobody. They don't even trust themselves no more. "You're workin' in a crooked system and you gotta be a crook." So the guy figures, I wouldn't do it for anybody else, why this guy? Another typical thing is: It won't work. You can't beat 'em. They're too big. The Teamsters are too big. The steel mills are too big. Everything's against us. If you fight it, you get hurt.

You gotta re-educate 'em, you gotta climb up on the cross every day. What you build, eventually, unfortunately, is a following that will follow you no matter what you do. That's why you end up with Hoffa, with them sayin' "I don't care if Jimmy stole a million dollars, he's okay with me." It's a shame that people are that much sheep.

We're not getting the grass-roots backing we'd like to have. They're too busy, they go to their families. Sometimes I wonder why I'm in this thing. But it's rewarding. There's nothing like dealing with people, dealing with situations. It's like a crash course to educate yourself. It's something I really enjoy doing because it's something I thought should have been done all these years. After eighteen years of trucking, a change to do this work. . . .

If I thought I could hand-tailor a job that I'd like to do, it's this job I'm doing right now. I never worked so hard at anything in my life. Most of this forty-six months has been seven days a week. I get weary but I never get tired of doing the job. I'm enjoying every minute of it. We're up against a lot of big people, big corporations. It has the feeling of playing chess with the top contender. It can affect people's lives, even people that don't even know.

If you win, the stakes are high. It's not just whether you're gonna make a buck. All of a sudden, you feel catapulted into these levels of decision-making that I never dreamed I'd ever reach. All of a sudden, you're no longer the guy smiling and putting up a front and waiting all the time in the truck. All of a sudden, you found your own sense of self-respect. The day's finally here. Now.

Marriage is a central life interest around which many persons seek to develop a distinctive life style. Although the life style of married people is considerably different from the life style of single people, there is no one single or married life style. Even this presumably important variable cannot explain a very large portion of variation in most people's life styles. One reason is that there are so many ways to be married or to be single. Although marriage means stability for some and nonmarriage means autonomy for others, not all married people enjoy stability nor do all nonmarried enjoy autonomy. Thus, even though marriage may be a central life interest of both an upper class suburban and an urban black housewife, their experiences with marriage largely reflect other dimensions of their life style.

The following articles make several important points. Married life styles are different than single life styles, but married and single life styles are affected by such factors as social class, age, and the size of the community in which an individual lives. Life styles thus do not only vary around a single factor but by a combination of two or more variables.

49 Million Singles Can't Be All Right

Susan Jacoby

Last year I bought a townhouse and two dogs and moved in with a girl I really loved. It was the first time I'd made a solid commitment to anyone. She decided it wasn't what she wanted, so here I am by myself — a suburban homeowner with two toy poodles and no woman.

    —A WASHINGTON DOCTOR

Swinging singles? They live somewhere else, not in this town. I've gone out on exactly three dates since my divorce a year-and-a-half ago.

    — A LANSING, MICH., SECRETARY

I'm my own woman and I like it just that way. I don't have to go down to a court and beg for child support my ex-husband won't pay anyhow. I drive my cab 12 hours a day, six days a week, and I bring home $150. I'm young, I'm tough, I do fine.

    —AN ATLANTA TAXI DRIVER

The diversity of single life in the United States contradicts both the old-fashioned image of unmarried people as lonely losers and the current media picture of "swingles" who cavort

From *The New York Times Magazine* (February 17, 1974). © 1974 by The New York Times Company. Reprinted by permission.

through an endless round of bars, parties and no-strings-attached sexual adventures. The adult single population, which jumped by two million a year during the nineteen-sixties, is now approaching 49 million. The estimate includes men and women who have never been married, widows and widowers, the divorced and legally separated — everyone from new college graduates savoring their first taste of independence to retired people who live together instead of getting married because they want to collect two Social Security checks. In between, there are millions of single parents who cope with the problems and pleasures of both family and unmarried life.

Like any newly discovered minority, singles tend to be viewed by the majority in misleading, monolithic terms. Stereotypes about the unmarried frequently seem as ludicrous as the image of a black populaton with a universal sense of rhythm and love for watermelon. Single men and women in different areas of the country expressed a combination of dismay, resentment and amusement when they were asked about their public image. "Five years ago I was used to hearing sorrowful comments about my 'loneliness,' " said a 34-year-old executive with the Coca-Cola Company in Atlanta. "Now I get lecherous envy. From reading the press, you'd think that every girl is 36-24-36, like the blonde on the cover of Newsweek, and every guy lounges by a pool-side and waits for the beautiful blondes to admire his rippling muscles. The truth just isn't very glamorous — some single people are happy and some aren't, just like married people."

The 1970 census attests to the dramatic growth of the single population, but the statistics do not support most of the hasty, widely publicized conclusions about marriage being on the way out and singlehood being the wave of the future. The post-World War II baby boom was a predictable factor in the singles increase of the mid-sixties, but the unpredictable and even more important factors include later marriages, a spiraling divorce rate and a marked trend against early remarriage after divorce. The number of adults who have never been married jumped from an estimated 12.9 million in 1960 to 16.2 million in 1970, but the under-25 age group accounted for the largest share of the growth. Among adults over 30, the percentage of people who have never been married has actually declined during the past 15 years.

The rise in the divorce rate — an 80 per cent increase between 1960 and 1972 — is well-known and well-documented. A less noticed phenomenon is the growing reluctance of divorced men and women to leap into early second marriages. By 1970, there were more than 1.3 million divorced people under 35 who had not remarried—double the number in 1960.

None of the people I interviewed fitted into a neat newsmagazine-style package of "the single life." Age, sex, location and economic status are major factors contributing to the diversity and complexity of single life. Twenty-year-old singles have no more in common with 40-year-old singles than newly married people do with middle-aged couples. Single life in small towns differs radically from single life in large cities. In some respects, economic status has an even more significant impact on the lives of singles than of married couples. Married people often add one small income — usually the woman's — to a larger income — the man's — and use the combination to push into a higher stratum of society. Singles of both sexes must go it alone, and take a heavier tax bite into the bargain.

Not surprisingly, single life seems to satisfy the upper middle class more than any other group. Affluent singles need never choose between a tacky studio apartment and putting up with three roommates; they are spared the penny-pinching which takes some of the "swing" out of the lives of $90-a-week file clerks and gas-station attendants. Money is especially useful in combating loneliness, the No. 1 bogeyman of many singles. "The most satisfying single lives are dotted with unhappy love affairs and sexual droughts — times when you just don't meet anyone worth seeing," says a 30-year-old Washington journalist. "If you have money, you can go to New York for a weekend or Europe for a month. It's not as easy to spend money to get yourself out of a rut when you're married. Maybe your mate isn't in the same mood you are and doesn't feel the need for a trip."

Without money, it is difficult to translate the theoretical freedoms afforded by the single life into reality. A 36-year-old New York lawyer emphasized this point as he described his plans to close out a highly successful law practice because he wants to travel and try to write fiction. "Most of my friends think I'm crazy," he said, "but I've already made enough money to support myself comfortably for several years. I've spent most of my adult life accumulating money or looking after other people's money; now I'm going to use it to free myself. I've always wanted to write, and I plan to settle somewhere in Europe and see if I have any talent. If I don't, I can pick up the law practice again. If I were married, I doubt that I would be able to break away and do this 'crazy' thing. Some of my friends have children who are only a few years away from college. How could I throw over a career in that situation?

"It's important to me that I've been successful at something and that I do have money. My friends say to me, 'But what if you're an absolute failure at writing?' Well, what if I am? I won't starve, anyway, and I'm not a failure as a lawyer. It's very bourgeois, and probably wrong, but I think most middle-class people fail to strike out in new directions because they are afraid of financial insecurity."

Small but growing numbers of upper-middle-class women are also enjoying the combination of money, success and single freedom that was formerly a male preserve. Unlike college-educated men, these women frequently seem surprised by their monetary and professional success. "I've been surprised to find myself making such a good salary," said a 30-year-old Washington woman with a demanding legislative staff job on Capitol Hill. "Freedom and security and money and power are all bound together in our society. Rightly or wrongly, I always thought that someone else would provide those things for me, although I was determined to become 'someone' myself."

Even when they make substantial salaries, single women are less likely than men to make the kinds of financial investments which would assure their future economic security and independence. I talked with a group of eight Washington women in their late 20's and early 30's, most of them making between $15,000 and $20,000 a year. Only two owned any stocks, and they attributed their investment to the relentless nagging of their parents. None owned houses or cooperative apartments. Several had jobs which offered an optional payroll-deduction pension plan, but none had taken the option. Their financial arrangements were typical of the single women I met throughout the country; most of the single men who were making $20,000 a year had investments to show for their salaries.

"Women aren't brought up to think about managing money alone," observed Ellen Sudo, who works for the Democratic Study Group in the House of Representatives. "Even when a single woman loves her work and knows she will always work regardless of marriage, there's a hangover from traditional upbringing. Until very recently, I've always thought of the single state as something impermanent. Now I feel that I want a home and I want it now — I don't want to wait for someone else to come along and make it for me. I have thought about buying a house, although I'm terrified of accumulating possessions. I've been renting a house for the last six months, and the landlord isn't sure he can let me have it next spring. I'd like to plant flower bulbs — it's a small thing but, damn it, I want to know whether I can have flowers next spring or not."

Upper-middle-class singles of both sexes talk constantly about choices — whether to travel or save money, buy houses or rent apartments, invest in stocks or pension plans, stay with the same company or change jobs. Such choices are as foreign to millions of blue-collar singles as they are to married people with six children. Most blue-collar workers do not hang out at Maxwell's Plum, and they do not live in expensive singles complexes with swimming pools, saunas and night clubs. In every city, singles are acutely aware of class distinctions in places of entertainment and residence. Just as the older crowd moves on when teeny-boppers invade a bar, professionals tend to abandon a favored hangout when file clerks and bank tellers seem to be moving in. "These people are pushy," said a young Atlanta engineer. "I've found two bars I really liked in the last year, and they were both taken over by swarms of girls looking for a 'college boy.' You want to be with your own kind of people."

Blue-collar singles look for their own kind of people in places like The Red Rail, a combination bar and dance hall on the outskirts of Lansing, Mich. — a city of 135,000, the state capital and home of the Oldsmobile division of General Motors. With no cover charge, 90-cent drinks and a country-and-western band, The Red Rail is jammed with file clerks and auto workers on weekend nights. There is no regional ambience; the bar might be in any American city large enough to support a modest amount of night life. The customers range in age from the early 20's through the mid-50's. Some are married people pretending to be single, but most of the older patrons are divorced. Many of the middle-aged men arrive in bowling shirts imprinted with the numbers of their union locals; the young men arrive in everything from turtlenecks to immaculately pressed suits, white shirts and ties. The women favor tight pants and tighter sweaters. Fifty-year-old men roam from table to table, trying not to wince when the younger women turn down their invitations to dance.

The band was winding down into a slow song as Peggy Ann Sears turned down an invitation from a middle-aged man whose greasy gray hair, wide bell-bottomed trousers and flashing ruby ring suggested a combination of Liberace and Elvis Presley. He hung around the table and cracked several dirty jokes, following Red Rail etiquette, which dictates that a man cannot slink away too quickly lest everyone know he has been rejected as a dance partner.

"He's a well-known creep — that's spelled C-R-E-E-P," Peggy Ann said after her unwanted admirer had moved on to another table. She looked both older and younger than her 29 years — older because she wore her hair in a page boy-and-bangs style reminiscent of the fifties, younger because she was only 5 feet tall and constantly chewed a wad of gum between swallows of gin-and-tonic. "You've gotta turn down the creeps on slow dances, unless you want to get squeezed and worked over like a tomato in a supermarket. I come here for one reason — because I love to dance — but what man will believe that?

"I laugh when I read about how exciting the single life is, what wonderful chances there are for a girl alone today. 'That Cosmopolitan Girl!' Wow! I'm a secretary to a man who owns a liquor store — the only other men I meet are married liquor dealers. If it hadn't been for my kids, I would've moved to a bigger town — maybe Detroit — when my husband took off. But I bring home $95 a week — before taxes, get that — and my mother takes care of my two little girls while I'm working. With my education, I wouldn't make much better money in a big city but a hunk of my check would go for day care. I just couldn't make it."

Before her divorce 10 months ago, Peggy Ann was taking night courses to qualify herself for a job as a court reporter. She dropped the classes when her husband left her. "I really liked court reporting, and it pays much better than what I'm doing now. But I had to go to work full time, and I didn't see how I could be gone every night too. It's too hard on the kids and my mom. Maybe when they get to be school age I can make it out of this dead-end job. Maybe."

Peggy Ann Sears illustrates a pervasive fact of life for many single women — they simply do not make enough money. The aggravating money shortages turn to suffocating hardship for those with children. An estimated 2,272,000 families fall into what the Census Bureau defines as the "near-poor" category — those who make between $4,274 and $5,345 a year. Of these families, nearly one-third are headed by women. They are the working poor, people who are usually too proud to go on welfare but find it difficult to make enough money for what the Department of Labor considers a "moderate" standard of living. "I don't especially want to get married again," Peggy Ann said in a defeated tone. "But if I can manage to meet someone decent, I probably will get married again for the sake of my kids. They've never had a man around the house. And I don't want them to grow up with what I can give them on my salary. But in my job, it's just not easy to meet anyone."

Because most blue-collar and low-level white-collar workers are trapped in sex-segregated "job ghettos," blue-collar men and women find it difficult to meet potential partners. "There aren't any girls on the assembly line," said a 25-year-old Oldsmobile worker. "I came here for work from a much smaller town, and I don't have any old girl friends from high school. So there's really no place to meet girls except in a bar, preferably with dancing. I have this dream, see. Someday I'll go to a Michigan State football game and there will be a nice girl sitting next to me. We'll be able to talk to each other like normal people, because we're both just there to watch the game and not to pick someone up. Everything will be just natural, like when you were sitting in the same algebra class with girls in high school. And I won't have to go to bars any more. But I've been to lots of football games and the girls beside me always have a date."

I did meet some blue-collar singles who enjoyed their lives and their freedom. Patricia Grant (a pseudonym), a 32-year-old Atlanta cab driver, is the

mother of 11- and 12-year-old boys.
She is usually on the streets by 6:30
A.M. so she can make it home in time
to spend the evening with her sons.
"I work harder than a man to make
do," she says. "This is still the South,
and people will pass up a cab driven
by a woman for one driven by a man.
I agree with Shirley Chisholm — I get
more static because I'm a woman than
because I'm black. Hell, all the cab
drivers in Atlanta are black. There are
men who get into my cab and give me
the business because I'm a woman —
they think I'm just a whore trying to
drum up clients. I set them straight,
and they give me bigger tips because
they're embarrassed."

Pat Grant has a "steady man," who
also drives a cab, and she met him
through her job. He works the same
hours and manages to bring home $25
more a week than she does. "It's true,"
he says, "I see it with Pat — it's just
tougher for a woman alone. I'm not
much of a swinger myself. My wife
split and left me with three kids. Yeah,
that's funny, it's the black man who's
supposed to be irresponsible according
to all those studies. People just ain't
studies. A lot of Pat's and my friends
ask us why we don't just get married
and combine the kids. We think about
it sometimes, but we're both a little
scared of marriage. Pat sure doesn't
want to be depending on anyone but
herself again, and maybe I don't want
to depend on a woman. But we help
each other out a lot, the way married
people do. Still, there's times when the
kids are in bed and I open a beer —
and I'm glad I'm alone." Pat is equally
cautious about trying marriage a second time, and she takes considerable

pride in the fact that she is making it
alone. Out of her $150-a-week earnings,
$10 goes into a savings account each
Friday. "That's over $1,500 in the last
three years," she says. "When my boys
are old enough for college, the money
is going to be there."

Socially, sexually and economically,
singles are usually better off in large
cities like Atlanta than in small ones
like Lansing. The sexual revolution has
not bypassed towns the size of Lansing, but it still causes much more
comment than it does in larger cities.

The middle-aged residents of an expensive apartment complex in East
Lansing — a university town of 60,000
— were surprised one afternoon when
a fellow tenant showed up at a pool-
side party with a woman he lived with
and whom everyone assumed was his
wife. When one of the neighbors introduced her as "Mrs. ———," the
man cut in and said, "No way." He is
a regional administrator for a well-
known religious organization, and the
incident was still a topic of conversation several months later.

The desire to escape gossip and social restrictions is an important factor
in the migration of singles from small
towns to medium-sized cities and from
medium-sized cities to larger metropolitan areas. Some fast-growing cities
like Atlanta and Dallas are special
meccas for divorced people who found
that small-town life began to pall when
they were without a mate. Pat Grant
moved from Macon to Atlanta six
years ago primarily because "I couldn't
have a boyfriend there without my
mama knowing. She and my daddy
were pillars of the Baptist Church. I
couldn't have had any normal life as

a woman without getting married again, even if the man took off the day after the ceremony. What you value most as a single person is people minding their own business, and you only get that in a big city."

Singles are at a particular social disadvantage in small cities with a sharply limited number of cultural activities, restaurants and public places of entertainment. Socializing goes on almost entirely in private homes and is controlled by married couples. The domination of social life by couples is irksome to older singles who have never been married, and especially to divorced people cut off from most of the friends they had when they were married. Beverly Cogbill, who works for the Georgia Labor Department, is another Atlanta refugee from Macon: "I kept running into my husband's friends all the time, and I was hardly ever included in anything. I sat there for four years, feeling sorry for myself. One Christmas, I cried and cried. When I was through crying, I decided it was my last Christmas in Macon. So I moved here, got a much better job and found a whole world of people like myself."

Social life is not the only area in which small-town prejudice surfaces against single people. A 34-year-old Michigan State University faculty member found it was virtually impossible for a single man to rent a house in East Lansing. "People just have this image of a single man as an irresponsible person who has beer busts and will probably break up the joint," he says. "I've tried and tried to rent houses, and I always get turned down when they find out I'm not married.

Lots of faculty members go away and rent their houses for the the summer, but I've never been able to get into one."

This experience typifies the reverse side of the swinging single stereotype: Whatever their age, sex, economic status or location, singles must contend with an image problem which frequently combines the old picture of the lonely loser with the new, excessively carefree stereotype. The special image of singles affects both their personal and professional lives.

A recent survey of 50 major corporations by the new national magazine Single found substantial evidence of discrimination against the unmarried. Although 80 per cent of the responding companies asserted that marriage was *not* essential to upward mobility, a majority indicated that only 2 per cent of their executives — including junior-management personnel — were single. More than 60 per cent of the respondents said that single executives tend to make snap judgments, and 25 per cent believed singles are generally "less stable" than their married counterparts.

Many single men in their mid-20's confirmed this corporate attitude; they told me job interviewers always asked them why they were still unmarried. One personnel officer with an insurance company asked a 27-year-old Detroit man whether or not he "liked girls." An executive with another company said, "You don't look like an irresponsible sort of guy, but you've been living in the same place for four years and haven't found a wife. Why?" The young man replied that he had not yet found anyone with whom he wanted to spend the rest of his life. The executive chortled and said, "You still like a good f——, that's it."

The single image does not work the same way for women in business. In general, executives seem to believe that marriage makes a man more reliable and a woman less reliable. Many middle-aged male bosses tend to assume that a woman will stay with a company forever if she has not married by her late 20's. They also assume that pregnancy will disrupt the careers of married women. When a 36-year-old editor in a New York publishing house received a major promotion two years ago, her boss told her: "You're a real career girl. I know that I can count on you not to go get married and leave us." The executive was taken aback when the woman told him she had already been married for three years.

The self-image of singles has improved substantially as a result of the unprecedented growth in the single population during the past decade. "I've gotten a lot of headaches from my family because I'm not married," said a 30-year-old Manhattan stockbroker. "A nice Jewish boy is supposed to get married as soon as he's out of college and started in business. I think there was always the unspoken thought lurking around: 'Could my baby boy be a homosexual?'

"Now, suddenly, I've become respectable again. All of the good little boys who got married are getting divorced. The other day my mother said to me, "Well, Paul, at least you've still got a clean slate in life.' I can even take a girl home to meet my parents now. They're really great people, but I used to hate having them meet any woman

I was dating because they'd start asking whether she was Reform, Conservative or Orthodox — or maybe not Jewish at all — and how the wedding ceremony could be performed if there were religious complications."

Jerry Zweig, a 43-year-old floor-covering distributor from Jersey City, N.J., remembers that "for the first year after my divorce, I was even embarrassed to say the word. I felt it was like talking about a terrible disease. Now there are so many people like me that I don't feel ashamed. I'm not opposed to marriage. I'd like to get married again, but I want to take time to learn some things about myself. I see this as a perfectly legitimate desire now. When I was in my 20's and early 30's, the idea would have been unthinkable."

It is probably too early to tell whether the sharp rise in the single population indicates a radically new life-style or simply a shift in the timing of marriages. Most of the singles I interviewed, including both the divorced and the never-married, expressed opposition to early and hasty marriages rather than to the idea of marriage itself.

The millions of young singles who are taking more time to choose their mates could contribute to greater marital stability in the nineteen-eighties and nineties (although this is only a hypothesis based on past marital patterns). Many men and women who had emerged from bitter divorces said they felt their marriages would never have failed if they had "grown up" as singles before they took on the responsibility of a family. "If I were just getting out of college today," said one woman, "I wouldn't be getting married right away. Fifteen years ago, I felt like a freak because I was 21 and unmarried. Now I have to do the growing up I should have done then, and I won't get married again until I feel I am fully mature. But I'm not afraid of trying a second marriage when I do reach that point of maturity."

It is certainly a mistake to assume that unattached men and women in their 20's will remain permanently in the singles fold. Managers of singles apartment complexes say they have a high tenant turnover primarily because so many residents leave them to get married. "There's a lot of charisma about the city," says an Atlanta man. "People come and live in the singles apartments after college, but after a while most of them will go back to being exactly what they would always have been."

Although there were exceptions, single men and women generally felt their attitudes toward marriage had become more positive as they had grown older. Never-married singles in their late 20's and early 30's usually expressed a deep interest in forming long-term relationships. "I don't necessarily want to marry," says 31-year-old Joel Pickelner, "but I'm certainly not ideologically opposed to the idea of marriage. I would like to setle down. I've had my

fill of a nomadic sort of life. If I met a girl I loved and she wanted to get married, I think I'd be glad to. If she didn't want to get married but just to live together, that would probably be all right too."

Members of both sexes frequently mentioned children as a reason for shifting from singlehood to marriage. "I think about kids all the time," said a 32-year-old man. "When I meet a new woman, there's always the question in the back of my mind: 'Could we be good enough together to be responsible for a new individual?'" Many singles echoed the views of 29-year-old Evelyn Wolfson, a Brooklyn teacher:

"If you'd asked me about being single four years ago, I would have said it was the greatest thing in the world. I still think it's great for a lot of people, especially in contrast to immature marriages. But quite frankly, I want to get married now. I want children, and I'm middle class enough to think I'd never have one while I wasn't married. Also, I love my work and I don't see how you could manage a child and a job without a mate to help you. I can be alone, often I want to be alone, but I don't want to stay alone for the rest of my life. I'm not desperate to get married, but marriage is the big, tantalizing unanswered question in my life."

How Fashionable Is Your Sex Life?
William Simon and John Gagnon

	Highbrow	Upper Middlebrow
How Girl Meets Boy	He was an usher at her best friend's wedding	At college, in the psychology lab
The Proposal	In his room during the Harvard-Princeton game	In the back seat of a Volkswagen
The Wedding	In her living room, by a federal judge	College chapel (nondenominational)
The Honeymoon	Mediterranean	Bahamas
Marriage Manual	*Kama Sutra*	*Sexual Efficiency in Marriage,* volumes I and II
Sex Novels She Reads	Jane Austen	*Lady Chatterley's Lover*
Sleeping Arrangements	Double bed	King-size bed or twin beds with one headboard
Sleeping Attire	He: nothing. She: nothing	He: red turtleneck nightshirt. She: gown with matching peignoir
Background Music	Ravi Shankar or the Beatles	Wagner
Turn-Ons	Pot	Champagne and oysters
The Schedule	Spontaneously, on an average of 2.5 weekly (that means 2 times one week and 3 times another)	Twice a week and when the kids go to the Sunday matinee
Number of Children	1 each by a previous marriage, or as many as God provides	2.4
Anniversary Celebrations	A weekend in Dublin	He gives her a new dishwasher. She gives him a power lawn mower
Quarrels	"I don't care what your analyst says"	"I don't care if he is your brother"
If the Marriage Needs Help	He consults her analyst. She consults his	They go (a) to a marriage counselor; (b) to the minister
The Affair	"But I assumed you knew"	"It was basically a problem in communication"
Sex Education	"Ask Doctor Grauber, dear, when you see him tomorrow"	"Well, you see, Daddy has something called a . . . etc. And Daddy and Mommy love each other very much"
Vacations	Europe in May. She takes the children to the Cape. He commutes	Europe in July. Family camping in Yosemite
Financial Arrangements	Separate trust funds	Joint checking account
Who Raises the Children	English nanny, boarding school, and Dr. Grauber	Mommy and Daddy, Cub Scouts, and Dr. Freud

From *McCall's*, 94 (October, 1968), pp. 58–59. Reprinted by permission.

Lower Middlebrow	Lowbrow
In the office, by the water cooler	On the block
After three drinks in an apartment he borrowed	In her home one night when Mom and Dad were at the movies
City Hall	Neighborhood church
Any Hilton hotel	Disneyland
Van de Velde	None
Myra Breckinridge and any novel by Harold Robbins	*Valley of the Dolls*
Twin beds with matching night tables	Double bed
He: pajamas. She: pajamas	He: underwear. She: nightgown
Sound track of *Dr. Zhivago*	Jackie Gleason and the Silver Strings
Manhattans and whisky sours	Beer
Twice a week and when the kids go to Sunday school	Twice on Saturday night
3	As many as God provides
Corsage and dinner out	Whitman Sampler and dinner at Howard Johnson's
"What do you think I'm made of?"	"Drop dead!"
He: to his successful brother. She: to her best friend	He: to the bartender. She: to her mother
"It was bigger than both of us"	"Some things no woman should have to put up with"
"Well, you see, Daddy puts the seed in Mommy's tummy, etc., etc."	"We got you at the hospital"
He hunts or fishes. She visits Mother with the children	They visit Brother Charlie in Des Moines
She budgets	He gets weekly allowance
Mom and Dad, the Little League, and Dr. Spock	Mom, the gang, Ann Landers, and good luck

SOCIAL STRATIFICATION AND LIFE STYLES

Social inequality is present in all societies. Sociologists generally refer to unequal categories of people as social classes; moreover, they generally recognize that people in different social classes differ in life style. The relationship between social inequality and life style variation is generally so clear and widely recognized that many sociologists have come to the conclusion that most life style variation within a society can be explained in terms of social inequality. Although this conclusion may be an overgeneralization, it is nevertheless true that many of the behavioral patterns we regard as components of life style vary according to inequality in income, education, and occupational standing.

Social class has traditionally been considered the most potent variable in explaining life style differences, and studies in sociology are regarded as lacking if they disregard it. Practically every aspect of life from sexual behavior* to pronunciation† has been demonstrated to be class-related. Currently there is debate regarding what social classes are. Some contend

* Alfred C. Kinsey, Wardell B. Pomeroy, and Clyde E. Martin, *Sexual Behavior in the Human Male* (Philadelphia: Saunders, 1948).

† William Labov, "Phonological Correlates of Social Stratification," *American Anthropologist,* 66 (December 1964, part 2), pp. 164–176.

that they are easily recognized and distinct entities, others believe that all boundaries are arbitrary and misleading.† Thus, when we use the term* social class *we do so cautiously.*

Market researchers are interested, for practical reasons, in delineating social classes. Frequently they get a sense of the market, that is, they identify the kinds of people who will buy a product by categorizing interviewees into social classes. Their categories may be crude, such as upper, upper-middle, middle, and lower class, but they prove to be useful even though they may be no more than a convenient fiction. Researchers make decisions about the category into which a respondent should be placed on the basis of available indicators such as a respondent's neighborhood, house type, or the furnishings within a living room. Other indicators from which the researcher infers social class may be the occupation or educational level of the respondent. Sometimes these factors are combined in a standardized index.‡

In the following article, Bensman and Vidich give us their overview of the American class system. There is not one life style within each social class but many. But it is also true that despite the differences, life styles within a social class are somewhat similar and are distinct from the life styles within other social classes.

* W. Lloyd Warner et al., *Social Class in America* (New York: Harper, 1960).

† Dennis H. Wrong, "Social Inequality Without Stratification," *Canadian Review of Sociology and Anthropology,* 1 (1964), pp. 5–16. For a more complete discussion of this issue, see Gerald W. Thielbar and Saul D. Feldman (eds.), *Issues in Social Inequality* (Boston: Little, Brown, 1972), pp. 1–104.

‡ For a discussion of measuring social class, see Thielbar and Feldman, pp. 371–451.

The New Class System and Its Life Styles

Joseph Bensman and
Arthur Vidich

If one took the characteristic life styles now visible in American society and assumed that they were to become the basis for forming the future life-style traditions of the different classes, what would the American class structure look like? Of course, classes do not simply disappear. . . . [E]ven with changes in their economic basis classes remain, though their psychology may be drastically altered. The same is true of life styles. New life styles may replace older ones even while the economic basis of both styles remains the same. More likely, however, new life styles will not completely replace old ones, but will simply become accretions on them. Any innovations in life styles thus increase the complexity of the class system because older classes and styles coexist with the new ones. Recognizing this, we can foresee not only new classes and styles but also a wide range of different life styles within each stratum.

THE UPP

The u
industr
was ac
and su
the 1
class
roads, su
automobiles. Some
names are du Pont, Whitney,
Harriman, Eaton, Rockefeller, Mellon, Duke, Pew, Manville, and Ford. These "groups" have survived a number of economic cycles over a variety of industrial phases and have remained at the top. Now that they are stable in their economic positions, they can afford a certain amount of patrician restraint and *noblesse oblige*. In both business and philanthropic activities they have sufficient confidence in their own social and economic positions to be able to allow paid professionals to manage their wealth. E. Digby Baltzell has been the major sociological chronicler of their mentality and life style, and the historian Gabriel Kolko has most carefully analyzed the mechanisms by which they have protected and maintained their wealth. In modern times no one has analyzed the administrative and legal structures by which the families making up this group are organized, though Robert Brady, in his book *Business as a System of Power*, suggested how this might be done.

This segment of the upper class has a long and continuing tradition of social intercourse with European nobility, Eastern Ivy League schools, and the exclusive New York City social and debutante life. Because both their

130

Socia
social and
internatio
viduals
minds
con
in

conomic activities have an
nal flavor, upper-class indi-
tend to be internationally
d, and they occasionally come in
act with and "use" world-minded
tellectuals as spokesmen for projects
consistent with worldwide business
interests.

Since the twenties, new sets of investment oportunities have accounted
for additions to this upper class. These
opportunites include Texas oil, space
industries, electronics, communications, real estate, air transport, and the
entire industrial expansion of the West.
Names like Hunt, Murchison, Getty,
Hughes, Giovanini, Kaiser, and Kennedy are most closely associated with
these opportunities. The older industrial aristocracy regards these groups
as *nouveau riche* and for this reason
the newer wealth has not been admitted into this class nor has it accepted
the patrician style. In being excluded
the new groups have tried to invent
their own styles, which include massive purchases of art, establishing
universities and other monuments, sub-
sidizing sons in political and journalistic enterprises, overcompeting in conspicuous philanthropy, and, above all,
linking themselves to the international
life of the jet and celebrity sets. These
styles of living and pleasure go beyond
the patrician style. For example, Howard Hughes distinguished himself by
his investments in Hollywood starlets
(Jane Russell) and Las Vegas real estate, and J. Paul Getty bought an English manorial estate. Grace Kelly married Prince Rainier and upheld a prin-
cipality, rejuvenated by this transfu-
sion of American beauty, aspiration,
and nouveau wealth.

But not all these nouveaux riches
have been internationally successful.
Where this wealth is not internationally minded or not successful enough
to become so, it will attempt to join
older regional elites from previous periods. In cities like St. Louis, Cleveland, and Milwaukee, post–World War
II real estate speculators may hobnob
with old German brewery families. Out
of such regional elites new national and
international elites may emerge, depending upon the future potential of
the industrial base off which they live.
It is difficult to foresee who from this
group will rise to the top, because
capital growth patterns are difficult to
predict.

In addition to the older industrial
aristocrats and the nouveaux riches,
there is a type of wealth based on a
wholly new kind of economic opportunity in American society. As we have
noted before, the federal bureaucracy
and the elite managerial class in modern industry are now in a position to
command important investment and
political decisions. These people have
the power to determine the distribution of contracts, subcontracts, and
great expenditures of money. These
upper-level bureaucrats and managers,
whose positions are based on talent,
hold key positions in the society and
are indispensable to its functioning. It
is "natural" that they should receive
a disproportionate share of the social
wealth. Through processes like stock
options, "kickbacks," "marrying the
boss's daughter," "taking over the
firm," "salvaging a declining corporation," and so on, the managers can
acquire wealth. We have in mind men
such as McNamara of Ford, the De-

fense Department, and the World Bank; Gruenwalt of du Pont, who married the boss's daughter; Litchfield, a professor whose consulting activities gained him control of a corporation and who later became president of a university; Theodore Sorenson, now with a New York law firm; and Leonard Bernstein, Sol Linowitz, Abe Fortas, Billie Sol Estes, and Bobbie Baker, the latter two having failed in mid-course. Though these men have not necessarily acquired massive wealth, they have established themselves in positions from which they may build substantial "equity." It is difficult to say which of them will accumulate the successful "portfolios," but, in the long run, wealth-holding follows the key positions to which they have access.

Insofar as the successful bureaucrats and managers aspire to upper-class social status, they are unique in that they constitute a new strata for recruitment into the upper class. As *potential* recruits, however, they face the problem of whose styles to emulate, and thus they have a choice. The choices available include the styles of the older social aristocracy, the nouveau riche style of the oil-electronics-space-industry types, the style of politically ascendant wealthy groups, or that of the socially minded international set. Specific choices will determine specific future fates, and the heirs of this generation of successes may or may not emerge at the top, depending on social and fiscal decisions made by the principals during this generation.

Related to the higher managerial and bureaucratic expert is the Ph.D. nouveau riche. The former Cal Tech, Columbia, MIT, Harvard, Berkeley, or Chicago academic or scientist-technician turned entrepreneur is a special case of a single idea related to space, electronics, data-control systems, or atomic energy being used to inaugurate an industry. These Ph.D. technicians add a wholly new dimension to potential upper-class life styles. Because their major life experience was in the university, they have an intellectual and literary bent which historically has not been characteristic of the American upper class. While the Ph.D. technicians are bookish and literary, they can also follow the stock market with mathematical precision. They have a talent which is highly remunerative, so they are appreciated even by old-style, upper-class business vulgarians. To the extent that they are admired by their economic superiors, they may be both accepted and emulated by them. Where that is the case, they may influence the future conventions of upper-class life styles.

All these groups — based on old wealth, massive wealth, vulgar wealth, intellectual wealth, and managerial-bureaucratic wealth — are joined by the international class of movie stars, sports heroes, artistic heroes, space heroes, and dramatized political heroes who through personal effort, skill, and talent have distinguished themselves in a special line of human endeavor. They are recognized because they are active, exciting, and proficient. Personal, physical, intellectual, or technical performance is impressive especially to old-line *rentier* wealth, which, because it has never been asked to do anything (after the first and second moneymaking generations), is overly impressed by any achievement. This provides the link between the old-line wealth and the celebrity.[1]

It seems likely that two dominant themes will be added to the styles of the traditional American upper class. One is the expansiveness of the Texas tycoon, whether oil businessman or political manipulator: in either case he steps out in a big way unself-consciously, confident that his manner will produce results because it has done so in the past in Texas. The gall of the Texan will continue to help shape in the future, as it has in the past, the leadership style of the United States on the world scene.

The other theme is provided by the Ph.D. intellectual-entrepreneur of space, science, and data-processing, who in his narrow instrumental rationality thinks of himself as an educated man. He is literate, reads and writes books, and thinks the problems of the world can be solved by his methods without knowing that once upon a time St. Simon, Comte, and Marx had similar visions. In the meantime, he has brought intellectuality to the life style of the American upper classes. The new technically based industries and Washington, with its big federal budgets, provide the basis for this emergent class. In its major outlines this class parallels emergent managerial, technical, and bureaucratic upper-class patterns that appear to be characteristic of modern Russia.

A major innovation in the United States, though not in Europe, has appeared among both new members of the upper class and the scions of the older upper class. This is upper-class radicalism. Not only is it appropriate for the upper class to engage in the degenerate sexuality described by Robert Graves in his Claudian novels, by Choderlos de Laclos in *Les Liaisons Dangereuses*, and by Federico Fellini in *La Dolce Vita*, but also in the use of drugs, as illustrated in De Quincey's *Anatomy of Melancholia*. Various forms of gambling and alcoholism are not new to the upper class, but "radical chic" in politics is. It involves an identification with the political movements of the lowest classes through social affairs which become prestigeful events designed to raise political funds for the downtrodden, the oppressed, and revolutionaries. To be sure, not all of this new politics comes from the old upper classes. Increasingly it is a means by which artistic social climbers demonstrate their liberalism, their modness — not madness — and their in-ness. Frequently they are so "in" that they are ahead of all others who by definition must be out. Of course, "radical politics," whether it represents new or old wealth, provides an ideology for personal liberation beyond politics. It may be sexual, personal, or cultural. It seeks to escape from the bonds of classes, but is usually enacted in the form of a class-based arrogance which justifies itself in the right of the indivi-

---

[1] The relatively simple, dull Babbittry of traditional business leadership has been reasserted in the public prominence given to it by the appointment of representatives of this class to major offices in the Nixon administration. It is not unusual that a leadership class may lag behind social and cultural elites in the same society. Differences in such styles, as we shall see, are increasing.

dual to such stylized behavior.[2] The best description of this in European society is in Dostoevsky's *The Possessed* or Turgenev's *Fathers and Sons*. Such behavior can be found in the old upper class in all societies, and at times in new classes where the acquisition of wealth is so great in a short time that the group has not had time to learn to be degenerate in more sophisticated ways.

The new "radical chic" includes, then, the sons and daughters of America's wealthiest families, some of whom financed the Students for a Democratic Society (SDS), the Weathermen, and the Columbia and Harvard riots. It

[2] See Renato Poggioli, *The Theory of the Avant-Garde* (Cambridge, Mass., 1968). Poggioli makes this point with respect to the avant-garde in the arts. some of his illustrations suggest that by the nineteenth century prestigeful modernism included experimentation with many contemporary forms of drugs: "And from the more or less conscious sense of that relationship there originated among romantic avant-garde artists the illusory hope of being able to attain aesthetic ecstasy, a mystic state of grace, by means of certain physiological and psychological stimulants: opium in the cases of De Quincey, Coleridge, Novalis, and Nerval; alcohol in the case of Poe; hashish in Baudelaire's case; absinthe in Verlaine's and Rimbaud's — in short, those drugs which give easy access to the 'artificial paradises' found in other heavens than that of art" (pp. 194–195).

To complete the comparisons between classes, we would add that drugs are instrumental to the overworked and underfed lower classes in that they provide a release from pain, especially from hunger. For the upper class, their "pain" is the emptiness of existence; their stylized vices serve to fill such emptiness.

also includes radical "think tanks" and journalistic ventures which have had the misfortune of being economically successful, though it is hard to determine whether this was an intention or a result.[3] As the new upper-class political style emerges, it becomes apparent that the new styles can be profitable and appropriate to all classes. One of the great virtues of commercial capitalism is that its market mentality and its permissiveness permit profit-making from all forms of self-destruction, whether political, narcotic, or alcoholic. Herbert Marcuse would argue that the promiscuity of such permissiveness is actually a permissive repression. We would disagree, arguing that such permissiveness represents the destruction of the older repressive culture and is really the new culture.

THE UPPER MIDDLE CLASS

The upper middle class historically has been the responsible backbone of the community because of its civic participation and its support of cultural affairs. All large and medium-sized cities can point to the older and distinguished residential suburbs (Westchester, Shaker Heights, West Hartford, The Main Line, Brookline, Scarsdale, Harrison, The North Shore) which date to the twenties and earlier. In some cities this upper middle class may be regarded as the upper crust, but this is true only from a local perspective. When this local upper crust is

[3] See Dennis H. Wrong, "The Case of the New York Review," *Commentary,* November 1970.

compared to the national and international upper class, it is clearly only an urban and regional upper middle class with an economic base in upper middle management — proprietors and executives in retailing and distribution, the more successful of the fee professionals, and so on. Since World War II, however, this older upper middle class has been joined by newcomers who have deviated from the older suburban style. The new segments of the upper middle class located in the greatly expanded suburbia and exurbia have added new dimensions to upper-middle-class life styles.

In the more sophisticated and advanced regional, suburban, and university centers, upper-class styles have penetrated the class system. With the development of mass media and mass communications, patterns of emulation have been diffused culturally and geographically throughout the society. The density of the new culture is determined by previous class position, social and cultural mobility and sensitivity, and access to the mass media. Radical chic, now an emerging style, will compete with and be partially absorbed by the following styles, some of which are themselves relatively new and unstabilized.

1. The style of the Country Gentleman includes the image of the serious-minded sportsman or the nautical devotee, or some combination of these. During leisure hours the advocate of this style retreats into his chosen pleasure and invests substantial portions of his earnings to maintain it. The country gentleman emphasizes the estate-like quality of his residence

with elaborate gardens, swimming pools, and other yard facilities. The nautical gentleman builds his life around a boat, nautical dress styles, and involvement in cup races. This sporting life is combined with fashionable, elaborate entertainment and membership in country or golf clubs which incorporate all members of the family into their activities. This outdoor, healthy, casual, and sophisticated approach carries with it only a minimum emphasis on culture, urban sophistication, and avant-gardism. Fresh air and sun are preferred to books and intellectually taxing activities, and so these groups are less likely to orient themselves to the city in their recreational patterns.

2. The style of the Culture-Vulture intellectual, as opposed to that of the Country Gentleman, emphasizes cultural consumption and quasi-avant-garde cultural sophistication. Books, talk, theater, music, and museum-going are standard fare. This group has been in the vanguard of the cultural revolution for the past fifteen years. It has embraced the avant-garde arts, the emphasis on movies as an art form, the theater of the absurd, multimedia experiments, new forms of music, pop and op art, and the new pornography. The publishing industry, book and record clubs, music groups, Broadway and off-Broadway theater, and the dance have all depended on the cultural demand created by this segment of the upper middle class. Authentic cultural producers frequently resent this group because they have destroyed the exclusivity of the arts. This group lives in the suburbs but closer to the city, in luxury apartments

bordering the city; or in the city itself, in upper-middle-class apartments if the children have gone to college or have not yet been born. Here we find studied bohemianism and the cocktail party circuit attended by artists or intellectuals in temporary captivity. Among this group are many people who, though they graduated from the university, have psychologically never left it. A high percentage of them, especially around the larger cities, are Jews.

3. The Cultured Academic may not be a professor, but he aspires to be both cultural and gentlemanly in a pastoral environment that finds the university setting to be the ideal place of residence. Thus businessmen, upper-level managers, and professionals have chosen to live in the vicinity of places like Cambridge, MIT, Princeton, Ann Arbor, UCLA, Berkeley, and almost any other major university environment. Princeton, New Jersey, as described in *Fortune*, is populated by upper-echelon Wall Street professionals who own reconstructed early-model luxury cars, attempt to participate in university-connected cultural events, maintain old school ties, and, in general, tone down their affluence in order to leave the impression of established, secure, genteel solidity. The Ph.D. *nouveau riche* contributes substantially to this style, for it offers a convenient compromise between an intellectual past and newly acquired economic success.

4. The Fun-Lover specializes in active social participation — sports, indoor and outdoor parties, dancing, discotheque, world travel, hunting safaris, flying, and skiing. This group in its focus on "fun" most obviously models itself on the jet set and is primarily concerned with movement, gaiety, and remaining eternally young. Though it may occasionally evidence a mild interest in culture, it does not take culture seriously because it does not wish to sit in any one place for too long.

A special, primarily occupational variant of this active group are the young men who specialize in being on the move and who convey the impression of being "in" — influential in science, technology, and administration. The type is exemplified in the world-traveling junior executive, the dashing astronaut, or the youthful college president. They appear to be in a hurry to get somewhere to solve some complex problem which is partially secret and very important, and their manner is always slightly boastful. Although they are likely to be quite a distance from the men at the very top, their life consists in advancing their contacts. Occasionally the right contact may pay off. These men, who are highly elastic to opportunity, represent the middle ranks of government and large-scale business.

5. Lastly there is the old-upper-middle-class Vulgarian who believes in conspicuous consumption. In the postwar period he is unable to crystallize a pattern of consumption because there is no single style he can understand. For the most part these are people who own their own businesses and who, not without diligence and hard work, have risen far beyond their expectations. They are ready to enjoy the benefits of their business success, but lack both a model to imitate and the sophistication to create their own

style. They are left holding a bundle of money, without knowing exactly what to do with it. Thus the plethora of Thunderbirds, Cadillacs, and Lincolns among middle-aged and older Iowa farmers, merchants, and small-town bankers, who, also, in the winter months take the two-week Caribbean cruise. The urban businessman in construction, retailing, or insurance, who invests in conspicuous consumption, is another example. For the most part, the necessity for hard work isolates this group from the life styles that would validate their small business successes.

THE LOWER MIDDLE CLASS

The lower middle class follows the themes indicated for the upper middle class, but it does so from a different historical base. Going to church, taking pride in property, being neat and orderly, and showing a capacity for moral indignation against corruption are the chief elements of the lower-middle-class legacy. These traditional lower-middle-class virtues are in conflict with modern upper-middle-class and university-bred sophistication, and are declining under the pressure of the new patterns.

This conflict in class values can be seen clearly in the older lower-middle-class and middle-class religious groups, for example, the Baptists, Methodists, Congregationalists, and the Church of the Latter Day Saints. The older generation which has lived through the moral epoch and into the modern epoch still wishes to uphold the older bible-loving Christian virtues. Yet in their older age and retirement they also wish

to loosen up a bit and enjoy themselves — so perhaps some drinking may be condoned, and perhaps even a trip to a wicked place like Las Vegas, a night on the town, a sexy movie, or a lascivious thought. The older moralists have relaxed their morality on the grounds of a deserved self-indulgence.

But they differ from the upper middle classes because they have not yet absorbed the newer life styles. This lack of acceptance of the new tone of the classes above them expresses itself in attitudes of resentment and moral indignation against the immorality of society. The older moralists point to the political and economic corruption of establishment leaders and to the degeneracy of the international celebrity set. Though they may still be actively religious in the old sense and, in their view, pursuing the way of Jesus, their moral indignation has largely been secularized. Now it is expressed in political protest and reform movements such as the John Birch Society, or organizations espousing such virtues as integrity, honesty, public service, citizenship, and opposition to corruption. Their resentments focus upon the Negro and upon white radical college students, whom they believe to be not only lacking in all of the traditional American virtues but actively attacking such virtues while expecting rewards for their vices. This group has sometimes been called the silent majority; it includes Southern Baptists such as Bobbie Baker and Billie Sol Estes (who was a lay preacher), who are at once exponents of the old virtues and examples of the fall from grace into secular corruption. No doubt this is one of the reasons why they played their roles as anti-heroes so successfully. The combination of middle-class fraud and Puritan righteous indignation is, of course, one of the basic elements of the American tradition.

The younger generation in the lower middle class presents a different problem. Although those in small towns and medium-sized cities may have been exposed to the morality and religiosity of their parents, they have been more thoroughly exposed to upper-middle-class patterns in youth magazines, television, and the cinema. Unlike their parents, this group will have had direct exposure to the new sophistication at the state university or city college, which is their instrument of mobility. The conflicts expressed by these youth are different from those of their parents.

The residues of virtue and morality which they carry with them are at odds with the secular world they live in. Their parents, in their view, have submitted to the system and show no concern for the world. The children point to flaws and weaknesses at all levels of society and see bureaucracy robbing them of their freedom and dignity. Like that of their parents, their moral indignation has been secularized, but in their case it is expressed as disgust with their parents, their elders, and with dehumanized bureaucracy. At present these youth often express themselves in protest, reform, peace, youth, religious revival, rock-festival revival, existentialist, or radical activities to save the world. If they are not liberated, they may join the hard-hats and express their resentment by attacking those who have succeeded in "liberating" themselves. In the lives of these young people, "liberation" can produce total reversals and inversions of social character in short periods of time.

For the youth of the lower middle class, especially those who go to college, the culturally stylized life of the upper middle class always represents an example if not an option. Their desire to go to college is itself an affirmation of a desire to ascend; but going to college delays the real issues of life for four years, and so for these years it is still possible to protest, reject, and remain morally uprighteous. The protest, criticism, and political activities of these youth are alternatives to the styles of life and morality displayed by the upper middle class. As these youth end their college careers, get married, have children, acquire mortgages, and hold down jobs, they may be forced to shed protest politics, civil rights and reform movements. It would appear that the protests of these youth groups represent the last measure of rebellion against their own cooptation into the upper middle class. Much of politics on the campus, then, is not politics in the usual sense at all, but only an expression for or against cooptation into the affluent middle class.

To carry the point one step further, once coopted the issue of cooptation and depoliticization is not wholly resolved. The education of the middle class often leads to unexpected success within the establishment. The largess of the corporate, publishing, and banking worlds as well as of universities and philanthropic institutions may lead to impressive incomes which the individual may find reprehensible in terms of his earlier rebellion. He must find a way to live with both his older radical idealism and his new success.

The resolution of this problem seems to lie in the pursuit of culture in such a way that radical ideals can be expressed without threatening the job. Thus a substantial radical political literature exists and a great number of morally, religiously, and sexually irreverent books and periodicals are published. Radical idealism and politics easily become intellectualized. Politics can become a cultural activity, like listening to fine music. In this way political intellectualism and cultural aspiration operate in the same direction. Culture becomes the opiate of the aspiring educated classes.

THE WORKING CLASSES

The working classes are in the most difficult position of all in American society. They do not have access to a university education, nor do they receive any training in the higher cultural forms. They are therefore cut off from the mainstream of the new culture. When they are exposed to the new culture, it is primarily through the mass media or casual personal contacts. Thus they are not able to emulate the new styles accurately, and when they try, their efforts result in caricatures. Only in small communities and in rural areas are members of the working classes coopted into middle-class activities. In those marginal areas the working classes may exhibit some of the middle-class styles, but this is only at the small-town level. For the most part the working-class style always falls short of providing an independent basis for a working-class life style.

Some authors have talked about a working-class or lower-class subculture as if it were independent from the rest of society and its classes. These authors have failed to notice that the poverty of lower-class culture is a result of its failure to be sufficiently emulative *because* it is outside the mainstream of society, and not because it has created something on its own.

To the extent that the working classes are aware of new life styles of which they are not a part, they are desperately conscious of their personal educational disadvantages. They resent the educated unless they are their own children. They become aware of the error of not having finished high school or of not having gone to college. Thousands of degree-giving institutes, including adult and evening education courses in universities, cater to this specific desperation.

Their awareness of their own educational deficiencies accentuates their desire to educate their children, some of whom will go to a city college or state university. Those who are successful will enter the middle class and thus affirm the American dream. The continuous expansion of the higher educational institutions in providing for an avenue of mobility keeps alive the older American equalitarian and success ethic. The working classes, though they are unsuccessful themselves, can feel vindicated if their children get an education.

Life for the working classes is not wholly dismal. They are offered a broad fare of engaging and distracting involvements: the mass media (Ed Sullivan, football and baseball games, space shots, "Hogan's Heroes," and so on);

fishing, hunting, and camping; unlimited home improvements by the do-it-yourself method; and Catholic religiosity, Protestant self-satisfaction, beer, and compulsiveness as outlets that allow them to make their compromise with life in an increasingly middle-class world to which they feel they do not belong. They can strive to belong, and even though their children do not go to college, they can get jobs and help in the acquisition of the American symbols of success: automobiles, garden tractors, houses, modern furniture, outboard motors, color TV sets, camping trailers, and a million other objects from American industry.

All of this is possible because for skilled and semiskilled white union members, life in America has not been at all bad. America has not suffered a major depression since World War II, and the recessions have been of short duration. Wage raises have remained reasonably in line with the rising cost of living, and there have been opportunities for overtime, moonlighting, and jobs for wives and unmarried children. Since most of these opportunities are, for the older generation, greater than they had expected in their depression-bound youth, they have some grounds for satisfaction. The new chances for consumption have given them a stake in American society. As union members they remain loyal insofar as the unions serve as bargaining agents; otherwise they are not much interested in labor's traditional causes. Their stake in society, protected by seniority and virtual job monopolies, makes them hostile to the aspirations of less-favored groups who seek economic and social equality. Organized workers, favored

by the relatively benign labor legislation and economic policies of the Kennedy and Johnson administrations, have become increasingly conservative. They have developed vested interests, and resist those below who would challenge their new prosperity and their claims to having made it in America. Some of them become adherents of racist arguments.

On issues of bread-and-butter unionism, they remain liberal. They are forced to use the rhetoric of patriotism and superpatriotism, especially in their reaction to the rebellion of middle-class college youth and the draft deferments these youth have received while their own children have been drafted. Perhaps part of their resentment is due to the fact that they lack both the psychological and verbal resources to protect their own children. If given the opportunity to express anonymously their attitude to the war in Vietnam, their identification with their children becomes apparent.[4]

THE SUBWORKING CLASSES

Subworking classes are committed to almost nothing except immediate pleasure. The original members of this class (hoboes, tramps, and bums) have been joined by cats, hippies, opouts, copouts, dropouts, surf bums, communards, and other economically marginal groups. Narcotics, alcohol, sex, or some other inarticulate activity short of suicide is used to absorb time, attention, and energy. Oddly, this style is itself an

[4] Harlan Hahn, "Dove Sentiments Among Blue-Collar Workers," *Dissent*, May–June 1970, pp. 202–205.

emulation of the jet-set and upper-middle-class fun and immorality ethic which in part derives from a kind of emulation of this same subworking-class style of life. Radical chic culture appears to be the common ground for these two extremes, allowing the upper and lower classes to have fun together *en passant*. Earlier forms of radical chic were the weekend meeting of the Vassar coed and the Negro cat, or the NYU Bronx bagel and the Tomcat, who could exploit each other in the name of civil rights. But such relationships can exist only in a make-believe world. The upper-discotheque and Ivy League girl can maintain the fiction (temporarily) much more easily than the cat or other outcast who after the weekend must go on living without a future. Of course, if she wishes, the Ivy League girl (or boy) can also drop out.

The major problem of pursuing such a life style is the need to accept the total inaccessibility of success as defined in the society at large, and the accompanying feeling of failure. No matter how much contact these subclasses have with the "slumming" coed, the well-intentioned civil rights worker, the Northern white liberal, the Jewish college radical, the well-meaning Protestant minister or Catholic priest, they have almost no way out of their situation. No matter how extensive the poverty programs, this class is stalemated. This is why violence and aggressiveness in such groups are erratic, unpredictable, and imperfectly contained. Violence is always possible, especially when triggered by community action programs and the emulation of peaceful civil rights demonstrations.

Protest movements, civil rights programs, and community action solutions are not simple attempts to deal with this uncontained aggression. Their meaning differs for two different groups of the subworking class:

1. There is, first, the traditional-minded subworking class which depends upon religion and religious ecstasy to provide a controlled release for emotion and resentment. The Southern Negro and the Harlem storefront minister are prime examples. Historically, since the time of the Romans, Christianity has served this function more efficiently than most have been willing to recognize. Religion in its Protestant variation has accomplished a similar function for the Negro in America, though lately the Catholics have seen that they too have an audience. Both the Protestant and the Catholic churches now offer themselves as a point of attachment for those members of the subworking class who would like to avoid descending to the very bottom of the social heap.

Yet religion, whether Catholic or Protestant, in its very nature a symbolic activity, is never wholly successful in pacifying the people. Martin Luther King, Jr., up to 1966, seems to have swayed the mass with his message of Christian nonviolence and to have prevented more civil violence than otherwise would have occurred. His assassination may have removed a major brake on potentially violent civil and political action among both organized and unorganized blacks. But extreme deprivation, provocation, or social contagion can always evoke hostility and aggression as a response to long-term, institutionally based deprivation. Nowadays among the subworking class, even the religious are not wholly predictable.

2. The older Christian ethic attempted to justify slavery and to reconcile the slave to his lot. It also justified and reconciled lower-class positions by emphasizing that the social world reflects God's will. The new wrinkle in this ethic is the secular politicizing of the subworking class, particularly urban blacks and Puerto Ricans. These new nationalist and protest groups have begun to accept the implications of direct action. Through movements of black nationalism, riots, urban guerilla warfare, and other forms of group assertion, their actions stand opposed to the religious forms of sublimation that until recently have controlled them.

The major issue for these secularized and politically prodded subworking classes is whether they can develop a leadership with the political skills and abilities to organize and sustain the process of politicization. This remains to be seen. If the process follows the classic American pattern, responsible Negro leadership will be coopted as it has been in the past, leaving the masses of blacks to their own devices. At best this means having to produce a continuous succession of new leaders, each of whom after five or ten years of struggle decides he too must think of himself and the needs of his family. All other ethnic groups in the American past have been bought off in this way, so it is not unreasonable to assume that the blacks and the Puerto Ricans can

suffer or enjoy a similar fate. If this happens, the aggressiveness and violence of the subworking-class movement will be turned against itself, with intermittent periods of crisis and disorder, particularly in the cities. On the other hand, if a measure of leadership stability can be achieved, a major new political force will have entered the scene of American politics, and no one can predict what the consequences might be. All in all, these pressures from below offer both creative and destructive possibilities for American society.

LIFE STYLES IN
THE HISTORICAL PROCESS

If the above analysis is correct, it is obvious that throughout American history there has been no life style capable of sustaining and reinforcing itself from the resources provided by its bearers' children. The great traditional life styles have been sustained primarily by immigrants from foreign shores, by internal immigrants mainly from rural areas, and by ascendant groups. All of these "immigrants," as strangers who lack confidence in their own past, have emulated upper classes and by so doing have given the emulated style a new vitality until their own children or grandchildren abandoned it. Why has this been so?

Throughout American history, and more recently in Europe as well, the rate of economic and political change has been so great that new patterns have been imposed on whole populations before those populations have had an opportunity to absorb and consolidate older life styles. An instability of life style appears in any period of fundamental institutional change, the case of Europe in its emergence from feudalism to capitalism being a prime example. (Veblen, in his *Imperial Germany and the Industrial Revolution*, made this a central point in his analysis of Germany and Japan.) If the United States, as a world model, fails to stabilize any single set of styles, there will likely be no permanent replacements in Europe and in the underdeveloped world for the traditional life styles now being forgotten and destroyed.

In much of our analysis there has been little evidence of total innovation in the creation of new life styles. In almost all cases where there has been some creation, it arises out of imperfect or overperfect emulation. Aspiring classes emulate the stereotyped life styles of distant and not directly observed groups, and thus introduce the possibility of distortion. Only selected elements of a total life style are emulated, enhanced, caricatured, and elaborated in the process of stereotyping. In this way meanings are introduced which were only minimally present. For example, the cultural patterns of the English urban middle classes are emphasized and exaggerated by aspirants who emulate that style: selected aspects of the original style take on a quality of completeness and totality they never had. In just this way the culture of the English upper classes has been fractionated into four dimensions of emulation by Americans. As we have described them, these are the gentlemanly style, the search for culture, the fun and immorality theme, and the diversions of the late aristocracy. Each of these dimensions has been the ob-

ject of emulation by a different group in American society, and each of these groups in turn polarizes the given style and creates a total way of life from it.

When the life style being emulated is distant, there is also the possibility that only a given historical stage of a life style may become the object of emulation. Thus an American elite will emulate the life style of European aristocracies at the exact point when that life style might collapse if it were not for the emulation. Neither group has a basis for its style, except for the fact that the style is validated by emulation. In this mirroring process the parties to the emulation validate each other, where otherwise the style would die.

This same process of emulation, accentuation, and distortion also takes place domestically. In periods of cultural revolution, the amount of distortion in the emulating process is almost unimaginable; but this distortion results in intense innovation and creativity. The rate of change within the last ten years accounts for what otherwise appear to be discontinuities in cultural traditions and life styles. It is for this reason that a book like *Catch-22* becomes understandable. For example, lower-class blacks, when attempting to emulate nonblack styles, caricature selective aspects of middle-class culture, both broadening them and investing them with a comic playfulness which in other situations is a "put-on." In so doing they suggest new and unanticipated possibilities for the middle-class fun morality, which in turn is emulated by the very groups who may have been the original source of that emulation. These circulating patterns of emulation add new and unanticipated dimensions to a life style, revitalize it, and change its characteristics.

The only limit to this ebb and flow of emulation is the social and psychological needs of those groups who do the emulating. These needs, as we have tried to indicate, are based on the collapse of older life styles and the ability of newer ones to give expression to the changes in the life position of the people involved. In the evolution of society, there would seem to be no end to this process.

As Bensman and Vidich pointed out in the last selection, there is not one "upper-class" life style but many. For one portion of the upper class, a central life interest is family in the broader sense of lineage. Members of this group tend to regard themselves and only themselves as legitimate members of the American aristocracy. You can only be born into such a group and not enter through acquisition of money, power, or knowledge. The old American upper class can trace its ancestry to the time of the American Revolution, knows its family lines and perpetuates its genealogies.

It is not by accident that one thinks of Philadelphia and Boston in connection with such an upper-class life style. Members of the old American aristocracy recognize each other and formalize this membership in volumes called social registers. Not all American cities have their own social registers. They are found in New York, Philadelphia, Boston, Washington, Chicago, Baltimore, St. Louis, San Francisco, Pittsburgh, Cincinnati, Buffalo, and Cleveland. These older American cities have enough history and sufficiently well established families to warrant a social register. Like many elite groups, they have their own institutions, from clubs to popular causes (often local orchestras or art museums), and their own educational institutions (from private schools to universities). In the following article, Charles MacNamara illustrates an upper-class social network and the life style associated with membership in such a network.

Social Register, Philadelphia 1969

Charles H. MacNamara

Assiduous observers of the Soviet hierarchy constantly study photographs of state functions. By noting relative positions of high-ranking personages, they are able to gauge who is moving to the center of power and who is on the way to managing cement factories in Kazakhstan.

For the study of society in Philadelphia there are similar techniques. There are those newspaper anachronisms, the society pages. One may note there the rise of young matrons by the company they keep in photos of charitable committees. At formal dress functions young protégés cling limpet-like to starchy elders of repute. And in the columns of type, alliances among first families are detailed in reports of engagement and marriage, followed at respectable intervals by announcement of heirs to the crossed bloodline.

To gain a little perspective for these minute stirrings in the pond of local society, however, there is nothing like the *Philadelphia Social Register*. The 1969 edition (its discreet black and orange binding looking like a course catalog for Princeton) has already been

From *Philadelphia Magazine,* 66 (March 1969), pp. 69ff. Reprinted by permission of Philadelphia Magazine.

resting for several months on telephone tables and escritoires from Delancey Place to Paoli and beyond. It is by careful gleaning of the *Social Register* that one is able to glimpse something of the flaky structure of Philadelphia's upper crust. It is not to be studied as photos of the Kremlin crowd, to discover the latest clue on who is close to the center occupied by the Biddles, Ingersolls, Morrises, Cadwaladers, Robertses and Wisters. For several generations it has been obvious that this space has been occupied by Scotts, Smiths, Cassatts, Lippincotts, Woods, Peppers, Pews, Disstons and the like. And since Wilmington is included in the *Philadelphia Social Register*, several hundred du Ponts, a sui generis family, must be reckoned with.

Beyond the solid nucleus of old-timers, observation becomes a fascinating parlor sport. Society may be dying as a directional force, but its members are spawning at a handsome rate. The first issue of the local *Register* in 1890 contained 135 families. By 1940 the count was 5,150. A calculated estimate of the current issue is that there are 7,400 households and approximately 20,000 individuals. (Young children are not listed.)

For the past year there were 350 marriages solemnized against only 200 deaths. To restructure Ripley's famous speculation on marching Chinese in "Believe It Or Not," one has the feeling that if everyone in the current *Social Register* were lined up two abreast on the tracks of the Main Line in Paoli and began marching in stately grace to the beat of Meyer Davis's orchestra playing "Pomp and Circumstance," they would reproduce at such a rate that they and their heirs would file through 30th Street Station for eternity.[1]

Although it can be held comfortably in one hand, the *Social Register* is by no means a pamphlet. For 573 pages it celebrates the virtues of blood and distinction. A typical listing goes something like this: family name and Christian name of male, maiden name of wife in parentheses, enumeration of approved clubs in cryptic abbreviation, college with year of graduation, phone number and address, listing of other adults in household, listing of juniors in household (males 14 to 20; misses 12 to 17).

For example: "Lippincott Mr & Mrs R Schuyler (Jones — Elizabeth W Hanger) Ph. Cr. Fw. Myf. Pc. Ac. Ncd. Pa '39; Juniors Misses E Hadley & Edith B Jones; Phone No CH 8-000. . . ."

This listing indicates that Mr. R. Schuyler Lippincott graduated from the University of Pennsylvania in 1939 and is now a member of the prestigious Philadelphia Club, Corinthian Yacht, the Military Order of Foreign Wars, Society of Mayflower Descendants, and Philadelphia Cricket. Mrs. Lippincott is a member of Acorn, considered the ultra women's club in Philadelphia. The two juniors listed are from Mrs. Lippincott's previous marriage to Mr. Jones. The phone number (altered here) and address (which we skipped) indicate that the family resides in

Chestnut Hill, a perfectly acceptable neighborhood for a *Social Register* family.

Despite the length of the *Social Register*, it is an exclusive listing. Keeping people *out* is half the fun. The easiest way to get into the *Social Register* is to be born into it. This way there is no social climbing and no subsequent guilt feelings.

The second method of entering is by marriage. The typical Philadelphia arrangement is for fresh money to marry old blood. The offspring of such marriages thereby combine the best of both worlds. This is as close to mixed marriage as society cares to contemplate.

The trickiest method of entering the elite is by application to the Social Register Association, publisher of the Philadelphia directory and 11 companion volumes for other cities. According to a Philadelphia social consultant (one who aids the elite in planning parties), "The *Social Register* is administered by a secret board in New York City, and anyone here who gives information is also kept under wraps." Those in the *Social Register* have the privilege of recommending new names for listing, and the quality of the recommender frequently droppeth as a gentle rain on the recommendee.

Gentility and status are the primary qualifications for listing — plus the backing of those who are already listed. Five or six endorsers of the application are sufficient, if they are the right ones. Time is relative. When Stuart Saunders moved to Philadelphia as chairman of the city's most social business institution, the Pennsylvania Railroad, everyone tripped over each other's patent leather pumps to get him into the

[1] "Main Line" refers to the main line of the commuter route of the Pennsylvania Railroad, which goes through "elite" communities such as Paoli, Haverford, and Bryn Mawr, ending in Philadelphia at the 30th Street Station. [Eds.]

Social Register and the best clubs in the area. The average social climber, however, may have to wait a decade or so before being rewarded. Some never make the grade.

Kicking people out can be great sport. There is no black-bordered card announcing the event, no braid stripped from a uniform to the slow roll of drums in Rittenhouse Square. One is simply not in the next edition of the *Register*. One is not surprised by this absence, because one has already noted a falling off of invitations to social affairs.

In truth, however, there are more voluntary delistings than purges. This can come about simply by neglecting to provide the information necessary for listing, particularly after a change in address or marital status.

Divorce, once considered a scandalous breach of the social ethic, is no longer reason for anything other than a change in listing. Nor, for that matter, are dipsomania, kleptomania, homosexuality or participation in sex orgies causes for exile — so long as these eccentricities are not indulged in a proletarian manner. Shoplifting at Bonwit's, for example, displays a sense of social form. Doing the same thing at Woolworth's exhibits a deplorable lack of class. Wife swapping in Levittown is separated by more than just a few miles from the high society cavortings of yore on Hound Dog Hill.

For public sins, exclusion may be the penalty. As with entrance, much depends on family. Members of peripheral families may be snuffed out with as little ceremony as guttering candles. A member of a family closer to the center of things may be allotted *two* messy scandals before the name disappears. It can be heartbreaking to older members of the family. Youth, of course, is rebellious in all strata today. One never knows when the child of a *Social Register* family will do something wild and crazy like joining the Communist Party, dating a Negro, or marrying a Jew.

Speaking of Jews, they are as likely to be found in the *Social Register* as rabbis officiating at the Church of the Holy Trinity.... After all, since they are excluded from most of the social clubs enumerated in the *Social Register*, it is only logical that they be excluded from society and from the book.

•   •   •

Whatever the occupation, coupon clipper or life insurance salesman (both are in the directory), it is a man's clubs that mark his station in society. These are recorded in the *Social Register* in a sometimes baffling (to outsiders) shorthand. Altogether there are 48 men's and women's clubs considered worthy of listing, from Ac (for Acorn) to Y (for Yale Club). Some are based on historical orientation, such as Ds (Descendants of Signers of the Declaration of Independence) and Sar (Sons of the American Revolution).

Others are social-suburban, such as Sg (Sunnybrook Golf) and Rh (Rose Tree Fox Hunt). Still others are social-city, the men's clubs such as Ph (Philadelphia Club) and R (Rittenhouse). A few are exclusive men's cooking clubs, Ssk (State in Schuylkill) and Rb (The Rabbit). For the political-business set there is the Republicans-only Union League. And for those with literary leanings there is the democratic Franklin Inn.

The club that has been most exclusive from its founding in the 18th century is the State in Schuylkill. Membership is limited to 40, vacancies being filled from apprentices, who have usually seen the shad broach the Delaware at least 50 springs before attaining full membership. So exclusive is the group that few Philadelphians, out of society's inner circle, would be able to identify a single member. And even when the names are known they will hardly jolt the response of memory.

•   •   •

While the clubs listed in the *Social Register* have remained the same for a generation, the colleges have not. When Digby Baltzell examined various *Social Registers* for his study *Philadelphia Gentlemen*, he noted that in 1940 the upper class in each directory favored the Big Three (Harvard, Yale, and Princeton). In addition the upper class of each city had a local school that it favored, the Philadelphia choice being the University of Pennsylvania. These four local schools still dominate the local *SR*. The circle is widening, however.

For years the choices beyond these four schools seemed to be limited to the East, roughly from Bowdoin in the north to the University of Virginia in the south. But today the thirst of the upper class for education is so great that its sons and daughters are attending schools unknown to the *SR* listings of a generation ago. At Main Line teas, matrons these days are proudly spreading the word that grandson J. Jared the Fourth has been accepted at New

Mexico, Miami, U. of Alaska, Colorado State, Santa Fe, or what have you. . . .

More static are the addresses of the elite listed in the *Register*. Their ghettos are shady, their homes from sound to magnificent. The presence of a single rat in the vicinity prompts a discreet call to an exterminator with an unmarked panel truck.

Chestnut Hill and center city are the only acceptable areas to live inside Philadelphia. The repetition of addresses in the suburbs seldom deviates from the expected — Devon, Berwyn, Penllyn, Wayne, Bryn Mawr, Villanova, Rosemont, Spring House, Paoli, Wawa, Uniontown. As is evident from the *Social Register*, the upper class feels stultified by street addresses. They may be necessary in Chestnut Hill, but in the outlying districts a list of properties echoes manorial names of the English squirearchy. There are Heathcote Farm and Fairthorne, Journey's Ended and Rebel Fox Farm, Pheasant Run and Spring Meadow Farm.

The most famous names are probably the Biddles' Andalusia and George Widener's Erdenheim Farm, a name known to horse players completely ignorant of the family's heartbreaking struggle to enter society at the turn of the century. For reasons known only to its editors, the names of estates appear in quotation marks in *SR*. At least the upper class has avoided that pitfall of the exurban bourgeoisie — picking out a cutesy or punny name for their 18th-century farmhouse-cum-plumbing and surrounding three acres of rabbit burrows.

Some families would not be caught with a street address if it could possibly be avoided. Perhaps an extreme example is that of the Woods family of Wawa. Various branches of the Woods may be addressed at Blossom Hill, Blossom Hill Cabin (even the elite subdivide), Tree Tops, Logtown Farm, and Hurricane Hollow (presumably located in the declivity between Blossom Hill and Forge Hill). All of this in Wawa, a Delaware County community that hardly matches the Ponderosa ranch in size.

As for location, it is not the suburban addresses that impress the reader of the *Social Register*. It is that Philadelphia society, as listed in the *SR*, is international in character. The listings begin with Mr. and Mrs. John Abbate in Perugia, Italy, and end with Mr. and Mrs. Alexandre Zvegintzov in Paris. There are in fact very few pages in the directory that do not contain an alien address. It is not just a du Pont plantation in South Carolina or a Dixon ranch in Wyoming. There are people living in New York City, Connecticut, Washington, Palm Beach, Rio de Janeiro, Dar es Salaam (Tanzania), and Ras Tanura (Saudi Arabia), who are considered and consider themselves members of Philadelphia society.

The mass of Philadelphians and suburbanites, the 4.5 million who are not listed in the *Social Register*, undoubtedly have very little concept of that world behind the closed doors of the clubs and nestled in the quiet confines of Berwyn and Paoli. How much relevance does the *Social Register* crowd have for society — not that introverted society, but for the society that forms the totality of our relationships? Does this self-perpetuating upper class actually provide motivating leadership? In *Philadelphia Gentlemen*, Baltzell matched the upper class of the 1940 *Social Register* with the listings in the 1940 *Who's Who*, which he accepted as a directory of the active elite leadership. Of the elite in *Who's Who* living in this area, he found that 29% were also listed in *SR*.

A partial check of the current *Who's Who* and the *Social Register* indicates that society is providing a diminishing role in leadership. In *Who's Who* there are 146 area residents with last names beginning with B. Only 30 of these are also listed in the *Social Register* (including Catherine Drinker Bowen, listed in *SR* as Mrs. T. McKean Downs). This is only 20% — a drop of nine points in a single generation. Such figures can have only one meaning to the investment bankers of social observation: family stock has been in decline as a factor in the market and shows little chance for rejuvenation. Management has refused to diversify or make significant merger with steadily rising, newer issues. Drop society from investment portfolios.

Americans have demonstrated a propensity to label themselves as middle-class when opinion surveys offered them the choice of calling themselves upper-, middle-, or lower-class. Even when "working-class" is added to the alternatives many still prefer to see themselves as middle-class.* This preference may be interpreted as a denial of class differences affirming a belief that the United States is a middle-class society in which class differences should have no part. Most Americans are neither rich nor poor, but somewhere in the middle. The middle class is the largest class and is becoming larger as a result of the expansion in the proportion of middle-class occupations that require technical skill or advanced education.

Because the term "middle-class" may be applied to so many people whose life styles are quite diverse, it may be useful to distinguish categories within the middle class — for example, "upper middle class," "middle middle class," and "lower middle class."

What is upper middle class? "The snobs. They're people with money. They look down on those that don't have as much as they do. They feel that money makes them better people, that anyone that has less than they do is beneath them," said P. H., a clerical job-seeker, in response to the question of the day in the San Francisco Chronicle,† *"What is your idea of the upper middle class?" C. W., another job-seeker, said, "Upper middle class implies wealth. Professional people. Usually means the silent majority. Upper middle class politically would mean the conservatives. But that's not always the case." Finally, W. E., a radio interviewer, stated: "The term upper middle class should be discarded. It's outmoded today. Upper middle class is someone who makes about three hundred dollars a week and lives beyond his means and is buying everything on time." Respondents did not agree on what it is to be upper middle-class, nor on who upper middle-class people are. But they did imply that to be upper middle-class is to have a particular life style.*

"Career" has been identified as the central life interest of the upper middle class.‡ But career patterns differ and so do their related life styles. A college professor or a physician differs from a corporation executive or a business owner, yet, on the basis of their occupation, all may be defined as "upper middle class." Especially in this category, life style, social class, and occupation are bound together. Other white-collar people,

---

* Richard Centers, *The Psychology of Social Classes* (Princeton, N.J.: Princeton Univ. Press, 1949); Raymond J. Murphy and Richard T. Morris, "Occupational Situs, Subjective Class Identification and Political Affiliation," *American Sociological Review,* 26 (1961), pp. 383–392.

† December 4, 1969.

‡ Joseph Kahl, *The American Class Structure* (New York: Holt, Rinehart and Winston, 1957), p. 193.

who lack the career orientation and autonomy of full professionals, are generally thought of as the lower middle class. They are people for whom work is less than a central life interest. They have the dignity of clean work but not the financial rewards of blue-collar occupations such as plumber, truck driver, and electrician. Their work lacks intrinsic gratification and they may fail to find gratification elsewhere. They are caught in the countertrends of embourgeoisement and proletarianization,* and, according to C. Wright Mills, are in a state of panic.

In a quiz directed at higher executives, "status points" were given to the executive for such things as being visited regularly in the office by a bootblack and not having to hang up his own coat; "status points" were deducted however, for using memo paper with the imprinted name of a supplier and for having artificial flowers in the office.†

A search for status may be even more intense among middle middle- and lower middle-class individuals. Below the professionals and above the low-status white-collar workers are semiprofessionals, who may be thought of as the middle middle class. Social workers, teachers, engineers, nurses, and pharmacists do not have the same degree of power, wealth, or prestige as physicians, lawyers, or higher executives. Semiprofessionals, more than any other group, are caught in a bind. Upward emulation may mean higher status with unequal salary, while emulation of occupations below them may mean a loss of professional status but a gain of income.

White-collar workers beneath the semiprofessionals often are indistinguishable in income from blue-collar workers, and their only compensation may be that they view their occupation as having more status. It is difficult to predict whether white-collar employees will move toward proletarianization (becoming more working-class) or embourgeoisement (becoming more middle-class). At this point there is still the struggle for status, discussed in the following article by C. Wright Mills.

* See James W. Rinehart, "Affluence and Embourgeoisement of the Working Class: A Critical Look," paper presented before the annual meeting of the American Sociological Association, Washington, D.C., August 1970. Embourgeoisement is the process of working-class people becoming more like the middle class.

† George P. Nicholas, "Executive Status Quiz," *TWA Ambassador,* 3 (October 1970) p. 20.

The Status Panic

C. Wright Mills

Prestige involves at least two persons: one to claim it and another to honor the claim. The bases on which various people raise prestige claims, and the reasons others honor these claims, include property and birth, occupation and education, income and power — in fact almost anything that may invidiously distinguish one person from another. In the status system of a society these claims are organized as rules and expectations which regulate who successfully claims prestige, from whom, in what ways, and on what basis. The level of self-esteem enjoyed by given individuals is more or less set by this status system.

The extent to which claims for prestige are honored, and by whom they are honored, may vary widely. Some of those from whom an individual claims prestige may honor his claims, others may not; some deferences that are given may express genuine feelings of esteem; others may be expedient strategies for ulterior ends. A society may, in fact, contain many hierarchies of prestige, each with its own typical bases and areas of bestowal, or one hierarchy in which everyone uniformly "knows his place" and is always in it.

From C. Wright Mills, *White Collar: The American Middle Classes* (New York: Oxford University Press, 1956), pp. 239–358. Reprinted by permission; copyright 1951 by Oxford University Press. Inc.

It is in the latter that prestige groups are most likely to be uniform and continuous.

Imagine a society in which everyone's prestige is absolutely set and unambivalent; every man's claims for prestige are balanced by the prestige he receives, and both his expression of claims and the ways these claims are honored by others are set forth in understood stereotypes. Moreover, the bases of the claims coincide with the reasons they are honored: those who claim prestige on the specific basis of property or birth are honored because of their property or birth. So the exact volume and types of deference expected between any two individuals are always known, expected, and given; and each individual's level and type of self-esteem are steady features of his inner life.

Now imagine the opposite society, in which prestige is highly unstable and ambivalent: the individual's claims are not usually honored by others. The way claims are expressed are not understood or acknowledged by those from whom deference is expected, and when others do bestow prestige, they do so unclearly. One man claims prestige on the basis of his income, but even if he is given prestige, it is not because of his income but rather, for example, his education or appearance. All the controlling devices by which the volume and type of deference might be directed are out of joint or simply do not exist. So the prestige system is no system, but a maze of misunderstanding, of sudden frustration and sudden indulgence, and the individual, as his self-esteem fluctuates, is under strain and full of anxiety.

American society in the middle of the twentieth century does not fit either of these projections absolutely, but it seems fairly clear that it is closer to the unstable and ambivalent model. This is not to say that there is no prestige system in the United States; given occupational levels, however caught in status ambivalence, do enjoy typical levels of prestige. It is to say, however, that the enjoyment of prestige is often disturbed and uneasy, that the bases of prestige, the expressions of prestige claims, and the ways these claims are honored, are now subject to great strain, a strain which often puts men and women in a virtual status panic.

WHITE-COLLAR PRESTIGE

The prestige position of white-collar employees has been one of the most arguable points about them as strata, the major point to be explained by those who would locate them in modern social structures. Although no one dimension of stratification can be adequate, the social esteem white-collar employees have successfully claimed is one of their important defining characteristics. In fact, their psychology can often be understood as the psychology of prestige striving. That it is often taken as their signal attribute probably reflects the effort, which we accept, to overcome the exclusively economic view of stratification; it also reflects the desire, which we reject, to encompass the entire group with a single slogan.

White-collar people's claims to prestige are expressed, as their label implies, by their style of appearance. Their occupations enable and require them to wear street clothes at work. Although they may be expected to dress somewhat somberly, still, their working attire is not a uniform, or distinct from clothing generally suitable for street wear. The standardization and mass production of fashionable clothing have wiped out many distinctions that were important up to the twentieth century, but they have not eliminated the distinctions still typical between white-collar and wage-worker. The wage-worker may wear standardized street clothes off the job, but the white-collar worker wears them on the job as well. This difference is revealed by the clothing budgets of wage-workers and white-collar people, especially of girls and women. After later adolescence, women working as clerks, compared with wage-working women of similar income, spend a good deal more on clothes; and the same is true of men, although to a lesser extent.

The class position of employed people depends on their chances in the labor market; their status position depends on their chances in the commodity market. Claims for prestige are raised on the basis of consumption; but since consumption is limited by income, class position and status position intersect. At this intersection, clothing expenditure is, of course, merely an index, although a very important one, to the style of appearance and the life-ways displayed by the white-collar strata.

Claims for prestige, however, expressed, must be honored by others, and, in the end, must rest upon more or less widely acknowledged bases, which distinguish the people of one social stratum from others. The prestige of any stratum, of course, is based upon its mutually recognized relations with other strata. The "middle position" of white-collar people between independent employers and wage-workers, "a negative characteristic — rather than definite technical functions," Emil Lederer wrote in 1912, "is the social mark of the salaried employees and establishes their social character in their own consciousness and in the estimation of the community."[1]

Salaried employees have been associated with entrepreneurs, and later with higher-ups in the managerial cadre, and they have borrowed prestige from both. In the latter nineteenth century, the foreman, the salesclerk, and the office man were widely viewed, and viewed themselves, as apprentices or assistants to old middle-class people. Drawing upon their future hopes to join these ranks, they were able to borrow the prestige of the people for whom they worked and with whom they were in close, often personal, contact. White-collar people intermarried with members of the old middle class and enjoyed common social activities; in many cases the salaried man represented the entrepreneur to the public and was recruited from the same social levels — mainly, the old rural middle class. All this — descent, association, and expectation — made it possible for earlier salaried employees to borrow status from the old middle class.

Today, in big city as well as small town, white-collar workers continue to

borrow such prestige. It is true that in larger concerns personal contacts with old middle-class entrepreneurs have been superseded by impersonal contacts with the lower rungs of the new managerial cadre. Still, all white-collar people do not lack personal contact with employers; not all of them are employed in the big layout, which, in many areas, is as yet the model of the future more than of present reality. The general images of the white-collar people, in terms of which they are often able to cash in claims for prestige, are drawn from present reality. Moreover, even in the big hierarchies, white-collar people often have more contact — and usually feel that they do — with higher-ups than do factory workers.

The prestige cleavage between "the shop" and "the front office" often seems to exist quite independently of the low income and routine character of many front-office jobs and the high pay and skills in the shop. For orders and pay checks come from the office and are associated with it; and those who are somehow part of it are endowed with some of the prestige that attends its function in the life of the wage-worker. The tendency of white-collar people to borrow status from higher elements is so strong that it has carried over to all social contacts and features of the workplace.

Salespeople in department stores, as we have already seen, frequently attempt, although often unsuccessfully, to borrow prestige from their contact with customers, and to cash it in among work colleagues as well as friends off the job. In the big city the girl who works on 34th Street cannot successfully claim as much prestige as the one who works on Fifth Avenue or 57th

[1] According to a recent National Opinion Research rating, on a scale running from 90.8 for government officials and 80.6 for professionals and semi-professionals (both free and salaried) to 45.8 for non-farm laborers, the whole group of "clerical, sales, and kindred workers" stand at 68.2, about on a par with the "craftsmen, foremen, and kindred workers."

Street. Writes one observer: "A sales-girl in Bonwit Teller's . . . will act and feel different from a salesgirl at Macy's. She will be more gracious, more help-ful, more charming . . . but at the same time she will have an air of dignity and distance about her, an air of distinc-tion, that implies, 'I am more impor-tant than you because my customers come from Park Avenue.' "

It is usually possible to know the prestige of salespeople in department stores in terms of the commodities they handle, ranked according to the "ex-pensiveness" of the people who typi-cally buy them. Prestige may be bor-rowed directly from the commodities themselves, although this is not as likely as borrowing from the type of customer.

If white-collar relations with super-visors and higher-ups, with customers or clients, become so impersonal as seriously to limit borrowing prestige from them, prestige is then often bor-rowed from the firm or the company itself. The fetishism of the enterprise, and identification with the firm, are often as relevant for the white-collar hirelings as for the managers. This iden-tification may be implemented by the fact that the work itself, as a set of activities, offers little chance for ex-ternal prestige claims and internal self-esteem. So the work one does is buried in the name of the firm. The typist or the salesgirl does not think of herself in terms of what she does, but as being "with Saks" or "working at *Time*." A $38-a-week clerk in a chrome and ma-hogany setting in Radio City will often successfully raise higher claims for pres-tige than a $50-a-week stenographer in a small, dingy office on Seventh Avenue.

Help-Wanted ads ("Beautifully Fur-nished Office in Rockefeller Center," "Large Nation-wide Concern," "Offices located on 32nd floor of Empire State Building") reveal conscious appeal to the status striving of the office worker. Such positions are often easier to fill, not because of higher salary and more rapid promotion, but because of the prestige of the firm's name or location.

In identifying with a firm, the young executive can sometimes line up his ca-reer expectations with it, and so iden-tify his own future with that of the firm's. But lower down the ranks, the identification has more to do with se-curity and prestige than with expecta-tions of success. In either case, of course, such feelings can be exploited in the interests of business loyalties.

In the impersonal white-collar hier-archies, employees often attempt to personalize their surroundings in order to identify with them more closely and draw prestige therefrom. In the per-sonnel literature, there are many illus-trations of an often pathetic striving for a sense of importance — for exam-ple, when a girl's chair is taken from her and she is given one thought more convenient for her work, her production drops. When questioned, she asks, "Why are you picking on me?" and explains that she had used the old chair for five years and it had her name plate on it. When the name plate is transferred to the new chair, it is ex-plained, her attitude changes, and her production comes up to normal. Similar observations have been made in con-nection with the arrangement of desks in an office, in which, unknown to man-agement, the old pattern had been in terms of seniority. Women are probably more alert to these prestige borrowings than men. The first consideration of one large group of women seeking employment had to do with "the office environment," the state of the equipment, the appearance of the place, the "class of people," working there. Periodical salary increases and initial salary were both ranked below such considerations. Of course, such prestige matters often involve the desire to be available on a market for more marriageable males, yet the material signs of the status environment are in themselves crucial to the white-collar sense of importance.

That white-collar work requires more mental capacity and less muscular effort than wage work has been a standard, historical basis for prestige claims. In the office, as we have seen, white-collar technology and social rationalization have definitely lessened technical differences between white-collar and factory work. Many white-collar people now operate light machinery at a pace and under conditions that are quite similar to those of light industrial operations, even if they do so while wearing street clothes rather than overalls. Still, the variety of operations and the degree of autonomous decision are taken as bases of white-collar prestige. And it is true that in thousands of offices and salesrooms, the receptionist, the salesgirl, the general secretary, and even the typist seems to perform a wide variety of different operations at her own pace and according to her own decisions.

The time required to learn white-collar skills and how they are learned has been an important basis for their prestige, even though as white-collar work is rationalized the time needed to acquire the necessary skills decreases. Some 80 percent of the people at work, it is frequently estimated, now perform work that can be learned in less than three months. Accompanying this rationalization of the work process, a stratum of highly skilled experts has arisen. Over the whole society, this stratum is popularly, even if erroneously, associated with "white-collar" work, while the semi-skilled is associated with wage work. So those white-collar workers who are in fact quite unskilled and routinized still borrow from the prestige of the skills.

More crucial, perhaps, than type of skill is the fact that many white-collar skills are still acquired at school rather than on the job. The two ways of learning working skills that carry most prestige have been combined in many white-collar areas, whereas neither is now prevalent among wage-workers. Apprenticeships, involving close contact with entrepreneurs or managerial levels, continued in white-collar occupations after they had ceased to exist in wage work; then, formal education, in high school and "business college," became the typical white-collar way.

The shift from small independent property to dependent occupations greatly increases the weight of formal education in determining life conditions. For the new middle class, education has replaced property as the insurance of social position. The saving and sacrifice of the new middle class to insure a "good education" for the child replace the saving and sacrifice of the old middle class to insure that the child may inherit "the good property" with which to earn his livelihood. The inheritance of occupational ambition, and of the education that is its condition, replaces the inheritance of property.

To acquire some white-collar skills requires twenty years of formal and expensive education; others may be learned in one day, and are more efficiently performed by those with little education. For some white-collar jobs, people above the grammar-school level are not wanted, for fear boredom would lead to slowdown by frustration; for others, only the Ph.D. is allowed to go to work. But the educational center around which the white-collar worlds revolve is the high school.

In 1890, only 7 out of every 100 boys and girls between 14 and 17 were enrolled in high schools; by 1940, 73 out of every 100 were. During these fifty years, the number of children of this age increased some 82 percent, the number of high-school enrollments, 1,888 percent. The white-collar people, the great depository of the High-School Culture implanted in U.S. youth, have completed an average of 12.4 years of school, compared with the free enterprisers' 8.4 and the wage-workers' 8.2 years.[2] On every occupational level, white-collar men and women are better educated, except for the single one of independent professionals, who, of course, lead educationally with 16.4 years of schooling. Many a clerk in a

small office has a less educated, although more experienced, boss; many a salesclerk in a small store is supervised by a higher-up not so well educated as she. Of course, the higher educational level of the white-collar people in part reflects their youthfulness; being younger, they have had more opportunities for education. But they have availed themselves of it; for in the white-collar pyramids education has "paid-off"; it has been a source of cash and a means of ascent. Here "knowledge," although not power, has been a basis for prestige.[3]

Even today, white-collar occupations contain the highest general average of educated people; but twenty-five years ago this was much more strongly the case; in large part, white-collar people monopolized intermediate and higher education. Twenty-five years ahead it will not necessarily be the case; in fact, all trends point to the continued narrowing of the educational gap between white-collar and wage-worker.

Fifty years ago the general labor market was almost entirely composed of grade-school graduates; today of high-school graduates; by the early fifties, nine and a half million college-educated youth will be in the labor market. Most of them will reach for the white-collar job, and many of them will not find routinized white-collar jobs a challenge, for, as H. K. Tootle has esti-

[2] The breakdown by detailed groups (median years of school completed, 1940): farmers, 7.6 years; businessmen, 9.9; free professionals, 16.4; managers, 10.8; salaried professionals, 14.9; salespeople, 12.1; office workers, 12.3; skilled workers, 8.5; semi-skilled, 8.4; unskilled, 8.2; rural workers, 7.3.

[3] No doubt some prestige accrues to white-collar people because of their youthfulness, first because if they are young they may, in the American ethos, still be hopefully seen as having more to win; and secondly, because youth itself often carries prestige, a prestige that is much advertised by displayed models and expected efficiency.

mated for an office-management association, "educated youth is being
challenged into business faster than
job satisfactions can be developed for
it. . . . As there are not enough stimulating jobs for the hordes of college
graduates we see descending upon us
in the years to come like swarms of
hungry locusts, they will have to take
jobs that satisfy, or perhaps even now
do not satisfy, the high-school graduate."

As the general educational level rises,
the level of education required or advisable for many white-collar jobs falls.
In the early twenties, personnel men
said: "I think it has become a principle with the majority of our progressive
offices that they will not take into the
office any person or candidate who has
not had the benefit of at least a high-
school education." But soon they began to say that too much education
was not advisable for many white-collar jobs. In fact, the educated intelligence has become penalized in routinized work, where the search is for
those who are less easily bored and
hence more cheerfully efficient. "When
you employ 2600 clerks," says one personnel supervisor, "you don't want all
college people. I much prefer the young
fellow who is fresh from high school,
or graduated from normal school, and
who is full of pep and ambition, and
wants to get ahead. We could not use
college men in many of our positions."
Education, in short, comes to be viewed
as a sort of frustrating trap.

The rationalization of office and store
undermines the special skills based on
experience and education. It makes the
employee easy to replace by shortening
the training he needs; it weakens not
only his bargaining power but his pres-

tige. It opens white-collar positions to
people with less education, thus destroying the educational prestige of
white-collar work, for there is no inherent prestige attached to the nature of
any work; it is, Hans Speier remarks,
the esteem the people doing it enjoy
that often lends prestige to the work
itself. Insofar as white-collar workers
base their claims for external prestige
and their own self-esteem upon educated skills, they open themselves to a
precarious psychological life.

In the United States, white-collar
people have been able to claim higher
prestige than wage-workers because of
racial, but to a greater extent and in
a more direct way, national origin.

The number of Negroes in white-
collar jobs is negligible, but especially
since World War I, considerable numbers have worked in unskilled and
semi-skilled factory jobs. The new middle class contains a greater proportion
of white people than any other occupational stratum: in 1940, some 99.5 percent of the white-collar, compared with
90 percent of free enterprisers, 87 percent of urban wage-workers, and 74
percent of rural workers.

Nativity and immigration differences
between white-collar and wage-work
are probably more direct bases of
white-collar prestige. When the "race
peril" literature was popular, the textbook myth about the lowly character
of newer immigrants was also widespread. Most of the major American
historians of the period between 1875
and 1925 belligerently declared the
superiority of "Anglo-Saxon" stock,
concludes Edward Saveth. Being of old
stock themselves, their "conception of
the immigrant reflected, in some de-

gree, their feeling that the newcomer somehow constituted a threat to what they held dear, ideologically and materially. . . ." Mass as well as academic publicity reflected and spread the fact of prestige distinctions between immigrant and native.

If the "American" stature of a group may be judged by the proportion of its native-born members, white-collar workers have been the most American of all occupational strata. In 1930, after mass immigration had been stopped, only 9 percent of the white population of the new middle class were foreign-born, compared to 16 percent of the free enterprisers and 21 percent of the wage-workers. But now there is no bulk immigration: soon, virtually all Americans will be American-born of American-born parents. Time will not automatically erase the prestige cleavages based on descent, but, for most white-collar and wage-workers, as they become more similar in origin, it probably will. In the meantime, nativity differences still underlie the prestige claims of white-collar groups.

Every basis on which the prestige claims of the bulk of the white-collar employees have historically rested has been declining in firmness and stability: the rationalization and downgrading of the work operations themselves and hence the lessening importance of education and experience in acquiring white-collar skills; the leveling down of white-collar and the raising of wage-worker incomes, so that the differences between them are decidedly less than they once were; the increased size of the white-collar labor market, as more people from lower

ranks receive high-school educations, so that any monopoly of formal training adequate to these jobs is no longer possible; the decline in the proportion of people of immigrant origin and the consequent narrowing of nativity differences between white-collar and wage-worker; the increased participation of white-collar people, along with wage-workers, in unemployment; and the increased economic and public power of wage-workers because of their union strength, as compared with that of white-collar workers.

All these tendencies for white-collar occupations to sink in prestige rest upon the numerical enlargement of the white-collar strata and the increase in prestige which the wage-workers have enjoyed. If everybody belongs to the fraternity, nobody gets any prestige from belonging. As the white-collar strata have expanded they have included more offspring of wage-worker origin; moreover, insofar as their prestige has rested upon their sharing the authority of those in charge of the enterprise, that authority has itself lost much of its prestige, having been successfully challenged at many points by unionized wage-workers.

Although trends should not be confused with accomplished facts, it is clear that many trends point to a "status proletarianization" of white-collar strata.

THE SMALLER CITY

To understand the prestige of white-collar people we must examine the kinds of people among whom they successfully raise claims for prestige. For different groups do not honor white-collar claims to the same extent; in fact, their estimates often clash, and there is much ambivalence about white-collar prestige.

White-collar workers are city people; in the smaller cities, they live on the right side of the tracks and work "uptown"; in the larger cities they often live in suburbs and work "downtown." The city is their milieu and they are shaped by its mass ways. As the city has expanded, more and more of its inhabitants have been white-collar people. And it is in cities of differing size that they must raise their claims for prestige.

In the smaller cities, lower classes sometimes use the term "white collar" to refer to everyone above themselves. Sometimes their attitude is that white-collar people are "pencil pushers" who "sit around and don't work and figure out ways of keeping wages cheap"; and sometimes it is that "the clerks are very essential. They are the ones who keep the ball rolling for the other guy. We would be lost if we didn't have the clerks." The upper classes, on the other hand, never acknowledge white-collar people as of the upper levels and sometimes even place them with "the laborers." An upper-class man in a city of 60,000, for instance, says: "Next after retailers, I would put the policemen, firemen, the average factory worker and the white-collar clerks.... I've lived in this town all my life and come to the bank every day but Sunday and I can't name five clerks downtown I know."

This situation of white-collar prestige in the smaller city is in part due to the fact that white-collar occupations are divided into higher and lower,

in terms of almost every basis on which prestige claims might be made: social origin, occupational history, income, education. Now, the images held of the white-collar people by upper-class groups seem to be derived, by and large, from the lower groups of these occupations, the "clerk" and the "salesperson." When upper-class individuals do focus upon higher-income salesmen, or professional and managerial employees, they think of them as part of "business" rather than as part of "white collar." Members of lower classes, on the other hand, tend to blend white collar, both higher and lower, into business and to make little distinction between them.

The ambiguous prestige of the smaller businessman in these smaller cities is explained, in part, by the "power" ascribed to him by lower groups but denied to him by the upper. Insofar as power is concerned, the ambiguous status position of the white-collar worker rests less upon complications in his power position than upon his lack of any power. White-collar employees have no leaders active as their representatives in civic efforts; they are not represented as a stratum in the councils; they have no autonomous organizations through which to strive for political and civic ends; they are seldom, if ever, in the publicity spotlight. No articulate leaders appeal directly to them, or draw strength from their support. In the organized power of the middle-sized city, there is no autonomous white-collar unit.

The few organizations in which white-collar employees are sometimes predominant — the Business and Professional Women's Clubs, the Junior

Chamber of Commerce, and the YWCA — are so tied in with business groups that they have little or no autonomy. Socially, the lower white-collar people are usually on "the Elk level," the higher in the No. 2 or 3 social club; in both they are part of a "middle-class mingling" pattern. They are "led," if at all, by higher-income salesmen and other "contact people," who are themselves identified with "business," and whose activities thus lend prestige to businessmen rather than to white-collar people.

Even in the smaller cities, then, there is no homogeneous social arena in which white-collar prestige is uniformly honored; in the big city this fact is the key to the character of white-collar prestige.

THE METROPOLIS

The rise of the big city has modified the prestige structure of modern society: it has greatly enlarged the social areas with reference to which prestige is claimed; it has split the individual from easily identifiable groups in which he might claim prestige and in which his claims might be acknowledged; it has given rise to many diverse, segregated areas in each of which the individual may advance claims; and it has made these areas impersonal. The prestige market of the big city is often a market of strangers, a milieu where contacts having relevance to prestige are often transitory and fleeting.

The neighbors of the small-town man know much of what is to be known

about him. The metropolitan man is a temporary focus of heterogeneous circles of casual acquaintances, rather than a fixed center of a few well-known groups. So personal snoopiness is replaced by formal indifference; one has contacts, rather than relations, and these contacts are shorter-lived and more superficial. "The more people one knows the easier it becomes to replace them."

The metropolitan man's biography is often unknown, his past apparent only to very limited groups, so the basis of his status is often hidden and ambivalent, revealed only in the fast-changing appearance of his mobile, anonymous existence. Intimacy and the personal touch, no longer intrinsic to his way of life, are often contrived devices of impersonal manipulation. Rather than cohesion there is uniformity, rather than descent or tradition, interests. Physically close, but socially distant, human relations become at once intense and impersonal — and in every detail, pecuniary.

Apart from educational opportunities, the status of most middle- and working-class people becomes individualized, one generation cut off from the other. Among the propertyless, status must be won anew by each generation. The small businessman's sons or the farmer's might look forward to the inheritance of a more or less secure property as a basis for their status; the floorwalker's sons or the assistant manager's cannot expect to inherit such family position.

The more transparent lives of people in smaller cities permit status bases, such as social origin, to be more readily transferred to various occupational levels. The nature of the opaque contacts characteristic of big-city life make this difficult: members of one occupational level may see or even contact members of others, but usually in a stereotyped rather than in a personal manner. They meet on impersonal terms and then retire into their socially insulated personal lives. In smaller cities and smaller enterprises, the status lines between white-collar and wage-worker are, perhaps, drawn most clearly. In metropolitan areas white-collar people seldom contact wage-workers; the physical layout of the city, the segregation of routes of travel for different occupations often restrict people to separate circles of acquaintances.

The mass media, primarily movies and radio, have further enlarged the whole prestige area and the means of status expression. In the media the life styles of the top levels are displayed to the bottom in a way and to an extent not previously the case.

Some communication system is needed to cover any prestige area, and in modern times, with the enlargement of prestige areas, "being seen" in the formal media is taken as a basis of status claims as well as a cashing of them. When national prestige was focused in local society, local newspapers used to be the principal media involved in the prestige of local society matrons. But since the 1920's, radio and especially motion pictures and TV have supplemented newspapers and have created a national status market in which the movie star, a status type

who suddenly acquires liquid assets and a lavish style of life, has replaced the local society matron. The deciders and originators in matters of the highest fashion and style of life have definitely passed from the old families of Boston, Philadelphia, Baltimore, and Newport to the stars of Hollywood and Radio City.

"In Newport, and on Fifth Avenue," Lloyd Morris has observed, "wealth had been a weapon indispensable to those who fought to win social power. In Hollywood, social prestige was an instrument essential to those determined to win wealth." The society reporters of all the eastern cities combined cannot compete with the several hundred journalists who cover Hollywood. Two dozen magazines are devoted to the film center; Louella Parsons reaches thirty million readers. Eighteen thousand movie houses are visited by ninety million people each week. The heterogeneous public appears avid for intimate details of the Hollywood elite. And the movies, which made them an elite, are set up to supply new images of them continuously. Not the society matron, but the movie star, becomes the model for the office girl.

The rich of previous eras could not so readily be known by the public, the way they lived being known only by hearsay and glimpses through curtained windows. But by the 1920's in America a democracy of status vision had come about; the area of prestige was truly national; now the bottom could see the top — at least that version of it that was put on display. It did not matter if this top was sometimes contrived and often a cloak. It did not matter if the real top was even more secluded and unseen than before. For those on the bottom, the top presented was real and it was dazzling.

The enlargement and animation, the anonymity and the transitoriness, the faster turnover and the increased visibility of the top, filling the individual's vision with a series of big close-ups — these changes have been paralleled by less noticed but equally intense changes in the prestige dynamics of the middle and lower strata.

THE STATUS PANIC

The historic bases of white-collar prestige are now infirm; the areas in which white-collar people must seek to have their claims honored are agitated. Both sides of the situation in which they are caught impel them to emphasize prestige and often to engage in a great striving for its symbols. In this, three mechanisms seem to be operating:

1. In the white-collar hierarchies, as we have seen, individuals are often segregated by minute gradations of rank, and, at the same time, subject to a fragmentation of skill. This bureaucratization often breaks up the occupational bases of their prestige. Since the individual may seize upon minute distinctions as bases for status, these distinctions operate against any status solidarity among the mass of employees, often lead to status estrangement from work associates, and to increased status competition. The employees are thus further alienated from work, for, in striving for the next rank, they come

to anticipate identification with it, so that now they are not *really* in their places. Like money, status that is exterior to one's present work does not lead to intrinsic work gratification. Only if present work leads to the anticipated goal by a progression of skills, and is thus given meaning, will status aspirations not alienate the worker. Status ascent within the hierarchy is a kind of illusionary success, for it does not necessarily increase income or the chance to learn superior skills. Above all, the hierarchy is often accompanied by a delirium for status merely because of its authoritarian shape: as Karl Mannheim has observed, people who are dependent for everything, including images of themselves, upon their place in an authoritarian hierarchy, will all the more frantically cling to claims of status.

The sharp split of residence from work place, characteristic of urban life since the Industrial Revolution, is most clearly manifested in the big-city suburb, where work associates are formally segregated from neighbors. This means that the subordinate may compete in two status worlds, that of workplace in the big city and that of residence in the suburb.

At the workplace, it is difficult, even in large enterprises, to inflate real occupational status, although great status tensions are likely to be lodged there. But actual job position is not so well known to those whom one meets away from work. It may be that to the extent that status aspirations and claims are frustrated at work, there is a more intense striving to realize them off the job. If the status struggle within the job hierarchy is lost the status struggle outside the job area shifts its ground: one hides his exact job, claims prestige from his title or firm, or makes up job, title, or firm. Among anonymous metropolitan throngs, one can make claims about one's job, as well as about other bases of prestige, which minimize or override actual occupational status.

The place of residence, which is a signal of income and style of life, limits this inflation of status; for neighbors, like job associates, will not readily cash in higher claims. But there are other areas. Anonymous and the just-known strangers who cannot so readily "place" one, may cash in one's claims. Among them, the first, often the only, impression one makes may permit a brief success in status claiming, sometimes as a sort of mutual deal.

2. "Under modern conditions," Thorstein Veblen wrote, "the struggle for existence has, in a very appreciable degree, been transformed into a struggle to keep up appearance." Personal worth and integrity may count for something, but "one's reputation for excellence in this direction does not penetrate far enough into the very wide environment to which a person is exposed in modern society to satisfy even a very modest craving for respectability. To sustain one's dignity — and to sustain one's self-respect — under the eyes of people who are not socially one's immediate neighbors, it is necessary to display the token of economic worth, which practically coincides . . . with economic success."

The leisure of many middle-class people is entirely taken up by attempts to gratify their status claims. Just as work is made empty by the processes of alienation, so leisure is made hollow by status snobbery and the demands of emulative consumption. It takes money to do something nice in one's off time — when there is an absence of inner resources and a status avoidance of cheaper or even costless forms of entertainment. With the urban breakdown of compact social groups in smaller communities, the prestige relations become impersonal; in the metropolis, when the job becomes an insecure basis or even a negative one, then the sphere of leisure and appearance become more crucial for status.

"One does not 'make much of a showing' in the eyes of the large majority of the people whom one meets with," Veblen continued, "except by unremitting demonstration of ability to pay. That is practically the only means which the average of us have of impressing our respectability on the many to whom we are personally unknown, but whose transient good opinion we would so gladly enjoy. So it comes about that the appearance of success is very much to be desired, and is even in many cases preferred to the substance . . . the modern industrial organization of society has practically narrowed the scope of emulation to this one line; and at the same time it has made the means of sustenance and comfort so much easier to obtain as very materially to widen the margin of human exertion that can be devoted to purposes of emulation."

Of an eighteenth-century nobility, Dickens could say that "dress was the one unfailing talisman and charm used for keeping all things in their places," but in a mass society without a stable system of status, with quick, cheap imitations, dress is often no talisman. The clerk who sees beautifully gowned women in the movies and on the streets may wear imitations if she works hard and, skipping the spiced ham sandwich, has only cokes for lunch. Her imitations are easily found out, but that is not to say they do not please her. Self-respectability is not the same as self-respect. On the personality markets, emotions become ceremonial gestures by which status is claimed, alienated from the inner feelings they supposedly express. Self-estrangement is thus inherent in the fetishism of appearance.

3. The prestige enjoyed by individual white-collar workers is not continuously fixed by large forces, for their prestige is not continuously the same. Many are involved in status cycles, which, as Tom Harrison has observed, often occur in a sort of rhythmic pattern. These cycles allow people in a lower class and status level to act like persons on higher levels and temporarily to get away with it.

During weekdays the white-collar employee receives a given volume of deference from a given set of people, work associates, friends, family members, and from the transient glimpses of strangers on transport lines and street. But over the weekend, or perhaps a weekend once a month, one can by plan raise oneself to higher status: clothing changes, the restaurant or type of food eaten changes, the best theater seats are had. One cannot well change one's residence over the weekend, but in the big city one can get away from it, and in the small town one can travel to the near-by city. Expressed claims of status may be raised, and more importantly those among whom one claims status may vary —

even if these others are other strangers in different locales. And every white-collar girl knows the value of a strict segregation of regular boyfriends, who might drop around the apartment any night of the week, from the special date for whom she always dresses and with whom she always goes out.

There may also be a more dramatic yearly status cycle, involving the vacation as its high point. Urban masses look forward to vacations not "just for the change," and not only for a "rest from work" — the meaning behind such phrases is often a lift in successful status claims. For on vacation, one can *buy* the feeling, even if only for a short time, of higher status. The expensive resort, where one is not known, the swank hotel, even if for three days and nights, the cruise first class — for a week. Much vacation apparatus is geared to these status cycles; the staffs as well as clientele play-act the whole set-up as if mutually consenting to be part of the successful illusion. For such experiences once a year, sacrifices are often made in long stretches of gray weekdays. The bright two weeks feed the dream life of the dull pull.

Psychologically, status cycles provide, for brief periods of time, a holiday image of self, which contrasts sharply with the self-image of everyday reality. They provide a temporary satisfaction of the person's prized image of self, thus permitting him to cling to a false consciousness of his status position. They are among the forces that rationalize and make life more bearable, compensate for economic inferiority by allowing temporary satisfaction of the ambition to consume.

Socially, status cycles blur the realities of class and prestige differences by offering respite from them. Talk of the "status fluidity of American life" often refers merely to status cycles, even though socially these cycles of higher display and holiday gratification do not modify the long-run reality of more fixed positions.

Status cycles further the tendency of economic ambition to be fragmented, made trivial, and temporarily satisfied in terms of commodities and their ostentatious display. The whole ebb and flow of saving and spending, of working and consuming, may be geared to them. Like those natives who stare until whales are tossed upon the beach, and then gorge, white-collar workers may suffer long privation of status until the month-end or year-end, and then splurge in an orgy of prestige gratification and consumption.

Between the high points of the status cycle and the machinery of amusement there is a coincidence: the holiday image of self derives from both. In the movie the white-collar girl vicariously plays the roles she thinks she would like to play, cashes in her claims for esteem. At the peak of her status cycle she crudely play-acts the higher levels, as she believes she would like to always. The machinery of amusement and the status cycle sustain the illusionary world in which many white-collar people now live.

The term "lower class" generally is taken to refer to those at the lower end of the occupational scale — skilled and unskilled workers, and those chronically unemployed and unemployable people outside the occupational structure. This large, inclusive category encompasses a variety of life styles. The life style of the stable working class, as typified by Kahl, is geared toward "getting by." * These are people who are likely to regard themselves as working class. A key question is: What does work mean to members of the working class? According to Fred Blum, who conducted a study of a Minnesota meat packing plant, work is something that kills time and is different from life. Life begins after work ends.† Harvey Swados, in his analysis of the automobile assembly-line worker, said simply that the worker felt his job was "mindless, endless, stupefying, sweaty, filthy, noisy, exhausting, insecure in its prospects, and practically without hope of advancement. The plain truth is that factory work is degrading." ‡ And Nathan Hurvitz has noted, "Although

* Joseph Kahl, *The American Class Structure* (New York: Holt, Rinehart, Winston, 1957), p. 205.

† Fred H. Blum, *Toward a Democratic Work Process* (New York: Harper, 1953).

‡ Harvey Swados, "The Myth of the Happy Worker," *The Nation* 185 (August 3, 1957), p. 67.

work and the work place are not central life interests, they are central life requirements." *

Life at home is also a source of strain. "Numerous studies have shown that divorce proneness is inversely related to husband's occupational rank." † *Marital problems begin early in marriage for working-class people. Unlike middle-class couples, husbands and wives in the lower working class have fewer friends, belong to fewer voluntary associations, and are less likely to share common interests. Blue-collar husbands are likely to share interests with their male friends rather than with their wives, but wives are likely to have close relationships only with female relatives. When blue-collar wives want to learn about sex and child-bearing, they are more likely to consult their mothers than professionals. Although women in the lower working class are less satisfied with their marriages than are spouses in any other stratum, they do not seek reform through women's liberation by attempting to modify their traditional sex role."* ‡

As dissatisfied as the blue-collar worker is with his job or marital situation or both, his situation is still better than that of the true American under class — the lower lower class. This subgroup, alienated from the rest of society, lives on poverty income, with no skills, a feeling of defeat, and no hopes for the future. Governmental financial assistance programs do not even provide them with subsistence income. This life style is not just trying to get by but an attempt at survival.§

An important hypothesis is that a distinctive life style develops under conditions of extreme poverty. This life style has been called the "culture of poverty" and occurs in many societies. In this view, the poor in Mexico, Italy, and the United States are all very similar. Poverty becomes the overriding determinant of life style, superseding race, age, region, ethnicity, and any other variable generally affecting one's way of life. Oscar Lewis, an anthropologist who wrote extensively about the poor, characterizes the culture or life style of poverty in the following essay.

---

* Nathan Hurvitz, "Marital Strain in the Blue-Collar Family," in Arthur B. Shostak and William Gomberg (eds.), *Blue-Collar World: Studies of the American Worker* (Englewood Cliffs, N.J.: Prentice-Hall, 1964), pp. 92–105.

† George Levinger, "Marital Cohesiveness and Dissolution: An Integrative Review," *Journal of Marriage and Family,* 27 (1965), pp. 19–28. See also William J. Goode, *After Divorce* (Glencoe, Ill.: Free Press, 1956); Thomas P. Monahan, "Divorce by Occupational Level," *Marriage and Family Living,* 17 (1955), pp. 323–324.

‡ Mirra Komarovsky, *Blue Collar Marriage* (New York, Random House, 1962).

§ See Charles Lebeaux, "Life on ADC: Budgets of Despair," *New University Thought* (Winter, 1963).

The Culture
of Poverty

Oscar Lewis

Although a great deal has been written about poverty and the poor, the concept of a culture of poverty is relatively new. I first suggested it in 1959, in my book *Five Families: Mexican Case Studies in the Culture of Poverty*. The phrase is a catchy one and has become widely used and misused.[1] Michael Harrington used it extensively in his book *The Other America* (1961), which played an important role in sparking the national anti-poverty program in the United States. However, he used it in a somewhat broader and less technical sense than I had intended. I shall try to define it more precisely as a conceptual model, with special emphasis upon the distinction between poverty and the culture of poverty.

From Oscar Lewis, *La Vida* (New York: Random House, 1966), pp. xlii–lii. Reprinted by permission of Random House, Inc. Copyright © 1966 by Oscar Lewis.

[1] There has been relatively little discussion of the culture of poverty concept in the professional journals, however. Two articles deal with the problem in some detail: Elizabeth Herzog, "Some Assumptions About the Poor," in *The Social Service Review*, December 1963, pp. 389–402; Lloyd Ohlin, "Inherited Poverty," Organization for Economic Cooperation and Development (no date), Paris.

The absence of intensive anthropological studies of poor families from a wide variety of national and cultural contexts, and especially from the socialist countries, is a serious handicap in formulating valid cross-cultural regularities. The model presented here is therefore provisional and subject to modification as new studies become available.

Throughout recorded history, in literature, in proverbs, and in popular sayings, we find two opposite evaluations of the nature of the poor. Some characterize the poor as blessed, virtuous, upright, serene, independent, honest, kind, and happy. Others characterize them as evil, mean, violent, sordid, and criminal. These contradictory and confusing evaluations are also reflected in the in-fighting that is going on in the current war against poverty. Some stress the great potential of the poor for self-help, leadership, and community organization, while others point to the sometimes irreversible, destructive effect of poverty upon individual character, and therefore emphasize the need for guidance and control to remain in the hands of the middle class, which presumably has better mental health.

These opposing views reflect a political power struggle between competing groups. However, some of the confusion results from the failure to distinguish between poverty per se and the culture of poverty, and the tendency to focus upon the individual personality rather than upon the group — that is, the family and the slum community.

As an anthropologist I have tried to understand poverty and its associated traits as a culture or, more accurately, as a subculture[2] with its own structure and rationale, as a way of life which is passed down from generation to generation along family lines. This view directs attention to the fact that the culture of poverty in modern nations is not only a matter of economic deprivation, of disorganization, or of the absence of something. It is also something positive and provides some rewards without which the poor could hardly carry on.

Elsewhere I have suggested that the culture of poverty transcends regional, rural-urban, and national differences and shows remarkable similarities in family structure, interpersonal relations, time orientation, value systems, and spending patterns. These cross-national similarities are examples of independent invention and convergence. They are common adaptations to common problems.

The culture of poverty can come into being in a variety of historical contexts. However, it tends to grow and flourish in societies with the following set of conditions: (1) a cash economy, wage labor, and production for profit; (2) a persistently high rate of unemployment and underemployment for unskilled labor; (3) low wages; (4) the failure to provide social, political, and economic organization, either on a voluntary basis or by government imposition, for the low-income population; (5) the existence of a bilateral kinship system rather than a unilateral one;[3]

and finally, (6) the existence of a set of values in the dominant class which stresses the accumulation of wealth and property, the possibility of upward mobility and thrift, and explains low economic status as the result of personal inadequacy or inferiority.

The way of life which develops among some of the poor under these conditions is the culture of poverty.

---

[2] While the term "subculture of poverty" is technically more accurate, I have used "culture of poverty" as a shorter form.

[3] In a unilineal kinship system, descent is reckoned either through males or through females. When traced exclusively through males it is called patrilineal or agnatic descent; when reckoned exclusively through females it is called matrilineal or uterine descent. In a bilateral or cognatic system, descent is traced through males and females without emphasis on either line.

In a unilineal system, the lineage consists of all the descendants of one ancestor. In a patrilineal system, the lineage is composed of all the descendants through males of one male ancestor. A matrilineage consists of all the descendants through females of one female ancestor. The lineage may thus contain a very large number of generations. If bilateral descent is reckoned, however, the number of generations that can be included in a social unit is limited, since the number of ancestors doubles every generation.

Unilineal descent groups ("lineages" or "clans" are corporate groups in the sense that the lineage or clan may act as a collectivity: it can take blood vengeance against another descent group, it can hold property, etc. However, the bilateral kin group (the "kindred") can rarely act as a collectivity because it is not a "group" except from the point of view of a particular individual, and, furthermore, has no continuity over time.

In a unilineal system, an individual is assigned to a group by virtue of his birth. In contrast, a person born into a bilateral system usually has a choice of relatives whom he chooses to recognize as "kin" and with whom he wants to associate. This generally leads to a greater diffuseness and fragmentation of ties with relatives over time.

It can best be studied in urban or rural slums and can be described in terms of some seventy interrelated social, economic, and psychological traits.[4] However, the number of traits and the relationships between them may vary from society to society and from family to family. For example, in a highly literate society, illiteracy may be more diagnostic of the culture of poverty than in a society where illiteracy is widespread and where even the well-to-do may be illiterate, as in some Mexican peasant villages before the revolution.

The culture of poverty is both an adaptation and a reaction of the poor to their marginal position in a class-stratified, highly individuated, capitalistic society. It represents an effort to cope with feelings of hopelessness and despair which develop from the realization of the improbability of achieving success in terms of the values and goals of the larger society. Indeed, many of the traits of the culture of poverty can be viewed as attempts at local solutions for problems not met by existing institutions and agencies because the people are not eligible for them, cannot afford them, or are ignorant or suspicious of them. For example, unable to obtain credit from banks, they are thrown upon their own resources and organize informal credit devices without interest.

The culture of poverty, however, is not only an adaptation to a set of objective conditions of the larger society.

[4] The "culture of poverty," in John J. TePaske and S. N. Fischer (eds.), *Explosive Forces in Latin America* (Columbus: Ohio State Univ. Press, 1964), pp. 149–173.

Once it comes into existence it tends to perpetuate itself from generation to generation because of its effect on the children. By the time slum children are age six or seven they have usually absorbed the basic values and attitudes of their subculture and are not psychologically geared to take full advantage of changing conditions or increased opportunities which may occur in their lifetime.

Most frequently the culture of poverty develops when a stratified social and economic system is breaking down or is being replaced by another, as in the case of the transition from feudalism to capitalism or during periods of rapid technological change. Often it results from imperial conquest in which the native social and economic structure is smashed and the natives are maintained in a servile colonial status, sometimes for many generations. It can also occur in the process of detribalization, such as that now going on in Africa.

The most likely candidates for the culture of poverty are the people who come from the lower strata of a rapidly changing society and are already partially alienated from it. Thus landless rural workers who migrate to the cities can be expected to develop a culture of poverty much more readily than migrants from stable peasant villages with a well-organized traditional culture. In this connection there is a striking contrast between Latin America, where the rural population long ago made the transition from a tribal to a peasant society, and Africa, which is still close to its tribal heritage. The more corporate nature of many of the African tribal societies, in contrast to Latin

American rural communities, and the persistence of village ties tend to inhibit or delay the formation of a full-blown culture of poverty in many of the African towns and cities. The special condition of apartheid in South Africa, where the migrants are segregated into separate "locations" and do not enjoy freedom of movement, create special problems. Here the institutionalization of repression and discrimination tend to develop a greater sense of identity and group consciousness.

The culture of poverty can be studied from various points of view: the relationship between the subculture and the larger society; the nature of the slum community; the nature of the family and the attitudes, values, and character structure of the individual.

1. The lack of effective participation and integration of the poor in the major institutions of the larger society is one of the crucial characteristics of the culture of poverty. This is a complex matter and results from a variety of factors which may include lack of economic resources, segregation and discrimination, fear, suspicion or apathy, and the development of local solutions for problems. However, "participation" in some of the institutions of the larger society — for example, in the jails, the army, and the public relief system — does not per se eliminate the traits of the culture of poverty. In the case of a relief system which barely keeps people alive, both the basic poverty and the sense of hopelessness are perpetuated rather than eliminated.

Low wages, chronic unemployment, and underemployment lead to low income, lack of property ownership, absence of savings, absence of food reserves in the home, and a chronic shortage of cash. These conditions reduce the possibility of effective participation in the larger economic system. And as a response to these conditions we find in the culture of poverty a high incidence of pawning of personal goods, borrowing from local moneylenders at usurious rates of interest, spontaneous informal credit devices organized by neighbors, the use of second-hand clothing and furniture, and the pattern of frequent buying of small quantities of food many times a day as the need arises.

People with a culture of poverty produce very little wealth and receive very little in return. They have a low level of literacy and education, usually do not belong to labor unions, are not members of political parties, generally do not participate in the national welfare agencies, and make very little use of banks, hospitals, department stores, museums, or art galleries. They have a critical attitude toward some of the basic institutions of the dominant classes, hatred of the police, mistrust of government and those in high position, and a cynicism which extends even to the church. This gives the culture of poverty a high potential for protest and for being used in political movements aimed against the existing social order.

People with a culture of poverty are aware of middle-class values, talk about them and even claim some of them as their own, but on the whole they do not live by them. Thus it is important to distinguish between what they say and what they do. For example, many will tell you that marriage by law, by the church, or by both, is the ideal form of marriage, but few will marry. To men who have no steady jobs or other sources of income, who do not own property and have no wealth to pass on to their children, who are present-time oriented and who want to avoid the expense and legal difficulties involved in formal marriage and divorce, free unions or consensual marriage makes a lot of sense. Women will often turn down offers of marriage because they feel it ties them down to men who are immature, punishing, and generally unreliable. Women feel that consensual union gives them a better break; it gives them some of the freedom and flexibility that men have. By not giving the fathers of their children legal status as husbands, the women have a stronger claim on their children if they decide to leave their men. It also gives women exclusive rights to a house or any other property they may own.

2. When we look at the culture of poverty on the local community level, we find poor housing conditions, crowding, gregariousness, but above all a minimum of organization beyond the level of the nuclear and extended family. Occasionally there are informal, temporary groupings or voluntary associations within slums. The existence of neighborhood gangs which cut across slum settlements represents a considerable advance beyond the zero point of the continuum that I have in mind. Indeed, it is the low level of organization which gives the culture of poverty its marginal and anachronistic quality in our highly complex, specialized, organized society. Most primitive peoples have achieved a higher level of sociocultural organization than our modern urban slum dwellers.

In spite of the generally low level of organization, there may be a sense of community and esprit de corps in urban slums and in slum neighborhoods. This can vary within a single city, or from region to region or country to country. The major factors influencing this variation are the size of the slum, its location and physical characteristics, length of residence, incidence of home and land ownership (versus squatter rights), rentals, ethnicity, kinship ties, and freedom or lack of freedom of movement. When slums are separated from the surrounding area by enclosing walls or other physical barriers, when rents are low and fixed and stability of residence is great (twenty or thirty years), when the population constitutes a distinct ethnic, racial, or language group, is bound by ties of kinship or *compadrazgo*, and when there are some internal voluntary associations, then the sense of local community approaches that of a village community. In many cases this combination of favorable conditions does not exist. However, even where internal organization and esprit de corps is at a bare minimum and people move around a great deal, a sense of territoriality develops which sets off the slum neighborhoods from the rest of the city. In Mexico City and San Juan this sense of territoriality results from the unavailability of low-income housing outside the slum areas. In South Africa the sense of territoriality grows out of the segregation enforced by the government, which confines the rural migrants to specific locations.

3. On the family level, the major traits of the culture of poverty are the absence of childhood as a specially prolonged and protected stage in the life cycle, early initiation into sex, free unions or consensual marriages, a

relatively high incidence of the abandonment of wives and children, a trend toward female- or mother-centered families and consequently a much greater knowledge of maternal relatives, a strong predisposition to authoritarianism, lack of privacy, verbal emphasis upon family solidarity which is only rarely achieved because of sibling rivalry, and competition for limited goods and maternal affection.

4. On the level of the individual, the major characteristics are a strong feeling of marginality, of helplessness, of dependence, and of inferiority. I found this to be true of slum dwellers in Mexico City and San Juan among families who do not constitute a distinct ethnic or racial group and who do not suffer from racial discrimination. In the United States, of course, the culture of poverty of the Negroes has the additional disadvantage of racial discrimination, but as I have already suggested, this additional disadvantage contains a great potential for revolutionary protest and organization which seems to be absent in the slums of Mexico City or among the poor whites in the South.

Other traits include a high incidence of maternal deprivation, of orality, of weak ego structure, confusion of sexual identification, a lack of impulse control, a strong present-time orientation with relatively little ability to defer gratification and to plan for the future, a sense of resignation and fatalism, a widespread belief in male superiority, and a high tolerance for psychological pathology of all sorts.

People with a culture of poverty are provincial and locally oriented and have very little sense of history. They know only their own troubles, their own local conditions, their own neighborhood, their own way of life. Usually they do not have the knowledge, the vision, or the ideology to see the similarities between their problems and those of their counterparts elsewhere in the world. They are not class-conscious, although they are very sensitive indeed to status distinctions.

When the poor become class-conscious or active members of trade-union organizations, or when they adopt an internationalist outlook on the world, they are no longer part of the culture of poverty, although they may still be desperately poor. Any movement, be it religious, pacifist, or revolutionary, which organizes and gives hope to the poor and effectively promotes solidarity and a sense of identification with larger groups, destroys the psychological and social core of the culture of poverty. In this connection, I suspect that the civil rights movement among the Negroes in the United States has done more to improve their self-image and self-respect than have their economic advances, although, without doubt, the two are mutually reinforcing.

The distinction between poverty and the culture of poverty is basic to the model described here. There are degrees of poverty and many kinds of poor people. The culture of poverty refers to one way of life shared by poor people in given historical and social contexts. The economic traits which I have listed for the culture of poverty are necessary but not sufficient to define the phenomena I have in mind. There are a number of historical examples of very poor segments of the population which do not have a way of life that I would describe as a subculture of poverty. Here I should like to give four examples:

1. Many of the primitive or preliterate peoples studied by anthropologists suffer from dire poverty which is the result of poor technology and/or poor natural resources, or of both, but they do not have the traits of the subculture of poverty. Indeed, they do not constitute a subculture because their societies are not highly stratified. In spite of their poverty they have a relatively integrated, satisfying, and self-sufficient culture. Even the simplest food-gathering and hunting tribes have a considerable amount of organization, bands and band chiefs, tribal councils and local self-government — traits which are not found in the culture of poverty.

2. In India the lower castes (the Chamars, the leather workers, and the Bhangis, the sweepers) may be desperately poor, both in the villages and in the cities, but most of them are integrated into the larger society and have their own *panchayat* [5] organizations which cut across village lines and give them a considerable amount of power.[6] In addition to the caste system, which gives individuals a sense of identity and belonging, there is still another factor, the clan system. Wherever there are unilateral kinship systems or clans one would not expect to find the culture of

poverty, because a clan system gives people a sense of belonging to a corporate body with a history and a life of its own, thereby providing a sense of continuity, a sense of a past and of a future.

3. The Jews of eastern Europe were very poor, but they did not have many of the traits of the culture of poverty because of their tradition of literacy, the great value placed upon learning, the organization of the community around the rabbi, the proliferation of local voluntary associations, and their religion which taught that they were the chosen people.

4. My fourth example is speculative and relates to socialism. On the basis of my limited experience in one socialist country — Cuba — and on the basis of my reading, I am inclined to believe that the culture of poverty does not exist in the socialist countries. I first went to Cuba in 1947 as a visiting professor for the State Department. At that time I began a study of a sugar plantation in Melena del Sur and of a slum in Havana. After the Castro Revolution I made my second trip to Cuba as a correspondent for a major magazine, and I revisited the same slum and some of the same families. The physical aspect of the slum had changed very little, except for a beautiful new nursery school. It was clear that the people were still desperately poor, but I found much less of the despair, apathy, and hopelessness which are so diagnostic of urban slums in the culture of poverty. They expressed great confidence in their leaders and hope for a better life in the future. The slum itself was now highly organized, with block committees, educational commit-

[5] A formal organization designed to provide caste leadership.

[6] It may be that in the slums of Calcutta and Bombay an incipient culture of poverty is developing. It would be highly desirable to do family studies there as a crucial test of the culture-of-poverty hypothesis.

tees, party committees. The people had a new sense of power and importance. They were armed and were given a doctrine which glorified the lower class as the hope of humanity. (I was told by one Cuban official that they had practically eliminated delinquency by giving arms to the delinquents!)

It is my impression that the Castro regime — unlike Marx and Engels — did not write off the so-called lumpen proletariat as an inherently reactionary and anti-revolutionary force, but rather saw its revolutionary potential and tried to utilize it. In this connection, Frantz Fanon makes a similar evaluation of the role of the lumpen proletariat based upon his experience in the Algerian struggle for independence. In his recently published book[7] he wrote:

> *It is within this mass of humanity, this people of the shanty towns, at the core of the lumpen proletariat, that the rebellion will find its urban spearhead. For the lumpen proletariat, that horde of starving men, uprooted from their tribe and from their clan, constitutes one of the most spontaneous and most radically revolutionary forces of a colonized people.*

My own studies of the urban poor in the slums of San Juan do not support the generalizations of Fanon. I have found very little revolutionary spirit or radical ideology among low-income Puerto Ricans. On the contrary, most of the families I studied were quite conservative politically and about half of

[7] Frantz Fanon, *The Wretched of the Earth* (New York: Grove Press, 1965), p. 103.

them were in favor of the Republican Statehood Party. It seems to me that the revolutionary potential of people with a culture of poverty will vary considerably according to the national context and the particular historical circumstances. In a country like Algeria which was fighting for its independence, the lumpen proletariat was drawn into the struggle and became a vital force. However, in countries like Puerto Rico, in which the movement for independence has very little mass support, and in countries like Mexico which achieved their independence a long time ago and are now in their postrevolutionary period, the lumpen proletariat is not a leading source of rebellion or of revolutionary spirit.

In effect, we find that in primitive societies and in caste societies, the culture of poverty does not develop. In socialist, fascist, and in highly developed capitalist societies with a welfare state, the culture of poverty tends to decline. I suspect that the culture of poverty flourishes in, and is generic to, the early free-enterprise stage of capitalism and that it is also endemic in colonialism.

It is important to distinguish between different profiles in the subculture of poverty depending upon the national context in which these subcultures are found. If we think of the culture of poverty primarily in terms of the factor of integration in the larger society and a sense of identification with the great tradition of that society, or with a new emerging revolutionary tradition, then we will not be surprised that some slum dwellers with a lower per capita income may have moved farther away from the core characteristics of the culture of poverty than others with a higher per capita income. For example, Puerto Rico has a much higher per capita income than Mexico, yet Mexicans have a deeper sense of identity.

I have listed fatalism and a low level of aspiration as one of the key traits for the subculture of poverty. Here too, however, the national context makes a big difference. Certainly the level of aspiration of even the poorest sector of the population in a country like the United States, with its traditional ideology of upward mobility and democracy is much higher than in more backward countries like Ecuador and Peru, where both the ideology and the actual possibilities of upward mobility are extremely limited and where authoritarian values still persist in both the urban and rural milieus.

Because of the advanced technology, high level of literacy, the development of mass media, and the relatively high aspiration level of all sectors of the population, especially when compared with underdeveloped nations, I believe that although there is still a great deal of poverty in the United States (estimates range from thirty to fifty million people), there is relatively little of what I would call the culture of poverty. My rough guess would be that only about 20 percent of the population below the poverty line (between six and ten million people) in the United States have characteristics which would justify classifying their way of life as that of a culture of poverty. Probably the largest sector within this group would consist of very low-income Negroes, Mexicans, Puerto Ricans, American Indians, and Southern poor whites. The relatively small number of people in the United States with a culture of poverty is a positive factor, because it is much more difficult to eliminate the culture of poverty than to eliminate poverty per se.

Middle-class people, and this would certainly include most social scientists, tend to concentrate on the negative aspects of the culture of poverty. They tend to associate negative valences to such traits as present-time orientation and concrete versus abstract orientation. I do not intend to idealize or romanticize the culture of poverty. As someone has said, "It is easier to praise poverty than to live in it"; yet some of the positive aspects which may flow from these traits must not be overlooked. Living in the present may develop a capacity for spontaneity and adventure, for the enjoyment of the sensual, the indulgence of impulse, which is often blunted in the middle-class, future-oriented man. Perhaps it is this reality of the moment which the existentialist writers are so desperately trying to recapture but which the culture of poverty experiences as natural, everyday phenomena. The frequent use of violence certainly provides a ready outlet for hostility, so that people in the culture of poverty suffer less from repression than does the middle class.

In the traditional view, anthropologists have said that culture provides human beings with a design for living, with a ready-made set of solutions for human problems so that individuals don't have to begin all over again each generation. That is, the core of culture is its positive adaptive function. I, too, have called attention to some of the adaptive mechanisms in the culture of poverty — for example, the low aspiration level helps to reduce frustration, the legitimization of short-range hedonism makes possible spontaneity and enjoyment. However, on the whole it seems to me that it is a relatively thin culture. There is a great deal of pathos, suffering, and emptiness among those who live in the culture of poverty. It does not provide much support or long-range satisfaction, and its encouragement of mistrust tends to magnify helplessness and isolation. Indeed, the poverty of culture is one of the crucial aspects of the culture of poverty.

The concept of the culture of poverty provides a high level of generalization which, hopefully, will unify and explain a number of phenomena viewed as distinctive characteristics of racial, national, or regional groups. For example, matrifocality, a high incidence of consensual unions, and a high percentage of households headed by women, which have been thought to be distinctive of Caribbean family organization or of Negro family life in the U.S.A., turn out to be traits of the culture of poverty and are found among diverse peoples in many parts of the world and among peoples who have had no history of slavery.

The concept of a cross-societal subculture of poverty enables us to see that many of the problems we think of as distinctively our own or distinctively Negro problems (or that of any other special racial or ethnic group) also exist in countries where there are no distinct ethnic minority groups. This suggests that the elimination of physical poverty per se may not be enough to eliminate the culture of poverty, which is a whole way of life.

What is the future of the culture of poverty? In considering this question, one must distinguish between those countries in which it represents a relatively small segment of the population and those in which it constitutes a very large one. Obviously the solutions will differ in these two situations. In the United States, the major solution proposed by planners and social workers in dealing with multiple-problem families and the so-called hard core of poverty has been to attempt slowly to raise their level of living and to incorporate them into the middle class. Wherever possible, there has been some reliance upon psychiatric treatment.

In the underdeveloped countries, however, where great masses of people live in the culture of poverty, a social-work solution does not seem feasible. Because of the magnitude of the problem, psychiatrists can hardly begin to cope with it. They have all they can do to care for their own growing middle class. In these countries, the people with a culture of poverty may seek a more revolutonary solution. By creating basic structural changes in society, by redistributing wealth, by organizing the poor and giving them a sense of belonging, of power, and of leadership, revolutions frequently succeed in abolishing some of the basic characteristics of the culture of poverty even when they do not succeed in abolishing poverty itself.

We have examined illustrative life styles from three social class divisions in the United States. Class lines are not rigid boundaries; many Americans desire to move up in the class system. In Part 2, we looked at the frustrations encountered by independent truckers in their quest for upward mobility. We also found that purchasers of encyclopedias believe that they are buying the symbols associated with an upward change in social class. Thus life style strategies may have upward mobility as a central life interest, but there are many different strategies for attaining this goal. One strategy involves cultivating and maintaining the "right" social contacts. Although this strategy is limited to only a small group of Americans, Sheila Johnson in the following article shows how well calculated such a strategy can be and how it can be manifested in routine aspects of everyday life.

Sociology of Christmas Cards

Sheila K. Johnson

Anyone who has ever composed a Christmas card list has pondered the inclusion and exclusion of names on the basis of a variety of fairly explicit considerations. Shall I send so-and-so a card this year, since he didn't send me one last year? Or, I *must* send so-and-so a card this year, even though he probably won't send me one, because I want to be remembered by him. Like the decisions we make about whom to vote for, we like to think of these choices as purely individual, rational matters. Nevertheless, sociologists have demonstrated that, regardless of how

From *Trans-action,* vol. 8, no. 3 (Jan. 1971). Reprinted by permission of Transaction, Inc. Copyright © 1971, by Transaction, Inc.

and why we choose a candidate, voting behavior can be analyzed as a function of one's socioeconomic status, mobility aspirations, ethnicity and religious affiliation. Similarly, it seems likely that the patterns in which people send and receive Christmas cards can also be explained in terms of certain social characteristics, especially their social status and mobility aspirations.

This proposition first occurred to me several years ago, as I was opening some Christmas cards and noticed that there was a strange disjunction between the cards we were receiving and the ones we had sent out. About half of the cards we received were from people to whom we had also sent cards, but the other half came from people to whom we had not sent cards and to whom we had had no intention of sending cards, and we ourselves had sent half of our cards to people from whom we had not expected to receive (and did not receive) a card in return. When I studied the names that fell into each of these three categories, it dawned on me that the people with whom we had exchanged cards reciprocally were either relatives or people with whom we were on an equal social footing — professional friends of my husband or personal friends in different but nevertheless comparable occupations. The cards we had sent but to which we had received no reply, I discovered, went invariably to individuals whom *we* wanted to cultivate — people with regard to whom we were, in sociological terms, "upwardly mobile," such as professional acquaintances who might someday prove useful or important or social acquaintances whom we wished we knew better. By the same token, the cards we received and to which we did not reply came from individuals who wanted to cultivate us — some of my husband's graduate students and office employees, the liquor store, the hairdresser and foreign scholars who obviously expected to visit the United States at some time in the future.

In order to test out my theory I telephoned several friends shortly after Christmas and asked them to sort the cards they had received into two piles — reciprocals and those to whom they had not sent cards — and also to count up the number of cards they had sent "upward." (Some of the incensed replies to this request would indicate that the nature of Christmas card sending is a very touchy subject indeed.) Those of my friends who continued to speak to me and who complied with my request corroborated my theory. Several couples in their late thirties or early forties who, although in different professions, were rather similar to ourselves in their mobility aspirations and in the number of people they knew who were upwardly mobile with regard

to them found that their Christmas cards could be grouped into equal thirds (one-third sent and not received, one-third sent and received and one-third received but not sent). However, a young graduate student reported that about 70 percent of his cards were reciprocal, with 30 percent sent upward and none received from people who were trying to curry favor with him. This is clearly the pattern for those with their foot on the bottom rung of the status ladder. At the other end, several retired people reported that 90 percent of their cards were reciprocal, with only 5 percent sent upward and 5 percent received from people who still regarded them as important. A man who had retired but taken a second job, however, reported that 70 percent of his cards were reciprocal but that 10 percent had been sent upward and 20 percent had come from people trying to cultivate him.

While the percentages of cards an individual sends and receives tell us a good deal about his mobility aspirations, the fact that he sends Christmas cards at all places him rather firmly in the middle class. Members of the upper class — particularly a closed upper class to which one gains admission by birth rather than through the acquisition of wealth — have no need to send cards upward, and sending cards to other members of the upper class is a formality that many are dispensing with. In England, for example, it is increasingly common for upper-class families to place an ad in the personal columns of the London *Times* stating that Lord and Lady So-and-So send warm greetings to all their friends for Christmas and the New Year as they will not be sending cards. (Several years ago an upper-class English wit poked fun at these ads by placing one asking *his* friends to send him Christmas cards as he would not be able to read the *Times* columns during December.) In the United States, because the upper class is more fluid than in England, and because the country is simply too large for all one's upper-class friends to read the same daily newspaper, the custom of sending cards among upper-class individuals has not died out. One would predict, however, that most of the private card sending of the upper class is reciprocal and that only its business Christmas cards are sent upward, since there is always room for upward mobility in the business world.

Lower-class and working-class individuals also send few or no Christmas cards, but for entirely different reasons. Sociologists have demonstrated that lower- and working-class individuals tend to rely upon tightly knit family networks and neighbors for their friendships and that they are less geographically mobile than the middle class. Thus a skilled union man will probably have a large number of relatives in the same town or same general area as he does, and he will be on friendly terms with many of his neighbors. There is no need to send these people Christmas cards, however, since he sees them nearly every day. He may be upwardly mobile in terms of his job, but this is handled by the union, and a Christmas card to the front office is not likely to do the trick. Only if he is upwardly mobile to the extent of trying to leave his stratum and become a white-collar worker may he take to sending Christmas cards to people who can help him. In that case he may

adopt other middle-class behavior patterns, such as joining various clubs and lodges, in which he will make a broader range of friends to whom he will also want to send cards at Christmas.

SENDERS AND RECIPIENTS

It is the middle class — particularly the upper middle class, consisting of high managerial and professional people — who are the Christmas card senders par excellence. These are the people who are both geographically and socially mobile — growing up in one place, going to college somewhere else and then moving about as success in one's firm or profession seems to dictate. Kinship ties tend to be far-flung and tenuous, since it would not be advantageous to be tied down to a given area by one's aging parents or embarrassed by the sudden appearance of a lower-class cousin. Friendships are formed among social equals — at school, at work, in professional or social organizations — but these, too, change as one moves up the ladder of success or to a different section of the country. Such are the ideal conditions for the exchange of Christmas cards. Friends and relatives are scattered widely, but one wants to keep "in touch," and there are vast sources of upward mobility to be tapped.

I realize that some people will object strenuously to this analysis of their Christmas card sending and receiving. While I was attempting to collect data on the subject, several of my friends declined to cooperate on the grounds that they did not fit into the pattern I had just described to them. "Really," one of them said self-righteously, "I keep an up-to-date Christmas list, and the only people I send cards to are people who send me cards. There is no upward sending or downward receiving in our family: it's strictly reciprocal." This is pure propaganda, nurtured by the myth of absolute social equality that exists in this country. Everyone can think of some acquaintances to whom he simply *has* to send cards, regardless of whether he gets one in return. The obligatory nature of the act is the real tip-off to the social pressures at work. As for people who receive cards they were not expecting — that is, cards being sent upwards to them — and who then shamefacedly rush out on Christmas Eve to mail the forgotten sender one of theirs, they are simply insecure in their status position. Imagine the president of Chase Manhattan Bank receiving a Christmas card from the janitor and saying remorsefully, "Oh, my God, and I didn't send *him* one." Yet thousands of people do roughly the same thing when they receive a card from someone who looks up to them. What should they do instead? The answer is nothing, except sit back and enjoy it. Of course, if the upward sender shows other indications of increased social status, it might be wise to send him a Christmas card next year, but that would depend on circumstances ranging far beyond the scope of this article.

In a recent film, "Diary of a Mad Housewife," the husband is shown counting the family's Christmas cards and remarking to his wife, "One-hundred-and-fifty-three. That's fine. Three more weeks to go until Christmas and we've already reached the half-way mark . . . We sent out 300." He then goes on to instruct his wife to note carefully who has sent cards to them, since there's "no point" in sending cards the following year to people who have not sent them one this year. Here the authors of the film have missed a bet, however, since the husband is depicted as a social climber of the first water who would clearly insist on sending Christmas cards to certain "important" people — the same people whom he invites to his abysmal party and tries to cultivate in other ways.

In addition to scrutinizing the number of Christmas cards people send and receive for signs of social status and mobility aspirations, one can also tell a good deal about the personality of the sender by the kind of card he chooses. There may still be a few rare individuals who choose every Christmas card individually to suit the *recipient* but for the most part those days went out with the advent of boxed cards. Somewhat more common is the tendency for people with two radically different constituencies — for example, businessmen who keep their business and private acquaintances well compartmentalized — to choose two different sets of cards. However, in such cases it is not at all clear whether the two sets of cards are chosen to suit the different sets of recipients or to reflect the different personality that the businessman wishes to convey to each group — sober and elegant cards for his business acquaintances and mod, swingerish cards for his personal friends. In general one may assume that cards reflect the sender rather than the receiver, and that a Madison Avenue executive would no more receive a museum card from his Aunt Emma in Vermont than he would send her a Hallmark Santa Claus with a rhymed poem inside.

How can one classify some of the cards that people consciously or subconsciously select to convey not only their Christmas wishes but also their personality? Among university types, whom I know best, there seem to be several distinct patterns. Well-established WASP professors tend to send museum cards or rather small studio cards of abstract design. Usually, the more powerful the professor, the smaller the card. (This appears to be a snobbish, willful inversion of the usual business pattern: the more important the executive, the bigger and more lavish the card. An academic friend argues that there are exceptions to this rule and cites Professor Henry Kissinger, from whom last year he received an absolutely gigantic Christmas card portraying both sides of the globe. I would maintain, however, that this Christmas card merely illustrates Professor Kissinger's defection from the academic ranks and his adoption of the big-business ethos of the Nixon administration.) Jewish and youngish, slightly left-of-center professors tend to send UNICEF cards, often choosing a design that reflects their area of academic interest — India specialists send the Indian-designed card, Africa specialists send the African-designed card and so forth. A similar tendency may be observed among government officials.

From professors who have (or think they have) artistic wives we get hand-screened, hand-blocked or otherwise handcrafted Christmas cards. From professors who have just had their first child we get (you guessed it) baby photographs, and from professors who are doing research abroad we often get photos of their children in native dress.

From professors abroad sans children, or from those who've been there before, we get interesting Chinese, Japanese or Thai renderings of the nativity. (The most fascinating Thai card we ever received, from a high-ranking Thai army officer, was a photograph of the gentleman himself posed proudly beside his new Jaguar XKE. *Joyeux Noel* indeed!)

People with strong political convictions tend to remind us of these at Christmas time. Thus we get our share of CORE and CND cards. From less political but equally morally outraged friends we get a strange assortment of messages: cards that say on them "printed by spastics" or "designed by the deaf" and cards depicting felled redwood trees or oil-stained beaches. From our wealthier, nonacademic friends we get cards supporting the Symphony Association and the Junior League.

In addition to all of these types of cards, we get, every year, a couple of photographs of houses. These are never from the academic world — although some professors I know live in very nice houses — because the houses displayed on Christmas cards have a special status significance. Most of the houses that I have seen on Christmas cards belonged to friends who had just retired to Florida or Hawaii, or they were the dream-come-true of people who had finally bought that acre in the country. Whatever the occasion, the house depicted is usually the visible sign of a major change in social status, and it is certainly no accident that the president's Christmas card almost always features the White House.

Finally, and perhaps hardest of all to pin down sociologically, there is the category of Christmas card known as the mimeographed Christmas letter. I would like to hold a contest sometime for the most fatuous Christmas letter, but I'm afraid I'd be deluged with entries. It is hard to attribute the Christmas letter to a particular type of person or a particular station in life, because almost everyone who has ever had an eventful year, taken an exciting trip, or accomplished a great deal has felt the urge to compose one. I have received them from internationally famous professors who were attempting to describe their world travels, from graduate students describing their Ph.D. research in the field and from relatives recounting the latest family gossip. Perhaps mimeographed Christmas letters should be used as a vanity indicator, since they expose those among us who yielded to, rather than resisted, the pervasive temptation to blow one's own horn.

A MATTER OF TONE

The chief defect of the Christmas letter is its tone — that peculiar half-personal, half-distant note that makes most of them sound as if they were addressed to mentally defective 13-year-olds. This tone is the inevitable result of trying to address a single letter to a score or more of different friends. As any letter writer knows, one usually manipulates the tone of a letter to convey a certain personal image to a specific correspondent. If it is often difficult to send the same *card* to business as well as personal acquaintances because of the image to be conveyed to each group, how much more difficult to compose a letter that will ring true to a variety of recipients.

Not only is the tone of Christmas letters muddled by the lack of a clearly defined recipient, but it also often lacks the unifying voice of a single sender. Most Christmas cards can convey the status and life style of a couple or a family as readily as they can those of an individual. But this is because cards deal in visual symbols, whereas letters traffic in words. It is always hard to believe that a mimeographed letter from "Betty and Bob" is really a joint verbal product, and so one looks for telltale "I's" and "he's" or "she's" to pin down the author. In a genuine Christmas letter, however, such slips never occur, and one is left to figure out for himself who is being the more sanctimonious from sentences that announce: "While Bob worked like a demon interviewing local politicians and village chiefs, Betty spent her time learning how to cook native dishes and teaching English to some of the wives and children." (For the full effect, one must trying substituting "I" for each of the proper nouns in turn.)

There are doubtless still other sociological and psychological facets to the sending and receiving of Christmas cards. However, having said all of this, I would not want readers to conclude that I am trying to denigrate Christmas cards or that I personally am above sending them. Far from it. Having already passed through my family photograph, foreign and UNICEF phases, I may even succumb to sending a Christmas letter one of these years. My card this year was a small, high-status museum number depicting a medieval knight being hoisted on his own petard. The motto on his banner reads: *Honi soit qui mal y pense.* I think it suits me rather well.

REGIONAL SUBCULTURES: GEOGRAPHIC DIMENSIONS OF LIFE STYLES

The News Banner, *the local newspaper of the small town of Wadsworth, Ohio, calls itself "the only newspaper in the whole wide world that cares about Wadsworth." Americans strongly identify with the place they live in. For some it is the city or state in which they live while for others it is the region of the country. As we can infer from the following article by Ben Bagdikian, Americans have a strong sense of local identity fostered through a tradition of local politics, local pride, and local media.*

Some Peculiarities of American News

Ben H. Bagdikian

Among world news systems, America's is peculiar.

In other countries there are national newspapers issued in one or two important urban centers and distributed as the primary serious journals throughout the country. Local papers are marginal and parochial, classified geographically and culturally as "the provincial press."

In most countries radio and television also are centralized, with few local originating facilities. Programs typically emanate from a central studio owned and controlled by a government monopoly.

In the United States, the typical American consumer receives all his daily printed and broadcast news from a local private enterprise. There are historical reasons for this unique pattern in the United States and social reasons why it should continue. Though there are contemporary trends diminishing local independence, compared to world systems the American news continues to be rooted in the local community.

The American news is even at odds with its own technological and corpo-

From Ben H. Bagdikian, *The Information Machines: Their Impact on Men and the Media,* pp. 68–85. Copyright © 1971 by the RAND Corporation. Reprinted by permission of Harper & Row, Publishers, Inc.

rate environment. It transmits most of its information through national monopolies, the telephone and telegraph systems. Its major suppliers of national and world news are two highly centralized national services, the Associated Press and United Press International. The newspaper industry as a whole is one of the country's largest and as such operates in an economic environment of corporate giantism and oligopoly. Yet the news itself continues to be dispensed through a highly fragmented collection of local firms.

In the United States no national newspaper is readily available in all parts of the country at its time of publication. *The New York Times* comes closest to being a national newspaper, but it is printed only in New York City and despite its considerable influence does not displace a significant portion of national newspaper reading.

The *Wall Street Journal* is published simultaneously in six different locations and is readily available in more cities than any other daily, but specializes in business and finance. The *Christian Science Monitor* of Boston is distributed nationally but its countrywide circulation is small.

Broadcasting in the United States also operates through local firms; national networks dominate prime-time television and are important in national broadcast news. But even the networks and their affiliates operate exclusively through local outlets.

No other country approaches this degree of localism in news institutions. In Russia, for example, metropolitan Moscow has less than 3 percent of total U.S.S.R. population, but Moscow-based dailies have 87 percent of all Russian daily circulation. In Japan, metropolitan Tokyo has 11 percent of national population, but Tokyo-based dailies have 70 percent of national circulation. In Britain, metropolitan London has 14 percent of population, but its dailies have 70 percent of national circulation.

In contrast, metropolitan New York and Washington, D.C., together have 6.6 percent of national population and together their daily papers supply only 9.6 percent of daily papers throughout the country.

Technical innovations in the coming years could change the fundamental pattern of public information distribution in the United States, and it is logical to ask whether the unique localism in the United States can or should be preserved. This question is worth asking because prevailing explanations for the absence of national news media in the United States seldom touch on its profound social basis.

The usual explanation for the lack of national newspapers is that the United States is so large geographically that it has been impossible to transport a paper speedily from its city of origin to all other cities. This has

been one influence. But if it were the controlling factor, it would be predictable that new technology would quickly eliminate the pattern of local newspapers, since remote reproduction of large quantities of documents will become increasingly fast and inexpensive. One need not even wait for future developments. Present technology permits effective centralized control of newspaper production over great distances. Russia is two and a half times larger than the United States but manages to control most of its papers from Moscow.

Still another explanation usually offered is national affluence that can support many papers. This, like geographical size, is a factor but not a controlling one. A number of countries have a higher rate of per-capita newspaper buying but support fewer individual papers [Table 1].

Note, for example, that Japan, with about half the population of the United States, sells about 50 percent more papers per capita, but has only one-tenth as many individual dailies.

The American broadcasting news system follows somewhat the same pat-

TABLE 1

Country	Daily papers sold per 100 population	Number of individual daily papers
Sweden	501	117
Britain	488	106
Japan	465	174
New Zealand	380	41
Australia	370	60
Denmark	347	67
Switzerland	344	126
West Germany	332	416
United States	312	1754

Source — *Statistical Abstract of the United States, 1968,* Table 1272, p. 862.

tern, with a large number of individual radio and television stations spread throughout the country. This is primarily the result of governmental regulatory policy rather than market mechanisms that govern placement of newspapers. But it is significant that government policy places a high value on localized radio and television stations. Governments of other industrialized countries favor centralized systems.

Centralizing radio broadcasting would be technically simple. Commercial radio signals ricochet between the surface of the earth and layers of the atmosphere during the evening, propelling themselves over very long distances in every direction. Thus, it would not be difficult to produce nighttime coverage of the entire continental United States from a single transmitter. As a matter of fact, this was done from 1934 to 1938 when WLW in Cincinnati was permitted to operate at 500,000 watts.

Daytime radio signals fade more quickly, but with easily achieved power and selected frequencies a single station can still be heard within ranges of several hundreds of miles, so that a few stations could easily cover the entire United States.

Despite this technical feasibility of a few stations covering the entire country, there are 6,200 commercial AM and FM radio stations operating in 2,672 separate American communities. The largest number of radio stations in a single area is 34.

If the only desired end in the distribution of radio stations were diversity on a national scale, this could be achieved more easily, economically,

and with greater variety than the present scattered locations. It would be possible, for example, to have 100 powerful radio transmitters that could reach every radio in the United States, rather than 6200 weaker ones reaching only their own locales. And the 100 centralized ones would provide more choice for the average listener, whose present maximum local stations are 34, with most communities able to receive far fewer. But the 100 centralized stations would not conform to the special force of localism in the United States.

Television cannot be so easily propagated from a few national transmitters because its carrier wave has a range less than a hundred miles and is even more disturbed than radio by intervening masses. But if national coverage with several channels were desired, it could be produced by several centralized studios whose programs would be relayed to each locality by relatively simple translator stations that are automatic. Instead, there are 639 commercial television transmitters in operation in 285 metropolitan areas, each with facilities for originating its own programs, rather than merely relaying national ones.

The fundamental reason for this persistent localism in American news institutions is a peculiarity in American political organization and the prevailing pattern of family money spending.

More governmental functions are left to the local level in the United States than in other developed countries. Schools, property taxes, land use, public health, large areas of business regulation, and many other political and social activities are controlled by locally elected and locally controlled bodies in the United States, while in other countries many of these are controlled by national governments or administered by national bureaucracies.

These locally controlled policies have maximum immediate impact on family life, such as schooling for children, design and location of homes, routes of local highways, and rates of personal property taxes. Such decisions are made by a complicated but highly localized set of political bodies. There are 18,000 municipalities and 17,000 townships. Within these are 500,000 local government units of one kind or another directly elected by local residents, 100,000 of these being directly elected local school boards, and 70,000 of the local jurisdictions possessing the power to impose taxes on their constituents.

No national newspaper or national broadcast news program can tell the local citizen what he needs or wants to know about these local activities that affect his family life. Furthermore, what is relevant to one local jurisdiction is only minimally significant for the next, since school systems, property taxes, and similar matters follow strictly local lines and cease to apply across the local boundary. Continuing information from relatively small districts is a unique imperative of the American social system.

Another powerful force for localism in the mass media is the large amount of local money spending by the average family. Mass purchasing power requires enough spending decisions to support advertising as a major economic activity.

American family income has been rising rapidly. From 1929 to 1962 average family personal income, measured in constant 1954 dollars, rose 70 percent. This, and the demands of modern urban and occupational life, have made necessities of some consumer goods that previously had been luxuries or nonexistent — refrigerators, cleaning compounds, formal city clothes. And, as national styles of work and social life evolved, other consumer goods became essential for coping efficiently with the environment — telephones, a family car, and electrical appliances like vacuum cleaners, radio and television sets. So, even at the lowest levels of income, the pressure for large-scale consumer purchasing became significant.

The great majority of this family money spending is done locally among competing enterprises. There are 1,700,000 retail stores in the United States. The average American family spends $5,000 a year in them. Many of these stores advertise in competition for this disposable family income, and most of their advertising is in the general locality of their stores, in the mass media of the region.

Thus, there is both a political and an economic base for the localized pattern of American news media.

But there are conflicting forces at work, some in the direction of the traditional fragmentation of news firms, and some in the direction of a more homogenized, national pattern of a few organizations dominating the country. At present, there seems to be a tenuous equilibrium between the forces, with a surprising degree of stability among small journalism units despite the national trend toward large national corporations. The nature of new technology and the way it is organized could be crucial to the fate of this equilibrium.

The stability and profit of small, local journalism firms are remarkable, considering their rarity in other countries. In the daily-newspaper business, for example, there is a common pattern of a few large firms controlling a disproportionate share of the total market. In the United States, 8 percent of the largest papers have over half of all circulation. The smaller papers, those under twenty-five thousand circulation, constitute 70 percent of all daily newspaper firms but they have less than 20 percent of national circulation [Table 2].

In the usual corporate trend, where in a field of 1,752 firms the top 2 percent have 30 percent of all the business, consolidation would proceed until most smaller operations would be absorbed by the giants. There is, in fact, a strong trend in the newspaper business toward consolidations, mergers, and chains, though these do not take

the conventional form of centralized production, planning, and sales and do not seem to enjoy the usual economies of scale. But, while consolidation grows, the distribtuion of the market among smaller papers remains fairly stable, thanks to the emphasis on local self-government and local merchandising.

Location of broadcasting stations is decided by the Federal Communications Commission, and though these decisions are influenced by market demand, they are more influenced by limitations of positions on the dial. And, since there is no simple measure of "customers" for broadcasting because the consumer does not pay directly for his broadcast, determining how stations share their market is somewhat blurred. The distribution of profitable stations, by size of their community, of the 2,624 AM and AM-FM stations reporting profits to the Federal Communications Commission in 1967 is shown [in Table 3].

Here, as with newspapers, one sees advantages with domination of larger

TABLE 2

Circulation of papers	Number of papers of this size	Percentage of all papers	Percentage of total market
500,001 and over	11	0.6	14.0
250,001 to 500,000	28	1.6	15.6
100,001 to 250,000	93	5.3	24.4
50,001 to 100,000	112	6.4	12.3
25,001 to 50,000	255	14.5	14.6
10,001 to 25,000	462	26.3	11.8
5,001 to 10,000	467	26.7	5.3
Less than 5,000	324	18.5	1.9
Total papers	1,752	100.0	100.0

Source — *Editor and Publisher Yearbook: 1969,* p. 17. Percentages of papers and of total market added.

markets, but relative stability in the smaller ones.

The pattern of economic activity of television stations by size is more difficult to discern in official data, since the Federal Communications Commission does not issue comparable information for television. There are fewer television stations nationally, and fewer per market. There are over two hundred television markets; the top ten markets have more than a third of all TV households in the country and the top forty markets have two-thirds. Since there is a narrow limit to the number of television stations in any market because of the frequency shortage in the air — seven is the VFH maximum — there is a poor fit between available audience and available stations. Pittsburgh, for example, has $23 million a year in advertising revenues for its three television stations. The

New York market has $130 million in television advertising revenues, or 5.6 times as much, which presumably would support 5.6 times as many stations, which would be sixteen or seventeen stations. But in New York there are only seven stations. Thus, the physical limitations of electro-magnetic space in broadcasting through the air distorts any tendency to let television broadcasting adjust itself to potential audience or demand for advertising.

The news media from the start were carriers of local merchandising information. The newspaper in the United States began as a printed extension of bulletin boards of taverns and coffeehouses, its content mainly of ship arrivals and their offerings of cargo. These papers sold for six cents each, a very high price in the eighteenth century, designed for the affluent in the local population. The nonadver-

TABLE 3

Population category of community where station is located	Number of stations in communities of this size	Average percent profit on gross per station before federal tax
2,000,000 or more	146	28%
1,000,000 to 2,000,000	106	27
500,000 to 1,000,000	217	19
250,000 to 500,000	241	15
200,000 to 250,000	58	15
150,000 to 200,000	89	13
100,000 to 150,000	116	13
50,000 to 100,000	71	11
25,000 to 50,000	239	13
10,000 to 25,000	465	11
5,000 to 10,000	457	13
2,500 to 5,000	294	12
Less than 2,500	125	12

Source — *AM-FM Broadcast Data, 1967*, F.C.C. Document 27306, February 7, 1969-B, Table 8. Percentages of profit added.

tising content consisted largely of re-printed stories from the English papers which arrived on the same ship as the merchandise. Until the Revolution, the most common name for American newspapers was *Advertiser*.

This pattern was enhanced by the absence of very large cities in the eighteenth-century North American continent. When the first dailies were established, the two largest cities, New York and Philadelphia, each had twenty-five thousand population.

Most of these early papers were published either by the local postmaster or by a local printer. Colonial postal service was crude and unreliable, a private monopoly granted by the Crown, and operating in only three cities. The population was a dispersed agricultural one, kept deliberately unindustrialized by the mother country, lacking the urbanization that might have encouraged a different press pattern.

As the country grew it developed a different demographic pattern from Europe, which already had its population clustered around large cities. The American frontier expanded and its population kept proliferating outward to virgin territory. A lively apprentice system produced many printers who had a reputation for itchy feet and parched throats, drifting drinkers who fell out of one job to another just beyond their reputation, but leaving behind the idea of a locally printed sheet.

Other factors helped create many small papers instead of a few large ones. One was the absence of a tax on papers. The European attempt to control the press through stamp taxes was so burdensome in many countries

that it inhibited new papers. This concentrated circulation in the few papers that were rich and stable enough to pay the heavy duty on individual editions, and that tended to be very establishmentarian.

In the United States there was both constitutional and statutory encouragement for a free and growing press. Congress was forbidden to make any law abridging the freedom of the press. And the new postal system set up by Benjamin Franklin, an ex-printer, and William Hunter favored local printers. Each subscriber to a newspaper was charged nine pence sterling a year for every fifty miles the paper had to be carried by the postal system. On the other hand, papers sent from one printer to another went free. Thus, the individual subscriber was penalized by distance while his local printer was not; this encouraged printers to clip and paste other papers from distant cities and reprint locally.

In 1833, the largest American daily, the New York *Courier and Enquirer*, had a circulation of forty-five hundred, and that probably exaggerated, and most other American papers had less than a thousand circulation. The same year, the London *Times* and at least two Paris papers had circulations of more than fifteen thousand each.

The most spectacular burgeoning of the press came in mid-nineteenth century, largely because of new communications technology, like paper production from wood, high-speed presses, railroads, and the telegraph. The prices of many papers dropped. It became possible to buy a daily paper for a penny. In 1800, there had been 235 individual newspapers in the country, by 1850, 2,300. By 1860, there were more than three times as many papers in the United States as in England and France. Always local merchandising and local government stimulated indigenous papers, and the number of dailies rose to a peak of 2,461 in 1916.

But with World War I the number of newspapers in the country began to decline and has continued to decline until today there are 1,750 papers, a drop of 30 percent. And since that time there has been a rise in strictly national news media, separate or nearly separate from the local papers and broadcast stations. The rise was slow until the last twenty years, during which it has become marked.

Since 1940, total daily newspaper circulation in the United States has risen about 50 percent, roughly the same as population. But the carriers of daily national news have outpaced this. The *Wall Street Journal*'s circulation in its home state increased 2,100 percent, but outside New York it went up 4,700 per cent. *The New York Times*'s circulation in greater New York rose 30 percent, outside its own city, 165 percent. The *Christian Science Monitor*'s circulation in its home city, Boston, actually dropped slightly, but elsewhere in the country it rose 26 percent.

National news magazines, an invention of the period, have gained even more rapidly. In the 1940–1968 period, *Time*, *Newsweek*, and *U.S. News and World Report* increased their circulation 585 percent.

Responding to the same growing appetite for national news, new special supplementary news services for daily papers concentrated on serious Wash-

ington and world reportage and analysis. The New York Times Service was going to 16 North American papers in 1956 and to 211 in 1969. The Los Angeles Times/Washington Post News Service started in 1962 with 21 papers and in 1969 had 189. *Congressional Quarterly*, a relatively sophisticated summary and statistical analysis of legislative activity in Washington, was subscribed to by 1 paper in 12 in 1955, but in 1968 by 1 paper in 6, even though it had a rival in a new service, Center for Political Research.

But, during the same period of marked growth of national news media, there was growth in strictly local ones. Hundreds of specialized papers, many classed as "underground," sprang up, with a circulation estimated at 4 million. "Establishmentarian" weeklies, mostly serving small areas, also grew. During the decade 1958–1967, daily newspaper circulation rose 5 percent, but circulation of standard commercial weeklies rose 51 percent. Some operators forecast even more spectacular growth. John E. Tilton, of Suburban Papers, Inc., of Minneapolis, said, "In the next 20 years, someone will start another 2000 suburban newspapers."

Nevertheless, commercial pressures for ever wider jurisdictions, made all the more tempting by easier and cheaper long-distance transmission of information, raise the possibility of increasing separation between local media and national.

Two factors push in this direction. One is the growth in popular consciousness of national and world affairs, the result both of increased cosmopolitanism and education and the enlargement of the role of the national government and world events in the life of the average family.

The other factor is the trend in contemporary advertising and merchandising reversing the historic role of rooting the local media to their immediate communities.

In the late nineteenth century, newspapers for the first time took seriously the possibility that at least one newspaper could be sold to each household each day. By then it was technically possible to manufacture enough papers for this kind of saturation. Advertising was becoming an important national economic activity and assuming an ever larger share of the newspaper's revenues. In 1867 $50 million a year was spent on ads; in 1900 this had gone up ten times, by 1950 a hundred times.

Merchants generally buy space or broadcasting time on the basis of the cost of exposing their advertising to a thousand persons, or cost-per-thousand. As individual newspaper production plants developed the capacity to print one complete newspaper for every house in the community, and advertisers clearly became indirect subsidizers of these plants, the working of the marketplace made it inevitable that it would be less expensive for the advertisers to support one plant in a community instead of two or three or a dozen. Even with the increased advertising rates that a local monopoly could charge, the cost-per-thousand was cheaper than advertising in two or more competing papers.

Since World War I the number of individual newspapers has declined, though the surviving papers have become fatter and devote a larger per-

centage of their space to advertisements. Since World War II advertising content in daily papers has gone from 52 percent to 61 percent, the size of papers from twenty-two pages a day, of which eleven were ads, to fifty pages in 1965 for the average daily, of which thirty were ads.

Fatter papers meant larger plants, more presses, more typesetting machines, and larger work forces. Processing of advertising is more demanding and expensive than that of news matter. Costs rose. But, once plates were on the presses, labor costs remained relatively level and the cost of added circulation was largely the cost of paper and ink. And, since advertising was placed more on the basis of cost-per-thousand than any other single factor, it was advantageous for a paper to increase its production, even if it meant extending its sales beyond the limits of its immediate city.

Conversion of newspapers into substantial manufacturing plants inhibited growth of new papers in new communities. Surviving papers gained monopolies in their own communities and pushed beyond the city limits to nearby communities. Consequently, the cost of starting new papers in the new communities at the edges of the metropolises was unattractive, since the established nearby papers were always prepared to produce papers for the new communities at small incremental cost. The country created more and more communities, and served them with fewer and fewer newspapers.

The consequences of this reversal of the traditional American tendency for each community to serve its self-governing functions with its own news medium are difficult to measure. But the change from 90 percent of urban places with their own daily paper to less than 30 percent [Table 4] is a radical one, and it may have radical consequences. It could be a contributing factor to the growing inability of municipalities to control their social and political affairs, to the psychological loss of community identity characteristic of newer towns and cities, and to the sluggishness with which urban governments responded to postwar social pathologies and the slowness with which this pathology, once felt, came to national attention.

The need for systematic community communication in the United States is self-evident from the number of important functions left to local decision. Jack Lyle, in his book *The News in Megalopolis*, notes that the local press is usually thought of as a watchdog over local government, and while this is true, there is a positive function as well: "... officials want to get information to the public ... because of the proliferation of public agencies, such bodies are actually competing for the attention of the individual citizen and for coverage within the news media."

Lyle's research showed that community communications depend more than anything else on the presence of a locally based printed news medium. When he asked local officials how frequently their activities were covered by news media, both city-government and school-district activities showed coverage in this way:

Local weeklies	53%
Local dailies	53
Metropolitan dailies	17
Radio and TV	0

Banfield and Wilson in *City Politics* note that a city like Chicago has 341

TABLE 4

Year	Daily papers	Cities with dailies	Percentage of daily cities with competing papers	Percentage of urban places with own dailies
1880	850	389	61	90
1910	2202	1207	57	53
1920	2042	1295	43	48
1930	1942	1402	21	44
1940	1878	1426	13	41
1945	1744	1396	8	—
1961	1763	1461	4	29
1968	1749	1500	3	—

Source — *Subcommittee on Antitrust and Monopoly*, "The Failing Newspaper Act," Part 6, p. 2842, Table 1, "Trends in Ownership of English-Language Dailies of General Circulation and Content in the United States, 1880–1968," percentage of daily cities with competing papers added. Number of urban places from *Historical Statistics of the United States*, p. 14, and *Statistical Abstract of the United States*, p. 16.

different officials with identifiable authority in city and county matters and "in most cases there is no formal mechanism by which all these governments can be brought together."

The growing number of radio and television stations has not relieved this trend because broadcasting pays little attention to systematic local reportage. Robert Paul Boynton and Deil S. Wright, in a study of council managers in cities of over 100,000 population, found that "Local news is the base of a newspaper's operation. A high percentage of its total space is allotted to community concerns. Radio and television have other primary interests."

Boynton and Wright polled city managers on their judgment of mass-media influence on municipal affairs, with . . . results [as given in Table 5].

This parallels a survey by the Bureau of Advertising of the ANPA which, in 1966, polled a cross-section of readers on the "best way" to find out about local affairs, to which 48 percent cited newspapers, 13 percent television, and 15 percent radio. Both the newsmakers and the news consumers depend on the local printed newspaper for important community information.

The basic causes for present community malaise in the United States can hardly be laid at the door of absent or delinquent news media. Even with ideal local attention to civic affairs, it would be difficult to cope with the bewildering maze of governmental and quasi-governmental units, often uncoordinated and frequently at cross-purposes. But apathy or frustration produced by this random agglomeration of civic functions is deepened by the lack of locally based news-media that even try to follow and publicize systematically the more important developments. In a country of 100,000 autonomous school districts and 400,000 other local governmental units, it is significant that fewer than 30 percent of the communities in whose boundaries they lie has any locally based news medium.

This poor fit between community units and news media comes largely because newspapers and radio and television stations, even though they carry a place name in their identification, do not arrange their output by civic boundaries but instead by merchandising territories. As the automobile determines the range for shopping, merchandising territories increasingly

TABLE 5

Degree of influence	Newspapers	Television	Radio
Highly influential	51%	8%	2%
Moderately influential	42	50	33
Limited influence	7	23	49
No apparent influence	0	20	16

Reprinted from "Communication Gap: Is Anybody Up There Listening?" by Robert Paul Boynton and Deil S. Wright, *Public Management,* March, 1968, p. 2, by special permission. © 1968, The International City Management Association.

ignore civic boundaries. And, as these shopping territories enlarge, the growing production power of the mass media follows them through communities whose civic affairs they largely ignore.

The effective boundary line of most newspapers is a territory called "retail trade zone," which varies in definition from place to place but commonly ends in neighborhoods where the paper's daily sales fall to between 5 and 20 percent of the total households.

Broadcasting stations occupy territories called "markets," which are usually the area of the effective range of their broadcast signal.

About 400 markets are calculated for daily newspapers and about 230 markets for broadcasting stations. Within these are most of the 500,000 units of local government. Given the total space for serious local news in newspapers, and the total time devoted in typical broadcasting stations, it would be impossible to give systematic reportage of all the important public-affairs developments in each of the significant public bodies within the market areas of individual news media.

In 1969 a majority of the FCC raised questions about the transfer in ownership of the only television station in Hutchinson, Kansas, KTVH, Channel 12. The Commission was concerned with concentration of ownerships, but KTVH is typical of other television stations in its jurisdiction, which represents problems regardless of ownership.

KTVH covers about 18,000 square miles with its strongest signal, with average penetration of 90 percent of the 344,000 homes. If the 23 counties for which KTVH is the primary station

have their share of all local governmental units in Kansas, they contain over 800 different governmental bodies, including 210 municipalities and 110 school boards. About 350 of them levy taxes.

If the station devotes typical TV time to local news (not including sports), and if each of the governmental bodies in its area made only one newsworthy decision a month, and if the station happened to cover this decision, and if the station devoted all of its local newscasts exclusively to the deliberations of these public bodies, each would have reportage of thirty seconds a month.

KTVH is part of the Kansas Broadcasting System for the purpose of selling commercials. This network of television stations advertises itself as "a 93 county major television market of 403,400 television homes, 1.3 million people in a five state area with a consumer spendable income of over $3.5 billion...."

For merchandisers, such a network is effective. As reporters of events within their boundaries, it reduces each civic function to a fraction of a minute per month.

Yet the merchandising function continues to favor ever larger geographical territories, so that the cost of reaching each consumer will drop. This is impelled not only by the larger shopping ranges made possible by the automobile, but also by the growth of unified national brands, commonly available "at your local" (anonymous) drug, department, or grocery store. Standard-brand cosmetics, food, and cigarettes do not need to specify particular stores or addresses in order to

stimulate sales by wide-area broadcasting or newspaper advertising.

Among newspapers, two categories
of standardized retail goods make up
42 percent of all newspaper advertising: automobiles with 28 percent, and
foods with 14 percent. In television, in
1970, four categories of nationally
standard brands made up almost 60
percent of all television advertising:
foods with 19 percent; toiletries, 17
percent; tobacco, 12 percent; and
drugs, 11 percent.

The retail outlets for these standardized items are also becoming regionally
and nationally standardized by a relatively small number of recognizable
and dominant firms. The combination
of near-universal recognition of both
store names and brand names means
that broad, homogenized advertising
becomes more effective, and the small
medium with a special audience less
competitive.

Especially with broadcasting, whose
entertainment and news also are increasingly produced in a national
source, the financial rewards lie with
enlargement of area and of gross population, even to the deliberate exclusion
of a station's immediate home base.

The Federal Communications Commission recently took note of this
tendency. "We have . . . noted that
there is a tendency on the part of stations in suburban communities in
metropolitan areas, to identify themselves with the entire metropolitan
area rather than with the particular
needs of their communities." The FCC
intervened when the only full-time
radio station in Camden, New Jersey,
was about to be sold to a Texas corporation which intended to eliminate all

local programming serving the 117,000
population of Camden in order to attract advertising for programming designed for the metropolitan Philadelphia area across the Delaware River,
although Philadelphia already had
twenty-eight of its own radio stations.

Technology helped eliminate the
idea of every community with a news
medium of its own. But even broadcasting once started as a local service.
When the British Broadcasting Corporation started in 1922, there was no
practical network system in existence.
Consequently it established twenty
strictly local stations with only 1/4 kw
power (American communities now
have stations with many times that
power). When communications technology improved, the BBC became a
centralized operation out of London.
Frank Gillard, managing director of
radio for the BBC, says that the result
has been that the former development
of local talent in discussion, entertainment, and culture atrophied as only
the highly professionalized work of
London reached the air, and that "democracy in the country breaks down
at the local level."

If England, which depends far less
on local decision making for the health
of its basic institutions than the United
States, is apprehensive about a breakdown at the local level for lack of local
media, the United States has cause for
concern. Although the United States
has far more local media than any
other country, it is far more dependent
on such media than any other country.
And these local media are expanding
their territories, largely at the expense
of neighborhood, community, and city
information and programming. The

commercial imperative is not news but to reach the largest possible undifferentiated gross numbers of audience for purposes of national and regional advertising. And this advertising is less and less tied to particular communities.

Regionalism is a dominant force in American life fostering different styles of life in different areas of the country. The pace of life in the southwest is different from that in New England. Beer and Brat Houses abound in Wisconsin and Illinois, but are nowhere to be found in California. Grits are served with breakfast eggs in the South, but potatoes are served with eggs in the North. A "regular" coffee to an Easterner means with cream and sugar, while to a Westerner it's black coffee. In Philadelphia, a sandwich with a variety of Italian meats is a "hoagie"; in other regions, a similar sandwich is called a "grinder," "torpedo," "poor boy," "submarine," or some other name.* Even names for common objects differ throughout the nation. Thus a creek may be called a "kill" or "run" in the East, a "branch" or "stream" in the upper Midwest, a "crick" or "bayou" in parts of the South, and a "gully" or "wash" in the West.† Pronunciation also differs in the United States: orange is pronounced "Awrange" in the West and "AREange" in the East; wash is pronounced "warsh" in parts of the Midwest; and we are all familiar with New York, Boston and Southern accents.

There are definitely regional differences; yet the United States does have a common culture. Patterns of culture shared by some individuals within a society but not by all members of that society are called subcultural patterns. There are within the United States not only regional subcultures but occupational, ethnic, deviant, college student subcultures, etc.

One of the reasons that life in Los Angeles is so different from life in New York City is that the cities differ geographically. The outdoor life can be enjoyed year round in many portions of the West, South, and Southwest while this type of activity is seasonal in the Midwest, and the East. Furthermore, regions have their unique history and patterns of in-migration and out-migration. With a vast in-migration of Cuban immigrants, the life style of Miami has become more Latinized than in the past. Miami still has a large Jewish population and a large popula-

---

* Edwin Eames and Howard Robby, "The Socio-Cultural Context of an Italian-American Dietary Item," *Cornell Journal of Social Relations*, 2 (Fall 1967), pp. 63–75.

† George Lundberg, Clarence Schrag, Otto Larsen, and William R. Catton, Jr. *Sociology, 4th ed.* (New York: Harper & Row, 1968), p. 255.

tion of retired people. Coupled with a warm climate, Miami offers a life style and a character found in no other city of the United States.

The life style of Miami however, is different from that of other parts of the South. The South was characterized by Mencken* as the American stronghold of the White Anglo-Saxon Protestant:

> He runs the whole South — and in the whole South, there are not as many first-rate men as in many a single city of the mongrel North. Wherever he is still firmly in the saddle, there Kukluxery flourishes and Fundamentalism, and lynching, and prohibition, and all of the other stupid and anti-social crazes of inferior men.

Historian J. G. Randall suggested that the uniqueness of the South is due to its white Anglo-Saxon settlers and the prevalence of a one-crop economy based on cotton.† U. B. Phillips summed up the uniqueness of the South as "above all, . . . a resolve indomitably maintained — that it is and shall remain a white man's country." ‡

A few cities and towns are recognized as the setting of a distinctive life style that sets their inhabitants apart from even their near neighbors. Minneapolis, unlike St. Paul, has a large Scandinavian population and every year Minneapolis annually observes a Swedish Day, a Danish Day, and a Norwegian Day.

Cities may recognize the geographic origins of their residents in other manners as well. In Seattle, there are state picnics (with an especially large Minnesota picnic) at which people who have migrated to Washington from other states may meet to reaffirm their regional origins.

San Francisco is perhaps the city in the United States which is most widely acclaimed as being subculturally distinctive. First, the city contains more than its share of ethnic, political, religious, occupational and deviant subcultures who seem to coexist in relative harmony. This harmony plus the unique nature of many of its social institutions (and distinct climate and topography) fosters a subculture of "professional San Franciscans" who strongly identify with the city and who may develop a life style whose central life interest is living in San Francisco.§

In the following article, Howard S. Becker and Irving Louis Horowitz describe San Francisco's life style as resulting from a soft official line on deviance, great diversity of actual behavior patterns and an accommodation of all persons in an urban culture of civility.

* H. L. Mencken, *Prejudices: Fourth Series* (New York: Knopf, 1924), p. 28.

† J. G. Randall, *The Civil War and Reconstruction* (Boston: Heath, 1937), pp. 2–26.

‡ U. B. Phillips, "The Central Theme in Southern History," *The American Historical Review* (October 1928), p. 31.

§ Many locals take umbrage at the term "Frisco" and feel it should be referred to as *San Francisco* or more preferably "The City."

The Culture of Civility

Howard S. Becker and
Irving Louis Horowitz

Deviants of many kinds live well in San
Francisco — natives and tourists alike
make that observation. The city's apparently casual and easygoing response
to "sex, dope and cheap thrills" (to
crib the suppressed full title of Janis
Joplin's famous album — itself a San
Francisco product) astounds visitors
from other parts of the country who
can scarcely credit either what they see
happening or the way natives stroll by
those same events unconcerned.

Walking in the Tenderloin on a summer evening, a block from the Hilton,
you hear a black whore cursing at a
policeman: "I wasn't either blocking
the sidewalk! Why don't you mother-
fucking fuzz mind your own goddamn
business!" The visiting New Yorker
expects to see her arrested, if not shot,
but the cop smiles goodnaturedly and
moves on, having got her back into the
doorway where she is supposed to be.

You enter one of the famous rock
ballrooms and, as you stand getting
used to the noise and lights, someone
puts a lit joint of marijuana in your
hand. The tourist looks for someplace
to hide, not wishing to be caught in

From *Trans-action*, vol. 7, no. 6 (April
1970). Reprinted by permission of Transaction, Inc. Copyright © 1970, by Transaction,
Inc.

the mass arrest he expects to follow.
No need to worry. The police will not
come in, knowing if they do they will
have to arrest people and create disorder.

Candidates for the city's Board of
Supervisors make their pitch for the
homosexual vote, estimated by some at
90,000. They will not be run out of
town; the candidates' remarks are duti-
fully reported in the daily paper, as
are the evaluations of them by representatives of SIR, the Society for Individual Rights.

The media report (tongue in cheek)
the annual Halloween Drag Ball, for
which hundreds of homosexuals turn
out at one of the city's major hotels in
full regalia, unharassed by police.

One sees long-haired, bearded hippies all over the city, not just in a few
preserves set aside for them. Straight
citizens do not remark their presence,
either by gawking, hostility or flight.

Nudie movies, frank enough to satisfy anyone's curiosity, are exhibited
in what must be the largest number of
specialty movie houses per capita in
the country. Periodic police attempts
to close them down (one of the few
occasions when repression has been attempted) fail.

The items can be multiplied indefi-
nitely, and their multiplicity demands
explanation. Most cities in the United
States refuse to let deviants indulge
themselves publicly, let alone tolerate
candidates who seek their bloc votes.
Quite the contrary. Other cities, New
York and Chicago being good examples,
would see events like these as signs of
serious trouble, omens of a real breakdown in law enforcement and deviance
control, the forerunner of saturnalia

and barbarian take-over. Because its politicians and police allow and can live with activities that would freak their opposite numbers elsewhere, San Francisco is a natural experiment in the consequences of tolerating deviance. We can see from its example what happens when we ignore the warnings of the custodians of conventional morality. We can learn too about the conditions under which problems that perhaps lie deeper than matters of morals or life style can be solved to the satisfaction of all the parties to them.

We can summarize this low-key approach to deviance in the phrase "a culture of civility." What are its components, and how does it maintain itself?

San Francisco prides itself on its sophistication, on being the most European of American cities, on its picturesque cosmopolitanism. The picturesque quality, indeed the quaintness, rests in part on physical beauty. As the filling of the Bay and the destruction of the skyline by high-rise buildings proceeds to destroy that beauty, the city has come to depend even more on the presence of undigested ethnic minorities. It is as though San Francisco did not wish its Italians, Chinese or Russians to assimilate and become standard Americans, preferring instead to maintain a panoply of ethnic differences: religious, cultural and culinary (especially culinary). A sophisticated, livable city, on this view, contains people, colonies and societies of all kinds. Their differences create a mosaic of life styles, the very difference of whose sight and smell give pleasure.

Like ethnic minorities, deviant minorities create enclaves whose differ-

ences add to the pleasure of city life. Natives enjoy the presence of hippies and take tourists to see their areas, just as they take them to see the gay area of Polk Street. Deviance, like difference, is a civic resource, enjoyed by tourist and resident alike.

To enjoy deviance instead of fearing it requires a surrender of some common sense notions about the world. Most people assume, when they see someone engaging in proscribed activity, that there is worse to come. "Anyone who would do that [take dope, dress in women's clothes, sell his body or whatever] would do anything" is the major premise of the syllogism. "If you break one law or convention, who knows where you'll stop." Common sense ignores the contrary cases around us everywhere: professional criminals often flourish a legionnaire's patriotism; housewives in every other respect conventional sometimes shoplift; homosexuals may be good family providers; some people who habitually use the rings from poptop cans to work the parking meter would not dream of taking dope, and vice versa. Deviance, like conforming behavior, is highly selective. San Francisco's culture of civility, accepting that premise, assumes that if I know that you steal or take dope or peddle your ass, that is all I *know*. There may be more to know; then again, there may be nothing. The deviant may be perfectly decent in every other respect. We are often enjoined, in a generalization of therapeutic doctrine, to treat other people as individuals; the prescription comes nearer to being filled in San Francisco than in most places in the United States.

Because of that tolerance, deviants find it possible to live somewhat more openly in San Francisco than elsewhere. People do not try so hard to catch them at their deviant activities and are less likely to punish them when caught. Because they live more openly, what they do is more visible to straight members of the community. An established canon of social psychology tells us that we find it harder to maintain negative stereotypes when our personal experience belies them. We see more clearly and believe more deeply that hippies or homosexuals are not dangerous when we confront them on the street day after day or live alongside them and realize that beard plus long hair does not equal a drug-crazed maniac, that limp wrist plus lisp does not equal child-molester.

When such notions become embodied in a culture of civility, the citizenry begins to sense that "everyone" feels that way. We cannot say at what critical point a population senses that sophistication about deviance is the norm, rather than a liberal fad. But San Francisco clearly has that critical mass. To come on as an anti-deviant, in a way that would probably win friends and influence votes in more parochial areas, risks laughter and ridicule in San Francisco. Conservatives who believe in law and order are thus inclined to keep their beliefs to themselves. The more people keep moralistic notions to themselves, the more everyone believes that tolerance is widespread. The culture maintains itself by convincing the populace that it is indeed the culture.

It gets help from public pronouncements of civic officials, who enunciate what will be taken as the collective sentiment of the city. San Francisco officials occasionally angle for the conservative vote that disapproves licentiousness. But they more frequently take the side of liberty, if not license. When the police, several years ago, felt compelled to close the first of the "topless joints," the judge threw the case out. He reasoned that Supreme Court decisions required him to take into account contemporary community standards. In his judgment San Francisco was not a prudish community; case dismissed. The city's major paper, the *Chronicle*, approved. Few protested.

Similarly, when California's leading Yahoo, Superintendent of Public Instruction Max Rafferty, threatened to revoke the teaching credentials of any San Francisco teacher who used the obscene materials listed in the standard high school curriculum (Eldridge Cleaver's *Soul on Ice* and LeRoi Jones' *Dutchman*), the City did not remove the offending books from its curriculum. Instead, it successfully sued to have Rafferty enjoined from interfering in its operation.

In short, San Franciscans know that they are supposed to be sophisticated and let that knowledge guide their publications, whatever their private feelings. According to another well-known law of social psychology, their private feelings often come to resemble their public actions, and they learn to delight in what frightens citizens of less civil cities.

We do not suggest that all kinds of deviation are tolerated endlessly. The police try, in San Francisco as elsewhere, to stamp out some vices and keep a ceiling on others. Some deviants frighten San Franciscans too, precisely because their activities seem to portend worse to come (most recently, users and purveyors of methedrine — "speed merchants" and "speed freaks" — whose drug use is popularly thought to result in violence and crime). But the line is drawn much farther over on the side of "toleration" in San Francisco than elsewhere. A vastly wider range of activities is publicly acceptable. Despite the wide range of visible freakiness, the citizenry takes it all in stride, without the fear and madness that permeates the conventional sectors of cities like Detroit, Chicago, New York, Washington, D.C. and similar centers of undaunted virtue.

How does a culture of civility arise? Here we can only speculate, and then fragmentarily, since so few cities in the United States have one that we cannot make the comparisons that might uncover the crucial conditions. San Francisco's history suggests a number of possibilities.

It has, for one thing, a Latin heritage. Always a major seaport, it has long tolerated the vice that caters to sailors typical of such ports. It grew at the time of the gold rush in an explosive way that burst through conventional social controls. It ceded to its ethnic minorities, particularly the Chinese, the right to engage in prostitution, gambling and other activities. Wickedness and high living form part of the prized past every "tourist" city constructs for itself; some minor downtown streets in San Francisco, for instance, are named for famous madames of the gold rush era.

Perhaps more important, a major potential source of repressive action —

the working class — is in San Francisco more libertarian and politically sophisticated than one might expect. Harry Bridges' longshoremen act as bellwethers. San Francisco is one of the few major American cities ever to experience a general strike and the event still reverberates. Working people who might support repression of others know by personal experience that the policeman may not be their friend. Trade unionism has a left-wing, honest base which gives the city a working-class democracy and even eccentricity, rather than the customary pattern of authoritarianism.

Finally, San Francisco is a town of single people. Whatever actual proportion of the adult population is married, the city's culture is oriented toward and organized for single people. As a consequence, citizens worry less about what public deviance will do to their children, for they don't have any and don't intend to, or they move from the city when they do. (Since there are, of course, plenty of families in the city, it may be more accurate to say that there are fewer white middle-class families, that being the stratum that would, if family-based, provide the greatest number of complaints about deviance. Black, chicano and oriental populations ordinarily have enough to worry about without becoming guardians of public morality.)

San Francisco is known across the country as a haven for deviants. Good homosexuals hope to go to San Francisco to stay when they die, if not before. Indeed, one of the problems of deviant communities in San Francisco is coping with the periodic influx of a new generation of bohemians who have heard that it is the place to be: the beatnik migration of the late fifties and the hippie hordes of 1967. But those problems should not obscure what is more important: that there are stable communities of some size there to be disrupted. It is the stable homosexual community that promises politicians 90,000 votes and the stable bohemian communities of several vintages that provide both personnel and customers for some important local industries (developing, recording and distributing rock music is now a business of sizeable proportions).

Stable communities are stable because their members have found enough of what they want to stay where they are for a while. If where they were proved totally unsatisfying, they presumably would move elsewhere, unless restrained. But no one forces deviants to live in San Francisco. They stay there because it offers them, via the culture of civility, a place to live where they are not shunned as fearsome or disgusting, where agents of control (police and others) do not regard them as unfortunate excrescences to be excised at the first opportunity. Because they have a place to stay that does not harass them, they sink roots like more conventional citizens: find jobs, buy houses, make friends, vote and take part in political activities and all other things that solid citizens do.

Sinking roots stabilizes deviants' lives, as it does the lives of conventional citizens. They find less need to act in the erratic ways deviants often behave elsewhere, less need to fulfill the prophecy that because they are

deviant in one respect they will be deviant in other, more dangerous ways. San Francisco employers know that homosexuals make good employees. Why not? They are not likely to be blackmailed by enterprising hustlers. The police seldom haul them off to jail for little reason or beat them because they feel like pushing some "queers" around. Homosexuals fear none of this in San Francisco, or fear it much less than in most places, and so are less given to the overcompensatory "camping" that gets their fellows into trouble elsewhere.

Police and others do not harass deviants because they have found, though they may deny it for public relations purposes, that looking the other way is sometimes a good policy. It is easier, when a Be-In is going on, to turn your back on the sight of open marijuana smoking than it is to charge into the crowd and try to arrest people who will destroy the evidence before you get there, give you a hard time, make a fool of you and earn you a bad press — and leave you with no conviction to show for it. At the same time, when you turn your back, nothing worse is likely to happen: no muggings, no thefts, no rapes, no riots. Police, more calculating than they seem, often choose just this kind of accommodation with stable deviant communities.

The accommodation works in circular fashion. When deviants can live decent lives, they find it possible to behave decently. Furthermore, they acquire the kind of stake they are often denied elsewhere in the present and future structure of the community. That stake constrains them to behave in ways that will not outrage nondeviants, for they do not want to lose what they have. They moderate their activities to what they think the community will stand for.

The community in turn, and especially the police, will put up with more than they might otherwise, because they understand that nothing else is forthcoming, and because they find that what they are confronted with is not so bad after all. If homosexuals have a Halloween Drag Ball, the community discovers it can treat it as a good-natured joke; those who are offended discover that they needn't go near the Hilton while it is happening.

No doubt neither party to such a bargain gets quite what he would like. Straight members of the community presumably would prefer not to have whores walking the downtown streets, would prefer not to have gay bars operating openly. Deviants of all kinds presumably would prefer not to have to make any concessions to straight sensibilities. Each gives up something and gets something, and to that degree the arrangement becomes stable, the stability itself something both prize.

What we have just described verges on the idyllic, Peace and Harmony in Camelot forever. Such a dream of perfection does not exist in San Francisco, though more deviants there have more of the advantages of such a bargain, perhaps, than in any other city in the United States. Nor is it clear that the system we described, even in its perfect form, would be such an idyll.

In San Francisco, as everywhere, the forces of decency and respectability draw the line somewhere and can be every bit as forceful and ruthless the other side of that line as the forces of decency and respectability anywhere else. When Haight-Ashbury got "out of hand" with the overcrowded transiency of 1967, the city moved in the police Tactical Squad, the City Health Department and all the other bureaucratic weapons usually used to rouse deviants. They did it again with the growth of violence in that area associated with the use and sale of methedrine. In general, the city has responded with great toughness to those deviants it believes will not be satisfied with something "reasonable." In particular, political dissent has sometimes been met with force, though San Francisco police have never indulged themselves in the way that has made Chicago police internationally detested.

The system has beauty only for those deviants who do not mind giving up some portion of their liberty, and then only if what they are willing to give up is the same as what the community wants given up. This no doubt is the reason an accommodative system works well with those whose deviant desires are narrowly circumscribed, and may have less utility with those whose wants can be accommodated only at the expense of others who will not easily give up their privileges. In fact, many current urban difficulties clearly result from the breakdown of accommodation.

These considerations indicate the more general importance of San Francisco's experiment in tolerating and accommodating to the minor forms of deviance encompassed in sex, dope and cheap thrills. How can a complex and differentiated society deal with variety and dissent and simultaneously with its own urges for centralized control? An accommodative relationship to difference, in which it is allowed to persist while paying some minimal dues to the whole, is what San Francisco recommends to us, suggesting that the amount of the dues and the breadth of the license be set where both parties will, for the time being, stand still for it. The resulting working arrangement will be at least temporarily stable and provide for all concerned a tranquility that permits one to go about his business unharmed that many will find attractive.

But is this no more than a clever trick, a way of buying off deviant populations with minor freedoms while still keeping them enslaved? Beneath the rhetoric, the analysis is the same. The more radical statement adds only that the people who accept such a bargain ought not to, presumably because they have, if they only knew it, deeper and more important interests and desires which remain unsatisfied in the accommodative arrangement. So, of course, do those who hold them in check. Perhaps that is the ultimate lesson of San Francisco: the price of civilization, civility and living together peacefully is not getting everything you want.

It is tempting to think that an accommodation based on civility and mutual interest provides a model for settling the conflicts now wracking our urban areas. Our analysis suggests that this is a possibility, but no more than that. Peace can occur through accommodation, the example of the potheads and pimps tells us, only under certain

not so easily attained conditions. Those conditions may not be present in the ethnic and political problems our major cities, San Francisco among them, are now experiencing.

Accommodation requires, as a first condition, that the parties involved prize peace and stability enough to give up some of what they want so that others may have their desires satisfied as well. But people take that point of view only when the accommodation leaves them enough of a share to want no more. Some urban groups no longer believe that they are getting that necessary minimum, either because they have learned to interpret their situation in a new light or because they have lost some advantages they once had.

Members of black communities may be no worse off than ever, but they are considerably worse off than whites and know it. For a variety of historical reasons, and as a matter of simple justice, some of them no longer regard the little they have as sufficient reason to keep the peace. All the discussion about how many blacks feel this way (is it 10 percent or 50 percent?) and how strongly they feel it (are they willing to fight?) is beside the main point: enough feel strongly enough to make a lot of trouble for the white community, thus changing the balance of costs to whites and insisting on a new division of rights as the price of stability.

Some members of white communities probably are objectively worse off and may resent it sufficiently to give up peace and stability in an effort to raise the costs to others and thus minimize their losses. Many whites in civil service positions, in the skilled trades and in similar protected occupational positions have lost or are in danger of losing competitive job advantages as governments act to do something about the injustice that afflicts black communities. Without a general expansion of the economy, which is *not* what blacks demand, injustices inflicted on blacks can be remedied only by taking something away from more favorably situated whites. It may be possible to improve the education of poor black children, for instance, only by taking away some of the privileges of white teachers. It may be possible to give black youths a chance at apprenticeships in skilled trades only by removing the privileged access to those positions of the sons of present white union members. When whites lose those privileges, they may feel strongly enough to fracture the consensus of civility.

The deviant communities of San Francisco show us cases in which the parties involved agree in a way that leaves each enough. But that may only be possible when the interests to be accommodated involve morals and life styles. When those interests include substantial economic prizes, major forms of privilege and real political power, it may be that nothing less than a real-life assessment of relative intensities of desire and ability to inflict costs on others will suffice. That assessment takes place in the marketplace of conflict.

This suggests a second, more procedural condition for the achievement of urban peace through accommodation and civility. Mechanisms and procedures must exist by which the conflicting desires and resources for bargaining can be brought together to produce a temporarily stable working arrangement. The accommodations of enforcement officials and deviants typically occur in a host of minor bargaining situations. Hassles are settled by the people immediately involved, and settled "on their own merits" — in a way, that is, that respects the strength of everyone's feelings and the amount of trouble each is prepared to make to have his way. The culture of civility works well because the myriad of separate local bargains respect and reflect what most of the involved parties want or are willing to settle for.

We do not allow ourselves this extreme degree of decentralized decision-making with respect to many important problems (though many critics have suggested we should). Instead, we allow federal, state or city bureaucracies to make general policies that inhibit local accommodation. While government might well intervene when circumstances make bargaining positions unequal, we know now that it is not ordinarily well equipped to reach accommodative agreements that will work at the grass roots. Unable to know what the people who inhabit local areas will want and settle for, officials turn to technocrats for solutions.

Thus, when we confront the problem of slums and urban renewal, we send for the planner and the bulldozer. But the lives of urban residents are not determined by the number or newness of buildings. The character of their relationships with one another and with the outside world does that. Planners and technocrats typically ignore those relationships, and their influence in shaping what people want, in constructing solutions. They define "slums" impersonally, using such impersonal criteria as density or deterioration, and fail to see how awakened group consciousness can turn a "slum" into a "ghetto," and a rise in moral repute turn a "ghetto" into a "neighborhood."

Too often, the search for "model cities" implies not so much a model as an ideology — a rationalistic vision of human interaction that implies a people whose consistency of behavior can nowhere be found. We already have "model cities": Brasilia at the bureaucratic end and Levittown at the residential end. And in both instances the force of human impulses had to break through the web of formal models to make these places inhabitable. In Brasilia the rise of shantytown dwellings outside the federal buildings made the place "a city," whereas the Levittowners had to break the middle-class mode and pass through a generation of conformity before they could produce a decent living arrangement. To design a city in conformity to "community standards" — which turn out to be little more than the prejudices of building inspectors, housing designers and absentee landlords — only reinforces patterns of frustration, violence and antagonism that now characterize so many of America's large cities. To think that the dismal failure of large housing projects will be resolved by their dismal replacement by small housing projects is nonsense. Minibuildings are no more a solution than maxibuildings are the problem.

In any event, centralized planning operating in this way does not produce

a mechanism through which the mutual desires, claims and threats of interested groups can sort themselves out and allow a modus vivendi, if one exists, to uncover itself. The centralized body makes bargains for everyone under its influence, without knowing their circumstances or wants, and so makes it impossible for the people involved to reach a stable accommodation. But centralized planning still remains a major solution proffered for urban problems of every kind.

Accommodations reached through the mechanism of old-fashioned city political machines work little better, for contemporary machines typically fail to encompass all the people whose interests are at stake. Richard Daley demonstrated that when the Chicago ghetto, supposedly solidly under his control, exploded and revealed some people his famed consensus had not included. Lyndon Johnson made the same discovery with respect to opponents of the Vietnam War. Insofar as centralized decision-making does not work, and interested parties are not allowed to make bargains at the local level, accommodative stability cannot occur.

So the example of San Francisco's handling of moral deviance may not provide the blueprint one would like for settling urban problems generally. Its requirements include a day-to-day working agreement among parties on the value of compromise and a procedure by which their immediate interests can be openly communicated and effectively adjusted. Those requirements are difficult to meet. Yet it may be that they are capable of being met in more places than we think, that even some of the knottier racial and political problems contain possibilities of accommodation, no more visible to us than the casual tolerance of deviance in San Francisco was thinkable to some of our prudish forebears.

Regional variation in the United States immediately suggests the importance of rural-urban differences, for one of the most notable differences among regions is the degree to which they are urbanized. The impact of this difference among regions is reflected in responses to public polls — for example, polls dealing with the importance of religion, orientation toward pornography, and use of drugs. Traditional virtues associated with rural residence are most strongly endorsed in less urbanized regions.* In general, the more urban the region, the more liberal the opinions regarding traditional values. Ruralism as opposed to urbanism, represents a cherished life style that some people seek to preserve within small towns in all regions of the country. A small town represents, to its residents, a bastion of defense against the intrusion of urban industrialized society.† Although regions of the United States differ, rural-urban differences are found throughout the nation and the patterns described by Peter Schrag are typical not only of the midwest but of many areas. Many rural values and ways of life are not shared by urban dwellers, and thus we see a rural subculture fostering a rural life style.

* In the urbanized East, for example, 38 percent of college students reported that organized religion was relevant to them; in the Midwest, 39 percent; in the West, 41 percent; and in the less urbanized South, 50 percent. From *The Gallup Opinion Index: The Student Revolution, Report No. 60* (Princeton, N.J.: The Gallup Organization, 1970), p. 18.

† Arthur Vidich and Joseph Bensman, *Small Town in Mass Society: Class, and Religion.* (Princeton: Princeton University Press, 1958).

Is Main Street Still There?

Peter Schrag

Mason City, Iowa, Pop. 32,642. Meat packing, Portland cement, brick and tile, beet sugar, dairy products, commercial feeds, soybean oil and meal, thermopane windows and mobile homes. At the intersection of Highways 18 and 65, 135 miles south of Minneapolis, 125 miles north of Des Moines. Three major railroads. Ozark Airlines. Daily newspaper, one local television station. Library, art museum.

It is hard to stay in any small American town for more than a few days and remain an outsider. There seems to be a common feeling that anyone — even a writer from New York — is, somewhere in his heart, a small-town boy come home. The light but unceasing stream of traffic that moves through Main Street — Federal Avenue in Mason City — north to Minneapolis and beyond, south to Des Moines, reinforces the belief that this flat, open place is part of a great American continuity extending through other Main Streets, across the fields of corn and beets, past tractor depots and filling stations, past grain elevators and loading pens to the very limits of the national imagination. Such a belief must make it difficult to conceive of

anyone as a total stranger, for being here — local pride notwithstanding — cannot seem very different from being anywhere else.

They take you in, absorb you, soak you up; they know where you've been, whom you've seen, what you've done. In Mississippi hamlets, the sheriff follows you around; here it is The Word. *Small towns co-opt* (you tell yourself), *and nice small towns co-opt absolutely.* But it is not just them, it's you. The things that you bring with you — your sense of yourself as a friendly sort, the wish to believe that the claims of small-town virtue are valid, your particular kind of chauvinism — all these things make you a willing collaborator. So maybe they're right. *Maybe we're all just small-town boys come home.* Yes, you're willing to come to dinner, to visit the Club, to suspend the suspicion that all this is some sort of do-it-yourself Chamber of Commerce trick. Later perhaps (says the Inner Voice of Reason) you will be able to sort things out, to distinguish Main Street from the fantasies that you and a lot of other people from New York have invented for it. Later.

You have come here to see what is happening to the heart of this country, to ask how the great flat democracy responds to Vietnam and Black Power, to marijuana and SDS, to see how it is taking technology and the Bomb — all the things that overwhelm the visible spectrum of public concern. Is there something here that can survive in New York and Chicago? Is there an Americanism that will endure, or will it perish with the farm and the small town? What, you ask, is happening to Main Street? Later. For the moment you are simply in it, listening to them worry about a proposed civic center, about the construction of a mall, about taxes and industrial development, and about something they call "the traffic problem," which seems, by even the more placid standards of New York, more imagined than real.

There are ghosts in this country — local ghosts, and ghosts that you bring with you, that refuse to stay behind: shades of brawling railroad workers and dispossessed farmers; frontiersmen and Babbitts; the old remembered tales of reaction and America First, of capital "R" Republicanism and the Ku Klux Klan; the romance of Jefferson and Frederick Jackson Turner, the yeoman farmer and the self-made man. As a place of literary irony, Middle America is celebrating its golden anniversary. "Main Street," wrote Sinclair Lewis in 1920, "is the climax of civilization. That this Ford car might stand in front of the Bon Ton Store, Hannibal invaded Rome and Erasmus wrote in Oxford cloisters. What Ole Jensen the grocer says to Ezra Stowbody the banker is the new law of London, Prague, and the unprofitable isles of the sea; whatsoever Ezra does not know and sanction, that thing is heresy, worthless for knowing and wicked to consider." But such irony, too, may be a ghost — now as much myth, perhaps, as the self-flattering cultural propositions invented to answer it. ("Right here in Mason City," someone tells you, "we sell 300 tickets each year for the Metropolitan Opera tour performances in Minneapolis.") The life of Babbittry, you tell yourself, follows the life (and art) of others. But the models are no longer clear. Main Street

once insisted on rising from Perfection (rural) to Progress (urban): Sauk Centre and Zenith were trying to do Chicago's "thing," but what does Chicago have to offer now? The Main Street boosters are still there, hanging signs across the road proclaiming "A Community on the March," but their days are numbered. How would Lewis have portrayed the three hundred marchers of the Vietnam Moratorium in Mason City? How would he deal with the growing number of long-haired, pot-smoking kids? Here, too, Mason City follows New York and Chicago. (The Mafia, you are told, controls the floating dice games that occasionally rumble through the back rooms of a local saloon.) The certainty of Lewis's kind of irony was directed to the provincial insularity that war, technology, and television are rendering obsolete. Main Street lives modern not in its dishwashers and combines — not even in Huntley-Brinkley and Walter Cronkite — but in its growing ambivalence about the America that creates them, the America that crosses the seas of beets and corn, and therefore about Main Street itself.

It is not a simple place, and perhaps never was. You see what you expect, and then begin to see (or imagine) what you did not. Standard America, yes: the Civil War monument in the square; the First National Bank; Osco's Self-Service Drugs; the shoe store and movie theaters; Damon's and Younkers' ("Satisfaction Always"); Maizes' and Penney's; Sears and Monkey Ward. Middle America the way it was supposed to be: the farmers coming to shop on Saturday afternoon; the hunting and fishing; the high school football game Friday night; the swimming and sailing at Clear Lake, a small resort nine miles to the west. You cannot pass through town without being told that Mason City is a good place to raise a family, without hearing praise for the schools, and without incessant reminders that Meredith Willson's musical play *The Music Man* was *about* Mason City, that Willson was born here, and that the town was almost renamed River City because of it. (There *is* a river, the Winnebago, which makes itself known only at times of flood.) Mr. Toot, the figure of a trombone-blowing bandsman (says a man at the Chamber of Commerce) is now the town symbol. "We hope," says the man, "that we can make our band festival into a major event." Someday, you imagine, this could be the band capital of the nation, the world, and maybe the whole wicked universe.

Mason City, they tell you, is a stable community: steady population, little unemployment, no race problem (there are, at most, 300 Negroes in town), clean water, and — with some huffy qualifications (dust from one of the cement plants, odor from the packing house) — clean air. A cliché. In the *Globe Gazette*, the editor, Bob Spiegel, suggests that the problems and resources of the large cities be dispersed to all the Mason Cities in America. A Jeffersonian, Mr. Spiegel, and a nice guy: "The smaller communities need the plants and the people that are polluting the urban centers — not in large doses, but steadily, surely. . . . The small communities are geared up. They have comprehensive plans. They know they can't stand still or they will be passed by." Stable, perhaps, but

what is stable in a relativistic universe? The very thing that Spiegel proposes seems to be happening in reverse. The community is becoming less pluralistic: it has fewer Negroes, fewer Jews, and fewer members of other minorities than it had twenty years ago. "After the war," said Nate Levinson, an attorney, who is president of the synagogue, "we had eighty Jewish families. Now we have forty. We can't afford a rabbi anymore." On the few occasions that Mason City has tried to attract Negro professionals, they refused to come or to stay. There is nobody to keep them company, and the subtle forms of discrimination — in housing and employment — are pervasive enough to discourage pioneers. ("My maid says if she hears any more about Black Power she'll scream. . . . I wouldn't mind one living next door, if he mowed the grass and kept the place neat.") The brighter kids — black and white — move away, off to college, off to the cities, and beneath that migration one can sense the fear that the city's declining agricultural base will not be replaced by enough industrial jobs to maintain even the stability that now exists.

Mason City is not a depressed town, although in its stagnating downtown shopping area it often looks like one. (Shopping centers are thriving on the periphery; the farmers come in to shop, but not all the way.) The city shares many of the attributes of other small Middle Western communities, competing with them for industry, counting, each week, another farm family that is selling out or giving up, counting the abandoned houses around the county, counting the number of acres (now exceeding 200) required for an efficient agricultural operation. An acre of land costs $500, a four-row combine $24,000. If you stop in such places as Plymouth, a town of 400, nine miles from Mason City, you hear the cadences of compromise and decline: men who have become part-time farmers and make ends meet, at $2.25 an hour, by working in the sugar mill in Mason City. Independence becomes, ever more, a hopeful illusion belied by abandoned shops and boarded windows, and by tales of success set in other places — an engineer in California, a chemist in Detroit, a teacher in Oregon.

Iowa, you realize, not just from statistics, but from faces, is a state of old people: "What do the kids here want to do? What do the kids in Mason City want to do? What do the kids in Iowa want to do? They want to get out. I'd get out, go to California if I could." There is a double migration, from farms into towns, from towns into cities, and out of the state. More than 10 per cent of Mason City's work force is employed at the Decker packing plant on the north side of town. (The plant is a division of Armour and Company.) At the moment the plant is prosperous; it pays good wages. (A hamboner — who does piece work — can make $6 to $7 an hour.) But what would happen, asked one of the city's corporate managers, if the place should succumb to the increasing efficiency of newer plants? "What'll we do the day — and don't quote me — when the place has to shut down?"

It is the fashion to worry slow, worry with a drawl. Urgency and crisis are not the style. Through most of its history, Mason City was dominated by a few families, and to some extent it still

is — not because they are so powerful, but because Federal Avenue once thought they were. Small towns create their own patriarchs, tall men who look even taller against the flatness of history, producing — inevitably — a belief that civic motion and inertia are the subtle work of Big Men: bankers, real estate operators, and corporate managers. Mason City still talks about the General, Hanford MacNider (banking, cement, real estate), who was an Assistant Secretary of War under Coolidge, ambassador to Canada, an aspirant for the 1940 Republican nomination for President, and, for a time, a supporter of America First. (In Mason City, MacNider was *Secretary* of War and barely missed becoming President.) The MacNiders gave the city land for parks, for the public library, and for a museum. (The General was also a founder of the Euchre and Cycle Club, a lunch-and-dinner club — all the best people — which still has no Jewish members, and he is remembered, among other things, as the man who did not lower his flag for thirty days after John F. Kennedy was killed.) "My father," said Jack MacNider, now president of the Northwestern States Portland Cement Company, "was quite a guy. Some people thought he was tough. To some he was a patron saint. You should have known him."

The General's shadow has survived him, and there are still people who are persuaded that nothing of major consequence can be accomplished in Mason City against the opposition of the MacNider family. Is that true, you ask Jack, sitting in his second-story office overlooking Federal Avenue. (There is a picture of the General, in full uniform, behind Jack's desk.) "I'm flattered," he answers, not defensively, but with some amusement, saying more between the lines than on the record, telling you — you imagine — that the MacNiders take the rap for a lot of small-town inertia they can't control, and that they suffer (or enjoy) a visibility for which they haven't asked. At this very moment, a young lawyer named Tom Jolas, a second generation Greek, is challenging the Establishment (such as it is) in his campaign for mayor; you both know that Jolas is likely to win (on November 4 he did win, handily) and that the city's style and mood are now determined as much by younger businessmen and professionals — and by hundreds of packing house workers and cement workers — as they are by the old families. "This must be a fish bowl for the MacNiders," you say, and Jack offers no argument. And when you speak about prejudice in Mason City, Jack agrees — yes, there is — but you can't be sure whether he means only against Catholics, Jews, and Negroes (or Greeks, and Chicanos), or also against the MacNiders. The shadow is still there, but the General is dead.

Mason City's traditional style of politics and political behavior was nicely represented by sixty-five-year-old George Mendon, who was mayor for sixteen years until Jolas beat him. Small towns always create the illusion of responsiveness — you can call any public official, any corporate manager, with little interference from secretaries who ask your business, your name, and your pedigree — and you thus can walk into Mendon's office unannounced and receive an audience. But you are never

sure that, once in, you have really arrived anywhere. The action must be someplace else. The room is almost bare, the desk virtually clean, the man without visible passion. Yes, jobs and industrial development are a problem, and Mason City has done pretty well, but there are 20,000 other towns trying to attract industry, and, you know, these things take time. Yes, they would like to hire some Negroes for the police force, but none has qualified. Yes, the MacNiders had been good to the city — all that land they'd given (and all those tax deductions?) but.... When Mendon was challenged during the campaign about operating an underpaid and undertrained police force, he answered that the city had the most modern equipment, including riot guns, Mace, and bulletproof vests. What are they for, you ask, and Mendon, rattling the change in his pocket, identifies himself. "Our colored population is peaceful," he said. "They wouldn't riot. But you never know when people from the outside might come in and try to start something." Mason City is prepared for Watts and Newark, and somewhere in its open heart there lurks an edge of apprehension that the fire next time might burn even here. But when Mendon spoke about his riot guns at an open meeting, the general response was tempered by considerable facetious amusement, and the people who were amused went out to vote against him, and beat him.

There is no single current running against the old style of politics, or against the Mendons and the Establishment they are supposed to represent. In 1968, Mason City voted for Nixon, for the conservative Congressman, H. R. Gross, and for Harold Hughes, a liberal Democrat, for the U.S. Senate. ("We helped elect Gross the first time he ran," said a union official, "and we've been sorry ever since.") Sociology and political calculations don't help much. "The issue here," said Bud Stewart, who runs a music store and worked for Jolas, "is generational," implying that whatever was young and progressive supported the challenger against the older Establishment. Jolas campaigned under the slogan "Time for a Change," including, among other things, concern for public housing (which the city does not have, but desperately needs), more attention to the problems of youth, and the creation of a modern police force that could meet what he called the rising rate of crime. (And which meant, I was told, getting rid of the reactionary police chief who had bought all the riot junk.) But what Jolas said was clearly not as important as what he is: young, energetic, and, beneath it all, ambiguously liberal, and unambiguously decent. "I had my hair long and wore sideburns," he tells you (two years ago, he managed a teen-age rock band), "but my friends said I couldn't win with it; so I cut it short. But maybe after the election I might get a notion and let it grow again."

Jolas's great political achievement before he ran for mayor was to force the state to reroute a projected interstate highway so that it would pass within a few miles of Mason City, but it was undoubtedly personality rather than politics that elected him. ("You know what they're saying about me?" he mused one day toward the end of the campaign. "They're saying that, if

I'm elected, the Greeks and the niggers are going to take over Mason City. I even had someone charge that I belong to the Mafia — the Greek Mafia.") More than anything else, Jolas seems to have a sense of concern about youth — not a program — but an awakening awareness of how kids are shortchanged by schools, by politicians, by adults. ("He knows," I wrote in my notes, "that the world screws kids.")

What Jolas can achieve is doubtful. He will not have a sympathetic city council nor perhaps even a sympathetic community, and his commitment to a downtown civic center and mall as a means of restoring the vitality of the central business area may be more the token of modernism than the substance of progress; yet it is clear that Jolas received the support, and represented the aspiration, of whatever liberalism (black, labor, professional) the city could muster. If you sit in his storefront headquarters long enough, you learn how far Main Street has come from Babbittry. You meet Marie Dresser, the recently widowed wife of a physician, who, as president of the Iowa League of Women Voters, carried a reapportionment fight through the legislature and who speaks of how, when their son decided to grow a mustache, she and her husband decided to back him against the school authorities and how, eventually, they won; Jean Beatty, the wife of a psychologist, answering phone calls and stuffing Jolas campaign envelopes, and shuttling between meetings of the league and the local branch of the NAACP, knowing that the organization should be run by black people, but knowing also that its precariously weak membership cannot sustain it without help; or Jim Shannon, the country Democratic chairman, who has worked for the Milwaukee Railroad all his life, and who has gone back to the local community college (working nights, studying economics during the day), speaking in his soft, laconic, infinitely American cadences about the campaign for Bobby Kennedy in 1968, about a decade of legislative fights, reminding you, without meaning to, or even mentioning it, that liberalism wasn't invented in New York, that the Phil Harts, the Frank Churches, the Fred Harrises, and the George McGoverns weren't elected by professors.

If that were all — if one could merely say that Mason City and Middle America are going modern — it would be easy, but it is not. (What, after all, is modern — uniquely modern — after technology has been dispensed with?) The national culture is there — mass cult, high, middle, and low, mod and trad: Bud Stewart in the Edwardian double-breasted suits that he orders from advertisements through the local stores; the elite trooping off to Minneapolis to hear the Met when it comes on tour, or to Ames to catch the New York Philharmonic (mostly, say the cynics, to be conspicuous, not for love of music); the rock on the radio and in the jukes (the Fifth Dimension, Blood, Sweat and Tears, new Dylan and old Baez, plus some leavening from the likes of Johnny Cash); the long hair and the short skirts, the drugs and the booze. (At the same time, beer, rather than pot, seems still to be the preponderant, though not the exclusive, form of adolescent sin.) But somehow what Mason City re-

ceives through the box and the tube — and from trips to Minneapolis and Des Moines, where some of the ladies do almost weekly shopping — Mason City seems to shape and reshape into its own forms. There is a tendency to mute the decibels of public controversy and social friction, perhaps because people are more tolerant and relaxed, perhaps because they are simply less crowded. There is talk about crime and violence, but the most common examples seem usually to involve the theft of bicycles and the destruction of Halloween pumpkins. (Another way of staking a claim on the modern?) If you ask long enough, you can get some of the blue-collar workers to speak about their resentment against welfare, taxes, and student demonstrators (not at Harvard, mind you, but at the State University of Iowa), but it is commonly only television and the newspapers that produce the talk. And so it tends to be dispassionate, distant, and somewhat abstract. Bumper stickers and decals are scarce; American flags are rarely seen on the rear windows of automobiles because, one might assume, there aren't many people at whom to wave them, not many devils to exorcise. The silent majority here is an abstraction, a collage of minorities, except when it comes to the normalcy of the ladies' study clubs and bridge clubs, the football, the hunting and fishing, and the trip to the lake. And every two years they go back, most of them, and vote for H. R. Gross.

And yet, here are the kids, high school students and students at the Community College, organizing a Moratorium march, running a little newspaper semi-underground within the high school, and with the blessing of the school authorities; here are the clergymen, not all, but a few, giving their support for the march from the pulpit (when she heard her minister that Sunday, one prominent parishioner promptly resigned from the church); and here are ordinary people responding to the critics of dissent with their own protest. In a letter to the *Globe Gazette:*

> *We supported the Moratorium Day demonstration. We have a son in Vietnam. We love our country. We fly the American flag.*
>
> *But we do not believe in blindly following our leader as the Germans did when their leader decided to exterminate the Jews, or as some Americans would do if our leader should decide to exterminate the Indians.*
>
> *We feel our country was wrong to send 40,000 of our boys to their death, not defending their own shores.*
>
> *Supporting the Moratorium was our way of saying we love our country right or wrong, and this time it was wrong.*

Given the reputation of the average small town in America, the greatest surprise is the school system, which, under Rod Bickert, the superintendent, and John Patzwald, the high school principal, has managed to move well beyond the expected, even in the conventional modern suburb. Mason City has abandoned dress codes in its high school, has instituted flexible-modular scheduling (meaning that students have only a limited number of formal lectures classes, and can do their own thing — in "skill" and study centers, in the library, or in the cafeteria — as

they will), and has begun to experiment, in the high school, with an "open mike" on which a student can talk to the entire school on anything he pleases. There are no bells, no monitors. As you walk through the halls (modern, sprawling, corporate style) with Patzwald, a Minnesotan, he explains that he first came to the school as a disciplinarian. "It was a conservative school, and I ran a tight ship." When he became principal, he turned things around. "We're something of an island, and when some of the parents first heard about it, they thought it was chaos. We had an open meeting — parents and students — to explain the flexmod schedule, but most of the parents wanted to know about dress. You know, we have everything here, including girls in miniskirts and pants suits. The students helped us carry it. They know that some sort of uproar could blow this thing right out of the water, but I think they can do the job."

Every day Patzwald spends a couple of hours visiting classes, asking students irreverent questions that are, at least tangentially, directed to the teachers. "I ask them why they're doing what they're doing. What's the significance of this? Why study it at all? Sure we have some weak teachers, but now when I hire people I role-play with them a little. I want to see how they take pressure. In the classroom it's too easy for the teachers always to be the last resort and to put the screws down. That's no way to improve the climate of learning." The conversation is frequently interrupted while Patzwald stops to talk with students (he knows many by name), and later he tells you about them. "Kids are my life," he says, rounding a corner after a brief encounter with two boys. "The whole point is to get them to appreciate the worth of an individual. We have to reach the ones who are overlooked, like one boy they were taunting and who talked about himself as 'a ball that they always kick around.' Those are the ones we have to reach. But I think we're coming."

The militant students seek you out. Mason City is still a confining place, and they find The Man from *Saturday Review*, the outsider, walking through the hall alone. The organizers of the Moratorium, the editors of the mimeographed paper, the *Bitter End* (not quite underground, not quite official), the activists are sons and daughters of affluent lawyers and doctors, all local people, not carpetbaggers from the East. The school, they say, is divided between "pointy heads like us" and "the animals." (A group passes through the hall after school, and the pointy heads, through a glass door, follow the herd with "moo-moo," "oink-oink.") The radicals still see the school as a fraud. "There is no way to get a decent education in a public school. Everybody's too up-tight." Like what? "Like being allowed to leave school during your unstructured time to make a movie. You can get a release to dish hamburgers at McDonald's; so why not to make movies?" One of them gets threatening letters for his part in the peace movement, another loses his allowance because he won't cut his hair. Their lives are no different — nor are their parents' — from those of similar people in Scarsdale or Shaker Heights or Winnetka.

(Some of them, said Patzwald, "have told their parents to go to hell.") What is surprising is that, although they are a lonely minority, they can be found in this community at all.

For the majority of the young, the concerns are universal: cars, dances, sports. You hear them in Vic's ("Real Dago Pizza"): "It's a '65 Chevy. I traded it for that car that was sitting in the grass by the Hub." "Paid $350 and put a new engine in it, and it runs great." They want to go to college, to get jobs; more than half the high school students work, so they can maintain those automobiles, and get married. The modest dream is to become an airline stewardess — "If I'm not too clumsy" — to enlist in the Army, to learn a trade. On Friday nights they cruise up and down Federal, shuttling from a root beer stand at the south end to a drive-in at the other. There is some talk about establishing a teen center, a Place Where Kids Can Go, but the proposal draws little enthusiasm from adults and less from the kids. And yet, even among the majority, the animals, the apathetic, something may be happening. The war perhaps, or television, or the music. There was a time, said a school administrator, "when the war seemed very distant." Mason City's enlistment rate was always high; the college students were exempt anyway, and the draft wasn't much of an issue. But in the past year eight recent graduates of Mason City High were killed in Vietnam, making death and change more personal. Nearly a hundred turned out to hear discussions about the war inside the school, and, while the patriotic speakers still come to address the assembly, other messages are being heard as well. The hair gets longer, the music a little harder, and the news is on everybody's set.

The young are slowly becoming mediators of the culture; they receive the signals from the outside and interpret the messages for the adults. And that's new for all America, not just for Mason City. "The kids are having an effect on their parents," said a mental health worker, apparently one of the few clinicians in town whom the adolescents are willing to trust. "People here are friendly and up-tight at the same time. Many of them take the attitude that the children should have their fun, that eventually they'll come around to their parents' view. But people have been jarred — by TV and by their own children — and they know, some of them at least, that they've got to listen. They're trying to become looser."

But becoming looser is still a struggle and, given the conditions of life, an imperative that can be deferred. ("I'm *not* going to send my son to Harvard," says a Harvard graduate. "An eighteen-year-old is not mature enough to handle SDS and all that other garbage.") The space, the land, the weather, the incessant reminders of physical normalcy make it possible to defer almost anything. Church on Sunday, football on Friday, and the cycle of parties, dinners, and cookouts remain more visible (not to say comprehensible) than the subtleties of cultural change or social injustice. If the churches and their ministers are losing some of their influence among the young (and if the call for psychiatrists

is increasing), they are still holding their members, and if the Catholic monsignor, Arthur Breen, has to schedule a folk mass at Holy Family every Sunday (in addition to four other masses) he nonetheless continues to pack them in.

What you see most of all (see is not a good word; feel, maybe) is a faith in the capacity of people and institutions to be responsive, the belief that, finally, things are pretty much what they seem, that Things Work. "This is just a big farm town," said a Mason City businessman. "You don't check people's credit here. You just assume they'll pay their bills. In Waterloo, which is really an industrial city, even though it isn't very big, you check everybody out." The answer to an economic problem is to work harder, to take a second job, or to send your wife to work, usually as a clerk or a waitress (Wages for women are extremely low.) On the radio, *Junior Achievement* makes its peace with modernism by setting its jingle to "Get With It" to a rock beat, but the message of adolescent enterprise (Babbittry?) is the same, and around the lunch tables at the Green Mill Restaurant or the bar at Tom MacNider's Chart House it is difficult to convince anyone that sometimes even people with the normal quota of ambition can't make it.

The advantages of that faith are obvious, but the price is high. "This is a nice town as long as you don't rock the boat," said Willis Haddix, a meat packer, who is president of the struggling Mason City chapter of NAACP. "What's wrong here is in the secret places": in subtle discrimination in housing and jobs; in the out-of-sight, dilapidated frame houses at the north and south ends of town, buildings surrounded with little piles of lumber, rusting metal chairs, decaying junk cars once slated for repair; in the lingering aroma of personal defeat; and in the cross between arrogance and apathy that declares "there are no poor people in this area." On Sundays, while most people are packing their campers for the trip home, or making the transition between church and television football, the old, who have little to do, wander into the Park Inn for lunch — hot roast beef sandwiches for $1.25 — and to talk about Medicare. And against theirs you hear other voices: Murray Lawson, for example, a civilized compassionate man, who represents Mason City in the legislature, saying, "We've been generous with education, but not so generous with the old. We've had a rough time with nursing homes"; Jim Shannon, who supports his wife and seven children on the salary of a railroad clerk and janitor, describing the effects of a regressive sales tax that victimizes the small man but makes little impact on the rich; the official of the local OEO poverty agency talking about the county's third welfare generation and reflecting that "an admission of poverty is an admission of failure, and people here don't do that"; Tom Jolas describing Mason City's enthusiasm for the New York Mets when they won the World Series after a ninth place finish in 1968, because "people believe in coming off the bottom."

And then you learn something else — about yourself, and about the phe-nomenon you choose to call Main Street. You hear them complain about Eastern, urban provincialism, about those people who cannot believe that Mason City has television ("You must get it from the West Coast"), let alone an art museum, a decent library, or a couple of go-go joints (or that you can buy Philip Roth, Malcolm X, and Henry Miller in the bookstore), and you begin to understand, almost by suggestion, what the barriers of comprehension are all about. Is it really surprising that Main Street cannot fully comprehend talk about police brutality, police rigidity, or social disillusionment? If the system works here, why doesn't it work everywhere else? Main Street's uniquely provincial vice lies in its excessive, unquestioning belief (in the Protestant ethic, hard work, honesty, and conventional politics); New York's in the conviction that most of the time nothing may make much difference, that institutions and public life are by their very nature unresponsive. And if New York has come to doubt the values and the beliefs of tradition, it still hasn't invented anything to replace them. The anger of the blue-collar worker — at welfare, students, Negroes — is rooted in the frustrated ethic of Main Street, frustrated in not only its encounters with urban problems and technology, but in the growing doubt of the Best people—Wallace's pointy heads, Agnew's effete impudent snobs — that it still has merit. Among the characteristic excesses of rural populism (whether expressed by William Jennings Bryant, Joe McCarthy, or Spiro Agnew) was a paranoia about Them: the bankers, the railroads, the Communists in government, the Eastern Establishment. But paranoia is surely also one of the characteristic defenses of almost every other inhabitant of New York. (If you try to explain the vicissitudes of dealing with Con Edison or the New York Telephone Company, most people in Mason City stare at you in disbelief; if you speak about rents and housing, they're certain you've gone mad.) Every rural or small-town vote against some proposal for the alleviation of a problem in New York or Chicago or Cleveland is not merely an act of self-interest (keeping taxes low, protecting the farmers) but a gesture of disbelief that Main Street's ethic and tactics — if they were really applied — would be ineffective in the Big City.

At the end, sitting in the waiting room at the Municipal Airport (all flights from Chicago, naturally, are late), you detach yourself. You hear, still, one of the Federal Avenue lawyers saying, "This town is solid. It's solid as a commercial center, and as a medical and cultural center for a large region." You see his nearly bare office, the brown wood furniture, the linoleum floors, and the fluorescent lights, see his partner in a sleeveless, gray pullover walking through the outer office (Clarence Darrow?), and hear the trucks stopping for the red light at the intersection below. You hear Jack MacNider speaking about the gradual movement of the "iron triangle" — the Midwestern industrial region — into north central Iowa, speaking about the ultimate industrialization of the area around the city. You see the high school homecoming queen, fragile and

uncomfortable in the back of an open convertible in the wind-chilled stadium; see the wide residential streets with their maples and time-threatened elms, the section of magnificent houses by Prairie School architects (one of them by Frank Lloyd Wright) and the crumbling streets at the south end, near the Brick and Tile; and you hear, in that same neighborhood, two NAACP ladies, one white, one Negro, discussing the phrasing of a letter to the school board politely protesting the use of *Little Black Sambo* in the elementary grades. And then, finally, you hear again all those people speaking about how good Mason City is for raising a family, and you wonder what kind of society it is that must separate growing up and the rearing of children from the places where most of its business is transacted, its ideals discussed, and its policies determined. And then you wonder, too, what would happen if something ever came seriously to disturb Main Street's normalcy, if direct demands were ever made, if the letters ceased being polite, if the dark places — the discrimination and disregard — were probed and, for the first time, tested. Small towns do co-opt, you think, not by what they do, not by their hospitality, but by what we wish they were — because all of us, big city boys and small, *want* to believe. And yet, when Ozark 974 rises from the runway, off to Dubuque, over the corn and beets, over the Mississippi, off to Chicago, you know that you can't go home again, that the world is elsewhere, and that every moment the distances grow not smaller but greater. Main Street is far away.

Political scientist James Q. Wilson has written:

Let two Birchite loud-mouths pop off anywhere else in the country and we rush out to sociology texts to see whether it is alienation or the decline of the small entrepreneur that is the cause; let two of them say the same thing in Los Angeles, and we just smile knowingly and murmur, "It figures." *

Just mentioning certain cities brings forth images of their life style. Cities such as Hollywood, New Orleans, and Boston each offer a unique style of life that in some cases characterizes not only the city but pervades the entire region. Some speak of the Hollywoodization of California, implying that the life style of Hollywood goes far beyond its border. Although Bagdikian is correct about the local press's pervasive influence within the city, that influence may go far beyond city borders. Minneapolis newspapers are delivered daily to the Dakotas, Seattle newspapers are circulated throughout Alaska, and Boston newspapers are found throughout New England. Powerful cities often dominate a region and have a great effect upon its life styles. In the following article by Terrence Flanagan, we see one man's view of such a process. To Flanagan, because of the domination of New York in the north and Philadelphia in the south, New Jersey is a state without a distinguishable life style.

* James Q. Wilson, "A Guide to Reagan Country: The Political Culture of Southern California," *Commentary* (May 1967), p. 371.

Guess What State's Initials Are N.J.?

Terrence J. Flanagan

New Jersey is a small state on the eastern seaboard halfway between

From *The New York Times Magazine* (February 21, 1973). © 1973 by The New York Times Company. Reprinted by permission.

Honest John Lindsay and the Liberty Bell. It is best known for its Turnpike, Atlantic City, Imamu Baraku, Newark Airport and the "Morro Castle" disaster. Most of its leaders are in jail for stealing money.

New Jersey does not have earthquakes. Its weather is mainly left over from Ontario and the Gulf of Mexico. It is a state custom to re-elect the Governor to a second term because the people are only getting used to his name by then. It is never clear which party he belongs to. Most of the residents are from Illinois, Maryland and Buffalo.

New Jersey's two major rivers, the Hudson and the Delaware, belong to New York and Pennsylvania, respectively. Its two minor rivers, the Passaic and the Raritan, are navigable for several hundred feet. The state's highest point is called High Point. Its two Senators have never served time. New Jersey has five million dump trucks.

New Jersey has no center. It is a neutral zone, penned between two bullies, and its development has been a form of vassalage to them. The New Jerseyan does not possess an exaggerated sense of statehood. If you insult the place he won't punch you. New Jersey has no big-league football or baseball. Her moderately sick are sent to New York or Philadelphia for diagnosis. New Jersey has six million insurance salesmen.

New Jerseyans do not discuss New Jersey; they are well informed about the rest of the world. New York and Pennsylvania TV channels — the only ones around — rarely mention New Jersey, and then only at the end of the weather report: "Meanwhile," the announcer smiles, "over in the Garden State . . ." and then we are shown another of our leaders entering prison. The Jersey Blues are National Guard soldiers, not symptoms of melancholia.

The New Jersey State Police is an élite corps of highly trained, professional lawmen. They are polite and restrained. The average trooper spends the prime of his life at the bottom of a hill waiting for speeders, with an occasional break to eat eggs-over-with-ketchup at a diner. Fine money goes to the state treasury. The most recent state treasurer is facing a long stretch for grand larceny. There are five million plumbers in New Jersey, and thirteen million pickup trucks.

New Jersey has never been considered — by the rest of the nation — a valid place to come from. When asked where they are from, out-of-state New Jerseyans have to give the relative distance of their home from New York and Philadelphia. You make people uncomfortable when you tell them you're from New Jersey. They are inclined to respond with "Oh!" or "Why?" Unlike the New England states, the South, etc., New Jersey has no indigenous cultural warts for an outsider to hang his cliché on. The New Jerseyan defies general analysis.

New Jersey has never inspired a musical. New Jersey does not have Bella Abzug, Disneyland, the Miami Dolphins or the San Andreas Fault. But it does have outstanding features such as Camden, Route 22 at Union, the Boonton Reservoir, the Cheesequake exit on the Parkway, Perth Amboy and the Paterson Plank Road. And it has hobos from all over the nation who claim it's the only state left where a guy down on his luck can get a decent handout.

And it has me.

SEX ROLES
AND LIFE STYLES

Women in the United States are not "supposed" to smoke cigars. People listed in the social register are not "supposed" to serve corned beef and cabbage and beer at a formal dinner party. Children (of all ages) are "supposed" to always love and respect their parents. But who says so? Patterns of "ideal behavior" are a reflection of a society's norms and values. For each position in society there is a pattern of behavior (implying rights and obligations) considered appropriate; this pattern of expected behavior is called a role. Thus a five-year-old child may slide down a bannister but not smoke a cigar; a forty-five-year-old man may smoke a cigar but not slide down a bannister.

At any given time, people hold a wide variety of roles. Persons are male or female; young, old, or in between; perhaps members of a racial or ethnic group; if one is a member of a certain age group, more than likely he will hold a job; and one is probably a family member as a father or mother, son or daughter, and/or husband or wife. For some people one role takes primacy above all the others and becomes a central life interest.* This does not mean that this individual is not affected by other

---

* This central life interest may then become a "master status." See Everett C. Hughes, "Dilemmas and Contradictions of Status," *American Journal of Sociology* 50 (March, 1945), 353–359.

roles but that this central role affects the way all other roles will be enacted. A nun may be a daughter, teacher, friend, and citizen but above all else she is a nun.

Since people hold many roles at the same time, different people may be making different demands upon the same individual. An individual may be at once a college student, son or daughter, friend and employee. At the same time professors may expect this student to study, parents may expect this child to attend a family celebration, friends may expect this friend to go out and drink beer, and a boss may expect this employee to be at work, whether or not there is an exam, a family party, or a group of friends getting together. You cannot enact all of these roles at the same time and one must choose among them. This role conflict is generally a matter of stress.

It is not necessary to hold a master status for some roles to be more important to them than others. Generally some important roles have a profound effect on a person's life style. Some of these, such as an occupational role or the role of being married or single, are more or less a matter of choice, but about other important roles, there are no choices. Old people are not "supposed" to enact the role of child, teenager, or young adult; and men are "supposed" to act like men and not women. Such behavior would be stigmatized or ridiculed, and may bring other sanctions. In general, sex, race, age, and other unalterable characteristics require a certain role to be enacted, regardless of a person's feelings about that role.

Every role, including required ones, has its obligations, but it also has its rights. A young child has an obligation to obey his or her parents but also has a right to be supported and protected. Persons who reach the age of majority have the rights of adults but also the obligation to accept the consequences of their own behavior.

This chapter deals with a particular role, that of being female, and with how it affects women's life styles. Women have traditionally been expected to be passive, nurturant, emotional, nonintellectual, and highly dependent upon men. Like children, women could expect to be supported and protected, but were obliged to be subservient to their male counterparts.

Women are taught to be idealistic rather than pragmatic,* accommodative rather than exploitative,† to be neater, more restrained, gentler, more emotionally demonstrative, more dependent, and more family

---

* William Bezdek and Fred L. Strodtbeck, "Sex Role Identity and Pragmatic Action," *American Sociological Review* 35 (1970), pp. 491–502.

† Thomas Uesugi and W. Edgar Vinacke, "Strategy in a Feminine Game," *Sociometry* 36 (1963), pp. 75–78.

oriented than men,* and to be less analytic† and less ambitious‡ than their male counterparts. Roger Brown describes the result of sex role differences as follows:

> In the United States, a real boy climbs trees, disdains girls, dirties his knees, plays with soldiers, and takes blue for his favorite color. A real girl dresses dolls, jumps rope, plays hopscotch, and takes pink for her favorite color. When they go to school, real girls like English and music and auditorium; real boys prefer manual training, gym, and arithmetic. In college the boys smoke pipes, drink beer, and major in engineering or physics; the girls chew Juicy Fruit gum, drink cherry Cokes, and major in the fine arts. The real boy matures into a man's man who plays poker, goes hunting, and drinks brandy, and dies in the war; the real girl becomes a "feminine" woman who loves children, embroiders handkerchiefs, drinks weak tea and "succumbs" to consumption.§

The traditional role of women dates back at least to Biblical times.‖ In many quarters, there are changing conceptions of this role but at the same time conservative forces are trying to prevent this change. In the article that follows, psychologists Sandra Bem and Daryl Bem examine the bases of the traditional view and barriers impeding change.¶

* Mirra Komarovsky, *Women in the Modern World* (Boston: Little, Brown, 1953), pp. 53–59.

† Eleanor Maccoby, "Feminine Intellect and the Demands of Science," *Impact of Science on Society* 20 (1970), pp. 13–28.

‡ Ralph Turner, "Some Aspects of Women's Ambition," *American Journal of Sociology* 70 (1964), pp. 271–285.

§ Roger Brown, *Social Psychology,* New York: Free Press (1965), p. 161.

‖ See Kate Millet, *Sexual Politics,* Garden City: Doubleday (1970), pp. 50–55.

¶ Good general discussions of sex roles may be found in Liam Hudson, *Frames of Mind,* London: Methuen, 1968; Eleanor Maccoby (ed.), *The Development of Sex Differences* (Stanford: Stanford University Press, 1966), Georgene Seward and Robert Williamson (eds.), *Sex Roles in a Changing Society* (New York: Random House, 1970), and Janet Saltzman Chafetz, *Masculine/Feminine or Human?* (Itasaca, Illinois: Peacock, 1974).

Homogenizing the American Woman: The Power of an Unconscious Ideology

Sandra L. Bem and Daryl J. Bem

In the beginning God created the heavens and the earth. . . . And God said, Let us make man in our image, after our likeness; and let him have dominion over the fish of the sea, and over the fowl of the air, and over the cattle, and over all the earth. . . . And the rib, which the Lord God had taken from man, made he a woman and brought her unto the man. . . . And the Lord God said unto the woman, What is this that thou hast done? And the woman said, The serpent beguiled me, and I did eat. . . . Unto the woman God said, I will greatly multiply thy sorrow and thy conception; in sorrow thou shalt bring forth children; and thy desire shall be to thy husband and he shall rule over thee. (Gen. 1, 2, 3)

There is a moral to that story. St. Paul spells it out even more clearly.

For a man . . . is the image and glory of God; but the woman is the glory of the man. For the man is not of the woman, but the woman of the man. Neither was the man created for the woman, but the woman for the man. (1 Cor. 11)

From Sandra L. Bem and Daryl J. Bem, "Homogenizing the American Woman" (October 1972). © Sandra L. Bem and Daryl J. Bem, 1973. Reprinted by permission.

Let the woman learn in silence with all subjection. But I suffer not a woman to teach, nor to usurp authority over the man, but to be in silence. For Adam was first formed and then Eve. And Adam was not deceived, but the woman, being deceived, was in the transgression. Notwithstanding, she shall be saved in childbearing, if they continue in faith and charity and holiness with sobriety. (1 Tim. 2)

Now one should not assume that only Christians have this kind of rich heritage of ideology about women. So consider now, the morning prayer of the Orthodox Jew:

Blessed art Thou, oh Lord our God, King of the Universe, that I was not born a gentile.

Blessed art Thou, oh Lord our God, King of the Universe, that I was not born a slave.

Blessed art Thou, oh Lord our God, King of the Universe, that I was not born a woman.

Or, consider the Koran, the sacred text of Islam:

Men are superior to women on account of the qualities in which God has given them pre-eminence.

Because they think they sense a decline in feminine "faith, charity, and holiness with sobriety," many people today jump to the conclusion that the ideology expressed in these passages is a relic of the past. Not so, of course. It has simply been obscured by an equalitarian veneer, and the same ideology has now become unconscious. That is, we remain unaware of it because alternative beliefs and attitudes about women, until very recently, have gone unimagined. We are very much like the fish who is unaware of the fact that his environment is wet. After all, what else could it be? Such is the nature of all unconscious ideologies in a society. Such, in particular, is the nature of America's ideology about women.

What we should like to do in this paper is to discuss today's version of this same ideology.

When a baby boy is born, it is difficult to predict what he will be doing 25 years later. We can't say whether he will be an artist, a doctor, a lawyer, a college professor, or a bricklayer, because he will be permitted to develop and fulfill his own unique potential — particularly, of course, if he happens to be white and middle class. But if that same newborn child happens to be a girl, we can predict with almost complete confidence how she is likely to be spending her time some 25 years later. Why can we do that? Because her individuality doesn't have to be considered. Her individuality is irrelevant. Time studies have shown that she will spend the equivalent of a full working day, 7.1 hours, in preparing meals, cleaning house, laundering, mending, shopping and doing other household tasks. In other words, 43% of her waking time will be spent in activity that would command an hourly wage on the open market well below the federally set minimum for menial industrial work.

Of course, the point really is not how little she would earn if she did these things in someone else's home. She will be doing them in her own home for free. The point is that this use of time is virtually the same for homemakers with college degrees and for homemakers with less than a grade school education, for women married to professional men and for women married to blue-collar workers. Actually, that's understating it slightly. What the time study really showed was that college-educated women spend slightly *more* time cleaning their houses than their less-educated counterparts!

Of course, it is not simply the full-time homemaker whose unique identity has been rendered largely irrelevant. Of the 31 million women who work outside the home in our society, 78% end up in dead-end jobs as clerical workers, service workers, factory workers, or sales clerks, compared to a comparable figure of 40% for men. Only 15% of all women workers in our society are classified by the Labor Department as professional or technical workers, and even this figure is misleading — for the single, poorly-paid occupation of non-college teacher absorbs half of these women, and the occupation of nurse absorbs an additional quarter. In other words, the two jobs of teacher and nurse absorb three-quarters of all women classified in our society as technical or professional. That means, then, that fewer than 5% of all professional women — fewer than 1% of all women workers — fill those positions which to most Americans connote "professional": physician, lawyer, engineer, scientist, college professor, journalist, writer, and so forth.

Even an I.Q. in the genius range does not guarantee that a woman's unique potential will find expression. There was a famous study of over 1300 boys and girls whose I.Q.'s averaged

151 (Terman & Oden, 1959). When the study began in the early 1900's, these highly gifted youngsters were only ten years old, and their careers have been followed ever since. Where are they today? 86% of the men have now achieved prominence in professional and managerial occupations. In contrast, only a minority of the women were even employed. Of those who were, 37% were nurses, librarians, social workers, and non-college teachers. An additional 26% were secretaries, stenographers, bookkeepers, and office workers! Only 11% entered the higher professions of law, medicine, college teaching, engineering, science, economics, and the like. And even at age 44, well after all their children had gone to school, 61% of these highly gifted women remained full-time homemakers. Talent, education, ability, interests, motivations: all irrelevant. In our society, being female uniquely qualifies an individual for domestic work — either by itself or in conjunction with typing, teaching, nursing, or (most often) unskilled labor. It is this homogenization of America's women which is the major consequence of our society's sex-role ideology.

It is true, of course, that most women have several hours of leisure time every day. And it is here, we are often told, that each woman can express her unique identity. Thus, politically interested women can join the League of Women Voters. Women with humane interests can become part-time Gray Ladies. Women who love music can raise money for the symphony. Protestant women play canasta; Jewish women play Mah Jongg; brighter women of all denominations and faculty wives play bridge.

But politically interested *men* serve in legislatures. *Men* with humane interests become physicians or clinical psychologists. *Men* who love music play in the symphony. In other words, why should a woman's unique identity determine only the periphery of her life rather than its central core?

Why? Why nurse rather than physician, secretary rather than executive, stewardess rather than pilot? Why faculty wife rather than faculty? Why doctor's mother rather than doctor? There are three basic answers to this question: (1) discrimination; (2) sex-role conditioning; and (3) the presumed incompatibility of family and career.

DISCRIMINATION

In 1968, the median income of full-time women workers was approximately $4500. The comparable figure for men was $3000 higher. Moreover, the gap is widening. Ten years ago, women earned 64% of what men did; that percentage has now shrunk to 58%. Today, a female college graduate working full time can expect to earn less per year than a male high school dropout.

There are two reasons for this pay differential. First, in every category of occupation, women are employed in the lesser-skilled, lower-paid positions. Even in the clerical field, where 73% of the workers are women, females are relegated to the lowest status positions and hence earn only 65% of what male clerical workers earn. The second reason for this pay differential is discrimination in its purest form: unequal pay for equal work. According to a survey of 206 companies in 1970, female college graduates were offered jobs which paid $43 per month less than those offered to their male counterparts in the same college major.

New laws should begin to correct both of these situations. The Equal Pay Act of 1963 prohibits employers from discriminating on the basis of sex in the payment of wages for equal work. In a landmark ruling on May 18, 1970, the U.S. Supereme Court ordered that $250,000 in back pay be paid to women employed by a single New Jersey glass company. This decision followed a two-year court battle by the Labor Department after it found that the company was paying men selector-packers 21.5 cents more per hour than women doing the same work. In a similar case, the Eighth Circuit Court of Appeals ordered a major can company to pay more than $100,000 in back wages to women doing equal work. According to the Labor Department, an estimated $17-million is owed to women in back pay. Since that estimate was made, a 1972 amendment extended the Act to cover executive, administrative and professional employees as well.

But to enjoy equal pay, women must also have access to equal jobs. Title VII of the 1964 Civil Rights Act prohibits discrimination in employment on the basis of race, color, religion, national origin — and sex. Although the sex provision was treated as a joke at the time (and was originally introduced by a Southern Congressman in an attempt to defeat the bill), the Equal Employment Opportunities Commission discovered in its first year of operation that 40% or more of the complaints warranting investigation charged discrimination on the basis of sex (Bird, 1969).

Title VII has served as one of the most effective instruments in helping to achieve sex equality in the world of work. According to a report by the E.E.O.C., nearly 6,000 charges of sex discrimination were filed with that agency in 1971 alone, a 62% increase over the previous year.

But the most significant legislative breakthrough in the area of sex equality was the passage of the Equal Rights Amendment by both houses of Congress in 1972. The ERA simply states that "Equality of rights under the law shall not be denied or abridged by the United States or by any state on account of sex." This amendment had been introduced into every session of Congress since 1923, and its passage now is clearly an indication of the changing role of the American woman. All of the various ramifications are hard to predict, but it is clear that it will have profound consequences in private as well as public life.

Many Americans assume that the recent drive for equality between the sexes is primarily for the benefit of the middle-class woman who wants to seek self-fulfillment in a professional career. But in many ways, it is the woman in more modest circumstances, the woman who *must* work for economic reasons, who stands to benefit most from the removal of discriminatory barriers. It is *she* who is hardest hit by unequal pay; it is *she* who so desperately needs adequate day-care facilities; it is *her* job which is often dead-ended while her male colleagues in the factory get trained and promoted into the skilled craft jobs. And if both she and her husband work at unfulfilling jobs eight hours a day just to make an adequate income, it is still *she* who carries the additional burden of domestic chores when they return home.

We think it is important to emphasize these points at the outset, for we have chosen to focus our remarks in this particular paper on those fortunate men and women who can afford the luxury of pursuing self-fulfillment through the world of work and career. But every societal reform advocated by the new feminist movement, whether it be the Equal Rights Amendment, the establishment of child-care centers, or basic changes in America's sex-role ideology, will affect the lives of men and women in every economic circumstance. Nevertheless, it is still economic discrimination which hits hardest at the largest group of women, and it is here that the drive for equality can be most successfully launched with legislative and judicial tools.

SEX-ROLE CONDITIONING

But even if all discrimination were to end tomorrow, nothing very drastic would change. For job discrimination is only part of the problem. It does impede women who choose to become lawyers or managers or physicians. But it does not, by itself, help us to understand why so many women "choose" to be secretaries or nurses rather than executives or physicians; why only 3% of 9th grade girls as compared to 25% of the boys "choose" careers in science or engineering; or why 63% of America's married women "choose" not to work at all. It certainly doesn't explain those young women whose vision of the

future includes only marriage, children, and living happily ever after; who may, at some point, "choose" to take a job, but who almost never "choose" to pursue a career. Discrimination frustrates choices already made. Something more pernicious perverts the motivation to choose.

That "something" is an unconscious ideology about the nature of the female sex, an ideology which constricts the emerging self-image of the female child and the nature of her aspirations from the very beginning; an ideology which leads even those Americans who agree that a black skin should not uniquely qualify *its* owner for a janitorial or domestic service to act as if the possession of a uterus uniquely qualifies *its* owner for precisely such service.

Consider, for example, the 1968 student rebellion at Columbia University. Students from the radical Left took over some administration buildings in the name of equalitarian ideals which they accused the university of flouting. Here were the most militant spokesmen one could hope to find in the cause of equalitarian ideals. But no sooner had they occupied the buildings than the male militants blandly turned to their sisters-in-arms and assigned them the task of preparing the food, while they — the menfolk — would presumably plan future strategy. The reply these males received was the reply that they deserved — we will leave that to your imagination — and the fact that domestic tasks behind the barricades were desegregated across the sex line that day is an everlasting tribute to the class consciousness of these ladies of the Left. And it was really on that day that the campus women's liberation movement got its start — when radical women finally realized that they were never going to get to make revolution, only coffee.

But these conscious co-eds are not typical, for the unconscious assumptions about a woman's "natural" talents (or lack of them) are at least as prevalent among women as they are among men. A psychologist named Phillip Goldberg (1968) demonstrated this by asking female college students to rate a number of professional articles from each of six fields. The articles were collated into two equal sets of booklets, and the names of the authors were changed so that the identical article was attributed to a male author (e.g., John T. McKay) in one booklet and to a female author (e.g., Joan T. McKay) in the other booklet. Each student was asked to read the articles in her booklet and to rate them for value, competence persuasiveness, writing style, and so forth.

As he had anticipated, Goldberg found that the identical article received significantly lower ratings when it was attributed to a female author than when it was attributed to a male author. He had predicted this result for articles from professional fields generally considered the province of men, like law or city planning, but to his surprise, these women also downgraded articles from the fields of dietetics and elementary school education when they were attributed to female authors. In other words, these students rated the male authors as better at everything, agreeing with Aristotle that "we should regard the female nature as afflicted with a natural defectiveness." Such is the nature of America's unconscious ideology about women.

When does this ideology begin to affect the life of a young girl? Research now tells us that from the day a newborn child is dressed in pink, she is given "special" treatment. Perhaps because they are thought to be more fragile, six-month-old infant girls are actually touched, spoken to, and hovered over more by their mothers while they are playing than are infant boys (Goldberg & Lewis, 1969). One study even showed that when mothers and babies are still in the hospital, mothers smile at, talk to, and touch their female infants more than their male infants at two days of age (Thoman, Leiderman, & Olson, 1972). Differential treatment can't begin much earlier than that.

As children begin to read, the storybook characters become the images and the models that little boys and little girls aspire to become. What kind of role does the female play in the world of children's literature? The fact is that there aren't even very many females in that world. One survey (Fisher, 1970) found that five times as many males as females appear in the titles of children's books; the fantasy world of Doctor Seuss is almost entirely male; and even animals and machines are represented as male. When females do appear, they are noteworthy primarily for what they do *not* do. They do not drive cars, and they seldom even ride bicycles. In one story in which a girl does ride a bicycle, it's a two-seater. Guess where the girl is seated! Boys in these stories climb trees and fish and roll in the leaves and skate. Girls watch, fall down, and get dizzy. Girls are never doctors, and although they may be nurses or librarians or teachers, they are never principals. There seemed to be only one children's book about mothers who work, and it concludes that what mothers love "best of all" is "being your very own Mommy and coming home to you." And although this is no doubt true of many daddies as well, no book about working fathers has ever found it necessary to apologize for working in quite the same way.

As children grow older, more explicit sex-role training is introduced. Boys are encouraged to take more of an interest in mathematics and science. Boys, not girls, are usually given chemistry sets and microscopes for Christmas. Moreover, all children quickly learn that mommy is proud to be a moron when it comes to math and science, whereas daddy is a little ashamed if he doesn't know all about such things. When a young boy returns from school all excited about biology, he is almost certain to be encouraged to think of becoming a physician. A girl with similar enthusiasm is usually told that she might want to consider nurse's training later on, so she can have "an interesting job to fall back upon in case — God forbid — she ever needs to support herself." A very different kind of encouragement. And any girl who doggedly persists in her enthusiasms for science is likely to find her parents as horrified by the prospect of a permanent love affair with physics as they would be either by the prospect of an interracial marriage or, horror of horrors, no marriage at all. Indeed, our graduate women report that their families seem convinced that the menopause must come at age 23.

These socialization practices take their toll. When they apply for college, boys and girls are about equal on verbal aptitude tests, but boys score significantly higher on mathematical aptitude tests — about 60 points higher on the College Board Exams, for example (Brown, 1965). Moreover, for those who are convinced that this is due to female hormones, it is relevant to know that girls improve their mathematical performance if the problems are simply reworded so that they deal with cooking and gardening, even though the abstract reasoning required for solution remains exactly the same (Milton, 1958). That's not hormones! Clearly, what has been undermined is not a woman's mathematical ability, but rather her confidence in that ability.

But these effects in mathematics and science are only part of the story. The most conspicuous outcome of all is that the majority of America's women become full-time homemakers. And of those who do work, nearly 80% end up in dead-end jobs as clerical workers, service workers, factory workers or sales clerks. Again, it is this "homogenization" of America's women which is the major consequence of America's sex-role ideology.

The important point is not that the role of homemaker is necessarily inferior, but rather that our society is managing to consign a large segment of its population to the role of homemaker — either with or without a dead-end job — solely on the basis of sex just as inexorably as it has in the past consigned the individual with a black skin to the role of janitor or domestic. The important point is that in spite of their unique identities, the majority of

American women end up in virtually the *same* role.

The socialization of the American male has closed off certain options for him, too. Men are discouraged from developing certain desirable traits such as tenderness and sensitivity, just as surely as women are discouraged from being assertive and, alas, "too bright." Young boys are encouraged to be incompetent at cooking and certainly child care, just as surely as young girls are urged to be incompetent at math and science. The elimination of sex-role stereotyping implies that each individual would be encouraged to "do his own thing." Men and women would no longer be stereotyped by society's definitions of masculine and feminine. If sensitivity, emotionality, and warmth are desirable *human* characteristics, then they are desirable for men as well as for women. If independence, assertiveness, and serious intellectual commitment are desirable *human* characteristics, then they are desirable for women as well as for men. Thus, we are not implying that men have all the goodies and that women can obtain self-fulfillment by acting like men. That is hardly the utopia implied by today's feminist movement. Rather, we envision a society which raises its children so flexibly and with sufficient respect for the integrity of individual uniqueness that some men might emerge with the motivation, the ability, and the opportunity to stay home and raise children without bearing the stigma of being peculiar. Indeed, if homemaking is as glamorous as women's magazines and television commercials would have us believe, then men, too, should have that option. And even if homemaking isn't all that glamorous, it would probably still be more fulfilling for some men than the jobs in which they now find themselves forced because of their role as breadwinner. Thus, it is true that a man's options are also limited by our society's sex-role ideology, but as the "predictability test" reveals, it is still the women in our society whose identity is rendered irrelevant by America's socialization practices.

FURTHER PSYCHOLOGICAL BARRIERS

But what of the woman who arrives at age 21 still motivated to be challenged and fulfilled by a growing career? Is she free to choose a career if she cares to do so? Or is there something standing even in her way?

There is. Even the woman who has managed to finesse society's attempt to rob her of her career motivations is likely to find herself blocked by society's trump card: the feeling that one cannot have a career and be a successful woman simultaneously. A competent and motivated woman is thus caught in a double-bind which few men have ever faced. She must worry not only about failure, but also about success.

This conflict was strikingly revealed in a study which required college women to complete the following story: "After first-term finals, Anne finds herself at the top of her medical-school class" (Horner, 1969). The stories were then examined for concern about the negative consequences of success. The women in this study all had high intellectual ability and histories of academic success. They were the very women who could have successful careers. And yet, over two-thirds of their stories revealed a clear-cut inability to cope with the concept of a feminine, yet career-oriented, woman.

The most common "fear-of-success" stories showed fears of social rejection as a result of success. The women in this group showed anxiety about becoming unpopular, unmarriageable, and lonely:

Anne starts proclaiming her surprise and joy. Her fellow classmates are so disgusted with her behavior that they jump on her in a body and beat her. She is maimed for life.

Anne is an acne-faced bookworm....
She studies twelve hours a day, and lives at home to save money. "Well, it certainly paid off. All the Friday and Saturday nights without dates, fun — I'll be the best woman doctor alive." And yet a twinge of sadness comes through — she wonders what she really has....

Anne doesn't want to be number one in her class.... She feels she shouldn't rank so high because of social reasons. She drops to ninth and then marries the boy who graduates number one.

In the second "fear-of-success" category were stories in which the women seemed concerned about definitions of womanhood. These stories expressed guilt and despair over success and doubts about their femininity and normality:

Unfortunately Anne no longer feels so certain that she really wants to be a doctor. She is worried about herself and wonders if perhaps she is not normal.... Anne decides not to continue

with her medical work but to take courses that have a deeper personal meaning for her.

Anne feels guilty.... She will finally have a nervous breakdown and quit medical school and marry a successful young doctor.

A third group of stories could not even face up to the conflict between having a career and being a woman. These stories simply denied the possibility that any woman could be so successful:

Anne is a code name for a nonexistent person created by a group of med students. They take turns writing for Anne....

Anne is really happy she's on top, though Tom is higher than she — though that's as it should be. Anne doesn't mind Tom winning.

Anne is talking to her counselor. Counselor says she will make a fine nurse.

By way of contrast, here is a typical story written not about Anne, but about John:

John has worked very hard and his long hours of study have paid off....
He is thinking about his girl, Cheri, whom he will marry at the end of med school. He realizes he can give her all the things she desires after he becomes established. He will go on in med school and be successful in the long run.

Nevertheless, there were a few women in the study who welcomed the prospect of success:

Anne is quite a lady — not only is she top academically, but she is liked and admired by her fellow students —

quite a trick in a man-dominated field. She is brilliant — but she is also a woman. She will continue to be at or near the top. And . . . always a lady.

Hopefully the day is approaching when as many "Anne" stories as "John" stories will have happy endings. But notice that even this story finds it necessary to affirm repeatedly that femininity is not necessarily destroyed by accomplishment. One would never encounter a comparable story written about John who, although brilliant and at the top of his class, is "still a man, still a man, still a man."

It seems unlikely that anyone in our society would view these "fear-of-success" stories as portraits of mental health. But even our concept of mental health has been distorted by America's sex-role stereotypes. Here we must indict our own profession of psychology. A recent survey of seventy-nine clinically-trained psychologists, psychiatrists, and social workers, both male and female, revealed a double standard of mental health (Broverman, Broverman, Clarkson, Rosenkrantz, & Vogel, 1970). That is, even professional clinicians have two different concepts of mental health, one for men and one for women; and these concepts parallel the sex-role stereotypes prevalent in our society. Thus, according to these clinicians, a woman is to be regarded as healthier and more mature if she is: more submissive, less independent, less adventurous, more easily influenced, less aggressive, less competitive, more excitable in minor crises, more susceptible to hurt feelings, more emotional, more conceited about her appearance, less objective, and more antagonistic toward math

and science! But this was the very same description which these clinicians used to characterize an unhealthy, immature man or an unhealthy, immature adult (sex unspecified)! The equation is clear: Mature woman equals immature adult.

Given this concept of a mature woman, is it any wonder that few women ever aspire toward challenging and fulfilling careers? In order to have a career, a woman will probably need to become relatively more dominant, independent, adventurous, aggressive, competitive, and objective, and relatively less excitable, emotional and conceited than our ideal of femininity requires. If she were a man (or an adult, sex unspecified), these would all be considered positive traits. But because she is a woman, these same traits will bring her disapproval. She must then either be strong enough to have her "femininity" questioned; or she must behave in the prescribed feminine manner and accept second-class status, as an adult and as a professional.

And, of course, should a woman faced with this conflict seek professional help, hoping to summon the strength she will need to pursue her career goals, the advice she is likely to receive will be of virtually no use. For, as this study reveals, even professional counselors have been contaminated by the sex-role ideology.

It is frequently argued that a 21-year-old woman is perfectly free to choose a career if she cares to do so. No one is standing in her way. But this argument conveniently overlooks the fact that our society has spent 20 years carefully marking the woman's ballot for her, and so it has nothing to lose in that 21st year by pretending to let her cast it for the alternative of her choice. Society has controlled not her alternatives (although discrimination does do that), but more importantly, it has controlled her motivation to choose any but one of those alternatives. The so-called "freedom-to choose" is illusory, and it cannot be invoked to justify a society which controls the woman's motivation to choose.

BIOLOGICAL CONSIDERATIONS

Up to this point, we have argued that the differing life patterns of men and women in our society can be chiefly accounted for by cultural conditioning. The most common counter argument to this view, of course, is the biological one. The biological argument suggests that there may really be inborn differences between men and women in, say, independence or mathematical ability. Or that there may be biological factors beyond the fact that women can become pregnant and nurse children which uniquely dictate that they, but not men, should stay home all day and shun serious outside commitment. What this argument suggests is that maybe female hormones really are responsible somehow. One difficulty with this argument, of course, is that female hormones would have to be different in the Soviet Union, where one-third of the engineers and 75% of the physicians are women (Dodge, 1966). In America, by way of contrast, women constitute less than 1% of the engineers and only 7% of the physicians. Female physiology *is* different, and it may account for some of the psychological differences between the sexes, but America's sex-role ideology still seems primarily responsible for the fact that so few women emerge from childhood with the motivation to seek out any role beyond the one that our society dictates.

But even if there really were biological differences between the sexes along these lines, the biological argument would still be irrelevant. The reason can best be illustrated with an analogy.

Suppose that every black American boy were to be socialized to become a jazz musician on the assumption that he has a "natural" talent in that direction; or suppose that parents and counselors should subtly discourage him from other pursuits because it is considered "inappropriate" for black men to become physicians or physicists. Most Americans would disapprove. But suppose that it *could* be demonstrated that black Americans, *on the average*, did possess an inborn better sense of rhythm than white Americans. Would *that* justify ignoring the unique characteristics of a *particular* black youngster from the very beginning and specifically socializing him to become a musician? We don't think so. Similarly, as long as a woman's socialization does not nurture her uniqueness, but treats her only as a member of a group on the basis of some assumed *average* characteristic, she will not be prepared to realize her own potential in the way that the values of individuality and self-fulfillment imply that she should.

THE PRESUMED INCOMPATIBILITY OF FAMILY AND CAREER

If we were to ask the average American woman why she is not pursuing a full-time career, she would probably not say that discrimination had discouraged her; nor would she be likely to recognize the pervasive effects of her own sex-role conditioning. What she probably would say is that a career, no matter how desirable, is simply incompatible with the role of wife and mother.

As recently as the turn of the century, and in less technological societies today, this incompatibility between career and family was, in fact, decisive. Women died in their forties and they were pregnant or nursing during most of their adult lives. Moreover, the work that a less technological society requires places a premium on mobility and physical strength, neither of which a pregnant woman has a great deal of. Thus, the historical division of labor between the sexes — the man away at work and the woman at home with the children — was a biological necessity. Today it is not.

Today, the work that our technological society requires is primarily mental in nature; women have virtually complete control over their reproductive lives; and most important of all, the average American woman now lives to age 74 and has her last child before age 30. This means that by the time a woman is 35 or so, her children all have more important things to do with their daytime hours than to spend them entertaining some adult woman who has nothing fulfilling to do during the entire second half of her life span.

But social forms have a way of outliving the necessities which gave rise to them. And today's female adolescent continues to plan for a 19th century life style in a 20th century world. A Gallup poll has found that young women give no thought whatever to

life after forty (Gallup & Hill, 1962). They plan to graduate from high school, perhaps go to college, and then get married. Period!

THE WOMAN AS WIFE

At some level, of course, this kind of planning is "realistic." Because most women do grow up to be wives and mothers, and because, for many women, this means that they will be leaving the labor force during the child-rearing years, a career is not really feasible. After all, a career involves long-term commitment and perhaps some sacrifice on the part of the family. Furthermore, as every "successful" woman knows, a wife's appropriate role is to encourage her husband in *his* career. The "good" wife puts her husband through school, endures the family's early financial difficulties without a whimper, and, if her husband's career should suddenly dictate a move to another city, she sees to it that the transition is accomplished as painlessly as possible. The good wife is selfless. And to be seriously concerned about one's own career is selfish — if one is female, that is. With these kinds of constraints imposed upon the work life of the married woman, perhaps it would be "unrealistic" for her to seriously aspire toward a career rather than a job.

There is some evidence of discontent among these "selfless" women, however. A 1962 Gallup poll (Gallup & Hill, 1962) revealed that only 10% of American women would want their daughters to live their lives the way they did. These mothers wanted their daughters to get more education and to marry later. And a 1970 study of women married to top Chicago-area business and professional men (Ringo, 1970) revealed that if these women could live their lives over again, they would pursue careers.

Accordingly, the traditional conception of the husband-wife relationship is now being challenged, not so much because of this widespread discontent among older, married women, but because it violates two of the most basic values of today's college generation. These values concern personal growth, on the one hand, and interpersonal relationships on the other. The first of these emphasizes individuality and self-fulfillment; the second stresses openness, honesty, and equality in all human relationships.

Because they see the traditional male-female relationship as incompatible with these basic values, today's young people are experimenting with alternatives to the traditional marriage pattern. Although a few are testing out ideas like communal living, most seem to be searching for satisfactory modifications of the husband-wife relationship, either in or out of the context of marriage. An increasing number of young people claim to be seeking fully equalitarian relationships and they cite examples like the following:

Both my wife and I earned college degrees in our respective disciplines. I turned down a superior job offer in Oregon and accepted a slightly less desirable position in New York where my wife would have more opportunities for part-time work in her specialty. Although I would have preferred to live in a suburb, we purchased a home near my wife's job so that she could have

an office at home where she would be when the children returned from school. Because my wife earns a good salary, she can easily afford to pay a housekeeper to do her major household chores. My wife and I share all other tasks around the house equally. For example, she cooks the meals, but I do the laundry for her and help her with many of her other household tasks.

Without questioning the basic happiness of such a marriage or its appropriateness for many couples, we can legitimately ask if such a marriage is, in fact, an instance of interpersonal equality. Have all the hidden assumptions about the woman's "natural" role really been eliminated? Have our visionary students really exorcised the traditional ideology as they claim? There is a very simple test. If the marriage is truly equalitarian, then its description should retain the same flavor and tone even if the roles of the husband and wife were to be reversed:

Both my husband and I earned college degrees in our respective disciplines. I turned down a superior job offer in Oregon and accepted a slightly less desirable position in New York where my husband would have more opportunities for part-time work in his specialty. Although I would have preferred to live in a suburb, we purchased a home near my husband's job so that he could have an office at home where he would be when the children returned from school. Because my husband earns a good salary, he can easily afford to pay a housekeeper to do his major household chores. My husband and I share all other tasks around the house equally. For example, he cooks the meals, but I do the laundry for him and help him with many of his other household tasks.

Somehow it sounds different, and yet only the pronouns have been changed to protect the powerful! Certainly no one would ever mistake the marriage *just* described as equalitarian or even very desirable, and thus it becomes apparent that the ideology about the woman's "natural" place unconsciously permeates the entire fabric of such "pseudo-equalitarian" marriages. It is true the wife gains some measure of equality when she can have a career rather than have a job and when her career can influence the final place of residence. But why is it the unquestioned assumption that the husband's career solely determines the initial set of alternatives that are to be considered? Why is it the wife who automatically seeks the part-time position? Why is it *her* housekeeper rather than *their* housekeeper? Why *her* household tasks? And so forth throughout the entire relationship.

The important point is not that such marriages are bad or that their basic assumptions of inequality produce unhappy, frustrated women. Quite the contrary. It is the very happiness of the wives in such marriages that reveals society's smashing success in socializing its women. It is a measure of the distance our society must yet traverse toward the goal of full equality that such marriages are widely characterized as utopian and fully equalitarian. It is a mark of how well the woman has been kept in her place that the husband in such a marriage is almost always idolized by women, including his wife. Why? Because he "permits her" to squeeze a career into the interstices of their marriage as long as his own career is not unduly inconvenienced. Thus is the white man blessed for exercising his power benignly while his "natural" right to that power forever remains unquestioned. Such is the subtlety of America's ideology about women.

In fact, however, even these "benign" inequities are now being challenged. More and more young couples really are entering marriages of full equality, marriages in which both partners pursue careers or outside commitments which carry equal weight when all important decisions are to be made, marriages in which both husband and wife accept some compromise in the growth of their respective careers for their mutual partnership. Certainly such marriages have more tactical difficulties than more traditional ones: It is simply more difficult to coordinate two independent lives rather than one-and-a-half. The point is that it is not possible to predict ahead of time *on the basis of sex*, who will be doing the compromising at any given point of decision.

It should be clear that the man or woman who places career above all else ought not to enter an equalitarian marriage. The man would do better to marry a traditional wife, a wife who will make whatever sacrifices his career necessitates. The woman who places career above all else would do better — in our present society — to remain single. For an equalitarian marriage is not designed for extra efficiency, but for double fulfillment.

The Woman as Mother

In all marriages, whether traditional, pseudo-equalitarian or fully-equalitarian, the real question surrounding a mother's career will probably continue to be the well-being of the children. All parents want to be certain that they are doing the very best for their children and that they are not depriving them in any important way, either materially or psychologically. What this has meant recently in most families that could afford it was that mother would devote herself to the children on a full-time basis. Women have been convinced — by their mothers and by the so-called experts — that there is something wrong with them if they even want to do otherwise.

For example, according to Dr. Spock (1963), any woman who finds full-time motherhood unfulfilling is showing "a residue of difficult relationships in her own childhood." If a vacation doesn't solve the problem, then she is probably having emotional problems which can be relieved "through regular counseling in a family social agency, or if severe, through psychiatric treatment. . . . Any mother of a pre-school child who is considering a job should discuss the issues with a social worker before making her decision." The message is clear: If you don't feel that your two-year-old is a stimulating, full-time companion, then you are probably neurotic.

In fact, research does not support the view that children suffer in any way when mother works. Although it came as a surprise to most researchers in the area, maternal employment in and of itself does not seem to have any negative effects on the children; and part-time work actually seems to benefit the children. Children of working mothers are no more likely than children of non-working mothers to be delinquent or nervous or withdrawn or anti-social; they are no more likely to show neurotic symptoms; they are no more likely to perform poorly in school; and they are no more likely to feel deprived of their mothers' love. Daughters of working mothers are more likely to want to work themselves, and, when asked to name the one woman in the world that they most admire, daughters of working mothers are more likely to name their own mothers! (Nye & Hoffman, 1963). This is one finding that we wish every working woman in America could hear, because the other thing that is true of almost every working mother is that she *thinks* she is hurting her children and she feels guilty. In fact, research has shown that the worst mothers are those who would like to work, but who stay home out of a sense of duty (Yarrow, Scott, de Leeuw, & Heinig, 1962). The major conclusion from all the research is really this: What matters is the quality of a mother's relationship with her children, not the time of day it happens to be administered. This conclusion should come as no surprise; successful fathers have been demonstrating it for years. Some fathers are great, some fathers stink, and they're all at work at least eight hours a day.

Similarly, it is true that the quality of substitute care that children receive while their parents are at work also matters. Young children do need security, and research has shown that it is not good to have a constant turnover of parent-substitutes, a rapid succession of changing baby-sitters or housekeepers (Maccoby, 1958). Clearly, this is why the establishment of child care centers is vitally important at the moment. This is why virtually every woman's group in the country, no matter how conservative or how radical, is in agreement on this one issue: that child care centers ought to be available to those who need them.

Once again, it is relevant to emphasize that child care centers, like the other reforms advocated, are not merely for the benefit of middle-class women who wish to pursue professional careers. Of the 31 million women in the labor force, nearly 40% of them are working mothers. In 1960, mothers constituted more than one-third of the total woman labor force. In March, 1971, more than 1 out of 3 working mothers (4.3 million of them) had children under 6 years of age, and about half of them had children under 3 years of age. And most of these women in the labor force — like most men — work because they cannot afford to do otherwise. Moreover, they cannot currently deduct the full costs of child care as a business expense as the executive can often deduct an expensive car. At the moment, the majority of these working women must simply "make do" with whatever child care arrangements they can manage. Only 6% of their children under 6 years of age currently receive group care in child care centers. *This* is why child-care centers are a central issue of the new feminist movement. This is why they are not just an additional luxury for the middle-class family with

a woman who wants to pursue a professional career.

But even the woman who is educationally and economically in a position to pursue a career must feel free to utilize these alternative arrangements for child care. For once again, America's sex-role ideology intrudes. Many people still assume that if a woman wants a full-time career, then children must be unimportant to her. But of course, no one makes this assumption about her husband. No one assumes that a father's interest in his career necessarily precludes a deep and abiding affection for his children or a vital interest in their development. Once again, America applies a double standard of judgment. Suppose that a father of small children suddenly lost his wife. No matter how much he loved his children, no one would expect him to sacrifice his career in order to stay home with them on a full-time basis — even if he had an independent source of income. No one would charge him with selfishness or lack of parental feeling if he sought professional care for his children during the day.

It is here that full equality between husband and wife assumes its ultimate importance. The fully equalitarian marriage abolishes this double standard and extends the same freedom to the mother. The equalitarian marriage provides the framework for both husband and wife to pursue careers which are challenging and fulfilling and, at the same time, to participate equally in the pleasures and responsibilities of child-rearing. Indeed, it is the equalitarian marriage which has the potential for giving children the love and concern of two parents rather than one. And it is the equalitarian marriage which has the most potential for giving parents the challenge and fulfillment of two worlds — family and career — rather than one.

In addition to providing this potential for equalized child care, a truly equalitarian marriage embraces a more general division of labor which satisfies what we like to call "the roommate test." That is, the labor is divided just as it is when two men or two women room together in college or set up a bachelor apartment together. Errands and domestic chores are assigned by preference, agreement, flipping a coin, alternated, given to hired help, or — perhaps most often the case — left undone.

It is significant that today's young people, so many of whom live precisely this way prior to marriage, find this kind of arrangement within marriage so foreign to their thinking. Consider an analogy. Suppose that a white male college student decided to room or set up a bachelor apartment with a black male friend. Surely the typical white student would not blithely assume that his black roommate was to handle all the domestic chores. Nor would his conscience allow him to do so even in the unlikely event that his roommate would say: "No, that's okay. I like doing housework. I'd be happy to do it." We suspect that the typical white student would still not be comfortable if he took advantage of this offer because he and America have finally realized that he would be taking advantage of the fact that such a roommate had been socialized by our society to be "happy" with such obvious

inequity. But change this hypothetical black roommate to a female marriage partner, and somehow the student's conscience goes to sleep. At most it is quickly tranquilized by the comforting thought that "she is happiest when she is ironing for her loved one." Such is the power of an unconscious ideology.

Of course, it may well be that she *is* happiest when she is ironing for her loved one.

Such, indeed, is the power of an unconscious ideology.

References

Bird, C. *Born Female: The High Cost of Keeping Women Down.* New York: Pocket Books, 1969.

Broverman, I. K., D. M. Broverman, F. E. Clarkson, P. S. Rosenkrantz, and S. R. Vogel. "Sex-Role Stereotypes and Clinical Judgments of Mental Health." *Journal of Consulting and Clinical Psychology,* 1970, 34, 1–7.

Brown, R. *Social Psychology.* New York: Free Press, 1965.

Dodge, N. D. *Women in the Soviet Economy.* Baltimore: Johns Hopkins Press, 1966.

Fisher, E. "The Second Sex, Junior Division." *The New York Times Book Review,* May, 1970.

Gallup, G., and E. Hill. "The American Woman." *The Saturday Evening Post,* December 22, 1962, pp. 15–32.

Goldberg, P. "Are Women Prejudiced Against Women?" *Transaction,* April, 1968, 5, 28–30.

Goldberg, S., and M. Lewis. "Play Behavior in the Year-Old Infant: Early Sex Differences." *Child Development,* 1969, 40, 21–31.

Horner, M. S. "Fail: Bright Women." *Psychology Today*, November 1969.

Maccoby, E. E. "Effects upon Children of Their Mothers' Outside Employment." In *Work in the Lives of Married Women*. New York: Columbia University Press, 1958.

Milton, G. A. "Sex Differences in Problem Solving as a Function of Role Appropriateness of the Problem Content." *Psychological Reports*, 1959, 5, 705–708.

Nye, F. I., and L. W. Hoffman. *The Employed Mother in America*. Chicago: Rand McNally, 1963.

Ringo, M. The Well-Placed Wife. Unpublished manuscript, John Paisios & Associates, 332 South Michigan Ave., Chicago, Illinois.

Spock, B. "Should Mothers Work?" *Ladies' Home Journal*, February 1963.

Terman, L. M., and M. H. Oden. *Genetic studies of genius, V. The gifted group at mid-life: Thirty-five years' follow-up of the superior child.* Stanford, Calif.: Stanford University Press, 1959.

Thoman, E. B., P. H. Leiderman, and J. P. Olson. "Neonate-Mother Interaction during Breast Feeding." *Developmental Psychology*, 1972, 6, 110–118.

U.S. Department of Labor, Wage and Labor Standards Administration, Women's Bureau. Fact sheet on the earnings gap, February, 1970.

U.S. Department of Labor, Wage and Labor Standards Administration, Women's Bureau. *Handbook on Women Workers*, 1969. Bulletin 294.

Yarrow, M. R., P. Scott, L. de Leeuw, and D. Heinig. "Child-Rearing in Families of Working and Non-Working Mothers." *Sociometry*, 1962, 25, 122–140.

In the traditional viewpoint, the central life interest for all women should be home and family. In the past, acceptance of this life style could generally be assumed, although there were always a few rebels in male dominated professions. In the 1920s there was a minor flourish of feminist activism; however, after women attained minor goals such as establishment of women's colleges, interest declined.*

Temporarily, during the 1940s, women assumed a more active role in the occupational structure; but when the men returned from war, women returned to their traditional life style. The 1950s and 1960s brought about increasing numbers of college-educated women, many of whom were not content to be educated housewives. Educated women in the occupational structure tended to be underpaid or overqualified for their jobs. Influenced by the success of other minority groups in attaining their rights, women began to organize a protest.

* Jessie Bernard, *Academic Women* (University Park, Pa.: Pennsylvania State University Press, 1964), pp. 36–37.

All women were not protesting their status. On the Boardwalk in At-lantic City, outside of Convention Hall, a group of militant women were burning their bras. Inside Convention Hall, women from throughout the United States were once again competing for the title of "Miss America."

The Miss America Pageant can be described as a commercialized cele-bration of the ideal life style of the young unmarried woman. According to the stereotype, she is a young Doris Day with a modicum of talent, an overabundance of wholesomeness, and great love for parents and country. But above all, she is a sincere believer that her fulfillment lies in a future of raising her children, encouraging her husband, and serving her community.

There She Is . . . Miss America

Judith Martin

"Anbody here over 35?" shouted Bert Parks.

"Yaaay" came back the answer from the crowd gathered in Atlantic City's Convention Hall last weekend to watch the Miss America Pageant.

They had come to cheer their idea of what youth should be like and 50 girls had tried all week to personify that idea. Miss America girls do not smoke, drink, date, discuss controversial topics or go around unchaperoned during the pageant — the winner agrees to be-have that way for a year — and they are very polite to their elders.

From *The Washington Post* (September 14, 1969). Reprinted by permission of the Washington Post.

They support their government, con-demn dissent, and set their goals on spending a year or two in traditional female occupations — modeling or ele-mentary school teaching — until the right man comes along.

Miss America of 1970, Pamela Anne Eldred of Detroit, gave a press con-ference in which she said she was a spokesman for her generation and she made a statement about the Establish-ment:

"I feel that the people who were voted into office must have the intel-ligence to know what to do and that everybody should have faith in them."

She said she did not object when pageant officials refused to let her speak on certain subjects. "I feel that they are older and wiser than I am and I can always learn something, espe-cially from someone who is older. If I am told I can't do something, I am told for a reason and I don't challenge it."

"God love you," said a state pageant official from Michigan.

Other pageant officials, the audience, and the judges all talked about how comforting it was to see this girl and the others like her. They called them "true representatives of American youth."

For a few magic days the drug scene, the sexual revolution, and the civil rights, antiwar, female liberation, and student protest movements seemed to them to have been just bad dreams populated by "a tiny minority of kooks."

Miss America told her admirers that the war was right because otherwise the government never would have gotten into it. Miss Minnesota, Judith Claire Mendenhall, a runner-up to the title, told them that women shouldn't try to run things "because they are more emotional and men can overcome their emotions with logic."

Miss Virginia, Sydney Lee Lewis, won a talent award for a speech in which she condemned student reform movements but lauded her generation for things like "conceiving the Rally for Decency."

The theme of this year's pageant was "the sound of youth." There was much talk in it about the new sound and then one talent winner sang "Get Happy" and another played "Bumble Boogie" on the piano.

"Each generation has its own translation of young, and this generation's is a search for the golden rainbow of peace and understanding," said Parks to introduce Miss America 1969, Judi Ford, who wore a Ginger Rogers white pleated chiffon dress and danced the kind of number which used to be the finale of motion picture musical comedies of the '40s.

The pastel chiffon dresses with sequined tops, which the girls wore with 18-button length white cotton gloves in the evening dress competition, had to be specially made. So did the one-piece solid-color, no-cutouts bathing suits, which are no longer stocked commercially. Spiked-heeled, pointed-toes shoes dyed to match were worn with the bathing suits.

Evening culottes were permitted during the talent competition, but most girls favored the sequined, drum majorette type of costume. Several chose mid-knee cocktail dresses just a shade longer than the new habits of a group of nuns who attended the preliminary competition one night.

Make-up was used in the shows to create the kewpie doll look of decades ago — bright red lipstick, blue eye shadow, and hair teased into beehives with wiglets of curls added.

Offstage, however, the girls were more contemporary, with shoulder-length hairstyles and little wool dresses which gave them the look of 50 Tricia Nixons.

The judges said they were gratified at what they saw and had a hard time picking a winner.

"It renews my faith in youth," said Hollywood make-up man Bud Westmore, a judge, whose wife was Miss California of 1952.

"We have a complete misconception of what is going on when we see the New York hippies who don't wash," said Leon Leonidoff, another judge, who has been staging Radio City Music Hall spectaculars since 1932. "This country is wholesome and healthy." His wife is a former Miss New Jersey, and he had been going around all week offering contracts to his favorite contestants.

"We really haven't got a thing to worry about," said judge Jane Pickens Langley, who describes herself as "singer, artist, and philanthropist."

"These aren't the girls you hear about, because there is never any scandal attached to them," said judge Zelma George, executive director of the Cleveland Job Corps Center for Women. "Someone should do a master's thesis on them."

"You don't hear about them later because basically they are not ambitious," said writer John Crosby, a judge. "They want to be good wives and mothers."

No one seemed to know, however, why most of the past Miss Americas have been divorced at least once.

The pageant officials expressed their delight with the way Miss America 1970 handled reporters' questions.

Topics on which she smiled and said "I really couldn't voice an opinion — I don't know enough about that" included drugs, nudity in the theater, unisex fashions, student unrest, what the priorities of America should be, and whether 18-year-olds should have

the vote. She also said that she was happy about the moon shot "which proves that the United States is a great country" and that her goal in life is "to be a nice person."

Her mother, Mrs. William B. Eldred, who broke in once just after the crowning to tell Miss America, "You are no expert," said that she and her daughter feel alike on all topics. "There is no generation gap," said Mrs. Eldred.

Miss America's one moment of confusion was when she was asked where her father works. He is an employe of Chrysler, and loyalty to the pageant's sponsors, one of which is Oldsmobile, is an important quality of Miss America.

Miss America 1969 said that, during her year, love of Toni hair products, Pepsi-Cola, and Oldsmobile became a spontaneous part of her.

The past and present Miss Americas looked very much alike—both with blond bouffant hairdos, green eyes, pale skin, and wide smiles. They are both, said Bert Parks, "composites of positive wonders. All Miss Americas are," he said.

In an era of questioning traditional sex-roles, the Miss America Pageant is still very much part of the American scene but there have been rumblings even from this conservative camp. Recently, some contestants stated that women should receive equal pay for equal work and at least one contestant spoke out in favor of abortion.

One's biological gender does not necessarily have to lock one into a particular mode of behavior. If change is to come however, what shall be the outcome of this change and where shall it come from? Some be-

lieve that both men and women will have to change so that sex role differences become more blurred. Others value and want to maintain these differences but strive for real equality between the two sexes.

And how does change come about? Partially through political pressure. Civil rights legislation prohibits hiring people for jobs on the basis of their sex, and in many traditionally male occupations, women are being hired instead of men. The law may create changes in the opportunity structure but can it bring about changes in attitudes toward sex roles? One goal of the women's movement has been to raise men's and women's consciousness about their sex roles and to make them more open to change. People are asked to examine themselves, and to compare their own lives to the lives of those who have been liberated from traditional sex role ideology. In the following deeply personal article, Sally Kempton discusses her transformation from traditional to non-traditional sex role attitudes.

Cutting Loose, 1970: A Private View of the Women's Uprising

Sally Kempton

Once another woman and I were talking about male resistance to Woman's Liberation, and she said that she didn't understand why men never worry about women taking their jobs away but worry only about the possibility that women may stop making love to them and bearing their children. And once

From *Esquire Magazine* (July 1970), pp. 53–57. Reprinted by permission of *Esquire Magazine.* © by Esquire, Inc.

I was arguing with a man I know about Woman's Liberation, and he said he wished he had a motorcycle gang with which to invade a Woman's Liberation meeting and rape everybody in it. There are times when I understand the reason for men's feelings. I have noticed that beyond the feminists' talk about the myth of the vaginal orgasm lies a radical resentment of their position in the sexual act. And I have noticed that when I feel most militantly feminist I am hardly at all interested in sex.

Almost one could generalize from that: the feminist impulse is anti-sexual, anti-male, just as the purposely all-male group is anti-female. There is often a sense of genuine cultural rebellion in the atmosphere of a Woman's Liberation meeting. Women sit with their legs apart, carelessly dressed, barely made-up, exhibiting their feelings or the holes at the knees of their jeans with an unprovocative candor which is hardly seen at all in the outside world. Of course, they are demonstrating by their postures that they are in effect off duty, absolved from the compulsion to make themselves attractive, and yet, as the world measures these things, such demonstrations could in themselves be seen as evidence of neurosis: we have all been brought up to believe that a woman who was "whole" would appear feminine even on the barricades.

The fact is that one cannot talk in feminist terms without revealing feelings which have traditionally been regarded as neurotic. One becomes concerned about women's rights, as Simone de Beauvoir noted, only when one perceives that there are few personal advantages to be gained from accepting the traditional women's roles. A woman who is satisfied with her life is not likely to be drawn into the Woman's Liberation movement: there must be advantages for her as a woman in a man's world. To be a feminist one must be to some degree maladjusted to that world, one must be, if you will, neurotic. And sometimes one must be anti-sexual, if only in reaction to masculine expectations. Men do not worry about women taking their jobs because they do not think that women could do their jobs; most men can only be threatened by a woman in bed. A woman who denies her sexuality, if only for an evening, denies her status as an object of male attention, as a supplicant, successful or not, for male favor. For a woman to deny her sexuality is to attack the enemy in his most valuable stronghold, which is her own need for him.

I became a feminist as an alternative to becoming a masochist. Actually, I always was a masochist; I became a feminist because to be masochist is intolerable. As I get older I recognize more and more that the psychoanalytical idea that women are natural masochists is at least metaphorically correct: my own masochism derived from an almost worshipful respect for masculine power. In my adolescence I screwed a lot of guys I didn't much like, and always felt abused by them, but I never felt free to refuse sex until after the initial encounter. My tactic, if you can call it a tactic, was to Do It once and then to refuse to see the boy again, and I think I succeeded, with my demonstrations of postcoital detachment, in making several of them feel as rejected by my lovemaking as I had felt by their desire to make love to me without love. Yet I found in those years that I had irretrievably marked myself a sexual rebel and I was given to making melodramatic statements like "I'm not the kind of girl men marry." Years later I realized that I had been playing a kind of game, the same game boys play at the age of sexual experimentation, except that, unlike a boy, I could not allow myself to choose my partners and admit that I had done so. In fact, I was never comfortable with a lover unless he had, so to speak, wronged me. Once during my senior year in high school I let a boy rape me (that is not, whatever you may think, a contradiction of terms) in the bedroom of his college suite while a party was going on next door; afterward I ran away down the stairs while he followed shouting apologies which became more and more abject as he realized that my revulsion was genuine, and I felt an exhilaration which I clearly recognized as triumph. By letting him abuse me I had won the right to tell him I hated him; I had won the right to hurt him.

I think most American adolescents hate and fear the opposite sex: in adolescence it seems that only one's lovers can hurt one, and I think that even young people who are entirely secure in other relations recognize and would, if they could, disarm the power the other sex has for them. But for adolescent boys, sexual success is not the sole measure of worth. It is assumed that they will grow up and work, that their most important tests will come in areas where criteria are extra-sexual. They can fail with girls without failing entirely, for there remains to them the public life, the male life.

But girls have no such comfort. Sex occupies even the economic center of our lives; it is, we have been brought up to feel, our life's work. Whatever else she may do, a woman is a failure if she fails to please men. The adolescent girl's situation is by definition dependent: she *must* attract, and therefore, however she may disguise it, she must compromise the sticky edges of her personality, she must arrange herself to conform with other people's ideas of what is valuable in a woman.

I was early trained to that position, trained, in the traditional manner, by my father. Like many men who are uncomfortable with adult women, my father saw his daughter as a potential antidote to his disappointment in her sex. I was someone who could be molded into a woman compatible with his needs, and also, unlike my mother,

I was too impressionable to talk back. So I became the vessel into which he fed his opinions about novels and politics and sex; he fed me also his most hopeful self-image. It reached a point where I later suspected him of nourishing a sort of eighteenth-century fantasy about our relationship, the one in which the count teaches his daughter to dread Virgil and ride like a man, and she grows up to be the perfect feminine companion, parroting him with such subtlety that it is impossible to tell that her thoughts and feelings, so perfectly coincident with his, are not original. I had three brothers, as it happened, and another sort of man might have chosen one of them to mold. But my father had himself a vast respect for masculine power. Boys grow up and have to kill their fathers, girls can be made to understand their place.

My father in his thirties was an attractive man, he was witty by adult standards and of course doubly so by mine, and he had a verbal facility with which he invariably demolished my mother in arguments. Masculine power in the intellectual classes is exercised verbally: it is the effort of the male supremacist intellectual to make his woman look clumsy and illogical beside him, to render her, as it were, dumb. His tactic is to goad the woman to attack him and then, resorting to rationality, to withdraw himself from the battle. In my childhood experience, subtlety appeared exclusively a masculine weapon. I never saw a woman argue except straightforwardly, and I never saw a woman best a man in a quarrel. My mother tried, but always with the conviction of ultimate failure.

She attacked with pinpricks to begin with; in the end, maddened invariably by my father's ostentatious mental absence, she yelled. He was assisted in these struggles by his natural passivity. Withdrawal came easily to him; he hated, as he told us over and over again, scenes. My mother, it seemed to me, was violent, my father cool. And since it also seemed to me that he preferred me, his daughter who never disagreed with him, to his wife who did (that was a fantasy, of course, but one to which my father devoted some effort toward keeping alive), I came to feel that male power, because uncoercible, could only be handled by seduction, and that the most comfortable relation between men and women was the relation between pupil and teacher, between parent and child.

My father taught me some tricks. From him I learned that it is pleasant and useful to get information from men, pleasant because it is easier than getting it for yourself, and useful because it is seductive: men like to give information, and sometimes love the inquirer, if she is pretty and asks intelligently. From him I also learned that women are by definition incapable of serious thought. This was a comforting lesson, although it made me feel obscurely doomed, for if I was to be automatically barred from participation in the life of high intellect, there was no reason why I should work to achieve it, and thinking, after all, is difficult work. When I was fifteen my father told me that I would never be a writer because I wasn't hungry enough, by which I think he meant that there would always be some man to feed me. I accepted his pronounce-

ment as I accepted, at that age, all pronouncements which had an air of finality, and began making other career plans.

My task, it seemed to me, was to find a man in whom there resided enough power to justify my acting the child, that is, to justify my acceptance of my own femininity. For I regarded myself as feminine only in my childlike aspect; when I presented myself as a thinking person I felt entirely sexless. The boys in my class regarded me as an intellectual and showed an almost unanimous distinterest in my company. When I was in the eighth grade I lived in trepidation lest I be cited as class bookworm, and defended myself against that threat by going steady with what surely must have been the dumbest boy in our set. He was no fonder of me than I was of him; we needed each other because you had to be part of a couple in order to get invited to parties.

I did not get the opportunity to demonstrate my skill as a child-woman until I became old enough to go out with college boys. My training had equipped me only to attract intelligent men, and a boy who was no brighter than I held no power for me. But for a man who could act as my teacher I could be submissive and seductive — I *felt* submissive and seductive; my awe of the male mind translated easily into an awe of the male person.

I was, I realize now, in tune with the demands of my time. This was in the late Fifties, Marilyn Monroe was the feminine archetype of the period, and Marilyn Monroe was sexy because of her childishness. It is not much of a step from seeing oneself as a child in relation to men to seeing oneself as their victim; obviously a child does not control its environment, obviously a child is powerless before adults. All children are potential victims, dependent upon the world's good-will. My sense of powerlessness, of feminine powerlessness, was so great that for years I trusted no man who had not indicated toward me a special favor, who had not fallen in love with me. And even toward those who had, I acted the victim, preferring to believe myself the one who loved most, for how could a man retain his power in loving me unless I gave it back to him through my submission? Years later I heard a story about how Bob Dyan so tormented a groupy that she jumped out a window while ten people looked on, and recognized the spirit of my adolescence. I never got myself into a situation even comparably extreme, my fundamental self-protectiveness having permitted me to allow only minor humiliations, but the will was there.

Masochism as clinically defined is more or less exclusively a sexual disorder: masochists are people who derive sexual pleasure from pain. Freudian psychiatrists claim that all women are to one degree or another masochistic in the sexual sense (the male penetrates the female, presumably he hurts her, and presumably she enjoys the pain as part of the pleasure), and many Freudian thinkers extend the use of the term out of the area of sex into the social area and argue that the womanly woman is correctly masochistic, must be masochistic in order to accept the male domination which is necessarily a part even of her extrasexual life. It seems to me more useful to define masochism, insofar as the word is to be used to describe a nonclinical emotional condition, as the doing of something which one does not enjoy because someone else demands it or even because one's conscience demands it. In this sense clinical masochism can be said to be non-masochistic: if one enjoys being whipped, one is acting directly upon one's own needs, whereas if one allows oneself to be whipped for someone else's pleasure without deriving any pleasure from the act, one is behaving masochistically. A person who acts upon someone else's will, or in accordance with someone else's image of her, or who judges herself by someone else's standards, has allowed herself to be made into an object. A masochist, as I define the term, is a person who consents to be made an object. It is in that sense that I think most women are, or have been at some time in their lives, masochists. For insofar as a woman lives by the standards of the world, she lives according to the standards set by men. Men have laid down the rules and definitions by which the world is run, and one of the objects of their definitions is woman. Men define intelligence, men define usefulness, men tell us what is beautiful, men even tell us what is womanly. Constance Chatterley was a male invention; Lawrence invented her, I used to think, specifically to make me feel guilty because I didn't have the right kind of orgasms.

Lionel Trilling wrote in an essay on Jane Austen that it is the presumption of our society that women's moral life is not as men's, and that therefore we do not expect from women, in fact do not condone in them, the same degree of self-love which we expect and encourage in men. What he meant, I think, was that since women are in a sense given their lives, since women customarily choose a life-style by choosing a man rather than a path, they do not need the self-love which is necessary to carry a man to the places he has to go. Self-love is indeed a handicap to a being whose primary function is supportive, for how is a woman adequately to support another ego when her self-love demands the primacy of her own? Women learn in many ways to suppress their selfishness, and by doing so they suppress also their self-esteem. If most men hold women in contempt it is no greater than the contempt in which women hold themselves. Self-love depressed becomes self-loathing. Men are brought up to command, women to seduce: to admit the necessity of seduction is to admit that one has not the strength to command. It is in fact to accept one's own objecthood, to internalize one's oppression.

Still, I picked up some interesting lore from men, while I was studying to please them. I learned about Eliot from one boy, and about Donne from another, and about Coltrane from a third. A lover turned me on to drugs and also showed me how you were supposed to act when you were high — that is, as if you were not high. I was not surprised that he was better at this than me, cool was beginning to seem more and more a masculine talent, and I had even taken to physical retaliation in arguments, having given up the idea that I would ever win anything by verbal means. I went to Sarah Lawrence instead of Barnard because my boyfriend thought that Sarah Lawrence was a more "feminine" school. My parents got divorced and I sided with my father, at least at first, because his appeared to me to be the winning side. Men, I believed, were automatically on the winning side, which was why my oldest brother could afford to withdraw in moral outrage from my father's advances; there was for *him* no danger of branding himself a loser by consorting with my mother. Yet I envied him his integrity. How could I maintain integrity when I was willing to sell out any principle for the sake of masculine attention?

I went to Sarah Lawrence and got to love it without ever taking it very seriously, which I also supposed was the way the boys I loved in those days felt about me. In fact, Sarah Lawrence appeared to me and to most of my friends there as a sort of symbol of ourselves: like the college, we were pretty and slightly prestigious and terribly self-serious in private, but just as we laughed at the school and felt embarrassed to be identified with it publicly (I always felt that if I had been a real student I would have gone to Barnard), so we laughed publicly at our own aspirations. "I like Nancy," a Princeton boy said to me, "except she always starts talking about Kafka promptly at midnight." And I laughed, god how I laughed, at Nancy — how *Sarah Lawrence* to carry on about Kafka — and, by implication, at myself. For I too expressed my intellectualism in effusions. Men expected the effusions, even found them charming, while treating them with friendly contempt. It was important to be charming. A passion for Marxism, stumblingly expressed, an interpretation of *Moby Dick*, these tokens we offered our lovers to prove we were not simply women, but people. Yet though we displayed strong feelings about art and politics, we behaved as if we had not really done the reading. To argue a point logically was to reveal yourself as unfeminine: a man might respect your mind, but he would not love you. Wit, we believed, is frightening in a woman.

In my senior year I met a girl who knew the editor of *The Village Voice*, and after graduation she got me a job there. I went to work as a reporter without having the slightest notion of how to conduct an interview and so, to cover myself, I made up a couple of pieces out of whole cloth. They were about drugs and hippies and homosexuals, the sort of scene pieces *The Voice* later specialized in, but nobody much was writing about that stuff in 1964, and I got several book offers and invitations to cocktail parties, and my father's friends started writing me letters full of sports analogies, saying it was time I entered a main event. In fact, I felt terribly guilty about writing those pieces because they seemed frivolous and sensationalistic, the sort of thing empty-headed girl reporters did when they were too dumb to write about politics, but on the other hand they got me attention, which writing about politics would never have done. I agonized all summer, publicly and privately, over this dilemma, often spending hours telling big strong male reporters how unworthy I felt. They seemed to like it.

I had never thought of myself as ambitious; actually I think I was too convinced of my basic incompetence to be constructively ambitious, but I quickly saw that a lady journalist has advantages denied to men. For one thing, she never has to pick up a check. For another thing, if she is even remotely serious, people praise her work much more than they would praise the work of a comparably talented man; they are amazed that a woman can write coherently on any subject not confined in interest to the readers of a woman's magazine. And finally, people tell her things they would not tell a man. Many men think the secrets they tell a woman are automatically off the record. They forget that the young woman hanging on their every word is taking it all down — often they confuse her attention with sexual interest. (That is not such an advantage. Some men, rock stars for instance, simply assumed that sex was what I had come for. They would expend a little flattery to assure me that they regarded me as a cut above other groupies, and then they would suggest that we get down to balling. They were often nasty when I refused.)

At any rate, the work was nice, and it gave me a higher status as a sexual object than I had ever had before. But it was also scary. If I was to do well at it I had to take it seriously, and the strongest belief I had retained from my childhood was my idea that nothing I could achieve was worth taking seriously. In the Autumn of 1964 I fell in love with a boy who was not sure he was in love with me, and by the time he decided he was I had quit my job and moved with him to Boston. He styled himself a revolutionary and thought the content of my work hardly worth the effort it took to produce it; I accepted his opinion with relief, telling myself that in any case I had not the emotional energy to handle both a lover and a job. My feeling for him evaporated fairly soon after I discovered that it was reciprocated, though I lived with him for several months after that, partly out of guilt and partly because living with a man made me feel grown-up in a way holding a job never could have done. But finally I left him and took a job as a staff writer on a national magazine, a classy job but underpaid. Instead of complaining about the salary, I took to not showing up for work, justifying my laziness by telling myself that I was selling out anyway by taking an uptown job and that the sooner I rid myself of it, the sooner I would regain my integrity.

In the meantime I had met a grown-up man who was powerful and smart and knocked out by my child act. We spent a few months seducing each other — "You're too young for me," he would say, and I would climb upon his lap, figuratively speaking, and protest that I was not. It was no more disgusting than most courtships. In the end we got married.

Of course, I had to marry a grown-up, a father figure if you will, and my husband, as it turned out, had to marry a child. That is, he had to have an intelligent woman, but one whose intelligence had been, as it were, castrated by some outside circumstances. My youth served that purpose; my other handicaps had not as yet emerged.

Anyway, our romantic personae lasted about a year. For a year he was kind to me and listened to my problems and put up with the psychosomatic diseases which marriage had induced in me, and for a year I brought joy and spontaneity into his drab grown-up existence. Then he began to get tired of being a father and I to resent being a child, and we began to act out what I think is a classic example of contemporary marriage.

It had turned out, I realized with horror, that I had done exactly what middle-class girls are supposed to do. I had worked for a year in the communications industry, and my glamorous job had enabled me to meet a respectable, hardworking man who made a lot of money at *his* glamorous job, and I had settled down (stopped screwing around) and straightened myself out (went into analysis), and all that was missing was babies. I defended myself by assuming that we would be divorced in a year, and sneered a lot at Design Research furniture and the other symbols of middle-class marriage, but still I could not escape the feeling that I had fallen not just into a trap but into a cliché. On the other hand, I loved my husband, and I was still a writer, that is to say, a privileged woman with a life of her own. I could afford, as I began to at that time, to read feminist literature without really applying it to my own situation.

My husband, although he is nice to women, is a male supremacist, very much in the style of Norman Mailer. That is, he invests women with more or less mystical powers of control over the inner workings of the world, but thinks that feminine power is strongest when exercised in child rearing and regards contraception as unnatural. When I had my first stirrings of feminist grievance, he pronounced the subject a bore: I used to follow him from room to room, torturing him with my recitals of the sexist atrocities I was beginning to find in my favorite novels, and when I complained that magazines were paying me less than they paid men, he accused me of trying to blame the world for my own crazy passivity. But we were engaged at that time in the usual internal power struggle, and my feminism seemed to both of us more an intellectual exercise than a genuine commitment. It was not until many months later that he began to accuse me of hating men.

We already knew that he hated women, even that he had good reasons for hating women, but I had up to that time put on such a good display of being cuddly, provocative, sexually uninhibited and altogether unlike those other women that the subject of my true feelings about men had never come up. He knew that I had a compulsion to seduce men, which argues a certain distrust of them, but as the seductions, since our marriage, were always intellectual rather than sexual, they could, if you didn't want to consider their implications, be put down simply to insecurity. I don't think even I realized how I felt. Once I told my husband about a rigmarole a friend and I had made up to dismiss men we didn't like — we would go through lists of names, pointing our fingers and saying, "Zap, you're sterile," and then collapse into giggles; my husband, who

has a psychoanalytical turn of mind, thought that was Terribly Revealing and I agreed that it was, but so what? And also, I agreed that it was Terribly Revealing that I liked to pinch and bite him, that I made small hostile jokes and took an almost malicious pleasure in becoming too involved in work to pay attention to him (but only briefly; I never for very long attempted to work when he had other plans), that I would go into week-long depressions during which the bed never got made nor the dishes washed. But the degree of my hostility didn't reveal itself to me until a pattern began to emerge around our quarrels.

We had, since early in the marriage, periodically engaged in bitter fights. Because my husband was the stronger, and because he tends to be judgmental, they usually started when he attempted to punish me (by withdrawing, of course) for some offense. I would dispute the validity of his complaint, and the quarrel would escalate into shouts and blows and then into decisions to terminate the marriage. In the first year my husband always beat me hollow in those battles. I used to dissolve into tears and beg his forgiveness after twenty minutes; I could not bear his rejection and I had no talent at all for conducting a quarrel. I won only when I succeeded in making him feel guilty; if he behaved badly enough I automatically achieved the moral upper hand for at least a week following the quarrel. But after a while, the honeymoon being over, he began to refuse to feel guilty and I began to resent his superior force. Things rested there until, in the third year of our marriage, we went to live in Los Angeles because of my husband's work. During the year we spent away from home I found that I could not work, and that he was always working, and we suddenly found ourselves frozen into the textbook attitudes of male-female opposition. We fought continually, and always about the same things. He accused me of making it impossible for him to work, I accused him of keeping me dangling, dependent upon him for all emotional sustenance, he accused me of spending too much money and of keeping the house badly, I accused him of expecting me continually to subordinate my needs to his. The difficulty, I realized over and over again without being able to do much about it, was that I had gotten myself into the classic housewife's position: I was living in a place I didn't want to be, and seeing people I didn't like because that was where my man was. I was living my husband's life and I hated him for it. And the reason this was so was that I was economically dependent upon him; having ceased to earn my living I could no longer claim the breadwinner's right to attention for my special needs.

My husband told me that I was grown-up now, twenty-six years old, there were certain realities which I had to face. He was the head of the household: I had never questioned that. He had to fulfill himself: I had never questioned that. He housed and fed me and paid for my clothes, he respected my opinions and refused all his opportunities to make love to other women, and my part of the bargain should have become clear to me by now. In exchange for those things, I was supposed to keep his house and save his money and understand that if he worked sixteen hours a day for a year it was no more than necessary for his self-fulfillment. Which was all quite true. Except that it was also necessary for his fulfillment that I should be there for those few hours when he had time for me, and not complain about the hours when he did not, and that I should adapt myself to his situation or else end the marriage. It never occurred to him to consider adapting himself to mine, and it never occurred to me. I only knew that his situation was bad for me, was alien, was in fact totally paralyzing, that it kept me from working, that it made me more unhappy than I had been in my life.

I knew that I was being selfish. But he was being selfish also, the only difference being that his selfishness was somehow all right, while mine was inexcusable. Selfishness was a privilege I had earned for a while by being a writer, that is, a person who had by male standards a worthwhile place to spend her time. As soon as I stopped functioning as a writer, I became to my husband and to everyone else a mere woman, somebody whose time was valueless, somebody who had no excuse for a selfish preoccupation with her own wants.

I used to lie in bed beside my husband after those fights and wish I had the courage to bash in his head with a frying pan. I would do it while he slept, since awake he would overpower me, disarm me. If only I dared, I would mutter to myself through clenched teeth, pushing back the realization that I didn't dare not because I was afraid of seriously hurting him — I would have loved to do that — but because even in the extremity of my anger I was afraid that if I cracked his head with a frying pan he would leave me. God, how absurd it was (god, how funny, I would mutter to myself, how amusing, oh wow, what a joke) that my whole life's effort had been directed toward keeping men from leaving me, toward placating them, submitting to them, demanding love from them in return for living in their style, and it all ended with me lying awake in the dark hating my husband, hating my father, hating all the men I had ever known. Probably I had always hated them. What I couldn't figure out was whether I hated them because I was afraid they would leave me or whether I was afraid they would leave me because I hated them.

Because one cannot for very long support such a rage without beginning to go crazy, I tried to think of the problem in political terms. It seemed to me too easy to say that my hatred for men was a true class hatred, that women hate men because women are an oppressed class hungering for freedom. And yet wherever there exists the display of power there is politics, and in women's relations with men there is a continual transfer of power, there is continually, politics. There are political analogies even to our deepest, our most banal fantasies. Freud maintains that the female terror of the penis is a primary fear, and that the male fear of castration by the vagina is merely a retaliatory fantasy, a guilty fear of punishment. The serf fears the overlord's knout, the overlord, guilty, fears the serf's revenge. Women are natural guerrillas. Scheming, we nestle into the enemy's bed, avoiding open warfare,

watching the options, playing the odds. High, and made paranoiac by his observance of my rage, my husband has the fantasy of woman with a knife. He sees her in sexual ecstasy with her eyes open to observe the ecstasy of her partner, with her consciousness awake, her consciousness the knife. It had often been my private boast that even in moments of greatest abandon, I always kept some part of my mind awake: I always searched for clues. Is he mine now, this monster? Have I disarmed him, and for how long? Men are beasts, we say, joking, parodying the Victorian rag, and then realize to our surprise that we believe it. The male has force almost beyond our overpowering, the force of laws, of science, of literature, the force of mathematics and skyscrapers and the Queensboro Bridge; the penis is only its symbol. We cannot share men's pride in the world they have mastered. If you follow that symbolism to its conclusion, we are ourselves that conquered world.

It is because they know that this is true, know it in their bones if not in their heads, that men fear the hatred of women. For women are the true maintenance class. Society is built upon their acquiescence, and upon their small and necessary labors. Restricted to the supportive role, conditioned to excel only at love, women hold for men the key to social order. It is a Marxist truism that the original exploitation, the enslavement which set the pattern for everything which came later, was the enslavement of women by men. Even the lowest worker rests upon the labor of his wife. Where no other claim to distinction exists, a man defines himself by his difference from the supportive sex: he may be a less than admirable man, but at least he is a man, at least he is not a woman.

And if women have fought, they have fought as guerrillas, in small hand-to-hand skirmishes, in pillow wars upon the marriage bed. When they attack frontally, when they come together in groups to protest their oppression, they raise psychic questions so profound as to be almost inadmissible. In E. E. Cummings' play *Him*, there is a scene in which two women sit in a Paris café and order men served up to them like plats du jour; it is an inexpressibly sinister sequence, and it has its counterparts elsewhere in the avant-garde literature of the Twenties. I do not imagine that Cummings approved of men using women like meat, but I am quite sure that he could not have treated the situation with such horror had the sexual roles been reversed. Cummings, like Leonid Andreyev and the other modernists who dealt in surreal images of female dominance, was writing during the early period of feminist protest, and I think they were expressing a fear basic to every man confronted with the idea of women's liberation. When men imagine a female uprising they imagine a world in which women rule men as men have ruled women: their guilt, which is the guilt of every ruling class, will allow them to see no middle ground. And it is a measure of the unconscious strength of our belief in natural male dominance that all of us, men and women, revolt from the image of woman with a whip, that the female sadist is is one of our most deep-rooted images of perversion.

And although I believe this male fantasy of feminine equality as a euphemism for feminine dominance to be evidence of the oppressors' neurosis rather than of any supporting fact, it was part of the character of my resentment that I once fancied wresting power from men as though nothing less than total annihilation would satisfy my rage. The true dramatic conclusion of this narrative should be the dissolution of my marriage; there is a part of me which believes that you cannot fight a sexist system while acknowledging your need for the love of a man, and perhaps if I had had the courage finally to tear apart my life I could write you about my hard-working independence, about my solitary self-respect, about the new society I hope to build. But in the end my husband and I did not divorce, although it seemed at one time as if we would. Instead I raged against him for many months and joined the Woman's Liberation Movement, and thought a great deal about myself, and about whether my problems were truly all women's problems, and decided that some of them were and that some of them were not. My sexual rage was the most powerful single emotion of my life, and the feminist analysis has become for me, as I think it will for most women of my generation, as significant an intellectual tool as Marxism was for generations of radicals. But it does not answer every question. To discover that something has been wrong is not necessarily to make it right: I would be lying if I said that my anger had taught me how to live. But my life has changed because of it. I think I am becoming in many small ways a woman who takes no shit. I am no longer submissive, no longer seductive; perhaps it is for that reason that my husband tells me sometimes that I have become hard, and that my hardness is unattractive. I would like it to be otherwise. I think that will take a long time.

My husband and I have to some degree worked out our differences; we are trying to be together as equals, to separate our human needs from the needs imposed upon us by our sex roles. But my hatred lies within me and between us, not wholly a personal hatred, but not entirely political either. And I wonder always whether it is possible to define myself as a feminist revolutionary and still remain in any sense a wife. There are moments when I still worry that he will leave me, that he will come to need a woman less preoccupied with her own rights, and when I worry about that I also fear that no man will ever love me again, that no man could ever love a woman who is angry. And that fear is a great source of trouble to me, for it means that in certain fundamental ways I have not changed at all.

I would like to be cold and clear and selfish, to demand satisfaction for my needs, to compel respect rather than affection. And yet there are moments, and perhaps there always will be, when I fall back upon the old cop-outs. Why should I trouble to win a chess game or a political argument when it is so much easier to lose charmingly? Why should I work when my husband can support me, why should I be a human being when I can get away with being a child?

Woman's Liberation is finally only personal. It is hard to fight an enemy who has outposts in your head.

There are few American men or women who are not aware of the presence and the goals of the women's movement. As Sally Kempton pointed out, those most involved are the women who have felt a personal need for change. It is not a matter of changing one person but of changing the values within society.

What women are most likely to feel oppressed? In large part, they are highly educated women already in the work force, who are seeking opportunities for advancement in their careers. Thus, the women's movement is largely middle-class in its composition. Blue-collar housewives have probably formed some opinion about women's rights, but it is not clear how opening employment opportunities for educated women will effect the lives of women with little education. If work is not a central life interest of blue-collar husbands, is there any reason for it to become so among blue-collar wives? Most blue-collar women who enter the labor forces have short-term jobs and it is unlikely that these jobs will be part of a lifelong career.

Some women choose to rally against the women's movement while others are genuinely disinterested. Women of all classes who prefer to remain traditional wives and mothers are largely unchanged by the movement, as illustrated by this letter to the editor of the Cleveland Press.

I'm sick and tired of hearing about male chauvinism and women's liberation. I have never felt fettered by just being me. During World War II, I worked in a defense plant. I was paid by incentive, as were the men. I earned what they did, by putting out the product, as they did.

My husband has never treated me as an acquired object. He is always aiding, unasked, where needed.

I like having doors held for me and being helped with my coat. I enjoy compliments on a good meal — that he provided. I like being "Mrs." I feel fulfilled, I am sure many, like me, would like to keep it this way.

In the following article, Brooke Shearer describes the life style of a disinterested woman, who happens to be the wife of the mayor of a large city.

At Home with Mama Perk

Brooke Shearer

It is late Monday morning, about 11 o'clock. Somewhere in the recesses of Gracie Mansion, overlooking the East River in New York, Mary Lindsay is probably just donning a subdued Halston shirtdress and pumps to attend a charity luncheon, or perhaps consulting with a cook for that evening's dinner party. Inside the brown clapboard

From *Cleveland Magazine*, vol. 2, no. 7, pp. 63–64. Reprinted by permission.

house which is Cleveland's current equivalent to the New York mayor's residence, and which is within smelling distance of the Cuyahoga, Lucille Perk is also busy — Monday is laundry day. Her husband left for work in the city's chauffered limousine hours ago. Now, dressed in a billowy flowered muumuu and rubber shower thongs, her bangs scotch-taped to her forehead, she is ironing the mayor's shirts.

"You can let his being away from home get to you," she says evenly, "but if you have a strong, loving family, he will always come back to you.... No, I don't let the thought of other women worry me. Ralph says that you can either play around or stay in politics and that you can't do both. Sure, it's true that some women throw themselves on politicians, and it is quite a temptation. . . . Women from all over love to give Ralph huge hugs. I say to them, 'It's all right for you to hug him where I can see you, but don't you get out of my sight.' "

It comes off as a statement of sheer faith from a woman whose husband hasn't been home for dinner since 1962, the year Ralph became county auditor. She'll be up past midnight, when he comes home to catch his usual six hours of sleep, but her customary eight hours will stretch past the time His Honor awakens to fix himself coffee and oatmeal.

"I can't say we see any less of Ralph at election time. He does the same thing all year round," says Lucille with the good nature that is by now anticipated. An outsider might expect an incumbent mayor's wife to see *more* of him as an election draws near, guessing she wouldn't escape the grind of aching smiles and tireless, if veneered, good grace. But Lucille knows she won't perfume the limousine's back seat as it zigzags around the city, and the mayor breaks only to sip something nonalcoholic, shake some hands, say some words and prepare for the next stop.

Of course, Mrs. Perk will attend a few requisite affairs — the big fundraising dinner, the party picnic, the traditional City Club debate in the last days of the campaign — with the mayor's chauffeur and confidant, Edward Harrison, and his bodyguard, Jim McHugh, at her side to engage her in genial chit-chat, steer her toward the crackers and cheese, and see that she doesn't develop any sudden interest in international politics. But before the handshaking gets heavy, the mayor will deliver a small tribute to his wife,

the keystone of his moral superstructure, as a preface to her cheerful parting wave. By the time her corsage begins to wilt, she will be on her way back to solid home turf, East 49th Street, the neighborhood that saw her grow up, sneak off to go dancing with Ralph Perk, another neighborhood kid, marry, and become the Italian-American Civic Club's 1965 Italian Mother of the Year.

And it seems that simply fulfilling that weighty testimonial is perhaps, in the end, the best Lucille could possibly do to please her husband — not to mention his middle and lower-middle class ethnic constituents. Certain of the mayor's cohorts, aides and media contacts are unabashedly relieved that she acts out her role on the political sidelines. As one veteran observer puts it, "Lucille knows her place. If she tried to thrust herself into Ralph's political life, she'd be a real liability. He keeps her in the background." But there's no denying that Mrs. Perk has in her very own way been a tangible help to her husband's career, ever since he entered politics three days after their wedding in May, 1940, by running, successfully, for Republican precinct committeeman. Witty banter and righteous speechifying are better left to Ralph's more articulate and adept supporters, but as Mama Perk and the darling of the Southeast Ladies' Bowling League, Lucille's performance is unsurpassed.

While plump, smiling women cluster around the mayor, keeping him well supplied with friendly kisses and kielbasa, they are warmed by the knowledge that plump, smiling Lucille is at home scrubbing the kitchen floor. Although Ralph's annual paycheck has increased from his councilmanic days to $35,000, the mayor's wife still does her own cooking, cleaning and shopping. She has part-time help, but when the cleaning lady broke her wrist this summer, Lucille didn't bother to look for a temporary replacement. And the only noticeable additions to the two-story four-bedroom Perk household in 27 years have been a color TV, a dishwasher, a refrigerator equipped with a gadget that spews ice cubes, and the air-conditioner that keeps out the noise and smell of the industrial Flats and Interstate 77, which runs some 400 yards from the porch of 3421 East 49th St.

Often, though, the housekeeping has to be squeezed in among other pressing matters. Lucille, having excelled in typing and shorthand at nearby South High School, still finds herself acting as an unpaid short-order secretary. And the phone! Even after Ralph became a councilman in 1953, he insisted on having his home number listed in the directory (883-3866) so voters could call with support, suggestions or gripes. And innumerable unseen advisers insist on talking, if not to the man himself, then at least to his wife, who has been within reach of a phone for the last 30 years. Resting her elbows on a crocheted tablecloth, she sighs, "People call to complain about bills, taxes, schoolteachers, issues they hear about on radio or TV. I get everything." She rubs her orange-frosted fingernails and glances at the pile of unironed shirts. "The callers let me do my wash on Monday, but the rest of the week the phone really rings. Sometimes I can hardly get supper started.

They even call as late as eleven or twelve at night."

She lights a filterless Kool and reaches for the iron again, a signal for the phone to begin ringing. Lucille answers in a voice so low it is barely audible, and moments later hangs up, shaking her head. "That woman calls me at least once a day, often three times. She has been calling me for a year and a half, and I don't know her name. She just called because she has company, and she wants to impress them by talking to the mayor's wife."

In the days when Ralph was first elected mayor, some of the non-congratulatory calls — especially the inevitable threats — would have Lucille nervously dialing City Hall for her husband's guidance and soothing words. But he has helped her calm down, so that now she can better relax and take things in her stride. Her eldest child, Virginia, explains that at first "Mom was in awe of the publicity and having a police guard. It was as though she was watching herself on a screen, but now things are back to normal."

Neither have things changed much for the three Perk sons still at home. Michael, 19, is retarded and works during the day at the Sheltered Workshop on the West Side. Seventeen-year-old Allen is now a senior at Central Catholic High School, where cross-country track keeps him busy. Ricky is 13, and has a *Cleveland Press* paper route to help earn his $100 tuition at nearby Our Lady of Lourdes grammar school, from which both his mother and father graduated.

Six months after their father was elected, two of the other five children, fraternal twins Kenneth and Thomas, now 24, dropped out of school to run for state representative from the eleventh and ninth districts, respectively. But they were both unsuccessful, and Ralph J. Perk, Jr., known as Rocky in Ward 15 where he grew up and is now, at 28, councilman, remains the only junior politician in the family. Kenneth now works as a computer programmer and attends Cleveland State University night classes; his twin, Thomas, goes to what his mother described as "some college in Washington, D.C." — actually, Northern Virginia Community College. Lucille's only daughter, Mrs. Virginia Bowers, is 29 and the mother of three.

Beyond attending phone, family and friends, and doing the weekly shopping at Gillombardo's Bi-Rite Super Market on Broadway, Mrs. Perk involves herself in club activities. She belongs to an Italian Club, through which she went to Europe in 1971 with her youngest son, Ricky. Then there is the Our Lady of Lourdes Parent-Teachers Union, and the Mission Circle of the Knights of Columbus, which raises money for Catholic missions in Africa. The most informal is the Birthday Club, seven women who get together several times a year just to go out, celebrate, and exchange gifts.

By now everyone knows Lucille is a bowler, especially after the story that circulated last December, after Ralph went solo to a White House dinner, that she had refused the Nixons' invitation rather than miss her regular Wednesday night game at the Golden Pin Recreation Center. "Actually," she counters, "Ralph forgot to tell me about the invitation until the day before, and I didn't have time to get my hair done or buy a new dress or get someone to care for the kids. Besides, I had a lot of Christmas shopping to do."

The story may have made her an overnight media heroine to her bowling team, sponsored by Vic's Florist Shop, and her bowling league, of which she is treasurer, but it has also made her more conscious of her game. "They tease me, so I have picked up my average and work at my game. I have to concentrate to improve now, whereas before I used to go bowling to relax."

Indeed, she finds little enough time for relaxation; with so many demands on her attention the days are for her crammed full. She manages to visit Ricco's Beauty Salon on Fleet Avenue only by juggling chores and appointments, and TV viewing is restricted to the 11 o'clock news. She flips quickly through the newspaper, skimming columns for articles or photos featuring her husband. Of national issues, and especially Watergate, she claims to be only vaguely aware. "I don't watch the hearings. I don't understand why they have to spend so much time reading their testimony. Why can't they speak from the heart? . . . I don't know what it is about. I cannot believe there has been such a big deal made about spying. All I know is they've bugged somebody."

On another day, Lucille is helping her sister, Kate Burger, in the kitchen. Kate and Lucille grew up with nine other brothers and sisters in the family of Salvatore Gagliardi, known in the neighborhood as Sam the Barber. And today Kate has taken a day off from her job as head cashier at Catalano's Stop & Shop in Mayfield Heights to prepare a barbecue supper in honor of a visiting out-of-town cousin. Lucille is lifting stuffed chicken breasts, manicotti, potato salad and lemon cream pie out of the refrigerator. In the adjoining den the 6 o'clock news flashes on the TV screen. A niece cries out over her shoulder, "Look who's on TV. It's Uncle Ralph!" Lucille moves quickly out of the kitchen and is immediately absorbed in the image on the set. Her eyes do not leave the screen until the mayor's face blurs into that of the sports announcer. Then she turns around and goes back into the kitchen.

SOCIALIZATION AND THE FAMILY: THE LIFE CYCLE AND LIFE STYLES

In the course of their lives, all Americans share some common experiences. They were all born, all will die, and in between most will attend school, marry, have children, and face middle age and then old age. Factors such as race, sex, and social class have a profound effect on the way Americans will encounter these phases of their lives. The very rich may be born in the best hospitals, attend elite private schools, have lavish weddings, hire governesses for their children, and eventually may retire to a warm sunny climate while the very poor may be born at home or in a county hospital, attend overcrowded public schools, be married by a justice of the peace or in a small neighborhood church, struggle to raise their children, and when old live on a small pension or in an overcrowded home for the aged.

Given that there is an American life style, there is a typically American life cycle. Most Americans experience a transition from family life to school life, from dependency to adulthood, from high school or college to the world of work, from single to married status, from childlessness to parenthood, from middle years to retirement, and from old age to death. Major stages in life are common to all Americans with our cultural norms establishing such points as (approximate) ages at which children enter school, leave secondary education, and attain the rights of adulthood.

When infants are born, they have no social skills. They cannot care for themselves, speak the language, or even understand what is going on around them. Their parents teach them these basic skills through the process of socialization. It is through this basic socialization that a child begins to develop a self-concept and a feeling of autonomy. By the time children are six years of age, most are ready for school where they learn further skills, interact with a wide variety of children, and develop a life that is not fully dependent upon their parents. Socialization goes beyond merely inculcating children with basic skills; and throughout their lives, people continue to undergo this process.

At each new stage in the life cycle, individuals develop somewhat different concepts of themselves. Children see the world and themselves differently than do teenagers, and middle-aged people see themselves differently than do the aged. How much change really has occurred is a point of debate among behavioral scientists. Freudian psychologists see little change after the first six years of a child's life; the basic self is set by age six and although there can be some changes, it is all a result of the first years of socialization. To illustrate this view of development of self by analogy: you can fry it, poach it, or hard boil it, but any way you look at it, it is still an egg.

A second view is that people spend their lives trying to discover who they are and to resolve uncertainties about their self concepts. A basic part of life is searching for and accepting one's true identity. This resolution may not come until old age, if ever.*

The third view, held by most sociologists is that of constant change. In this view, there is no fixed or final self; rather, there is a self that is constantly changing with each socialization situation. Each new socialization experience is dependent upon what went on before and will change things for what happens afterwards.†

Up to the time of entry into school, children may have very little firsthand information about the diversity of life styles in America since their experiences were almost entirely shaped by their family and their

---

* See for example, Erik Erikson, *Identity: Youth and Crisis,* (New York: Norton, 1968).

† A specific discussion of these three perspectives may be found in Anselm Straus, *Mirrors and Masks* (San Francisco: Sociology Press, 1969).

family's race, social class, religion, and other factors.* Schools perform an important function by further initiating children into the American life style; it is here that they may have their first experiences with regimentation. They learn to follow orders from an impersonal authority, comply with routines, and are no longer the center of attention but just one of many children in the classroom. School not only teaches children basic language and mathematical skills but it also socializes them into the bureaucratic world within which all Americans function. School routines are generally much more rigid than the routines the child was used to at home. School also takes up a major part of a child's day and may present real change in a child's style of life. It is the first of many transitions that people will undergo in their lives.

* Children do learn something (although perhaps of a stereotypical nature) of the variety of American life styles through their exposure to the mass media. See for example Wilbur Schramm, Jack Lyle, and E. B. Parker, *Television in the Lives of our Children* (Stanford: Stanford University Press, 1961); Melvin De Fleur and Lois De Fleur, "The Relative Contribution of Television as a Learning Source for Children's Occupational Knowledge," *American Sociological Review* 32 (1967), pp. 777–789; and the United States Surgeon General's five volume report, *Television and Social Behavior* (Washington: USGPO, 1972).

Learning the Student Role: Kindergarten as Academic Boot Camp

Harry L. Gracey

INTRODUCTION

Education must be considered one of the major institutions of social life today. Along with the family and orga-

Reprinted by permission of Macmillan Publishing Co., Inc. from *Readings in Introductory Sociology* by Dennis Wrong and Harry Gracey. Copyright © 1972 by Macmillan Publishing Co., Inc.

nized religion, however, it is a "secondary institution," one in which people are prepared for life in society as it is presently organized. The main dimensions of modern life, that is, the nature of society as a whole, is determined principally by the "primary institutions," which today are the economy, the political system, and the military establishment. Education has been defined by sociologists, classical and contemporary, as an institution which serves society by socializing people into it through a formalized, standardized procedure. At the beginning of this century Emile Durkheim told student teachers at the University of Paris that education "consists of a methodical socialization of the younger generation." He went on to add:

It is the influence exercised by adult generations on those that are not ready for social life. Its objects is to arouse and to develop in the child a certain number of physical, intellectual, and moral states that are demanded of him by the political society as a whole and by the special milieu for which he is specifically destined. . . . To the egoistic and asocial being that has just been born, [society] must, as rapidly as possible, add another, capable of leading a moral and social life. Such is the work of education.[1]

The educational process, Durkheim said, "is above all the means by which society perpetually recreates the conditions of its very existence." [2] The contemporary educational sociologist, Wilbur Brookover, offers a similar formulation in his recent textbook definition of education:

Actually, therefore, in the broadest sense education is synonymous with socialization. It includes any social behavior that assists in the induction of the child into membership in the society or any behavior by which the society perpetuates itself through the next generation.[3]

The educational institution is, then, one of the ways in which society is perpetuated through the systematic socialization of the young, while the nature of the society which is being perpetuated — its organization and operation, its values, beliefs and ways of living — are determined by the primary institutions. The educational system, like other secondary institutions, *serves* the society which is *created* by the operation of the economy, the political system, and the military establishment.

Schools, the social organizations of the educational institution, are today for the most part large bureaucracies run by specially trained and certified people. There are few places left in modern societies where formal teaching and learning is carried on in small, isolated groups, like the rural, one-room schoolhouses of the last century. Schools are large, formal organizations which tend to be parts of larger organizations, local community School Districts. These School Districts are bureaucratically organized and their operations are supervised by state and local governments. In this context, as Brookover says:

the term education is used . . . to refer to a system of schools, in which specifically designated persons are expected to teach children and youth certain types of acceptable behavior. The school system becomes a . . . unit in the total social structure and is recognized by the members of the society as a separate social institution. Within this structure a portion of the total socialization process occurs.[4]

Education is the part of the socialization process which takes place in the schools; and these are, more and more today, bureaucracies within bureaucracies.

[1] Emile Durkheim, *Sociology and Education* (New York: The Free Press, 1956), pp. 71–72.

[2] Ibid., p. 123.

[3] Wilber Brookover, *The Sociology of Education* (New York: American Book Company, 1957), p. 4.

[4] Ibid., p. 6.

Kindergarten is generally conceived by educators as a year of preparation for school. It is thought of as a year in which small children, five or six years old, are prepared socially and emotionally for the academic learning which will take place over the next twelve years. It is expected that a foundation of behavior and attitudes will be laid in kindergarten on which the children can acquire the skills and knowledge they will be taught in the grades. A booklet prepared for parents by the staff of a suburban New York school system says that the kindergarten experience will stimulate the child's desire to learn and cultivate the skills he will need for learning in the rest of his school career. It claims that the child will find opportunities for physical growth, for satisfying his "need for self-expression," acquire some knowledge, and provide opportunities for creative activity. It concludes, "The most important benefit that your five-year-old will receive from kindergarten is the opportunity to live and grow happily and purposefully with others in a small society." The kindergarten teachers in one of the elementary schools in this community, one we shall call the Wilbur Wright School, said their goals were to see that the children "grew" in all ways: physically, of course, emotionally, socially, and academically. They said they wanted children to like school as a result of their kindergarten experiences and that they wanted them to learn to get along with others.

None of these goals, however, is unique to kindergarten; each of them is held to some extent by teachers in the other six grades at the Wright School. And growth would occur, but differently, even if the child did not attend school. The children already know how to get along with others, in their families and their play groups. The unique job of the kindergarten in the educational division of labor seems rather to be teaching children the student role. The student role is the repertoire of behavior and attitudes regarded by educators as appropriate to children in school. Observation in the kindergartens of the Wilbur Wright School revealed a great variety of activities through which children are shown and then drilled in the behavior and attitudes defined as appropriate for school and thereby induced to learn the role of student. Observations of the kindergartens and interviews with the teachers both pointed to the teaching and learning of classroom routines as the main element of the student role. The teachers expended most of their efforts, for the first half of the year at least, in training the children to follow the routines which teachers created. The children were, in a very real sense, *drilled* in tasks and activities created by the teachers for their own purposes and beginning and ending quite arbitrarily (from the child's point of view) at the command of the teacher. One teacher remarked that she hated September, because during the first month "everything has to be done rigidly, and repeatedly, until they know exactly what they're supposed to do." However, "by January," she said, "they know exactly what to do [during the day] and I don't have to be after them all the time." Classroom routines were introduced gradually from the beginning of the year in all the kindergartens, and the children were drilled in them as long as was necessary to achieve regular compliance. By the end of the school year, the successful kindergarten teacher has a well-organized group of children. They follow classroom routines automatically, having learned all the command signals and the expected responses to them. They have, in our terms, learned the student role. The following observation shows one such classroom operating at optimum organization on an afternoon late in May. It is the class of an experienced and respected kindergarten teacher.

At about 12:20 in the afternoon on a day in the last week of May, Edith Kerr leaves the teachers' room where she has been having lunch and walks to her classroom at the far end of the primary wing of Wright School. A group of five- and six-year-olds peers at her through the glass doors leading from the hall cloakroom to the play area outside. Entering her room, she straightens some material in the "book corner" of the room, arranges music on the piano, takes colored paper from her closet and places it on one of the shelves under the window. Her room is divided into a number of activity areas through the arrangement of furniture and play equipment. Two easels and a paint table near the door create a kind of passageway inside the room. A wedge-shaped area just inside the front door is made into a teacher's area by the placing of "her" things there: her desk, file, and piano. To the left is the book corner, marked off from the rest of the room by a puppet stage and a movable chalkboard. In it are a display rack of picture books, a record player, and a stack of children's records. To

the right of the entrance are the sink and clean-up area. Four large round tables with six chairs at each for the children are placed near the walls about halfway down the length of the room, two on each side, leaving a large open area in the center for group games, block building, and toy truck driving. Windows stretch down the length of both walls, starting about three feet from the floor and extending almost to the high ceilings. Under the windows are long shelves on which are kept all the toys, games, blocks, paper, paints and other equipment of the kindergarten. The left rear corner of the room is a play store with shelves, merchandise, and cash register; the right rear corner is a play kitchen with stove, sink, ironing board, and bassinette with baby dolls in it. This area is partly shielded from the rest of the room by a large standing display rack for posters and children's art work. A sandbox is found against the back wall between these two areas. The room is light, brightly colored and filled with things adults feel five- and six-year-olds will find interesting and pleasing.

At 12:25 Edith opens the outside door and admits the waiting children. They hang their sweaters on hooks outside the door and then go to the center of the room and arrange themselves in a semi-circle on the floor, facing the teacher's chair which she has placed in the center of the floor. Edith follows them in and sits in her chair checking attendance while waiting for the bell to ring. When she has finished attendance, which she takes by sight, she asks the children what the date is, what day and month it is, how many children are enrolled in the class, how many are present, and how many are absent.

The bell rings at 12:30 and the teacher puts away her attendance book. She introduces a visitor, who is sitting against the right wall taking notes, as someone who wants to learn about schools and children. She then goes to the back of the room and takes down a large chart labeled "Helping Hands." Bringing it to the center of the room, she tells the children it is time to change jobs. Each child is assigned some task on the chart by placing his name, lettered on a paper "hand," next to a picture signifying the task — e.g., a broom, a blackboard, a milk bottle, a flag, and a Bible. She asks the children who wants each of the jobs and rearranges their "hands" accordingly. Returning to her chair, Edith announces, "One person should tell us what happened to Mark." A girl raises her hand, and when called on says, "Mark fell and hit his head and had to go to the hospital." The teacher adds that Mark's mother had written saying he was in the hospital.

During this time the children have been interacting among themselves, as well as with Edith. Children have whispered to their neighbors, poked one another, made general comments to the group, waved to friends on the other side of the circle. None of this has been disruptive, and the teacher has ignored it for the most part. The children seem to know just how much of each kind of interaction is permitted — they may greet in a soft voice someone who sits next to them, for example, but may not shout greetings to a friend who sits across the circle, so they confine themselves to waving and remain well within understood limits.

At 12:35 two children arrive. Edith asks them why they are late and then sends them to join the circle on the floor. The other children vie with each other to tell the newcomers what happened to Mark. When this leads to a general disorder Edith asks, "Who has serious time?" The children become quiet and a girl raises her hand. Edith nods and the child gets a Bible and hands it to Edith. She reads the Twenty-third Psalm while the children sit quietly. Edith helps the child in charge begin reciting the Lord's Prayer, the other children follow along for the first unit of sounds, and then trail off as Edith finishes for them. Everyone stands and faces the American flag hung to the right of the door. Edith leads the pledge to the flag, with the children again following the familiar sounds as far as they remember them. Edith then asks the girl in charge what song she wants and the child replies, "My Country." Edith goes to the piano and plays "America," singing as the children follow her words.

Edith returns to her chair in the center of the room and the children sit again in the semi-circle on the floor. It is 12:40 when she tells the children, "Let's have boys' sharing time first." She calls the name of the first boy sitting on the end of the circle, and he comes up to her with a toy helicopter. He turns and holds it up for the other children to see. He says, "It's a helicopter." Edith asks, "What is it used for?" and he replies, "For the army. Carry men. For the war." Other children join in, "For shooting submarines." "To bring back men from space when they are in the ocean." Edith sends the boy back to the circle and asks the next boy if he has something. He replies "No" and she passes on to the next. He says "Yes" and brings a bird's nest to her. He holds it for the class to see, and the teacher asks, "What kind of bird made the nest?" The boy replies, "My friend says a rain bird made it." Edith asks what the nest is made of and different children reply, "mud," "leaves" and "sticks." There is also a bit of moss woven into the nest and Edith tries to describe it to the children. They, however, are more interested in seeing if anything is inside it, and Edith lets the boy carry it around the semi-circle showing the children its insides. Edith tells the children of some baby robins in a nest in her yard, and some of the children tell about baby birds they have seen. Some children are asking about a small object in the nest which they say looks like an egg, but all have seen the nest now and Edith calls on the next boy. A number of children say, "I know what Michael has, but I'm not telling." Michael brings a book to the teacher and then goes back to his place in the circle of children. Edith reads the last page of the book to the class. Some children tell of books which they have at home. Edith calls the next boy, and three children call out, "I know what David has." "He always has the same thing." "It's a bang-bang." David goes to his table and gets a box which he brings to Edith. He opens it and shows the teacher a scale-model of an old-fashioned dueling pistol. When David does not turn around to the class, Edith tells him, "Show it to the children," and he does. One child says, "Mr. Johnson [the principal] said no guns." Edith replies, "Yes, how many of you know that?" Most of the children in the circle raise their hands. She continues, "That you aren't supposed to bring

guns to school?" She calls the next boy on the circle and he brings two large toy soldiers to her which the children enthusiastically identify as being from "Babes in Toyland." The next boy brings an American flag to Edith and shows it to the class. She asks him what the stars and stripes stand for and admonishes him to treat it carefully. "Why should you treat it carefully?" she asks the boy. "Because it's our flag," he replies. She congratulates him, saying, "That's right."

"Show and Tell" lasted twenty minutes and during the last ten one girl in particular announced that she knew what each child called upon had to show. Edith asked her to be quiet each time she spoke out, but she was not content, continuing to offer her comment at each "show." Four children from other classes had come into the room to bring something from another teacher or to ask for something from Edith. Those with requests were asked to return later if the item wasn't readily available.

Edith now asks if any of the children told their mothers about their trip to the local zoo the previous day. Many children raise their hands. As Edith calls on them, they tell what they liked in the zoo. Some children cannot wait to be called on, and they call out things to the teacher, who asks them to be quiet. After a few of the animals are mentioned, one child says, "I liked the spooky house," and the others chime in to agree with him, some pantomiming fear and horror. Edith is puzzled, and asks what this was. When half the children try to tell her at once, she raises her hand for quiet, then calls on individual children. One says, "The house with nobody in it"; another, "The dark little house." Edith asks where it was in the zoo, but the children cannot describe its location in any way which she can understand. Edith makes some jokes but they involve adult abstractions which the children cannot grasp. The children have become quite noisy now, speaking out to make both relevant and irrelevant comments, and three little girls have become particularly assertive.

Edith gets up from her seat at 1:10 and goes to the book corner, where she puts a record on the player. As it begins a story about the trip to the zoo, she returns to the circle and asks the children to go sit at the tables. She divides them among the tables in such a way as to indicate that they don't have regular seats. When the children are all seated at the four tables, five or six to a table, the teacher asks, "Who wants to be the first one?" One of the noisy girls comes to the center of the room. The voice on the record is giving directions for imitating an ostrich and the girl follows them, walking around the center of the room holding her ankles with her hands. Edith replays the record, and all the children, table by table, imitate ostriches down the center of the room and back. Edith removes her shoes and shows that she can be an ostrich too. This is apparently a familiar game, for a number of children are calling out, "Can we have the crab?" Edith asks one of the children to do a crab "so we can all remember how," and then plays the part of the record with music for imitating crabs by. The children from the first table line up across the room, hands and feet on the floor and faces pointing

toward the ceiling. After they have "walked" down the room and back in this posture they sit at their table and the children of the next table play "crab." The children love this; they run from their tables, dance about on the floor waiting for their turns and are generally exuberant. Children ask for the "inch worm" and the game is played again with the children squirming down the floor. As a conclusion Edith shows them a new animal imitation, the "lame dog." The children all hobble down the floor, table by table, to the accompaniment of the record.

At 1:30 Edith has the children line up in the center of the room; she says, "Table one, line up in front of me," and children ask, "What are we going to do?" Then she moves a few steps to the side and says, "Table two over here, line up next to table one," and more children ask, "What for?" She does this for table three and table four and each time the children ask, "Why, what are we going to do?" When the children are lined up in four lines of five each, spaced so that they are not touching one another, Edith puts on a new record leads the class in calisthenics, to the accompaniment of the record. The children just jump around every which way in their places instead of doing the exercises, and by the time the record is finished, Edith, the only one following it, seems exhausted. She is apparently adopting the President's new "Physical Fitness" program in her classroom.

At 1:35 Edith pulls her chair to the easels and calls the children to sit on the floor in front of her, table by table. When they are all seated she asks,

"What are you going to do for work-time today?" Different children raise their hands and tell Edith what they are going to draw. Most are going to make pictures of animals they saw in the zoo. Edith asks if they want to make pictures to send to Mark in the hospital, and the children agree to this. Edith gives drawing paper to the children, calling them to her one by one. After getting a piece of paper, the children go to the crayon box on the right-hand shelves, select a number of colors, and go to the tables, where they begin drawing. Edith is again trying to quiet the perpetually talking girls. She keeps two of them standing by her so they won't disrupt the others. She asks them, "Why do you feel you have to talk all the time," and then scolds them for not listening to her. Then she sends them to their tables to draw.

Most of the children are drawing at their tables, sitting or kneeling in their chairs. They are all working very industriously and, engrossed in their work, very quietly. Three girls have chosen to paint at the easels, and having donned their smocks, they are busily mixing colors and intently applying them to their pictures. If the children at the tables are primitives and neo-realists in their animal depictions, these girls at the easels are the class abstract-expressionists, with their broad-stroked, colorful paintings.

Edith asks of the children generally, "What color should I make the cover of Mark's book?" Brown and green are suggested by some children "because Mark likes them." The other children are puzzled as to just what is going on and ask, "What book?" or "What does she mean?" Edith explains what she thought was clear to them already, that they are all going to put their pictures together in a "book" to be sent to Mark. She goes to a small table in the play-kitchen corner and tells the children to bring her their pictures when they are finished and she will write their message for Mark on them.

By 1:50 most children have finished their pictures and given them to Edith. She talks with some of them as she ties the bundle of pictures together — answering questions, listening, carrying on conversations. The children are playing in various parts of the room with toys, games and blocks which they have taken off the shelves. They also move from table to table examining each other's pictures, offering compliments and suggestions. Three girls at a table are cutting up colored paper for a collage. Another girl is walking about the room in a pair of high heels with a woman's purse over her arm. Three boys are playing in the center of the room with the large block set, with which they are building walk-ways and walking on them. Edith is very much concerned about their safety and comes over a number of times to fuss over them. Two or three other boys are driving trucks around the center of the room, and mild altercations occur when they drive through the block constructions. Some boys and girls are playing at the toy store, two girls are serving "tea" in the play kitchen and one is washing a doll baby. Two boys have elected to clean the room, and with large sponges they wash the movable blackboard, the puppet stage, and then begin on the tables. They run into resistance from the children who are working with construction toys on the tables and do not want to dismantle their structures. The class is like a room full of bees, each intent on pursuing some activity, occasionally bumping into one another, but just veering off in another direction without serious altercation. At 2:05 the custodian arrives pushing a cart loaded with half-pint milk containers. He places a tray of cartons on the counter next to the sink, then leaves. His coming and going is unnoticed in the room (as, incidentally, is the presence of the observer, who is completely ignored by the children for the entire afternoon).

At 2:15 Edith walks to the entrance of the room, switches off the lights, and sits at the piano and plays. The children begin spontaneously singing the song, which is "Clean up, clean up. Everybody clean up." Edith walks around the room supervising the cleanup. Some children put their toys, the blocks, puzzles, games, and so on back on their shelves under the windows. The children making a collage keep right on working. A child from another class comes in to borrow the 45-rpm adaptor for the record player. At more urging from Edith the rest of the children shelve their toys and work. The children are sitting around their tables now and Edith asks, "What record would you like to hear while you have your milk?" There is some confusion and no general consensus, so Edith drops the subject and begins to call the children, table by table, to come get their milk. "Table one," she says, and the five children come to the sink, wash their hands and dry them, pick up a carton of milk and a straw, and take

it back to their table. Two talking girls wander about the room interfering with the children getting their milk and Edith calls out to them to "settle down." As the children sit many of them call out to Edith the name of the record they want to hear. When all the children are seated at tables with milk, Edith plays one of these records called "Bozo and the Birds" and shows the children pictures in a book which go with the record. The record recites, and the book shows the adventures of a clown, Bozo, as he walks through a woods meeting many different kinds of birds who, of course, display the characteristics of many kinds of people or, more accurately, different stereotypes. As children finish their milk they take blankets or pads from the shelves under the windows and lie on them in the center of the room, where Edith sits on her chair showing the pictures. By 2:30 half the class is lying on the floor on their blankets, the record is still playing and the teacher is turning the pages of the book. The child who came in previously returns the 45-rpm adaptor, and one of the kindergarteners tells Edith what the boy's name is and where he lives.

The record ends at 2:40. Edith says, "Children, down on your blankets." All the class is lying on blankets now. Edith refuses to answer the various questions individual children put to her because, she tells them, "it's rest time now." Instead she talks very softly about what they will do tomorrow. They are going to work with clay, she says. The children lie quietly and listen. One of the boys raises his hand and when called on tells Edith, "The animals in the zoo looked so hungry yesterday." Edith asks the children what they think about this and a number try to volunteer opinions, but Edith accepts only those offered in a "rest-time tone," that is, softly and quietly. After a brief discussion of animal feeding, Edith calls the names of the two children on milk detail and has them collect empty milk cartons from the tables and return them to the tray. She asks the two children on clean-up detail to clean up the room. Then she gets up from her chair and goes to the door to turn on the lights. At this signal the children all get up from the floor and return their blankets and pads to the shelf. It is raining (the reason for no outside play this afternoon) and cars driven by mothers clog the school drive and line up along the street. One of the talkative little girls comes over to Edith and pointing out the window says, "Mrs. Kerr, see my mother in the new Cadillac?"

At 2:50 Edith sits at the piano and plays. The children sit on the floor in the center of the room and sing. They have a repertoire of songs about animals, including one in which each child sings a refrain alone. They know these by heart and sing along through the ringing of the 2:55 bell. When the song is finished, Edith gets up and coming to the group says, "Okay, rhyming words to get your coats today." The children raise their hands and as Edith calls on them, they tell her two rhyming words, after which they are allowed to go into the hall to get their coats and sweaters. They return to the room with these and sit at their tables. At 2:59 Edith says, "When you have your coats on, you may line up at the door." Half of the children go to the door and stand in a long line. When the

three o'clock bell rings, Edith returns to the piano and plays. The children sing a song called "Goodbye," after which Edith sends them out.

TRAINING FOR LEARNING AND FOR LIFE

The day in kindergarten at Wright School illustrates both the content of the student role as it has been learned by these children and the processes by which the teacher has brought about this learning, or, "taught" them the student role. The children have learned to go through routines and to follow orders with unquestioning obedience, even when these make no sense to them. They have been disciplined to do as they are told by an authoritative person without significant protest. Edith has developed this discipline in the children by creating and enforcing a rigid social structure in the classroom through which she effectively controls the behavior of most of the children for most of the school day. The "living with others in a small society" which the school pamphlet tells parents is the most important thing the children will learn in kindergarten can be seen now in its operational meaning, which is learning to live by the routines imposed by the school. This learning appears to be the principal content of the student role.

Children who submit to school-imposed discipline and come to identify with it so that being a "good student" comes to be an important part of their developing identities, *become* the good students by the school's definitions. Those who submit to the routines of the school but do not come to identify with them will be adequate students who find the more important part of their identities elsewhere, such as in the play group outside school. Children who refuse to submit to the school routines are rebels, who become known as "bad students" and often "problem children" in the school, for they do not learn the academic curriculum and their behavior is often disruptive in the classroom. Today schools engage clinical psychologists in part to help teachers deal with such children.

In looking at Edith's kindergarten at Wright School, it is interesting to ask how the children learn this role of student — come to accept school-imposed routines — and what, exactly, it involves in terms of behavior and attitudes. The most prominent features of the classroom are its physical and social structures. The room is carefully furnished and arranged in ways adults feel will interest children. The play store and play kitchen in the back of the room, for example, imply that children are interested in mimicking these activities of the adult world. The only space left for the children to create something of their own is the empty center of the room, and the materials at their disposal are the blocks, whose use causes anxiety on the part of the teacher. The room, being carefully organized physically by the adults, leaves little room for the creation of physical organization on the part of the children.

The social structure created by Edith is a far more powerful and subtle force for fitting the children to the student role. This structure is established by the very rigid and tightly controlled set of rituals and routines through which the children are put during the day. There is first the rigid "locating procedure" in which the children are asked to find themselves in terms of the month, date, day of the week, and the number of the class who are present and absent. This puts them solidly in the real world as defined by adults. The day is then divided into six periods whose activties are for the most part determined by the teacher. In Edith's kindergarten the children went through Serious Time, which opens the school day, Sharing Time, Play Time (which in clear weather would be spent outside), Work Time, Clean-up Time, after which they have their milk, and Rest Time, after which they go home. The teacher has programmed activities for each of these Times.

Occasionally the class is allowed limited discretion to choose between proffered activities, such as stories or records, but original ideas for activities are never solicited from them. Opportunity for free individual action is open only once in the day, during the part of Work Time left after the general class assignment has been completed (on the day reported the class assignment was drawing animal pictures for the absent Mark). Spontaneous interests or observations from the children are never developed by the teacher. It seems that her schedule just does not allow room for developing such unplanned events. During Sharing Time, for example, the child who brought a bird's nest told Edith, in reply to her question of what kind of bird made it, "My friend say it's a rain bird." Edith does not think to ask about this bird, probably because the answer is "childish," that is, not given in accepted adult categories of birds. The children then express great interest in an object in the nest, but the teacher ignores this interest, probably because the object is uninteresting to her. The soldiers from "Babes in Toyland" strike a responsive note in the children, but this is not used for a discussion of any kind. The soldiers are treated in the same way as objects which bring little interest from the children. Finally, at the end of Sharing Time the child-world of perception literally erupts in the class with the recollection of "the spooky house" at the zoo. Apparently this made more of an impression on the children than did any of the animals, but Edith is unable to make any sense of it for herself. The tightly imposed order of the class begins to break down as the children discover a universe of discourse of their own and begin talking excitedly with one another. The teacher is effectively excluded from this child's world of perception and for a moment she fails to dominate the classroom situation. She reasserts control, however, by taking the children to the next activity she has planned for the day. It seems never to have occurred to Edith that there might be a meaningful learning experience for the children in re-creating the "spooky house" in the classroom. It seems fair to say that this would have offered an exercise in spontaneous self-expression and an opportunity for real creativity on the part of the children. Instead, they are taken through a canned animal imitation procedure, an activity which they apparently enjoy, but which is also imposed upon them rather than created by them.

While children's perceptions of the world and opportunities for genuine spontaneity and creativity are being systematically eliminated from the kindergarten, unquestioned obedience to authority and rote learning of meaningless material are being encouraged. When the children are called to line up in the center of the room they ask "Why?" and "What for?" as they are in the very process of complying. They have learned to go smoothly through a programmed day, regardless of whether parts of the program make any sense to them or not. Here the student role involves what might be called "doing what you're told and never mind why." Activities which might "make sense" to the children are effectively ruled out and they are forced or induced to participate in activities which may be "senseless," such as the calisthenics.

At the same time the children are being taught by rote meaningless sounds in the ritual oaths and songs, such as the Lord's Prayer, the Pledge to the Flag, and "America." As they go through the grades children learn more and more of the sounds of these ritual oaths, but the fact that they have often learned meaningless sounds rather than meaningful statements is shown when they are asked to write these out in the sixth grade; they write them as groups of sounds rather than as a series of words, according to the sixth grade teachers at Wright School. Probably much learning in the elementary grades is of this character, that is, having no intrinsic meaning to the children, but rather being tasks inexplicably required of them by authoritative adults. Listening to sixth grade children read social studies reports, for example, in which they have copied material from encyclopedias about a particular country, an observer often gets the feeling that he is watching an activity which has no intrinsic meaning for the child. The child who reads, "Switzerland grows wheat and cows and grass and makes a lot of cheese" knows the dictionary meaning of each of these words but may very well have no conception at all of this "thing" called Switzerland. He is simply carrying out a task assigned by the teacher *because* it is assigned, and this may be its only "meaning" for him.

Another type of learning which takes place in kindergarten is seen in children who take advantage of the "holes" in the adult social structure to create activities of their own, during Work Time or out-of-doors during Play Time. Here the children are learning to carve out a small world of their own within the world created by adults. They very quickly learn that if they keep within permissible limits of noise and action they can play much as they please. Small groups of children formed during the year in Edith's kindergarten who played together at these times, developing semi-independent little groups in which they created their own worlds in the interstices of the adult-imposed physical and social world. These groups remind the sociological observer very much of the so-called "informal groups" which adults develop in factories and offices of large bureaucracies.[5] Here too, within au-

thoritatively imposed social organizations people find "holes" to create little sub-worlds which support informal, friendly, nonofficial behavior. Forming and participating in such groups seems to be as much part of the student role as it is of the role of bureaucrat.

The kindergarten has been conceived of here as the year in which children are prepared for their schooling by learning the role of student. In the classrooms of the rest of the school grades, the children will be asked to submit to systems and routines imposed by the teachers and the curriculum. The days will be much like those of kindergarten, except that academic subjects will be substituted for the activities of the kindergarten. Once out of the school system, young adults will more than likely find themselves working in large-scale bureaucratic organizations, perhaps on the assembly line in the factory, perhaps in the paper routines of the white collar occupations, where they will be required to submit to rigid routines imposed by "the company" which may make little sense to them. Those who can operate well in this situation will be successful bureaucratic functionaries. Kindergarten, therefore, can be seen as preparing children not only for participation in the bureaucratic organization of large modern school systems, but also for the large-scale occupational bureaucracies of modern society.

[5] See, for example, Peter M. Blau, *Bureaucracy in Modern Society* (New York: Random House, 1956), Chapter 3.

As children become older, they become more independent. School, although still a major part of their lives, becomes a predictable routine activity. Friendship patterns develop and peer influence becomes a major factor shaping their life style. Peer values are often at odds with parental values and teenagers especially become aware of conflicting sets of expectations between friends and parents. High school becomes the locus of a variety of age-graded subcultures, each with their own set of central life interests. Burton Clark notes that within high school there are subcultures of delinquents, academically oriented students, and students who are just out to have a good time. *

Adolescents today are viewed as a major market and a whole industry has developed around them. This was equally true when Bennett Berger wrote the following article. American marketing exploits this age group, selling youth oriented clothing, cosmetics, food, and music — items that are important symbols of youthful life style. A common interest in such commodities helps to create and maintain a subculture whose main interest may be in the consumption of these products. Autonomy is furthered as teenagers become independent consumers (and as they become workers at part-time jobs to help pay for their purchases). Although marketing practices are geared toward a particular age group, youth culture is emulated by those younger and older. It is not uncommon to find eleven-year-olds going steady or thirty-year-olds affecting the clothing, mannerisms, and the interests of people fifteen years younger.

Not all adolescents adopt youth-centered life styles. Some perpetuate the life styles of their families. Many middle-class adolescents concentrate on good grades and the reward of professional occupations. Blue collar adolescents may perpetuate their parents' life styles by enrolling in vocational training courses. Although the deviance inherent in youthful subculture does not turn most adolescents into delinquents, some do develop a deviant life style that leads to a life-long career as a law violator. Whether through identification with youth culture, a vocation, academic achievement, or deviance, adolescents are in a crucial stage of their life style. It is during this period that people begin to face the prospect of choosing among alternative life styles.

* Burton Clark, *Educating the Expert Society* (San Francisco: Chandler, 1962), pp. 202–243. Many high school students are not members of any student subculture or may be involved in subcultures that are unrelated to school.

On the Youthfulness of Youth Cultures

Bennett Berger

For more than twenty years now, sociologists have increasingly concerned themselves with the study of "youth culture." Talcott Parsons' very influential article, published in 1942, with its much quoted characterization of youth culture as "more or less specifically irresponsible" has become a point of departure for an enormous amount of research and discussion on youth.[1] Parsons' characterization of youth culture, however, inadvertently suggests that whatever it is that constitutes the "youthfulness" of youth culture may have less to do with chronology than with culture. To characterize youth culture as "irresponsible," to describe its "dominant note" as "having a good time," or to say that it has "a strong tendency to develop in directions which are on the borderline of parental approval or beyond the pale..." clearly excludes those large numbers of adolescents who have had no important experiences in anything remotely resembling such a milieu. Many, and probably most young persons, while they experience the classic problems of adolescent psychology described in the textbooks, seem to make their way through to full adult status without grave cultural damage, without getting into serious trouble, without a dominating hedonism, and without generalized attitudes of rebellion toward parents and the world.

These introductory remarks are not intended as a preface to a "defense" of adolescents against the bad press they have been getting in recent years. I intend, rather, to suggest (1) that "youth culture" should refer to the normative systems of *youthful* persons, not necessarily of young ones; (2) that whatever it is that is normatively distinctive about youth culture is probably not characteristic of all or even most adolescents, and therefore is not attributable solely or even primarily to chronological age; and hence (3) that the definitive characteristics of youth culture are relevant to groups other than the age-grade we call adolescence.

While Frederick Elkin and William A. Westley believe they have exploded "The Myth of Adolescent Culture"[2] with survey data showing that a sample of middle-class adolescents comply with the norms of deferred gratification and get along well with their parents, without hostility or resentful feelings that "they don't understand us," what they have actually done is present evidence that certain adolescents do not share the norms of youth culture. By thus implicitly distinguishing the facts of chronological age from the phenomena of culture, they invite

A revised version of a talk given at the annual banquet of Alpha Kappa Delta, Purdue University, May 19, 1961. From *Social Research,* vol. 30, no. 3 (Autumn 1963), pp. 319–342. Reprinted by permission.

[1] "Age and Sex in the Social Structure of the United States," *American Sociological Review* (October 1942).

[2] *American Sociological Review* (December 1955).

us to consider the hypothesis that what we are in the habit of calling "youth culture" is the creature of some young and some not so young persons. If hedonism or irresponsibility or rebelliousness are essential features of youth culture, then it may be unwise as well as unnecessary to restrict the consideration of youth culture to adolescent groups, for these qualities are dominant in several adult groups as well — and the fact that this is so is probably not fortuitous. I am suggesting, in short, that youthfulness, like fertility, is unequally distributed in society, and that it cannot be explained satisfactorily by reference to chronological age. This essay is an attempt to explore theoretically some of the conceptual problems that an investigation of the structure and dynamics of youth culture will encounter.

YOUTH CULTURES OF THE YOUNG

Two Images of the Young: "Teenagers" and "American Youth" [3]

To begin, let us note a recurrent ambiguity in the images with which American adolescents are usually conceived. The "teen-agers" are those who, in Dwight McDonald's apt ethnography,[4] spend an hour a day on the phone and two hours a day listening to disc jockeys; they are the most assiduous moviegoers in the nation, preferring especially films about monsters,

rock and roll music, and teenagers like themselves. More than half of them "go steady" and practice the sexual or protosexual intimacies implied by that phrase. The boys are very car-conscious, and spend a good deal of their leisure reading about, talking about, and working on hot rods. They read *Mad*, and its imitators *Frenzy* and *Thimk;* they don't read the Bible, don't go to church regularly, are bored by politics, ignorant of the Bill of Rights, and so on.

If one shifts one's perspective for a moment, and begins to think of the adolescents who populate Boy Scouts, Youth for Christ, 4-H clubs, Future Farmers of America, and other groups of this sort, McDonald's characterization (based in part upon the results of Remmers' work[5] and Eugene Gilbert's youth polls) has a rather jarring effect. These doers of good deeds and raisers of prize pigs and winners of essay contests on Americanism are clearly not the adolescents who have seemingly become a permanent "problem" on the American scene.

"Teen-agers" and "American youth" are, of course, images, and as such, they may be little more than stereotypes; we may, and likely will, find rock and rollers belonging to the FFA. But it is also likely that these distinctive images express differences in social and demographic variables like class, region, ethnicity, and religion. In any case, the initial distinction between "teen-agers" (the adolescents publicly worried about) and "Ameri-

---

[3] I am indebted to Barbara Williams for the terms of this distinction.

[4] See his two-part "profile" of Eugent Gilbert in *The New Yorker* (November 22 and 29, 1958).

[5] H. H. Remmers and D. H. Radler, *The American Teenager* (Indianapolis, Ind.: Bobbs-Merrill, 1957).

can youth" (the adolescents publicly praised) does suggest the useful banality that some adolescents engage in ways of life essentially at odds with or indifferent to the official desires and expectations of "responsible" adults, whereas other adolescents comply with or actively pursue the aims and expectations set down for youth by adult authorities.

Transitional Stage and Subculture

One way of extending this distinction between types of adolescents is to contrast two ideas that are frequently used in psychological and sociological discussions of youth. Most standard works on the social psychology of adolescence speak of it as a "transitional stage" between childhood and adulthood, a period ridden with conflicts and tensions stemming partly from an acceleration in the individual's physical and cultural growth but also from the age-grading norms of our society that withhold from adolescents most of the opportunities, rights, and responsibilities of adults. When sexual desires are more powerful than they will ever again be, sexual opportunities are fewest; obedience and submission are asked of adolescents at precisely the time when their strength, energy, and desire for autonomy are ascendant; responsible participation in the major institutions are denied them at the moment when their interest in the world has been poignantly awakened.[6]

---

[6] These are a few of the "discontinuities" made famous by Ruth Benedict in her celebrated article "Continuities and Discontinuities in Cultural Conditioning," *Psychiatry*

Such tensions, generated by our age-grading system and exacerbated by a decline in parental control and a world in a state of permanent crisis, are frequently cited as the major source of adolescent difficulty. Conceived as a "transitional stage," adolescence is a very difficult period: it is described (and caricatured) as a time of awkwardness and embarrassment and trouble and pain — something to be got out of as soon as possible by orienting oneself primarily toward eventual membership in "the" adult community.

For many years, apparently, this conception of adolescence as a difficult transitional stage was the dominant framework in which adolescent problems were discussed. In 1944, Caroline Tryon could write, "we have a tendency to disregard or to minimize the educational significance of the child's experience in his peer group." [7] Today this statement strikes the eye as incredible; certainly it is no longer true. Very few contemporary discussions of youth fail to mention the significance of the involvement of young persons in their own age-graded peer groups. The emphasis in these discussions is quite different from that in discussions of adolescence as a transitional stage; the stress is on the orientation of adolescents to their peers. From this per-

---

(May 1938). See also Kingsley Davis' related discussions: "Adolescence and the Social Structure," *The Annals* (November 1944) and "The Sociology of Parent-Youth Conflict," *American Sociological Review* (August 1940).

[7] "The Adolescent Peer Culture," *43rd Yearbook of the National Society for the Study of Education* (Chicago, Ill.: University of Chicago Press, 1944).

spective emerged the idea of an adolescent subculture[8] as a relatively autonomous "way of life," controlled internally by a system of norms and sanctions largely antithetical or indifferent to that offered by parents, teachers, and clergymen — the official representatives of the adult world.

By itself, the subcultural view of adolescence suggests nothing *inherently* transitional, except in the sense that all experience is transitional, representing, as it does, the passage from what one was to what one is about to become. But oddly enough, it is precisely the concern for consequences that is missing from the conventional usage of the concept of "transitional stage." To suggest that adolescence is a "stage they go through" — something that adolescents "grow out of" — is to violate much of what we know about the permanent effects of socialized experience. It is as if adolescence, frequently designated "the formative years," formed nothing, but was simply a rather uncomfortable period of biding one's time until the advent of one's twenty-first birthday or until one's graduation from school induced the adult world to extend a symbolic invitation to join it. But if the transitional view of adolescence minimizes the permanent influences of adolescent experience, the subcultural view exag-

gerates the degree to which adolescents create an insulated, autonomous milieu in which they may with impunity practice their alleged antiadult rites. *No large scale study of high school youth, for example, has successfully demonstrated the existence of a really deviant system of norms which governs adolescent life.*[9]

The point I wish to stress here, however, is that our understanding of the varieties of adolescent experience depends heavily upon whether adolescent group life is primarily conceived in the vocabulary of developmental psychology as a transitional stage, or in the sociological vocabulary of subcultures. Conceived as a transitional stage, adolescence is typically described in ways which make its termination devoutly to be wished by adolescents as well as adults.[10] When adolescence is discussed in subcultural terms, no such implication is carried with it. The literature on youth culture most consistently describes it in terms of hedonistic, irresponsible, and "expressive" behavior. Although most adults may believe that this behavior and the norms that constrain it *ought* to be terminated at the

---

[8] This is not the place to go into the problems of applying the concept of "subculture," developed on ethnic models, to age groups. See J. Milton Yinger, "Contraculture and Subculture," *American Sociological Review* (October 1960) and my own comments in "Adolescence and Beyond" (p. 43).

[9] The most ambitious attempts to demonstrate this is James Coleman's *The Adolescent Society* (Glencoe, Ill.: The Free Press, 1961).

[10] The characterization of adolescence as "the awkward age" full of pimples and embarrassment has validity only for the very early teen years. It may merely be a survival from a period when adolescents were completely dependent and completely subordinate. Today, high school students, free and relatively affluent, frequently feel that they are currently living what they expect will be the best years of their lives.

threshold of adulthood, it is by no means self-evident that a group which can "get away with" a life of hedonism (read: fun, kicks), irresponsibility (read: freedom, license), and expressiveness (read: immediate gratification, ego enhancement) may be expected to terminate this life easily in exchange for the mixed blessings of recognition as adults, and the sometimes baleful responsibilities that this entails. Objectively — and at the very least, adolescence is a portion of a life lived — *formative* attitudes and orientations, talents and commitments, capacities *and incapacities* develop that affect adolescents' various modes of adaptation into adult worlds, which more or less facilitate or obstruct their eventual recruitment into a specific adult milieu. If the child is father to the man, an understanding of the varieties of experience adolescents undergo, the varieties of milieux they touch, should contribute to the understanding of the kind of adults they are likely to become — and *not* become.

Chronological Age and Youthfulness

Before attempting to describe the groups that might fit the categories of "teen-agers" and "American youth," and the groups that might be usefully analyzed with the concepts of "transitional stage" and "subculture," I wish to make explicit one more distinction alluded to earlier which is conceptually parallel to the two sets of distinctions I have already made. To say that youthfulness is far from perfectly correlated with chronological age is to imply that some adolescents are more

youthful than others. Once the distinction is made, we can speak categorically of youthful young men, unyouthful young men, youthful old men, and unyouthful old men. This fourfold classification suggests, perhaps oversharply, that chronological age and the culture–personality variables associated with it may be analytically separated. To render the distinction fruitful, however, it is necessary to specify what is meant by youthfulness. It seems wise to approach this problem indirectly, by contrasting youthfulness with the relative lack of it in "American youth."

In this connection, let me again draw attention to *The Vanishing Adolescent* in which Edgar Friedenberg argues that adolescence as a stormy decade of identity-seeking and as a distinctive stage of human development is disappearing in the United States largely as a result of premature socialization primarily in the high schools. Without replacing my earlier discussion of Friedenberg's thesis, we *can* say that we have all known adolescents of the kind about which he is concerned. They do well enough in school, are "well adjusted," popular with their peers, have few great conflicts with their parents or other authorities, and in general have few if any serious quarrels with the value system into which they are being socialized or with the institutions representing these values. Grant this image some validity; then let us ask, In what sense are these young persons youthful? Certainly they are young and probably inexperienced in the affairs of the world. But adolescents who respond docilely to the expectations of school authorities, who accept as legitimate the limits imposed upon them by their parents,[11] who engage in the activities that are deemed appropriate by adult authorities, are more aptly described as going through the final phase of their pre-adult socialization, as junior grown-ups, rather than as incarnations of youthfulness. For when, in common usage, we describe persons as "youthful," we mean not primarily that they are obviously young, and hence relatively naive and inexperienced; we mean that they tend to manifest certain qualities in their behavior, and that although these qualities do seem to be empirically *associated* with tender years, they are not *exclusively* age-graded.

Regardless of chronological age, youthful persons tend to be impulsive, spontaneous, energetic, exploratory, venturesome, and vivacious; they tend to be candid, colorful, blunt in speech (having not acquired the skill and habit of dissmulation); they are often irreverent, frequently disrespectful, extreme, immoderate, they know no golden mean; they are "action seekers"[12] rather than seekers of stable routine. They joke a lot; the play motif dominates much of their activity, which they tend to transform into games,

even in the most apparently unpropitious of circumstances. Lacking caution and judiciousness, they tend to throw themselves with full passion and sexually alert intensity into those activities that promise thrills and excitement, which they tend to pursue with little regard for consequences.

Notice that these are primarily the qualities of persons, not roles, and certainly not rationalized bureaucratic roles — although they may become quasi-institutionalized as "deviant" roles. Notice too that they are all very active — one might say erotic. When abstracted from behavior and made conscious, qualities such as these assert themselves on *ideological* grounds. When, that is, they take on the character of moral imperatives, we can properly speak of a system of subcultural norms.[13] Such norms underlie the content of youth culture. Clearly, they are dangerous. From the perspective of the major institutions of social order, youthfulness is excess; it is implicit or incipient disorder; for society, it is a "problem" that requires handling, control, cooperation, or channeling in socially approved directions.

Society has at its disposal a great armory of means to control this implicit threat of disorder. I mean not the police and the courts or the more informal sanctions wielded by parents and other authorities; I mean the com-

---

[11] There actually are many adolescents who respond to questionnaires with the opinion that teenagers are not really old enough to smoke or drink or in general to know what is good for them.

[12] The term "action seeker" is taken from Herbert Gans' characterization of some working-class Bostonians. See his *The Urban Villagers* (New York: The Free Press of Glencoe, 1962).

[13] For modern formulations of this theology, see Norman Brown, *Life Against Death* (New York: Random House, 1960); Herbert Marcuse, *Eros and Civilization* (Boston, Mass.: Beacon, 1959) and Paul Goodman, *Growing up Absurd,* (New York: Random House, 1960).

munity youth center, the chaperoned dance, organized sports, school-sponsored extracurricular clubs, and the junior auxiliaries of business, religious, fraternal and veterans' associations — for adults have learned that adolescents will frequently accept from their peers the same norms they may reject from adults. But the effectiveness of these organizational weapons in coping with youth varies with the location of particular youths in the social structure. Where, for example, adult leadership is poor and community facilities limited, as in urban slums and certain new suburbs; or where sudden discontinuities in style of life create inter-generation tensions and anxieties and disqualify parents as models worthy of emulation and respect, as frequently occurs in immigrant or highly mobile families; or where failure or anticipated failure in academic competition leaves the failed with the perception of a bleak future and with no approved alternative sources of self-respect, as frequently occurs among ethnic and working-class boys in schools dominated by middle-class norms — where these and other early experiences of incipient social disaffection can mobilize ideological supports and some degree of structural insulation from the major institutions, there we are likely to find fertile ground in which the seeds of youthful excess and disorder can grow, and, eventually, bear the exotic flower called "youth culture."

Varieties of Youth Culture

The flower has many blooms; the varieties of youth culture are as wide as the variety of cultural contexts and opportunity systems offered by a pluralistic society. At its broadest and most innocuous, the youth cultures of the young touch the fringes of what is called "teen-age culture": popular songs, rock and roll, disc jockeys, juke boxes, portable phonographs, movie stars, dating, and romantic love; hot rods, motorcycles, drag racing, and sports cars, panty raids and water fights, drive-in hamburgers and clandestine drinking, football games, basketball games, dances and parties, and clubs and cliques, and lovers' lanes. At its delinquent extreme, youth culture is black leather jackets, gang rumbles and switch blades, malicious mischief, and joy riding in stolen cars. Politically, it is expressed in sit-ins, freedom rides, peace marches, and folk songs; it is jazz at Newport, vacations at Fort Lauderdale — and their attendant riots. And it is also bohemians and beatniks and beards and hipsters, and coffee house desperadoes plotting everything from literary magazines to assaults on the House Committee on Un-American Activities.[14]

I intend by this apparently formless catalogue of symbols to suggest how wide a variety of group styles and expressions the youth cultures of the young include. Intimations[15] of youth

[14] For a very similar formulation, see David Matza, "Subterranean Traditions of Youth," *The Annals* (November 1961) in which Matza argues that radicalism, bohemianism, and delinquency are the three basic forms which subterranean traditions (that is, subcultures) of youth take.
[15] I say "intimations" because "teen-age culture" is what David Matza calls a "conventionalized version" of what I would call a genuine youth culture.

culture will be found more frequently among "teen-agers" than
among "American youth," more frequently among "conflict" and "retreatist" delinquent gangs than among
the "rational" criminal delinquents,[16]
more among "bohemian" and "collegiate" undergraduates than among
academically or vocationally oriented
college students,[17] and more among
politically militant and extreme student groups than among the student
adherents of "moderate" sentiment
within the two major political parties.
The wide social spectrum represented
by these groups should reassure the
skeptic that I have no ideological axes
to grind; few of those prone to moral
judgments of youth could unambiguously approve or disapprove of *all* of
these groups at the same time. But
what delinquents and bohemians and
campus radicals and even some high
school hot rodders and college fraternity boys have in common is, I am
suggesting, their youthfulness, that is,
their tendency to behave in patterned
ways normatively hedonistic, irresponsible, and expressive.

In spite of the wide variety of dissimilar forms in which it is expressed,
it seems reasonable and useful — and
also more objective — initially to designate this normative behavior as
"youthful" (rather than, say, "deviant" or "delinquent" or "alienated,"
although it may *become* these) because it is in large part the autonomous creature of subsocieties of the
recalcitrant young. However, as I have
suggested above and will argue at
some length below, it is also selected
from, supported by, and modeled after
a long cultural tradition, nourished by
several contemporary subcultures of
adults, and is hence in principle viable
into adulthood and beyond. The youth
cultures of the young man are an adaptive response by *some* adolescents to
problems presented to them by their
parent society and culture (for example, contradictions or imbalances in
norms, blockage of opportunity, inade-
quately defined roles, ambiguities of
age-grading, the prospect of meaningless work), and *the forms they take in
specific groups reflect a choice from
traditions available to them.* To see the
matter this way takes account of both
the autonomous character of the subculture and its linkage to important
traditions which antedate it. The significance of the adjective in the term
"youth culture," however, rests not in
the fact that many of its participants
are young, but in the fact that their
selective interaction with one another,
under the difficult conditions generated
by our age-grading norms and in contexts that limit the exercise of adult
supervision and control, may sustain
a set of more or less counter-norms
which encourage and support, however
ambivalently, a pattern of behavior at
odds with the official norms of the culture in which it is located, but *adaptive* in the sense that it can provide —
not just temporarily — a more or less
viable way of life.

[16] See Richard Cloward and Lloyd Ohlin,
Delinquency and Opportunity, (Glencoe,
Ill.: The Free Press, 1960) for a discussion
of these types of gangs.

[17] See the typology of college student
orientations in Martin A. Trow and Burton
Clark, "The Organizational Context," in
College Peer Groups, T. M. Newcomb and
E. K. Wilson, eds. (Chicago, Ill.: Aldine,
1966).

ADULT YOUTH CULTURES

The Preservation of Youth Culture: Its Links with the Adult World

Earlier, I criticized the usage of the concept of "transitional stage" because it did not sufficiently specify the differential impact of adolescent experience upon subsequent careers. We already know that adolescents eventually become adults; but we do not know much about the ways in which variations in adolescent experience affect subsequent adult adaptations. The concept of "transitional stage" is often employed largely as a palliative for society's functional problems of recruiting and integrating youth into adult worlds: if it's merely "a stage they're going through," then adults need not frankly confront the problems their behavior raises, because, after all, "they'll grow out of it."

Most of them, it is true, do grow out of it, and the fact that they do is testimony not only to the power of adult agencies of socialization but to the vulnerability to co-optation of "teen-age culture" — to its lack of resources to sustain it in crisis and insulate it from attack.[18] But some do not or cannot grow out of it. What becomes of

[18] It is this lack which distinguishes "teen-age culture" from more genuine subcultures such as ethnic communities, delinquent gangs in urban slums, and bohemias. Ethnic communities frequently have a full blown institutional structure to shield its members from the society's encroachments; delinquent gangs emphasize the inviolability of "turf" for good sociological reason; bohemias are usually ecological communities as well as subcultures; and even political radicals have, at the very least, a strong ideology to sustain them. Teen-agers have very little.

those young persons whose "youthful rebelliousness" turns out to be not "a stage they're going through," but a series of subculturally rewarding experiences that subjectively validate their initial opposition to or irritation with the official demands of adults? And what becomes of those whose participation in political, delinquent, and bohemian forms of youth culture leaves permanent stigmata that render them permanently visible to a henceforth skeptical and suspicious world? Delinquency statistics, the beatnik craze (and its successor, the hippie movement), student militance and riots suggest that for substantial numbers (how many, no one knows) adolescence is not simply an awkward but benign transitional stage, and it is these facts to which we refer when we speak of youth and their growing up as a "social problem." To the extent that we can conceive of growing up as a *career* (and in this psychoanalytical age it is not difficult to do so), "*not growing up*" (that is, the preservation of the essential features of youth culture in later life) can also be considered as a career. Although there is a certain joylessness in the idea of "maturity" (identified, as it is, with sober responsibilities and solemn commitments), there are relatively few niches in the adult social structure where "youthfulness" does not receive severe negative sanctions, and those adolescents whose peer group experience has developed in them incapacities for growing up or perhaps even conscientious objections to it may be expected to gravitate toward those niches.

Those adolescents whose youthful attributes are weakest — for example, those studied by Elkin and Westley,

the prematurely socialized type described by Friedenberg, and the bulk
of adolescents only superficially involved in teenage culture — will probably have the least difficulty in making
the transition to the typical adult
careers offered in a highly industrialized, bureaucratized society. On the
other hand, those in whom youthful
attributes are strong will have the
greatest difficulty in making those sacrifices of youthfulness that most executive and professional and other prestigious adult careers require.

What kinds of adult occupations and
milieu are likely to reward or at least
tolerate youthfulness, and thus normatively support an attempt not to
grow up or an inability to grow up?
If it is true that some adolescents are
more youthful than others, it is also
true that some adults are more youthful than others, and it is likely that
some of the important forces that sustain youthfulness in those who are no
longer young may be found in the
norms of the occupations they choose
(or which choose them) and in the
milieu that those norms help create.[19]
What are some of these types of occupations?

YOUTHFUL CAREERS

I submit the following short list for
illustrative purposes. My best hope is
that it will be taken as suggestive of

one way of theoretically linking the
content of adolescent youth cultures
with important subterranean or deviant traditions in the adult world, and
hence of linking certain kinds of youthful experience in the adolescent milieu
with the subsequent taking up of adult
careers.

Bohemian business: By bohemian
businessmen, I mean the proprietors or
managers of small enterprises that cater
to the needs, tastes, and desires of bohemians. These enterprises range all
the way from those that are central to
bohemian subcultures (espresso coffee
houses, small art galleries, sandal and
leather shops, pottery shops, jewelry
shops, and so on) to other marginal
businesses serving other markets as
well ("art" theaters, paperback bookstores, small night clubs specializing in
modern jazz, accessory and specialty
shops for women, and so on). Wherever
a "deviant" community exists (in this
case a bohemian community), a business community is likely to exist to
supply the wants that symbolize and
define its deviance — in a sense anal-
ogous to that in which organized crime
is symbiotically interrelated with government, law enforcement agencies, and
parts of the legitimate business community. Bohemian business enterprise
is one of the relatively few types of careers available to persons who, having
had their basic orientations to the
world shaped by experience in an adolescent subculture, have developed
trained incapacities for pursuing more
conventional kinds of business or professional or "bourgeois" careers — although the ironic and economically
"reactionary" character of bohemian
enterprise is that it gives its entrepreneurs the status of shopkeeper.

[19] Statuses other than occupational ones,
of course, may also help sustain youthfulness: bachelor, divorcé(e), student, for example. Periodicals such as *Esquire* and
Playboy are apparently directed at youthful adult audiences, and an analysis of their
readers might provide evidence of youthful
adult statuses.

But their status as shopkeepers is less important and less revealing than the fact that they are likely to be bohemians. Bohemian businessmen, that is, are more like their customers than like other small businessmen. Even in their strictly economic capacities, bohemian businessmen are likely to reflect the habits of their customers. They may, for example, be expected to keep irregular hours, to open their shops late in the day and remain open late in the evening. Located primarily in the "Latin quarter" of large cities or near university campuses, they frequently take long summer vacations or move their shops to summer resorts of the "art colony" type. They are not likely to keep rigorous books and their prices are frequently not standardized — sometimes because their wares are not. Often, they do not have a primarily commercial or instrumental orientation to what they sell, but rather an expressive one.[20] Dealing mainly in beauty — in esthetic objects or experience — they are not likely to think of themselves primarily as businessmen, but either as craftsmen or as esthetic functionaries performing services for the community of avant-garde good taste. However they think of themselves, bohemian businessmen (recruited largely from the student bohemian world of craftsmen, failed or insufficiently talented artists, and hangers-on and camp followers of the

cultural avant-garde) live in a milieu that tolerates and rewards a youthful adaptation to the world. Bohemian business offers a moderately viable niche in the adult world for those unable or unwilling to grow out of youth culture.

Perhaps an *image* of a viable niche in the world would be a more accurate statement. For it is, of course, true that the actual opportunities for a successful career in bohemian business are probably not very good. Although it is a theoretically open milieu, the rate of business failure is high, and the population of bohemia is probably not large enough to support the commercial enterprises of very many of those young persons who are more or less successfully resisting or evading middle-class socialization. Nevertheless, the image of an adult bohemian life is culturally fertile and ambiguously seductive to many. Bohemia is always newsworthy; its consistent coverage in the mass media, its consistent status as a "tourist attraction" means that it is of great interest to the vicarious lives of large numbers of people. For every core bohemian there are probably five fringe bohemians; for every fringe bohemian there are probably five "weekend bohemians"; and for every weekend bohemian there are probably scores of Walter Mittys each of whom might be secretly flattered to have one of his perhaps idiosyncratic habits labeled "bohemian" by a suspicious and surly neighbor. My point is simply that although full-time bohemianism as a career may not be viable very long for very many, its part-time or fantasy appeal is apparently much stronger than the actual opportunities it offers. But it is the existence of this appeal and

[20] An example: a customer walks into an "art mart" to purchase a teapot that goes with a set of china that the customer knows the shop stocks. With some hauteur, the proprietress informs the customer that she does not sell the teapot (although she sells all the other pieces in the set) because it is "poorly designed."

the ambiguous possibilities represented by it that enable it to serve for the youthful as a *milieu of orientation* tolerant of their behavior and to which they may look for permanent sustenance.

Show business: Many actors, singers, dancers, musicians, comedians, and other entertainers inhabit a world suffused by the myth of youth — a world in which grandmothers and grandfathers are noted for their sex appeal. The professional milieu of jazz musicians interpenetrates with the hip and bohemian varieties of youth culture, bonded by a common antipathy to "squares." Much like the jazz milieu, the world of the off-Broadway theater is heavily populated with aspiring actors and actresses, committed to their expressive art, who live on the fringe of bohemia. The celebrity world of Hollywood stars is, for public consumption at least, "La Dolce Vita," with its dominating motifs of sex, speed, alcohol, drugs, and perversion set in a context of luxury. Most of the "new" American comedians have come up from the dark basement clubs catering to bohemian-intellectual audiences into the bright glare of the legitimate stage and the TV studio to continue, somewhat diluted, their savage satires of the routine, the usual, the ordinary (that is, the "adult") — but now to the masochistic audience upon whose lives and opinions their material is based. Finally, teen-age pop singers, despite their ritual affirmation of God, Home, and Mother, and their pious promises to "continue their education" (directed, one supposes, at the parents of their admirers), create a professional image compounded of thinly disguised erotica and forlorn adolescent aliena-

tion, and, with the help of publicity, transform their slum or otherwise poverty-stricken backgrounds into a romantic determination to "be somebody." ("I want to become a really good actor instead of just a teen-age singer.")

That show business careers and similar occupations are in fact subject to much the same economic circumstances and bureaucratic controls as are other occupations, and that many show folk in fact live model middle-class lives are less important than the carefully nurtured Dionysian images of show business life, the persistent myth that careers are made "overnight," that its durable stars are ageless, and that "expressive" opportunities are offered by the public spotlight. Like other "creative" occupations, show business tends to be tolerant of irregular, spontaneous, unpredictable, exhibitionistic behavior — indeed, these are sometimes built into the very conditions of employment; more, show business expects this kind of behavior, and sometimes rewards it (in publicity, if nothing else — and publicity is seldom nothing else), at least among its stars. The hedonism and public irresponsibility of show business celebrities is disingenuously mythologized as "artistic temperament," suggesting that in those industries in which "creativity" is a basic commodity, perversities of other sorts must also be accepted: great beauty, great talent, great acclaim imply great vices. Thus Ava Gardner (a living Lady Brett) leaves a trail of discarded lovers across the bull rings of Spain; thus Maria Callas sails the Mediterranean in her Greek billionaire's yacht, telling the press at Riviera ports that they are "just friends"; thus

Ingrid Bergman conceives an illegitimate child on a volcanic Aegean island to the merely temporary dismay of her fans; thus Lana Turner rears a daughter who becomes the killer of her mother's gangster-lover; thus Eddie leaves Debbie for Liz and Liz leaves Eddie for Richard to a breathless watching world of column readers. Billie Holiday, the greatest jazz singer of the era, wasted from years of addiction to heroin, dies under guard in a hospital; idols of teenage girls get picked up for homosexuality; Dean Martin nurtures a lucrative public image built on a reputation for alcoholism, and the Frank Sinatra clique spread across the night life of the country their money, their liquor, their arrogance, and their talent to delight the press.

With this newsreel, I intended neither a documentation of the lurid nor a righteous cry of decadence but only a vivid suggestion that, manufactured or not, the image of show business careers exists in a milieu in which Dionysian excess has a long tradition and an honored place — a cautious and implicit honor (given its dependence on the whims of public opinion), but a milieu in which one neither loses face nor gets fired for scandalous behavior, a milieu in which the only bad publicity is no publicity at all. The extremes to which the public behavior of show business celebrities is constrained are, like that of gang delinquents, justified by the "rep" it engenders; the Dionysian comings and goings of middle-aged Frank Sinatra and his middle-aged friends are apparently regarded by the public with the same mock severity reserved for the pranks of teenagers. There is a normative kinship between the Dionysian motifs of the celebrity world of show biz and the hedonistic, expressive values of youth culture. A substantial part of the material content of youth culture is provided and sustained by the industries of mass entertainment and a large part of the entertainment business depends upon youth for its markets. Notice also that show business careers (and satellite show business careers such as disc jockeying and modeling) are virtually the *only* occupations or occupational images offered to adolescents in the pages of the "teen-age magazines." Like bohemian business, show business offers the image of a career to talented young people with trained incapacities for business or the bureaucratized professions. People with "artistic talent" have, according to legend, no "business sense," and show business careers are often said to require the kind of single-minded dedication that is unable even to imagine another kind of future. Like bohemian business, show business tolerates or rewards a youthful orientation to the world and offers the inducement of "romantic" or "glamorous" careers to those unable or unwilling to "grow up." [21]

Like bohemian business too, show business has an important component of vicarious appeal: there is a sense in

---

[21] Moss Hart, who should know, writes, "I would hazard a guess . . . that the temperament, the tantrums, and the utter childishness of theater people in general, is neither accidental nor a necessary weapon of their profession. It has nothing to do with so-called 'artistic temperament.' The explanation, I think, is a far simpler one. For the most part they are impaled in childhood like a fly in amber." *Act One* (New York: Random House, 1959).

which show business is everyman's vicarious business; there are probably thousands of Americans who sit in front of their TV sets quietly confident that they can sing as well, dance as well, tell jokes as well, ride a horse and sling a gun as well as those merely lucky ones on the screen. Show business not only involves the audience in the imaginary worlds it creates, it involves them vicariously in show business itself. This may be one of the reasons for the proverbial interest of Americans in the private lives of celebrities, and why professional, in-group banter and jokes about show business is virtually the only kind of esoteric humor of interest to out-groups. So that in addition to the promise of an actual career, show business, again like bohemia, offers an abundance of vicarious careers to the imperfectly socialized, and is thus, in an oddly perverse sense, functional to the extent that, by mollifying largely unfulfilled yearnings for a freer, more spontaneous, that is, more youthful life, it softens the tensions and frustrations engendered by socialization without internalization. Like the Horatio Alger myth, which told us that we too could succeed, the myths of the adult milieux which combine the exciting with the unsavory tell us that our lives need not be routine and colorless. The Alger myth succored an age of economic growth preoccupied with objective success; the youthfulness myth succors an age of psychology preoccupied with subjective "fulfillment."

Working-class occupations: Many of the adolescents whom I have called "youthful" — the high school rebels, the flouters of adult authority, the claimers of autonomy for adolescents — are likely to be of working-class background, especially ethnics, culturally "deprived," without much talent, who drop out of high school or do poorly in it, and are probably headed not for the glamorous careers I have mentioned but for the lower reaches of the manual labor force. Nevertheless, there are good reasons for believing that many working-class occupations and the subcultural norms associated with some of them are more supportive of youthful orientations than most middle-class occupations.

Several otherwise disparate intellectual traditions converge in their characterizations of working-class life in terms akin to my conception of youthfulness. The Marxist tradition, for example, confers upon labor the innocent dignity of useful work, the tragedy of exploitation and alienation, and the heroic mission of carrying within it the seeds of a bright and revolutionary future. Having nothing else to lose but their chains, the proletariat can take dramatic and passionate steps in its own interest. Sabotage, walk-outs, general strikes, the Marxist myth of a militant working class — bold, defiant, resentful of its oppressors, impatient to bring down the system of authority which victimizes it — strikingly partake of much the same spirit and imagery as rebellious adolescents vis-à-vis the world of adults. Both groups claim for themselves, in the strident tones characteristic of those without a parliamentary voice, autonomy: freedom from their illegitimate subordination to an authority they never chose, from consignment to a future they do not want.

There is also a literary tradition more than 150 years old that bestows upon laborers — especially rural laborers — greater energy, vitality, and sexuality than it does to the pale, thin, beardless, repressed pencil pushers who inhabit the offices of the world. In this literary tradition, workers are impulsive, strong, intuitive, passionate — capable of great anger and great tenderness; above all, they are, like adolescents, *personal*, largely alienated from and disgusted with the rationales and rationalizing of the impersonal bureaucratic world.

Paralleling these two romanticisms of working-class life is a third intellectual tradition that emphasizes the common values and long history of both the highest and the lowest classes of traditional Europe, which the despised, calculating minds of the *arriviste* middle class could never share: aristocrats and peasants share a tendency to violence, to alcoholic excesses, and to blood sports. This kinship between the highest and the lowest may be rather forced, but the peculiar combination of aristocratic and vulgar motifs, or elite and egalitarian themes which crystallize around a disdain for middle-class life has persisted for nearly 200 years.[22] The intellectual core of this tradition is the belief that the powers, privileges, and immunities of aristocratic life, and passion, desperation, and anarchy of life in the depths are both preferable to the calculated moderation and mediocrity inherent in bourgeois definitions of maturity and responsibility. Each extreme is, in its different way, transcendent; the middle class is forever earthbound. Translating this tradition into my own terms, the lower classes and the upper classes are more youthful than the middle classes.

Finally, recent empirical descriptions of working-class culture by sociologists lend considerable support to these romanticized versions of working-class life. These studies show a highly remarkable but generally unremarked upon similarity to standard descriptions of youth culture. Thus workers tend to be hedonistic, unable or unwilling to plan ahead or defer gratification; they are highly expressive rather than instrumental in their basic orientations, given to violent and extreme views, irrational, anti-intellectual, "person-centered" (rather than "role-centered"), and generally indifferent to their civic responsibilities.[23] Certain working-class occupations, then, especially *lower* ones, are likely to require much less in the way of sacrifice of youthfulness than most other occupations, and it should come as no sur-

[22] Especially strongly in the bohemian tradition from, say, Diderot to Norman Mailer. One is reminded that "teddy boys" affect the garments of Edwardian gentlemen and the manners of hoodlums. Leslie Fiedler has argued at some length that "highbrow" and "lowbrow" culture have more in common than either has with "middlebrow" culture. See his, "Both Ends Against the Middle," reprinted in *Mass Culture*, Rosenberg and White, eds. (Glencoe, Ill.: The Free Press, 1957).

[23] See, for example, William F. Whyte, *Street Corner Society* (Chicago, Ill.: University of Chicago Press, 1943); S. M. Miller and Frank Riessman, "The Working Class Subculture," *Social Problems* (Summer 1961); Richard Hoggart, *The Uses of Literacy* (London: Chatto and Windus, 1957); A. K. Cohen and H. M. Hodges, "Characteristics of the Lower-Blue-Collar Class," *Social Problems* (Spring 1963); Herbert J. Gans (note 13); and Seymour Martin Lipset, "Working Class Authoritarianism," in *Social Controversy*, W. Petersen and D. Matza, eds. (Belmont, Calif.: Wadsworth Publishing Co., 1963).

prise that recalcitrant youth without academic ability or usable deviant talents should gravitate toward these jobs.

CONCLUSION

What I have offered here is in a sense a conceptual model for the analysis of adolescent behavior and the youthful adult milieu to which, under certain conditions, it may lead. There are youthful occupations and milieu other than those I have described. I have not, for example, mentioned free lance art or the military or professional sports, nor have I mentioned several niches in the academic and intellectual worlds that support youthful orientations. But I think that by now my major point should be clear. I have tried to suggest that the successful socialization of children into the dominant value system is always problematic especially in pluralistic societies; that recalcitrance can be spotted early; and that what I have called youth culture begins when adolescent rebellion against dominant adult norms takes on ideological supports from existing deviant adult traditions. For many adolescents, of course, this is only "a stage they go through," and most of them eventually internalize or at least comply with the norms constrained on them by the major agencies of socialization. At the same time, it is important to recognize that many adolescents do not, that the experience of many in adolescent subcultures shapes their futures by incapacitating them for bureaucratic roles. Most of these, it is true, wind up at the lower end of the occupational hierarchy, especially those

who are unable to survive high school. But those who do survive and who are fortunate enough to discover the other face of their trained incapacities — in college or elsewhere — are uniquely enabled to take advantage of the few sheltered places a pluralistic society offers in its occupational structure which will permit them, as adults, to sustain that normative variation without which pluralism is emptied of its cultural meaning, leaving a society highly differentiated on the level of social structure but homogeneous on the level of culture.

With this analysis, I am not offering only a more differentiated view of socialization — substituting a frame of reference emphasizing conformity to milieu rather than to general cultural norms. I mean also to emphasize that groups differ in the extent to which they tolerate or encourage normative dissension, and the extent to which this is true is directly relevant to the *roles* that inveterate dissenters can find in the social structure. In groups which require a high degree of uniformity, dissenters are constrained to yield or to withdraw from active participation; but in groups that place a high value on innovation — and many youthful groups are prominent among these — dissenters are much more likely to be able to retain the privileges of active association.[24]

This analysis also bears upon the problem of adaptation to failure, and casts a little light on the ingenious way in which society provides for the com-

[24] For empirical data on this point, see Yrjo Littunen, "Deviance and Passivity in Radio Listener Groups," *Acta Sociologia* vol. 4, no. 3 (1959), pp. 17–26.

fort of its failures, while using its own failure to socialize some of its members as a way of easing the tensions engendered by its excessive success with others: those who are relegated to the bottom of the occupational heap, for example, are heir to a ready-made ideology, a myth that invidiously contrasts their own vigor, vitality, and authentic humanity with the repressions, the desk-boundness, and the futile status-seeking of the successful. Society uses the luckier ones too — those who are able to find loftier, more glamorous, youthful adult niches. These feed the vicarious appetites of the nation, and are living testimony to the bored, the alienated from work, and the otherwise vaguely dissatisfied that exciting careers *do* exist. And the definition of these careers as newsworthy by the mass media peculiarly fits them for the strategic role they play in the vicarious lives of others.

High school graduation (or termination) brings about another life style transition. Some enter college while others take a job. The teen years bring with them dating and courtship which for many will lead to marriage. Changes may occur in many spheres of life during this transition. Often weddings are timed to coincide with graduation from college or high school. Hence, people may enter several new roles at once, bringing a radical shift in life style for them. Still others choose to remain single, fostering a variety of single life styles (see the article by Susan Jacoby in Part 2). A whole book could deal with various phases of the life cycle and life style changes; in this section we can only illustrate some possible situations. All people do not enter or leave various roles at the same time. And some people never participate in youth culture; some people never become parents; and some people never retire.

It is not unusual for young adults to change their plans, disengaging themselves from bad career choices or members of the opposite sex who prove to be a disappointment. In American society it is expected that by the time people reach 25 or 30, if not before, they should have opted for a stable marriage and rearing a family. If parenthood turns out to be less enjoyable than was anticipated, one must make the best of it. Child rearing is held to be so important that it must not be approached casually by fathers and especially not by mothers. Hence parenthood entails a major commitment to a stable and socially approved life style for both adult men and women. Alice Rossi contends that parenthood is a crisis. It represents a point of radical change in life style, from autonomy to responsibility, from freedom of time and movement to restrictions that come from the tasks of child care. It means alternatives foregone in favor of an unalterable long-term commitment.

Transition
to Parenthood

Alice S. Rossi

THE PROBLEM

The central concern in this sociological analysis of parenthood will be with two closely related questions. (1) What is involved in the transition to parenthood: what must be learned and what readjustments of other role commitments must take place in order to move smoothly through the transition from a childless married state to parenthood? (2) What is the effect of parenthood on the adult: in what ways do parents, and in particular mothers, change as a result of their parental experiences?

To get a firmer conceptual handle on the problem, I shall first specify the stages in the development of the parental role and then explore several of the most salient features of the parental role by comparing it with the two other major adult social roles — the marital and work role. Throughout the discussion, special attention will be given to the social changes that have taken place during the past few decades which facilitate or complicate the transition to and the experience of parenthood among young American adults.

From *Journal of Marriage and the Family* (February 1968), pp. 26–39. Reprinted by permission.

FROM CHILD TO PARENT: AN EXAMPLE

What is unique about this perspective on parenthood is the focus on the adult parent rather than the child. Until quite recent years, concern in the behavioral sciences with the parent-child relationship has been confined almost exclusively to the child. Whether a psychological study such as Ferreira's on the influence of the pregnant woman's attitude to maternity upon postnatal behavior of the neonate,[1] Sears and Maccoby's survey of child-rearing practices,[2] or Brody's detailed observations of mothering,[3] the long tradition of studies of maternal deprivation[4] and more recently of maternal employment,[5] the child has been the center of attention. The design of such research has assumed that, if enough were known about what parents were like and what they in fact did in rearing their children, much of

[1] Antonio J. Ferreira, "The Pregnant Woman's Emotional Attitude and its Reflection on the Newborn," *American Journal of Orthopsychiatry,* 30 (1960), pp. 553–561.

[2] Robert Sears, E. Maccoby, and H. Levin, *Patterns of Child-Rearing,* Evanston, Illinois: Row, Peterson, 1957.

[3] Sylvia Brody, *Patterns of Mothering: Maternal Influences during Infancy,* New York: International Universities Press, 1956.

[4] Leon J. Yarrow, "Maternal Deprivation: Toward an Empirical and Conceptual Reevaluation," *Psychological Bulletin,* 58:6 (1961), pp. 459–490.

[5] F. Ivan Nye and L. W. Hoffman, *The Employed Mother in America,* Chicago: Rand McNally, 1963; Alice S. Rossi, "Equality Between the Sexes: An Immodest Proposal," *Daedalus,* 93:2 (1964), pp. 607–652.

the variation among children could be accounted for.[6]

The very different order of questions which emerge when the parent replaces the child as the primary focus of analytic attention can best be shown with an illustration. Let us take, as our example, the point Benedek makes that the child's need for mothering is *absolute* while the need of an adult woman to mother is *relative*.[7] From a concern for the child, this discrepancy in need leads to an analysis of the impact on the child of separation from the mother or inadequacy of mothering. Family systems that provide numerous adults to care for the young child can make up for this discrepancy in need between mother and child, which may be why ethnographic accounts give little

evidence of postpartum depression following childbirth in simpler societies. Yet our family system of isolated households, increasingly distant from kinswomen to assist in mothering, requires that new mothers shoulder total responsibility for the infant precisely for that stage of the child's life when his need for mothering is far in excess of the mother's need for the child.

From the perspective of the mother, the question has therefore become: what does maternity deprive her of? Are the intrinsic gratifications of maternity sufficient to compensate for shelving or reducing a woman's involvement in non-family interests and social roles? The literature on maternal deprivation cannot answer such questions, because the concept, even in the careful specification Yarrow has given it,[8] has never meant anything but the effect on the child of various kinds of insufficient mothering. Yet what has been seen as a failure or inadequacy of individual women may in fact be a failure of the society to provide institutionalized substitutes for the extended kin to assist in the care of infants and young children. It may be that the role requirements of maternity in the American family system extract too high a price of deprivation for young adult women reared with highly diversified interests and social expectations concerning adult life. Here, as at several points in the course of this paper, familiar problems take on a new and suggestive research dimension when the focus is on the parent rather than the child.

[6] The younger the child, the more was this the accepted view. It is only in recent years that research has paid any attention to the initiating role of the infant in the development of his attachment to maternal and other adult figures, as in Ainsworth's research which showed that infants become attached to the mother, not solely because she is instrumental in satisfying their primary visceral drives, but through a chain of behavioral interchange between the infant and the mother, thus supporting Bowlby's rejection of the secondary drive theory of the infant's ties to his mother. Mary D. Ainsworth, "Patterns of Attachment Behavior Shown by the Infant in Interaction with his Mother." *Merrill-Palmer Quarterly,* 10:1 (1964), pp. 51–58; John Bowlby, "The Nature of the Child's Tie to His Mother," *International Journal of Psychoanalysis,* 39 (1958), pp. 1–34.

[7] Theresa Benedek, "Parenthood as a Developmental Phase," *Journal of American Psychoanalytic Association,* 7:8 (1959), pp. 389–417.

[8] Yarrow, op. cit.

Background

Since it is a relatively recent development to focus on the parent side of the parent-child relationship, some preliminary attention to the emergence of this focus on parenthood is in order. Several developments in the behavioral sciences paved the way to this perspective. Of perhaps most importance have been the development of ego psychology and the problem of adaptation of Murray[9] and Hartmann,[10] in the interpersonal focus of Sullivan's psychoanalytic theories,[11] and the life cycle approach to identity of Erikson.[12] These have been fundamental to the growth of the human development perspective: that personality is not a stable given but a constantly changing phenomenon, that the individual changes along the life line as he lives through critical life experiences. The transition to parenthood, or the impact of parenthood upon the adult, is part of the heightened contemporary interest in adult socialization.

A second and related development has been the growing concern of behavioral scientists with crossing levels of analysis to adequately comprehend social and individual phenomena and to build theories appropriate to a complex social system. In the past, social anthropologists focused as purely on the level of prescriptive normative variables as psychologists had concentrated on intrapsychic processes at the individual level or sociologists on social-structural and institutional variables. These are adequate, perhaps, when societies are in a stable state of equilibrium and the social sciences were at early stages of conceptual development, but they become inadequate when the societies we study are undergoing rapid social change and we have an increasing amount of individual and subgroup variance to account for.

Psychology and anthropology were the first to join theoretical forces in their concern for the connections between culture and personality. The question of how culture is transmitted across the generations and finds its manifestations in the personality structure and social roles of the individual has brought renewed research attention to the primary institutions of the family and the schools, which provide the intermediary contexts through which culture is transmitted and built into personality structure.

It is no longer possible for a psychologist or a therapist to neglect the social environment of the individual subject or patient, nor is the "family" they are concerned with any longer confined to the family of origin, for current theory and therapy view the adult individual in the context of his current family of procreation. So too it is no longer possible for the sociologist to focus exclusively on the current family relationships of the individual. The incor-

---

[9] Henry A. Murray, *Explorations in Personality,* New York: Oxford University Press, 1938.

[10] Heinz Hartmann, *Ego Psychology and the Problem of Adaptation,* New York: International Universities Press, Inc., 1958.

[11] Patrick Mullahy (ed.), *The Contributions of Harry Stack Sullivan,* New York: Hermitage House, 1952.

[12] E. Erikson, "Identity and the Life Cycle: Selected Papers," *Psychological Issues,* 1 (1959), pp. 1–171.

poration of psychoanalytic theory into the informal, if not the formal, training of the sociologist has led to an increasing concern for the quality of relationships in the family of origin as determinants of the adult attitudes, values, and behavior which the sociologist studies.

Quite another tradition of research has led to the formulation of "normal crises of parenthood." "Crisis" research began with the studies of individuals undergoing traumatic experiences, such as that by Tyhurst on natural catastrophes,[13] Caplan on parental responses to premature births,[14] Lindemann on grief and bereavement,[15] and Janis on surgery.[16] In these studies attention was on differential response to stress — how and why individuals vary in the ease with which they coped with the stressful experience and achieved some reintegration. Sociological interest has been piqued as these studies were built upon by Rhona and Robert Rapoport's research on the honeymoon and the engagement as normal crises in the role transitions to marriage and their theoretical attempt to build a conceptual bridge between family and occupational

research from a "transition task" perspective.[17] LeMasters, Dyer, and Hobbs have each conducted studies of parenthood precisely as a crisis or disruptive event in family life.[18]

I think, however, that the time is now ripe to drop the concept of "normal crises" and to speak directly, instead, of the transition to and impact of parenthood. There is an uncomfortable incongruity in speaking of any crisis as normal. If the transition is achieved and if a successful reintegration of personality or social role occurs, then crisis is a misnomer. To confine attention to "normal crises" suggests, even if it is not logically implied, successful outcome, thus excluding from

[17] Rhona Rapoport, "Normal Crises, Family Structure and Mental Health," *Family Process*, 2:1 (1963), pp. 68–80; Rhona Rapoport and Robert Rapoport, "New Light on the Honeymoon," *Human Relations*, 17:1 (1964), pp. 33–56; Rhona Rapoport, "The Transition from Engagement to Marriage," *Acta Sociologica*, 8, fasc. 1–2 (1964), pp. 36–55; and Robert Rapoport and Rhona Rapoport, "Work and Family in Contemporary Society," *American Sociological Review*, 30:3 (1965), pp. 381–394.

[18] E. E. LeMasters, "Parenthood as Crisis," *Marriage and Family Living*, 19 (1957), pp. 352–355; Everett D. Dyer, "Parenthood as Crisis: A Re-Study," *Marriage and Family Living*, 25 (1963), pp. 196–201; and Daniel F. Hobbs, Jr., "Parenthood as Crisis: A Third Study," *Journal of Marriage and the Family*, 27:3 (1963), pp. 367–372. LeMasters and Dyer both report the first experience of parenthood involves extensive to severe crises in the lives of their young parent respondents. Hobbs's study does not show first parenthood to be a crisis experience, but this may be due to the fact that his couples have very young (seven-week-old) first babies and are therefore still experiencing the euphoric honeymoon stage of parenthood.

[13] J. Tyhurst, "Individual Reactions to Community Disaster," *American Journal of Psychiatry*, 107 (1951), pp. 764–769.

[14] G. Caplan, "Patterns of Parental Response to the Crisis of Premature Birth: A Preliminary Approach to Modifying the Mental Health Outcome," *Psychiatry*, 23 (1960), pp. 365–374.

[15] E. Lindemann, "Symptomatology and Management of Acute Grief," *American Journal of Psychiatry*, 101 (1944), pp. 141–148.

[16] Irving Janis, *Psychological Stress*, New York: John Wiley, 1958.

our analysis the deviant instances in which failure occurs.

Sociologists have been just as prone as psychologists to dichotomize normality and pathology. We have had one set of theories to deal with deviance, social problems, and conflict and quite another set in theoretical analyses of a normal system — whether a family or a society. In the latter case our theories seldom include categories to cover deviance, strain, dysfunction, or failure. Thus, Parsons and Bales's systems find "task-leaders" oriented to problem solution, but not instrumental leaders attempting to undercut or destroy the goal of the group, and "sociometric stars" who play a positive integrative function in cementing ties among group members, but not negatively expressive persons with hostile aims of reducing or destroying such intragroup ties.[19]

Parsons' analysis of the experience of parenthood as a step in maturation and personality growth does not allow for negative outcome. In this view either parents show little or no positive impact upon themselves of their parental role experiences, or they show a new level of maturity. Yet many women, whose interests and values made a congenial combination of wifehood and work role, may find that the addition of maternal responsibilities has the consequence of a fundamental and undesired change in both their relationships to their husbands and their involvements outside the family. Still other women, who might have kept a precarious hold on adequate functioning as adults had they *not* become parents, suffer severe retrogression with pregnancy and childbearing, because the reactivation of older unresolved conflicts with their own mothers is not favorably resolved but in fact leads to personality deterioration[20] and the

[19] Parsons' theoretical analysis of the family system builds directly on Bales's research on small groups. The latter are typically comprised of volunteers willing to attempt the single task put to the group. This positive orientation is most apt to yield the empirical discovery of "sociometric stars" and "task leaders," least apt to sensitize the researcher or theorist to the effect of hostile non-acceptance of the group task. Talcott Parsons and R. F. Bales, *Family, Socialization and Interaction Process,* New York: The Free Press, a division of the Macmillan Co., 1955.

Yet the same limited definition of the key variables is found in the important attempts by Straus to develop the theory that every social system, as every personality, requires a circumplex model with two independent axes of authority and support. His discussion and examples indicate a variable definition with limited range: support is defined as High (+) or Low (−), but

"low" covers both the absence of high support and the presence of negative support; there is love or neutrality in this system, but not hate. Applied to actual families, this groups destructive mothers with low-supportive mothers, much as the non-authoritarian pole on the Authoritarian Personality Scale includes both mere nonauthoritarians and vigorously anti-authoritarian personalities. Murray A. Straus, "Power and Support Structure of the Family in Relation to Socialization," *Journal of Marriage and the Family,* 26:3 (1964), pp. 318–326.

[20] Mabel Blake Cohen, "Personal Identity and Sexual Identity," *Psychiatry,* 29:1 (1966), pp. 1–14; Joseph C. Rheingold, *The Fear of Being a Woman: A Theory of Maternal Destructiveness,* New York: Grune and Stratton, 1964.

transmission of pathology to their children.[21]

Where cultural pressure is very great to assume a particular adult role, as it is for American women to bear and rear children, latent desire and psychological readiness for parenthood may often be at odds with manifest desire and actual ability to perform adequately as parents. Clinicians and therapists are aware, as perhaps many sociologists are not, that failure, hostility, and destructiveness are as much a part of the family system and the relationships among family members as success, love, and solidarity are.[22]

A conceptual system which can deal with both successful and unsuccessful role transitions, or positive and negative impact of parenthood upon adult men and women, is thus more powerful than one built to handle success but not failure or vice versa. For these reasons I have concluded that it is misleading and restrictive to perpetuate the use of the concept of "normal crisis." A more fruitful point of departure is to build upon the stage-task concepts of Erikson, viewing parenthood as a developmental stage, as Benedek[23] and Hill[24] have done, a perspective carried into the research of Raush, Goodrich, and Campbell[25] and of Rhona and Robert Rapoport[26] on adaptation to the early years of marriage and that of Cohen, Fearing et al.[27] on the adjustments involved in pregnancy.

ROLE CYCLE STAGES

A discussion of the impact of parenthood upon the parent will be assisted by two analytic devices. One is to follow a comparative approach, by asking in what basic structural ways the parental role differs from other primary adult roles. The marital and occupational roles will be used for this comparison. A second device is to specify the phases in the development of a social role. If the total life span may be said to have a cycle, each stage with its unique tasks, then by analogy a role may be said to have a cycle and each stage in that role cycle, to have its unique tasks and problems of adjustment. Four broad stages of a role cycle may be specified:

1. *Anticipatory stage.* All major adult roles have a long history of anticipatory training for them, since parental and school socialization of children is dedicated precisely to this task of producing the kind of competent adult valued by the culture. For our present purposes, however, a narrower conception of the anticipatory stage is preferable: the engagement period in

---

[21] Theodore Lidz, S. Fleck, and A. Cornelison, *Schizophrenia and the Family,* New York: International Universities Press, Inc., 1965; Rheingold, op. cit.

[22] Cf. the long review of studies Rheingold covers in his book on maternal destructiveness, op. cit.

[23] Benedek, op. cit.

[24] Reuben Hill and D. A. Hansen, "The Identification of a Conceptual Framework Utilized in Family Study," *Marriage and Family Living,* 22 (1960), pp. 299–311.

[25] Harold L. Raush, W. Goodrich, and J. D. Campbell, "Adaptation to the First Years of Marriage," *Psychiatry,* 26:4 (1963), pp. 368–380.

[26] Rapoport, op. cit.

[27] Cohen, op. cit.

the case of the marital role, pregnancy in the case of the parental role, and the last stages of highly vocationally oriented schooling or on-the-job apprenticeship in the case of an occupational role.

2. *Honeymoon stage.* This is the time period immediately following the full assumption of the adult role. The inception of this stage is more easily defined than its termination. In the case of the marital role, the honeymoon stage extends from the marriage ceremony itself through the literal honeymoon and on through an unspecified and individually varying period of time. Raush[28] has caught this stage of the marital role in his description of the "psychic honeymoon": that extended postmarital period when, through close intimacy and joint activity, the couple can explore each other's capacities and limitations. I shall arbitrarily consider the onset of pregnancy as marking the end of the honeymoon stage of the marital role. This stage of the parental role may involve an equivalent psychic honeymoon, that postchildbirth period during which, through intimacy and prolonged contact, an attachment between parent and child is laid down. There is a crucial difference, however, from the marital role in this stage. A woman knows her husband as a unique real person when she enters the honeymoon stage of marriage. A good deal of preparatory adjustment on a firm reality-base is possible during the engagement period which is not possible in the equivalent pregnancy period. Fantasy is not corrected by the reality of a specific individual child until the birth of the child. The "quick-

ening" is psychologically of special significance to women precisely because it marks the first evidence of a real baby rather than a purely fantasized one. On this basis alone there is greater interpersonal adjustment and learning during the honeymoon stage of the parental role than of the marital role.

3. *Plateau stage.* This is the protracted middle period of a role cycle during which the role is fully exercised. Depending on the specific problem under analysis, one would obviously subdivide this large plateau stage further. For my present purposes it is not necessary to do so, since my focus is on the earlier anticipatory and honeymoon stages of the parental role and the overall impact of parenthood on adults.

4. *Disengagement-termination stage.* This period immediately precedes and includes the actual termination of the role. Marriage ends with the death of the spouse or, just as definitively, with separation and divorce. A unique characteristic of parental role termination is the fact that it is not clearly marked by any specific act but is an attenuated process of termination with little cultural prescription about when the authority and obligations of a parent end. Many parents, however, experience the marriage of the child as a psychological termination of the active parental role.

UNIQUE FEATURES OF PARENTAL ROLE

With this role cycle suggestion as a broader framework, we can narrow our focus to what are the unique and most salient features of the parental role. In doing so, special attention will be given

[28] Raush et al., op. cit.

to two further questions: (1) the impact of social changes over the past few decades in facilitating or complicating the transition to and experience of parenthood and (2) the new interpretations or new research suggested by the focus on the parent rather than the child.

Cultural Pressure to Assume the Role

On the level of cultural values, men have no freedom of choice where work is concerned: They must work to secure their status as adult men. The equivalent for women has been maternity. There is considerable pressure upon the growing girl and young woman to consider maternity necessary for a woman's fulfillment as an individual and to secure her status as an adult.[29]

This is not to say there are no fluctuations over time in the intensity of the cultural pressure to parenthood. During the depression years of the 1930's, there was more widespread awareness of the economic hardships parenthood can entail, and many demographic experts believe there was a great increase in illegal abortions during those years. Bird has discussed the

[29] The greater the cultural pressure to assume a given adult social role, the greater will be the tendency for individual negative feelings toward that role to be expressed covertly. Men may complain about a given job but not about working per se, and hence their work dissatisfactions are often displaced to the non-work sphere, as psychosomatic complaints or irritation and dominance at home. An equivalent displacement for women of the ambivalence many may feel toward maternity is to dissatisfactions with the homemaker role.

dread with which a suspected pregnancy was viewed by many American women in the 1930's.[30] Quite a different set of pressures were at work during the 1950's, when the general societal tendency was toward withdrawal from active engagement with the issues of the larger society and a turning in to the gratifications of the private sphere of home and family life. Important in the background were the general affluence of the period and the expanded room and ease of child rearing that go with suburban living. For the past five years, there has been a drop in the birth rate in general, fourth and higher-order births in particular. During this same period there has been increased concern and debate about women's participation in politics and work, with more women now returning to work rather than conceiving the third or fourth child.[31]

Inception of the Parental Role

The decision to marry and the choice of a mate are voluntary acts of individuals in our family system. Engagements are therefore consciously considered, freely entered, and freely terminated if increased familiarity de-

[30] Caroline Bird, *The Invisible Scar,* New York: David McKay Company, 1966.
[31] When it is realized that a mean family size of 3.5 would double the population in 40 years, while a mean of 2.5 would yield a stable population in the same period, the social importance of withholding praise for procreative prowess is clear. At the same time, a drop in the birth rate may reduce the number of unwanted babies born, for such a drop would mean more efficient contraceptive usage and a closer correspondence between desired and attained family size.

creases, rather than increases, intimacy and commitment to the choice. The inception of a pregnancy, unlike the engagement, is not always a voluntary decision, for it may be the unintended consequence of a sexual act that was recreative in intent rather than procreative. Secondly, and again unlike the engagement, the termination of a pregnancy is not socially sanctioned, as shown by current resistance to abortion-law reform.

The implication of this difference is a much higher probability of unwanted pregnancies than of unwanted marriages in our family system. Coupled with the ample clinical evidence of parental rejection and sometimes cruelty to children, it is all the more surprising that there has not been more consistent research attention to the problem of *parental satisfaction*, as there has for long been on *marital satisfaction* or *work satisfaction*. Only the extreme iceberg tip of the parental satisfaction continuum is clearly demarcated and researched, as in the growing concern with "battered babies." Cultural and psychological resistance to the image of a non-nurturant woman may afflict social scientists as well as the American public.

The timing of a first pregnancy is critical to the manner in which parental responsibilities are joined to the marital relationship. The single most important change over the past few decades is extensive and efficient contraceptive usage, since this has meant for a growing proportion of new marriages, the possibility of and increasing preference for some postponement of childbearing after marriage. When pregnancy was likely to follow shortly after marriage, the major transition point in a woman's life was marriage itself. *This transition point is increasingly the first pregnancy rather than marriage.* It is accepted and increasingly expected that women will work after marriage, while household furnishings are acquired and spouses complete their advanced training or gain a foothold in their work.[32] This provides an early marriage period in which the fact of a wife's employment presses for a greater egalitarian relationship between husband and wife in decision-making, commonality of experience, and sharing of household responsibilities.

The balance between individual autonomy and couple mutuality that develops during the honeymoon stage of such a marriage may be important in establishing a pattern that will later affect the quality of the parent-child relationship and the extent of sex-role segregation of duties between the parents. It is only in the context of a growing egalitarian base to the marital relationship that one could find, as Gavron has,[33] a tendency for parents to establish some barriers between themselves and their children, a marital defense against the institution of parenthood as she describes it. This may eventually replace the typical coalition in more traditional families of mother and children against husband-father. Parenthood will continue for some time to impose a degree of temporary segregation of primary respon-

[32] James A. Davis, *Stipends and Spouses: The Finances of American Arts and Sciences Graduate Students,* Chicago: University of Chicago Press, 1962.

[33] Hannah Gavron, *The Captive Wife,* London: Routledge & Kegan Paul, 1966.

sibilities between husband and wife, but, when this takes place in the context of a previously established egalitarian relationship between the husband and wife, such role segregation may become blurred, with greater recognition of the wife's need for autonomy and the husband's role in the routines of home and child rearing.[34]

There is one further significant social change that has important implications for the changed relationship between husband and wife: the in-

creasing departure from an old pattern of role-inception phasing in which the young person first completed his schooling, then established himself in the world of work, then married and began his family. Marriage and parenthood are increasingly taking place *before* the schooling of the husband, and often of the wife, has been completed.[35] An important reason for this trend lies in the fact that, during the same decades in which the average age of physical-sexual maturation has dropped, the average amount of education which young people obtain has been on the increase. Particularly for the college and graduate or professional school population, family roles are often assumed before the degrees needed to enter careers have been obtained.

Just how long it now takes young people to complete their higher education has been investigated only recently in several longitudinal studies of college-graduate cohorts.[36] College is far less uniformly a four-year period

---

[34] The recent increase in natural childbirth, prenatal courses for expectant fathers, and greater participation of men during childbirth and postnatal care of the infant may therefore be a *consequence* of greater sharing between husband and wife when both work and jointly maintain their new households during the early months of marriage. Indeed, natural childbirth builds directly on this shifted base to the marital relationship. Goshen-Gottstein has found in an Israeli sample that women with a "traditional" orientation to marriage far exceed women with a "modern" orientation to marriage in menstrual difficulty, dislike of sexual intercourse, and pregnancy disorders and complaints such as vomiting. She argues that traditional women demand and expect little from their husbands and become demanding and narcissistic by means of their children, as shown in pregnancy by an over-exaggeration of symptoms and attention-seeking. Esther R. Goshen-Gottstein, *Marriage and First Pregnancy: Cultural Influences on Attitudes of Israeli Women,* London: Tavistock Publications, 1966. A prolonged psychic honeymoon uncomplicated by an early pregnancy, and with the new acceptance of married women's employment, may help to cement the egalitarian relationship in the marriage and reduce both the tendency to pregnancy difficulties and the need for a narcissistic focus on the children. Such a background is fruitful ground for sympathy toward and acceptance of the natural childbirth ideology.

[35] James A. Davis, *Stipends and Spouses: The Finances of American Arts and Sciences Graduate Students,* op. cit.; James A. Davis, *Great Aspirations,* Chicago: Aldine Publishing Company, 1964; Eli Ginsberg, *Life Styles of Educated Women,* New York: Columbia University Press, 1966; Ginsberg, *Educated American Women: Self Portraits,* New York: Columbia University Press, 1967; National Science Foundation, *Two Years After the College Degree — Work and Further Study Patterns,* Washington, D.C.: Government Printing Office, NSF 63-26, 1963.

[36] Davis, *Great Aspirations,* op. cit.; Laure Sharp, "Graduate Study and Its Relation to Careers: The Experience of a Recent Cohort of College Graduates," *Journal of Human Resources,* 1:2 (1966), pp. 41–58.

than high school is. A full third of
the college freshmen in one study had
been out of high school a year or more
before entering college.[37] In a large
sample of college graduates in 1961,
one in five were over 25 years of age
at graduation.[38] Thus, financial difficulties, military service, change of career plans, and marriage itself all tend
to create interruptions in the college
attendance of a significant proportion
of college graduates. At the graduate
and professional school level, this is
even more marked: the mean age of
men receiving the doctorate, for example, is 32, and of women, 36.[39] It is
the exception rather than the rule for
men and women who seek graduate
degrees to go directly from college to
graduate school and remain there until
they secure their degrees.[40]

The major implication of this change
is that more men and women are
achieving full adult status in family
roles while they are still less than fully
adult in status terms in the occupational system. Graduate students are,
increasingly, men and women with full
family responsibilities. Within the family many more husbands and fathers
are still students, often quite dependent on the earnings of their wives to

see them through their advanced training.[41] No matter what the couple's desires and preferences are, this fact alone
presses for more egalitarian relations
between husband and wife, just as
the adult family status of graduate
students presses for more egalitarian relations between students and
faculty.

Irrevocability

If marriages do not work out, there
is now widespread acceptance of divorce and remarriage as a solution. The
same point applies to the work world:
we are free to leave an unsatisfactory
job and seek another. But once a pregnancy occurs, there is little possibility
of undoing the commitment to parenthood implicit in conception except in
the rare instance of placing children
for adoption. We can have ex-spouses
and ex-jobs but not ex-children. This
being so, it is scarcely surprising to
find marked differences between the
relationship of a parent and one child
and the relationship of the same parent
with another child. If the culture does
not permit pregnancy termination, the
equivalent to giving up a child is psychological withdrawal on the part of
the parent.

This taps an important area in which
a focus on the parent rather than the
child may contribute a new interpre-
tive dimension to an old problem: the
long history of interest, in the social
sciences, in differences among children
associated with their sex-birth-order
position in their sibling set. Research

[37] James D. Cowhig and C. Nam, "Educational Status, College Plans and Occupational Status of Farm and Nonfarm Youths,"
U.S. Bureau of the Census Series ERS (P-
27), No. 30, 1961.

[38] Davis, *Great Aspirations,* op. cit.

[39] Lindsey R. Harmon, *Profiles of Ph.D.'s
in the Sciences: Summary Report on Follow-
up of Doctorate Cohorts, 1935–1960,* Washington, D.C.: National Research Council,
Publication 1293, 1965.

[40] Sharp, op. cit.

[41] Davis, *Stipends and Spouses, The Finances of American Arts and Sciences Graduate Students,* op. cit.

has largely been based on data gathered about and/or from the children, and interpretations make inferences back to the "probable" quality of the child's relation to a parent and how a parent might differ in relating to a first-born compared to a last-born child. The relevant research, directed at the parents (mothers in particular), remains to be done, but at least a few examples can be suggested of the different order of interpretation that flows from a focus on the parent.

Some birth-order research stresses the influence of sibs upon other sibs, as in Koch's finding that second-born boys with an older sister are more feminine than second-born boys with an older brother.[42] A similar sib-influence interpretation is offered in the major common finding of birth-order correlates, that sociability is greater among last-borns[43] and achievement among first-borns.[44] It has been suggested that

last-borns use social skills to increase acceptance by their older sibs or are more peer-oriented because they receive less adult stimulation from parents. The tendency of first-borns to greater achievement has been interpreted in a corollary way, as a reflection of early assumption of responsibility for younger sibs, greater adult stimulation during the time the oldest was the only child in the family,[45] and the greater significance of the first-born for the larger kinship network of the family.[46]

Sociologists have shown increasing interest in structural family variables in recent years, a primary variable being family size. From Bossard's descriptive work on the large family[47] to more methodologically sophisticated work such as that by Rosen,[48] Elder and Bowerman,[49] Boocock,[50] and Nisbet,[51] the question posed is: what is

[42] Orville G. Brim, "Family Structure and Sex-Role Learning by Children," *Sociometry,* 21 (1958), pp. 1–16; H. L. Koch, "Sissiness and Tomboyishness in Relation to Sibling Characteristics," *Journal of Genetic Psychology,* 88 (1956), pp. 231–244.

[43] Charles MacArthur, "Personalities of First and Second Children," *Psychiatry,* 19 (1956), pp. 47–54; S. Schachter, "Birth Order and Sociometric Choice," *Journal of Abnormal and Social Psychology,* 68 (1964), pp. 453–456.

[44] Irving Harris, *The Promised Seed,* New York: The Free Press, a division of the Macmillan Co., 1964; Bernard Rosen, "Family Structure and Achievement Motivation," *American Sociological Review,* 26 (1961), pp. 574–585; Alice S. Rossi, "Naming Children in Middle-Class Families," *American Sociological Review,* 30:4 (1965), pp. 499–513; Stanley Schachter, "Birth Order, Eminence and Higher Education," *American Sociological Review,* 28 (1963), pp. 757–768.

[45] Harris, op. cit.

[46] Rossi, "Naming Children in Middle-Class Families," op. cit.

[47] James H. Bossard, *Parent and Child,* Philadelphia; University of Pennsylvania Press, 1953; James H. Bossard and E. Boll, *The Large Family System,* Philadelphia: University of Pennsylvania, 1956.

[48] Rosen, op. cit.

[49] Glen H. J. Elder and C. Bowerman, "Family Structure and Child Rearing Patterns: The Effect of Family Size and Sex Composition on Child-Rearing Practices," *American Sociological Review,* 28 (1963), pp. 891–905.

[50] Sarane S. Boocock, "Toward a Sociology of Learning: A Selective Review of Existing Research," *Sociology of Education,* 39:1 (1966), pp. 1–45.

[51] John Nisbet, "Family Environment and Intelligence," in *Education, Economy and Society,* ed. by Halsey et al. New York: The Free Press, a division of the Macmillan Company, 1961.

the effect of growing up in a small family, compared with a large family, that is attributable to this group-size variable? Unfortunately, the theoretical point of departure for sociologists' expectations of the effect of the family-size variables is the Durkheim-Simmel tradition of the differential effect of group size or population density upon members or inhabitants.[52] In the case of the family, however, this overlooks the very important fact that family size is determined by the key figures *within* the group, i.e., the parents. To find that children in small families differ from children in large families is not simply due to the impact of group size upon individual members but to the very different involvement of the parent with the children and to relations between the parents themselves in small versus large families.

An important clue to a new interpretation can be gained by examining family size from the perspective of parental motivation toward having children. A small family is small for one of two primary reasons: either the parents wanted a small family and achieved their desired size, or they wanted a large family but were not able to attain it. In either case, there is a low probability of unwanted children. Indeed, in the latter eventuality they may take particularly great interest in the children they do have. Small

families are therefore most likely to contain parents with a strong and positive orientation to each of the children they have. A large family, by contrast, is large either because the parents achieved the size they desired or because they have more children than they in fact wanted. Large families therefore have a higher probability than small families of including unwanted and unloved children. Consistent with this are Nye's finding that adolescents in small families have better relations with their parents than those in large families[53] and Sears and Maccoby's finding that mothers of large families are more restrictive toward their children than mothers of small families.[54]

This also means that last-born children are more likely to be unwanted than first- or middle-born children, particularly in large families. This is consistent with what is known of abortion patterns among married women, who typically resort to abortion only when they have achieved the number of children they want or feel they can afford to have. Only a small proportion of women faced with such unwanted pregnancies actually resort to abortion. *This suggests the possibility that the last-born child's reliance on social skills may be his device for securing the attention and loving involvement of a parent less positively predisposed to him than to his older siblings.*

In developing this interpretation,

---

[52] Thus Rosen writes: "Considering the sociologist's traditional and continuing concern with group size as an independent variable (from Simmel and Durkheim to the recent experimental studies of small groups), there have been surprisingly few studies of the influence of group size upon the nature of interaction in the family," op. cit., p. 576.

[53] Ivan Nye, "Adolescent-Parent Adjustment: Age, Sex, Sibling, Number, Broken Homes, and Employed Mothers as Variables," *Marriage and Family Living,* 14 (1952), pp. 327–332.

[54] Sears et al., op. cit.

rather extreme cases have been stressed. Closer to the normal range, of families in which even the last-born child was desired and planned for, there is still another element which may contribute to the greater sociability of the last-born child. Most parents are themselves aware of the greater ease with which they face the care of a third fragile newborn than the first; clearly, parental skills and confidence are greater with last-born children than with first-born children. But this does not mean that the attitude of the parent is more positive toward the care of the third child than the first. There is no necessary correlation between skills in an area and enjoyment of that area. Searls[55] found that older homemakers are *more* skillful in domestic tasks but experience *less* enjoyment of them than younger homemakers, pointing to a declining euphoria for a particular role with the passage of time. In the same way, older people rate their marriages as "very happy" less often than younger people do.[56] It is perhaps culturally and psychologically more difficult to face the possibility that women may find less enjoyment of the maternal role with the passage of time, though women themselves know the difference between the romantic expectation concerning child care and the incorporation of the first baby into the household and the more realistic expectation and sharper assessment of

their own abilities to do an adequate job of mothering as they face a third confinement. Last-born children may experience not only less verbal stimulation from their parents than first-born children but also less prompt and enthusiastic response to their demands — from feeding and diaper-change as infants to requests for stories read at three or a college education at eighteen — simply because the parents experience less intense gratification from the parent role with the third child than they did with the first. The child's response to this might well be to cultivate winning, pleasing manners in early childhood that blossom as charm and sociability in later life, showing both a greater need to be loved and greater pressure to seek approval.

One last point may be appropriately developed at this juncture. Mention was made earlier that for many women the personal outcome of experience in the parent role is not a higher level of maturation but the negative outcome of a depressed sense of self-worth, if not actual personality deterioration. There is considerable evidence that this is more prevalent than we recognize. On a qualitative level, a close reading of the portrait of the working-class wife in Rainwater,[57] Newsom,[58] Komarovsky,[59] Gavron,[60] or Zweig[61]

[55] Laura G. Searls, "Leisure Role Emphasis of College Graduate Homemakers," *Journal of Marriage and the Family,* 28:1 (1966), pp. 77–82.

[56] Norman Bradburn and D. Caplovitz, *Reports on Happiness,* Chicago: Aldine Publishing, 1965.

[57] Lee Rainwater, R. Coleman, and G. Handel, *Workingman's Wife,* New York: Oceana Publications, 1959.

[58] John Newsom and E. Newsom, *Infant Care in an Urban Community,* New York: International Universities Press, 1963.

[59] Mirra Komarovsky, *Blue Collar Marriage,* New York: Random House, 1962.

[60] Gavron, op. cit.

[61] Ferdinand Zweig, *Woman's Life and Labor,* London: Camelot Press, 1952.

gives little suggestion that maternity has provided these women with opportunities for personal growth and development. So too, Cohen[62] notes with some surprise that in her sample of middle-class educated couples, as in Pavenstadt's study of lower-income women in Boston, there were more emotional difficulty and lower levels of maturation among multiparous women than primiparous women. On a more extensive sample basis, in Gurin's survey of Americans viewing their mental health,[63] as an Bradburn's reports on happiness,[64] single men are less happy and less active than single women, but among the married respondents the women are unhappier, have more problems, feel inadequate as parents, have a more negative and passive outlook on life, and show a more negative self-image. All of these characteristics increase with age among married women but show no relationship to age among men. While it may be true, as Gurin argues, that women are more introspective and hence more attuned to the psychological facets of experience than men are, this point does not account for the fact that the things which the women report are all on the negative side; few are on the positive side, indicative of euphoric sensitivity and pleasure. The possibility must be faced, and at some point researched, that women lose ground in personal devel-

opment and self-esteem during the early and middle years of adulthood, whereas men gain ground in these respects during the same years. The retention of a high level of self-esteem may depend upon the adequacy of earlier preparation for major adult roles: men's training adequately prepares them for their primary adult roles in the occupational system, as it does for those women who opt to participate significantly in the work world. Training in the qualities and skills needed for family roles in contemporary society may be inadequate for both sexes, but the lowering of self-esteem occurs only among women because their primary adult roles are within the family system.

Preparation for Parenthood

Four factors may be given special attention on the question of what preparation American couples bring to parenthood.

1. *Paucity of preparation.* Our educational system is dedicated to the cognitive development of the young, and our primary teaching approach is the pragmatic one of learning by doing. How much one knows and how well he can apply what he knows are the standards by which the child is judged in school, as the employee is judged at work. The child can learn by doing in such subjects as science, mathematics, art work, or shop, but not in the subjects most relevant to successful family life: sex, home maintenance, child care, interpersonal competence, and empathy. If the home is deficient in training in these areas, the child is left with no preparation for a major segment of

---

[62] Cohen, op. cit.

[63] Gerald Gurin, J. Veroff, and S. Feld, *Americans View Their Mental Health,* New York: Basic Books, Monograph Series No. 4, Joint Commission on Mental Illness and Health, 1960.

[64] Bradburn and Caplovitz, op. cit.

his adult life. A doctor facing his first patient in private practice has treated numerous patients under close supervision during his internship, but probably a majority of American mothers approach maternity with no previous child-care experience beyond sporadic baby-sitting, perhaps a course in child psychology, or occasional care of younger siblings.

2. *Limited learning during pregnancy.* A second important point makes adjustment to parenthood potentially more stressful than marital adjustment. This is the lack of any realistic training for parenthood during the anticipatory stage of pregnancy. By contrast, during the engagement period preceding marriage, an individual has opportunities to develop the skills and make the adjustments which ease the transition to marriage. Through discussions of values and life goals, through sexual experimentation, shared social experiences as an engaged couple with friends and relatives, and planning and furnishing an apartment, the engaged couple can make considerable progress in developing mutuality in advance of the marriage itself.[65] No such headstart is possible in the case of pregnancy. What preparation exists is confined to reading, consultation with friends and parents, discussions between husband and wife, and a minor nesting phase in which a place and the equipment for a baby are prepared in the household.[66]

3. *Abruptness of transition.* Thirdly, the birth of a child is not followed by any gradual taking on of responsibility, as in the case of a professional work role. It is as if the woman shifted from a graduate student to a full professor with little intervening apprenticeship experience of slowly increasing responsibility. The new mother starts out immediately on 24-hour duty, with responsibility for a fragile and mysterious infant totally dependent on her care.

If marital adjustment is more difficult for very young brides than more mature ones,[67] adjustment to motherhood may be even more difficult. A woman can adapt a passive dependence on a husband and still have a successful marriage, but a young mother with strong dependency needs is in for difficulty in maternal adjustment, because the role precludes such dependency. This situation was well described in Cohen's study[68] in a case

---

life rather than pregnancy, a good deal of anticipatory "nesting" behavior took place from the time of conception. Now more women work through a considerable portion of the first pregnancy, and such nesting behavior as exists may be confined to a few shopping expeditions or baby showers, thus adding to the abruptness of the transition and the difficulty of adjustment following the birth of a first child.

[67] Lee G. Burchinal, "Adolescent Role Deprivation and High School Marriage," *Marriage and Family Living,* 21 (1959), pp. 378–384; Floyd M. Martinson, "Ego Deficiency as a Factor in Marriage," *American Sociological Review,* 22 (1955), pp. 161–164; J. Joel Moss and Ruby Gingles, "The Relationship of Personality to the Incidence of Early Marriage," *Marriage and Family Living,* 21 (1959) pp. 373–377.

[68] Cohen, op. cit.

[65] Rapoport, "The Transition from Engagement to Marriage," op. cit.; Raush et al., op. cit.

[66] During the period when marriage was the critical transition in the adult woman's

of a young wife with a background of co-ed popularity and a passive dependent relationship to her admired and admiring husband, who collapsed into restricted incapacity when faced with the responsibilities of maintaining a home and caring for a child.

4. *Lack of guidelines to successful parenthood.* If the central task of parenthood is the rearing of children to become the kind of competent adults valued by the society, then an important question facing any parent is what he or she specifically can do to create such a competent adult. This is where the parent is left with few or no guidelines from the expert. Parents can readily inform themselves concerning the young infant's nutritional, clothing, and medical needs and follow the general prescription that a child needs loving physical contact and emotional support. Such advice may be sufficient to produce a healthy, happy, and well-adjusted preschooler, but adult competency is quite another matter.

In fact, the adults who do "succeed" in American society show a complex of characteristics as children that current experts in child-care would evaluate as "poor" to "bad." Biographies of leading authors and artists, as well as the more rigorous research inquiries of creativity among architects[69] or scientists,[70] do not portray childhoods with

characteristics currently endorsed by mental health and child-care authorities. Indeed, there is often a predominance of tension in childhood family relations and traumatic loss rather than loving parental support, intense channeling of energy in one area of interest rather than an all-round profile of diverse interests, and social withdrawal and preference for loner activities rather than gregarious sociability. Thus, the stress in current child-rearing advice on a high level of loving support but a low level of discipline or restriction on the behavior of the child — the "developmental" family type as Duvall calls it [71] — is a profile consistent with the focus on mental health, sociability, and adjustment. Yet the combination of both high support and high authority on the part of parents is most strongly related to the child's sense of responsibility, leadership quality, and achievement level, as found in Bronfenbrenner's studies[72] and that of Mussen and Distler.[73]

---

[69] Donald W. MacKinnon, "Creativity and Images of the Self," in *The Study of Lives,* ed. by Robert W. White, New York: Atherton Press, 1963.

[70] Anne Roe, "A Psychological Study of Eminent Biologists," *Psychological Monographs,* 65:14 (1951), 68 pages; Anne Roe, "A Psychological Study of Physical Scien-

tists," *Genetic Psychology Monographs,* 43 (1951), pp. 121–239; Anne Roe, "Crucial Life Experiences in the Development of Scientists," in *Talent and Education,* ed. by E. P. Torrance, Minneapolis: University of Minnesota Press, 1960.

[71] Evelyn M. Duvall, "Conceptions of Parenthood," *American Journal of Sociology,* 52 (1946), pp. 193–203.

[72] Urie Bronfenbrenner, "Some Familial Antecedents of Responsibility and Leadership in Adolescents," in *Studies in Leadership,* ed. by L. Petrullo and B. Bass, New York: Holt, Rinehart, and Winston, 1960.

[73] Paul Mussen and L. Distler, "Masculinity, Identification and Father-Son Relationships," *Journal of Abnormal and Social Psychology,* 59 (1959), pp. 350–356.

Brim points out [74] that we are a long way from being able to say just what parent role prescriptions have what effect on the adult characteristics of the child. We know even less about how such parental prescriptions should be changed to adapt to changed conceptions of competency in adulthood. In such an ambiguous context, the great interest parents take in school reports on their children or the pediatrician's assessment of the child's developmental progress should be seen as among the few indices parents have of how well *they* are doing as parents.

System and Role Requirements: Instrumentality and Integration

Typological dichotomies and unidimensional scales have loomed large in the search by social scientists for the most economical and general principles to account for some significant portion of the complex human behavior or social organization they study. Thus, for example, the European dichotomy of *Gemeinschaft* and *Gesellschaft* became the American sociological distinction between rural and urban sociology, subfields that have outlasted their conceptual utility now that the rural environment has become urbanized and the interstices between country and city are swelling with suburban developments.

In recent years a new dichotomy has gained more acceptance in sociological circles — the Parsonian distinction between *instrumental* and *expressive*, an

[74] Orville G. Brim, "The Parent-Child Relation as a Social System: I. Parent and Child Roles," *Child Development*, 28:3 (1957), pp. 343–364.

interesting dichotomy that is unfortunately applied in an indiscriminate way to all manner of social phenomena including the analysis of teacher role conflict, occupational choice, the contrast between the family system and the occupational system, and the primary roles or personality tendencies of men compared to women.

On a system level, for example, the "instrumental" occupational system is characterized by rationality, efficiency, rejection of tradition, and depression of interpersonal loyalty, while the "expressive" family system is characterized by nurturance, integration, tension-management, ritual, and interpersonal solidarity. Applied to sex roles within the family, the husband-father emerges as the instrumental rational leader, a symbolic representative of the outside world, and the wife-mother emerges as the expressive, nurturant, affective center of the family. Such distinctions may be useful in the attempt to capture some general tendency of a system or a role, but they lead to more distortion than illumination when applied to the actual functioning of a specific system or social role or to the actual behavior of a given individual in a particular role.

Take, for example, the husband-father as the instrumental role within the family on the assumption that men are the major breadwinners and therefore carry the instrumentality associated with work into their roles within the family. To begin with, the family is not an experimental one-task small group but a complex, ongoing 24-hour entity with many tasks that must be performed. Secondly, we really know very little about how occupational roles affect the performance of family roles.[75] An aggressive courtroom lawyer or a shrewd business executive are not lawyers and businessmen at home but husbands and fathers. Unless shown to be in error, we should proceed on the assumption that behavior is role-specific. (Indeed, Brim[76] argues that even personality is role-specific.) A strict teacher may be an

indulgent mother at home; a submissive wife may be a dominant mother; a dictatorial father may be an exploited and passive worker on the assembly line; or, as in some of Lidz's schizophrenic patients' families,[77] a passive dependent husband at home may be a successful dominant lawyer away from home.

There is, however, a more fundamental level to the criticism that the dichotomous usage of instrumentality and expressiveness, linked to sex and applied to intrafamily roles, leads to more distortion than illumination. The logic of my argument starts with the premise that every social system, group, or role has two primary, independent, structural axes. Whether these axes are called "authority and support," as in Straus's circumplex model,[78] or "instrumental and expressive," as by Parsons,[79] there are tasks to be performed and affective support to be given in all the cases cited. There must be discipline, rules, and division of labor in the nation-state as in the family or a business enterprise *and* there must be solidarity among the units comprising these same systems in order for the system to function adequately. *This means that the role of father, husband, wife, or mother each has these two independent dimensions of authority and support, instrumentality and expressiveness, work and love.* Little is gained by trying to stretch empirical results to fit the father role to the instrumental cate-

[75] Miller and Swanson have suggested a connection between the trend toward bureaucratic structure in the occupational world and the shift in child-rearing practices toward permissiveness and a greater stress on personal adjustment of children. These findings are suggestive rather than definitive, however, and no hard research has subjected this question to empirical inquiry. Daniel R. Miller and G. Swanson, *The Changing American Parent,* New York: John Wiley & Sons, 1958.

The same suggestive but nondefinitive clues are to be found in von Merings study of the contrast between professional and nonprofessional women as mothers. She shows that the professionally active woman in her mother role tends toward a greater stress on discipline rather than indulgence and has a larger number of rules with fewer choices or suggestions to the child: the emphasis is in equipping the child to cope effectively with rules and techniques of his culture. The nonprofessional mother, by contrast, has a greater value stress on insuring the child's emotional security, tending to take the role of the clinician in an attempt to diagnose the child's problems and behavior. Faye H. von Mering, "Professional and Non-Professional Women as Mothers," *Journal of Social Psychology,* 42 (1955), pp. 21–34.

[76] Orville G., Brim, "Personality Development as Role-learning," in *Personality Development in Children,* ed. by Ira Iscoe and Harold Stevenson, University of Texas Press, 1960.

[77] Lidz et al., op. cit.
[78] Straus, op. cit.
[79] Parsons and Bales, op. cit.

gory, as Brim[80] has done, or the mother role to the expressive category, as Zelditch has done.[81]

In taking a next logical step from this premise, the critical issue, both theoretically and empirically, becomes gauging the *balance* between these two dimensions of the system or of the role. Roles or systems could be compared in terms of the average difference among them in the direction and extent of the discrepancy between authority and support; or individuals could be compared in terms of the variation among them in the discrepancy between the two dimensions in a given role.

An example may clarify these points. A teacher who is all loving, warm support to her students and plans many occasions to evoke integrative ties among them but who is incompetent in the exercise of authority or knowledge of the subjects she teachers would be judged by any school principal as an inadequate teacher. The same judgment of inadequacy would apply to a strict disciplinarian teacher, competent and informed about her subjects but totally lacking in any personal quality of warmth or ability to encourage integrative and cooperative responses among her students. Maximum adequacy of teacher performance requires a relatively high positive level on both of these two dimensions of the teacher role.

To claim that teachers have a basic conflict in approaching their role because they are required to be a "bi-sexual parent, permissive giver of love and harsh disciplinarian with a masculine intellectual grasp of the world," as Jackson and Moscovici[82] have argued, at least recognizes the two dimensions of the teacher role, though it shares the view of many sociologists that role *conflict* is inherent wherever these seeming polarities are required. Why conflict is predicted hinges on the assumed invariance of the linkage of the male to authority and the female to the expressive-integrative roles.

It is this latter assumed difference between the sexes that restricts theory-building in family sociology and produces so much puzzlement on the part of researchers into marriage and parenthood, sex-role socialization, or personality tendencies toward masculinity or femininity. Let me give one example of recent findings in this latter topic and then move on to apply the two-dimension concept to the parental role. Vincent[83] administered the Gough Femininity Scale along with several other scale batteries from the California Personality Inventory to several hundred college men and women. He found that women *low* on femininity were higher in the Class I scale which measures poise, ascendancy, and self-assurance, and men *high* in femininity were higher in dominance, capacity for status, and responsibility. Successful

[80] Brim, "The Parent-Child Relation as a Social System: I. Parent and Child Roles," op. cit.

[81] Parsons and Bales, op. cit.

[82] Philip Jackson and F. Moscovici, "The Teacher-to-be: A Study of Embryonic Identification with a Professional Role," *School Review,* 71:1 (1963), pp. 41–65.

[83] Clark E. Vincent, "Implications of Changes in Male-Female Role Expectations for Interpreting M-F Scores," *Journal of Marriage and the Family,* 28:2 (1966), pp. 196–199.

adult men in a technological society
are rarely interested in racing cars,
soldiering, or hunting; they are cautious, subtle, and psychologically attuned to others. So too, contemporary
adult women who fear windstorms, the
dark, strange places, automobile accidents, excitement, crowded parties, or
practical jokes (and are therefore high
on femininity in the Gough scale) will
be inadequate for the task of managing an isolated household with neither
men nor kinswomen close by to help
them through daily crises, for the assumption of leadership roles in community organizations, or for holding
down supplementary breadwinning or
cakewinning jobs.

When Deutsch[84] and Escalona[85]
point out that today's "neurotic"
woman is not an assertive dominant
person but a passive dependent one,
the reason may be found in the social
change in role expectations concerning competence among adult women,
not that there has been a social change
in the characteristics of neurotic
women. In the past an assertive, dominant woman might have defined herself and been defined by her analyst
as "neurotic" because she could not
fill the expectations then held for adequacy among adult women. Today, it
is the passive dependent woman who
will be judged "neurotic" because she
cannot fill adequately the expectations

now set for and by her. What is really
meant when we say that sex role definitions have become increasingly blurred
is that men are now required to show
more integrative skills than in the
past, and women more instrumental
skills. This incurs potential sex-role
"confusion" only by the standards of
the past, not by the standards of what
is required for contemporary adult
competence in family and work roles.

Once freed from the assumption of
a single bipolar continuum of mascu-
linity-femininity,[86] authority-integra-
tion, or even independence-depen-
dence,[87] one can observe increased

---

[84] Helene Deutsch, *The Psychology of Women: A Psychoanalytic Interpretation,* Vol. 1, New York: Grune and Stratton, 1944.

[85] Sibylle Escalona, "The Psychological Situation of Mother and Child Upon Return from the Hospital," in *Problems of Infancy and Childhood: Transactions of the Third Conference,* ed. by Milton Senn, 1949.

[86] Several authors have recently pointed out the inadequacy of social science usage of the masculinity-feminity concept. Landreth, in a study of parent-role appropriateness in giving physical care and companionship to the child, found her four-year-old subjects, particularly in New Zealand, made no simple linkage of activity to mother as opposed to father. Catherine Landreth, "Four-Year-Olds' Notions about Sex Appropriateness of Parental Care and Companionship Activities," *Merrill-Palmer Quarterly,* 9:3 (1963), pp. 175–182. She comments that in New Zealand "masculinity and feminity appear to be comfortably relegated to chromosome rather than to contrived activity" (p. 176). Lansky, in a study of the effect of the sex of the children upon the parents' own sex-identification, calls for devising tests which look at masculinity and femininity as two dimensions rather than a single continuum. Leonard M. Lansky, "The Family Structure also Affects the Model: Sex-Role Identification in Parents of Preschool Children," *Merrill-Palmer Quarterly,* 10:1 (1964), pp. 39–50.

[87] Beller has already shown the value of such an approach, in a study that defined independence and dependence as two separate dimensions rather than the extremes of a bipolar continuum. He found, as hy-

instrumentality in a role with no implication of necessarily decreased integration, and vice versa. Thus, an increasing rationality in the care of children, the maintenance of a household, or meal planning for a family does not imply a decreasing level of integrative support associated with the wife-mother role. So, too, the increased involvement of a young father in playful encounters with his toddler carries no necessary implication of a change in the instrumental dimension of his role.

The two-dimensional approach also frees our analysis of parenthood on two other important questions. Brim has reviewed much of the research on the parent-child relationship[88] and noted the necessity of specifying not only the sex of the parent but the sex of the child and whether a given parent-child dyad is a cross-sex or same-sex pair. It is clear from his review that fathers and mothers relate differently to their sons and daughters: fathers have been found to be stricter with their sons than with their daughters, and mothers stricter with their daughters than with their sons. Thus, a two-dimensional approach to the parent role is more appropriate to what is already empirically known about the parent-child relationship.

Secondly, only on a very general overview level does a parent maintain a particular level of support and of discipline toward a given child: situational variation is an important determinant of parental response to a child. A father with a general tendency toward relatively little emotional support of his son may offer a good deal of comfort if the child is hurt. An indulgent and loving mother may show an extreme degree of discipline when the same child misbehaves. Landreth found that her four-year-olds gave more mother responses on a care item concerning food than on bath-time or bedtime care and suggests, as Brim has,[89] that "any generalizations on parent roles should be made in terms of the role activities studied."[90]

Let me illustrate the utility of the two-dimensional concept by applying it to the parental role. Clearly there are a number of expressive requirements for adequate performance in this role: spontaneity and flexibility, the ability to be tender and loving and to respond to tenderness and love from a child, to take pleasure in tactile contact and in play, and to forget one's adultness and unself-consciously respond to the sensitivities and fantasies of a child. Equally important are the instrumental requirements for adequate performance in the parental role: firmness and consistency; the ability to manage time and energy; to plan and organize activities involving the child; to teach and to train the child in body controls, motor and language skills, and knowledge of the natural and social world; and interpersonal and value discriminations.

---

pothesized, a very *low* negative correlation between the two measures. E. K. Beller, "Exploratory Studies of Dependency," trans., *N.Y. Academy of Science,* 21 (1959), pp. 414–426.

[88] Brim, "The Parent-Child Relation as a Social System: I. Parent and Child Roles," op. cit.

[89] Ibid.

[90] Landreth, op. cit., p. 181.

Assuming we had empirical measures of these two dimensions of the parental role, one could then compare individual women both by their levels on each of these dimensions and by the extent to which the discrepancy in level on the two dimensions was tipped toward a high expressive or instrumental dimension. This makes no assumptions about what the balance "should" be; that remains an empirical question awaiting a test in the form of output variables — the characteristics of children we deem to be critical for their competence as adults. Indeed, I would predict that an exhaustive count of the actual components of both the marital and parental roles would show a very high proportion of instrumental components in the parental role and a low proportion in the marital role and that this is an underlying reason why maternal role adjustment is more difficult for women than marital role adjustment. It also leaves as an open, empirical question what the variance is, among fathers, in the level of expressiveness and instrumentality in their paternal role performance and how the profile of fathers compares with that of mothers.

It would not surprise many of us, of course, if women scored higher than men on the expressive dimension and men scored higher on the instrumental dimension of the parental role. Yet quite the opposite might actually result. Men spend relatively little time with their children, and it is time of a particular kind: evenings, weekends, and vacations, when the activities and mood of the family are heavily on the expressive side. Women carry the major burden of the instrumental dimension of parenting. If, as Mable Cohen[91] suggests, the rearing of American boys is inadequate on the social and sexual dimension of development and the rearing of American girls is inadequate on the personal dimension of development, then from the perspective of adequate parenthood performance, we have indeed cause to reexamine the socialization of boys and girls in families and schools. Our current practices appear adequate as preparation for occupational life for men but not women, and inadequate as preparation for family life for both sexes.

However, this is to look too far ahead. At the present, this analysis of parenthood suggests we have much to rethink and much to research before we develop policy recommendations in this area.

[91] Cohen, op. cit.

Families, like individuals, have life cycles. They dissolve through death, divorce, and departure of grown children, often leaving individual family members to face their later years alone. This may mean a change in life style. Aging itself may affect the pace and style of a person's life. For these reasons many questions can be raised about how older persons live, how they cope with problems of this particular phase of the life cycle. Influenced by cultural emphasis on production and on youth, social scientists were not until recently much interested in the study of older people. Popular generalizations like those which follow are often made about older people: they are incapable of caring for themselves; they are disinterested in the world around them; they are sick a great deal of the time; and they tend to be childlike. Research supports none of these generalizations.

Some older people may find the central life interest of being a "senior citizen" thrust upon them, especially if they are in retirement villages or in old age homes. Others remain in the larger community living with people in many age groups. These people are less likely to have their "senior citizen status" as a central life interest.

Bernice Neugarten reports in the following article on a long-term study of 2,000 persons over seventy and finds that for many old age is still a period of growth. The ways people cope with biological changes of aging may depend upon their prior life styles more than upon their chronological ages.

Grow Old Along with Me! The Best is Yet to Be

Bernice L. Neugarten

Most of us have a half-conscious and irrational fear that one day we will find ourselves old, as if suddenly we will fall off a cliff, and that what we *will be* then has little to do with what *are* now. Recent research has shown,

however, that nothing could be farther from the truth.

It would be a gross over-simplification, of course, to say that no changes occur in personality as people move from middle age through old age, just as it would be a distortion to say that life-styles always remain consistent. But within broad limits — and with no overwhelming biological accidents — the pattern of aging is predictable for the individual if we know his personality in middle age and how he has dealt with earlier life events.

ARC

Several years' research that I and other investigators have done at the University of Chicago has led us to conclude that aging should be seen as one part of the continuous life cycle. It is shaped by the individual's past — his childhood, adolescence and adulthood. Like earlier periods in life, aging brings new situations and new problems. It calls for new adaptations.

Middle age and old age are eventful periods, and grandparenthood, retirement, widowhood, illness, and the recognition of approaching death can be as dramatic as anything that happens earlier. In adapting to the biological changes that are going on inside and to the social changes that are going on outside, the aging person draws upon what he has been as well as what he is. How else shall we account for the fact that one person copes well, another poorly, with the succession of late-life events?

Nevertheless, most people see aging as alien to the self and tend to deny or repress the associated feelings of distaste and anxiety. We have an irrational fear of aging and, as a result, we maintain a psychological distance between ourselves and older persons.

This irrational fear has its basis in our stereotypical thinking about age groups. Stereotypes about the young, the middle-aged and the old influence our behavior in subtle ways. They affect our perceptions of appropriate and inappropriate behavior in ourselves and in other persons. They constrain our attitudes and our actions. They make it difficult to improve relationships among persons of various ages.

ANIMUS

While the stereotyping of any age group is full of pitfalls, we are just now beginning to realize that stereo-types about aging and the aged create a particularly complex set of problems. In addition to making us fear aging, the stereotypes lead to a divisiveness in society at large that has been called ageism — that is, negative or hostile attitudes between age groups that lead to socially destructive competition. So long as we believe that old persons are poor, isolated, sick and unhappy (or, to the contrary, powerful, rigid and reactionary), we find the prospect of old age particularly unattractive. We can then separate ourselves comfortably from older persons and relegate them to inferior status.

Conflict between generations probably is a universal theme in history, but the intensity of the conflict and the focus of the hostility obviously fluctuate according to historical, social and economic factors. Some social scientists are alarmed that generational conflicts are increasing in the 1970s. Although the generation gap has been described mainly as a gap between the young and everybody else, it is entirely possible that conflicts will also appear in the other direction — that is, between the old and everybody else.

Anger toward the old may be on the rise. One of every 10 Americans is now 65 or older, and an industrialized society whose citizens live increasingly longer becomes in many ways a gerontocratic society. Older persons occupy an increasing proportion of power positions in judicial, legislative, economic and professional areas, and the young and the middle-aged often resent them. Older persons themselves are learning the politics of confrontation. The appeal to Senior Power and the recent growth of national organizations that act as advocates for older persons suggest that the conflict is being joined by those who might otherwise be its victims.

Stereotypes of the aged are difficult to dispel, largely because research on aging is a recent development in both the biological and the social sciences and research findings reach the public at a snail's pace. Many widely held but inaccurate images, inadvertently repeated through the mass media, come from social workers who serve the poor, the lonely and the isolated, and from physicians and psychiatrists who see the physically ill and the mentally ill. Thus we base many of our current stereotypes on a picture of the needy rather than on a picture of the typical older person.

Studies of large and representative samples of older persons are now appearing, however, and they go far toward exploding some of our outmoded images. For example, old persons do not become isolated and neglected by their families, although both generations prefer separate households. Old persons are not dumped into mental hospitals by cruel or indifferent children. They are not necessarily lonely or desolate if they live alone. Few of them ever show overt signs of mental deterioration or senility, and only a small proportion ever become mentally ill. For those who do, psychological and psychiatric treatment is by no means futile.

Retirement and widowhood do not lead to mental illness, nor does social isolation. Retirement is not necessarily bad: some men and women want to keep on working, but more and more choose to retire earlier and earlier. Increasing proportions of the population evidently value leisure more than they value work. Nor do retired persons sicken physically from idleness and feelings of worthlessness. Three fourths of the persons questioned in a recent national sample reported that they were satisfied or very satisfied with their lives since retirement. This is in line with earlier surveys. Most persons over 65 think of themselves as being in good health and they act accordingly, no matter what their physicians think.

CUT-OFF

The belief that 65 is a useful marker of old age is another stereotype. It was historical accident that set 65 as the age of eligibility for Social-Security payments. The decision reflected the economic situation and the manpower needs of the country in the 1930s. Age 65 otherwise has no reality as a turning point in the life of the individual. Because people are beginning to retire at earlier ages, perhaps we should call 60 or 55 the beginning of old age. Or, on the other hand, because 65-year-olds are generally more youthful today than their fathers were, and because longevity is increasing, perhaps we should use 75 as the marker. (The 1970 U.S. census shows that in the last 10 years the number of persons aged 75 and over increased three times as fast as the number of those aged 65 to 74.)

But the most insidious stereotype of all, in many ways, puts the old (or, for that matter, the young or the middle-aged) into a distinct category or a distinct group. There is, in truth, no such thing as "the" young, or "the" old. People *do* differ; they also become increasingly different over time, as each person accumulates an idiosyncratic set of experiences and becomes committed to a unique set of people, things, interests and activities. One has only to recall, for instance, the range of differences among the members of one's high-school graduating class and then to see these persons at a class reunion 25 years later. They are much more varied as 40-year-olds than they were as 18-year-olds. In a society as complex as ours, with increasing social permissiveness for people to follow their own bents, a good case can be made that — despite the counterpressures that create conformity — increased differentiation occurs over the life cycle.

To put the same point another way, calendar age or chronological age is a poor basis for grouping people who have attained biological maturity. Study after study of the happiness, intelligence, personality or health of adults has shown that age is a poor index of the differences between people.

PROBE

Older persons are not a homogeneous group, then, no matter from what perspective we look at them. This fact has become particularly clear to our group at Chicago in carrying out a long line of studies of middle age and aging over the past 15 years: studies of personality, of adaptational patterns, of career lines, of age-norms, of attitudes and values across social-class and generational lines. The number of

men and women who have participated now totals more than 2,000. We based each study in the series upon a relatively large sample of normal persons; none was a volunteer and all were living in one or another metropolitan community in the Midwest.

One study that illustrates the point about heterogeneity focused on persons aged 70 to 79. We were pursuing these questions: Would retired persons who stayed actively engaged in various family and community activities be happier than those who were relatively inactive? How would longstanding personality differences affect these relationships? To find out, we gathered various psychological test data and conducted home interviews repeatedly over a seven-year period. We made systematic assessments in three areas: personality, degree of satisfaction with life, and extent of social-role activity.

In the area of personality, we assessed each person on 45 dimensions. Then, by appropriate statistical methods, we derived four major personality types, which we called *integrated, defended, passive-dependent,* and *disintegrated.*

POINTS

Our life-satisfaction measure involved five components. We rated an individual high to the extent that he 1) took pleasure from the round of activities that constituted his everyday life — the person who enjoyed sitting at home watching television could rate as high as the one who enjoyed his job; 2) regarded his life as meaningful and accepted responsibility for what his life had been; 3) felt he had succeeded in achieving his major goals; 4) held a positive self-image; and 5) maintained optimistic attitudes and moods.

For role-activity, we rated both the extent and the intensity of activity (that is, the amount of time and energy invested and the emotional significance attached) in each of 11 social roles: parent, spouse, grandparent, kin-group member, worker, homemaker, citizen, friend, neighbor, club-and-association member, and church member. For example, with regard to the role of spouse, we rated a man low if he lived with his wife but shared few activities with her other than perfunctory routines such as eating his meals in her presence. A man who planned and carried out most of his day's activities in the company of his wife rated high. We summed the ratings in the 11 roles to obtain a role-activity score.

We also asked about an individual's activities in each role area when he had been age 60, then systematically assessed the differences that had developed as time passed. For this group as a whole, activity levels had decreased and members showed levels of social interaction that were lower than they were when they were 60. Yet the more dramatic finding was the great range of differences in terms of present activity patterns and life-styles. Using our various sets of data for each person, we found eight major patterns among the four major personality types that follow:

1. *Integrated.* The majority of these 70-year-olds remained integrated personalities — well-functioning persons with complex inner lives, intact cognitive abilities and competent egos. They accepted and maintained a comfortable degree of control over their impulses; they were flexible and open to new stimuli, mellow and mature. All were high in life satisfaction. At the same time, they differed among themselves with regard to role activity and therefore showed different patterns of aging.

One pattern we called the *reorganizers*, competent people who were engaged in a wide variety of activities. They were the optimum agers in some respects — at least in the American culture, which places a high value on continuing to be active. These persons substituted new activities for lost ones; when they retired from work, they gave time to community affairs or to the church or to other associations. They reorganized their patterns of activity. One such person was a retired schoolteacher who, at 75, was selling life insurance and making more money than ever. He held elective office in an association of retirees, attended concerts and the theater with his wife, and visited regularly with friends.

Another group of complex and well-integrated personalities we called the *focused* because they had become selective in their activities, devoting energy to the few roles that were important to them. One was an emeritus university professor who, at 75, was still teaching, but only those courses she wanted to teach. She had withdrawn from organizations that she felt were needlessly time-consuming; she felt free to accept or decline invitations at will. It was a relief to have her husband at home now, because he did things around the house that she had had to do earlier, but otherwise, he played a very secondary role in her life. She seldom saw her children and liked it that way. She was glad to be free of responsibility, and to invest all her energies in her work.

A third pattern we called the *disengaged*. These were also well-integrated personalities with high life satisfaction, but with low activity; they had moved away voluntarily from role commitments, not in response to external losses or physical deficits, but because of preference. These were self-directed, though not shallow, persons. They were interested in the world, but they were not imbedded in networks of social interaction. They had high feelings of self-regard, just as the first two groups did, but they had chosen the "rocking-chair" approach to old age — a calm, withdrawn, but contented pattern. One was a retired man who had dropped his club memberships, seldom saw his former work colleagues or friends, and welcomed the opportunity to lead a relaxed life at home, visiting with his children and grandchildren, gardening a little, and occasionally helping his wife around the house.

2. *Defended.* In the next major personality category were men and women whom we called "armored" or "defended." These were the striving, ambitious, and achievement-oriented persons who drove themselves hard. They had high defenses against anxiety and needed to maintain tight control over impulse life. This personality group provided two patterns of aging.

The *holding-on* pattern included the persons who said, "So long as you keep busy, you'll get along all right," or "I'll work until I drop." This group had medium to high life satisfaction because they managed to maintain relatively high levels of activity. One such woman had been an office worker all her life, had never married, and regarded herself as strong and tough. She said that when she was younger she was much too busy to feel lonely; now that she was retired, she kept busy as the historian and recording secretary for the local DAR. She had arteriosclerosis and had suffered a heart attack five years earlier, but she said that she did not let her illness get her down: "You can't slow down just because you happen to have some physical limitations."

The other group of defended personalities we called the *constricted*. These persons were busy defending themselves against aging; preoccupied with losses and deficits, they constricted their social interactions and shut out new experiences, fending off what they seemed to regard as imminent collapse. Given their personalities, their approach to the world worked fairly well, and they had medium or even high levels of satisfaction and contentment. Mr. B, for example, had worked out elaborate rituals for maintaining his health. He talked of little else. He and his wife spent hours shopping for just the right foods, and they made vegetable juices fresh every day. He took long drives into the country each week to bring back pure spring water. He was not much different now, he said, from when he was younger. All his life he had been cautious about himself, and even as a young man he "always thought twice before making any rash decisions."

3. *Passive dependent.* Among members of the passive-dependent group, there were also two patterns of aging.

The *succorance-seeking* were those persons with strong dependency needs who sought responsiveness from others. They showed medium levels of activity, for the most part, and medium satisfaction with life; they did fairly well so long as each had at least one or two other persons to lean on. One woman, for example, looked back to the time when her husband was alive because he always took such good care of her. Now she was diabetic and felt particularly helpless. But she said she counted on her son, who lived in the same city and visited her every day. He took her shopping on Saturdays, paid all her bills and saw to it that she took her medicine.

There were a small number of the *apathetic*, those in whom passivity was the most striking personality feature. They had few activities and very little interaction with others; they showed little interest in the world about them. Life was hard, they said, and there was never much that could be done about it, was there? One, for instance, was a woman who limited her activities entirely to meeting her physical needs and caring for her two cats. She seldom interacted even with her brother and sister-in-law, who lived on the floor above her, because, as she said, "They are old and sick, too, and don't go anywhere."

4. *Disintegrated.* Finally, there were a few whom we called the disintegrated or *disorganized*, persons who showed gross defects in psychological functions and deterioration in thought processes. They managed to maintain themselves in the community, either because of protective families or because of the forbearance of the people around them. Mr. G, for instance, was a paranoid, isolated man who lived in a run-down section of the city. He did a little janitorial work around the building in exchange for a room in the basement.

OTHERS

These eight patterns do not exhaust the variations we found in this group of 70-year-olds, and the group itself did not include the full range. There are, of course, some persons in their 70s who are too ill to be interviewed, a small number who live in hospitals and homes for the aged, and a few who have moved to leisure communities in the South and Southwest.

But it is the variation rather than the similarity among 70-year-olds that is impressive. And the diversity is likely to become even greater in the future. At present, there is an over-representation of the foreign-born, the poorly educated and the poor among those who are 65 and over. In future decades, with better health, more education and more financial resources, older men and women will have greater freedom to choose life-styles that suit them.

Another point is equally important. The individuals we studied in such great detail over seven years seemed to show relatively consistent patterns of coping and adjustment. Although we had no systematic data gathered when these persons were young or middle-aged, we knew a great deal about their life histories and we had information from family members. The general picture was one of personality continuities over time.

BRIDGE

Looked at realistically, then, and with the stereotypes dispelled, aging is not a leveler of individual differences. For most people it brings no sudden and drastic transformation of personality. This being so, aging will not separate the individual's present from his future self. Just as every person changes as he grows up, he will continue to change as he grows old. But aging will not destroy the continuities between what he has been, what he is, and what he will be. Recognition of this fact should lessen the fear of growing old. At the social level, the knowledge that our stereotypes are ill-founded should make older persons seem less distant and less alien, and should help to bridge the psychological barriers between people of different ages.

SOCIAL CHANGE AND SOCIAL MOVEMENTS: TEMPORAL DIMENSIONS OF LIFE STYLES

During the two hundred years that the United States has been an independent nation, there has been continuous change in American life styles. The life of an American in 1776 bears little resemblance to an American's life in 1976. Forces such as technology, migration, the economy, and the state of our relations with other nations have all set the context within which Americans have led their lives.

The study of social change by social scientists has for the most part been limited to the analysis of long-range trends, e.g., the transition within a particular society from an agricultural to an industrial economy. Life styles change drastically during such dramatic transitions. Sociologists demonstrate that there is sweeping social change by documenting the alterations in life styles during such major periods of transition. In this instance, sociologists are most interested in long-range changes in a nation's life style, such as major shifts in occupational and family patterns.*

* See, for example, Richard P. Applebaum, *Theories of Social Change,* Chicago (Markham, 1970) and Kenneth E. Boulding, *A Primer on Social Dynamics: History as Dialectics and Development* (New York: Free Press, 1970).

It is easy to document the difference between life in America today and two hundred years ago, but there have also been many significant changes in American life styles in the past thirty-five years. We shall limit our discussion to this shorter period of time. To many current college students, social concerns of even the recent past seem strangely remote. Yesterday's problems become quickly forgotten, and the life style of Americans even a few years before one was born is just another facet of history.

For instance, less than twenty years ago, Americans anticipated the beginning of World War III and prepared for this event by building home and public bomb shelters and by holding air raids in public schools. At the time bomb shelters were being constructed, another major fear was that Communists were infiltrating American institutions paving the way for a Russian takeover. It never happened. Now it is hard to believe that it could seriously have been expected. More recently, many saw hippies and radical college students as the major threat to American society, but college life settled back to its plodding routine of lectures and term papers. Not long before college radicals were perceived as a major threat, the invasion of the white middle-class world by blacks was seen by many whites as a national emergency. Now that that crisis has passed and at least some blacks have entered into the main stream of American life, fear of a black "invasion" has decreased.

The concerns of most Americans has shifted over the past thirty-five years. One example is Americans' orientations toward our natural resources. During World War II, many valued commodities were rationed or unavailable either because they were expended for the war effort or because the nation that was the source of these goods was fighting a war. Americans accepted scarcity as part of their life style as Richard Lingeman discusses in the following article. After the war, and up to the mid-sixties, scarcity was forgotten until a few people started pointing out that many of our national resources were limited. There is only so much coal, oil, and other essential natural resources available and we must conserve these essential commodities. The scarcity in the future may not be a temporary one and may affect the life style not only of all Americans but of all inhabitants of the planet earth.

Remembrance of Rationing Past

Richard R. Lingeman

As I cut into my $1.99-a-pound pork chop and think of the depleted beef section at the supermarket, I summon up remembrances of things past. How many in the class remember World War II rationing? The reason I ask is that as each day seems to bring with it a new shortage — whether gasoline, fuel oil, wheat, soybeans, canned goods — it seems we stood and talked like this before and I can remember where or when.

During the Second World War just about everything was scarce at one time or another and the Government instituted a variety of measures to keep the factories running and the population fed and clothed. On the industry level, the War Production Board allocated scarce raw materials among factories by a priority system. Goods for the civilian populace were distributed under a rationing system or simply sold on a first-come-first-served basis, which meant an awful lot of standing in line at times. To oversimplify, we had guns but we did not have a whole lot of butter (per capita butter consumption dropped from 17 pounds in the thirties to 11 pounds in 1943).

A random catalogue of items that fell short will give an impression: silk stockings, nylons, shellac for phonograph records, wool, shoe leather, rubber, alarm clocks, toothpaste tubes, zippers, whisky, kapok, tung oil, hog bristle, any appliance, champagne, bicycles, flashlights, garbage cans, razor blades, tea, tin cans, Lucky Strike green, chicle, sliced bread and metal caskets. As a result, women painted their legs, records were made from scrap, men's suits were cuffless and flapless, tires were recapped, "Victory" alarm clocks (with many metal parts replaced by plastic) were invented, flies were buttoned, cigarettes had names like Juleps or Coffeetone, people drank potato whisky and Australian champagne, life jackets were stuffed with milkweed fluff and toothpicks were used instead of hairpins in beauty shops.

Substitutes, stretching or plain doing without were one way the nation coped with shortages; rationing and price controls were another. The first necessity to be rationed was tires. In January, 1942, the Office of Price Administration issued a tire-rationing plan and called upon anyone owning more than five tires to turn the excess in. The shortage was caused by Japanese conquests in Malaya and Java, which cut off practically all of our rubber supply. Americans met the challenge by slowly driving their tires down to the rims while visions of synthetic rubber danced in their heads; but synthetic rubber was only a 12,000-ton gleam in the eye in 1941 and the nation consumed 700,000 tons annually. (Indeed, it was not until 1945 that synthetic rubber production was sufficient to meet civilian needs.) Meantime people recapped their tires or put their cars up on blocks "for the duration" or bought tires on the black market. The Administration ordered a massive rubber drive that had every man, woman and child rummaging through closets for old galoshes, but this reclaimed rubber was not any good for tires. Women felt the, ahem, pinch as much as men: rubberless girdles employing whalebone or piano wire were cinched into service. As an advertisement of the time proudly proclaimed: "The corset and brassière creators of America faced — and met — a challenging situation in the midst of a desperate rubber shortage."

Directly related to the rubber shortage was gas rationing. It took a year before this sacrifice could be extracted from the American people by a timid Congress and Administration. Eventually a national commission headed by the prototypical elder statesman Bernard Baruch had to be drafted to give the bad news that gasoline should be rationed and unnecessary driving cut out. By this time, the East Coast was already experiencing a fuel shortage because German submarines, operating almost within sight of the Eastern seaboard were sinking tankers almost as fast as they were sent up from the Caribbean oil fields. Gas stations periodically ran dry. Drivers took to following fuel trucks making deliveries, and when the word spread that a station had gas, lines of as many as 350 cars would form.

Nationwide gas rationing went into effect on Dec. 1, 1942. Each car owner was issued an A, B or C sticker for his windshield and a book of coupons to be exchanged for gas. The basic allotment for the A-card holder was 3 gallons a week. B's — those who used their cars to drive to work — received an extra allotment based on mileage. C's used their cars in their business — for example, doctors and salesmen — and got an even larger allotment. It was estimated that nearly half of all American drivers wangled B or C stickers, even though a Gallup Poll revealed that of the 45 per cent of American workers who drove their cars to work, three-fourths said they could get to work some other way. A national speed limit of 35 miles an hour was also set and patriotic motorists who kept within the limit threw dirty looks at speeders and muttered imprecations about "joy-riding war workers."

The tire-gas conservation campaign included a ban on "pleasure driving." Even those limited to 3 gallons had to be on "essential business," which was defined as "necessary" shopping, attending church services or funerals, securing medical attention, meeting emergencies involving a "threat to life, health or property" or trips for family or occupational necessities. The O.P.A. ruled that a driver might sample nonessential pleasures on an essential trip (such as stopping for a soft drink) so long as he did not "add as much as one foot to the distance traveled in his car for such a purpose."

To enforce this Draconian code, O.P.A. inspectors posted themselves at turnpike and bridge exits asking drivers where the hell they were going or hung around racetracks and stadiums copying down license numbers. The ban on pleasure driving was so difficult to enforce that it was dropped in September, 1943. Nonetheless, long trips by car virtually ceased, except for the favored few and people who used counterfeit ration coupons (counterfeiting of money dropped tenfold between 1939 and 1944, evidence that the old pros had turned to ration coupons). Gas rationing meant that one could drive up a city street with barely a halt for traffic; highways were uncrowded and the annual Labor Day carnage was halved.

The alternatives to driving were few. Trains and buses were crowded and you had to have a priority to fly. If you rode a bicycle — well, you could hardly get a bicycle any more. It required a certificate of necessity from one's ration board to acquire one.

In food rationing, sugar was the first to go — a casualty of shipping shortages and the loss of the Philippines, which supplied one-sixth of our sugar. In May, 1942, Americans trooped to their local schools and were issued War Ration Book One, one book for each member of the family. Already, people were buying 100-pound bags of sugar and some grocers set a limit of 10 pounds to a customer. Each person receiving a ration book was required to swear how much sugar he or she had on hand; stamps equivalent to this stockpile were torn from their books. Every man jack of them, of course, told the truth, and the story about the housewife whose husband, as a prank, impersonated an O.P.A. man over the phone and asked her about the 100-pound bag she had on hand, causing her to pour it all down the drain, was, of course, apocryphal. The sugar ration averaged out to 8 (later 12) ounces

per week, no great hardship. Still, pocketing a few lumps from a restaurant sugar bowl became a common practice.

In November, 1942, came coffee rationing. This, too, had been anticipated and a good deal of hoarding (one of the great pejorative words of both World War I and II) was engaged in. The coffee ration was one pound per person every five weeks, which averaged about a cup a day, the Government figured. Coffee rationing lasted only until July, 1943; they had, after all, an awful lot of coffee in Brazil — lack of cargo space had caused the shortage. A funny thing happened when coffee became unrationed, however; coffee sales temporarily dropped. Apparently its scarcity had increased its desirability.

More serious was the rationing of meat and canned goods in 1943. When the O.P.A. announced a freeze on sales of canned meat and fish prior to rationing, housewives swarmed into stores with wagons, perambulators, go-carts — anything with wheels — and pillaged the shelves of all shiny cylindrical objects. The grand champion hoarder was said to be the California woman who declared 8,400 cans when she appeared to receive her ration book (you had to return half the equivalent stamp value of the cans you had on hand, which did not exactly discourage hoarding). There was poetic justice in the account of another woman who had stored hundreds of cans in her basement, only to have a flood wash off all the labels. But there didn't seem to be quite the stigma attached to canned-goods hoarding — while the O.P.A. was publicly condemning hoarding, the newsletter of the Government Printing Office was praising the office's dietitian for her coup in laying in an ample supply of cans.

In the week prior to meat rationing, a similar panic took place. In Columbus, Ohio, 18 policemen had to be called in to control a punching, shoving crowd. A mob of 50,000 people milled around three big markets in Cleveland; in Chicago, policemen stationed in stores admitted only one customer at a time as long as the supply lasted. Some stores simply hung up signs reading CLOSED — NO MORE MEAT and shut down for the remainder of the week. At least one store that didn't close was the Man o' War Market in Milwaukee; it sold 8,000 pounds of horse meat in the first day and a half of business.

Things settled down when meat rationing went into effect in March, 1943. War Ration Book Two contained rows of red and blue stamps, marked A, B, C, D, each eventually worth 10 points. The blue stamps were for processed foods, the red ones were for meats, cheese and fats. Later, plastic tokens were given in change for stamps. Goods in the stores were assigned a point value by the O.P.A. on the basis of relative scarcity — scarce items cost a lot of points, abundant items only a few. Each person had 48 blue points to spend each month. A 1-pound can of beans cost eight points in 1943, a 16-ounce can of peaches, 18. There was a run on baby food because it was point cheap. The system added to the shopper's burdens, since one had to eye not only the price tag but the point tag as well. Newspapers printed reminders to aid the harassed housewife:

"Tomorrow — *Coffee* coupon No. 25 expires. Last day to use No. 4 A coupon, good for four gallons of *gasoline*. . . .

"March 31 — Last day to use A, B, and C point coupons for processed foods in Ration Book No. 2. Deadline for first *tire inspection* for A cards. . . .

"June 15 — Last day for coupon No. 17 good for one pair of *shoes*."

The meat ration was supposed to average out to 28 ounces of meat and 4 ounces of cheese weekly. This would come to a little more than 100 pounds of meat and cheese a year. Actually, however, per capita meat consumption in 1943 was 128.9 pounds, compared with an average of 126 pounds during the 1935–39 period; this figure rose to 140 pounds the next year. Since meat production rose 50 per cent by 1943, the chief cause of the meat shortage was simply overheated consumer demand (plus the needs of the armed forces and the lend-lease program to aid our Allies). The national income had risen from $72.5-billion in 1939 to $181-billion in 1944. Further, wartime migration to the production centers placed a strain on the O.P.A.'s area-allotment system because quotas for some congested towns had been figured on the basis of pre-war population. Everywhere there were periodic meat shortages; bacon might disappear altogether; butter was generally always scarce. Under the variable point system, a half pound of butter might cost an entire week's red points.

Butchers saved their choice cuts for old customers or those willing to pay under the table. Many people discovered tripe, lungs or kidneys for the first time. Eggs were usually plentiful, and the wartime hotdog contained enough filler to choke three Ralph Naders.

There was a roaring black market in meat, a practice confined mostly to legitimate businessmen. As O.P.A. Administrator Chester Bowles said, "We meet professional criminals only in a few limited areas — notably the gasoline black market. Most of our activity is concerned with violations on the part of hitherto reputable individuals or firms, and with violations that frequently result from indifference or carelessness rather than criminal intent." Enforcement was spotty by the undermanned O.P.A. staff: Each investigator had more than 1,000 businesses to inspect. If by "black market" we mean any transaction in violation of price ceilings or the rationing law — tie-in sales, cash paid on the side, shortweighting, upgrading, etc — then the black market was truly widespread, though figures differ. The Department of Agriculture estimated that 20 per cent of all meat found its way into the black market, while Joint Livestock Commission officials estimated that 90 per cent of all meat transactions at the wholesale and slaughterhouse level were in excess of legal ceilings. Overcharges to the housewife were estimated at up to 20 per cent and 83 per cent of the stores surveyed by the American Meat Institute sold at over-the-ceiling prices. So much poultry was being siphoned off by the black

market in Delaware that the Army stationed soldiers on the highways with orders to stop any trucks carrying chickens. If it was determined that the cargo was headed for the black market, the soldiers commandeered it, paying the ceiling price.

A postwar study by sociologist Marshall Clinard estimated that one in 15 of the nation's three million businesses were prosecuted by the O.P.A. for ceiling-price or rationing violations and one in five received warnings. Still, to a Gallup Poll which asked the question, "Do you think buying at black market prices is sometimes justified?" 74 per cent of the respondents answered, "No." Other polls consistently showed more than 90 per cent of the people supporting price controls.

Rationing had its inequities and it was a headache to merchants who had to stay abreast of changing point values and keep track of all those stamps and plastic tokens (which, incidentally, were made from soybeans; with the price of soybeans what it is these days maybe we could revive them as money). Still the idea of apportioning a fair share of scarce items to every citizen and preventing hoarding was a noble one, and to those who raise the specter of those awful World War II price controls it might be pointed out that between May, 1943, and the end of the war the cost of living rose only 3.3 per cent — by official figures anyway. How much has it gone up in the last two years or so? Just asking.

The end of World War II saw many changes in American life styles. During the war, there was a scarcity of skilled labor, and many women filled what would have been men's jobs, had the men not been off fighting a war. "Rosie the Riveter" went back to the kitchen and the men went back to work, manufacturing the consumer products that were unobtainable during the war. The United States was in an era of prosperity. Annual family income increased and job opportunities were abundant for college graduates. This was the period during which the majority of American families purchased televisions. There was a population shift from the city to suburbia. Social critics worried about the blandness of suburban life and the complacency of college students. Birth rates were high and nobody worried about overpopulation, the environment, or oppression of minorities.

For a few years in the early fifties there was a war (called a "police action") in Korea but that had relatively little effect on life back home. High school and college students were not protesting the war. Politics was far from their central life interest. Youth culture reflected much of the values of the fifties, and these values were manifest in the language teenagers spoke and the way many approached their college education.

As They Used to Say in the 1950s ...

Howard Junker

When the time comes, it may not be easy, despite the rebirth of Richard Nixon and Elvis Presley, to muster nostalgia for the Fifties. (Davy Crockett and Roy Cohn, Grace Kelly and

From *Esquire,* 72 (August, 1969), pp. 70–71, 141. Reprinted by permission of *Esquire* Magazine. Copyright © 1969 by Esquire, Inc.

the Playboy Bunny, *My Fair Lady* and adult Westerns, filter tips and instant coffee, Zen and the art of the Roller Derby, Ban the Bomb and togetherness, Harry Belafonte, Jack Kerouac, Dr. Kinsey, and The Golden Age of Television.)

But some of the words we used to use already have the power to charm, so great is the distance between then and now.

Jargonwise, the Fifties spoke a finalized version of advertisingese. Euphemists offered: the Police Action, peaceful coexistence, nuclear blackmail, freedom fighter, creeping Momism, desegregation, payola, cleavage, recession, pinko. Korea did little to enrich the language (brainwashing, gook).

But from Russia came Sputnik, hence beatnik, jetnik. . . .

One kind of nostalgia for the Eisenhower Era looks back to an age of innocence. But this apparent innocence was protected at a cost. Irony, ambiguity, complexity were academic passwords that sophomores enacted as apathy. The common language was designed to not say what was meant: Would you like to have a cup of coffee/come up for a drink? (In the Sixties, *pace* Lenny Bruce: Let's ball.) Sarcasm (Wanna lose ten ugly pounds? Cut off your head) and innuendo (I have here the names) were basic modes of conversation. Much literary imagination went toward developing acceptable variations on Mailer's (1948) fuggin, as in effing, frigging. Sick jokes finally mentioned other unmentionables, and with *Lady Chatterley's Lover* (1959) the unprintable became available in drugstores and at your local supermarket.

Beneath much of the (dirty) white buck, saccharine, other-directed innocence of the Fifties lurked a smug obliviousness. You could still say colored. (Ixnay, ofay). Niggerlipping didn't seem such a terrible way to describe wetting the end of a cigarette. A riot was really funny. A soul kiss involved the tongue. The ghetto was where the Jews had escaped from. Race as in arms, rat, and drag. A pill was like a dope. A bust was a pair of knockers, as in M.M., B.B., and Diana Dors. A joint was maybe a bar.

Getting stoned meant hitting the hard stuff (not horse, booze). A quick brew: quaff a foamy. Whales' tails, Thumper. Here's to the Cardinal once. Chug-a-lug. Getting blotto, stinko, loaded, smashed, plowed, bombed out of your ever-loving mind. Then: heaving, tossing, blowing your lunch (cookies). Upchuck, barf, puke. The problem of youth was getting served. Do you have proof (an I.D.)? Churchkey.

In short, in the Fifties, culture still enjoyed a literary base. Words (the novel) still mattered. Awareness was limited, not electronically total. And regionalisms, celebrated during the Thirties when the middle class stayed home, were not yet erased by television, which went coast to coast in 1951, and commercial jets, which crossed the Atlantic in 1958. Have gun, will travel.

In the Fifties, it was dangerous to take anyone at face value. (Are you for real?) In conformist times, you worried about Image (status), doubly anxious because words functioned as costume: are you hip?

Now you're talking (speaking my language). Certain key terms, dig, became juvenile gestures: L7 equaled square (cube or octagon meant supersquare). The three-ring sign indicated cool; screwy was the finger twirled at the temple, then flung at the nut.

Status was divvied up into geographical dualisms: in, out; with it, from squaresville. Hepcat. Beat/Jazz contributed: daddy-o, pad, bread, gig, slip me some skin. And all that, like, well, you know, man, incoherence. (Holden Caulfield, Marty, Brando and the Method, action painting, the silent generation, Nichols and May, taking the fifth.)

Don't hand me any of that jazz. Take five.

Alienation was the absurd egghead bit. (Did Adlai sell out?) Psychology was Krazy, man, like, I nearly flipped. The best minds. The orgone box. Or, as the get-well card said: I'm glad you're sick, but I'm sorry you're ill. You only got hung up when somebody flaked out on you. If you psyched a test, you had it made. What, me worry?

Yes, above all, anti-frantic. Stay cool. Hang loose. No sweat (negative perspiration). Under control. Made in the shade. Big deal.

Duhhhh!

The antithesis of cool was the slow burn, indicated by touching the index finger to the tongue, extending it toward the unfortunate victim, and announcing "Psss" as if touching a hot stove. A variation: same gesture: Chalk one up for me! Tuftittie. The way the cookie crumbles. The Royal Screw, hence The Royal Shaft, hence The King's Elevator. Up the creek without a paddle.

Cruising for a bruising. Don't give me any grief. You want a knuckle sandwich. Get Bent. Your ass is grass. Blast off. Suck gas. Wise up. Don't bug me. Drop dead. DDT. Finally gonna shut you down. Dump all over you. How's that grab you? Forty lashes with a wet noodle.

Who cut the cheese? The true clue: he who smelt it dealt it. Silent but deadly.

Hardeeharhar.

Antlers in the Treetop or Who Goosed the Moose.

That went over like a pregnant pole vaulter with a broken stick.

What a fake out.

Almost everything was a drag (negative attitude), although some guys did get a charge (some kicks). Have a blast. Really hairy. Going ape. Bad,

Mean, Wicked, Evil. Bitchin. I eat her up. She sends me. Gone, man, gone. Into the air, junior birdmen.

If you weren't grounded, you could take off. And hack, screw, mess around. Goof off.

Where did you go? (Take me to your leader.) I donno, waddya wanna do? Catch some rays. (Shades.) Play charades, spin-the-bottle, Frisbee, pogo stick, Hula-Hoop, bowling, knock-knock, why did the moron?

Precisely at age thirteen, you became a teen-ager. And there were pajama parties and sock hops with a thumbful of 45's. Only bird dogs cut in on a slow dance. Every party has a pooper, that's why we invited you. They tried to tell us we're too young. Grow up.

Certain college studs stuffed phone booths, smashed pianos and, from automobiles, displayed their naked asses to passersby, an act variously called dropping trou, mooning, handing out the b.a. gotcha. Slipping them some pressed ham involved pressing one's bare butt against the window. In the city, you could nerf a cab, i.e., bump it gently at a light. On the highway: chicken.

M*I*C*K*E*Y*M*O*U*S*E

The J.D.'s emerged. The hood. The Rock. (Don't knock the Rock.) Badd-ass. Tough as nails. Switchblade and zip gun for stomping, mixing it up, rumbles. (Squeezing a beer can.) Pegged pants and a greasy D.A.

Or: butch, crew cut, flat top. Charcoal-grey flannel, belt-in-the-back, paisley, Shetland, Madras, bermudas. Our fine-quality pink button-down. Tweedy and preppy.

The common ground: blue jeans, as

in the one and only Levi's. (I'm wise to the rise in your Levi's.) As in shrink 'em in the bathtub. As in James Dean lives. As in engineer boots. Classy.

With a digression to honor circle pins, knee socks, saddle shoes, fruit boots, straight skirts, ponytails. On the one hand. On the other: beards, sandals, and leotards — not yet called tights. Who wears short shorts? If you wore green on Thursday. . . .

As for sex, there was going steady (I.D. bracelet, ring-on-the-necklace, letter or sweater or jacket). And breaking up. But mostly the eternal search for a little action, etc. Bedroom eyes. Hot lips.

The first thing a make-out artist asked: Is she fast? (Nice or good.) Does she put out? Lay it on the line? Do the deed?

He, of course, was always horny. When really hard up, he would even overlook her b.o., cooties, flat chest. (Scuzzy, grungy.) Her zits.

It was suspected that sometimes she, too, was climbing up the wall. Hot to trot.

In that case, if he didn't get shot down (stood up), he might suggest catching a flick. The passion pit. Parking. Let's go watch the submarines race.

For openers, a snow job. Coming on like Gang Busters. Are you trying to feed me a line?

She might come across if he were a big wheel, a B.M.O.C. On the ball, divine, clean-cut, casual, snazzy, a really good (great) guy, the living end. Cute. Neat. Smooth. Peachy keen. A hunk. Hey, bobo. She would certainly be turned off if he were grubby, a phony, a sex fiend, bad news, out to lunch, a

banana, weenie, yo-yo, turkey, spastic, nebbish. Gross. A fink. With a bad case of the uglies. A dumb cluck. A loser, creep, simp. A nothing. Of course, if he were a straight arrow, there'd be no danger of his trying to go too far. (Goodnight kiss. Heavy petting.) Meanwhile, awaiting his chance to go all the way, a circular bulge etched itself into his wallet.

Back with the guys, he would be asked, especially if he had a rep as a hot ticket: Get much?

And at school next day, where the brains were grinds and usually brown-nosers, her friends noticed the hickey on her neck.

Which brings us to that ultimate, fabulous Fifties' experence: wheels.

Bombing around.

In a '49 Ford.

A '55 Chevy.

A Merc.

T-Bird.

Vette.

Coming and going in a Studey.

(Edsel.)

Stick shift, as in grind me a pound. Hang a left.

Fins and tails and two-tone and one year there was a three-tone.

Raked and flamed, decked and lowered, chopped and channeled.

Duals.

Glass pack.

Fuelie. Frenched lights. Coon tail.

I don't care if it rains or freezes, long as I've got my plastic Jesus.

A No. 4.56 rear end.

Driver ed.

I got to cut out. Peel out, lay rubber.

Take it easy.

Anyway I can get it.

See you later, alligator.

University of Texas 1953

Willie Morris

What strikes me most in reading books like Alfred Kazin's haunting poetic reminiscences of boyhood in an immigrant Jewish neighborhood in the East, is the vast gulf which separates that kind of growing up and the childhood and adolescence of those of us who came out of the towns of the American South and Southwest a generation later. With the Eastern Jewish intellectuals who play such a substantial part in American cultural life, perhaps in the late 1960s a dominant part, the struggle as they grew up in the 1930s was for one set of ideas over others, for a fierce acceptance or rejection of one man's theories or another man's poetry — and with all this a driving determination to master the language which had not been their parents' and to find a place in a culture not quite theirs. For other Eastern intellectuals and writers whom I later was to know, going to the Ivy League schools involved, if not a finishing, then a deepening of perceptions, or of learning, or culture.

But for so many of us who converged on Austin, Texas, in the early 1950s, from places like Karnes City or Big Spring or Abilene or Rockdale or Yazoo

City, the awakening we were to experience, or to have jolted into us, or to undergo by some more subtle chemistry, did not mean a mere finishing or deepening, and most emphatically did not imply the victory of one set of ideologies over another, one way of viewing literature or politics over another, but something more basic and simple. This was the acceptance of ideas themselves as something worth living by. It was a matter, at the age of eighteen or nineteen, not of discovering *certain* books, but the simple *presence* of books, not the nuances of idea and feeling, but idea and feeling on their own terms. It is this late coming to this kind of awareness that still gives the intellectuals from the small towns of our region a hungry naive quality, as opposed to the sharp-elbowed over-intellectuality of some Easterners, as if those from down there who made it were lucky, or chosen, out of all the disastrous alternatives of their isolated lower- or middle-class upbringings, to enjoy and benefit from the fruits of simply being educated and liberal-minded.

What we brought to the University of Texas in the 1950s, to an enormous, only partially formed state university, was a great awe before the splendid quotations on its buildings and the walls of its libraries, along with an absolutely prodigious insensitivity as to what they implied beyond decoration. Minds awakened slowly, painfully, and with pretentious and damaging inner searches. Where an Alfred Kazin at the age of nineteen might become aroused in the subway by reading a review by John Chamberlain in the *New York Times* and rush to his office to

From Willie Morris, *North Toward Home* (Boston: Houghton Mifflin, 1967), pp. 149–162. Reprinted by permission of Houghton Mifflin Company. Copyright 1967 by Willie Morris.

complain, we at eighteen or nineteen were only barely beginning to learn that there *were* ideas, much less ideas to arouse one from one's self. If places like City College or Columbia galvanized the young New York intellectuals already drenched in literature and polemics, the University of Texas had, in its halting, unsure, and often frivolous way, to teach those of us with good minds and small-town high school diplomas that we were intelligent human beings, with minds and hearts of our own that we might learn to call our own, that there were some things, many things — ideas, values, choices of action — worth commiting one's self to and fighting for, that a man in some instances might become morally committed to honoring every manifestation of individual conscience and courage. Yet the hardest task at the University of Texas, as many of us were to learn, was to separate all the extraneous and empty things that can drown a young person there, as all big universities can drown its young people, from the few simple things that are worth living a life by. Without wishing to sound histrionic, I believe I am thinking of something approaching the Western cultural tradition; yet if someone had suggested that to me that September night in 1952, as I stepped off the bus in Austin to be greeted by three fraternity men anxious to look me over, I would have thought him either a fool or a con man.

I emerged from that bus frightened and tired, after having come 500 miles non-stop over the red hills of Louisiana and the pine forests of East Texas. The three men who met me — appalled, I was told later, by my green

trousers and the National Honor Society medal on my gold-plated watch chain — were the kind that I briefly liked and admired, for their facility at small talk, their clothes, their manner, but whom I soon grew to deplore and finally to be bored by. They were the kind who made fraternities tick, the favorites of the Dean of Men at the time, respectable B or C-plus students, tolerable athletes, good with the Thetas or the Pi Phis; but one would find later, lurking there inside of them despite — or maybe because of — their good fun and jollity, the ideals of the insurance salesman and an aggressive distrust of anything approaching thought. One of them later told me, with the seriousness of an early disciple, that my table manners had become a source of acute embarrassment to all of them. That night they drove me around the campus, and they were impressed that I knew from my map-reading where the University library was, for two of them were not sure.

It was early fall, with that crispness in the air that awakened one's senses and seemed to make everything wondrously alive. My first days there I wandered about the enormous campus, mingling silently with its thousands of nameless students. I walked past the fraternity and sorority houses, which were like palaces to me with their broad porches and columns and patios, and down "The Drag" with its bookstores and restaurants, a perfectly contained little city of its own. On a slight rise dominating the place was a thirty-story skyscraper called the "Tower," topped with an edifice that was a mock Greek temple; the words carved on the white sandstone said, *"Ye Shall Know the Truth and the Truth Shall Make You Free,"* causing me to catch my breath in wonder and bafflement. That first morning I took the elevator to the top, and looked out on those majestic purple hills to the west, changing to lighter shades of blue or a deeper purple as wisps of autumn clouds drifted around the sun; this, they would tell me, was the Great Balcones Divide, where the South ended and the West began, with its stark, severe landscape so different from any I had known before. I saw the state capitol, only a few blocks to the south, set on its sloping green acres, its pink granite catching the morning light, and away to the east the baseball field dug into the native rock, and the football stadium, the largest and most awesome I had ever seen. Then down again the campus, where all the furious construction and demolition was going on, and where the swarms of students back for another year greeted each other with such shouts and screams of delight, war-whoops, and hoohaws and wild embracing, and twangy "hello there's" with the "r's" exploited as nowhere else in the South, that I suddenly felt unbearably displaced and alone. Everything around me was brisk, burgeoning, *metropolitan.* It was bigger than Memphis when I was twelve.

I was a desperately homesick Mississippi boy of seventeen, and the life I saw about me was richer and more flamboyant than anything I had known before. There was a kind of liberality of spirit there, an *expansiveness* which, as I was one day to learn, is one of the most distinctive qualities of Texans, even though it can be directed toward

things that do not deserve being expansive about. There was something frenetic, almost driven, about the organized pursuits of these Texas students; even by the gregarious standards of my own high school there was not enough loneliness in them, not enough disaffection; they moved about in packs, and they would organize a committee — a service committee, a social committee, a committee on committees — on the merest excuse. Today this characteristic, which reaches far into adult life, seems most curious in a state which in most established quarters glorifies, perhaps more than any other region of America, some mystical individualism, with sources more contemporaneous with Goldwater and Buckley than Rousseau.

Yet I myself shared that compulsion to join, and join I did, everything from the Freshman Council to student government to the ROTC Band. This, I thought, was the mark of success, something one assumed without dispute. Versatility, gregariousness, the social graces, these were the important things, just as they had been in Yazoo; these were what the University of Texas could provide, only bigger and better. Yet as time passed I would grow progressively more lonely, more contemptuous of this organized anarchy, more despairing of the ritualized childishness and grasping narcissism of the fraternity life.

This taste of fraternities had a curious effect. The experience of seeing grown men twisting paper-maché into flowers for a float, or of social lions advising how best to impress the sorority girls, at least gave one some early insight into priorities. And in that day this fraternity was the best one there; the further one got down the scale, the more insufferable were the practices. The new members who had not been initiated were called out at all hours, for "exercise rallies," "walks," or "serenades," the latter custom consisting of group singing at midnight to some sorority; while the idiotic fraternity songs were sung, the girls on their balconies or porches would giggle or squeal their approval, with proper gradations of intensity depending on how close to the top those doing the serenading came on the social register. Some fraternities beat their new members with paddles and other instruments, or gave elaborate "pig" parties, in which each member was expected to bring the ugliest girl he could manage to get for the evening. Around the campus one got to know of the "perennial" fraternity boys; one in particular was over thirty years old, registered each semester for the minimum of courses and seldom if ever went to class, his purpose being to indulge as freely as possible in all aspects of the Greek Life. He escorted girls twelve years his junior, and gave bright little lectures on how to handle yourself in the best social circumstances. Once he turned on me for some minor trespass and said, "I wonder when you're going to grow up." Another "perennial" came to school each fall semester on what amounted to an athletic scholarship; he ran a service station in San Antonio, and because he was adept at throwing a football, his group paid his tuition so he could play on the intramural touch football team. Then he would drop out of school after the season and just before examinations.

I was unhappy and insecure with the fraternity men. I and another young country boy from a small South Texas town walked the six blocks from Brackenridge Hall for dinner with the brothers each evening, dreading what organized torments they might have in store for us next. Our talk was bitter, but mainly frightened. He had the courage of his fear to get out, but I did not, for it would have implied some failure in me, and I would not admit failure even when I felt it. I simply went less and less and became more unhappy, until late in my junior year when I was beginning to campaign for the editorship of the student newspaper; with cynicism in my heart and the tally of the fraternity and sorority vote in my secret ledger, I sought their support. The difference was that in my first year I would not have had the self-awareness to be cynical, because I did not know that cynicism existed.

Some excellent men were involved in this debilitating preoccupation. Their names were Mohr, Little, Penn, Nagle, Jacoby, Higgins, Eastland, Eckert, Williams, Dahlin, Finch, Bailey, Ogden, Schmucker, Voekel, and a dozen others, most with appropriately vivid and wildly Texan nicknames — they were better by far as individuals than the organization to which they gave allegiance. For the organization itself, within the broader social framework of the fraternity and sorority system on a big state university campus, was pernicious and destructive — too encouraging of petty provincial snobbism, simple human waste, and downright prejudice, too demanding on its immature young people of social appurtenances and the trappings of respectability. At its worst this system could be cruel and despicably smug; at its best it was merely an easy substitute for more intelligent and mature forms of energy.

Early in that year I was taken on my first "walk" by a campus "service organization." It was late on a Saturday night in the fall; the members blindfolded me and put me in their car. We drove for miles, until the concrete gave out, and down some interminable gravel road until we stopped. They took all my clothes, including my shoes, and tied me to a tree. After I heard the car drive away, I worked the rope loose and started down the road, walking in the middle of it to avoid beer cans, broken whiskey bottles, and other debris that always clutter the sides of Texas roads. It was the last indignity: homesick, cold, alone, naked, and lost, off on some meaningless adolescent charade.

That afternoon I had escorted to the football game a gat-toothed brunette they had picked out for me, from a "wealthy family in Dallas" the thirty-two-year-old perennial had said, and she had spent the whole time making fun of the way I drawled! Finally, at the top of a lonely hill, I got my bearings. Looking down from the hill I caught sight of Austin in the cold night air: the Tower, lit orange because of the day's football victory, and the state capitol, and the curved boulevards faintly outlined in the pale blue artificial moonlight from the old street lamps. There it all was, miles away, and I was bruised and tired, but that skyline almost struck me over with its strange open beauty, the clear open beauty of the Southwest plains. Then,

all of a sudden, I got mad, probably the maddest I had ever been in my whole life — at homesickness, at blond majorettes, at gat-toothed Dallas girls, at fraternities, at twangy accents, at my own helpless condition. *"I'm better than this sorry place,"* I said to myself, several times, and be damned if I didn't believe it. Then I started walking again, having made a kind of toga of a greasy piece of canvas I had found by the side of the road. Two hours later I reached the concrete and flagged down the third car that came past, and got back to my dormitory just as the sun began to appear.

After an appropriate time for this kind of activity, there was a fraternity institution known as "hell week," a four-day ordeal of petty torture and sadism which preceded "initation" as a full-fledged brother. As victims of this institution, we were made to go sleepless for most of the four days, and were forced to wear burlap under our usual clothes when we went to class during the daytime, causing a most agonizing itch that would have made any lecture intolerable. At night the established brothers amused themselves with a great variety of entertainment. One night we were herded into a large room, and for an hour or more our seniors, who had chosen as usual not to be in libraries or at lectures, poured molasses, castor oil, chicken feed, and sand on us. Then several hundred eggs were brought in, in large cardboard boxes, and from the far side of the room the brothers used us as moving targets. I was chosen as the special object for this diversion; a relentless stream of eggs smashed against me, and I was covered with the oozing yellow yolk, which struck against the molasses and chicken feed and castor oil in a great soggy mess. Finally the brothers, having sated themselves, began drifting out of the room to watch television. The last to leave was an ex-Marine who chose to spend as much of his leisure time as possible on such scholarly pursuits. He was about to depart on what was colloquially known as a "fuck-date," and hence he was dressed immaculately in a navy-blue suit and bow tie. As we were being herded out of another door, I sighted an unbroken egg on the floor near me. I picked it up, took aim on the ex-Marine just as he was departing, let the egg fly, dashed through the back door, and heard the words: *"Hot —* damned!" The egg had smashed against the back of his neck, and the yolk had oozed under his shirt. This accomplishment proved to be the noblest of my first semester.

On the last night of "hell week" I was again blindfolded and taken on a drive by three of the senior members. Again we went up a gravel road, and I was led from the car and up a grassy, rolling hill. "Kneel right here," one of them said, in the tones of a Baptist preacher announcing a hymn. "Don't take the blindfold off for three minutes, and then when you see where you are, meditate for a while. Meditate *seriously*. This is your last responsibility as a pledge. Tomorrow you become one of us." I followed his instructions: when I heard the car leave I took off the blindfold. I was in the middle of a cemetery, kneeling on a grave; the gravestone identified the occupant as one of the founding members of the fraternity. "Well, hot shit," I said to myself, and went home to sleep for the first time in four days.

The next day the initiation was a traditional ceremony handed down by the generations. It was full of such garbled mumbo-jumboes and high-flown adolescent sputterings, all thrown together in some uneasy overlay of illiteracy, that I was reminded of the way Huck Finn and Tom Sawyer had negotiated their own private blood-oaths as pirates. It was so juvenile that the Ku Klux Klan, in contrast, might have resembled the American Associaton of Unversity Professors. But when the new brothers were lined up and presented with fraternity pins, I noticed that several of my fellow novitiates were crying, apparently from the impressiveness of it all. I could not avoid admitting to myself that, even though I was fresh out of a small town in the Mississippi delta, I was either smarter than everyone else in the room or a damned sight less emotionally involved.

It was two things, and the bare suggestion of a third, that made my lonely and superficially gregarious freshman year tolerable, and helped shape my knowledge of that campus.

One was the mad, rudimentary life of the dormitory. Old Brackenridge Hall, a yellow-brick affair with Spanish stucco roofs, stood right at the edge of the long intramural field, only a quarter of a mile from the capitol, and just across a narrow street from a line of dingy shops and greasy cafés. We called it "The Slum Area," not only for its general dinginess but for its violence, both organized and sporadic, which erupted inevitably on the weekend nights after the beer houses across the street closed down. Brackenridge Hall was where life was, stripped of its pretenses, where one saw every day the lonely, the pathetic, the hopeless young men — often poor though sometimes not, often ignorant but not always, but never anything if not various. Here a fairly sensitive boy could not avoid a confrontation with his basic and bare-boned self, and see a big state university in its true dimensions. My first roommate, who flunked out soon enough with five F's and a D-plus, was an alcoholic from Dallas who saw giant roaches in the middle of the night, though the roaches may have been for my benefit. He would throw his slide rule against the wall, or piss in the trashcan from a range of six feet. As I sat in front of my typewriter composing my pieces for the *Daily Texan*, he and his friends played poker and drank rot-gut bourbon on the other side of the table, interrupting themselves occasionally to make fun of my literary output which, when they read it, to their eternal honor, they did not appreciate.

I lived on the fourth floor, with a room overlooking the intramural field and the entire Slum Area, and down on the third floor lived the baseball players. I became a sort of poet laureate of that group, the resident egghead, it may have been, because I at least tried to study my books, and I actually did try to write for the student paper, which they called "The Daily Wipe."

Their floor was unquestionably the filthiest establishment I have ever seen, and from it emanated the most savage and grotesque, though until now unrecorded, happenings at the University of Texas in the 1950s. It was the decade of McCarthy, of Eisenhower and Dulles, the decade of students that David Riesman would characterize for posterity as outer-directed, the silent generation, I think it was called. These were promising labels, but they missed the closer truth, for real life at the University of Texas in the 1950s was like a circle with many rings — the smallest ring in the middle consisting of those students who were conscious of the labels and what they meant, the other inner circles progressively less aware. At the outside of that ring, the farthest out of all, was the third floor of Brackenridge Hall. They came from small ranch towns and middle-sized cities on the plains, and it was their decade right along with Ike's. Old newspapers covered the floors, and two of their number slept on cots in the hall so that one room could be a combination TV room, bar, and pornography library. Every so often they had rummage sales there, and for bargain prices tried to get rid of old water-wings, empty bottles, stale socks, and waterlogged baseballs. Dust and dirt covered the newspapers and the walls. Held most in contempt there were leaders of student government, fraternities, and deans, and they could smell out a stuffed shirt fifty yards away.

They wandered around at night in the pipes under the campus, breaking into office buildings through the sewage system in search of examination papers. Somewhere under there they found the mechanism which controlled the big clock on top of the Tower, and whenever the chimes struck eighteen, twenty, or twenty-four, I knew they were down there again. One afternoon

I went up to the top of the Tower with one of them and his girl; when we were on the observation deck he suddenly climbed over the barrier, balanced himself on a rainpipe, looked toward the ground thirty stories below, and shouted: *"Hee-haw:* Sani-Flush!"* They would spend hours on cheat notes, for they felt that an elaborate and successful set of cheat notes was a work of art, and in itself a kind of intellectual achievement. These were cunningly indexed with rubber bands for manual maneuvering, so that for a quick look at the Causes of the American Revolution one had only to flick the rubber band to C — and there, sure enough, were all seven causes, and in the right order. On a history identification test, one of them, his cheat notes not working, identified Daniel Webster as as a colored Senator from Arkansas.

Once they caught several cadets from Texas A&M, the rival school out in the boondocks, marauding around the campus at night, and summoned aid from the whole dormitory; they shaved the Aggies' heads, painted them in orange and white enamel, paraded them at close drill around the intramural field, and in an unexpected burst of Christian charity sent them home in time for reveille. For fifty cents they would take anyone to see the cadavers in the Biology Building. They had a public address system which they would occasionally place in the window of the third floor and turn on at full blast. Once I was standing at rigid attention in the ranks of the ROTC on the intramural field while in total silence the troops were being reviewed by a general from San Antonio. Suddenly I heard a booming

voice down the field, loud enough to be heard all the way to the capital building: "Private Morris, Private Willie Morris, Company D, Squad C, take charge of your troops and dismiss them!" At another ROTC drill I noticed them up in the window again, fiddling with the loudspeaker, and I feared the worst, but the voice merely said: "The War is over, boys! General Lee just gave his sword to ol' Grant! Go home to your families and your crops!"

They spied on parked cars behind the baseball field, sneaking right up to the windows and looking inside, then startling the passionate couples by setting off firecrackers under the cars and shouting and circling around like Apache Indians. Some two dozen of them, myself included, hiding in the grass under the bleachers at the baseball field late one night, watched while the starting pitcher for next day's game performed the act of love on a waitress on the pitcher's mound. The only times I saw them attentive, or ruminative, was during "Dragnet," or "The Ed Sullivan Show," or when they were listening to telephone conversations with an elaborate device that tapped the dormitory switchboard. All this was far more representative of the American state university generation in the 1950s than deans would likely have admitted. Nihilism was more articulate than silence, and more colorful than respectability. In the souls of all of us is anarchy, and it can erupt on a whim — especially in the young. That is why college administrators, like politicians, would have us believe they have had a glimpse of the higher truth. They need every defense they can get.

The decade of the 1960s was also a prosperous one. For the American middle class, this meant an unprecedented level of consumption. Two-car families became commonplace and middle-class suburbia continued to expand its boundaries. Nevertheless, annoying social problems persisted. There were still poor people, fatherless families, old people, and blacks who did not share in the prosperity. At the national level politicians optimistically believed at the beginning of this decade that American ingenuity could solve these problems. When blacks began to stage sit-ins at lunch counters and on segregated city buses, the problem of racial tensions became a dominant theme in American life. Some whites reacted with militant opposition to integration of schools and neighborhoods while others sought to foster changes in our society so that all would have equal opportunities.

There was the pervasive belief that the problem of racial tensions could be solved. It was believed that social science research could help in solving our social problems, and unprecedented funds were given for this purpose. Social science expanded during the sixties and so did awareness of social problems (although probably not as a result of social science research).

By the end of the decade, the hoped-for resolution of social problems had not been attained. It turned out to be easier to fly to the moon than to eliminate poverty or racial tensions. The domestic war was disrupted by a foreign one. The Vietnam war was seen by many in the United States as the major injustice. The nation's social problem frontier seemed to expand uncontrollably and for many young people, both black and white, the 1960s ended as a decade of political awakening. Political radicalization was accompanied by a radicalization of life styles.

Social movements developed from spontaneous responses to the problems of the 1960s. Blacks organized to improve their economic, political, and social standing. They were emulated by other minorities, American Indians, Chicanos, and Puerto Ricans. For some, social movements became a way of life. This became true for women, homosexuals, political radicals, and other racial and ethnic minorities. On college campuses student interests were more affected by political events than were college students of any previous era. Their effect was felt partly because there were more of them than at any previous time in our history. Students protested by staging sit-ins, striking, and rioting. Fear of students as a political force brought reaction and confrontation between them and agencies of law enforcement. Tragic events such as the killing of unarmed students at Kent State University raised questions for many. Serious questioning of American political, social and economic institutions accompanied the violent end of the 1960s.

The article that follows is a discussion of life styles that ensued as a result of the sixties. Not all people were activists during this period, and many were unaffected by the seemingly rapid social change around them. For others, this period was significant. Activism today is no longer as widespread, but many of the activists of the sixties still perpetuate their radicalized life style. To some of them, life today means continued interest in effecting change in the social system through political activity. It may not be the militancy of the sixties but many are still concerned and involved in politics. Their central life interest was in the sixties one of working toward social change; this central life interest continues, in a somewhat modified form. Others seek an alternative life style — one that is not a reflection of what they believe to be America's dominant values. Some who seek an alternative life style turn to others with similar interest and form communes. These communes may be geared toward working for social change, for retreating from mainstream society, or merely to create an atmosphere in which people with unconventional interests may find social support among those who hold similar unconventional world views.

Radicals Revisited: Long Range Effects of Student Protest

James M. Fendrich

This study focuses on the long range consequences of involvement in the student protest movement. It has been estimated that as many as 350,000 students became radicalized during the sixties (Lipset and Ladd, 1972). A movement of this size and scope has attracted a great deal of scholarly at-

Reprinted with permission from the *Journal of Voluntary Action Research,* published by the Association of Voluntary Action Scholars, Box G-55, Boston College, Chestnut Hill, Mass. 02167.

tention. The correlates of student protest have been extensively investigated and there are beginning attempts to evaluate the long range effects of the movement on both the participants and the larger society (Altbach and Laufer, 1972; Aronowitz et al, 1970; Flacks, 1971; Foster and Long, 1970; Matthews and Prothro, 1966; Pinkney, 1968; Peterson, 1968; Oppenheimer, 1970; Skolnick, 1969; and Weinberg and Walker, 1969). The contributions of student protesters to winding-down the Vietnam War, civil rights, the environmental movement and the reform efforts in the Democratic party are well known. However, precious little is known about what happens to activists once they graduate from college. Are they upwardly mobile in some traditional career, living in the suburbs, raising a family and voting as "liberal" Democrats? Or do they, because of the movement's apparent failures, seek out retreatist or escapist movements in drug subcultures or develop new life-styles in university ghettoes or rural communes? Or, to use the phrase Rudi Dutschke coined, have former activists begun that "long march through all the institutions of society"?

The paucity of studies for the sixties lends weak support to each of the three alternatives. Lipset and Ladd (1972) analyzed a series of public opinion surveys of different age cohorts of former college students in the United States. They found that the variations in political orientations among college generations over the last fifty years follow an essentially linear and age-related progression, despite such major upheavals as the Depression or World War II. Older college graduates were more conservative than younger graduates. They concluded:

In essence, in so far as we can generalize from the available data, they suggest that Aristotle's emphasis on the moderating effects of experience and aging turns out to be more predictive than Mannheim's stress on the long-term consequences of the formation of generation-units among the young (p. 84).

Unfortunately these data do not consist of long range panel studies that would permit the tracing of political opinions of the same individuals. Random samples of masses of college students with no knowledge of the level of student activism or political ideology while they attended college makes it difficult to determine effects. A fifty-year-old college graduate who is conservative may also have been

conservative at twenty, and a thirty-year-old liberal may also have been liberal at twenty.

The second alternative suggests that activists when compared to other college graduates would not be pursuing careers. Instead, they would be supporting themselves in menial, low-skilled occupations and living in ghettoes or communes. If this alternative is correct, we would expect to find former activists working in construction, hawking papers or perhaps even waiting tables. The evidence to support the alternative that former activists have become drop-outs in retreatist subcultures is inconclusive. Richard Blum et al (1970) found that experimentation with marijuana and drugs was found to be highly associated with left-wing student politics. However, they did not consider experimentation an escape mechanism, but a form of behavior more consistent with family background factors and current ideologies of student activists. Although no empirical evidence is presented, Mankoff and Flacks (1972) state that a number of early civil rights activists found solace with "acid" after burning themselves out in Mississippi. Carey (1968) studied marijuana and drug use in a new bohemia called the "Colony" near the Berkeley campus. He found one feature in common among approximately eighty drug users was a deep sense of disillusionment. Many of the most committed to the Colony's new life-style were former student activists who became disillusioned with any real hope of rearranging the social order.

The belief has emerged that the only change for which one can work is change within oneself, and that massive change can come only from individual transformations. This is the fundamental precondition for improving the world (pp. 17–18).

Although Carey's data are suggestive, the population base from which the respondents were selected makes it difficult to assess his findings. It would have been more useful to trace the careers of both activists and non-activists to discover what proportion of each became disillusioned and experimented with drugs both within and outside youth ghettoes. To know that those former activists who lived in the new bohemia were heavy drug users reveals nothing about activists living outside such communities. Moreover, there were enough disillusioning events during the sixties to motivate non-activists to become heavy drug users.

The only published information that supports the third alternative is two reports by journalists who have interviewed former members of the Berkeley Free Speech Movement. Greene (1970) interviewed twelve of the participants in the Sproul Hall demonstrations five years later. Neither the leaders nor rank-and-file participants were randomly selected. The former activists although knowledgeable about drugs and communal life-styles were not involved in retreatist movements; neither were they upwardly mobile in some traditional career, living in the suburbs, raising a family and voting Democratic. The "squarest" person interviewed in terms of conventional consumptive behavior was Matthew Halliman who at the time was the education director of the National Communist party. Most of the twelve re-

mained in close contact with the university as teachers, students or members of the youth ghetto. They remained politically active. Mario Savio was arrested in 1966 for taking part in a sit-in against the Navy recruiter at Berkeley and he ran for the State Senate on the Peace and Freedom ticket. Carl and Myra Riskin were new instructors at Columbia University.

Maidenberg and Meyer (1970) completed a larger study of the Berkeley Free Speech Movement five years later. They interviewed thirteen participants and analyzed 230 questionnaires sent to 400 of those who were arrested for occupying Sproul Hall. They found half of the respondents working. Of those working 27 percent were teaching, 13 percent were in social work and 10 percent were doing some form of clerical work. Of the remainder, 35 percent were still students and 13 percent were not in the labor force. They also found activists to be more radical five years later than they were before joining the Free Speech Movement. Moreover, more than half continued to participate in some form of protest.

Although these two studies provide some support for the third alternative, they share a number of weaknesses. There are no control groups to compare the career developments of non-activists with activists. The studies were undertaken before enough time had elapsed to accurately determine political and occupational pursuits. A large percentage had not completed their formal education and/or developed occupational commitments. Finally, the journalists did not probe deeply into current activities. For example, to know that 27 percent of the activists were teaching reveals nothing about the level or subject matter taught.

Krauss (1972) completed a more careful study of former Japanese activists who participated in anti-American demonstrations in 1960. He found that activists tended to go into teaching, journalism and the professions, while non-activists were more likely to enter business firms. There was also little change in political beliefs with most of the activists remaining politically alienated and left-wing. These data run counter to the commonly held but empirically unsupported views that Japanese youth totally reject their political commitments and settle down to become good bureaucrats or businessmen; however, the different cultural and political setting makes it difficult to generalize Krauss' findings to the United States.

This project is an initial exploratory effort to study more systematically the effects of student activism. Since it was impossible to project into the future it was necessary to go back to the earliest phase of student activism in order to select research subjects. The time period of student activism is the civil rights movement from 1960 to 1964. Although our primary focus was on former civil rights activists, it was decided to sample two additional generational units for comparison. One was students active in student government and the other a cross-section of undergraduates. Therefore, our independent variable was composed of three categories: (1) civil rights activists who were involved in issue oriented politics, confronting institutional structures that supported segregation; (2) student government members involved in consensual politics; and (3) a control group representing a sample of apolitical undergraduates who represented the large majority of students.

The first task in data gathering was defining and identifying student civil rights activists. Operationally they were considered to be those students who took direct action by marching and picketing or those students who publicly identified themselves as supporters of the specific actions of demonstrators. There were two periods of activism. One was the attempt to desegregate lunch counters in downtown department stores in Tallahassee in 1960. The second was the attempt to desegregate downtown movie theatres and eating establishments surrounding Florida State University campus in 1963. During 1960 only token white student support was involved as black Florida A&M University students provided most of the manpower and inspiration; five whites were arrested along with thirty-four blacks. During 1963 white students were more involved in the movie theatre and especially the restaurant boycotting and picketing. For their troubles white student activists were jailed, beaten, egged and harassed by hostile crowds. The chief university law enforcement officer stated publicly he could not provide protection for the activists from hostile crowds and the Dean of Students temporarily suspended students who were arrested. The demonstrations occurred over a period of weeks — even months. During that time there was legal action, administrative hearings, frequent meetings among demonstrators, third-party interventions and finally negotiations. The student newspaper was filled with articles, editorials (generally supportive) and letters (generally unsupportive) surrounding the events.

The list of names of civil rights activists was developed through interviews with faculty and graduate students at Florida State University who were present during the 1960–1964 period and through content analysis of student and local newspapers. Fifty males were selected for each of the three groups. Questionnaires with stamped, self-addressed envelopes were sent. This was followed by a reminder postcard and second wave of questionnaires. The response rates were 28 (56 percent) for the civil rights activists; 31 (62 percent) for the student government members and 36 (72 percent) for the apolitical undergraduates.

FINDINGS

Since this study was exploratory, it was decided to investigate the occupational and political orientations, marital status, income and voluntary organizational commitments of the three groups in order to determine whether the actions that civil rights demonstrators took while in college is having lasting effects. The current occupations were classified along a continuum ranging from those that offered monetary and status rewards in the private sector of the economy to those that offered the opportunity to express creativity and the opportunity for humanistic service. Occupations were classified into five categories: (1) proprietors, managers, officials and salesmen in the private sec-

tor; (2) private practice professionals, e.g., lawyers, etc.; (3) government workers; (4) academic professionals; and (5) social service and creative occupations.

Activists are highly concentrated in the academic profession (54 percent) and social service and creative occupations (29 percent). Student government members are found in the private sector of the economy (42 percent) and the professions (29 percent) with some representation in both governmental and academic professions. The apolitical undergraduates are heavily concentrated in the private sector of the economy (67 percent) and have some representation in the professional (11 percent) and governmental (17 percent) occupations. The civil rights activists are quite dissimilar from the two control groups. The former are pursuing careers in universities and the human service industries. Thirteen of the 15 educators taught at the university level. The apolitical worked in corporate, entrepreneurial and private practice professional occupations. The student government leaders are similar to the apolitical except for small representation in academic careers. When the occupational data is collapsed into private vs. public sector occupations, the activists are highly concentrated in the public sector (89 percent). Student government (71 percent) and the apolitical undergraduates (78 percent) are concentrated in the private sector.

There is a certain amount of variation within occupational categories. In the private sector, the apolitical have greater representation in ownership of private business and public accountants than the student government members. The student government members in comparison to the other two groups are overrepresented in the legal profession. In the government category the civil rights activists and student government members hold political appointments; in contrast the apolitical are military officers or technical officials in government programs. In the academic professional category civil rights activists are more concentrated in the social sciences than the student government members. Finally, in the social service and creative independent occupations we find an even split among activists. One activist listed his occupation as a full-time revolutionary. These data lend support to the uniqueness of the career development of former activists. Even within the same occupational categories the generational unit of activists are more likely to select occupations that complement the commitments they established in college.

A second measure related to occupational choice is the occupational values that the three groups of former students consider important. Rosenberg's (1957) study of occupational values profiles consists of ten occupational values that divided into three separate clusters: (1) self-expression which involves creativity, originality and the opportunity to use special abilities; (2) people-oriented values involving the opportunity to be helpful and work with people; and, (3) extrinsic rewards involving status, earning a good deal of money and having a stable secure future. We found that the only value cluster that distinguished between the three groups was the extrinsic-reward values. Activists

placed little importance on these values and the other two groups valued them highly. Only 21 percent of the activists highly valued the opportunity to make a good deal of money compared to 72 percent for student government and 44 percent for the apolitical undergraduates. The apolitical were the most interested in job security (53 percent) followed by the student government (37 percent) and the activists (14 percent). Although no clear occupational value profile emerged for the activists, they were distinctive in their lack of concern for the extrinsic rewards. The information on occupational choice suggests that activists are a distinctive generational unit of young adults who have not dropped out or pursued the traditional career interests of their contemporary classmates. They are concentrated in the educational and human service industries in the public sector of the economy.

The differences in occupational choice and occupational values is reflected in the current incomes of the three groups. The median annual income for activists was $13,500. There were 11 percent who made less than $5,000 a year and 15 percent who made more than $25,000. The former student government members had the highest median income, $18,635. They were followed by the apolitical undergraduates whose median was $15,725. Although former activists are by no means poor the other two groups are substantially better off. Part of the difference in earning power may be due to the fact that a number of activists have only recently entered the job market after completing advanced degrees. They are also concentrated in occupations that traditionally do not provide the same level of financial reward.

Two measures used to determine the current political involvement of the three groups were political self-identification and a five item scale measuring political behavior. In order to measure political self-identification respondents were asked to select one of thirteen political identifications. For purposes of analysis the thirteen were reduced to four categories: conservatives, moderates, liberals and radicals. There were major differences among the three groups. Activists professed to be radicals (54 percent), liberals (25 percent) and moderates (22 percent). The student government members had a strong preference for a moderate position (71 percent) with some conservatives (19 percent) and a few liberals (10 percent). The apolitical undergraduates were further right than the other groups. Their distribution was conservative (38 percent), moderates (47 percent) and liberals (15 percent). The activists' current political identification is heavily concentrated at the left end of the political spectrum. Former student government officers strongly prefer the moderate position, e.g., moderate Democrats or moderate Republicans or Independents. The apolitical undergraduates have a large minority who are conservatives.

The second measure of political involvement is a political behavioral scale that focuses on five political activities: following political events in the media, voting, involvement in political programs and campaigns, participation in peaceful demonstrations

and participation in illegal political protest. On the first item activists (89 percent) and student government members (86 percent) regularly follow political events in the media in comparison to 56 percent for the apolitical undergraduates. All three groups have about the same percentage that vote regularly in elections. The range was from 74 percent for the activists to 82 percent for student government members. Of the remaining three types of political behavior activists have the highest level of participation. Sixty-seven percent were involved in political organizational work, 74 percent have participated in peaceful demonstrations and 41 percent have been involved in illegal protest since graduating from college. For student government the percentages are: 57 percent for organizational work, 4 percent for demonstrations and no illegal participation. Lastly, the percentages for the apolitical undergraduates are: 37 percent for organizational work, 10 percent demonstrations and 3 percent involvement in illegal protest.

The single most interesting finding is the high level of activists' involvement in both institutional and non-institutional forms of political expression. If the first three items are considered to be expressions of institutional political involvement, activists as a group are the most involved. Given their political self-identification, they probably support different issues and candidates than the other two groups. Activists have also retained their commitments to participate in non-institutional political involvement. Although their absolute numbers are small in comparison to the other two groups, the level of political involvement for the activists is greater, suggesting that they could have a disproportionate impact on the political process.

The remaining two life-style variables are marital status and voluntary organizational involvement. Activists have not settled down by getting married and having children. Only 25 percent of the activists are currently married and have children. The comparable figures for the other groups are: 61 percent for student government and 86 percent for the apolitical undergraduates. Thirty-nine percent of the activists are married and do not have children compared to 29 percent for student government and 6 percent for the apolitical. Activists are more likely to have remained single (21 percent) compared to 7 percent for student government and 3 percent for the apolitical; or, they are more likely to be divorced (14 percent) compared to 3 percent for student government members and 6 percent for the apolitical. If being married and having children is a moderating effect on adult political expression, former activists have avoided that process even though at the time of the study most of them were in their early thirties.

The political commitments are also reflected in their organizational involvement. Members of all three groups are active in professional or occupational affiliated organizations with student government members being the most active (52 percent). Both student government members (35 percent) and the apolitical undergraduates (33 percent) are members of civic organizations such as Jaycees, Rotary,

Masons, YMCA, etc. in contrast to only 11 percent of the activists. The civil rights activists, however, manifest their civic responsibilities in other ways. They are members of leftist political organizations (21 percent), antiwar (11 percent), environmental (14 percent), and civil liberties organizations (11 percent). The lack of formal affiliation with civil rights organizations is puzzling. It may be due to a variety of reasons, e.g., existing civil rights organizations are not considered effective, or former activists may feel that only blacks can exercise an effective role in these organizations, or they have developed commitments to new causes since graduating. The level of participation in traditional two-party political organizations is different for the three groups. Former activists are most active (28 percent) followed by student government members (13 percent) and the apolitical (6 percent). These data confirm the earlier findings that former activists maintain commitments to both institutional and noninstitutional politics.

SUMMARY AND CONCLUSIONS

The patterns revealed in the analysis clearly indicate that former civil rights activists are a distinctive generational unit. Instead of saying activists are radical at 20 and moderate at 40, it is more accurate to describe this sample as moderate at 20 and liberal to radical at 35. When the activists first became involved in protest they were living in a Kennedy "New Frontier" era. They were naive and idealistic, thinking demonstrations would produce major structural changes with relatively low levels of personal costs. The experience of protesting and the harsh reaction it produced radicalized these young reformers. It was probably their most intensive set of experiences while attending college, and it has produced lasting effects on their life-styles. In contrast, the former members of student government and the apolitical undergraduates have more conventional life-styles as expressed in occupational careers, political attitudes and behavior and marital status. Occupationally the activists are heavily concentrated in the knowledge and human service industries while the former student government members and the apolitical are concentrated in the private sector of the economy. Even within broad occupational categories the activists perform different types of work. For example, in the academic profession they are more heavily concentrated in the social sciences. The second largest concentration of activists is in the social service and creative occupations. They are social workers and free-lance writers. The concentration of activists in a relatively small number of careers largely in the public sector may reveal two characteristics of their career pursuits. First, they are following through on their commitments that were developed as civil rights activists in selecting careers that provide some opportunity for creative and human service. Second, the limited scope of occupations activists pursued may reflect the restricted opportunity structures that tolerate the expression of anti-establishment sentiments and activities. For example, we found that approxi-

mately 71 percent of the activists have taken part in demonstrations since graduating from college. In many of the occupational careers chosen by non-activists this type of participation would not be permitted during working hours or would be negatively sanctioned if it were discovered by immediate colleagues or superiors.

Occupational careers, like migratory patterns, have both push and pull factors associated with selection. The opportunity for autonomy, humanistic service and creativity are all part of the pull toward the "new working class." On the other hand, activists are rejecting the traditional occupations and occupational values that only offer conventional rewards such as money, status and security. In fact they are pursuing careers that offer substantially less financial reward. The activists are looking for and demanding that institutions provide the opportunity to realize radical humanistic commitments. With growing pressures to provide both economically and socially for themselves, the activists have tried to balance these forces and their ethical obligations by working in the system while still trying to change and to humanize the social institutions with which they come in contact. In one sense the long march through a limited range of institutions has begun. The range of occupations in which activists are able to incorporate these seemingly conflicting demands is still very limited, and this is undoubtedly reflected in the narrow scope of occupations they have selected.

The radical, humanistic commitment of the activists is demonstrated in their political as well as their occupational activities. They participate actively in institutionalized and non-institutionalized politics, with their distinctive orientation setting them apart from the former student government members or the apolitical undergraduates. The activists identify themselves almost exclusively as radicals and liberals while the other groups are mostly moderates and conservatives. The activists follow political events in the media, vote, and do political organizational work to win elections. Yet this does not mean that the activists have allowed the pressures of "making it" simply to co-opt them. We suspect much of this effort in institutionalized politics is at the local level where attempts are being made to replace the power of the business community in the local politics or in reforming the Democratic party, thus re-orienting the political structure on more humanistic lines. This perspective sets the activists apart, so that within the traditional two-party system they are likely to support different issues and candidates than the other two groups. Moreover the activists alone are likely to demonstrate and participate in illegal political activities. The orientation of politics and of political commitments is part of a broader change in the obligations to the community. While student government people and the noninvolved are members of civic groups like the Jaycees, Rotary Clubs, YMCA and other voluntary groups which tend to reinforce the social institutions of the community and society, the activists join the American Socialist Party, Veterans Against the War, Friends of Earth and the American Civil Liberties Union — organiza-

tions that are attempting to reorder the priorities of the community and societal institutions. One interesting finding is the lack of current involvement in civil rights organizations. Although puzzling, we suspect this finding is due to the acceptance of a black power emphasis in militant or nationalist organizations and more established civil rights organizations being perceived as too conservative. Although these activists initially became involved in the civil rights movement, they have gravitated to other issues and causes.

In sum, the activists have not been co-opted during the ten years since they became involved in civil rights protests. They have resisted the moderating influences of getting married and having children. Nor have they allowed themselves to drift into a retreatist life-style. Instead they have combined ideological commitments with their occupational and political orientations. It remains uncertain as to the extent of the struggle with established authorities within institutions that will be necessary in the future. Indeed, many former activists may be engaged in heated conflict with university administrations or other bureaucracies which they eventually may loose. Yet one impression is becoming more and more focused. The actions activists took in college are still related to their life-style today. A distinctive generational unit was formed out of their protest. This small generational unit continues to march to a different drummer. Their effectiveness in the future will be contingent upon the type of viable movement organizations they can develop and influence and upon the foothold they can gain in established institutions as they challenge "business as usual" decision-making policies.

REFERENCES

Altbach, Philip G., and Robert S. Laufer (eds.), *The New Pilgrims: Youth Protest in Transition*. New York: David McKay Company, 1972.

Aronowitz, Stanley, et al. "Strategies for Radical Social Change." *Social Policy*, 1 (November–December 1970): 9–24.

Bell, Daniel. *Marxian Socialism in the United States*. Princeton, N.J.: Princeton Univ. Press, 1967.

Blum, Richard H., et. al. *Drugs and Society*. San Francisco: Jossey-Bass, 1970.

Carey, James T. *The College Drug Scene*. Englewood Cliffs, N.J.: Prentice-Hall, 1968.

Green, Wade. "Where Are the Savios of Yesteryear"? *The New York Times Magazine*, VI (July 12, 1970): 6–10.

Flacks, Richard. "Strategies for Radical Social Change." *Social Policy*, 1 (March–April 1970): 7–14.

Foster, Julian, and Durward Long. "The Dynamics of Institutional Response." In *Protest: Student Activism in America*. New York: William Morrow and Company, 1970.

Krauss, Ellis. "Radicals Revisited: A Longitudinal Political Study of Japanese Student Activists." Ph.D. Dissertation, Stanford University, 1972.

Lipset, Seymour Martin, and Everett C. Ladd, Jr. "The Political Future of Activist Generations." In Philip G. Alt-

bach and Robert S. Laufer (eds.), *The New Pilgrims: Youth Protest in Transition*. New York: David McKay Company, 1972.

Mankoff, Milton, and Richard Flacks. "The Changing Social Base of the American Student Movement." In Philip G. Altbach and Robert S. Laufer (eds.), *The New Pilgrims: Youth Protest in Transition*. New York: David McKay Company, 1972.

Maidenberg, Michael, and Philip Meyer. "The Berkeley Rebels: Five Years Later." Presented at the Annual Meeting of the American Association for Public Opinion Research, abstracted in *Public Opinion Quarterly*, 24 (Fall 1970): 477–478.

Matthews, Donald, and James Prothro. *Negroes and the New Southern Politics*. New York: Harcourt, Brace and World, 1966.

Oppenheimer, Martin. "White Collar Revisited: The Making of a New Working Class." *Social Policy*, 1 (July–August 1970): 27–32.

Peterson, Richard E. *The Scope of Organized Student Protest in 1967–1968*. Princeton, N.J.: Educational Testing Service, 1968.

Pinkney, Alphonso. *The Committed: White Activists in the Civil Rights Movement*. New Haven: College and University Press, 1968.

Skolnick, Jerome. *The Politics of Protest*. New York: Simon and Schuster, 1969.

Weinberg, Ian, and Kenneth N. Walker. "Student Politics and Political Systems: Toward a Typology." *American Journal of Sociology*, 75 (July 1969): 77–96.

In the 1970s, some social critics looked at quieter college campuses and concluded that the fifties had returned. Students appeared less socially concerned, fraternities and sororities were making a comeback, and more students were career oriented than their counterparts a decade ago. However, the forces of recent social change have shaped the current generation of college students. Life on college campuses is different from that of the fifties as well as that of the sixties. In the seventies, fraternities and sororities are more racially integrated. The "deviants" of the fifties and sixties now seem less deviant, with homosexuality and "unconventional" living arrangements more open, many college students smoking marijuana, and greater political participation of college students in local and national politics.

The changes among people of college age are evidenced by a recent study completed by survey researcher Daniel Yankelovich* which showed significant changes among this group in just a few years. For instance, in 1971 45 percent of a national sample of college students felt that "This is a sick society," while 35 percent of college students in 1973 agreed with this. In 1971 only 57 percent identified themselves as being either a Democrat or Republican as compared to 73 percent in 1973. In 1971 49 percent stated that they anticipated no great difficulty in accepting the kind of life that society has to offer, while 60 percent felt that way in 1973. Longer range data indicates the fall and rise of certain beliefs among college students. In 1968, 69 percent believed that hard work pays off. This figure fell to 56 percent in 1969 and bottomed out at 39 percent in 1971, but by 1973 this attitude was becoming more prevalent as 44 percent in that year agreed with this statement.

Changes in values spread to non-college youth as well. For instance, in 1969, 34 percent of college students and 57 percent of non-college youth felt that casual premarital sexual relations were morally wrong. By 1973, only 22 percent of college students and 34 percent of non-college youth felt that this was so. In 1969, 38 percent of college students and 64 percent of the non-college sample felt that religion was an important personal value, but in 1973, only 28 percent of college students and 42 percent of non-college believed this.

Many believe that social change is cyclical. We go to a point of radical change and then revert back to previous modes of behavior. In the forties and fifties, virginity was highly regarded among many women. During the sixties, with social change, increased birth control technology, and greater independence of college students, many believed that a "sexual revolution" was taking place. The "deviants" were the virgins.

* These data are from Daniel Yankelovich, *The New Morality: A Profile of American Youth in the 70s* (New York: McGraw Hill, 1974) and are used with the permission of the author.

In the seventies most college campuses offer birth control information to their students, and most dormitories have few regulations; yet there are those who believe that virginity is making a comeback, since people will always return to the "traditional" values.

In the article that follows Mike Mallowe intimates that virginity may be reestablished as a value and adhered to as a fact; however, there is no evidence one way or another that this is the case since the data are so impressionistic. Virgins may now be more outspoken (in light of the fact that college students are more tolerant of those with different ideas); or college students may be becoming more conservative; or the well documented change in attitudes may be more superficial than we realize.

Quick, Name Three Virgins

Mike Mallowe

It all started with a *Daily News* headline: SOUTH PHILLY'S VIRGIN TERRITORY. According to a lady doctor from Jefferson Hospital, Dr. Mirta Mulhare, the cult of virginity, which most of us had already written off along with the cult of Baal, was hanging tough downtown.

Italian working-class prudery, the Catholic Church and the daughter-should-live-at-home-till-marriage standard of the neighborhood combined to keep Angela and Maria from the couches of Tony and Vito until the mating was religiously blessed and

From *Philadelphia Magazine* (April 1974), pp. 69–75. Reprinted by permission.

properly celebrated at the Fiesta Ballroom or Venus Lounge. Dr. Mulhare was making the point that, except for isolated ethnic strongholds, premarital chastity is about as common as an earthquake.

That was definitely a clip-and-save item for virgin-watchers like myself. There aren't many of us around, and it's hard to spot one, but there are some clues. We hum along with the music at weddings, cringe when the secretaries at the office swap off-color stories, ramble on about the old values and conscientiously record every reported incident of a girl who says "no."

In recent years, of course, it's been all downhill in the virgin-watching business. Ever since the mid '60s when *Time* magazine declared that God was dead, the last shreds of religious sanctions have all but disappeared. The best thing that can be said for the chaste is that they do seem chic in their own antiquated way. At singles parties the suspected virgin is a nice counterbalance to everybody else. The tolerance of virgins is also a widely accepted symbol of the host's finely practiced liberalism.

In the 1960s they used to throw kinky fund-raisers for Black Panthers in Park Avenue apartments, but now that the wind has shifted from radical to reactionary chic, the virginal are stealing the limelight. The pendulum hasn't swung completely from the promiscuous to the prudish, but the arc is widening by degrees and the era of the New Chastity may soon be upon us.

I got hooked on virgin-watching almost by accident. A couple of times I innocently let it slip out that I intended to marry a virgin. Being very Catholic and very chauvinistic, this seemed natural enough, but then I realized that my statement had violated an unwritten code of conduct. Nobody in recent years expects to marry a virgin and nobody, but nobody, ever *says* so in public.

I'm convinced that with all our openness and neurotic need to kiss and tell, virginity is still the last conversational taboo. We talk about death and dying with more frankness than we consider the case for chastity.

Once upon a time we talked about hippies and flower power and actually believed all that swill about the counterculture. That's when sex was really sensational and the people who had an impact on our lives were sexually molesting everything in sight from *grandes dames* to Great Danes. The heroes and heroines out there, among the shock troops of our own home-grown Red Guard, were the sexual libertarians of their day.

But the movement is past now and life isn't guerrilla theater anymore.

Embarrassing as it is, we finally have to admit that the only difference between flower children and flappers is that the modern version dressed with a lot less elegance and got high with a little less style.

The irony is that now that it's classy to be conservative, the closed little minds can't shift gears fast enough. The true individualists of the '70s are the ones who aren't up for orgies twice a week. That kind of sex is not, as they say, where it's at. And this is what virgin-watching is all about. It's just an exercise in observation that measures the morality of the day.

Nobody, not even virgin-watchers, would argue that the New Chastity is at hand. Virgins of either sex are still infinitesimal statistical minorities. Birth control pills aren't going stale on the shelf and there's still more action in coed dorms than in brothels. But this is just the recent past catching up with itself. The present and the future look cloudy for sexual liberationists.

Julie is a tall, beautiful young woman who is nervously unaccustomed to talking about her virginity. At 22 she's heard all the arguments and replied to all the lines. She works in an almost all-girl office in Delaware County. Julie's not prepared to say that her views are straight out of *Little Women*, but she accepts the fact that most of her friends and co-workers see her as something of a rarity.

"Virginity's the greatest gift a girl

can give to her husband. I've always felt that way and I'm not changing.

"They always tell me they can't understand how I can live without it. I just say, how can you miss something you've never had?

"I'm a virgin and I'm engaged. We intend to wait. I know this can't work for everybody, but for me it's the best thing. I don't get involved in any religious or psychological reasons. I'm a simple person. I just want to give myself to the guy I'm in love with and married to, and not pass myself around beforehand."

Dr. Elaine Pierson, a gynecologist and sex researcher at the student clinic at the University of Pennsylvania, doesn't know Julie, but she does know that more and more young women are justifying their action with just as much candor.

" 'Virgin' is a bad word with negative connotations. I prefer to call them the non–sexually active. The cult of virginity is still meaningful for some people. There's no doubt about it.

"Women used to apologize for virginity three or four years ago, because of the pressure to be sexually active. But not any more. They say no intercourse and that's it. There's no blushing about it. Women's lib has had a lot to do with it, I imagine. But I deal with some girls that are 23, 24, 25 who are not lesbians, who are just not active. Now they have the ability to verbalize their actions and say 'no.' "

While Dr. Pierson hesitates to suggest that the New Chastity is really about to storm the campus, she's quite certain that the sexual evolution — not the revolution that has had its day —

of society is a process that offers increasing options for all extremes.

There's no more militancy or noise about sexuality — no more demands for coed dorms. People are comfortable with whatever they are and they've stopped apologizing for it. Dr. Pierson thinks that this may be more the result of common sense than anything else.

"Sex complicates life tremendously. It opens up new emotions and new feelings and new problems from pregnancy to guilt that the virgin never has to deal with. The celibate life is just so much simpler and the attitude on campus today so geared to taking the simple, easy way out that a lot of students are willing to let a sexual relationship come naturally through a conventional setup like marriage of one type or another."

Dr. Pierson has published several editions of a sex education handbook, *Sex Is Never An Emergency*, which is designed primarily for those who are sexually active on a physical level, but naïve when it comes to repercussions. She has a section in the beginning which cautions virgins of both sexes not to apologize or shrink from their chosen course. But after her years of research and counseling she feels that it's necessary to broadly expand the traditional concept of virginity.

"I really do believe that there is a 'new virginity,' but of course it hasn't anything to do with remaining non–sexually active. It's something that I call the 'non-orgasmic female.' The girl who feels that since nothing really happened in intercourse because she didn't allow anything to happen often considers herself a virgin despite the fact that she has violated all the old definitions. I can't come up with anything comparable for males."

Jaws somewhat agape, increasing numbers of local teachers, counselors and older students report that 1950s-style dating, baiting and mating is reviving. It's a return to the world of happier times: the litany of get good grades, get a good girl, get a good job, and get a good pension.

A freshman at Northwestern spelled out the ground rules for the classes of '77, '78, '79 and '80 when he recently told a reporter from the New York *Times* that his goal in life was simple, "I want to make money so I can smoke good pot and wear $200 suits."

That's a reordering of priorities that even his Victorian great-grandfather could be proud of.

In keeping with the American tradition, the New Chastity is more pragmatic than idealistic. And a lot of input has been supplied by the women's movement.

At least, that's the message that virgin-watchers are reading into a very significant document that recently emerged from the sociology department of St. Joseph's College.

Dr. Sylvia Clavan, an attractive, talented mother of college-age children who likes to refer to herself as a "returned woman," is the author of the thesis.

Dr. Clavan returned from hearth and home in 1971 to earn her doctorate and resume a career in sociology that had been in suspended animation while she fulfilled the roles of

wife and mother that her generation expected.

According to her theories, sexually speaking, it's always been a woman's world and always will be. Man, the predatory hunter and tireless seducer, has always demanded sex any way he could get it. Depending on his degree of enlightenment, he viewed women as either receptacles for his seed or useful companions, but in any case, his motives and desires remained the same.

The female, on the other hand, has been the active, changing element in the sexual game. Sexual civilities and social mores change according to *her* preferences — not *his*. When she decided to barter her virginity for a profitable marriage the old guidelines of chastity were in effect. And, conversely, when *she* chose to ignore the marriage contract and its code of conduct, virgins became scarcer than an open gas station on Sunday.

With the new accent on materialism and all the goodies that money can buy, it looks like women will once again decide on their own to alter the politics of sex. All the while, in the finest tradition of women's liberation, men are off on the sidelines, reacting to the actions of the female and performing in accordance with her whims and her socioeconomic decisions.

It's a rather unconventional position to emerge from conservative St. Joseph's College, but then Dr. Clavan is anything but a traditional Mrs. Chips.

When discussing the subject of virginity among the coeds on the St. Joe's campus, she frowns very primly, explains that her unbringing was one of middle-class prudishness and then, almost sadly, begins to explain how times have changed.

"I have to accept the statistics coming out that a majority of young women getting married are not virgins. I don't choose this type of behavior and didn't for myself. It was unheard of. But I just have to accept their behavior. They insist that they have more honest sexual relationships and, even with the economic depression, I don't see a swing back."

The trend, according to Dr. Clavan, has been irreversible since the two World Wars and, virgin-watchers notwithstanding, she just doesn't think that chastity has a chance.

Fortunately, she hasn't won over the whole faculty to her conclusions. Nick Robak, one of Dr. Clavan's colleagues at St. Joe's, insists that the New Chastity is already upon us.

"I can see it everywhere. The kids coming in in these classes as freshmen are so much more conservative than their older brothers and sisters that it's hard to believe. It's not just politics, either. When I start to talk about sex some of them actually get embarrassed. I admit that the phenomenon hasn't been going on long enough to measure it, but I get the feeling and the indications that it's changing.

"When I went back to Penn to do graduate work it was the same story there. It was more like the campus of the '50s than the '70s. I'm not saying they act like brothers and sisters when they live together in the campus setup, but the frantic urgency to get back at the establishment through sex is gone."

Even sociologists can't agree on how sex is really shaping up. They usually get hung up on two words — attitude and behavior. The attitude of promiscuity that Dr. Clavan sees may be an unstoppable trend, but it's a long way from attitude to behavior and that's what virgin-watchers are really out to gauge. It's easy enough to talk a good fight but when it comes to putting their bodies where their behavior is, it's a slightly different story.

For the last several years men have had to accept the de facto shortage of virgins. A 1973 survey of Jewish and Catholic sons and fathers conducted by Clavan and Robak in the Philadelphia area covering several college campuses revealed that a virgin bride was as elusive as the Golden Fleece.

This sampling, which the researchers thought would still show a demand for chastity by potential bridegrooms, shocked everyone by going the Kinsey reports a few percentage points better. Nearly 80% of the sons indicated that virginity in a woman would *not* be a determining factor in contracting a marriage.

At Penn State University virgin-watching is also being put on a very scientific basis. After beating the bushes from Lancaster to Erie, 80 female virgins between 17 and 23 years of age were rounded up and matched with 80 non-virgins. All were contemplating marriage before or shortly after graduation. The girls were given a 300-item test called the Adams Marital Happiness Prediction Inventory in addition to other forms of analysis and evaluation. The point of the study was an attempt to determine the value of virginity in marriage. Dr. David Shope, the grand inquisitor, issued a startling old-fashioned final conclusion: ". . . a virgin will be a better wife not because she is technically a virgin but because the very qualities that kept her a virgin are also those qualities that give her a greater chance for marital happiness."

Needless to say, Dr. Shope is being blasted for witchcraft, heresy and incorrigibility by all the scientific investigators who refuse to accept the possibility that virginity may be worthwhile. But as Shope's followers point out, at least he has the scientific evidence that academia demands.

It's an Alice-in-Wonderland world. The sex researchers are going at it hammer and tong trying to prove or disprove the need for a species that until recently has been facing extinction. Fascinating as their conjectures are, it's all a lot of statistical nonsense unless people really begin conforming to their predictions and projections. Somewhere or other chastity will have to make a comeback, or virgin-watchers will be placed in the category of irrelevant wishful thinkers.

In the real world it's still a toss-up. But one thing's for sure. More and more sexually active people are demanding some kind of commitment of exclusivity from each other. Alternate family lifestyles, like communal living and all the other varieties that involve sex outside of marriage, are flourishing here and there in artificial settings, but for most people traditional marriage or at least one-on-one living is still the usual alternative.

We know from the hoopla-hype of the 76ers that sex is still the Number One indoor sport. But the subtleties of the game have almost been lost in the complexity and confusion of rule changes in the last several years. Hard-nosed virgins, bartering their virtue for a safe, solid, professional man in the penny-pinching months and years to come, may get everyone back to basics. This could finally get virgin-watchers out of the bush leagues.

We have discussed how life styles have changed over the past thirty-five years. Armchair theorists, whether sociologists, journalists, or anybody else, may speculate on the forces that shaped our current life styles and what our life styles will be in the future. However, this speculation may be nothing more than an intellectual exercise.* There is also very little that may help us to see what forces will shape our life styles in the future or to accurately predict what future life styles will be like. Few in the sixties accurately predicted what the life style of the seventies would be like, and all of the tools of social science may not aid us in predicting the life styles of the eighties.

---

* For instance, there is very little evidence to back up Professor Clavan's contention that women have always been in control, giving their sexual favors at points in history when it would be to their advantage.

RACE AND ETHNICITY: ETHNIC LIFE STYLES

"An ethnic group consists of those who conceive of themselves as being alike by virtue of their common ancestry, real or fictitious, and who are so regarded by others."* Thus the American upper class, as discussed by MacNamara in Part 3 of this book, is an ethnic group, as are Jews, Italians, blacks and Indians. The only way to gain membership in an ethnic group is to be born into it. It does not matter how devout a convert one is, or how well one has mastered the group's life style; full membership in an ethnic group can occur only through ascription. By definition, then, an ethnic life style is genetically influenced — a life style to which one is predisposed at birth and which is perpetuated by intramarriage. Thus sanctions for failing to engage in the ethnic life style cannot be meted to converts or nonethnics; but sanctions may be imposed upon an ethnic who does not choose to engage in the ethnic life style.

Ethnicity in America poses a dilemma: Is the preferred American life style attained through membership in one of the many groups that make up the ethnic mix in America and perpetuating separate ethnic

* Tomatsu Shibutani and Kian M. Kwan, *Ethnic Stratification* (New York: Macmillan, 1965).

367

life styles? Or is the preferred American life style that of conforming to the middle-majority (nonethnic) life style? We can distinguish between cultural pluralism (the process of preserving separate ethnic life styles) or Anglo-conformity (the process by which ethnic groups disappear through adherence to the white Anglo-Saxon standard).*

Ethnic culture affects many aspects of an individual's life from food to friendship patterns, to aspirations. The following article by Mark Zborowski demonstrates the far-ranging impact of ethnic culture — it even extends to the way people react to the physiological process of pain. Zborowski studied Italian Americans, Jewish Americans, and Old Americans, noting how they reacted to pain in public and in private, both in the hospital and in the family setting. The three ethnic groups studied attributed different meanings to pain, and thus experienced the physiological process differently.

* See Milton Gordon, *Assimilation in American Life* (New York: Oxford University Press, 1964): 88–114.

Cultural Components in Responses to Pain

Mark Zborowski

From *Journal of Social Issues,* 8 (1951), pp. 16–30. Reprinted by permission; copyright © by the Society for the Psychological Study of Social Issues. This paper is based upon material collected as part of the study "Cultural Components in Attitudes toward Pain," under a grant of the U.S. Public Health Service.

SOME BASIC DISTINCTIONS

In human societies, biological processes vital for man's survival acquire social and cultural significance. Intake of food, sexual intercourse, or elimination — physiological phenomena which are universal for the entire living world — become institutions regulated by cultural and social norms, thus fulfilling not only biological functions but social and cultural ones as well. Metabolic and endocrinal changes in the human organism may provoke hunger and sexual desire, but culture and society dictate to man the kind of food he may eat, the social setting for eating, or the adequate partner for mating.

Moreover, the role of cultural and social patterns in human physiological activities is so great that they may in specific situations act against the direct biological needs of the individual, even to the point of endangering his survival. Only a human being may prefer starvation to the breaking of a religious dietary law or may abstain from sexual intercourse because of specific incest regulations. Voluntary fasting and celibacy exist only where food and sex fulfill more than strictly physiological functions.

Thus, the understanding of the significance and role of social and cultural patterns in human physiology is necessary to clarify those aspects of human experience which remain puzzling if studied only within the physiological frame of reference.

Pain is basically a physiological phenomenon and as such has been studied by physiologists and neurologists such as Harold Wolff, James Hardy, Helen Goodell, C. S. Lewis, W. K. Livingston, and others. By using the most ingenious methods of investigation they have succeeded in clarifying complex problems of the physiology of pain. Many aspects of perception and reaction to pain were studied in experimental situations involving most careful preparation and complicated equipment. These investigators have come to the conclusion that "from the physiological point of view pain qualifies as a sensation of importance to the self-preservation of the individual." [1] The biological function of pain is to provoke special reactive patterns directed toward avoidance of the noxious stimulus which presents a threat to the individual. In this respect the function of pain is basically the same for man as for the rest of the animal world.

However, the physiology of pain and

the understanding of the biological function of pain do not explain other aspects of what Wolff, Hardy, and Goodell call the *pain experience*, which includes not only the pain sensation and certain automatic reactive responses but also certain "associated feeling states." [2] It would not explain, for example, the acceptance of intense pain in torture which is part of the initiation rites of many primitive societies, nor will it explain the strong emotional reactions of certain individuals to the slight sting of the hypodermic needle.

In human society, pain, like so many other physiological phenomena, acquires specific social and cultural significance, and accordingly, certain reactions to pain can be understood in the light of this significance. As Drs. Hardy, Wolff, and Goodell state in their recent book, "... the culture in which a man finds himself becomes the conditioning influence in the formation of the individual reaction patterns to pain. ... A knowledge of group attitudes toward pain is extremely important to an understanding of the individual reaction." [3]

In analyzing pain it is useful to distinguish between self-inflicted, other-inflicted, and spontaneous pain. Self-inflicted pain is defined as deliberately self-inflicted. It is experienced as a result of injuries performed voluntarily upon oneself, e.g., self-mutilation. Usually these injuries have a culturally defined purpose, such as achieving a special status in the society. It can be observed not only in primitive cultures

[1] James D. Hardy, Harold G. Wolff, and Helen Goodell, *Pain Sensations and Reactions* (Baltimore: Williams and Wilkins, 1952), p. 23.

[2] Ibid., p. 204.
[3] Ibid., p. 262.

but also in contemporary societies on a higher level of civilization. In Germany, for instance, members of certain student or military organizations would cut their faces with a razor in order to acquire scars which would identify them as members of a distinctive social group. By other-inflicted pain is meant pain inflicted upon the individual in the process of culturally accepted and expected activities (regardless of whether approved or disapproved), such as sports, fights, war, etc. To this category belongs also pain inflicted by the physician in the process of medical treatment. Spontaneous pain usually denotes the pain sensation which results from disease or injury. This term also covers pains of phychogenic nature.

Members of different cultures may assume differing attitudes towards these various types of pain. Two of these attitudes may be described as pain expectancy and pain acceptance. Pain expectancy is anticipation of pain as being unavoidable in a given situation, for instance, in childbirth, in sports activities, or in battle. Pain acceptance is characterized by a willingness to experience pain. This attitude is manifested mostly as an inevitable component of culturally accepted experiences, for instance, as part of initiation rites or part of medical treatment. The following example will help to clarify the differences between pain expectancy and pain acceptance: Labor pain is expected as part of childbirth, but while in one culture, such as in the United States, it is not accepted and therefore various means are used to alleviate it, in some other cultures, for instance in Poland, it is not only expected but also accepted,

and consequently nothing or little is done to relieve it. Similarly, cultures which emphasize military achievements expect and accept battle wounds, while cultures which emphasize pacifistic values may expect them but will not accept them.

In the process of investigating cultural attitudes toward pain, it is also important to distinguish between pain apprehension and pain anxiety. Pain apprehension reflects the tendency to avoid the pain sensation as such, regardless of whether the pain is spontaneous or inflicted, whether it is accepted or not. Pain anxiety, on the other hand, is a state of anxiety provoked by the pain experience, focused upon various aspects of the causes of pain, the meaning of pain, or its significance for the welfare of the individual.

Moreover, members of various cultures may react differently in terms of their manifest behavior toward various pain experiences, and this behavior is often dictated by the culture, which provides specific norms according to the age, sex, and social position of the individual.

The fact that other elements as well as cultural factors are involved in the response to a spontaneous pain should be taken into consideration. These other factors are the pathological aspect of pain, the specific physiological characteristics of the pain experience, such as the intensity, the duration, and the quality of the pain sensation, and, finally, the personality of the individual. Nevertheless, it was felt that in the process of a careful investigation it would be possible to detect the role of the cultural components in the pain experience.

THE RESEARCH SETTING

In setting up the research we were interested not only in the purely theoretical aspects of the findings in terms of possible contribution to the understanding of the pain experience in general; we also had in mind the practical goal of a contribution to the field of medicine. In the relationship between the doctor and his patient the respective attitudes toward pain may play a crucial role, especially when the doctor feels that the patient exaggerates his pain while the patient feels that the doctor minimizes his suffering. The same may be true, for instance, in a hospital, where the members of the medical and nursing staff may have attitudes toward pain different from those held by the patient, or when they expect a certain pattern of behavior according to their cultural background while the patient may manifest a behavior pattern which is acceptable in his culture. These differences may play an important part in the evaluation of the individual pain experience, in dealing with pain at home and in the hospital, in administration of analgesics, etc. Moreover, we expected that this study of pain would offer opportunities to gain insight into related attitudes toward health, disease, medication, hospitalization, medicine in general, etc.

With these aims in mind, the project was set up at the Kingsbridge Veterans Hospital, Bronx, New York,[4] where

four ethno-cultural groups were selected for an intensive study. These groups included patients of Jewish, Italian, Irish, and "Old American" stock. Three groups — Jews, Italians, and Irish — were selected because they were described by medical people as manifesting striking differences in their reaction to pain. Italians and Jews were described as tending to "exaggerate" their pain, while the Irish were often depicted as stoical individuals who are able to take a great deal of pain. The fourth group, the "Old Americans," were chosen because the values and attitudes of this group dominate in the country and are held by many members of the medical profession and by many descendants of the immigrants who, in the process of Americanization, tend to adopt American patterns of behavior. The members of this group can be defined as white, native-born individuals, usually Protestant, whose grandparents, at least, were born in the United States and who do not identify themselves with any foreign group, either nationally, socially, or culturally.

The Kingsbridge Veterans Hospital was chosen because its population represents roughly the ethnic composition of New York City, thus offering access to a fair sample of the four selected groups, and also because various age groups were represented among the hospitalized veterans of World War I, World War II, and the Korean War. In one major respect this hospital was

[4] I should like to take the opportunity to express my appreciation to Dr. Harold G. Wolff, Professor of Neurology, Cornell University Medical College; Dr. Hiland Flowers, Chief of Neuropsychiatric Service; Dr. Robert Morrow, Chief of Clinical Psychology Section; Dr. Louis Berlin, Chief of Neurology Section; and the management of the hospital for their cooperation in the setting up of the research at the Kingsbridge Veterans Hospital.

not adequate, namely, in not offering the opportunity to investigate sex differences in attitude toward pain. This aspect of research will be carried out in a hospital with a large female population.

In setting up this project we were mainly interested in discovering certain regularities in reactions and attitudes toward pain characteristic of the four groups. Therefore, the study has a qualitative character, and the efforts of the researchers were not directed toward a collection of material suitable for quantitative analysis. The main techniques used in the collection of the material were interviews with patients of the selected groups, observation of their behavior when in pain, and discussion of the individual cases with doctors, nurses, and other people directly or indirectly involved in the pain experience of the individual. In addition to the interviews with patients, "healthy" members of the respective groups were interviewed on their attitudes toward pain, because in terms of the original hypothesis those attitudes and reactions which are displayed by the patients of the given cultural groups are held by all members of the group regardless of whether or not they are in pain, although in pain these attitudes may come more sharply into focus. In certain cases the researchers have interviewed a member of the patient's immediate family in order to check the report of the patient on his pain experience and in order to find out what are the attitudes and reactions of the family toward the patient's experience.

These interviews, based on a series of open-ended questions, were focused upon the past and present pain experiences of the interviewee. However, many other areas were considered important for the understanding of this experience. For instance, it was felt that complaints of pain may play an important role in manipulating relationships in the family and the larger social environment. It was also felt that in order to understand the specific reactive patterns in controlling pain, it is important to know certain aspects of child-rearing in the culture, relationships between parents and children, the role of infliction of pain in punishment, the attitudes of various members of the family toward specific expected, accepted pain experiences, and so on. The interviews were recorded on wire and transcribed verbatim for an ultimate detailed analysis. The interviews usually lasted for approximately two hours, the time being limited by the condition of the interviewee and by the amount and quality of his answers. When it was considered necessary, an interview was repeated. In most of the cases the study of the interviewee was followed by informal conversations and by observation of his behavior in the hospital.

The information gathered from the interviews was discussed with members of the medical staff, especially in the areas related to the medical aspects of the problem, in order to get their evaluation of the pain experience of the patient. Information as to the personality of the patient was checked against results of psychological testing by members of the psychological staff of the hospital when these were available.

The discussion of the material presented in this paper is based on interviews with 103 respondents, including 87 hospital patients in pain and 16 healthy subjects. According to their ethnocultural background the respondents are distributed as follows: "Old Americans," 26; Italians, 24; Jews, 31; Irish, 11; and others, 11.[5] In addition, there were the collateral interviews and conversations noted above with the family members, doctors, nurses, and other members of the hospital staff.

With regard to the pathological causes of pain, the majority of the interviewees fall into the group of patients suffering from neurological diseases, mainly herniated discs and spinal lesions. The focusing upon a group of patients suffering from a similar pathology offered the opportunity to investigate reactions and attitudes toward spontaneous pain which is symptomatic of one group of diseases. Nevertheless, a number of patients suffering from other diseases were also interviewed.

This paper is based upon the material collected during the first stage of study. The generalizations are to a great extent tentative formulations on a descriptive level. There has been no attempt as yet to integrate the results with the value system and the cultural pattern of the group, though here and there there will be indications to the effect that they are part of the culture pattern. The discussions will be lim-

[5] Italian respondents are mainly of South Italian origin; the Jewish respondents, with one exception, are all of East European origin. Whenever the Jews are mentioned they are spoken of in terms of the culture they represent and not in terms of their religion.

ited to main regularities within three groups, namely, the Italians, the Jews, and the "Old Americans." Factors related to variations within each group will be discussed after the main prevailing patterns have been presented.

Pain Among Patients of Jewish and Italian Origin

As already mentioned, the Jews and Italians were selected mainly because interviews with medical experts suggested that they display similar reactions to pain. The investigation of this similarity provided the opportunity to check a rather popular assumption that similar reactions reflect similar attitudes. The differences between the Italian and Jewish culture are great enough to suggest that if the attitudes are related to cultural pattern they will also be different, despite the apparent similarity in manifest behavior.

Members of both groups were described as being very emotional in their responses to pain. They were described as tending to exaggerate their pain experience and being very sensitive to pain. Some of the doctors stated that in their opinion Jews and Italians have a lower threshold of pain than members of other ethnic groups, especially members of the so-called Nordic group. This statement seems to indicate a certain confusion as to the concept of the threshold of pain. According to people who have studied the problem of the threshold of pain, for instance Harold Wolff and his associates, the threshold of pain is more or less the same for all human beings regardless of nationality, sex, or age.

In the course of the investigation, the general impressions of doctors were confirmed to a great extent by the interview material and by the observation of the patients' behavior. However, even a superficial study of the interviews has revealed that though reactions to pain appear to be similar, the underlying attitudes toward pain are different in the two groups. While the Italian patients seemed to be mainly concerned with the immediacy of the pain experience and were disturbed by the actual pain sensation which they experienced in a given situation, the concern of patients of Jewish origin was focused mainly upon the symptomatic meaning of pain and upon the significance of pain in relation to their health, welfare, and, eventually, for the welfare of their families. The Italian patient expressed in his behavior and in his complaints the discomfort caused by pain as such, and he manifested his emotions with regard to the effects of this pain experience upon his immediate situation in terms of occupation, economic situation, and so on; the Jewish patient expressed primarily his worries and anxieties as to the extent to which the pain indicated a threat to his health. In this connection it is worth mentioning that one of the Jewish words to describe strong pain is *yessurim*, a word which is also used to describe worries and anxieties.

Attitudes of Italian and Jewish patients toward pain-relieving drugs can serve as an indication of their attitude toward pain. When in pain the Italian calls for pain relief and is mainly concerned with the analgesic effects of the drugs which are administered to him.

Once the pain is relieved the Italian patient easily forgets his sufferings and manifests a happy and joyful disposition. The Jewish patient, however, often is reluctant to accept the drug, and he explains this reluctance in terms of concern about the effects of the drug upon his health in general. He is apprehensive about the habit-forming aspects of the analgesic. Moreover, he feels that the drug relieves his pain only temporarily and does not cure him of the disease which may cause the pain. Nurses and doctors have reported cases in which patients would hide the pill which was given to them to relieve their pain and would prefer to suffer. These reports were confirmed in the interviews with the patients. It was also observed that many Jewish patients, after being relieved from pain, often continued to display the same depressed and worried behavior, because they felt that though the pain was currently absent it might recur as long as the disease was not cured completely. From these observations it appears that when one deals with a Jewish and an Italian patient in pain, in the first case it is more important to relieve the anxieties with regard to the sources of pain, while in the second it is more important to relieve the actual pain.

Another indication as to the significance of pain for Jewish and Italian patients is their respective attitudes toward the doctor. The Italian patient seems to display a most confident attitude toward the doctor, which is usually reinforced after the doctor has succeeded in relieving pain; whereas the Jewish patient manifests a skeptical attitude, feeling that the fact that the doctor has relieved his pain by some drug does not mean at all that he is skillful enough to take care of the basic illness. Consequently, even when the pain is relieved, he tends to check the diagnosis and the treatment of one doctor against the opinions of other specialists in the field. Summarizing the difference between the Italian and Jewish attitudes, one can say that the Italian attitude is characterized by a present-oriented apprehension with regard to the actual sensation of pain, and the Jew tends to manifest a future-oriented anxiety as to the symptomatic and general meaning of the pain experience.

It has been stated that the Italians and Jews tend to manifest similar behavior in terms of their reactions to pain. As both cultures allow for free expression of feelings and emotions by words, sounds, and gestures, both the Italians and Jews feel free to talk about their pain, complain about it and manifest their sufferings by groaning, moaning, crying, etc. They are not ashamed of this expression. They admit willingly that when they are in pain they do complain a great deal, call for help, and expect sympathy and assistance from other members of their immediate social environment, especially from members of their family. When in pain they are reluctant to be alone and prefer the presence and attention of other people. This behavior, which is expected, accepted, and approved by the Italian and Jewish cultures, often conflicts with the patterns of behavior expected from a patient by American or Americanized medical people. Thus they tend to describe the behavior of the Italian and Jewish pa-

tient as exaggerated and over-emotional. The material suggests that they do tend to minimize the actual pain experiences of the Italian and Jewish patient, regardless of whether they have the objective criteria for evaluating the actual amount of pain which the patient experiences. It seems that the uninhibited display of reaction to pain as manifested by the Jewish and Italian patient provokes distrust in American culture instead of provoking sympathy.

Despite the close similarity between the manifest reactions among Jews and Italians, there seem to be differences in emphasis, especially with regard to what the patient achieves by these reactions and as to the specific manifestations of these reactions in the various social settings. For instance, they differ in their behavior at home and in the hospital. The Italian husband, who is aware of his role as an adult male, tends to avoid verbal complaining at home, leaving this type of behavior to the women. In the hospital, where he is less concerned with his role as a male, he tends to be more verbal and more emotional. The Jewish patient, on the contrary, seems to be more calm in the hospital than at home. Traditionally the Jewish male does not emphasize his masculinity through such traits as stoicism, and he does not equate verbal complaints with weakness. Moreover, the Jewish culture allows the patient to be demanding and complaining. Therefore, he tends more to use his pain in order to control interpersonal relationships within the family. Though similar use of pain to manipulate the relationships between members of the family may be present also in some other cultures, it seems that in the Jewish culture this is not disapproved, while in others it is.

In the hospital one can also distinguish variations in the reactive patterns among Jews and Italians. Upon his admission to the hospital and in the presence of the doctor the Jewish patient tends to complain, ask for help, be emotional even to the point of crying. However, as soon as he feels that adequate care is given to him he becomes more restrained. This suggests that the display of pain reaction serves less as an indication of the amount of pain experienced than as a means to create an atmosphere and setting in which the pathological causes of pain will be best taken care of. The Italian patient, on the other hand, seems to be less concerned with setting up a favorable situation for treatment. He takes for granted that adequate care will be given to him, and in the presence of the doctor he seems to be somewhat calmer than the Jewish patient. The mere presence of the doctor reassures the Italian patient, while the skepticism of the Jewish patient limits the reassuring role of the physician.

To summarize the description of the reactive patterns of the Jewish and Italian patients, the material suggests that on a semi-conscious level the Jewish patient tends to provoke worry and concern in his social environment as to the state of his health and the symptomatic character of his pain, while the Italian tends to provoke sympathy toward his suffering. In one case the function of the pain reaction will be the mobilization of the efforts of the family and the doctors toward a complete cure, while in the second case the function of the reaction will be focused upon the mobilization of effort toward relieving the pain sensation.

On the basis of the discussion of the Jewish and Italian material, two generalizations can be made:

1. Similar reactions to pain manifested by members of different ethnocultural groups do not necessarily reflect similar attitudes to pain.

2. Reactive patterns similar in terms of their manifestations may have different functions and serve different purposes in various cultures.

PAIN AMONG PATIENTS OF
"OLD AMERICAN" ORIGIN

There is little emphasis on emotional complaining about pain among "Old American" patients. Their complaints about pain can best be described as reporting on pain. In describing his pain, the "Old American" patient tries to find the most appropriate ways of defining the quality of pain, its localization, duration, etc. When examined by the doctor he gives the impression of trying to assume the detached role of an unemotional observer who gives the most efficient description of his state for a correct diagnosis and treatment. The interviewees repeatedly state that there is no point in complaining and groaning and moaning, etc., because "it won't help anybody." However, they readily admit that when pain is unbearable they may react strongly, even to the point of crying, but they tend to do it when they are alone. Withdrawal from society seems to be a frequent reaction to strong pain.

There seem to be different patterns in reacting to pain depending on the situation. One pattern, manifested in the presence of members of the family, friends, etc., consists of attempts to minimize pain, to avoid complaining and provoking pity; when pain becomes too strong there is a tendency to withdraw and express freely such reactions as groaning, moaning, etc. A different pattern is manifested in the presence of people who, on account of their profession, should know the character of the pain experience because they are expected to make the appropriate diagnosis, advise the proper cure, and give the adequate help. The tendency to avoid deviation from certain expected patterns of behavior plays an important role in the reaction to pain. This is also controlled by the desire to seek approval on the part of the social environment, especially in the hospital, where the "Old American" patient tries to avoid being a "nuisance" on the ward. He seems to be, more than any other patient, aware of an ideal pattern of behavior which is identified as "American," and he tends to conform to it. This was characteristically expressed by a patient who answered the question how he reacts to pain by saying, "I react like a good American."

An important element in controlling the pain reaction is the wish of the patient to cooperate with those who are expected to take care of him. The situation is often viewed as a team composed of the patient, the doctor, the nurse, the attendant, etc., and in this team everybody has a function and is supposed to do his share in order to achieve the most successful result.

Emotionality is seen as a purposeless and hindering factor in a situation which calls for knowledge, skill, training, and efficiency. It is important to note that this behavior is also expected by American or Americanized members of the medical or nursing staff, and the patients who do not fall into this pattern are viewed as deviants, hypochondriacs, and neurotics.

As in the case of the Jewish patients, the American attitude toward pain can be best defined as a future-oriented anxiety. The "Old American" patient is also concerned with the symptomatic significance of pain, which is correlated with a pronounced health-consciousness. It seems that the "Old American" is conscious of various threats to his health which are present in his environment and therefore feels vulnerable and is prone to interpret his pain sensation as a warning signal indicating that something is wrong with his health and therefore must be reported to the physician. With some exceptions, pain is considered bad and unnecessary and therefore must be immediately taken care of. In those situations where pain is expected and accepted, such as in the process of medical treatment or as a result of sports activities, there is less concern with the pain sensation. In general, however, there is a feeling that suffering pain is unnecessary when there are means of relieving it.

Though the attitudes of the Jewish and "Old American" patients can be defined as pain anxiety, they differ greatly. The future-oriented anxiety of the Jewish interviewee is characterized by pessimism or, at best, by skepticism, while the "Old American" patient is rather optimistic in his future-orientation. This attitude is fostered by the mechanistic approach to the body and its functions and by the confidence in the skill of the expert which are so frequent in the American culture. The body is often viewed as a machine which has to be well taken care of, be periodically checked for disfunctioning, and eventually, when out of order, be taken to an expert who will "fix" the defect. In the case of pain the expert is the medical man who has the "know-how" because of his training and experience and therefore is entitled to full confidence. An important element in the optimistic outlook is faith in the progress of science. Patients with intractable pain often stated that though at the present moment the doctors do not have the "drug" they will eventually discover it, and they give the examples of sulpha, penicillin, etc.

The anxieties of a pain-experiencing "Old American" patient are greatly relieved when he feels that something is being done about it in terms of specific activities involved in the treatment. It seems that his security and confidence increase in direct proportion to the number of tests, x-rays, examinations, injections, etc., that are given to him. Accordingly, "Old American" patients seem to have a positive attitude toward hospitalization, because the hospital is the adequate institution which is equipped for the necessary treatment. While a Jewish and an Italian patient seem to be disturbed by the impersonal character of the hospital and by the necessity of being treated there instead of at home, the "Old American" patient, on the contrary,

prefers the hospital treatment to the home treatment, and neither he nor his family seems to be disturbed by hospitalization.

To summarize the attitude of the "Old American" toward pain, he is disturbed by the symptomatic aspect of pain and is concerned with its incapacitating aspects, but he tends to view the future in rather optimistic colors, having confidence in the science and skill of the professional people who treat his condition.

SOME SOURCES OF INTRA-GROUP VARIATION

In the description of the reactive patterns and attitudes toward pain among patients of Jewish and "Old American" origin, certain regularities have been observed for each particular group regardless of individual differences and variations. This does not mean that each individual in each group manifests the same reactions and attitudes. Individual variations are often due to specific aspects of pain experience, to the character of the disease which causes the pain, or to elements in the personality of the patient. However, there are also other factors that are instrumental in provoking these differences and which can still be traced back to the cultural backgrounds of the individual patients. Such variables as the degree of Americanization of the patient, his socioeconomic background, education, and religiosity may play an important role in shaping individual variations in the reactive patterns. For instance, it was found that the patterns described are manifested most consistently among immigrants, while their descendants tend to differ in terms of adopting American forms of behavior and American attitudes toward the role of the medical expert, medical institutions, and equipment in controlling pain.

It is safe to say that the further the individual from the immigrant generation, the more American is his behavior. This is less true for the attitudes toward pain, which seem to persist to a great extent even among members of the third generation and even though the reactive patterns are radically changed. A Jewish or Italian patient born in this country of American-born parents tends to *behave* like an "Old American," but often expresses *attitudes* similar to those which are expressed by the Jewish or Italian people. They try to appear unemotional and efficient in situations where the immigrant would be excited and disturbed. However, in the process of the interview, if a patient is of Jewish origin he is likely to express attitudes of anxiety as to the meaning of his pain, and if he is an Italian he is likely to be rather unconcerned about the significance of his pain for his future.

The occupational factor plays an important role when pain affects a specific area of the body. For instance, manual workers with herniated discs are more disturbed by their pain than are professional or business people with a similar disease, because of the immediate significance of this particular pain for their respective abilities to earn a living. It was also observed that headaches cause more concern among intellectuals than among manual workers.

The educational background of the patient also plays an important role in his attitude with regard to the symptomatic meaning of a pain sensation. The more educated patients are more health-conscious and more aware of pain as a possible symptom of a dangerous disease. However, this factor plays a less important role than might be expected. The less educated "Old American" or Jewish patient is still more health-conscious than the more educated Italian. On the other hand, the less educated Jew is as much worried about the significance of pain as the more educated one. The education of the patient seems to be an important factor in fostering specific reactive patterns. The more educated patient, who may have more anxiety with regard to illness, may be more reserved in specific reactions to pain than an unsophisticated individual, who feels free to express his feelings and emotions.

THE TRANSMISSION OF CULTURAL ATTITUDES TOWARD PAIN

In interpreting the differences which may be attributed to different socioeconomic and educational backgrounds, there is enough evidence to conclude that these differences appear mainly on the manifest and behavioral level, whereas attitudinal patterns toward pain tend to be more uniform and to be common to most of the members of the group regardless of their specific backgrounds.

These attitudes toward pain and the expected reactive patterns are acquired by the individual members of the society from earliest childhood, along with other cultural attitudes and values which are learned from the parents, parent-substitutes, siblings, peer groups, etc. Each culture offers to its members an ideal pattern of attitudes and reactions, which may differ for various subcultures in a given society, and each individual is expected to conform to this ideal pattern. Here, the role of the family seems to be of primary importance. Directly and indirectly the family environment affects the individual's ultimate response to pain. In each culture the parents teach the child how to react to pain, and by approval or disapproval they promote specific forms of behavior. This conclusion is amply supported by the interviews. Thus, the Jewish and Italian respondents are unanimous in relating how their parents, especially mothers, manifested overprotective and overconcerned attitudes toward the child's health, participation in sports, games, fights, etc. In these families the child is constantly reminded of the advisability of avoiding colds, injuries, fights and other threatening situations. Crying in complaint is responded to by the parents with sympathy, concern, and help. By their overprotective and worried attitude they foster complaining and tears. The child learns to pay attention to each painful experience and to look for help and sympathy which are readily given to him.

In Jewish families, where not only a slight sensation of pain but also each deviation from the child's normal behavior is looked upon as a sign of illness, the child is prone to acquire anxieties with regard to the meaning and significance of these manifestations. The Italian parents do not seem to be concerned with the symptomatic meaning of the child's pains and aches,

but instead there is a great deal of verbal expression of emotions and feelings of sympathy toward the "poor child" who happens to be in discomfort because of illness or because of an injury in play. In these families a child is praised when he avoids physical injuries and is scolded when he does not pay enough attention to bad weather or drafts, or when he takes part in rough games and fights. The injury and pain are often interpreted to the child as punishment for the wrong behavior, and physical punishment is the usual consequence of misbehavior.

In the "Old American" family the parental attitude is quite different. The child is told not to "run to mother with every little thing." He is told to take pain "like a man," not to be a "sissy," not to cry. The child's participation in physical sports and games is not only approved but is also strongly stimulated. Moreover, the child is taught to expect to be hurt in sports and games and is taught to fight back if he happens to be attacked by other boys. However, it seems that the American parents are conscious of the threats to the child's health, and they teach the child to take immediate care of an injury. When hurt, the right thing to do is not to cry and get emotional but to avoid unnecessary pain and prevent unpleasant consequences by applying the proper first aid medicine and by calling a doctor.

Often attitudes and behavior fostered in a family conflict with those patterns which are accepted by the larger social environment. This is especially true in the case of children of immigrants. The Italian or Jewish immigrant parents promote patterns which they consider correct, while the peer groups in the street and in the school criticize this behavior and foster a different one. In consequence, the child may acquire the attitudes which are part of his home-life but may also adopt behavior patterns which conform to those of his friends.

The direct promotion of certain behavior described as part of the child-rearing explains only in part the influence of the general family environment and the specific role of the parents in shaping responses to pain. They are also formed indirectly by observing the behavior of other members of the family and by imitating their responses to pain. Moreover, attitudes toward pain are also influenced by various aspects of parent-child relationship in a culture. The material suggests that differences in attitudes toward pain in Jewish, Italian, and "Old American" families are closely related to the role and image of the father in the respective cultures in terms of his authority and masculinity. Often the father and mother assume different roles in promoting specific patterns of behavior and specific attitudes. For example, it seems that in the "Old American" family it is chiefly the mother who stimulates the child's ability to resist pain, thus emphasizing his masculinity. In the Italian family it seems that the mother is the one who inspires the child's emotionality, while in the Jewish family both parents express attitudes of worry and concern which are transmitted to the children.

Specific deviations from expected reactive and attitudinal patterns can often be understood in terms of a par-

ticular structure of the family. This became especially clear from the interviews of two Italian patients and one Jewish patient. All three subjects revealed reactions and attitudes diametrically opposite to those which the investigator would expect on the basis of his experience. In the process of the interview, however, it appeared that one of the Italian patients was adopted into an Italian family, found out about his adoption at the age of fourteen, created a phantasy of being of Anglo-Saxon origin because of his physical appearance, and accordingly began to eradicate everything "Italian" in his personality and behavior. For instance, he denied knowledge of the Italian language despite the fact that he always spoke Italian in the family, and even learned to abstain from smiling, because he felt that being happy and joyful is an indication of Italian origin. The other Italian patient lost his family at a very early age because of family disorganization and was brought up in an Irish foster home. The Jewish patient consciously adopted a "non-Jewish" pattern of behavior and attitude because of strong sibling rivalry. According to the respondent, his brother, a favored son in the immigrant Jewish family, always manifested "typical" Jewish reactions toward disease, and the patient, who strongly disliked the brother and was jealous of him, decided to be "completely different."

This analysis of cultural factors in responses to pain is tentative and incomplete. It is based upon only one year of research, which has been devoted exclusively to collection of raw material and formulation of working hypotheses. A detailed analysis of the interviews may call for revisions and reformulations of certain observations described in this paper. Nevertheless, the first objectives of our research have been attained in establishing the importance of the role of cultural factors in an area relatively little explored by the social sciences. We hope that in the course of further research we shall be able to expand our investigation into other areas of the pain problem, such as sex differences in attitudes toward pain, the role of age differences and the role of religious beliefs in the pain experience. We hope also that the final findings of the study will contribute to the growing field of collaboration between the social sciences and medicine for the better understanding of human problems.

From birth, people are socialized to the life styles of their ethnic group, and people tend to take the ethnic component of their life styles for granted. Since so much of ethnic life styles is really an ingroup phenomenon, outgroups may see ethnic life styles through popular stereotypes. Outsiders tend to develop distorted generalizations about all members of ethnic groups. There is a pervasive view that Italians are likely to have connections with organized crime, that all Poles are blue-collar, and that many Irish are alcoholics. Stereotypes tend to be selective and distorted with stereotypers tending not to see the same characteristic when it is present in other ethnic groups.*

The American Indian's life style has been stereotyped for years in novels, movies, and television shows. The Hollywood version of Indian life styles has become a commercialized attraction; in Indian settlements from Cherokee, North Carolina, to Pueblo, Colorado, and beyond, tourists purchase symbols of Indian life style in the form of orlon Indian blankets and plastic Japanese-made tepees. The life style of Indians, either on isolated reservations or urban ghettos, is still poorly understood by most Americans. In the following article, Donald Jewell shows that the Indian way of life is so alien, even to "experts," that it may be taken as a sign of mental illness.

---

* For a comprehensive review of the literature on stereotyping behavior, see Howard J. Ehrlich, *The Social Psychology of Prejudice* (New York: Wiley, 1973), pp. 20–60.

A Case of a "Psychotic" Navaho Indian Male

Donald P. Jewell

Increased psychological and ethnological rapprochement has resulted in a greater understanding of American subgroups and the processes of acculturation. Examples of this integrated approach are to be seen in Barnouw's study of Chippewa Indian acculturation[1] and, on the individual level, Devereux's psychotherapy of an alcoholic Sioux.[2]

Sometimes identified as the "culture-personality" orientation, this approach has reached a degree of clarification which justifies consistent designation. It is suggested here that it be defined as ethnopsychological. It is an approach which, as Kluckhohn has shown, has about a century of development.[3] Ethnopsychology has generally concerned itself with a definition of general normal personality characteristics of other cultures, only occasionally with the neurotic individual, and rarely with the psychotic.

PURPOSE OF THIS STUDY

The writer had the opportunity recently to make a rather extensive observation of a Navaho Indian institutionalized as a psychotic in a California state mental hospital. By drawing from the literature of Navaho ethnopsychology and the writer's own experience among the Navaho people, it was hoped that the dynamics of the patient's maladjustment would be revealed. It was also anticipated that some sort of psychotherapy would evolve.

This report is a summary of those endeavors to understand and assist the Navaho patient. Cultural and linguistic obstacles prohibited an ideal approach, but enough was accomplished to permit considerable insight into the patient's behavior. There were features about the patient's personality which would not fit harmoniously with concepts of psychiatric symptomatology derived from European culture, those concepts dealing particularly with the dynamics of the diagnosis of catatonic schizophrenia. The unique characteristics of this individual's personality lead, in fact, to the question as to what extent he should be considered psychotic, and whether that consideration should be viewed from Navaho or Anglo perspective.

During his many interviews with the patient, some of them with the aid of a Navaho interpreter, the writer developed an increasing awareness that to

Reprinted by permission of the Society for Applied Anthropology from *Human Organization,* vol. 11, no. 1 (Spring 1952), pp. 31–36.

[1] Barnouw, V., "Acculturation and Personality Among the Wisconsin Chippewa," *American Anthropologist,* Memoir Number 72, Vol. 52, 1950.

[2] Devereux, G., *Reality and Dream* (International Universities Press, 1950).

[3] Kluckhohn, C., "The Influence of Psychiatry on Anthropology in America During the Past One Hundred Years," in J. K. Hall, G. Zilboorg, and E. A. Bunker (eds.), *One Hundred Years of American Psychiatry* (Columbia University Press, 1947), pp. 589–617.

TABLE 1   SUMMARY OF SURVEY OF NAVAHO INDIAN MENTAL PATIENTS HOSPITALIZED
IN SOUTHWESTERN UNITED STATES, EXCLUDING MENTAL DEFECTIVES[a]

Diagnosis	Number	Sex and age
Psychosis with syphilis of the C.N.C.	2	1f: 47; 1m: 31
Psychosis with cerebral arteriosclerosis	1	1f: 62
Psychosis due to trauma (organic)	1	1m: 47
Epilepsy	8	6 m: 20, 24, 29, 33 37, 39; 2f: 20, 32
Schizophrenia, simple type	1	1m: 25
Schizophrenia, mixed type	1	1f: 25
Schizophrenia, hebephrenic type	1	1f: 30
Schizophrenia, catatonic type	7	4m: 26, 28, 28, 36; 3f: 20, 30, 38
Depressed state	1	1f: 37
Manic-depressive psychosis, manic type	1	1m: 42

[a] Acknowledgement of the hospitals cooperating in this survey must be regretfully omitted, due to the need to protect the identity of the patients.

call the patient psychotic was an arbitrary matter. When this Navaho is referred to as psychotic, then, it is merely because he carried such a diagnosis during his 18 months of hospitalization as a mental patient.

ORIENTATION

Considerable literary attention has been given to the general psychological characteristics of Navaho Indians.[4] These have related psychological findings to ethnological contexts, and so offer a background against which the atypical Navaho individual may be examined.

[4] Henry, W., "The Thematic Apperception Technique in the Study of Culture-Personality Relations," *Genetic Psychology Monographs*, Vol. 35, 1947, pp. 3–135; Kluckhohn, C., and Leighton, D., *Children of the People* (Harvard University Press, 1948).

On the behavioral level, the Navahos are in many ways unique, not only with respect to white people but other Indian tribes as well. One of their most characteristic traits may be seen in crisis situations. Kluckhohn and Leighton describe it as a passive resistance, the individual masking his fear by quiet unmovingness, an appearance of stoicism. If forced into action, the response is a mechanical, apparently uncomprehending behavior.[5]

Another form of withdrawal is often expressed in periods of depression, apparently a morbid preoccupation with health.[6]

These being salient aspects of the typical Navaho personality, the question now arises as to how those traits would be characterized on the psychotic level. Under prolonged psycho-

[5] Kluckhohn and Leighton, ibid., p. 108.
[6] Ibid., p. 110.

logical stress, what would develop from the stoicism and moods of morbid pre-occupation?

In an endeavor to answer this question a survey was made of those mental hospitals which would most likely be caring for Navaho patients. The Bureau of Indian Affairs' policy is not to concentrate Indian patients, but to subsidize their care in whatever hospital they may have been committed. It is thus possible that a few Navahos may be hospitalized some distance from their reservation area of New Mexico, Utah, and Arizona, and have not been located in this survey. It is felt, however, that a survey of those mental hospitals in the Southwest only would be adequate to show general trends. The findings are summarized in Table 1.

Elimination of the organic psychoses leaves one manic, one depressive, and 10 schizophrenics. Of the schizophrenics, seven are catatonic. This is an unusually high incidence of catatonic schizophrenia, and seems to indicate that Navahos are predisposed toward that particular psychosis. This immediately suggests that the above-described stoicism has been carried to pathological extremes, and possibly that the stoicism is actually a transient form of catatonia. It was with this problem in mind that the Navaho patient discussed in this report was studied.

THE PATIENT

The patient was a 26-year-old Navaho male. For purposes of anonymity he will be referred to as Bill. He came to the writer's attention through a survey of Indian patients at the hospital. He was the only Navaho of 13 Indian patients scattered throughout the various wards and cottages, and of the 4,000 general-patient population.

The outlook for examination and therapy seemed at first quite discouraging. The patient was in a cottage ordinarily reserved for the most regressed patients. Unlike most of the others in this cottage, however, he was not there because of repeated failure of such routine therapies as shock treatment, occupational therapy, etc. It was unusual for a patient in his condition, who had been at the hospital for eight months, not to have received at least electric shock treatment.

A preliminary period was spent at the cottage, observing Bill's behavior. He was very withdrawn. Most of his day was spent in inactive sitting or sleeping. He would rouse himself only for eating or attending to other personal needs. He would assist with floor waxing, dish washing, or other activities the attendants might require of him, but in a perfunctory and apathetic manner. His behavior was not patently catatonic, but certainly suggestive of it.

Most of the attendants reported never having heard Bill speak. A few, however, indicated that Bill would occasionally approach them and, in almost unintelligible English, ask if he could go home.

Shortly thereafter Bill was brought to the writer's office where he was greeted in Navaho. Bill responded in that language, glancing briefly at the writer before returning his gaze to the floor.

This closer inspection of Bill revealed occipital flattening, resulting from the cradle board as a child, and the pierced ear lobes of a conservative Navaho. During this first interview he complained about the close haircuts he received at the hospital, further evidence that he belonged to the old-fashioned, "long-hair" conservatives of the reservation.

The interview proceeded very slowly, but gradually a system of communication began to evolve. By utilizing mutually understood Navaho and English words, by means of pantomime, and with the aid of penciled sketches, the system became increasingly refined during the following interviews.

Bill was seen three hours a week for three months. The writer then took an eight-month leave of absence from the hospital, during which time he spent several months in Bill's home area near Shiprock, New Mexico.

While in the Shiprock area, the writer endeavored to locate Bill's family to advise them of the patient's circumstances. Bill had previously drawn a map indicating the approximate location of his family's *hogans* (dwellings), but it proved impossible to find them. The hogans were located about five miles from the nearest road, and even if a horse and interpreter had been available, the chances of locating the specific hogans were slight. The situation was complicated by the fact that the family did not have American names and the writer did not know their Navaho names. Missionaries and Bureau of Indian Affairs personnel were consequently given the problem of finding the family, but several months elapsed before they were

equipped with sufficient information to do so.

Although he could not communicate with Bill's family, the writer succeeded in talking with several Navahos who had known Bill, and in obtaining ecological and further case-history material.

Shortly after the writer's return to the hospital a Navaho interpreter was brought in from the Sherman Institute, a large Indian school not far from the hospital. Interviews with the patient through the interpreter corroborated the case history material obtained, and further satisfied the writer in his clinical evaluation of the patient. Both of these areas are separately discussed in the following text.

CASE HISTORY

The gathering of Bill's history extended over a period of 11 months, and was obtained piecemeal from a variety of sources. In summarizing, however, this material will be integrated for greater coherency.

Bill was born in a part of the reservation noted for being both very conservative and poverty-striken. Only 50 miles away is the markedly contrasting community of Shiprock, considered to be one of the most acculturated Navaho communities. It is also prospering from recently developed uranium operations in the region.

During his early years Bill saw very little of Shiprock, and was reared in the traditional Navaho way. He was born during an eclipse (it is not known whether of the sun or moon), and was thus destined to take part in a periodic

ceremony identified to the writer as the "Breath of Life" sing. The first of this series of ceremonies was held while he was still an infant, the second about six years ago. During the ceremony he inhales the breath of a great deity, and is thus assured of continued good health in the respiratory and vocal organs.

Bill lived with his immediate family until he was six years of age. He had only one younger sister at that time, although the family was later to include seven living siblings. He did not become well acquainted with his family, however, as he was given to his grandfather when he was six years old. The grandfather, a widower, lived several miles deeper into the reservation and required Bill's assistance as a sheep herder.

Bill worked for his grandfather as a sheep herder until he was 17, except for one interruption when, at the age of 15, he spent 50 days in the Shiprock hospital with a back ailment. Bill reports that the old man never talked to him.

At his grandfather's death Bill went to work for the railroad in Colorado. This was cut short by an illness which confined him to the Navaho Medical Center in Fort Defiance, Arizona. The illness was diagnosed as tuberculosis, pulmonary, moderately advanced. He was in the hospital for eight months and was discharged in the summer of 1944.

Bill returned to railroad employment, and worked in Utah, Oregon, and Nebraska. He was always part of Navaho crews and thus never exposed to acculturative influences. His father and a younger brother were also part of these crews.

Bill returned home for a brief visit in 1949, accompanied by his brother and father. He had saved $1,022. Subsequently, he went to Phoenix, Arizona, to pick cotton, a job that had been found for him by the employment agency at Shiprock. This was his first trip from home without a family member.

The employment at Phoenix did not last long and in December, 1949, on the advice of an Indian friend he went to Barstow, California, seeking railroad employment. At the section camp there his attempt to find work was unsuccessful, and after three days he started by bus back to Phoenix.

On this return trip he stopped for dinner at Colton. A white man he met there promised to obtain railroad employment for him. The stranger said that he required funds for this effort and in some way relieved Bill of his savings, which had now dwindled to $725.

Bill returned home penniless, pawned some jewelry, borrowed some money, and returned to Colton to try to find the man who had taken his savings. He also looked for Navahos who might have information about employment. The many hours of waiting around the bus station searching for his man apparently caused suspicion, for he was arrested for vagrancy.

In jail he met some Navahos with whom he went to Barstow after his release. But in Barstow he was still unable to find employment, and after six days he was completely out of funds. He started walking toward Phoenix, and was picked up by a man driving a truck. This man gave Bill one day's employment, which allowed funds for a return to Barstow and another attempt to find work.

He managed to raise a little money doing odd jobs about the section camp near Barstow, and then returned to San Bernardino on the first lap of his return to Phoenix and home. It occurred to him that if he could get to a hospital, the officials there would send him to a reservation hospital, from whence he would be sent home. This was logical thinking: on the reservations, the hospitals, schools, and trading posts are the major source of assistance in all sorts of troubles.

As this idea occurred to Bill, he noticed a woman dressed in white whom he took to be a nurse. He approached her and endeavored to explain that he was sick, but his endeavors were misinterpreted and he was taken to jail.

At the county jail Bill was apparently mistaken for a Mexican, since a Mexican interpreter had tried to interview him. When the interview failed he was transferred to the psychopathic ward. Interviewed by the medical examiner there, he reportedly demonstrated an anguished appearance and repeated, "Me sick." He was diagnosed as Schizophrenia, Catatonic Type, and delivered to the state mental hospital.

Upon admission to the hospital, Bill was first taken to be a Filipino. The psychiatric admission note indicated that he was "... confused, dull, and preoccupied. He has a look of anguish and appears to be hallucinating. . . . He repeats 'I don't know.' " He was diagnosed as Dementia Praecox, which was later specified as Hebephrenic Type.

Several months later the psychiatrist on Bill's cottage tested him for *cerea flexibilitas* (waxy flexibility) and, finding it to be present, altered the diagnosis to Catatonic Type.

Eight months after his admittance he was discovered by the writer.

PSYCHOLOGICAL ASPECTS

Concomitant with gathering the case history material presented above, endeavors were made to evaluate the patient's intelligence and personality. The lack of culturally-biased examining techniques made this extremely difficult.

Bill's performance on the various tests that were administered led to a conclusion that his probable I.Q. was in the vicinity of 80. This had to take into consideration the patient's slowness. At best, a Navaho refuses to be put under pressure of time, and to what extent Bill's slowness was cultural rather than psychotically pathological was a question of primary concern.

Bill's apathetic and withdrawn behavior has already been described. For diagnostic purposes, however, this syndrome is confused by cultural factors. It is common for Navahos, with their morbid fear of hospitals, to demonstrate just such a withdrawal patterning.[7] It is not known whether or not this would reach a stage of *cerea flexibilitas* or how long this behavior will persist. Accordingly it was concluded that Bill's apparent catatonia should not be accepted as a symptom of schizophrenia until underlying signs

[7] Ibid., pp. 108–109.

of schizophrenic processes could be detected.

During the first interview Bill was given the Draw A Person Test. The figure he drew was indistinct and without facial features and clearly reflected his withdrawal.

On the seventh interview the test was again given. Compared with the earlier attempt, the second drawing clearly reflected an improvement. It probably indicated the therapeutic benefits derived from the extensive individual treatment the patient was receiving.

The second drawing filled the paper, the facial features were portrayed, the arms were extended, and the drawing generally implied those signs which are held to indicate good contact with reality.

Although Bill's second drawing seems to infer considerable personality change, no changes could be observed in his behavior. He continued to appear apathetic and withdrawn. On several occasions he indicated his reluctance to talk because "me no good this place," pointing to his chest. This suggested the characteristic organ cathexes of schizophrenia. However, the patient's thinking behind this statement was made clear during the later interviews through an interpreter.

Bill was concerned about the fact that he had not completed the second series of the "Breath of Life" ceremony. This matter had gone too long unattended, and he assumed that he must conserve his vocal energies until they could be supplemented by the breath of the deity. He expressed a great need to return home to pursue the ceremony.

In continued endeavor to detect schizophrenic underlay of his apparent catatonia, Bill was given a series of tests, none of which revealed responses normally associated with schizophrenia.

During the early course of the interviews with Bill, although not satisfied that the patient was not psychotic, the writer recommended that the best therapeutic environment for him would be his own home. This recommendation was not acted upon, partly because no one knew where his home was, or how he could be supervised there, but chiefly because he continued to appear catatonic.

Later, as the writer became convinced that the catatonia — if such it could be termed — was not symptomatic of underlying schizophrenia, efforts were renewed to release the patient. The outcome of these endeavors is summarized in the following section.

Outcome

As mentioned earlier, the final interviews with Bill were carried on with the aid of a Navaho interpreter. Bill conversed quite freely with the other Navahos and expressed gratitude at being able to talk to someone in his own language. The conversations did not add much to the history and understanding previously gained, but did offer an opportunity to inquire for the presence of hallucinations, delusions, and more subtle clues of schizophrenic thinking. Unless Bill's anxiety regarding the uncompleted "Breath of Life" ceremony could be considered bizarre, nothing of significance was elicited.

The interpreter's reaction to the interviews represented their most significant outcome. He was a professional interpreter, with vast experience in interviewing Navaho youths in strange environments. He expressed a strong conviction that Bill's behavior and attitudes were not unusual under the circumstances.

The interpreter communicated his feelings to the superintendent of the Sherman Institute, who took an immediate and active interest in the case. After several interviews with Bill, satisfied that he could observe nothing about Bill's behavior which could be considered atypical under the circumstances, the superintendent offered to accept him into the flexible program of the Sherman Institute.

Bill was accordingly released under custody of the superintendent and careful plans were made to assure his adjustment at the school. At first, he was quartered in the school hospital, but allowed to participate in the school's social and recreational activities. He was employed with the animal husbandry and gardening program.

The writer's last visit to the Sherman Institute disclosed that Bill's adjustment had been quite rapid. He had put on weight and after about two weeks announced that he "felt right at home, now."

It had been difficult at first, because in spite of all precautions the students had learned something of Bill's past hospitalization. To the Navahos the hospital symbolizes death, and death is particularly abhorrent to them as they have no clearly structured concepts of an after-life. The students consequently shied away from Bill a

little when he arrived, but he has since found acceptance.

He will go back to the reservation in the spring, at the close of the school year, and attend to the unfinished business of the "Breath of Life" ceremony.

CONCLUDING DISCUSSION

In the course of this Navaho's commitment and 18 months of hospitalization, he was routinely examined by several psychiatrists, all of whom concurred with the diagnosis of schizophrenia. Without verbal communication with the patient, diagnosis was necessarily derived from observation of his overt behavior. Diagnosis was apparently confident as the patient was not referred to staff clinic or for psychological testing, the normal procedure with questionable cases.

Most of the psychiatrists' diagnostic observations were based on information received from the attendants of Bill's cottage, who reported the patient's withdrawn and apathetic behavior. Upon closer examination the patient would demonstrate *cerea flexibilitas*. Because of these factors the patient was assumed to be catatonic and hence schizophrenic.

Actually, many of the classic symptoms of catatonia were not present in this patient. He was not markedly stuporous or mute; he was clean in his personal habits and would eat willingly; he tended to doze as he sat rather than stare fixedly into space as does the typical catatonic. The writer, too, examined Bill for *cerea flexibilitas*, but learned later that the patient held grotesque positions because he thought it was expected of him.

With the assumption, however, that the patient's overt behavior could be interpreted as symptomatic of catatonic schizophrenia, it remains to be explained why testing and closer observation did not reveal the underlying ego disintegration which should be expected.

General personality traits of the Navaho people, as briefly reviewed earlier in this paper, could possibly infer a potential for schizophrenic disintegration. Navahos do not have the imaginative activity and the inner control which is so important to adjustment in the Anglo world. The scales are balanced, however, by a defense of rigidity and construction. In a threatening situation they strive to maintain ego structure by psychic withdrawal.

The few tests that were applicable in examining Bill did not permit a very intensive examination of the dynamics of his withdrawal, but all indications were that he continued to maintain ego strength. He could account for his acts rationally, he performed very well with conceptualization, he maintained orientation for time and place, and could hold in mind simultaneously various aspects of situations or problems. His visuo-motor performance exhibited no signs of distorted perspective. Many of his expressions could be considered naive, but hardly bizarre.

The apparent incongruity between the patient's overt behavior and underlying personality dynamics, although not fully understood psychologically, should not be considered as psychotic manifestation. Culturally derived, it can probably be explained as a defense mechanism characterized by an extreme and sustained withdrawal.

To what extent Bill's case may be typical of other Navaho patients diagnosed as catatonic schizophrenia cannot, of course, be proposed. It would be necessary to know if those patients were similarly diagnosed on the basis of overt behavior alone.

It is also unknown to what degree Bill may personify on-reservation Navaho youth. Superficially at least, his history appears quite typical. His lack of school, his years as a sheep herder for his grandfather, his attack of tuberculosis, and his railroad employment, are circumstances and events common to many Navahos. His grandfather's apparent lack of affection implies an almost feral existence for the growing boy, but even this situation is not unusual. It is, in fact, difficult to discern some way in which this patient could be atypical as evaluated against his cultural background. Except for his possible low intelligence, he appears to represent a typical Navaho youth, a fact heavy with implication when his 18 months of hospitalization as a mental patient is considered.

The previously cited survey of hospitalized Navaho mental patients shows an amazingly small percentage of the total Navaho population (which is about 65,000). This is probably because few Navahos are currently coming in very close contact with Anglo structure.

Of the catatonic schizophrenics, it would be of value to know more about the details of their admission. If they were referred from the reservation it probably meant that they were considered psychotic within the Navaho milieu; if, on the other hand, they were referred by agencies off the reservation (as was Bill), it would imply an evaluation derived from Anglo perspective. This will become a more poignant problem with increasing off-reservation movement of the Navaho people.

In addition to what this study may infer with respect to the Navaho Indians, it is hoped also that it may illustrate the need to consider the influence of cultural environment in any study of individual personality. The psychiatric approach usually concerns itself with the abnormal personality, and evaluates the individual according to concepts of what constitutes the normal personality. Too often these concepts are preconceived and stereotyped, giving very little consideration to the individual's cultural frame of reference.

This factor naturally varies in proportion to the degree of the individual's acculturation.

The cultural factor seems to be particularly important in reconciling overt behavior with covert personality dynamics. This is often a difficult reconciliation even with patients of the general American cultural patterning, and becomes increasingly more difficult the farther removed the individual is from acculturation.

The need to consider emotional maladjustment with respect to cultural factors has long been recognized. It has, however, been somewhat of an academic acknowledgement which demands greater practical application on the clinical level.

Urban Americans are more likely to have contact with selected aspects of Chinese culture (mainly food) than with American Indian culture, but their information about the life style of Chinese Americans is likely to be little better than their knowledge of the American Indian's life style. Even frequent visitors to Chinatowns do not have much of an opportunity to learn about the life styles of its residents. As Charles Choy Wong points out in the following article, Chinatowns are slums, many Chinese Americans are poor, often exploited, and limited in their occupational choices.

Immigrant Life in American Chinatowns

Charles Choy Wong

Chinatown communities in America are slums in dire need of assistance, but that is not the way they are viewed by middle-class visitors. Old myths die hard. In the glare of neon lights, visitors see only novelty shops and Cantonese restaurants where they eat chow mein; they do not notice overcrowding, substandard housing, or garment sweat shops. Occasional visits do not reveal the insufficient and inadequate health and recreational facilities, endemic tuberculosis, or suicide and infant mortality that are prevalent. However, in these slums the number of street gangs and crimes is increasing. Unemployment and underemployment are seriously growing problems, and the median family income is far below the national average.[1]

This article was prepared especially for this volume. Copyright © 1975 by Charles Choy Wong.

[1] For specific studies completed, see: Action for Boston Community Development, Inc. (ABCD), *The Chinese in Boston, 1970* (Boston: ABCD, 1970); Chinatown Study Group, *Chinatown Report,* 1969 (New York: East Asian Institute, Columbia University, 1970); Cattell, Stuart H., *Health, Welfare, and Social Organization in Chinatown, New York City* (New York: Department of Public Affairs, 1962); and *Report of the San Francisco Chinese Community Citizens' Survey and Fact-Finding Committee,* Abridged Edition, Lim P. Lee, et al (San Francisco:

The social conditions of American Chinatowns are the end product of decades of hostile discrimination in the general labor market that turned Chinese in desperation to self-employment in small businesses. When anti-Chinese agitation, legislation, and prejudice prevented them from entering more desirable occupations they were forced to do hand laundry or establish other retail businesses. Those who had to survive in the Chinatown subeconomy resigned themselves to its low wages and poor working conditions. Until recently, however, the native born were able to leave in sufficient numbers to alleviate the plight of the entrapped who remained. But a substantial increase in the number of Chinese immigrants occurred with the Nationalization and Immigration Act of 1965. When the new law struck down the old national origin quota that admitted 105 Chinese each year, Chinese immigration jumped to 4,769 that year. By the time the new law became fully effective in 1968, annual immigration had increased to 25,096. Between 1965 and 1972 a total of 128,692 Chinese had immigrated to the United States. The Chinese population in America grew from 237,000 to 436,000 between 1960 and 1970. Post-1965 immigration accounted for 46 percent of the 198,000 increase.[2]

Most recent immigrants came from Hong Kong. Like their predecessors most settled in Chinatown communi-

Chinese Community Citizens' Survey and Fact-Finding Committee, 1969).

[2] Annual Reports of the U.S. Immigration and Naturalization Service, Tables 6, 6A, and 6B.

TABLE 1   CHINESE IMMIGRATION TO THE UNITED STATES, 1965–72

	1965	1966	1967	1968	1969	1970	1971	1972	Total
Immigrants admitted	4,769	17,608	25,096	16,434	20,893	17,956	17,622	21,730	142,108
Aliens adjusted to permanent resident status	2,088	11,300	13,094	5,973	4,737	6,416	7,155	8,329	59,092
Immigrants admitted by last place of permanent residence (China, Taiwan, Hong Kong)	3,860	16,751	22,857	14,689	19,404	16,147	15,557	19,427	128,692
Non-immigrants admitted	17,508	20,245	22,111	31,062	39,476	47,080	54,560	64,281	296,323

SOURCE— Annual Reports of the U.S. Immigration and Naturalization Service. Tables 6, 6A, 6B.

ties. The physical boundaries of China-towns have expanded somewhat to accommodate the increased population; however, the expansion has not kept pace with population growth, so that population density increased tremendously, reaching the saturation point. For example, San Francisco's Chinatown population density of 150 persons per acre is second only to Manhattan's.[3] Beginning their immigration in the 1850's, the Chinese were the first non-white group voluntarily to immigrate to the United States. Since Chinese have remained at the point of their first settlement, their communities are now located in the oldest sections of the inner cities. It is here that recent immigration intensified existing problems.

Housing is frequently so overcrowded that tenants must line up in the morning to use toilets and bathrooms; and cooking must be done in shifts. Hence communal living is a way of life in the deteriorating tenements of American Chinatowns. Chinatown residents also contend with rats and cockroaches so numerous that ordinary pest-control measures cannot reduce their number.

Increased population and a shortage of housing has forced rent prices upward. Impoverished residents of Chinatown typically pay higher rents for their inferior accommodations than do other city dwellers. Intense demand for rentals benefits the family associations and *tongs* which own most of Chinatown rental properties. In turn high rents eliminate any incentive of business leaders to seek the construc-

[3] Lim, et al, op. cit., p. 51.

TABLE 2   CHINESE POPULATION OF THE UNITED STATES AND OF SELECTED
STANDARD METROPOLITAN STATISTICAL AREAS WITH PERCENTAGE
OF INCREASE FOR THE DECADE 1960–1970

	1960	1970	Percentage increase
San Francisco–Oakland	52,984	88,108	166
New York	36,129	76,208	211
Los Angeles–Long Beach	19,730	40,798	207
Chicago	6,214	12,653	204
Boston	5,811	12,025	210
Sacramento	6,770	10,444	154
Philadelphia	2,644	4,882	185
United States, total	237,000	435,000	184

SOURCE — U.S. Bureau of the Census, *Census of Population: 1970. General Population Characteristics. Final Report* PC (1) Bl. *United States Summary.* Washington: U.S. Government Printing Office, 1972, Table 67, p. 32 ff.; *idem., Census of Population: 1960.* Vol. I. *Characteristics of the Population.* Part 6. *California.* Washington: U.S. Government Printing Office, 1963, Table 21, p. 127.

tion of needed public housing.[4] In San Francisco, the largest public housing project is the 428-unit Ping Yuen. Even before it was opened, there were 778 families on the apartment waiting list. Vacancies seldom occur.

Chinatowns' employed residents either work in the restaurant-based tourist establishments or in the garment industry. They are disproportionately foreign-born, and non–English speaking, and they generally lack marketable skills. For these reasons, jobs in Chinatown are virtually the only ones available to recent immigrants. If local jobs ceased, the struggling immigrants who eke out a subsistence would not likely find employment outside of Chinatown.

The problems of Chinatown today result directly from recent immigration that worsened ghetto conditions and exacerbated existing social and economic problems. However, it is a mistake to overemphasize recent immigration by failing to view it in the context of previously existing conditions.[5] Such

[4] In November, 1972 the Department of Housing and Urban Development allocated 1.3 million dollars toward construction of additional low-income public housing in San Francisco's Chinatown. This allocation came in response to the pressure of Democratic politicians in San Francisco and a militant demonstration in Washington by Self-Help for the Elderly, an OEO-funded group, not Chinatown business leaders. See "$1.3 million comes through for housing," *East/West*, November 1, 1972, p. 1.

[5] A significant example of the social implications of this "immigration thesis" was the blatantly distorted document entitled, "Triad: Mafia of the Far East," issued in the July, 1973 Criminal Intelligence Bulletin. The document was prepared by the California Department of Justice under the direction of Attorney General Evelle Younger and distributed to all law enforcement agencies throughout the State. The case is now under litigation in the courts.

overemphasis merely revives a "yellow peril" hysteria, implying that remedial governmental action to curtail immigration of 20,000 Chinese per year is a solution. A basic cause of conditions in Chinatown is found within the social structure that preceded recent immigration. The garment and tourist industries that have long been the economic base of Chinatown impose cruel demands upon the working class. Recent immigrants find themselves trapped by the tourist-garment economy. That is important background to understanding the impact of recent immigration.

CHINATOWN'S GARMENT INDUSTRY

For immigrant Chinese women, by far the most important source of employment is the small garment factory. These establishments inconspicuously dot the community. Women immigrants say, "It is the only kind of job we can get." [6] They are a cheap source of labor. Chinese women are forced to do piece work as non-union seamstresses for as little as fifty cents an hour. In New York, there are over 250 garment factories; in San Francisco, over 150; in Los Angeles about 70. Even in Boston's small Chinatown there are more than twenty garment factories. The buildings in which they are located are usually in need of repair and lack adequate heating. A typical firm employs about twenty-five machine operators, who work in close

proximity. These factories, as "culturally modified" sweat shops, require a six-day week without overtime pay, but permit frequent breaks to allow women employees to get children off to school or prepare a family meal. Under the piece rate system, for each item of clothing completed the seamstress receives a fee, typically from $.10 to $1.50 depending upon the complexity of the task.[7]

The rapid growth of non-union garment shops is a direct result of the availability of cheap labor. Female immigrants must find work to supplement a family's meager income. They become the victims of exploitation by other Chinese. In New York, as in San Francisco and Los Angeles, investigatory agencies have accused employers of failure to keep accurate wage records, in effect, of cheating their workers.[8] In New York, the Department of Labor reported that Chinatown garment workers were one of the most exploited groups in the city. In San Francisco, the city's Human Rights Commission uncovered in one Chinatown factory twenty Chinese seamstresses who had worked as much as six months without being paid.[9] These women feared that they would be fired for daring to demand their wages. As one dissident resident stated,

---

[6] Nee, Victor and Brett De Bary Nee, *Longtime Californ'* (New York: Random House, 1972), p. 291.

[7] Ibid., p. 306.

[8] "U.S. jury awards $3310 to seamstress," *East/West*, July 28, 1971, p. 1; "Garment Industry Exposed," *Getting Together,* June 10, 1972, p. 1–2.

[9] "The Other Face of Chinatown," *San Francisco Examiner,* August 14, 1967. Reprinted by the International Ladies Garment Workers Union (ILGWU).

The ones who are lucky enough to own a sewing factory or something, just go on and make more and more money for themselves, and the Chinese workers can't do much. If they complain, well, the boss can always kick them out. They don't even have to do it directly, they can do it indirectly, like by making the worker do her sewing all over, and by complaining about every single stitch. My mom used to work at a sewing factory. Now her health is failing so she can't work at all.[10]

Some eventually quit, as Sharen Chew did after 15 years of substandard wages. One of her paystubs showed a gross income of $41.30 for sewing 118 blouses, at $4.20 per dozen, and $14.00 for 28 ladies dresses at $6.00 per dozen. Mrs. Chew, a mother of five, said it took her 100 hours to do the work for which her wages averaged 55¢ an hour.[11]

Advocates of the price rate system, chiefly the owners, insist that it has definite redeeming values; the clothing may be taken home to be sewn; there are no strict hours to inhibit the worker's duties as a housewife and mother. A worker may bring her children to the shop and take care of them herself; and the shop provides a socializing setting for the immigrant women who could not otherwise have such an opportunity in their daily lives, and a fast worker can make over $100 a week easily. The fact remains, however, that the owner benefits greatly from this wage arrangement. The "slower"

workers must take home their pre-cut patterns to do in the evenings, not because they want to, but because they have to. Because work can be done at home on the family sewing machine, the shop-owner can secure greater numbers of immigrant workers without having to provide the capital investment needed for the larger work site and machines. In short, piece rate is more economical for the boss than hourly wages.

The employers who own and operate sweatshops do not have ultimate control over wages. In fact, they often are crouched over a sewing machine themselves. In the garment-industry production system, the subcontractor is a middleman; he is over the workers in authority, but under the clothing producers who subcontract with him and in turn market the finished clothing. Big orders are subcontracted by clothing producers to big factories located elsewhere, leaving the less desirable small orders and "excess work" to the Chinatown shopowners who profit less.

Manufacturers, such as Arnelle, Fritz of California, Grant Avenue Fashions, or Levi Strauss, deliver pre-cut patterns of dresses, blouses, and shifts in tied bundles to be sewed and later picked up. This system, which is over a century old in America, produces clothing without the clothing producers having to be responsible for the personnel and management of the garment shops. Hence they are able to avoid paying workers at union scale or taking responsibility for working conditions over which in the last analysis they have controlling influence. When claims are brought against Chinese shopowners, the manufacturers often

[10] Nee and Nee, op. cit., p. 311–312.
[11] International Ladies Garment Workers Union, op. cit., p. 5.

intervene to settle out of court and thereby ward off adverse publicity. The Chinese shopowner becomes the visible target in the daily struggle between workers and bosses. Clothing firms extract maximum profit by setting low prices for contracted work. Their power comes from exploiting intense competition among subcontractors to drive contract prices down further and from seeking even cheaper sources of labor in immigrant and poverty communities. The contract work system is utilized by the manufacturers, as the piece rate is used by the shopowners. This is the most profitable method of production for them.

As is seen in the broader context of the American garment industry, Chinatown seamstresses and shopowners are both exploited. They share a sense of solidarity as both see low wages and unsteady income as coming from the seasonal nature of the industry that directly results from the flow of contracts negotiated with the clothing production firms. The Chinatown shopowner cannot insist upon higher rates; the manufacturer would cut off contracts completely. As a result of shared experience, a paternalistic feeling develops between workers and shopowners.

Loyalty and obligations to relatives who own or work in sweatshops intensifies this paternalism. As one shopowner described:

Suppose there is a thirty-year-old woman, an immigrant who just came from Hong Kong. Her husband sent for her and she can't speak English. Now suppose her husband makes a little money, but not enough for the family, so she goes out and looks for a job. She finds it's no good, she can't get a job anywhere. She begins to feel very worried. Then her husband comes to me. O.K., now downtown they would put a woman like that through a test for one or two weeks before they hire her. If she doesn't suit the job, she's out of luck. But in Chinatown we don't operate like that. . . . If you ask me for something and I won't do a favor for you, I feel ashamed. Especially if this man is my relative. . . . He'll walk all over town and tell my other cousins, "Gee, Chuck didn't help me. What kind of cousin is he?"

Even after arrival in America, workers continue to respect obligations to their extended families in Hong Kong. They regularly send money to Hong Kong out of their meager earnings. Against all odds they nevertheless aspire to improve their lot. For most, escape from the Chinatown ghetto and subeconomy is only an illusion. One resident gave this matter-of-fact summary of immigrant entrapment:

They come over, they don't speak English. He gets a job in a restaurant and the woman in a garment factory down here. In a few years, they think they will learn English, save some money, and move out. Everyone talks about that. But you look at someone like my mother, or most of the women in Ping Yuen, they've lived in Chinatown ten or twenty years. They earn just enough to keep going, they're too tired to study at night. The job they got to tide them over ends up as a lifetime occupation. It's like a vicious cycle. If they didn't have the garment industry, or those restaurant jobs, a lot of people in Chinatown wouldn't make it. But (ironically) as long as they have those jobs, they'll never get out of here.[12]

[12] Nee and Nee, op. cit., p. 317.

Therefore immigration, although it is an immediate cause of crowding and attendant social ills, is only one of the factors that shape life in Chinatown. Discrimination and economic exploitation established the garment sweatshop as a key element in the social structure of Chinatown ghettos. This arrangement has been developing for over one hundred years.

CHINATOWN'S TOURIST INDUSTRY

Restaurants, tourist shops, grocery stores, and delicatessens line the main thoroughfares of American Chinatowns. Directly or indirectly, they all are economically dependent upon the restaurants, which attract tourists to the community. San Francisco's Chinatown has 80 restaurants in 17 core blocks.[13] The same situation also prevails in eastern and midwestern Chinatowns where working-class residents are also dependent upon the restaurant trade for a livelihood. New York City's Chinatown now has over 200 restaurants and the number is still increasing as newer immigrants open family-owned and operated restaurants.[14] Over half of all working men in New York Chinatown are directly employed in restaurant-related occupations, as cooks, dishwashers, but mostly as waiters.[15] The waiters are of two distinct

age groups. If the waiter is young, he is probably a recent immigrant from Hong Kong and living alone or with relatives. If he is old, he has probably worked at the restaurant for twenty years or more and supports a family of two to five children. They both labor up to ten hours a day, six days a week, for wages as low as $350 a month. Intense competition in the restaurant business is directly felt by employer and employee alike. As worker's comments reveal, they have few alternatives:

There's too many restaurants, too much competition here. The Chinese have nothing (else) to do. What can you do? You run a restaurant here (in Chinatown), or you work long hours and get low pay. But if you go outside, you won't find anything.[16]

Using the appeal of novelty and low cost, Chinatown merchants have made a success of selling Chinatown tourism. Because tourism is a highly competitive industry, Chinatown must be made economically attractive to the American public; no admission charges, penny arcades, free browsing through exotic merchandise in candy stores and grocery stores. For an evening out, Chinatown is quite reasonable. The balance of the cost, however, must come from somewhere: In order for Chinatown to compete with other attractions, its low prices are achieved largely at the expense of the immigrant's survival wages and long, odd working hours. Things oriental benefit from the advantage of inherent novelty to westerners. Chinatown's mass appeal rests upon a presumed authentic-

[13] Leary, Mary Ellen, "San Francisco's Chinatown," *Atlantic Monthly,* 225 (March 1970), p. 40.
[14] Chin, Rocky, "New York Chinatown Today: Community in Crisis," in Amy Tachiki, et al, eds., *Roots: An Asian American Reader* (Los Angeles: Asian American Studies Center, University of California, 1971), p. 287.
[15] Chinatown Study Group, op. cit., p. 40.

[16] Nee and Nee, op. cit., p. 282.

ity of its community as a natural slice of immigrant life.[17] Chinatown is not generally perceived as an artifically contrived attraction such as Disneyland. Where tourists normally come in contact with the community, this is not true. Tourists who dine on "Authentic Chinese Food" are usually unaware that their beef chow mein, chicken chop suey, and egg flower soup result from many years of careful adulteration of authentic Chinese food in a careful effort to make it palatable to western tastes. In fact, most of the delicacies of authentic Chinese dishes such as sea cucumbers, bird's nest soup, and Joong (a kind of Chinese tamale wrapped in corn leaves) are not on the English language menus at all. Similarly, tourists expect to participate in genuine folk culture in celebrations of Chinese holidays and festivals. What occurs instead is a transformation of community events into controlled and commercialized novelty directed primarily toward the tourists.

CHINATOWN'S TOURIST FACADE

Instead of destroying and laying to rest the misconceptions and myths about Chinatown and its people, Chinatown tourism requires their perpetuation. Myths such as the idea that the Chinese community does not have serious social problems and needs are propagated. For example, in 1969–1971 some $32 million was appropri-

ated for community projects for the elderly.[18] Of this amount, not one cent was given to Asian American communities for their needy aged persons. The reason, according to the U.S. government, was that Asian Americans do not have problems. And even if they did, a second myth holds that they can take care of them themselves. As a result of these misconceptions, Chinatown communities are the only pockets of poverty in the country that also manage to be major tourist attractions. Some studies have concluded that the elderly of immigrant background, in fact, are more severely impaired emotionally by old age than the American-born elderly.[19] For most Chinese immigrants, old age is the culmination of a lifetime of personal sacrifice in which their expectations were not met. It is indeed ironic that one of America's most wretched slums should have its deplorable social conditions masked and disguised by the image of a tourist haven.

Chinatown was created for the tourist's familiarity and enjoyment. In order to achieve this, Chinatown was

---

[17] For a tourist's perspective of Chinatown, see for example, McHugh, Vincent, "San Francisco: Little China," *Holiday* 29 (April 1961), p. 100 ff; Clifford, William, "Little Wonder Restaurants of New York's Chinatown," *Holiday* 45 (April), p. 72 ff.

[18] 1971 White House Conference on Aging, *The Asian American Elderly* (Washington: U.S. Government Printing Office), p. 6.

[19] Berk, Bernard, and Lucie C. Hirata, "Mental Illness Among the Chinese: Myth or Reality?" *Journal of Social Issues,* 29 (1973), pp. 149–166; Kalish, Richard A. and Sharon Moriwaki, "The World of the Elderly Asian American," *Journal of Social Issues,* 29 (1973), pp. 187–209; Kalish, Richard A. and Yuen S., "Americans of East Asian Ancestry: Aging and the Aged," *The Gerontologist,* 11 (Spring, 1971), pp. 36–47; and Sue, S. and Sue, D. W., "Chinese American Personality and Mental Health," *Amerasia Journal,* 1 (1971).

outwardly purged of its criminal elements and vice; then, landscaped and superficially reconstructed by the Chinese Chamber of Commerce. Symbolic of American Chinatown's manufactured image is the central archway that leads to Los Angeles' New Chinatown and was built in the early 1930's. It came straight from the movie set of *The Good Earth*. Chinatown businessmen have for decades worked to package Chinatown as a quaint, wholesome, and family-oriented community attraction.

Trade is primarily dependent upon non-Chinese patrons, therefore, businessmen are very sensitive to the public's changing attitudes and images of Chinatown. These same merchants, who own the major restaurants, apartments, and other businesses, control the Chinese Consolidated Benevolent Association, more commonly known as the Chinese Six Companies. This organization exists in every major Chinatown in America. Its president is popularly called the "mayor" of Chinatown. To make a successful case for Federal Aid, these established leaders would need to present a dramatic account of the deteriorating ghetto conditions and social problems of Chinatown. After all, only "ghettos" qualify for Federal poverty assistance. Unwilling to declare their communities social disaster areas, business leaders instead have taken stern measures to suppress the Chinese street gangs and keep the lid on community dissent.[20] They have ini-

tiated no problem-probing studies in Chinatown nor have they done anything to publicize its squalor. When confronted by questions about social problems in Chinatown, Six Companies' representatives have answered that they have no real problems.[21] In summary, the business leadership has acted to prevent the American public from learning about poverty, crime, health, and housing problems in Chinatown. What information has been made public is despite Six Companies' efforts to prevent such news leakage.[22]

As a result of this deliberate deception, Chinatowns in America have spectacularly failed to obtain Federal welfare funds. No Chinatown in the United States benefits from the Model Cities Program, even though 150 cities have developed such programs. The case of Los Angeles' Chinatown is typical. In Los Angeles, the Model Cit-

---

[20] "Militant Charge Cop Harassments," *East/West*, February 17, 1971, p. 1; Rose, Pat, "Chinatown Arrest Brutality Charged,"

San Francisco *Chronicle*, October 25, 1972, p. 5; Seidenbaum, Art, "Hong Kong People Pong," *Los Angeles Times*, August 23, 1972, p. II, 1; Yee, Min S., "Cracks in the Great Wall of Chinatown," *Ramparts* (October 1972), p. 34.

[21] Light, Ivan H., *Ethnic Enterprise in America* (Berkeley: University of California Press, 1972), p. 182; Chu, George, "Chinatown: stereotypes and myths have made this the only pocket of poverty in the United States to be a major tourist attraction," *San Francisco Magazine*, 13 (1969), p. 38.

[22] Smith, Dave, "Gang Terror: San Francisco's Chinese Afraid for Their Lives," *Los Angeles Times*, July 7, 1972, p. I, 24; Reston, Richard, "Drug Smuggling: It's the Chinese Connection Now," *Los Angeles Times*, July 15, 1972, p. I, 1; "Police Charge New York Chinese in Heroin Case," *Los Angeles Times*, August 24, 1972, p. I, 7.

ies redevelopment area ends abruptly at the boundary of Chinatown, along the Los Angeles river. Chinatown's geographical neighbors, Lincoln Heights and Boyle Heights, predominantly Mexican-American, are safely within the renewal zone. The Master Plan for Central City Los Angeles also excludes Chinatown redevelopment. What governmental aid does penetrate the Chinese community, despite the Six Companies, is unsystematic, insufficient, and subject to yearly renewal. Los Angeles' Chinatown's only federally-funded program, the Chinatown Teen Post, began operations in September, 1971. Disapproving Teen Post's services to the unemployed and pre-delinquent youth, the Chinatown establishment encouraged the Los Angeles police to keep the storefront under close surveillance.[23] Federal funding of Teen Post quickly terminated.

The Six Companies today are under considerable pressure from within the community to revise their conservative position. Native-born, educated Chinese complain that Chinatown communities are not receiving a just share of jobs, welfare, and housing that Blacks and other protesting minorities receive. Educated persons in the community see no reason why impoverished Chinese Americans should nobly deprive themselves of sorely needed funds and programs available to other ethnic minorities.

Chinese merchants, however, are confronted with a difficult-to-resolve economic dilemma. Dilapidated housing, garbage cans lining the narrow sidewalks, contagious disease, and street crime all contribute to development of a slum community. Unfortunately, squalid slum conditions do not attract tourists. Tourism in Chinatown was able to flourish only after its merchants got rid of the vice in Chinatown and could offer clean surroundings and personal safety to its patrons. In order to build a public case for public aid in the Chinatown ghetto, the Six Companies would find it necessary first to make a public spectacle of Chinatown's misery and deplorable ghetto conditions. This publicity would drastically undermine countless Chinatown businesses and livelihoods.

In safeguarding their tourists from street gangs, Six Companies' merchants have been particularly sensitive to the economic threat to tourism. Unemployed Hong Kong youths first began to congregate on streets in named gangs during the late sixties. The largest of these gangs is the loosely knit Wah Ching in San Francisco which claims about 400 members. The Wah Ching have Brother Wah Ching and Baby Wah Ching organizations in other major Chinatowns as do the Suey Sing and Yu Li, their chief rivals. Smaller San Francisco gangs are the Raiders, Brothers Ten, Country Club Boys, the Drifters Motorcycle Club, the White Eagles, and Le Ways.[24] The

[23] Haynes, Roy, "Police Harassment in Chinatown Gang Inquiry Charged," *Los Angeles Times,* August 17, 1972, p. II, 4. Teen Post is now funded by the county.

[24] State of California Department of Justice, Organized Crime and Criminal Intelligence Branch, "Annual Report to the California Legislature," 1972, p. 6; Lyman, Stanford, *The Asian in the West* (Reno and Las Vegas: Desert Research Institute, University of Nevada, 1970), p. 106.

recent increasingly criminal activities in gangs or individually unavoidably created a disastrous situation for the tourist business. For the most part, gangs only harass tourists, stopping short of robbery or mugging. Usually this harassment is limited to shouting derisive slogans such as "Off the honkies" or "Get out of the ghetto, baby." [25] Sometimes, however, roving youths have robbed and beaten white tourists.[26] They have also extorted money and free meals from Chinatown merchants. And finally, tourists have been horrified witnesses to clashes between rival gangs and to murders on Chinatown streets. In 1971, an 18-year-old male Hong Kong entertainer was shot to death by three Chinese assailants in front of 644 Jackson Street in the heart of San Francisco's Chinatown.[27] Two years later in New York's Chinatown similar violence erupted. This time two members of the Ghost Shadows Gang were shot by members of the rival Flying Dragons gang; both gangs are composed of immigrant youths.[28] Such violent incidents need not make front-page headlines in order to have a deleterious effect upon Chinatown tourism.

But when the sordid news does crop up in headlines, the impact upon

Chinatown business is swift and disastrous. So, for example, the *Los Angeles Times* reported the slaying of Tong Fung, a Hong Kong entertainer, in a Chinatown restaurant on July 18, 1972 after he had refused the extortion demands by members of the local Wah Ching. The restaurant's business fell off markedly for several days following the *Times* report. A newspaper article entitled, "Chinatown's new dragon; street gangs," similarly had a devastating effect upon the entire restaurant trade of Los Angeles' Chinatown. In addition to a prolonged slowdown in walk-in business, lucrative banquets and meetings were canceled for months in advance.

Now calling themselves "merchant associations," Chinatown's historic tongs have extensive investments in restaurants and tourist-oriented businesses. As voting members of the Chinese Six Companies in most Chinatowns, the tongs have played the most brutal role in dealing with the economic threat posed by the street gangs. By admitting some of the leading gang members into their ranks, Chinatown's tongs were able to defuse dissent and ignore the grievances of some Hong Kong youths. These youths in turn employed their "muscle" thereafter to safeguard the tourist trade and its public order. The tongs have also threatened to apply their greater strongarm resources against the gangs. In 1971, the Bing Kong Tong, the largest on the Pacific Coast, made clear the organization's position in a public edict which read:

Due to the current lawlessness in the Chinese community, we issue this bul-

[25] Yee, Min, "Chinatown in Crisis," *Newsweek,* February 23, 1970, p. 57.

[26] Davis, R. W. "Major Crimes Rate Up in Chinatown," *East/West,* March 1, 1972, p. 1.

[27] "Young Man Murdered on Sunny Afternoon," *East/West*, October 6, 1971, p. 1.

[28] Crane, Robert, et. al., "Chinatown Gang Members Shoot Five," *New York Daily News,* August 17, 1973, p. 3.

letin to all of our brothers and sisters to obey the law, to observe the customs, and to desist from all the unruly behavior harmful to the commercial and social life of our community. If you persist in this antisocial conduct, our Tong will never interfere in your behalf. If you dare to damage any of the business enterprises owned by a member of our Tong, we will go after you all the way.[29]

Chinatown Militancy

Angered by police repression and by the unwillingness of the Six Companies to pursue a more aggressive position on matters of social welfare, the more militant Chinatown youths turned to street demonstrations as a means of bringing attention to the community's ghetto conditions. The most militant of these have been I Wor Kuen in New York and the Red Guards in San Francisco, both Marxist-Maoist groups. In 1970, I Wor Kuen staged an anti-tourist demonstration in New York City's Chinatown.[30] In the course of this demonstration, members of the radical group snapped cameras, shouted Maoist slogans, and shook their fists in anger at bewildered tourists descending from a Gray Line bus. I Wor Kuen also distributed leaflets charging the Chinese Six Companies with imposing news blackouts on Chinatown vice and poverty in order to keep the lower east community attractive to tourists. Similarly in San Francisco, the Red Guards had hoped by staging speeches, meetings and demonstrations

to awaken interest in Chinatown's many problems. As with I Wor Kuen, the Red Guards published their own newspaper and carried out community programs like the free breakfast program patterned after the Black Panthers Party. Confrontation between the Six Companies and the Red Guards came to a head when on October 1, 1969, the anniversary of the People's Republic of China, the Red Guards tried to raise the Communist Chinese five star red and yellow flag in Chinatown's Portsmouth Square. The pro-China rally turned into a free-for-all fisticuff between participants and tong strongmen.[31]

Besides pressuring the Chinatown establishment, radical demonstrations also frighten the working-class population of Chinatown, who fear for their tourist-dependent livelihoods. The adverse reaction of Chinatown workers, not just businessmen, to demonstrations has forced radical groups in Chinatown to change their political strategies and tactics. Today, the Red Guards are no longer active and I Wor Kuen has closed down their brightly painted red and yellow storefront while reassessing future direction.

Chinatown in Transition

Following violent confrontations, there has now emerged in Chinatown a more profound understanding of the life chances and predicaments of Chinatown immigrant life. The rhetoric of

[29] De Vere, Edmund, "Tong War Looms as Hoods Invade Chinatown," Los Angeles *Citizen News,* September 9, 1971, p. 1.

[30] Chin, Rocky, op. cit., p. 287.

[31] Lai, H. M., "A Historical Survey of Organizations of the Left Among the Chinese in America," *Bulletin of Concerned Asian Scholars,* 4 (Fall 1972), p. 10–20.

the left has accommodated itself to the realistic conditions of ghetto existence.[32] Unlike the Black poor, the Chinese poverty-stricken immigrants are under the subjugation of both the white power structure and the Chinatown merchants.

The realization of this contradiction among the left in Chinatown has resulted in numerous "serve the people" programs ranging from legal to immigration aid to child care and health clinics to sewing and food co-operatives in all of our major Chinatowns. As never before, Chinatown life is undergoing a period of rapid and massive transition. The short-range struggles are over issues of survival and responses to ghetto existence. The long-range struggle is over the eventual political direction of American Chinatowns.

[32] Wong, Paul, "The Emergence of the Asian American Movement," *Bridge,* 2 (1972), p. 32–39.

The context of insurgence has historically been accompanied by the historic changes in the motherland, China, and the severity of exploitation and discrimination in America. So it has been that the left movement in Chinatowns has been strongest during the periods of China's founding of the Republic (1911), the split between Mao Tse-tung's Communists and Chiang Kai Shek's Kuomintang and the ensuing civil war (1927), and the hardships emanating from the depression (1930's). Conversely, insurgence was stifled most during the post-war years of Communist victory and McCarthyism.[33] The most important factor that will affect the strength of movement toward change in American Chinatown communities is future relations between the U.S. and the People's Republic of China. How this will turn out is anybody's guess.

[33] Lai, H. M., op. cit.

Jewell and Wong demonstrate how much is to be learned about many of the ethnic groups in the United States. All members of ethnic groups are not alike, and within all groups there are rich and poor, law abiders and criminals, those with a high degree of ethnic identity and those with no ethnic identity at all.

*Among the dangers of stereotyping is that characteristics attributed to the life style of one group may be characteristic of other groups as well. One group may be praised for its aggressive behavior in the world of work while another group may be condemned for this same behavior — "an ingroup virtue may also be an outgroup vice." ***

* Robert Merton, "The Self Fulfilling Prophecy" in Robert Merton, *Social Theory and Social Structure* (New York: Free Press, 1957), pp. 421–438.

The black experience in the United States has been characterized by a past history of legal restrictions, segregated housing and schooling, and an American tradition of white racism.* Because blacks are easily identifiable and because of our racist history, white Americans may be quicker to stereotype blacks than any other racial or ethnic group,† yet, just as there is no one middle-class life style or no one life style of unmarried people, there is no one black life style. In the following article, Charles Willie shows the importance of sociological variables other than race in determining the variety of black life styles.

* See especially Otto Kerner (chmn.), *Report of the National Advisory Commission on Civil Disorders* (New York: Bantam, 1968).

† There are more ethnophalisms (derogatory terms about racial or ethnic groups) in the American vocabulary about blacks than about any other racial or ethnic group. See Erdman B. Palmore, "Ethnophalisms and Ethnocentrism," *American Journal of Sociology* 67 (January 1962), pp. 442–445.

Life Styles of Black Families: Variations by Social Class

Charles V. Willie

It has been difficult to understand the black family in America because most writers fail to deal with it on its own terms. Usually the black family is compared to or contrasted with the white family.

Scholars who follow this approach do so, they say, because racism is a

From *The American Journal of Orthopsychiatry* (January 1974). Copyright © 1974, The American Orthopsychiatric Association, Inc. Reproduced by permission.

pervasive experience in the United States which none can escape. But the author's upbringing, in a black community in Dallas, Texas, taught him that all blacks did was not necessarily a reaction to the actions of whites.

Indeed, reference groups for many blacks consisted of other blacks — black family members, black neighbors, black friends, black church members, and black club members. Social sanctions, norms, and behavior standards were generated by these groups.

The Sunday School Superintendent of the church attended by the family of orientation of the author organized Christmas parties at the church for the children and Labor Day picnics in the country for the teenagers and young adults. He gave neckties to boys who graduated from high school and went on to college and saved cereal box tops for the young. He delivered chicken dinners, which were prepared by the women of the church, to the homes of neighbors. He was a janitor in a building where automobiles were sold and serviced. He was an ordained clergyman with limited training of less than a high school education. His limited education and unskilled occupation were probably a manifestation of racism. But in Oak Cliff, a black community in Dallas, he was never looked upon as a victim. To the children in the author's community he was the Reverend J. I. Farrar — a decent, kind, and courteous gentleman, a man interested in children, and a man to whom one could always turn for help. It was the Reverend Farrar's love for the church, community, and children that was partly responsible for teaching them how to love others, despite the presence of racism. The interaction between the Reverend Farrar and his community is a common story about local black leaders throughout this nation; it is not necessarily a reaction to whites.

My interest in understanding the way of life of blacks independent of any reference to the way of life of whites is due to a desire 1) to extricate the social and behavioral sciences from a white ethnocentric perspective, and 2) to increase their contribution to the understanding of social change. Innovations in life-styles, including family life-styles, often develop among minority populations in the society before they are adopted by the majority. Such innovations may not be recognized when the way of life of the majority is looked upon as the "ideal type" and the behavior of others is considered deviant.

METHOD

During the past few years we have compiled approximately 200 case studies of black families, many southern migrants or descendants of southern migrants who now live in the northeastern region of the United States. The case studies were obtained as an assignment for students enrolled in a course on "The Black Family." The responsibility for locating a black family was that of each student. Many students interviewed families in their home towns scattered throughout the region. They interviewed families who were friends, referred to them by friends, referred by an agency, or selected at random by knocking on the door of a stranger. Students were provided with an interview schedule that requested specific information about economic, social and demographic characteristics, family customs, aspirations of parents for children, and patterns of authority within the family. Interviewers were black and white undergraduate students.

Out of the 200 or more case studies, nine were selected for detailed analysis in this paper as a composite representation of three income groups. Household income was the primary basis for more or less arbitrarily selecting three families each for middle-income, marginal-income, and lower-income groups. Utilized in this study were the student reports that contained the most complete and detailed descriptions. We cannot claim to have randomly selected the families for analysis. But we can say that the bias of the investigator was not the basic factor that determined whether or not a family was included among the nine for intensive study. The income groups studied ranged from $3000 to $6000 (low-income), $6000 to $10,000 (marginal-income), and $10,000 to $20,000 (middle income). Essentially, this study is an example of inductive analysis. Two variables — race and economic status — were used. Since blacks often are referred to as if they were a homogeneous group, nine families of the same race but of different income groups were studied to determine if, in fact, their way of life, customs, and practices were similar. Probability sampling, of course, would be necessary if the goal had been to make generalizations about the frequency of certain behavior forms within the total black population. This was not our goal. Thus, less rigor in the process of selecting the families for intensive analysis was possible.

Social class refers to style of life as well as economic resources. No operational definition of social class was developed for this study. The middle-class, working-class, and lower-class categories referred to later in this paper were derived from the analysis. The composite picture for the three families in each of the income groups was different from the style of life of black families in other income groups. Only the composite picture of the style of life for a social class is given. Detailed information on each of the nine families is presented elsewhere in a book-length manuscript.[1] The three social classes included in this study represent about 75% of all blacks. Not

[1] C. Willie, *A New Look at Black Families* (In press).

included are the upper middle class and the upper class, probably few in number, and at the other end of the stratification hierarchy, the under class — 20% to 25% of all blacks.

FINDINGS

Middle Class: The Affluent Conformists

Middle-class status for most black families is a function of dual employment of husband and wife. Black men and women have relied heavily on the public sector for employment at livable wages.

The public school has been an employment haven for black working wives. It has provided steady and continuous work and often has been the one occupational role in the family which has enabled it to lay claim to a professional style of life. Because of educational requirements, black female teachers of middle-class families are likely to be more highly educated than their male spouses. The length of employment of professional working wives is likely to be as long as that of their husbands, with only brief interruptions for childbearing. The numbers of children in black middle-class families tend to be small, ranging from one to three, but more often two or less. Thus, the black woman, in a public sector job with prescribed yearly increments and retirement benefits and with only a few interruptions in her labor force status, tends to draw a decent income by the time she reaches middle age.

Continuity in employment also is a characteristic of black men in middle-class families. Public sector jobs, especially in the postal service, have been a source of support and security over the years. Some black men have, however, received financially rewarding professional positions in industry.

The economic foundation for middle-class black families is a product of the cooperation of the husband and wife. Their way of life is a genuine illustration of a team effort. Few, if any, family functions, including cooking, cleaning, and buying, are considered to be the exclusive prerogative of the husband or wife. Probably the best example of the liberated wife in American society is the wife in the black middle-class family. She and her husband have acted as partners out of necessity and thus have carved out an equalitarian pattern of interaction in which neither husband nor wife has ultimate authority. He or she alone could not achieve a comfortable style of life, because of racial discrimination and the resulting income limitations of the kinds of jobs available to most blacks. Together they are able to make it, and this they have done. In the 1970s middle-class black families earned $10,000 to $20,000 a year — the joint income of husband and wife.

Such income is lavishly spent on a home and on the education of children. Unless restricted by racial discrimination, middle-class black families tend to trade in older homes for new structures as their income and savings increase. Thus, families in the income range mentioned above are likely to be found in houses valued from $25,000 to $35,000. The real expense in housing, however, is in the up-to-date furnishings and modern appliances. For most middle-class black families, their home is their castle and it is outfitted as such.

Because work is so consuming for the husband and wife, little time is left for socializing. Most families have nearby relatives — usually the reason for migrating to a particular city. They visit relatives occasionally, may hold membership in a social organization, participate regularly in church activities, and spend the remainder of their free time in household upkeep and maintenance chores.

In most middle-class black families, one member almost always has attended college. Often both have attended college. The husband and wife struggled and made great sacrifices to complete their formal education. Not infrequently, college and graduate school are completed on a part-time basis after adulthood and while the husband or wife, who also may be a parent, is employed full-time. Parents who have experienced these struggles and hardships know that their middle-class status, which usually is not achieved until middle age, is directly correlated with their increased education. New jobs, especially public school teaching, and salary increments can be traced directly to the added schooling. Education has been a major contributor to upward mobility for blacks.

Because education and, consequently, economic affluence are so closely tied together for middle-class black households, parents tend to go all out for their offspring. Particularly do they wish their children to go to college immediately after graduating from high school so that they will not have to struggle as long as did their parents whom middle-class status eluded during young-adult years. An ambition of most parents is to give to their children opportunities they did not have.

As a starter, almost all children in middle-class households are given music lessons. Daughters, in particular, are expected to learn to play a musical instrument, usually the piano. Recreational skills are developed, too. Most children in middle-class black families are expected to work around the house for an allowance. Families try to inculcate in their children positive attitudes toward work and thrift.

Active involvement in community affairs that take on the characteristics of a movement is not the cup of tea for most black middle-class, middle-aged adults. Their adolescent children may be deeply involved in various liberation movements but seldom are the parents.

Middle-class black families in America, probably more so than any other population group in this society, manifest the Puritan orientation toward work and success that is characteristic of our basic values. For them, work is a consuming experience. Little time is left for recreation and other kinds of community participation, except regular involvement in church affairs. The way of life of black middle-class Americans is a scenario patterned after Weber,[2] except that most blacks have little capital other than the house they own, which, of course, is their primary symbol of success.

[2] M. Weber, *The Protestant Ethic and the Spirit of Capitalism* (London: George Allen and Unwin, 1948).

Working Class: The Innovative Marginals

Family life in the black working class is a struggle for survival that requires the cooperative efforts of all — husband, wife, and children. Income for black working-class families ranged from $6000 to $10,000 during the 1970s. This is hardly enough for luxury living when the family size is considered. Black working-class families tend to be larger families, consisting of five or more children.

There is some indication that the size of the family is a source of pride for the parents, especially the father and maybe the mother too. The bearing and rearing of children are considered to be an important responsibility, so much so that black working-class parents make great personal sacrifices for their families. They tend to look upon children as their unique contribution to society, a contribution they are unable to make through their work roles, which at best are semi-skilled. The family size of the black working-class also may be a function of age at marriage, usually before twenty-one for the wife and mother and often during the late teens. Husbands tend to assume parenthood responsibilities early too; often they are only one or two years older than their spouses.

The cohesion of the black working-class family results not so much from understanding and tenderness shown by one for the other as from the joint and heroic effort to stave off adversity. Without the income of either parent or the contributions of children from part-time employment, the family would topple back into poverty.

The parents in black working-class families are literate but of limited education. Most have completed elementary school but may be high school drop-outs. Seldom do any have more than a high school education. This is the educational level they wish their children to achieve, although some families hope that one or two of the smarter children in their brood will go on to college. The jobs they wish for their children also are those that require only a high school or junior college education, like work as a secretary, nurse, mechanic, or bank messenger.

Racial discrimination, on the one hand, and insufficient education, on the other, have teamed up to delimit the employment opportunities for black working-class families. Their mobility from rural to urban areas and from the South to the North usually has been in search for a better life. Families tend to be attracted to a particular community because of the presence of other relatives who sometimes provided temporary housing.

In general, the moves have opened up new opportunities and modest advancement such as from gas station attendant to truck driver, or from farm laborer to dairy tanker. The northern migration has resulted in some disappointments, too. On balance, new employment opportunities have resulted from the move from South to North, particularly for wives who have found work in institutional settings, such as hospitals, more profitable than private household work. Nursing aide and cooking jobs have been outlets for women and have enabled them to supplement the family income.

One sacrifice that the members of black working-class families have made so as to pull out of and stay beyond the clutches of poverty is to give up on doing things together as a family. Long working hours and sometimes two jobs leave little time for the father to interact with family members. In some households, the husband works during the daytime and the wife works during the evening hours. In other families, children work up to twenty hours a week after school and on weekends. These kinds of work schedules mean that the family as a unit is not able to share any meals together, except possibly on Sunday.

Despite the hardships, there is a constancy among the members of black working-class families that tends to pull them through. Some husbands and wives have been married more than two decades; they tend to have been residents of their neighborhoods for ten or more years and to have worked for the same employer over a long period of time. Though their earnings are modest, this continuity in area of residence and in other experiences has stabilized these families and enabled their members to accumulate the makings of a tolerable existence without the losses that come from frequent stops and starts.

Another stabilizing experience is the home that some black working-class families own. Rather than renting, many are paying mortgages. Their homes may range in value from $10,000 to $15,000, may be located in isolated rural or unsightly urban areas, and may be in a poor state of exterior repair but neat and clean on the inside. Home ownership for black working-class families is not so much a symbol of success as an indicator of respectability.

Black working-class parents boast of the fact that their children are good and have not been in trouble with the police. They also have a strong sense of morality, which emphasizes "clean living." The home they own is part of their claim to respectability. The owned home is one blessing that can be counted. It is a haven from the harsh and sometimes unfriendly world.

There is little time for community activities for black working-class families. Most spare time is devoted to associating with household members, or with nearby relatives. Religion is important; but participation in church activities is limited to regular or occasional attendance at Sunday worship services. The mother in such families tries to maintain tenuous contacts with at least one community institution, such as the school. She even may be a member of the Parents-Teachers Association but is not deeply involved in organizational maintenance work as a volunteer.

Black working-class parents do well by their children if no special problems are presented. Their comprehension of psychological maladaption, however, is limited. These problems are dealt with by a series of intended remedial actions that seem to be of little assistance in solving the child's real problem and usually result in frustration both for the parent and for the offspring. Black working-class families have learned to endure; and so they bear with the afflictions of their members — those they do not understand as well as those with obvious sources of causation.

Cooperation for survival is so basic in black working-class families that relationships between the husband and wife take on an equalitarian character. Each knows that his or her destiny is dependent upon the actions of the other. Within the family, however, husbands and wives tend to have assigned roles, although in time of crisis, these roles can change. The husband tends to make decisions about financial expenditures, including the spending of money for furniture. He also has basic responsibility for household upkeep. The father is the chief advisor for the boys. The mother tends to be responsible for the cooking and cleaning, although she may delegate these chores to the children. She is the chief advisor for the girls. She also maintains a liaison relationship with the school and may be the adult link between the family and the church if the father is not inclined to participate.

We tend to think in terms of upward mobility in American society. Indeed, this is what many working-class families are — households moving out of poverty into respectability; households that emphasize mobility, goal, and purpose; households committed to making a contribution to society by raising and maintaining a family of good citizens. This, of course, involves a struggle. But the struggle may be a function of the ending of good times rather than the overcoming of adversity. A black working-class family may be of a lower-income household on its way up or a middle-income household on its way down. A middle-income family beset with illness, for example, could slip into the working-class status due to reduction in income and the requirement for change in style of living. How often this occurs, we do not know. It does occur often enough to keep the working class from becoming a homogeneous lot. For this and other reasons, one should not expect to find a common philosophical orientation within the working-class.

Lower Class: The Struggling Poor

The most important fact about black lower-class families is their low-income status; it forces them to make a number of clever, ingenious, and sometimes foolish arrangements to exist. These range from extended households consisting of several generations under one roof to taking in boarders or foster children for pay. Boyfriend-girlfriend relationships between adults often assume some parental functions when children are involved, while the participants maintain their autonomy unfettered by marital bonds. Because every penny counts, poor households often do whatever they must do to bring money in. Conventional practices of morality may be set aside for expedient arrangements that offer the hope of a livable existence. The struggle among poor families is a struggle for existence. All else is secondary. Family income tends to vary from $3000 to $6000, and more often than not the household does not receive public welfare.

The struggle is severe and there is little margin for error. Black low-income families learn to live with contingency. They hope for little and expect less. Parents love their children but seldom understand them. Men and women become sexually involved but are afraid to entrust their futures

to each other. There is much disappointment. The parents in broken families often have broken spirits — too broken to risk a new disappointment. For this reason, black lower-class parents often appear to be uncommitted to anyone or to anything when in actuality they are afraid to trust.

Movement is constant, as if one were afraid to stay put and settle down. Jobs, houses, and cities are changed; so are spouses and boyfriends and girlfriends. Unemployment is a constant specter. The womenfolk in the household usually find employment as maids or private household workers. The males are unskilled factory workers or maintenance men between periods of no work at all.

Marriage may occur at an early age, as early as sixteen years for some girls. The first child is sometimes born before the first marriage. Others tend to come in rapid succession. Some families have as many as eight or more children, while others are smaller. When the burdens of child care, illness, and unemployment strike at the same time, they often are overwhelming. Drinking, gambling, and other escape behavior may increase. A fragile love and capacity for endurance are shattered, and the man in the house moves out, no longer able to take it. One more failure is experienced.

The parents in black lower-class families are grade school or high school dropouts. Neither spouse has more education than the other. Thus, parents in lower-class families sometimes hold themselves up to their children as failures, as negative images of what not to do. There is only limited ability to give guidance concerning what ought to be done. Thus, children are advised not to marry early, not to drop out of school, and not to do this and not to do that. There is admonition but little concrete effort at prevention.

Scapegoating is a common way of explaining deviant behavior in children. Juvenile delinquency may be attributed to the disreputable parent. The mother on location seldom knows what to do. Although little love may exist between parents, there is fierce loyalty between mothers and offspring, and between grandmothers and children. The children come first. Mothers will extend every effort to take care of their sons and daughters, even into adulthood. Grandparents are excellent babysitters. They are expected to teach their grandchildren good manners and other fundamentals.

A strong custom of brothers and sisters helping each other exists in the lower class. The problem is that siblings are struggling too. About the most one can do for the other is share already overcrowded living quarters when a new member comes to town or when a two-parent family breaks down. The move from one city to another often is for the purpose of being near kinsmen. There is strong loyalty between siblings and a standing obligation to help.

Little participation in any community association is seen. Religion is important for some black lower-class families. But for others, it is no more than a delusion. Those who attend church regularly tend to engulf their lives with religion and especially with affirmations about its saving grace and reward system after death. Some shy away from the church as one more disappointing promise that has copped out on the poor without really helping. Black lower-class people are seldom lukewarm about religion. They are either all for it or all against it, although the latter are reluctant to deny their children religious experience, just in case there is more to it than was realized.

It is hard for a poor black family to overcome poverty; so much is lined up against it. If illness or unemployment do not drain away resources, there is a high probability that old age will.

Conclusion

We turn now to a theoretical discussion of the differences that have been observed. In his classical article, "Social Structure and Anomie," Robert Merton[3] identified five kinds of adaptations by individuals to social organizations: conformity, innovation, ritualism, retreatism, and rebellion. We shall discuss three of the adaptations to explain the way of life of the three different social classes. The conformist acknowledges the legitimacy of societal values and goals and also accepts the means that are sanctioned and prescribed for achieving them. The innovationist believes in the socially sanctioned goals but must improvise new and different means. The retreatist gives up on the socially sanctioned values and goals as well as the means and, therefore, is declared to be in a state of anomie or normlessness. This the-

---

[3] R. Merton, *Social Structure and Social Theory* (New York: Free Press, 1949), p. 133.

oretical formulation provides a helpful way for conceptually approaching an understanding of the differences between middle-class, working-class, and lower-class black families.

Middle-class black families subscribe to the basic values and goals in American society and utilize appropriately prescribed means for their achievement. Its members are success-oriented, upwardly mobile, materialistic, and equalitarian. They consume themselves in work and leave little time for leisure. Education, hard work, and thrift are accepted as the means for the achievement of success. Property, especially residential property, is a major symbol of success. This is the American way and the prevailing way of life to which the middle-class black family in America conforms. Thus, its members may be called conformists.

Black working-class families also have internalized the basic values and goals of this nation. They too are success-oriented and upwardly mobile. However, their symbol of success differs from that of the black middle class. The welfare of the total family is the principal measure of effective functioning. A black working-class family is successful if it is respectable. A family is respectable when its members are well-fed, well-clothed, and well-housed, and do not get into trouble with the police.

The location and value of a house is not so important. Home ownership is important but home value is something else. In the latter respect, the black working class differs from the black middle class, in which an expensive home is the symbol of success.

Almost everything that the black working-class parents do to achieve success and respectability is extraordinary, compared with the black middle class. Their education is limited; their occupations are unskilled; their income is modest; and their families are relatively larger. Yet they dream the impossible dreams about doing for their children what they could not do for themselves. By hook or crook, they — the parents — manage to do it when others said it couldn't be done. The members of the working class are the creative innovationists of our times. They strive to achieve the societal values and goals, are deficient in the possession of socially sanctioned means, but somehow overcome.

The black lower class is fatalistic. No note of hope does it sing. Failure and disappointment recur repeatedly, as if they were a refrain. Unable to deal with the difficulties presented, black lower-class families withdraw. The parents appear to be uninvolved with anyone or anything. They have retreated from social organizations but not necessarily from all social relations for we know of their loyalty to their children.

The retreatist behavior of black lower-class families is sometimes described as being in opposition to the basic values and goals of social organization — a rejection of that which is socially sanctioned. This may not be the case, however, but only the way it appears. Presumably, lower-class households, like the working class, wish for family cohesion. The tie between mother and offspring is a residual family relationship indicative of this desire. Presumably, also, lower-class families, like the middle class, wish for material comforts and new experiences. Spending sprees and impulse traveling are indicative of these desires.

Because of inadequate resources, lower-class families dare not hope for the fulfillment of their wishes in a systematic and regularized way. To protect themselves from more disappointment, denial of the wish for improvement is one approach and poking fun at the struggle for social mobility is another.

A fuller explanation of the retreatist behavior of the lower class requires examination of the interaction between objective and subjective dimensions of social structure. Despite the rhetoric about self-reliance and self-sufficiency, the family members of the working class and the middle class did not make it on their own unassisted by the social system. They acknowledged their interdependence, and asked for and received help when they needed it. Upward social mobility involves giving and receiving from others. The poor are given precious little in our society and so their capacity to receive is underdeveloped. In the giving of help, we learn to love. In the receiving of assistance, we learn to trust. Because the poor have been given so little in society, the poor have not learned how to receive — which is to say, the poor have not learned how to trust.

We learn to trust before we learn to love. Love involves commitment to persons, social groups, and social organizations. The members of lower-class families can commit themselves to persons, especially the mothers to their offspring and the siblings to each other; but they cannot commit them-

selves to a society they have never learned to trust. Thus, the retreatist behavior of the lower-class may be a manifestation of the absence of trust rather than a rejection of social organization in favor or social disorganization.

This paper clearly demonstrates that it is inappropriate to say, "a black family is a black family is a black family." Styles of life do vary among blacks by social class. Recognition of this should serve as a corrective against stereotyping black ways of life.

The neat way in which the different black family life-styles by social class fit into the theoretical model developed by Robert Merton for explaining variation in adaptations to the social organization also suggests that all black families, including the middle-class, the working-class, and the lower-class, participate in a common system of values shared by all families, including blacks and whites in the United States.

Finally, there was evidence of limited opportunities available to blacks due largely to racial discrimination. This was a common experience of most black families of all social classes. A frequent manifestation of racial discrimination was the delimitation of economic opportunity. Inadequate financial resources frequently resulted in the joint participation of husband and wife in the labor force — a circumstance more or less pervasive among black families, especially those who were upwardly mobile.

On the basis of this analysis, one may conclude 1) that black and white families in America share a common value system, 2) that they adapt to the society and its values in different ways, largely because of racial discrimination, and 3) that the unique adaptation by blacks is further differentiated by variations in style of life by social class.

Our initial assumption that the way of life of blacks in America can be understood independent of their involvement with whites appears to be unwarranted. Moreover, the life-styles of different social classes cannot be understood apart from the rest of society.

Referring to the interdependence of blacks and whites in America, this paper ends with the statement of a modified version of the wisdom of Eliza Doolittle, created by George Bernard Shaw. She said that she discovered the difference between a flower girl and a lady is not so much how she acts but how she is treated. Our revised version emphasizes *both* personal action *and* social reaction. We assert that the difference between the families of racial groups in the United States, and the difference between the families of various social classes within the racial groups are a result of how each family acts *as well as* how each family is treated.

Just as long as ethnic groups remain visible minorities, ethnic life styles persist. Nevertheless, there seems to be a fusion of some previously distinct ethnic minorities now recognized by the general designation "ethnic." This term refers especially to the southern and east European immigrants who were among the last Europeans to enter this country in large numbers at the end of the nineteenth and the beginning of the twentieth century. Included in this group are Poles, Italians, Greeks, Slavs, Armenians, Serbs, Czechs, Slovaks, Lithuanians, and Portuguese. Some might also include Germans and Irish in this group but these groups were already gaining a foothold in mainstream America at the time of the arrival of these other ethnic groups.* These groups have common characteristics — they tend to be blue-collar Catholics living together in their own identifiable neighborhoods in large cities. They have comparatively low rates of social mobility and were the people who felt most threatened by what they perceived to be a "black invasion." These people have been called by Michael Novak, the "unmeltable ethnics" and by Peter Binzen as the "Whitetowners." Binzen's description of Philadelphia's Whitetowner's applies as well to similar groups in other cities. Whitetowners tend to marry among themselves (although

* Michael Novak, *The Rise of the Unmeltable Ethnics* (New York: Macmillan, 1972), pp. 46–48.

perhaps out of their own original nationality group) and are starting to become an important force in American politics. We see the creation of a new potent ethnic group in our society, which has its own unique life style.

The Whitetowners

Peter Binzen

The Whitetowner's row house is fourteen feet wide.

Five rooms on two floors with a postage-stamp yard out back. One of hundreds of small properties in a vast, dreary industrial landscape — clogged streets, drafty factories, fouled air, a noisy elevated line. Hardly a tree. And the few tiny parks are littered with broken bottles.

The Whitetowner was born and raised in this section and his parents still live near by. They don't think of moving out. Neither does he.

The Whitetowner is a steady worker and a family man. He quit school in tenth grade to get a job. His wife, also a native of the area, dropped out to marry him two months before her graduation. She was a better student than he was. She manages the family finances. Their house and car are paid for.

It is evening. The Whitetowner's wife is in the front room with their three children watching a bang-bang TV show. Her hair is in pink plastic curlers. The television set is a big new color model. The house is neat and better furnished than its plain gray exterior would lead one to expect. On the wall behind the TV is a proud affirmation in needle point: A MAN'S HOME IS HIS CASTLE. On the kitchen wall is the prayerful GOD BLESS OUR HOME. In both rooms are religious ornaments and bouquets of plastic flowers.

The Whitetowner sits in the kitchen answering the questions of an outsider who is trying to find out what makes Whitetown tick. The questions bear on things that concern the Whitetowner deeply. Despite his lack of formal education, he expresses himself forcefully. Asked if he favors Bible reading in public schools, he says Yes and adds, "The Bible is the beginning of knowledge. A *must* for all!" He supports physical punishment of pupils but explains, "I also believe fairness should be shown and two sides of a story told."

He doubts that his children will go to college. He doesn't really want them to. "It would be a waste of money," he says, "with all this riot nonsense." He thinks the United States would be improved "if people with *guts* were in high places." He complains that his city's schools are too lax on discipline, too political, and too lenient toward student demonstrations.

Proudly, he describes his community:

Whitetown people are, and have been as long as I can remember, people who like to pay their own way. To be sure, there are a lot of "renters" moving in, but they aren't the result of Whitetown. They come from God only knows where. Whitetown may look run-down to an outsider, but the politicians are to blame for its condition. Compared to other sections, it is a decent place to raise children and to live. If outsiders would stop condemning Whitetown and her people, her future would become brighter. We have a minority that drink too much, but ninety per cent are social drinkers.

Asked to comment on Whitetown's reputation as a "provincial, backward section with strong prejudices," the Whitetowner swings both fists:

Who gave it the reputation you stated? And, anyway, just what is wrong with being provincial, backward (if that means opposing someone else's ideas), and having strong prejudices? Rich people have children that commit suicide, drive like maniacs, and are unruly. Rich people live on high parties and are social climbers, the mental hospitals are full of them. Why aren't the Negroes living in the suburbs? The suburbs are full of Whitetown people that are loaded down with high mortgages.

We are honest hard-working people with children we love dearly. If the Negro moves into Whitetown it will only be to push this issue of integration — and the people here are sick of

having it shoved down our throats. We are sick of reading in the paper where looters, arsonists, and murderers are allowed to do whatever they damn well please. We don't want them, they would ruin our community and our community and our property values would drop.

And, then, in a parting shot, the Whitetowner asks:

Why the sudden interest in our community? Could it be to help these poor lazy slobs get rent-free houses? Whitetown does have a future. When you eggheads run out of surveys to take and the dust begins to settle, we will be able to enjoy the life we have always known and feel contented with.

I don't know this Whitetowner's age or even his occupation. He might be a truck driver or a policeman, a turret-lathe operator or a white-collar office worker. All I know for sure is that he is white, he makes between five and ten thousand dollars a year, he owns his house, and he speaks his mind. (The comments are his; I've changed the name of his community.) I'm also certain that he speaks for a vast army of white American workingmen in Boston's Charlestown, New York's Belmont, and Philadelphia's Kensington; in Chicago's Southwest Side, Cleveland's West Side, and San Francisco's Eureka Valley. Law and order is their watchword and, for many, George Wallace was their candidate for President in 1968.

Not long ago this white workingman was almost a folk hero in our national life. He was the honest, respectable, law-abiding citizen, the backbone of the community. More than likely, he was the son or grandson of immigrants, and the melting pot was his kettle. Whether of Irish, Italian, German, Polish, Russian, or Ukrainian extraction, he was a hundred per cent American and proud of it. From Belleau Wood to Anzio and the Choisin Reservoir he fought for his country. He supported his church (usually Roman Catholic), backed his local political leaders (usually Democrats), and provided the votes for most of the progressive domestic and internationalist legislation enacted in Congress.

All this has now changed. Today the white workingman always seems to be *against* things. He's *against* open housing, *against* school bussing, *against* hippies, Yippies, and draft dodgers. He's *against* letting Negroes into unions, and China into the United Nations. He's even *against* his own church when it gets embroiled in civil-rights causes.

In the drama of a nation striving for interracial justice, for true equality in education, housing, and employment, Whitetowners often emerge as deep-dyed racists. While some are silent protesters, others have made spectacles of themselves. In recent years Whitetowners have rioted half a dozen times. Their strong feelings are potentially as explosive as the force that detonated Watts, Hough, Detroit, and Newark.

Who are these people? What are their origins? What makes them act as they do? Robert C. Wood, former Undersecretary of the United States Department of Housing and Urban Development, describes[1] the White-

[1] In a speech at Lincoln, Mass., on. Dec. 8, 1967.

towner as the "working American — the average white ethnic male ... the ordinary employee in factory and office, blue collar and white," who lives in the "gray area" fringe of central cities and constitutes the majority of the nation's work force.

The New York Times labels him the $8,000-a-year shoe clerk." During the 1968 Presidential election campaign, Richard M. Nixon called him "the forgotten American" and George C. Wallace identified him as "the little man." The American Jewish Committee speaks of him as "the reacting American," writer Elizabeth Hardwick considers him "the cheerless American," *Newsweek* magazine describes him as "the troubled American," and social scientist David Riesman rates him "the man in the middle." More recently he's been identified as part of that amorphous mass known as the "silent majority."

By whatever name, the people we are talking about are drawn mainly from the ethnic groups that differ from the basic white Protestant Anglo-Saxon settlers in religion, language, and culture. Many of these "ethnics" are among the thirty-four million foreign-stock Americans — that is, immigrants themselves or having at least one immigrant parent. Most are descendants of Eastern and Southern European peasants. Many others are Irish. Of course, not all white Anglo-Saxon Protestants have made their fortunes and moved to the suburbs. Especially in the South but also in Northern cities sizable numbers of Protestants, often fundamentalist or evangelical, are struggling to keep their heads above water. Conversely, a great many immigrants and immigrants' children have enjoyed success beyond their dreams and wouldn't deign to set foot in Whitetown. More often than not, however, the Whitetowns of America are populated by the ethnics and by first- and second-generation (and often third-generation) immigrants.

Whitetowns come in all ages, shapes, and sizes. Chicago's Scottsdale is new. It sprang up after World War II on former prairie in Chicago's extreme southwest corner, ten miles from the Loop. In neat single houses with pink flamingos on front lawns and two cars in many garages live fourteen thousand militant Caucasians, who are, says Scottsdale's school principal, "united in their determination to keep their community segregated." Many Scottsdalers are municipal employees required by ordinance to live within the city limits. For them Scottsdale, which extends to the city boundary, is the end of the line. They've run as far as they can. There appears to be no real poverty in Scottsdale, but many men hold two jobs to make ends meet, and average income there was last estimated at just over eight thousand dollars.

Boston's Charlestown is old. Its working-class whites cluster in drab surroundings at the foot of Bunker Hill, which dominates the area. The Boston Navy Yard is near by and many Charlestonians work there. It was in grimy, faded Charlestown that John F. Kennedy began his political career in 1948, and it was to Charlestown that he returned to start every subsequent campaign. Charlestown has poverty and it has Negroes — a

few living in public housing. Now it is engaged in a mighty renewal effort, with help from Washington and with the knowledge that along with new schools, new housing, a beautiful community college, will come meaningful racial integration.

New York's Belmont, in the Fordham section of the Bronx, is a small city of twenty-five thousand people, ninety-five per cent of them first- and second-generation Italians. Theirs is a classic ethnic enclave holding out against pressure from Negroes moving north from Manhattan. Curiously, some of the proudest and bitterest Belmonters are those who have moved to suburban Whitetowns but return regularly to Belmont's markets and its church and desperately want always to be able to do so. Every year brings another three hundred families to Belmont from Italy. Belmont's Our Lady of Mount Carmel Roman Catholic Church is an Italian national parish with six million dollars invested in the neighborhood. As Father Mario Zicarelli says with a smile, "While I take care of all Italians, whatever their color, maybe I have to be interested in my community."

In Cleveland's Near West Side, in Chicago's Uptown, and in sections of Detroit are examples of festering Anglo-Saxon poverty. Here live Appalachian white migrants from the hills of Tennessee, Kentucky, and West Virginia. These are truly forgotten people, just as miscast for city life as the most backward plantation Negroes. And often more miserable because they cannot blame their pigmentation for holding them back. Tough, mean sections of burned-out

pride, homesickness, and contention
as bitter as that in the hillbilly ballad:

> *Fight like dogs,*
> *If you ain't no kin,*
> *If you kill one another,*
> *It ain't no sin.*

Philadelphia's Kensington is a nine-
teenth-century mill area, a Dickensian
factory town. Here you find working-
class whites in their fourteen-foot-wide
row houses. Here you also find middle-
class workers with boats and summer
places at the Jersey shore, still living in
Kensington because it is home and
they are proud of it. There are many
pensioners just scraping by. And elderly widows. And, increasingly, poor
white families moving in from mixed
sections downtown. To the established
homeowners of Kensington these new-
coming renters are white trash. The
clash between these two groups is almost as bitter and traumatic as the
racial collision.

Poverty, we should note, doesn't
draw the color line in America's big
cities. The 1960 United States census
counted almost twice as many poor
white families in metropolitan areas as
poor nonwhite families. Poverty was
then considered to be three thousand
dollars a year for a family of four. By
this definition, there were 10.7 million
impoverished white families in urban
America and 5.6 million impoverished
nonwhite families. The 1960 census
did not reach all the nonwhites, its
figures were not very reliable and they
are now out of date. Furthermore,
since whites in the general population
outnumber nonwhites by about ten to
one while white poor outnumber nonwhite poor by less than two to one, the

poverty problem is obviously greater
among nonwhites. But the message of
the 1960 census still holds: In American urban areas, life is desperately
difficult for great numbers of whites
and blacks alike.[2]

What Whitetowners of different
classes, sections, backgrounds, occupations, religions, national origins, and
even political parties — for they cut
across party lines — share is their
alienation from the American "mainstream." This alienation is reflected in
distrust of most politicians, in contempt for white rich and black poor,
in a bristling defensiveness and a
yearning for the recent past when life
was simpler and loyalties less complex, when children were reared by the
Bible and the beltstrap, when the
schools stuck to the three R's, and
when patriotism meant "My country
right or wrong." . . .

I'm heading now for Wanda's house.
Wanda — I've made up the name but
not the person — is a short sharp-
featured, gray-haired Fishtowner, one

[2] The very existence of poor whites sometimes seems to be intentionally obscured. A
case in point is the March 1968 Report of
the National Advisory Commission on Civil
Disorders, the Kerner Report. It used 1960
census data to show that in the Milwaukee
Standard Metropolitan Statistical Area the
proportion of poor nonwhites was three
times that of poor whites. That is, 26.1 per
cent of the nonwhite families had incomes
under three thousand dollars a year compared with only 8.8 per cent of the white
families. A valid point. The report failed to
note, however, that in actual numbers the
poverty problem in Milwaukee was largely
a poor-white problem: 30,026 poor whites to
4,191 poor non-whites.

of its many Polish immigrants. I've been renting a room in her house in order to learn more about this distinctive community. The house is typical of many in Fishtown: a front room and kitchen, where Wanda eats, on the first floor, two bedrooms and a bathroom on the second. Wanda is sixty-two, lives alone, and keeps the house spotless. There are no books or magazines in the living room, but a big color-TV set stands in one corner, as well as bouquets of plastic flowers, religious figurines, and embroidered exhortations to God to bless this house.

In some ways I have found Wanda to be a typical Whitetowner and in other ways not so typical, but in all ways she is a gritty human being. She's at work when I open her front door with my key, and I have time to reflect on some of the things she has told me about herself.

She was the second oldest of twelve children of poor Polish peasants. Neither of her parents had had any formal schooling in Poland and her mother never did learn to read or write. When Wanda was young — and before most of the other children were born — the family emigrated from eastern Poland to Pennsylvania's hard-coal country around Scranton. Her father took a job in the mines. He labored as a miner for a number of years — Wanda wasn't sure how many — until a "big explosion" in No. 11 mine caused injuries from which he never fully recovered. After the family moved to Philadelphia, Wanda's father died of the dreaded "black lung" disease that continues to strike miners even today.

As the oldest girl in the family, Wanda had to stay home whenever anybody got sick. Still, she managed to get through four years of school before her mother forced her to find a job. She was twelve years old. ("Among the Polish people, you know," she had told me, "they don't think you need school.") She took work in the mills of Kensington, and for the next fifty years, with time out for bearing three children of her own, she toiled as a millhand. When I met her she was still working five days a week from two o'clock in the afternoon until ten at night, on a stand-up job twisting, reeling and winding carpet yarn. Eight hours on her feet was exhausting, Wanda acknowledged, and her boss must have been trained in Dickens-era sweatshops. But she stuck with it.

Wanda had lived in Fishtown for thirty-three years and in the house where I found her for seven. Her husband was dead and her three children were grown. One of her two sons, after a stint in the Marines that "made a man of him," had moved west with his wife and four children. He was runing a repair garage near Hollywood and was apparently living quite comfortably. Or so it seemed to his mother the millhand. The younger son, also married and with children, was a mechanic in a Philadelphia repair garage. Wanda also had a married daughter who lived in Connecticut. The daughter had eight children — the oldest boy was attending college. Wanda didn't know what college, but she was pleased. This grandson was the first member of her family, as far as anyone could remember, who had ever gone to college. And what's more, he was planning to become an English teacher. Wanda thought that was wonderful.

From her husband's savings and her own economies, Wanda had built a modest nest egg. She was making only a dollar-ninety-seven an hour at the mill, yet she had spent more than six thousand dollars on improvements to her small house. She knew she'd never get that much money out of the house if she sold it, but that didn't seem to trouble her. The house suited her and that was enough. She planned to retire at sixty-five and thought she would have enough money to live without burdening her children. Much depended on her health, which wasn't good; she had a liver ailment that required treatment from time to time. The doctor said she shouldn't be working on her feet eight hours a day, but that couldn't be helped. And, anyway, she wasn't complaining.

I am still musing about Wanda's life in Whitetown when she walks in. After completing her eight-hour stint, she's had to take two buses — thirty cents for the first ride, five cents for the transfer (and don't forget to have exact change!). Far less taxing than Orwell's miners crawling five miles back to the mine shaft, but wearisome enough for a fifty-year veteran of the mills. Wanda's tired, her feet hurt, and if I weren't there she'd probably flick on the TV. But she seems to welcome somebody to talk to. We go into her small kitchen. Living alone as she does, she keeps her housekeeping as simple as possible. Instead of squeezing oranges for juice in the morning, she puts a spoonful of Tang in a glass of cold water. Now, instead of percolating coffee, she boils water for instant. We sit at the breakfast table a few feet from the gas stove and talk. I ask about Fishtown. She laughs and says the place doesn't seem to have changed much in all the years she's been here.

"What do you like about it?"

"Well, I've lived here so long. No colored."

"Why don't you want to live with colored?"

"I've got nothing against colored. I've worked with colored girls. They're very nice. I wouldn't have nothing against them. As long as they left me alone. That's all I want. I work with colored girls and colored men, and they're very nice."

When I ask Wanda about Fishtown's deficiencies, she cites the shortage of recreation facilities for young people. "It doesn't even have a playground," she says. "That's what they should have around here, a playground. The poor kids. When they play on the street, why, they get chased. Where else are they gonna play? And people holler. In the summer, people holler. Well, I never sit outside. I don't have any time. But other people holler."

Wanda is pleased that there are very few beatniks or hippies in Fishtown. Most of the youngsters, she says, are just "normal boys." They're all "very nice boys" and quite a few have never been downtown on the Frankford El. "They couldn't even get there," says Wanda, laughing again. "They'd get lost. As far as they get is Front Street [at Fishtown's western extremity]. You can do all your shopping on Front Street. To tell you the truth, I ain't been in town in two years — up until last week. I went to the doctor's and then I stopped at Eighth Street and did some shopping. I ain't been down there for two years."

Still, Wanda sees a generation gap.

Even in Fishtown, the children are different. "We're old-fashioned," she says of the parents. "They [the children] want more. They want to live better." None of this impresses Wanda. She doesn't play bingo, as so many Fishtowners do. She doesn't play cards ("Too dumb," she explains with another laugh). She doesn't have many friends and doesn't want many. "I don't like anybody running in and out of my house. I think it's my business. I don't have time for coffee breaks and all that stuff."

Wanda acknowledges that Fishtown might not be as safe a place to live as it once was. "When I lived on Cabot [pronounced ka-BOTT] Street," she says, "I never even closed the door. The door was always open. This was fifteen years ago. We never even had a key. Everybody did that then." Now she never leaves her house unlocked. She'd be afraid to because of "the stuff that you read in the papers." You know, "sometimes you're not safe in your own house."

Despite its inadequacies, though, Fishtown suits Wanda. She has a house, a job, reasonably good health, and a certain pride that goes with being self-sufficient. She has achieved an admirable peace of mind in Fishtown that she might have lacked elsewhere. "I'm contented here," she says. "I think I've done pretty good for only going as far as fourth grade."

I go up to bed. And as I mount the stairs I think that Wanda *has* "done pretty good." Much of what is exciting and stimulating about America has passed her by, but she has kept a firm grip on her sanity while making ends meet. Given the handicaps under which she has labored all her life, perhaps

that is all one could hope for or expect.

My bedroom is at the head of the stairs. It has no door — you simply walk into it. Across the entranceway, Wanda has strung a curtain for privacy. Beside the bed is a long, plain dresser against one wall. The single overhead light is so weak that I can't read in bed without straining my eyes, but everything is tidy and I sleep well.

Tidiness is on my mind next morning when I awake. Tidiness, in fact, is the hallmark of Wanda's house — tidiness and a kind of mausoleum *décor*. These are common characteristics of the better Whitetown houses. In the larger ones you sometimes see completely furnished rooms that seem never to have been lived in. You find upholstered chairs and sofas carefully covered with plastic and obviously not intended for use. Their importance seems to lie in their simply being symbols of a secure and stable household and evidence of material wellbeing.

There is no mirror in Wanda's upstairs bathroom, so I go to the basement to shave over a laundry tub. The basement, too, is far cleaner than my dirty cellar in suburbia.

Wanda is still asleep. I boil an egg over her gas stove and make some instant coffee. Stacking the dishes in the sink — something I suspect Wanda would never do since she seems to clean up after every meal or snack — I leave the house and resume my wanderings.

A dozen blocks from Wanda's house is a particularly slummy section of Kensington, where wooden houses built on stilts look ready to collapse or to burn up at the striking of a match. It is drizzling as I walk down this street. In one house a family is preparing to move out. Children are carrying kitchen supplies down the long, wobbly outside staircase to a ten-year-old station wagon with a rented trailer hooked to the back. Standing on the sidewalk directing the packing is a small, hollow-cheeked man with a dead cigarette stuck onto his bottom lip in the manner of a French workman. I fall into conversation with the man and he tells this story:

He is a house painter. He and his wife and seven children formerly lived in Cleveland. Each of the past several winters he had come east alone to work in Philadelphia, where he found he could earn a hundred and sixty dollars a week against a hundred at home. The previous fall, rather than make the trip by himself again, he decided to relocate his entire family and take up a new life in the East. The family moved to Kensington. Four children were enrolled in the neighborhood elementary school and two in junior high. The oldest child, a seventeen-year-old boy, got a job.

Within two months, the couple's dream of happy family life in Kensington had turned into a nightmare. The oldest son took to drinking and cutting up. He couldn't hold a job. The junior-high kids played hooky, hung on corners, hid in vacant stores to smoke and sniff glue. School authorities warned the parents about the need of controlling their children. But the painter and his wife, also pale and tired, simply could not cope. Finally, the two junior-high youngsters disappeared for three days. Police picked them up downtown in the company of pot-smoking hippies.

For the harried parents that was the last straw. They decided to go back home. And as I walk by they are loading their battered furniture, their kitchen gear, and their seven children into their ancient auto for the drive west. I go inside the house and find a disaster area. Holes in the walls, trash and garbage strewn on the floor. Junky pieces of furniture left behind. Wanda would have been appalled.

As for the parents, they look like Okies from the 1930s dust bowl. And the older children could be bit players in *Bonnie and Clyde*. Just before getting behind the wheel, the father steps over to me. We shake hands in the rain and I wish him well. He hangs his head in despair.

"They just went wild," he says of the kids, now all peacefully assembled in the car and eager to begin their trip. "We'd never seen anything like it back home. Now we're goin' back. And with that, he gets into his car. I wave goodby to them and they drive off.

I keep walking and soon reach one of Kensington's main arteries. Not far along this wide avenue is the house and law office of a man I'll call Tom. Tom is a third-generation Irish Kensingtonian, a rare bird who not only graduated from high school but went on to "the University" (in Philadelphia, that's Penn) and Temple Law. Tom was first in his Kensington parochial-school class, and he caught hell for it. Academic eager beavers were disliked by their classmates. Tom is one of those Kensingtonians who continue to live in Kensington not because they're trapped but because they love it.

Tom invites me into his house, which is something to see. There are fine carpets, a nicely paneled basement children's rumpus room, three beautifully furnished bedrooms. No mortgage, no grounds to keep up, no hidden costs. So Tom is banking thousands of dollars each year for the future college education of his five children. Like many Kensingtonians, he doesn't believe in credit buying or charge accounts. When he needed a new car recently, he withdrew the money from the bank and paid the dealer in cash.

Tom has another law office downtown. Many of his clients are Kensingtonians, and he notes, as Wanda had done, that they are often lost and bewildered when they leave Kensington. "About once a month," says Tom, "I get a phone call from someone who can't find my office. Many of them just don't know their way around the city."

But his neighbors' provincialism doesn't dismay Tom. Nor, apparently, does it trouble his wife. Tom says that, although she grew up on the Main Line, she likes Kensington for the same reasons he does. Besides their comfortable house just three blocks from Tom's parents and two blocks from the site of the old grocery that his grandparents ran for years, they have a place at the Jersey shore and a growing bank account. Meanwhile, most of their suburban friends, says Tom, are weighted down with big mortgages. In the spring and summer they have a lot of grass to cut (Tom has none) and all year round they have a long commute to town. Tom concedes that only one of the fellows he grew up with is still living in Philadelphia. But Tom is "damn

proud" of Kensington, think it's a "great neighborhood," and plans never to move out. "To get some of us out of this neighborhood," he says, "they're going to have to carry us feet first in a box."

A client comes in to see Tom and I leave.

I abandon the main drag and walk up into another residential section of Kensington. Suddenly a beer truck whips around the corner and I recognize the driver's assistant. He is a public-school teacher whom I had met previously. I had known this teacher worked on a beer truck on Saturdays but had never before seen him on the job.

Unlike Tom, the teacher, whom I'll call Ed, is a native Kensingtonian who has moved out. He grew up in a Ukrainian section and attended a Ukrainian parochial school. When he yawned in class one afternoon, he once told me, the nun threatened to crack him in the mouth. To this day, Ed never fails to cover his mouth while yawning.

Ed's father is a welder and his mother is a sewing-machine operator. Both had ninth-grade educations. They still live in a conventional row house thirteen feet wide. His parents remember the Great Depression and continue to worry about money. Not Ed. He seems much more relaxed and sure of himself. He has reason to be more self-assured: he and his wife are making more money than Ed's parents. His wife works for a bank and Ed, in addition to his regular teaching job, also teaches summer school and works Saturdays and holidays on the beer truck. He and his wife moved from Kensington to a $14,000 house in Philadelphia's lower-middle-class Northeast. Before World War II, this section was largely farmland. Now it is filled with thousands of houses. It is almost entirely white. Many of its homeowners fled from Kensington or lower-income "changing neighborhoods" closer to the center of the city.

Ed isn't worried about finances, even though "all my neighbors are in debt." He says, " I don't believe in killing myself over money. After we have children we want to be home with them." For the present, though, Ed wears several hats. He enjoys hustling cases of beer into Kensington houses. Often his customers give him an earful. "The bigotry is tremendous," he says. "You have to hear it to believe it."

As the beer truck disappears down the street, I head over to Kensington Avenue and walk under the El. I'm in the neighborhood now where I'd been drinking beer with Al, the right-handed foreman, last night. Because of the rain this morning, Saturday business is poor in the shopping district. This is old-school shopping — no giant department stores or sleek plazas, just block after block of small storefronts. Kresge's, candies, shoes, shoes, shoes, shirts, shoes, a five-and-ten (where nothing costs a nickel or a dime any more), fashions, shoes, fashions, wigs, lamps, drugs, loans, lunch, flowers, frocks, paints, gifts, shirts, a bar — in fact, the bar I was in last night.

I leave the avenue again and walk several blocks to one of Kensington's typical elementary schools. It's a three-story monstrosity that should have been torn down years ago, but the sec-

tion didn't complain very much. Nothing would have been done had it not been for a young Protestant minister serving a small church in the area. He and his wife, who had two children in the school, mounted a drive to get it replaced. Their case was so convincing that the Board of Education revised its capital building program to speed up the school's replacement. But the new building is still three or four or five years away.

Directly across the street from the school live a couple whom I'll name John and Connie. I've gotten to know them through the minister who recruited them to help in the new-school campaign. John is thirty-six, Polish, a $165-a-week machinist at a Federal installation. His mother completed four years of school in Poland, his father six years in Philadelphia. John went through Catholic high school. His wife, a few years younger than John, is English and also a high-school graduate. They have two children in elementary school.

They urge me to come in out of the rain. In size and shape, their house is almost identical to Wanda's, but with children living there its furnishings and atmosphere are totally different. In the living room, their son's bicycle is leaning precariously against one wall. No other place to put it, John explains, unless you take it down to the basement. And it's a pain in the neck getting the bike down the cellar stairs. Also, John and Connie have interests far different from Wanda's. They have books, records, camping gear, a rock collection.

John and Connie are more middle class in living style and outlook than many Kensingtonians. Yet John, a husky, thoughtful man with glasses, hasn't tried to break out and maybe he never will. We sit in the kitchen drinking coffee and he talks about it. He speaks slowly, picking his words carefully and forming perfect sentences.

"We couldn't afford that tent we have," he says, "if we lived in another neighborhood. We couldn't afford the car I had to buy. For myself, I would like to move out. We stay here primarily because our parents are here. They're old and no one else stayed so we stayed. This is my wife's rationalization for staying. This angers me. I would like to move out. But the reality is: Why bring up a family fight over nothing? I do have it good here. There are some minor things. I can go down in my basement and bang my head against the pipes. Every time it happens, I swear, I curse. I love flowers. I love dirt. I don't have anything. If I go out in the yard, it's all cement. But generally I can be a little freer with the dollar than if I did move out.

"My anger is not with the poorer people moving in. It's with the older people who don't want change. These people are passive. They won't get involved. They're so old that they're afraid. All the fight has been driven out of them. It's not fear that you should be ashamed of, it's inaction. My anger with these people is that they let their fear master them. There are ways of overcoming fear and one of them is facing up to it. I was never as active as I am right now. There was a couple of times when I spoke before the whole auditorium of people over in school. I was terrified but still I did it.

I felt there was a need for it and when I get up again I'll be terrified again."

John says that he grew up frightened of Authority and cowed by it, whether that Authority was the mother superior or the cop on the beat. Those in authority never sought out his views on anything. Now he finds the public school doing just that: inviting the people in and soliciting their opinions on whether a new school should be built and where and how big.

"Whether they listen or not, to me with my background," John says, "I would say that this is amazing. To be able to talk back to Authority — this is something that I have to get used to. And this is one of the things also that retards me as a leader — that I cannot talk to Authority without any feelings of fear or whatever, whatever feelings I have. It's a compound feeling, not only fear, respect for Authority and everything else."

John may be too introspective to be the prototype Whitetowner. But he understands Whitetowners. He does not know his neighbors well, but he shares their feelings on many issues.

On city politics: "People feel they are being shortchanged. I think it's more than a suspicion. I feel that people . . . my attitude is that in a political year they'll take from one to give to another. My feeling is that this is a political reality. Whether it's necessary or not I don't know. I'm angered by this. I don't like it. But I don't know what to do about it."

On Negro gains: "The colored are evening up a big score. They're getting a lot more attention. My feeling is that we [Whitetowners] don't squawk enough. The squeaky wheel gets the oil, and it's a Depression axiom. Why should you have to scream and holler to get things done? If you lack leadership, if you lack drive, you won't get things yourself. It's not just feeling that the Negro is getting it. There's also a feeling that the richer whites are getting it."

On patriotism: "I'm an American and proud of it. When I put on a uniform [John was a draftee, serving from 1952 to 1954], it was an American uniform. People may call me a Pollack and I'll laugh at them, but I don't feel myself as being Polish. I'm an American. If you were to come with a [peace] placard down Kensington Avenue, this would get people mad enough to throw rocks at you."

On ethnic relations: "A race riot when I was a child was trouble between the Polish and the Italians. The Italians came up from South Philly and they fought right on our street corner. And there was a big fight. Now the Polish and the Italians intermarry. My sister married an Italian. And values change. Not that I would like to see the whites and colored — I still have that feeling — I don't know that I would like to see it. But, like I say, values change and they're not as horrifying when the change does come as the way people fantasize them."

On integrating Kensington: "I find myself being prejudiced. I do have the feeling that if the Negro comes in that it will deteriorate. The professional class will not move into this neighborhood. The middle class wants to move to Germantown. So what we are going to get is the lower class. I don't hate the Negro, I don't love him. But he's got to prove himself. And I don't feel that he's proving himself.

Before leaving Kensington there's one more stop to make. It's in tiny Fishtown, at the lower end of the Kensington district and just a couple of blocks from Wanda. It is the house of one of the leaders of Fishtown's unit of the Neighborhood Schools Association. She and her husband, a construction worker, have spearheaded the drive to keep Fishtown just as it is and to keep Fishtown's elementary school as it is.

The couple is expecting me. They are ready to give me an earful. With them are a construction worker whose children are grown up but whose feelings run high, and a repair-garage operator who is Jewish and a Mummer and whose children attend parochial school because his wife is Catholic.

The talk goes on for four hours. They express themselves with varying degrees of vehemence, but it all adds up to the same thing: they don't want any outsiders tinkering with their lives or with their schools.

My hostess and her husband are Italian-Americans from South Philly. They are converts to Fishtown and, just as converts to a religion often are more rabidly devout than the birthright faithful, they are more loyal to Fishtown and its traditions and prejudices than most native Fishtowners.

I had previously met a fourth-generation Fishtowner whose great-grandfather had seen Abraham Lincoln's funeral train pass through Philadelphia and through Kensington on its way to New York. This young man was thoroughly embittered. "Everything we have here," he had told me, "is anti — anti-Negro, anti-Jew, anti-everything. I don't see anything but doomsday as far as keeping the Negro out is concerned. There will be violence — blood on the sidewalk. There has been already."

But the people I'm talking to today, while acknowledging the possibility, even likelihood of violence, make no apologies for it.

Construction worker: "No son of a bitch — when it comes down to plain language, pardon me — no son of a bitch is going to tell me who I have to sell my house to. I'm not prejudiced against the colored race, believe me. I believe a man has a right to live, to make a living, a decent living, a decent home to live in — but to live decently, too. Not to be foul mouthed, and not to be a bunch of booze hounds, which three-quarters of them are. They haven't got a stick of furniture in the house, but they've got a brand-new car out there, a television in the house, and that's it. And you're trying to ram down my throat that I have to rent to one of them, or sell to one of them, no."

My hostess: "I think all intellectuals should stick their heads in a bucket of mud. It's you intellectuals that are trying to tell us we should change. And I don't think we should change. I think there's nothing wrong with trying to be a true-blue American."

Her husband: "I want my children to grow up to be good Americans, get a nice, fair education. I don't want them to have the best; I don't expect my kids to be Einsteins. I want them to live a normal life. I want them to come home to me after school [he has two daughters] and not tell me that someone molested them. And I worked in a lot of schools where I saw a lot of white girls being molested, buddy.

And God forbid if my kid should ever come home and tell me that one kid laid a hand on her."

Construction worker: "What gets me is this here business you read in the newspaper, you hear it all over the place — it actually gets under my skin and irritates me — that the Negro doesn't get the same education as the white person. I've been in those schools. I've seen whole classes doin' nothin' but reading comic books because the teacher couldn't tolerate them. They didn't want to hear the teacher. They go crazy.

"I was workin' down at Seventeenth and Wharton, the Barrett School, when they snuck that bird in from down South there, that King. They kept it quiet till he came in there, but that school went crazy when they brought that bird in. Now why should a school bring somebody like him into our district here? Let him be praised when he flaunts the law as much as he does. You mean I should respect him when he gets away with the stuff he pulls?"

Before going into Fishtown, I had been told that it was probably the most bigoted neighborhood in Philadelphia. "It's isolated and insulated," a school principal had told me. "There has never been an effort on the part of Fishtowners to do anything — except keep Negroes out." The conversation in the living room is not reassuring. The picture I get is of people who like their neighborhood, like it overly much, really, but that is because they are under attack and hence defensive. They like it white, they're afraid of the implications of integration. They tend to reduce all Negroes to the lowest common denominator since it is the lowest-common-denominator Negroes whom they see most often. And so they stand firm against change and against integration. It's almost as simple as that. They can talk in generalities, as my hostess does: "People in this neighborhood want to keep it provincial. There's a very dyed-in-the-wool atmosphere where a mother can reach out and see all her chicks." Or they can spell out their opposition to integration in dollars and cents, as the garage owner does: "My mother bought her home for six thousand dollars. She put five thousand dollars into it and eight years later she sold the home for twenty-one hundred to get out of the neighborhood."

These are bitter, suspicious people with very evident prejudices. It seems clear that the attitudes one finds in Fishtown go back a long way, not only to past ethnic conflicts there but back to attitudes that George Orwell saw in *Wigan Pier*. What Orwell said of English middle-class attitudes toward English workers fits perfectly, I think, lower-middle-class Fishtown's atti-

tudes toward black working-class North Philadelpha.

"Every middle-class person," wrote Orwell, "has a dormant class-prejudice which needs only a small thing to arouse it; and if he is over forty he probably has a firm conviction that his own class has been sacrificed to the class below. . . . In his eyes the workers are not a submerged race of slaves, they are a sinister flood creeping forward upwards to engulf himself and his friends and his family and to sweep all culture and all decency out of existence."

The conflict that Orwell analyzed in Britain in 1937 in terms of social-class differences is both a class and racial conflict in the United States in 1970. Since a person can change his class but not his color, the conflict is more firmly rooted here. It is much more difficult to resolve here and much less likely to wither away. For this reason, I conclude, as I bid my hosts good-by, the spirit of Fishtown is likely to long endure even if the neighborhood itself disintegrates.

DEVIANT BEHAVIOR: DEVIANT LIFE STYLES

What do the following people have in common: rapists, Republicans, blind people, marijuana smokers, homosexuals, Christian Scientists, schizophrenics, virgins, alcoholics, college professors, and murderers? All are considered by at least some portion of American society as deviant. No behavior is inherently deviant. It only becomes so if people for some reason label that behavior as deviant, and treat as deviant, people who exhibit that behavior.*

Sociology has studied deviant behavior from two different perspectives. One perspective holds that we should study the people who label behavior as deviant rather than the deviants themselves. This labeling school† maintains that we should concentrate on the community in which the deviant lives to learn how certain behaviors get to be labeled

---

* John Kitsuse, "Societal Reaction to Deviant Behavior: Problems of Theory and Method." *Social Problems* 9 (Winter 1962), pp. 247–257.

† See for example, Frank Tannenbaum, *Crime and The Community* (New York: Columbia University Press, 1938); Thomas Scheff, *Being Mentally Ill* (Chicago: Aldine, 1966); and Edwin Schur, *Labeling Deviant Behavior* (New York: Harper and Row, 1971).

as deviant. The deviant should be studied mainly to see how he or she reacts to the deviant label.*

Another perspective focuses on why individuals become deviant. The effects of labeling are seen as less important than other factors and the major focus is upon the individual deviant. There are three variations on this perspective. One viewpoint is that people become deviant because they lack the personal or social controls which are necessary to prevent people from becoming deviant.† A second view is that all people want certain things from life but some cannot attain them through "legitimate" means. They react to their frustration by becoming deviant.‡ A third viewpoint is that what is deviant in one group may be conformity to another group. If an individual conforms to the standards of one group, he or she may at the same time be violating the standards of the larger society. Behavior that is conforming within a given subculture may be deviant to the rest of society.§

A deviant is a person who has violated somebody's norm, and people react strongly to norm violators. Being labeled a deviant has a major effect on people's life styles and they are often forced into a situation in which deviance becomes their principal role and the major component affecting their life style.

Deviant life styles may be thought of as those that are discredited and stigmatized by the middle majority.‖ The labels "wino," "whore," "faggot," and "bum" are used to designate and degrade those whose life styles are regarded as deviant. Using their power, the middle ma-

---

* See for example, Edward Sagarin, *Odd Man In: Societies of Deviants in America* (New York: Quadrangle, 1969); Robert A. Scott, *The Making of Blind Men* (New York: Russell Sage, 1969); and, Richard Quinney, *The Social Reality of Crime* (Boston: Little, Brown, 1970), pp. 234–276.

† See for example, Scott Briar and Irving Piliavin, "Delinquency, Situational Inducements, and Commitment to Conformity." *Social Problems* 13 (Summer 1965), pp. 35–45; Walter Reckless, *The Crime Problem* (New York: Appleton-Century-Crofts, 1967), pp. 469–483; and Travis Hirschi, *Causes of Delinquency* (Berkeley: University of California Press, 1969).

‡ See for example, Robert K. Merton, "Social Structure and Anomie," *American Sociological Review* 3 (1938), pp. 672–682; Albert Cohen, *Delinquent Boys* (New York: Free Press, 1955); and Marshall Clinard (ed.), *Anomie and Deviant Behavior.* (New York: Free Press, 1964).

§ See for example, Paul Lerman, "Gangs, Networks, and Subcultural Delinquency," *American Journal of Sociology* 73 (1967), pp. 63–72; Edwin Sutherland and Donald Cressey, *Criminology: 8th Edition* (Philadelphia: Lipincott, 1970), pp. 71–93; and the article by David Matza and Gresham Sykes in this section.

‖ Erving Goffman, *Stigma: Notes on the Management of Spoiled Identity* (Englewood Cliffs, N.J.: Prentice-Hall, 1963), pp. 1–40.

*jority enacts laws against deviants, while they use other laws, such as
those against loitering, as a means of repression and control.**

*Secrecy is frequently an important aspect of deviant life styles. Some
individuals may secretly utilize the services of deviant groups — for example, the suburbanites who attend a strip show or the conventioneers
who pick up prostitutes. Other individuals are secret members of subcultures,† appearing to be part of the straight world while maintaining
membership in a deviant group. Leznoff and Westley‡ studied the homosexual community of a large Canadian city and found that secret homosexuals were more likely to be in the professions, management or sales
positions than overt homosexuals. The covert homosexuals maintained
their secrecy for fear of job dismissal or ridicule, or to protect their families. Overt homosexuals were more likely to come from lower-status
occupations or those that have traditionally accepted homosexual behavior, such as the fine arts or hairdressing.*

*Merle Miller, novelist, journalist and script writer, made public the
fact that for years he had been a homosexual while masquerading as part
of the "straight" community. The following letter in the* San Francisco
Chronicle *in response to Miller, vividly describes the life style dilemmas
of secret deviants.*§

JUST HIDING

To The Editor — Merle Miller is very lucky that he no longer has to
masquerade as a heterosexual. Many of us have to live a masquerade for
at least eight hours a day just to earn a living. And living in the web of
lies and pretense of this masquerade is not easy.

I am a college-educated, under-30 homosexual worming my way up in
a large corporation. I do not expect to get too far, though. My career will
probably stop at the lower end of middle management. To go any farther I
would have to be married, to a woman.

I have been married for the past three years, but to a man. The company
considers me single. I certainly would not tell them I am married. Yet marriage is a very significant fact of my life. And it is my biggest problem.
Marriages between men is very hard in this world that requires people to
seem heterosexual.

For eight hours a day I must pretend that I am single; straight and single. Our kind of marriage does not exist at work. Any upsets, any financial

* Richard Quinney, op. cit., pp. 3–25.
† Howard S. Becker, *Outsiders* (New York: Free Press, 1963), pp. 19–39.
‡ Maurice Leznoff and William Westley, "The Homosexual Community," *Social
Problems,* 3 (April 1956), pp. 257–263.
§ © Chronicle Publishing Co., 1971.

problems, any crises of our marriage do not exist either. I must be very careful not to say anything that would make my roommate and me sound "too" close.

When I was transferred from another city some time ago, I had to hide the fact that my roommate came along; and then weave a fabric of lies to explain why he was here when I accidentally mentioned him. And we are married! If he had been a woman, the company would have given me extra money to bring him here.

How often people tell me I act like a married man. Most of them find out I am single later on. Then the fun begins. The young women at work think I am a good prospect ("with a bright future"). They expect me to be interested in them — but I am married!

I must join in "stag" talk with the fellows. It is a big bore, but I had better not show it. To satisfy my boss' curiosity about my life I must intimate that a good friend of mine, who happens to be female, is having an affair with me.

I am trapped in a cage of pretending. I do not look at all different. How is anyone to know I am a homosexual? I do not look one bit different from other respectable, aggressive, married young men.

ANONYMOUS

Thus there is a public and a private deviant community. The public deviant community consists of those who are known deviants, while the larger deviant community consists of those who are public deviants, secret deviants, and consumers of deviance. The private deviant community may consist of those who are deviant in behavior but not in public identity. A distinct life style develops around public membership in the deviant community — the deviant role becomes a central life interest.

In response to repression launched against them, deviant groups become organized into close-knit communities with their own language, set of values, and behavior patterns. These shared language, value, and behavior patterns create a feeling of solidarity to insulate the deviant in-group from the pressures bombarding it from the outside world. The public may call them "bums," * "queers," or "whores," but they call themselves "tramps," "gay people," or "exotic dancers."

No matter what their characteristics, anybody can be labeled a deviant by some segment of society. Most would agree that rapists and murderers are deviant but this is not true of all law violators. In general, people react more strongly to crimes that have an identifiable victim

---

* Spradley notes that for those who call themselves tramps, there is a popular identity of bums, a sociological identity of alcoholics, and a legal identity of drunks or vagrants. James P. Spradley, *You Owe Yourself a Drunk* (Boston: Little, Brown, 1970), pp. 65–68.

than to "victimless" crimes such as marijuana smoking or homosexuality among consenting adults.* But obviously, one does not have to be a law violator to be considered deviant. To a religious zealot there may be no more deviant person than an avowed atheist. To an atheist there may be no more deviant person than a religious zealot. Erving Goffman has noted that "there is only one complete unblushing male in America: a young, married, white, urban, northern, heterosexual Protestant father of college education, fully employed, of good complexion, weight, and height, and a recent records in sports." † As Goffman intimates, those who lack even one of these characteristics may be considered deviant.

* See Edwin Schur, *Crimes Without Victims* (Englewood Cliffs, N.J.: Prentice-Hall, 1965).

† Erving Goffman, *Stigma* (Englewood Cliffs, N.J.: Prentice-Hall, 1963), p. 128.

The Presentation of Shortness in Everyday Life — Height and Heightism in American Society: Toward a Sociology of Stature

Saul D. Feldman

Physical stature is a variable that has generally been ignored by social scientists.[1] American society is a so-ciety with a heightist premise: to be tall is to be good and to be short is to be stigmatized.[2] This paper will examine the heightist emphasis within American society as it is manifest in aspects of everyday life.

VOCABULARY

The rhetoric of the joys of being tall and the evils of being short are well demonstrated in our daily language. When we degrade people we "put them down" or "belittle" them. Even when we inquire about an individual's physical stature, we ask, "How tall are you?" The ideal man is viewed as *tall*, dark and handsome. Impractical people are "shortsighted," dishonest cashiers "short-change" customers, losers get the "short end of the stick," elec-

[1] An early notable exception is Pirtim A. Sorokin, *Social and Cultural Mobility* (New York: Harper, 1927), pp. 215–253.

[2] For a good general discussion of stigmatization, see Erving Goffman, *Stigma* (Englewood Cliffs: Prentice Hall, 1963).

trical failures are known as "short circuits," and individuals with little money, no matter their height will state of their impecuniousness, "I'm short." A few years ago, a well-known politician spoke at a midwest liberal arts college and referred to a former head of the Federal Bureau of Investigation as "that short little pervert in Washington." It is rare that one hears of tall perverts for in many respects, just to be short is to be a "pervert." [3]

Male-Female Relationships

Sociologists of the family have demonstrated that most marriages are homogamous with regard to race, ethnicity, religion, social class, age range of partners, etc.[4] but most marriages are also homogamous by height. After similar ethnicity, age or social class, probably what most individuals seek in a mate is an individual of compatible height. For a woman, it means marrying an individual somewhat taller than she, and for a male it means being certain that he may be able to look down upon his mate. For many short males, courtship becomes problematic. Unlike taller males, they feel that their

range of potential partners is a lot more limited and generally does not include females of even equal height. Problems are created as well for short females and a new variety of heightism may be fostered as illustrated by this statement from a short female at a midwestern state university.

I don't like going out with short guys. It's not that I have anything against them but I think they're only going out with me because of my height and nothing else.

Figure 1 designates four possible stature situations. It is interesting to note that individuals in cell D share many problems with individuals in cell A. Tall women are limited to men taller than they; any attempt at a relationship with individuals in cell A (which in their case is quite large) is met with powerful weapons of informal social pressure.

The relationship between height and mate selection is indicative of the status of women in our society. Males are supposed to be more dominant and to have more power than females, and one way that a man may express his dominance is by being taller than his mate. If the women's movement has an impact, it may be manifested in such aspects of everyday life as the comparative heights of couples. In the future, if no sex will dominate, then more and more couples should not be matched on height. Tall couples tend to have tall children, and short couples tend to have short children. If height does become more of a random factor in mate selection, children of future generations may become "average" in

---

[3] There are in our vocabulary many words which are used to degrade short people such as "runt," "shrimp," "pipsqueak" and the ubiquitous "shorty."

[4] See for example, Ruth S. Cavan, *The American Family, 4th Edition* (New York: Crowell, 1969), pp. 317–349; Gerald Leslie, *The Family in Social Context, 2nd Edition* (New York: Oxford, 1973), pp. 418–458; and J. Richard Udry, *The Social Context of Marriage* (Philadelphia: Lippincott, 1966), pp. 230–256.

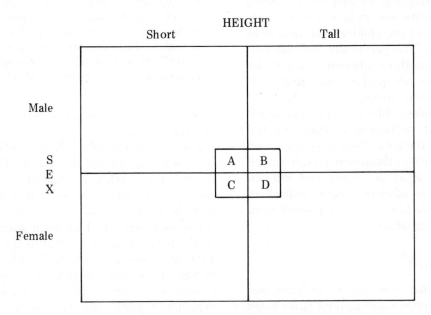

FIGURE 1   POSSIBLE STATURE SITUATIONS

height — i.e., not particularly tall or short.[5]

POLITICAL LIFE

Height has been an important aspect of the American political scene. Is it by chance that almost every American president elected since 1900 has been the taller of the two major candidates? [6] It has been hypothesized that the more favorably disposed peo-

ple are toward an incumbent of a political office, the taller they will think he is.

At another level, the American political ideology has been one of domination of shorter peoples and societies. The United States has attempted to express its dominance over shorter peoples in Vietnam, the Philippines, and in Latin America. It has however been unsuccessful in dominating taller peoples. Witness for example, its lack of success with tall African nations.

Within the United States there are height regulations concerning becoming duly authorized agents of political authority — namely policemen and firemen. In Washington D.C. for example, all policemen and firemen must be at least 5'7" while in Washington State policemen and firemen under 5'8" are ineligible for pension cover-

[5] In England, legend had it that certain parents want their children to become jockeys and thus stunt their growth by feeding them cigarettes and gin. Some militant short people have suggested this as a strategy for all tall parents, to prevent future generations of taller people.

[6] See "Heightism," *Time* (October 4, 1971), p. 64. The 1972 election was an exception to this pattern.

ages.[7] Height is viewed as the badge of authority and in fact from elementary school on, children are taught to "look up" to policemen and firemen. There is nothing inherent in the duties of either occupation that really requires their incumbents to be tall.[8] Nevertheless, life is more dangerous for short policemen. A study by the Atlanta Regional Commission showed that although there were no differences between short policemen and tall policemen in efficiency, short policemen were more likely to be assaulted than were taller officers.[9]

ECONOMIC LIFE

The fact that the short man has been discriminated against is no more evident than in the business world. A survey of University of Pittsburgh business graduates found that tall men (six feet two inches and above) received a starting salary 12.4% higher than graduates of the same school who were under six feet.[10] The Wall Street Journal [11] reported on a study which demonstrated that shorter men may even have more difficulty in obtaining a job than taller men:

David Kurtz, an Eastern Michigan University marketing professor, asked 140 recruiters to make a hypothetical hiring choice between two equally qualified applicants — one six feet one inches tall and the other five-five, for a sales job. Seventy-two percent "hired" the tall one, 27% expressed no preference, and 1% chose the short one.

The short man who becomes successful in politics or business is often viewed as an anomaly. Thus, a review of a book on the life of Andrew Carnegie began, "When he rose up to his full majestic height, he was all of five feet three inches tall." [12] It is so rare for a short male to become a success in the business world (or political life) that his success is coupled with his height. Assumption of political or economic power for a tall individual is considered admirable, but let an individual of less than average stature, such as Andrew Carnegie or Fiorello H. LaGuardia, assume power and he is viewed as having a Napoleon complex. For example, note this following description of industrialist Armand Hammer, "He stood before the analysts less than five-and-a-half feet tall, smiling as if he had swallowed an entire aviary." [13]

Because of the stigma of shortness, individuals may go to elaborate charades to attempt to disguise their height. Fashion coordinators advise short men on how to dress to create the illusion of being taller. American capitalism, quick to exploit any stigma, created the elevator shoe; but neither

---

[7] *Seattle Times* (October 7, 1971).

[8] Short firemen and policemen in fact, are better able to crawl into smaller spaces.

[9] *New York Times* (May 2, 1974).

[10] Leland Deck, "Short Workers of the World Unite," *Psychology Today* 5 (August 1971), p. 102.

[11] (November 25, 1969), p. 1.

[12] Milton R. Konvitz, "Review of *Andrew Carnegie* by Joseph F. Wall," *Saturday Review* (September 21, 1970), p. 34.

[13] Laurence Leamer, "The Go-Between," *New Times* (May 31, 1974), p. 46.

the Adler Shoe Corporation nor Charles Atlas have really had much effect.[14]

POPULAR CULTURE

Perhaps nowhere is America's obsession with height more evident than in the area of popular culture. Games such as basketball glorify height. Few baseball or football players are short. Boxing interest is not among flyweights or bantam weights but among taller middleweights and heavyweights. The one sport that is associated with short people is horse racing — the most popular spectator sport in America. In this sport, however, the short jockey is given second place to a horse, is bet upon by taller individuals, and despite the great popularity of horse racing, a jockey's face has never appeared on a bubblegum card. (Jockeys, unlike football, baseball, or basketball players, however, do appear across the nation as plaster lawn ornaments.)

In the movies the short actor is rarely the romantic lead. The average American cannot identify with the hero unless he rides "tall in the saddle." Thus, the short actor is reduced to playing the buffoon (e.g. Mickey Rooney), the arch-villain (e.g. Peter Lorre), or the small tough guy with the big Napoleon complex (e.g. Edward G. Robinson).

CONCLUSION: HEIGHT AND DEGRADATION OF THE SELF

An article in a major metropolitan newspaper[15] dealt with revitalizing urban centers throughout the United States. The article stated in part:

In Chicago, pudgy little Mayor Daley has been so concerned by the industrial exodus, he has taken the political stump to get a new airport near the city line to get firms that want to have easy access to air travel.

In an attempt to discredit Richard Daley and his program, comment in this article was directed not toward his politics but toward his physical stature. The media cannot make adverse comments about a person's race, religion, sex, or ethnicity but they can make adverse remarks about their height. Thus one newspaper referred to Lt. William Calley, commander at the My Lai massacre, as a "stubby little former platoon commander" [16] while another paper called George Wallace a "bumptious little governor." [17]

People do react strongly to an individual's height and make invidious distinctions on this basis. In a social psychological experiment, five groups of students were asked to judge the height of the same individual. In each of the five groups, he was introduced as having a different academic rank. The higher the academic status at-

[14] To illustrate at least one job for which it is believed that short people are especially suited, note should be taken of an advertisement in the student newspaper of Southern Methodist University. Applicants, to appear as clown Ronald McDonald, had to be under six feet.

[15] *San Francisco Examiner* (December 20, 1970), p. 11.
[16] *Dallas Times Herald* (February 24, 1971), p. 15.
[17] *San Francisco Examiner and Chronicle* (August 15, 1971), p. A1

tributed to this person, the taller the student subjects thought he was. Status and height were highly correlated.[18]

Thus, even on chance encounters, people may react strongly to a person's height. When the San Francisco Chronicle roving reporter asked "What would you do if a stranger smiled at you?" E. C., a secretary, stated:

> *It depends. If they were nice, I'd smile back. If they were really beady eyed and creepy looking, I'd ignore them. But if they were tall [emphasis mine] and good looking and well dressed, then I'd smile back.*

Since height and lack of it, is such a visible variable, it is surprising that sociologists have not dealt with it to this point. In a society directed toward overabundance and glorification of anything above average, individuals of less than average height are almost universally known as "Shorty," short adults purchase much of their clothing in children's departments,[19] and in short, are stigmatized. Stigmatization did not begin as an adult. As short children they were often lined up in elementary classrooms according to height. As teenagers, they learned the courtship problems of short people. As adults, discreditization of their stature became magnified in economic and political life, in popular culture, and in other aspects of daily life.

Shortness may be a virtue in academic papers, but as we have pointed out, to be of less than average height in American society is to fall short of the mark in almost all aspects of everyday life.

---

[18] Paul R. Wilson, "The Perceptual Distortion of Height as a Function of Ascribed Academic Status," *Journal of Social Psychology* 74 (1968), pp. 97–102.

[19] There is inequity in the market place even if adults buy their clothing from an adult clothing department. Even though there is far less cloth in a 36 short jacket than in a 46 long, short people and tall people pay the same price.

People have been using marijuana as an intoxicant since before the birth of Christ, and it has been used recreationally by some Americans since the founding of this nation.* As late as 1930, the use of marijuana was illegal in only 16 states† but by 1937 all states but two had laws against the use, sale, or possession of marijuana.‡ Despite its illegality, mari-

---

* For a history of marijuana use, see Edward Brecher and the Editors of Consumers Reports, *Licit and Illicit Drugs* (Boston: Little, Brown, 1972), pp. 397–472.
† Becker, Howard S., *Outsiders* (New York: Free Press, 1963), p. 135.
‡ Brecher et al, op. cit., p. 413.

juana was used within some deviant subcultures — especially jazz musicians and some lower-class black groups. The sixties saw a major increase in the use of marijuana and other drugs — not only on college campuses but throughout the United States. Youth culture had as one theme the use of drugs — not only marijuana but drugs such as LSD, barbiturates, amphetamines, cocaine, and heroin. Drugs were associated with youth culture and youth culture was associated with college (and high school) students. (According to a Gallup Poll of March, 1974, 55% of all college students surveyed stated that they had at least tried marijuana).

Subcultures form around drugs. These subcultures may pool money to obtain drugs, may use them together, and may band together for mutual protection and support. Not all drug users are members of subcultures, and not all people who use drugs have this as a central life interest. But among many heavy drug users, drug use is a central life interest. There are drug subcultures among college students, among professionals, and among working-class individuals.

Neither Heads nor Freaks: Working Class Drug Subculture

Gary Schwartz,
Paul Turner,
and Emil Peluso

THE PROBLEM

Until quite recently, adolescent social life in stable working class communities was sociological terra incognita.

Reprinted from *Urban Life and Culture*, vol. 2, no. 3 (Oct. 1973), pp. 288–314, by permission of the publisher, Sage Publications, Inc.

Social scientists did not pay much attention to working class youth unless they were delinquent or dropped out of school. Almost inadvertently, one thinks of working class youth as colorless replicas of their parents — fully committed to the routines and amusements of a blue-collar existence.

This paper examines a new phenomenon in American life: serious drug use among youth groups in stable, white working class communities, and the concomitant rise of a new actor on the working class youth scene, the hippie greaser. The term hippie greaser is the authors'. The group of working class polydrug users we shall discuss do not use it. In fact, they have not coined a word that refers to their niche in the local youth culture. Unlike their more conventional peers, they do not cultivate a public identity that advertises their pre-eminence in a particular sphere of activity. These young drug users do not boast about their expertise or prowess in the consumption of drugs. Nor do they self-consciously appropriate the insignia which the mass media provides young people who wish to adopt a generalized hippie stance so as to distinguish themselves from their "straight" peers. The hippie greasers' dress and demeanor is a careless amalgam of hippie and greaser styles.

The hippie greaser is anomalous in another respect. He represents a highly improbable fusion of two youthful styles that have opposing ideological connotations (Schwartz, 1972). The greaser is a tough-minded realist. As far as he is concerned, power is one of the elemental forces in human affairs, and everyone has to come to terms with this fact sooner or later. He admires manliness and believes in "rugged individualism." For the greaser, then, the strength of character that enables a person to control the things and persons that constitute his immediate environment is of paramount importance. The hippie, on the other hand, values self actualization and with or without drugs, continually monitors subtle changes in his own mood and in his perceptions of significant others. He tries to transform this heightened awareness of self into communion with others and with nature. This search for and receptivity to the intimate and personal dimensions of existence is thought to activate universal forms of human solidarity. The hippie believes in an organic community. The hippie greaser ignores these ideological contrasts. He combines the greaser's street

wisdom and personal toughness with the hippie's dedication to drugs and rock music without any regard for the ostensibly contradictory meanings of these two orientations toward life.

The specific meanings young people attribute to one of the prime cultural elements of youth culture, hallucinogenic drugs, depends upon their class background, their position in the local youth social system and the political atmosphere of the community. As the title of this paper implies, the participants in a working class drug subculture do not conform to the middle class "hippie" model (Davis, 1971). They are not "freaks" whose quest for intense methedrine highs ultimately destroys their friendships, nor are they self-searching "heads" (Davis, 1968). This paper focuses on the meanings the participants in a working class drug subculture impute to the drug experience in the context of peer group activity and what this *kind* of drug use implies about their attitudes toward the everyday world. Moreover, we shall show that the ideological implications of a serious commitment to drugs are quite paradoxical, at least for those who associate drugs with racial tolerance and other humane attitudes.

MODALITIES OF MIDDLE CLASS DRUG USE

Before we can discuss the meaning of the working class drug experience, we must first establish a solid point of comparison. To this end we shall briefly outline the principal modalities of middle class drug experience. Here the data come from a study of youth culture in an urban, solidly middle class community. Although the participants in drug subcultures are somewhat older in the working class community (18 and 19) than in the middle class community (16 thru 18), the differences in age do not strike us as consequential. Both groups of young people were firmly embedded in peer group worlds and neither had made the sort of commitment to careers or jobs that usually removes a young person from the youth culture.

A somewhat rare but still extant type of middle class drug user is ironically called the "love child." For the love child, drugs make one more open to other people and to nature. Drugs are said to bring a person into harmony with himself and the world. This search for inner peace is usually couched in a vague mystical or religious terminology. Love children talk about their "karma" and their astrological charts in the same breath. They adopt a passive, non-judgmental stance toward those persons who interfere with their activities or disapprove of their life style.

The next two types are actually interchangeable interpretative frameworks for talking about drug experiences rather than concrete life styles. There are no folk labels for the person who approaches drugs in the following ways, but the themes that dominate each type are heightened self awareness and pleasure in moderation. Both modes of drug use acknowledge the prior claims of everyday life over the delights of using consciousness altering substances.

It is difficult to tell, on the basis of appearance, whether middle class youth use drugs. For many, hippie garb is passé or optional. Nonetheless, they draw upon some elements of the hippie ideology to rationalize or explain their own drug experience. Hallucinogenic drugs enable these young people to "get into their own heads." Drug-induced sensations and moods connect vivid perceptual imagery to affects associated with one's past. In contrast to the love child, this remembrance of things past is not, for these drug users, a passive experience. It is, rather, an active attempt to "figure out where your head is at," and to do this, one explores insights (or so they seem when one is "high") into one's relationships with other people.

The recreational approach to drug use is closely allied to this emphasis on awareness of self. The underlying theme of this style might be phrased as follows: "We do this because it is fun and it is fun because we do it once in awhile." Part of the fun derives from the illicit and illegal nature of drugs. A young person can defy his parents and the law at the same time without doing anything, as he sees it, intrinsically more dangerous or immoral than drinking alcohol. The other pleasurable aspect of using drugs comes from the control recreational users exercise over a substance they know consumes the lives of their peers who use it with abandon. In other words, their sense of self control is strengthened by the fact that drugs are not their raison d'etre. Finally, for the temperate user, drugs are a convenient and often superior substitute for alcohol. They are a very reliable aid to sociability.

The last type resembles but is not identical to the working class drug style. We do not know whether the term is used elsewhere but, in the community from which our middle class data comes, this type frequently is referred to as a "bust out." Though the term "bust out" resonates with the meaning of being "strung out" on drugs, its primary meaning refers to the "bust out's" rejection of all conventional career patterns. He drops out of or marks time in school, very often going to class "high." Moreover, he refuses to hedge his bets and devotes himself totally to a way of life that has no viable links to ordinary society or to a regular source of income. There is a strong measure of contempt for middle class rationality in this style. It certainly ignores the warning that middle class schools and families give to adolescents: plan for the future.

However, there is one element in this style that distinguishes it from working class drug subcultures. It is our impression that the middle class "bust out" is a romantic figure at heart. Though it is usually very difficult for him to provide a coherent rationale for his total commitment to drugs, he seems to feel that drugs will somehow lead him to a fixed point of orientation for his life. Consequently, like other middle class drug users, the meaning of drugs revolves around the discovery of self for the "bust out."

THE COMMUNITY

The working class drug subculture we studied is located in a predominantly blue-collar suburb in the metropolitan region of a large American city. We shall call this suburb, Commerce-

ville.[1] It is distinguished by tree-lined, extremely clean streets of modest, very well kept, frame and brick houses, most of which were built in the 1920s and 30s. Commerceville is bordered on three sides by heavy industry. Its "open" border shades into Coldwind, a community with which it is commonly identified politically in the minds of the inhabitants of both communities as well as by others who are familiar with its reputation. Commerceville feels threatened by an urban Black population that has moved close to one of its industrial borders. It is well-known for its instant and militant

[1] The data for this paper come from thirteen months of field work in this community, from July of 1971 to August, 1972. Although the field worker maintained contact with the working class drug group for almost a year, it was not until eight months had gone by that they began to acknowledge his presence as an independent person. Before that, he was seen as someone who accompanied another member of the group. His identity was of little or no interest to them, even though he repeatedly explained what he was doing in the community and why he was interested in young people. Except for the informant who provided access to the group, the idea of a disinterested study of youth never had any meaning to the group members They accepted the field worker when it became apparent that he was not merely a tourist looking for exotic sights but was willing to share their underground existence and that he did not fish for information about their personal lives which they were unwilling to reveal in ordinary conversation. Consequently, formal, in-depth interviewing was not possible in this setting nor was it ever possible to systematically question anyone (except the field worker's collegiate informant) about his activities outside the group. All names of persons and places are pseudonyms.

reaction to any "intrusion" of Black persons into the area.

Most of the people who live in this community are first and second generation descendants of families that came to this country from Eastern or Southern Europe. Unlike suburban blue-collar communities built after World War II, friendships and associational ties are still formed along ethnic lines. In this respect, the community retains many of the qualities of inner-city ethnic communities that look inward to their cultural heritage rather than outward to the mass media for the symbols that organize informal social patterns (compare Suttles, 1968).

The political outlook of this community is decidely conservative and its political organization is very tight — nothing seems to happen without the knowledge and approval of city hall. Outside organizations and agencies that have a liberal, social welfare bias are told in no uncertain terms that their programs are unwanted and unnecessary. Local schools and churches are silent on all controversial issues. The local community college, for example, offers no anthropology courses because they deal with questions about race.

The political atmosphere is monolithic. There is no organized dissent from the prevailing conservative ideology that informs all decisions made by the political elites. Local citizens' groups, homeowners associations, political parties and the police carefully scrutinize public places and events for signs of trouble. In the local idiom, "outside agitators" are not allowed to stir up trouble. This community effec-tively prohibits any overt expression of opposition to the norms and values of mainstream America (compare Schwartz, 1972).

THE LOCAL YOUTH SOCIAL SYSTEM

The social categories that organize the local youth system are comparable to those used elsewhere (Schwartz and Merten, 1967). Young people in this community agree about the personal attributes which identify the adherents of a particular youth style. There is much less agreement about the relative worth of each style. Yet everybody judges the adherents of one style as better or worse than another, and the local high school is the place where the proponents of various youth styles come together.

Sterling East is the high school that serves Commerceville and "grease" is its predominant youth style. Greasers affect the tough, hyper-masculine stance traditionally associated with the "cornerboy." They dress in black leather jackets and pointed shoes. They usually take school lightly and rarely think of going to a four-year college. Yet they accept the adult world for what it is and make no bones about the fact that they will have to find a place in it. During the period before they get a full-time job or join the army, they spend much of their free time perfecting the manly arts of fighting, drinking, working on fast cars, and womanizing. Though some greasers wear long hair and use drugs occasionally, they do not have the cosmopolitan outlook of hippies. The greaser remains closely tied to the traditions of his neighborhood and community. In the eyes of youth less given to face-to-face confrontations, a greaser seems to interpret every non-deferential gesture as an insult and as grounds for physical retaliation. For greasers, personal honor and one's social identity are intimately connected to peer group friendships. These relationships, however, do not follow the middle class code for friendship. Loyalties are not rationalized in terms of common interests nor are friendships subjected to the norms of continuous mutuality and reciprocity. A greaser's commitment to his friends is simply taken for granted as the only basis upon which he can move freely in the peer group world.

As far as teachers and most adults are concerned, the "jocks" and what we will call "good kids" (for Simon et al, 1971, these include family-oriented and collegiate types) are the most laudable young people in the area. Jocks, as the term implies, are athletes. This label applies to more than the members of school teams, however. It refers to anyone who has the right kind of competitive school spirit and who treats athletics as the American equivalent of a semi-sacred morality play. Young people who participate in the extra-curricular activities of the school show the sort of ambition and social responsibility that appeal to the East European adults in this community. Jocks and good kids cause less trouble in school and show up for class more often than do greasers. They take seriously their parents' desire to have them graduate and, in general, show all the signs of wanting to get ahead in the world via the conventional routes of upward mobility.

The good kids and jocks are distinguished by their willingness to abide by the rules of the game set by adults and the greasers are distinguished by their propensity to impose whatever rules strike their fancy on peers who intrude on their "territory." Non-conventional youth (see below) are distinguished by their disinterest in and disregard for the proprieties and traditions of their community. The social identities of non-conventional youth do not coalesce around neighborhood or community values. In their eyes, the values of their parents and their more staid peers are depressingly provincial or simply irrelevant to anything that matters to them. They live in the community but are not of it. They remain there because they cannot afford to leave or because they have yet to find another place that is more comfortable or convenient. (However, even for the "collegiate" member of the drug subculture, there is an unspoken reason for returning to or residing in one's natal community. In very much the greaser spirit, these youth find it very difficult to break the ties they formed in childhood and adolescence.)

To adults, jocks, good kids, and greasers are all acceptable youth styles. Adults may not like a particular group of young people, but they never question the styles themselves as legitimate ways of life. But below these strata in the youth social system is a subterranean youth culture that is not so acceptable to adults. This youth culture is unified by its devotion to drugs, but split by the degree to which its participants are sympathetic to greaser attitudes or incorporate these attitudes in their own life style. The following distinctions are tentative inasmuch as the lines between the categories are often blurred by personal relationships.

There are what we call "arts and crafts hippies" who adopt the costume and demeanor of the hippie as he is portrayed by the mass media. Arts and crafts hippies usually dislike and avoid greasers. These youth sometimes are active in local theater and similar pursuits, and they may have the professional ambitions, artistic talent or musical ability that will ultimately bring them into the larger society, though perhaps not in the way their parents would prefer. In any event, their present mode of life derides the sort of respectability their parents admire.

At the very bottom of the youth world are hippie greasers and "burnt out" hippies. The latter term is used to describe those participants in the drug subculture who have become wholly dependent on drugs. Hippie greasers were originally part of the grease world but their attachment to drugs and rock music came to override their interest in anything else. In the eyes of conventional greasers, these youth have gone over into the hippie world, and, for awhile, they were fair game for harassment. What the less tolerant greasers did not count on was that some of the tougher "bikers" would find that they enjoyed the drug subculture and quickly spread the word that attacks on their friends would not be appreciated.

The Drug Subculture

The drug subculture, as represented by the group we studied, is literally as well as figuratively subterranean. The nightly drug taking routines of this group occur in the basement of a home owned by the parents of one of its members. One gains admittance to the group and the basement only through the personal recommendation of a regular member. This group is subterranean in another sense. Beyond the fact that its activities are illegal and violate the moral sensibilities of the community, the very category, "hippie greaser," defies all "normal" expectations about how the youth world is constituted. In other words, adults and most young people understand how one becomes a jock, greaser or good kid, and hippies are seen as alien beings whose way of life is inimical. This knowledge is grounded in taken-for-granted assumptions about what makes these categories recognizable life styles. However, the category hippie greaser questions the intelligibility of conventional distinctions between different types of youth groups. Thus, the hippie greaser violates the boundaries between distinct social categories, and, for this reason, his behavior is seen as suspect or weird by his more conventional contemporaries.

The basement in which this group gathers almost every evening is the relatively private apartment of one of the core members of the group and the place where his mother does the laundry. The basement is an L shaped room whose concrete walls are panelled with unfinished wood boards that reach only part way up the wall. The rest of the walls and the windows are painted in psychedelic colors. Besides a stove, sink and refrigerator, the room contains large floor pillows and an old couch, some wood-crate tables, and a regular table decorated with candles and an electric light that changes colors. There is a bedroom at the top of the L that is separated from the rest of the room by a curtain, and it contains a large waterbed and a television set. The walls are decorated with drug oriented posters and designs. One of the posters, for example, shows the man from Glad (the reference is to a television commercial) with a "lid" of marijuana in a glad bag saying, "It seals in the freshness." *Bent, Freak Brothers, National Lampoon, Mad* and *Zap* are spread around the room.

With the exception of Alice, the wife of one of the group's most active members, the core members are all male. Women are often present in the basement and partake in the drug using sessions, but, to use Simon's (1971) terminology, the atmosphere is markedly homosocial.[2] Women do not ordinarily decide how or where the group will spend its time and they rarely express an opinion on any subject unless asked. The group, which has no name

and whose members eschew all social formalities let alone formal organization, was formed during the junior and senior high school years. During this period, the regular members of the group gradually discovered their mutual attraction to drugs and rock music. For quite awhile, some were active in the same rock band, and to this day music along with drugs is the focus of the group's activities.

On the surface, the interests and affiliations of the regular members are extremely diverse. One is currently a student in excellent academic standing at a prestigious local university; another is the leader of a local street gang; others are bikers who spend much of their time working on their oversize motorcycles; half-hearted junior college students whose dedication to academic goals is evidenced by their nightly (and sometimes afternoon) sessions of getting totally "stoned" in the basement; and itinerant unskilled or semi-skilled workers. Some try to get by with doing nothing at all, and a few live wholly or partly on the proceeds of selling drugs (though none is a truly professional dealer).[3]

[2] Our data on the attitudes of these young men toward sex roles is thin but provocative. For instance, when a member brings one of his many girl friends to the basement, he introduces her by saying, "This is X, who wants to screw her." On the surface, this looks like the traditional working class "machismo." But the exaggerated, sardonic manner in which these youth joke about sexual conquest belies the low key and relatively open way they actually deal with women. We suspect that at this point they are uncertain how they want to view relationships with women but are unwilling to allow traditional conceptions of the "war between the sexes" to disrupt their personal lives. In other words, the issue of personal dominance in heterosexual relations does not seem to be salient for these young people.

[3] The "core" group who spent a good deal of time in the basement, often showing up every night for weeks on end, consisted of 17 people. In terms of their outside activities, this included three "collegiates," five "bikers," three musicians and six people for whom drugs were an all consuming interest.

The number of persons present in the basement scene varied widely from night to night and over the course of a particular evening. Some evenings only four or five people would be present and on many other occasions a stream of "regulars" would show up with their friends, stay awhile and then leave. On the average the group consisted of eight or nine persons.

What brings this rather strange cast of characters together for their nightly act of goodfellowship? The answer is twofold. The first deals with the nature of the personal ties that define a greaser's loyalty to his origins and to his past. Although these young people lead different lives outside of the basement, the simple fact that they grew up together and have had similar problems with their parents is enough to ratify their present union. However, their friendship rests on something more than a body of shared experience. Each member, in his own way, lives delicately balanced between going along with the standardized routines of the larger society and losing the ability to manipulate the world to his own advantage. This is a matter of one's personal motives and values and has little to do with how one looks to conventional society. A few members of this group look rather successful (this certainly applies to the "collegiate" member of the group and perhaps to the drummer in a rock band that has become prominent locally). Some are seen as failures by most adults in the community, and others fall somewhere in between (e.g., the junior college students). Yet all of these young people feel either ambivalent about or antagonistic toward societal structures that interfere with their personal freedom. Open rebellion against the representatives of societal authority — parents, teachers, employers and police — and passive acquiescence to their strictures are seen as equally abhorrent. They are unmoved by the threats and promises that their parents and others use to get them to act "responsibly." Whether they keep a foot in, or turn their back

on, respectable society, they all feel that only a lesser human being yields to the pressure. To do so means one either becomes totally dependent on drugs (a "burn out" who cannot honor commitments to friends or negotiate a difficult course through a world bent on molding him to its specifications) or becomes "straight" and follows a course approved of by one's parents and the community.

The second element of group solidarity arises out of the drug experience. Before we can grasp the meaning of getting "high" for these youth, we must first understand their attitude toward work and the "straight" world. Here we will characterize their "typical" attitude toward work: The way they evaluate work per se, that is, their feelings about the intrinsic value of work. We will look at the job histories of some of the core members of the group and only mention peripheral participants in passing.

Dave was one of the original members of the rock band formed in high school with Sid, Bee, Fred and a few others. The band lasted three years but the friendships they made during this time continue to the present. About the time the band was formed, they met Dream and Fox, who in turn, introduced some of their friends to the group. (Even now, people "join" or "leave" the group in this informal manner.) Dave is a drop-out from the local high school. He was kicked out of school for having long hair but when the American Civil Liberties Union won court cases reinstating the rights of long-haired young people to an education, he decided that it was not worth the trouble to return. Dave links some of the participants in this group who otherwise have little to do with one another and everyone likes and respects him although he is not the leader.[4]

Dave's work history is brief and episodic. He has worked at various odd jobs — watching a newspaper stand in the summer, for example. He says he took this job because you can get "high" all day. When asked what he would do if he got a regular job, Dave

[4] It makes little sense to talk about informal patterns of leadership in this group. Personal influence is important, of course, as when a subdued discussion about what music they will listen to that evening takes place or when they decided to go somewhere together. However, no one ever tells anyone else what to do or how to do it. This is not to say that they agree about everything or that they do not engage in those adolescent rituals that are meant to reveal one's superiority to one's peers (compare Schwartz and Merten, 1968). There are spirited arguments about which of the latest modifications for their motorcycles will work, and they "one-up" each other by making increasingly grotesque and denigrating remarks about Blacks and other minority groups. Even though Fox — a massive, muscular young man who is known as one of the most formidable street fighters in the community — and Butts — a physically imposing biker who is known for never backing away from a confrontation — are members of the group, there is an unwritten law that coercion of any kind is totally objectionable. The idea that anyone (except for two brothers who cannot contain their fratricidal hatred for one another) would use force against anyone else in the basement is unthinkable. While the hippie slogan, "everybody does his own thing," is alien to their style, they, nonetheless, protect the completely relaxed atmosphere of the basement. In matters of personal choice or taste, persuasion is rare and direct confrontation nonexistent.

replied that being a mailman would be all right. In Dave's opinion, a mailman does not work hard, he can get "high" while delivering the mail, and he is out-of-doors all day. Dave looks for a job on occasion, though hardly enthusiastically. He reports that the jobs that might interest him require too much education and that the jobs open to him require too much hard work. When talking to Dandy (Alice's husband, who works intermittently at manual labor until he has enough money to purchase a large supply of drugs), Dave and he agreed that one of the few jobs that would really interest them is working in a factory that makes musical instruments.

It would be wrong to conclude that someone like Dave merely feels apathy or revulsion when he thinks about making a living. For those who subscribe to the Protestant ethic, working and making a living are synonomous. For someone like Dave, they are not. He knows that he will eventually have to make a living; he hopes to do it without working at a boring job. If it would not diminish his personal freedom or make him dependent on people he despises, he is interested in the possibilities of "free enterprise." For instance, when a youth-serving agency made an effort to start a coffee house and then gave up without a fight when community pressures against it began, Dave and some of his friends investigated the possibility of opening a place on their own. They looked at some store-fronts and, excited by the idea, tried, unsuccessfully, to raise the necessary capital.

Dandy feels responsible for his wife Alice, works to support her and yet refuses to take a steady job. He has no desire to have Alice work, and she does not want a job even though they have no children. During the summer he works for the father of Mark, another member of the group. Mary, like many of the group, is an anathema to his parents. His father likes Dandy and offered to build him a house if he would stay with him, but Dandy preferred his freedom. Dandy views work solely as a necessity. If he and Alice could get "high" regularly without working they would do so. They dream of moving to Jamaica where they would live by selling the very high grade and easily obtainable local "grass" to their friends in the States. Although Dandy works, he feels no compunctions about "ripping off" food and other daily necessities from large chain stores. He draws the line at stealing from small businessmen because they cannot afford to take the loss, but views stealing from chain stores as merely taking back some of the money they "rip off" from ordinary people. However, such stealing has no revolutionary overtones for Dandy or for other members of this group. They do it simply as a matter of quid pro quo.

At first glance, Bee looks like an upwardly mobile working class youth. He has spent a half year in junior college and talks about going back. He presently works as a mailboy for a large building in the center of the city. He wanders about the building "high" as he delivers the mail. One of the people in his office noticed that he drew very well and said that he would have no trouble getting a job in the commercial art department of an adver-

tising agency in the building. He was excited about the possibility of making a living by drawing, and although his office promised to arrange to get it for him, the job never materialized. While Bee talks about "making it," he clearly intends to continue getting "stoned" every night in the basement. He is cynical about the "straight" world, believing that one should try to get ahead, but should not sacrifice one's freedom to dull office routines.

The job histories of other members of the group are similar. Mark, for example, drives a cab because he can do it while he is "high." Jinx, Mark's closest friend, attends the local junior college but rarely goes to class and spends most of his time getting "stoned" in the basement with Mark. The same is true for Fred, Don and Jack. Butts steals and was involved in a motorcycle theft gang. Butts and his friends, Val and Chuck, occasionally sell drugs. Although the bikers have a well deserved reputation for treating viciously those for whom they feel contempt, they are uniformly honest and generous in drug transactions with others in the basement.

In sum, these youth disengage themselves from or are disinterested in a conventional occupational career. Since it is impossible for most working class youth to avoid work altogether, they adopt a very flexible attitude toward jobs. If something comes along that really interests them, they will take it. Otherwise they try to get by the best they can. For some, this means taking the risks involved in theft and drug dealing. For others, it means short-term unskilled jobs or work that soon bores and frustrates them. Some hope that a junior college degree (which most expect to get without attending class) will somehow deliver them from the likely prospect of working at boring jobs. A few refuse to bend at all. For instance, Ken goes to job interviews dressed in the same jeans and work shirt he wears every day. It is just "too bad," he says, if a prospective employer does not like the way he dresses.

There are three exceptions to this pattern. Nick, an original member of the group, now departed for the West coast and living in a commune, was a self-styled radical who worked in a factory. While the group ridiculed his political rhetoric, they liked Nick personally and now joke about his search for the "cosmic High." They do not believe there is an ideological solution to their situation. Instead they take as given what the occupational system has to offer and try to slip through its interstices without getting caught up in its machinery.

Dream was also an original member of the group and, although he is now very active in the rock music business, he drops by the basement regularly to get "high" with old friends. Like them, Dream has serious conflicts with his parents and feels that "straight" society is, at best, a "drag." But, unlike them, he is quite successful at something they all would like to do. Moreover, he epitomizes, for them, a human virtue that few people can ever hope to embody. Dream absolutely refuses to let the world "bug" him. He neither tries to meet difficult situations head on nor tries to rise above them. He simply will not take them seriously. In the eyes of the group, he is a com-

pletely free spirit, the apotheosis of the rock drummer — supremely self-confident, self-contained and in tune with the very pulse of life itself. The group often talks, for example, about the time Dream was "busted" on a drug charge. What struck them as admirable and remarkable was that, indifferent to the risk and certain that his personal charm would carry the day, Dream went to his court appearance "high." (While this runs somewhat ahead of our argument, it is important to note here that Dream does not get "high" in the same manner as do his friends. He does not seek the state of passive withdrawal that characterizes the drug experience of this group and usually leaves the basement before the evening reaches its anti-climax.)

Sid, in contrast, clearly has not severed his ties to conventional society and works hard at his studies. Superficially, he is testament to the achievement motive and upward mobility. Yet while Sid has considerable self discipline and schedules most of his activities in the basement on weekends and vacations, getting "stoned" with his friends has more than marginal significance in his life. He deliberately seeks the kind of drug experience that appears to contradict his professional aspirations. And it is impossible to account for his persistent return to the basement merely as a sentimental reaffirmation of old school ties.

Sid has a relatively clear idea of what he wants to do with his life; he wants to use his mind creatively, and, currently, college teaching looks promising to him. He also wants many of the things that go with upward mobility, especially the freedom and self-respect that accompanies professional status. He knows as well what he does not want to do: he does not want to become the doctor his father very much wants him to become.

Along with losing himself in his studies, getting "stoned" in the basement allows him to resist family pressures. More important, it symbolically restates the major personal dilemma of his life: how to get ahead without giving in. Thus, he seeks the euphoric passivity of drugs because his very inactivity, the feeling of being totally immobilized, represents resistance to the authorities — familiar and otherwise — that he views as having arbitrarily tried to dictate a pattern for his life. Additionally, this experience is inimical to the sort of impersonal competition that sustains those societal structures (including universities) that Sid feels put people into pigeonholes.

Sid's involvement in the drug subculture is temporary. He realizes that he is set on a different course than the other members of the group and he has no illusions about the fact that they are "going nowhere." Yet unlike his friends, Millard and Frank, who are from the same community, go to the same university and occasionally visit the basement, Sid's commitment to the basement is more than a superficial gesture of rebellion. His sense of personal integrity does not allow him, unlike Millard, to follow his parents' directives while pretending to be his own man. Nor does it allow him, unlike Frank, to accept the idea that what one is paid for doing a job justifies the kind of work it entails.

However, in the short-term at least, it is not his occupational goals that are pulling him away from the basement, but his desire to find a more sophisticated, romantic heterosexual relationship. Sid is learning how to fall in love and he believes that this is not quite the same thing as simply having steady sexual relations with a girl. In fact, romance of one variety or another is the drug culture's vulnerable point. Most of its members will probably become part of the labor force; it is hard to see any other alternatives open to them. It is not the lure of a secure income, however, but involvements with women that may eventually break the group's spell over its members. The hippie greaser cannot look to his parents for models of open heterosexual relationships. And we suspect that a generation raised on the lyrics of rock music cannot easily accept the sex-role segregation that characterizes their parents' marriages. For better or worse, they too are influenced by the youth culture's insistence that personal happiness and romantic relationships somehow go together. Though the issue is very ambiguous at this point and most of the participants in this subculture have not overtly abandoned the standard working class conceptions of sex roles, we suspect that love, or at least some sort of permanent relationship with a woman, will ultimately bind them to societal structures such as families and steady jobs that now seem antithetical to their very being.

Like many members of his generation, the hippie greaser has not lost his taste for the products of industrial technology. But neither is he captivated by the standard American image of the good life: a home, two cars, an attractive wife and family, and so forth. For him, the material symbols of success simply do not justify a life whose predictable routines are broken only on weekends. The hippie greaser experiences, perhaps in an exaggerated way, a dilemma that confronts many young working class men. The cultural rationales that induced their parents to accept the rigors of blue collar work are less compelling to many of the younger generation and outside of economic necessity, they see few reasons to submit to the discipline of the assembly line.

These youth invert their parents' attitudes toward the basic requirements for a decent life. Instead of finishing school or getting the training for a skilled job, they make it a point of honor not to take work seriously, when they take it at all. Their implicit motto is that it is better to get by than to get ahead, and if one can get by without submitting to the drudgery of the forty hour week, one is a fool not to do so. Although they are, for the most part, disinterested in a criminal career, stealing and dealing dope are viewed as two of the least onerous ways of supporting one's more pleasurable activities. Some of these youth take romantic involvements seriously and others are interested only in casual sexual relations. But none openly acknowledges the fact that relationships with women often lead to a *settled* married life.

Yet, despite all this, they retain many of their parents' political and social attitudes, especially their hostility to Blacks. Their social conservatism is apparent in the way they react to authorities who impinge on their lives (notably the schools and police) and

in the way they respond to contemporary forms of youthful social protest and political idealism.

These young people view the world as a tough place. To survive, one needs an inner hardness. As they see it, one takes the pleasures one can get, avoids as many "hassles" with police, schools and parents as possible, and learns to bear misfortune without exaggerated self pity. Although the subject was rarely discussed, they seem to view the utopian morality of the adherents of communes and radical politics as a way of ignoring the hard facts of life.

Unlike middle class youth, they express little moral outrage when they are the targets of the animus of school administrators or police. And they are always ready to point out that people on welfare are inherently incapable of doing anything to change their situation. At the same time, evidence that minority groups are actively trying to improve their political and economic position elicits negative commentary about people who don't know where they belong. Thus, these young people subscribe to one of the key tenets of their parents' morality: One gets what one deserves in this world and the only way to change things is by your own efforts — no one else is going to do it for you. And, like their parents, they believe in the universal efficacy of "clout": it takes influence and "connections" to get those things that are theoretically available to everyone.

THE DRUG EXPERIENCE

The most remarkable thing about the drug experience of this group is how little the participants have to say about it. This does not mean that getting "stoned" literally "out of one's mind" every night is not an intense experience. Yet the tone of this activity is very sedate. It certainly pales in comparison with the cerebral and orgiastic modes of drug use that are part of the popular conception of the hippie world.

The evening's activities in the basement begin in a low key and move toward total quiescence. People drop by on an informal basis. Only very rarely are arrangements made in advance and members of the group do not keep track of one another's whereabouts. Those present greet each other in a friendly manner but do not inquire about the other person's activities since their last meeting. "What's happening" is a purely formal greeting. Everyone sits down and someone says, "what are we going to do tonight." Then someone jokingly replies, "you know what we are going to do tonight, what we do every night." Someone may look through a newspaper for ads for movies and rock concerts in town, but most of the time they decide it is not worth the effort to go anywhere. Then someone rolls the "joints" or distributes whatever drugs are available. The norm is one of sharing; hoarding drugs is extremely bad manners. "Downers" (barbituates) are currently very popular, and a barbituate "high" (or, more accurately, "low") most closely approximates the state these users want to achieve.

One ritual, however, is important. Whatever else they do, they always listen to rock music. Choosing the records is not taken lightly. Someone will suggest the music he wants to listen

to that evening, and if someone else disagrees, he will say, "That's cool but why don't we listen to . . ." There are never any heated arguments over music.

The way these young people use drugs is quite straightforward. They get "stoned" to the point of physical immobility, a state they describe as "vegetating" or "nodding." It is important to understand that the emotional state they use drugs to achieve is completely inward. Very little talking or joking occurs after they seriously begin to get "high" and they do not stop using drugs until they reach a state of near somnambulence. Passivity and withdrawal from everything except extremely simple and pleasant physical stimuli characterize this drug experience. This mood of inner drift and quietude — a state of pure disassociation from all social and psychological object relations other than those of perception — is sought solely for its own sake. It is not rationalized or explained, nor is it a means to some other end: it creates an aura of pure nothingness.

A number of means, in addition to drugs, are employed to achieve this state. One of their favorite devices is to turn off the television sound and watch the pictures while listening to music. Another is to adjust the dials of a color television so that only electrical lines and colors appear on the screen. One of the group's favorite games is called a "smoke out." In a "smoke out" everyone smokes marijuana or hashish until the "winner" is the only one left who can move or speak. At the end of an evening nearly everyone is "nodding."

From an outsider's perspective being "high" for the members of this group must look like an assiduously cultivated state of ennui. But the situation is just the reverse. They feel bored when they are "straight." For most, not having at least half a "joint" in the morning casts gloom over the day. Some complain about not being "high" as other people might complain about missing breakfast. This desire to constantly recreate an emotional state of total removal from the "hassles" of everyday life becomes apparent in the way they play and the way they handle frustration.

For this group, play connotes an idyllic return to the pleasures of childhood. One plays those games that have no consequential outcome (for example, no gambling) and no competitive overtones (for example, no football). Their favorite games are riding ten speed bicycles through the woods, throwing a frisbee around, and driving around in cars or motorcycles when "high." They also play cards, but not for money, and, in general, studiously avoid all those games that require concentration and sustained effort.

Finally, it is evident in many situations that most members of the group only feel relaxed and at ease with the world when they are "high." And they usually feel tense and "uptight" when a situation demands compliance in a way that allows them little room to maneuver — an argument with parents being the prototypical situation. To take a prosaic but typical example, the record player broke down one evening and everyone was quite upset. Someone immediately suggested that they ought to smoke some more dope so that they would not care whether the record player worked or not.

Conclusion

It is clear that the young people involved in this working class drug subculture will not readily accept the constraints of an ordinary nine to five job. Rather than commit themselves to what they feel are meaningless jobs, they reject the idea that a person must find a place in the occupational system and then try to improve his position in it. In other words, these hippie greasers are alienated from many of traditional working class values that revolve around a steady job and a good income. In our opinion, their disenchantment with the American dream is not part of the pattern of sowing one's wild oats while young and then settling down to raise a family. Their disaffection from their parents' material values is based on a realistic appraisal of what the industrial system has to offer them.

Commentators on the drug scene often seem mesmerized by the counter culture. Gouldner (1970: 78), for example, talks about "psychedelic culture" as one of the ideological spearheads of the new left. In our opinion, these scholars frequently confuse middle class modes of drug use with genuine transformations of political consciousness. In light of this working class drug subculture, it is difficult to see how the use of hallucinogenic drugs alone could create a radical political outlook when the latter is not already part of the cultural background of the user.

In this paper we have seen that at least one group of working class youth dismiss the discipline that constrains those who join the labor force and yet do not question the ideological superstructure that supports the occupational system. Instead, they escape into a realm beyond time and place which is strangely devoid of fantasy. Rather than dreaming about a better world or a more perfect mode of existence, their political and social attitudes remain definitely anti-utopian. Their response to their amorphous position in the "real" world is to "vegetate." They deal with the reality of of having to work at boring jobs by denying it. Of course, they probably will have to get a job, but it is very doubtful whether they will ever be able to justify the kind of work they do in terms of the money they make.

These young people represent only a small segment of the working class population in this country and we do not know to what extent they are like other working class youth who are seriously involved in drug subcultures. Yet there are some signs of change in working class youth cultures. Drugs, as part of a larger subcultural complex, are not without ramifications for the ordinary existence of its devotees. Though the evidence at hand is only suggestive, it appears that conventional working class definitions of appropriate sex roles, which are predicated upon the economic status of men as primary "bread winners," are no longer completely convincing to these young people. Whether this will induce working class participants in the drug subculture to move toward middle class definitions of sex roles is an open ques-

tion, but it is a possibility that bears watching.

Though the hippie greaser is a "dropout" in the eyes of mainstream America, he has not assimilated the hippie world-view (Davis, 1971). Instead of becoming a new satellite in the hippie firmament, the hippie greaser remains a marginal figure in the working class world. He does not justify his anomolous position in a world where a regular job is a measure of a man's worth. Nor does he couple his refusal to work regularly with an implacable hostility to all of those values hippies feel are corrupt. In other words, bourgeois materialism does not bother him but bourgeois morality does. Despite his distaste for the "work ethic," many of his social and political attitudes are consistent with the values that legitimate a highly competitive, achievement-oriented society.

Even though these young people do not oppose an impersonal technocratic society as a matter of principle, their disdain for the work-a-day world is not without ideological supports. The hippie subculture grounds its rejection of the larger society in metaphors of self discovery and self renewal. Here one knows that the larger society is corrupt because one has encountered another realm of being that regenerates profound human values. As we have seen, the participants in this working class drug subculture are not given to talking about the inner meaning of their drug experiences, let alone searching for ultimate values. Nevertheless, they are quite attentive to those aspects pects of popular culture that undermine the legitimacy of standard moral virtues (for example, punctuality, honesty, and so forth) and tacitly counsel people not to take anything at face value. In this respect, these working class youth subscribe to the credo of the youth culture: that one only fully experiences those things that truly matter within the confines of an age graded world — those symbols that articulate the central meanings of one's experience can only be fully shared with peers.

A glance at the favorite reading matter of hippie greasers locates what is perhaps the primary source of their resistance to conventional interpretations of the realities of American life. Magazines like *Mad* and the *National Lampoon* dwell on what the editors apparently feel is the absurdity of American culture. Venality and willful stupidity are the driving forces of a world in which just about everyone takes the inanities of advertising at face value. Here political leaders, celebrities and ordinary people speak a cliché-ridden language that ineffectively masks their insane lust for power, money, and so forth. Public morality is nothing more than a handy set of self-serving platitudes useful to those who need to rationalize their meaningless lives or irrational behavior. Violence and deception are so endemic that no one notices the most outrageous acts of cruelty.

The deliberate perversity of more arcane literature such as *Bent* comics seems designed to destroy the last vestiges of sexual hypocrisy and romantic sentimentality in this society. Yet these magazines carry what they see as a pervasive violent streak in the American character to the logical extreme. Ordinary sociability is no longer the arena for the "polite" forms of status aggrandizement one sees in *Mad* and kindred magazines. Instead sexuality becomes the master metaphor for the rapacious, sadistic impulses that underlie the competitive surface of American life. Here sexuality is so fused with unrestrained aggression that relations between people are depicted as a war of body parts (principally genitalia) disassociated from any image of human beings as persons.

All of these satirical publications are fascinated with, as well as revulsed by, the trivialities of American popular culture. Yet, despite their ironic tone, these magazines do not offer their readers any alternative to a world populated by cartoon characters. This vision of the ridiculous underside of social reality definitely strikes a responsive chord among hippie greasers. But while this attitude is consonant with their native skepticsim about the motives of those who speak in behalf of public morality, it has not moved them toward the ideological posture of the counter culture.

REFERENCES

Davis, F. *On Youth Subcultures: The Hippie Variant*. New York: General Learning, 1971.
——— "Heads and freaks: patterns and meanings of drug use among hippies" (with L. Munoz). *J. of Health and Social Behavior* 9 (1968): 156–164.
Gouldner, A. *The Coming Crisis of Western Sociology*. New York: Basic Books, 1970.

Simon, W. et al. "Son of Joe: continuity and change among white working-class adolescents." *J. of Youth and Adolescence* 1 (1971): 13–34.

Schwartz, G. *Youth Culture: An Anthropological Approach.* Reading, Mass.: Addison-Wesley, 1972.

———— and D. Merten "Social identity and expressive symbols: the meaning of an initiation ritual." *Amer. Anthropologist* 70 (1968): 1117–1131.

———— "The language of adolescence." *Amer. J. of Sociology* 72 (1967): 453–468.

Skid row areas are gradually disappearing within the United States. For example, the winter population of the Bowery, in New York City, was estimated at about 7,000 people in 1963. By 1971 this figure was expected to drop to about 3,000.* Reasons for the decline include greater economic prosperity and changing welfare policies that "induce men to live elsewhere".†

James Spradley and others‡ have noted that, although inhabitants of skid row are homeless, they are not without a sense of community. Like other deviant groups, they have an argot and unique values, most of which center around the central life interest of obtaining and consuming alcohol or its equivalents.§ Earl Rubington has noted the tacit set of norms centering around group alcohol consumption on skid row. Norms specify the number of "swigs" each person takes before passing the bottle, what people say to each other while drinking, and rules for disposing of the empty.‖ James Spradley, an anthropologist, notes in the following essay that a crucial aspect of skid row life style focuses on obtaining alcohol. This life style shows a greater sense of resourcefulness and a higher degree of social organization than would be expected from the popular stereotype of tramps.

* Howard M. Bahr, "The Gradual Disappearance of Skid Row," *Social Problems,* 15 (1967), pp. 41–45.

† Ibid., p. 43.

‡ Spradley, op. cit.; Samuel Wallace, *Skid Row as a Way of Life* (Totowa, N.J.: Bedminister Press, 1965); Earl Rubington, "Variations in Bottle-Gang Controls," in Earl Rubington and Martin Weinberg (eds.), *Deviance: The Interactionist Perspective* (New York: Macmillan, 1968), pp. 308–316.

§ Samuel Wallace has noted, "To be fully integrated and acculturated on Skid Row is to be a drunk...." Samuel Wallace, "The Road to Skid Row," *Social Problems,* 16 (1968), pp. 92–105.

‖ Rubington, op. cit., p. 311. Rubington studied an Eastern city of about 165,000. He also notes that "bottle-gang" norms on the East Coast differ from those in other regions.

Down and Out
on Skid Road

James P. Spradley

He moves slowly down the street, and everything about him announces to the world that he is down and out. Ill-fitting clothes cover a hollow chest and sagging muscles. The lines in his face, half hidden beneath the shadow of a faded hat, suggest that he is old before his time. His shoes are cracked with age and exposure to the weather. An overcoat, pocket bulging from a half-empty bottle, covers a sports jacket which long ago found its way to the secondhand clothing store. His course is unsteady, his face unshaven, and those who pass him by are assaulted by the odor of cheap wine. An outstretched hand with a few coins is thrust toward the affluent who have entered his world that morning from a distant suburb. Who is this man? A bum to be pitied? A vagrant to be jailed? A homeless man to be rehabilitated? An alcoholic in need of medical treatment? He must be down on his luck and out of resources — one who can no longer organize his behavior or achieve goals. He is adrift at the bottom of society, cut off from a life style ordered by cultural rules. In the minds of many he is even beneath the tribal

From Saul D. Feldman and Gerald W. Thielbar (eds.), *Life Styles: Diversity in American Society,* pp. 340-350. Reprinted by permission of Little, Brown and Company (Inc.).

savage whose way of life may be different, but not derelict. But let us look more closely at this man and the thousands like him who live in every large American city.

Anthropologists have long emphasized the importance of discovering the native point of view for their descriptions of non-Western cultures. This simple but difficult perspective is even more important in the study of urban subcultures. Recent developments in anthropology, known as ethnoscience, have proved especially useful for discovering the way insiders conceptualize their own life style. The goal of ethnoscience is to discover the characteristic ways in which members of a subculture categorize, code, and define their experiences. In every society "reality" is socially constructed, and this definition of the situation is used by individuals to organize their behavior. Those who live by other cultures do not identify their religion as "pagan superstition," their parents' brothers as "uncles," nor do they divide the rainbow into seven distinct colors. In a similar manner we shall misconstrue the culture of Skid Road men unless we enter their world and see life from their point of view. An understanding of those with different life styles must begin with a description of the cognitive maps they employ in everyday life.

In order to tap the cognitive and symbolic world of the down-and-outers, it was necessary to study their language. Although language does not exhaust the system of symbols for a particular culture, it certainly involves a central portion of it. In the study of a non-western society, the researcher is forced to learn their language before he can make headway in his studies. At first this did not appear to be the case with the population on Skid Road. The informants I encountered spoke a dialect of English which was similar to my own in both sound and grammar. After several months of participant observation and listening, however, I discovered that the semantic aspect of their language was very different. The questions which were relevant to informants had not been anticipated. The terms which they used to categorize and identify the objects in their environment would not have been included on a pretested survey questionnaire. It soon became clear that these men could only be considered "down and out" by those who did not not understand their perspective. Their behavior became comprehensible in terms of the meaning systems which they had learned and were using to order their daily activties. After a brief description of the major features in this culture, we shall examine one set of strategies used to achieve the goals which these men consider appropriate.

THE CULTURE OF TRAMPS

There are five major scenes where these men carry out their activities: buckets (jails), farms (treatment centers), jungles (encampments), skids (Skid Roads), and freights (railroad cars). The most important identity which a man has in all of these scenes is referred to as "tramp." There were more than fifteen different kinds of tramps recognized by informants. For example, a "box-car tramp" is an in-dependent person who is arrested often and travels by means of freight trains. A "bindle stiff" is a tramp who travels on freight cars but always carries a bed-roll and a few personal belongings. A "mission stiff" travels from mission to mission, drawing upon their resources for his needs. A semantic analysis of the terms for various tramps led to the discovery that the criteria for distinguishing among tramps were mobility-related. This reflects the importance of the nomadic style of life which tramps follow. This category system constitutes only one of the social-identity domains in this subculture.

When a man is arrested and placed in jail, usually on the charge of public intoxication, he assumes the identity of inmate. There are five major kinds of inmates which a man may become, the most important of which is *trusty*. In the particular jail studied there were over sixty different kinds of trusties. In this capacity nearly 150 men provided janitorial services for the city hall, outlying police precincts, and the jail. They assisted in the preparation of food, maintained the firing range, cared for police vehicles, and did numerous other tasks. Many tramps felt they were arrested and charged with public drunkenness, not because they were inebriated, but in order to provide cheap labor for the police department.

In each of the major scenes in this subculture there are specialized modes of action for solving common problems. For example, when a man is in jail, he discovers that his freedom is restricted and he often lacks food, cigarettes, and clothing. One solution to these problems is to engage in actions which tramps refer to as "hustling." This is a cover term for a large number of specific actions or plans which tramps group into the following equivalent classes: "conning," "peddling," "kissing ass," "making a run," "taking a rake-off," "playing cards," "bumming," "running a game," "making a pay-off," "beating," and "making a phone call." A knowledge of the different ways to "hustle" can mean the difference between doing "hard time" and "easy time." One younger tramp who was a college graduate gave the following description of hustling:

> *Speaking of survival in jail, there are various ways, of course. If you come in with some money, of course you have commissary twice a week. That way you can get eight packages of cigarettes and eight candy bars, toothbrush, toothpaste, that's about the limit of what you can buy, and of course postage stamps. If you do not have commissary you have to find other means if you wish to have more than two packs of Bull Durham a week. In any case you are shaking for the first few days from nothing more than malnutrition, and so one asks the doctors who come around twice a day, you might ask him for some librium or some phenobarbital to quiet you, or whatever you might be able to get from him, cold pills even (conning), but the wise drunk who has no money at all will just go through the whole thing cold turkey, suffer though he will, he'll save his pills and trade two quarter-grain phenobarbital for a package of Bull Durham or 1.25 mg. librium for a pack of Bull Durham (peddling). Some of them will even do push-ups or something like that before the doctor comes, just to be shaking and sweating (conning). But in gen-*

> *eral, within a very short time, 4–5 days, you're shut off completely from any of that. So then you have to find another way. By that time you've eaten enough so you're in pretty good balance and then you can make sandwiches. Sometimes you get a tray at night, which is your big meal, and you can barely make a sandwich out of it using the whole tray. But in any case you can trade them for a package of Bull Durham if that's what you need. Of course the ideal thing, if you are going to be sentenced, is to become a trusty if possible.*

It might be necessary to "make a pay-off" in order to become a trusty, but once in this position a man has many more opportunities to hustle.

When a tramp is out of jail, he usually refers to goals in a specific manner, and the techniques used to attain the goal will be classified as "ways of making it." In contrast to the view that these men are "down and out," they have numerous resources in the form of survival strategies which are compatible with a life style of mobility. These "ways of making it" are employed in the pursuit of many objectives, including the following: "I'm trying to make a flop," "I need something to eat," "I pled guilty in order not to do dead time," and "Let's make the mission for some clothes."

An important activity for most tramps is the drinking of alcoholic beverages. In part, this drinking has great social significance and binds together men with spoiled identities. Many men spend months at a time in jail, and when released they feel they owe themselves a drunk. Others drink to solve personal problems, and many admit they do not know why they drink.

Whatever the reason, one of the recurring goals in this culture is the acquisition of some alcoholic beverage, conceptualized by tramps as "making a jug." In the remainder of this paper, we shall examine the cultural techniques used by men who are "down and out" to achieve this goal.

WAYS TO MAKE A JUG

Every language functions to identify objects, events, and actions which are part of experience. Linguistic labels allow man to treat his experience symbolically. This involves continuous categorization, cognitive acts whereby different things are treated as equivalent. Thus, a group of individuals on a college campus, all of whom are unique, are treated as equivalent and labeled "students." A student engages in different activities which are identified as "studying." A knowledge of different "ways to study" is of great value to the student for organizing his behavior and achieving certain academic objectives. Whether one is a student or a tramp, the use of categories and linguistic labels is necessary if we are to simplify and organize our experience.

It may not seem very significant to have discovered that tramps identify their actions for obtaining alcoholic beverages as "ways to make a jug." But many other questions could be asked which would not lead to the exhaustive mapping of the cognitive world of informants. For example, it would have been possible — indeed, numerous researchers have done so — to ask these men about their income, type of employment, and where they live. On the basis of what was *significant to informants* the following question was used: "Are there different ways to make a jug?" The various techniques elicited by this question make up the following taxonomy of ways to make a jug.

Ways to Make a Jug

1. Making the blood bank
2. Bumming
   a. Panhandling (stemming)
   b. Making a 'Frisco Circle
   c. Bumming
3. Stealing
   a. Boosting
   b. Rolling
      (1) Rolling
      (2) Jackrolling
   c. Beating
   d. Clipping
4. Peddling
5. Taking a rake-off
6. Pooling
7. Cutting in on a jug
8. Borrowing
9. Buying
10. Making your own
    a. Making pruno
    b. Making raisin jack
    c. Making sweet lucy
    d. Squeezing heat
    e. Squeezing shoe polish
    f. Making home brew
    g. Straining shellac
    h. Mixing bay rum
    i. Mixing solax
    j. Mixing shaving lotion
    k. Mixing ruby-dub
    l. Mixing gasoline
11. Meeting a live one
12. Hustling a queer
13. Hustling a broad

14. Making a run
15. Spot jobbing
16. Making the mission
17. Making the V.A.
18. Junking

These ways to get an alcoholic beverage provide an exhaustive mapping of the strategies which tramps learn in their culture for meeting this particular need. Let us consider several ways to make a jug in more detail, for they clearly demonstrate the skill and resourcefulness which are present in this culture.

"Making the blood bank" is a common way to make a jug. In response to this behavior, there are blood banks in the Skid Road districts of many cities. One informant described this strategy:

Well, in my case I have too much blood and I'm a regular blood donor, but on the average a guy will make the blood bank for money to buy a bottle. Fifty percent of the guys that sells blood does it for a bottle. They give you about $5 a time. Whole blood you can only sell once every eight weeks unless you know how to lie and get by. Plasma you can sell from two to three times a week. I'll be drinking with a group and some guy will say, "You gonna make the blood bank today?" Or, "When's your day at the blood bank?" They're open from 7 til 5, but you got to be in there by three in the afternoon or you're out. See, if you went into the blood bank in the morning or any time during the day and you didn't have an appointment, you have to wait. You could go in there at seven in the morning and wait two or three hours. I come in and go right up there because I have an appointment. It only

takes fifteen minutes or a half hour at the most to give whole blood, it all depends on the person. For plasma it will take from an hour to two hours, and if you're in a hurry or got something to do, you want to give whole blood. A lot of guys might not be able to give plasma when they could give whole blood, because if you lay on the table for an hour or two hours, you might fall asleep or pass out where you're not supposed to.

Actually, they ain't supposed to take your blood if you're too sick or drinking, but at some places where you walk into and your blood pressure is high or low or your temperature isn't right, maybe you haven't slept good, or maybe you ain't eating right, or maybe you've climbed a hill too fast on the way there, there are different reasons why your pressure may be up anyway, if you take a shot of wine it will make you normal, it calms your nerves. The doctors tell you it isn't so, but I know it works. That's why a lot of tramps will take one or two shots of wine before going to give blood. If you've been drinking for a time and have the shakes, the girls at the blood bank will see you're shaking and nervous and so you can't give blood. But if they know you and see you got the shakes and need a drink, they'll sometimes say, "Well, here's 75¢, go down and get yourself a bottle and drink it and then come back." They get to know you after a while, and if they give you money to get a drink first, they just take it out of the $5 you get from your blood later. That's a good way to make a jug.

Another strategy frequently employed by tramps is "bumming." There are many specific acts involved in bumming, but tramps classify them as panhandling, making a 'Frisco Circle, and bumming. Some tramps become very skilled in these activities, and may even become "professional panhandlers," a kind of tramp known to some as a "ding." One informant reported:

> Bob and I went stemming in Chinatown yesterday. While he was stemming the street corners, I would be bumming the bars. You are stemming strictly for money. Panhandling is the same as stemming. You are always on the streets, and the best place is where there are a lot of tourists. Now you can be bumming anyplace, you can go to a grocery store or a business place or some church, on on the street or even a bar, you could be anyplace. You could be bumming for clothes, or groceries, or money, or drinks; but if you're panhandling, you're doing it strictly for money. Before you start bumming you have to have a drink to get your courage up, some guys cannot stem unless they do have a drink, they just haven't got the nerve.

Another informant reported the strategies which he used to induce a man on the street to give him some money to buy something to drink.

> Most generally you hit for the right tourists, you start bummin' where there's a lot of tourists, or you get downtown where the business person is. If I want a bottle, if I'm bummin' for a drink, I'll tell a man I'm sick and need a drink, or I'm short on a bottle, and nine times out of ten I'll get it. But if I tell a person I'm hungry and want something to eat, or wanted a place to sleep, nine times out of ten he'd turn me down, he wouldn't give it to me. You gotta use psychology, now like a good professional panhandler will go around in ragged clothes, some

> of them are misers and some of them bum all the time. Now an ordinary panhandler, just an ordinary guy bummin', he's just gonna get his drink and go get drunk. He might get more than he needs right at that one time, but he won't keep on. The other guy will keep on. I don't mind askin' others, a working man or something, I try to pick somebody who looks like he has a little something and can afford to share a little bit.

"Making a 'Frisco Circle" is a unique kind of bumming where one tramp stands in a bar or on the street and with a piece of chalk draws a circle on the ground or on the floor. He then asks others to toss into the 'Frisco Circle, or to "help out the circle." When there is sufficient money, those who contributed will share a drink together.

Since begging is against the law in many states, there is some degree of risk involved in bumming. One man reported his strategy for circumventing this risk or reducing it.

> It's getting to where it's generally two that prefers to panhandle. I'm walking down the street, I'm gonna stop those people and bum, and I got another guy on the other side of the street, or behind me a ways, and if he sees a cop or the fuzz, plain-clothes ragpicker, why he's gonna high-sign me and let me know — because I got my mind on you and the public, and I'm not exactly watching for the law.

The risk of arrest is not always as easily avoided. Consider the experience of another tramp:

> A ragpicker would see you with change and ask you, "Are you short?" and I'd say, "Yeah, fifteen cents, can you spare

*it?" and he would say, "Yes," give you
fifteen cents and then show you his
badge and get you for bumming, or
stemming.*

There are a variety of laws which a
tramp can violate and end up in jail.
Bumming and stealing are only two of
them. In addition, a man may be arrested for being drunk in public,
drinking in public, urinating in public,
and for purchasing liquor during days
or hours when its sale is illegal. This
latter case sometimes involves the ragpickers, as one man pointed out:

*You know, one sorry deal is those rag-
pickers. That's a sorry-ass goddam
deal, those ragpickers picking these
tramps up. They'll come down there
dressed like a tramp and come up and
say, "Hey, you know where I can get a
bottle?" and you show him where he
can get a bottle, maybe the guy's trying
to make him some money or something.
I don't give a damn, if I want a drink
and I have to pay out a little more I'll
pay it, but they'll come down and get
you to do something and know that it's
wrong and turn around and arrest your
ass. He gives you the loot to buy the
bottle and you buy the bottle and he'll
throw your ass in jail.*

Tramps survive in part by "stealing." In their culture this involves a
variety of acts which are classified into
different categories. "Rolling" almost
always involves theft from an individual who has passed out from too much
alcohol or who must be overcome by
the use of force. "Beating" involves
stealing from a person or institution. A
man in jail will beat another man for
his money. For example, a drunk in
the drunk tank will ask a trusty to
bring him a package of cigarettes and

give him $5, expecting change. The
trusty may take the money and never
return, thus beating the drunk for his
money, which he will use to purchase
a bottle upon release. "Clipping" is
stealing by stealth. In a bar when one
has placed money on the table, a
tramp might clip him for it without his
awareness.

"Boosting" almost always involves
stealing articles which can then be
sold or "peddled" from stores or other
business establishments. One informant reported:

*Boosting out of a parked car or boost-
ing out of a store, a lot of them call the
store "shoplifting" instead of "boosting," but both would be the same thing.
Like Sears and Roebucks, that's one of
their main places where guys shoplift
and boost. I got a buddy, and the only
thing he would boost is measuring
tapes. He would get a pocket full of
them, they're three- or four-dollar
tapes, and come down and get his wine
and come back. Some of them tramps
go in for tools or most anything you
can put in your pocket or shirt. Like a
good booster, he can steal T.V.'s or
radios or anything else, he'll walk into
a store, most generally there's two guys
or a guy and a woman; one will be
buying something and keep the clerk
busy, and the other will pick up something and walk off with it.*

Tramps find little difficulty in peddling
on the street those things which they
have boosted. In fact, tools, transistor
radios, shirts and other clothing are all
items which can be sold fast on the
street. One informant reported:

*The main thing is getting what you
know you can sell and get rid of fast,
and if you're selling them fast on a*

streetcorner, like clothes or tools, why then most generally there's two of you and one keeps their eye out for the fuzz, while the other one is talking, or if you go into a bar, it's the same thing. Wrist watches and pocket watches is another thing that you boost because they are easy to sell, particularly in a bar or on a streetcorner. You will get more money selling them in a bar or on the street than you will if you take it into a hock shop, and there ain't as much risk.

The risk involved in peddling makes some men shy away from it. Even when there is no evidence that the item was stolen, it is possible to get arrested. One man reported:

On April 3, 1968, I was in a hock shop on First and Pike trying to pawn my radio. When I came out I met a cop and he said I stole the radio but he could not prove it. So he booked me as drunk in the city jail.

Some tramps are future-oriented and when they do have money from working in the harvest, or at a spot job, they will purchase items which can be peddled at some later date. One man summarized this practice:

Well, most generally, like a fruit tramp, when they get paid they will buy a pile of expensive stuff, knowing that sooner or later they will go broke and they will always have something that they can take and hock, or peddle to get ready cash for it. They'll go in for expensive rings or wrist watches to do this.

The strategies which a tramp uses are not the impulses of a derelict. Indeed, each way to make a jug requires the processing of a great deal of information. The man who is bumming must learn effective approaches, evaluate people that he would beg from, and be on the alert for the police. The individual who makes the blood bank must keep track of when he was there last and how well those in the blood bank know him. He must be aware of his own physical condition in case he has to use subterfuge in order to sell his blood. Stealing of one sort or another involves careful calculations regarding other people and the chances of selling the item boosted. As a man begins a day in pursuit of a jug of wine, this map is especially useful for achieving his goal.

Many of the strategies for making a jug involve cooperation with other tramps. One of the myths that has grown up about Skid Road men, "the down-and-outers," is that they are friendless, isolated and alone. This study revealed that many of the ways to make a jug involve cooperative action with other men. Panhandling will often be done in pairs, as well as stealing and peddling, in order to reduce the risk of arrest. Both "pooling" and "cutting in on a jug" involve a group of men who are usually willing to share with other men who are looking for some alcohol. In fact, the question is raised as to whether drinking is the prime need one feels when he pools or cuts in on a jug. It may well be that one is seeking human companionship among other men, who, like himself, have been stigmatizd by the larger society.

"Meeting a live one" also involves other people and shows the bonds that exist between tramps as well as the generosity of this culture. A live one is defined by these men as anyone who will purchase a drink for you or give you a larger amount of money than the usual person on the street. A tramp walking down the street may have someone come up to him and say, "I'll buy you a drink." This is usually someone who just seeks to talk. Tramps often become "live ones" to other tramps, and when they have money they share it. One man reported the following experience:

> *He came out of Firland's (T.B. sanitarium) and he came down there drunk. Well, he pieced me off and he pieced Charlies off. He had four hundred bucks, he had three one-hundred-dollar bills. He took us up to the Morrison Hotel and paid for our dinner and all that and he bought us a jug. Then he went out and got racked up and you know, he wakes up in the morning and he's got twenty dollars in his property box in the jail.*

Another man who had returned from the harvest related his experience of being a live one:

> *I was over picking apples in the apple harvest and I stayed over after the harvest was done and worked on and they gave me a bonus. And I came to Seattle and had $299. I bought a bus ticket for $5 and came to Seattle. When I got to Seattle everyone was getting off the bus and there was a big crowd and they were headed in to get their luggage and I wanted a drink pretty bad, so I didn't even pick up my suitcase. I had gotten some new clothes and I headed right downtown to the Pike Street area where there's a liquor store that closes kind of early. I got myself a room and paid for two nights, got a bottle of Jim Beam and got a chaser and was headed back to my room when I met a fellow, an Indian boy, who I had known. We'd*

> *been in the same little shack where we lived, and he and I talked and he'd lost all his money, spent it and lost it in some way. So I gave him some money and bought him a room and we got something to eat. And I'd had a couple drinks by then but I wasn't blacking out or even staggering or anything like that, I knew what I was doing. I got picked up by the police coming out of the restaurant.*

Many tramps have learned to make their own in one way or another. This may be done in order to have a large supply, or because they do not have money or resources to get a bottle that has been made commercially. One man reported:

> *I know guys who drink nothing but beer, but if you've been on a drunk it's just like pop or water. Some drink nothing but apple wine. That generally makes me sick, and before I'd take apple wine, I'd rather make my own jug — sterno, bay rum, ruby-dub, or something else. If you get the sterno or canned heat in a red can it's o.k., but the one in the gray wrapper is poison. You squeeze the canned heat through a handkerchief, sock, or even an old rag to get out the alcohol. One big can of sterno makes a fifth of a pretty good drink after you cut it with water or coke. You can also mix bay rum and water, rubbing alcohol and orange juice, shaving lotion and water, or so-lax and coke. There are tramps who will go to the filling station after it closes and get the drips of gasoline which are left in the hose and mix it with sweet milk to make a jug. Others will strain shellac or shoe polish through a loaf of bread to get the impurities out and mix what's left with something for a drink.*

It takes a good deal of knowledge and care to mix your own, and just as much to make pruno, raisin jack, or sweet lucy. One man described his recipe as follows:

> *For raisin jack you take two pounds of raisins, seven pounds of sugar, one cake of yeast, and put it in a large plastic bucket. You can use a glass bottle, but a can or a pan is liable to give you ptomaine poisoning. You put warm water in with all the stuff and let it sit for 72 hours. When it's done you get about nine gallons of raisin jack that's 14–20% alcohol. A guy on the road usually won't make pruno, but take a couple guys who are staying in town or living in a jungle, they can make out pretty well making their own that way.*

Conclusion

In this paper we have discussed life styles of men on Skid Road — but it is important to point out that this description is not based on observation. Instead, using the techniques of ethnoscience, I attempted to elicit their perception of their own behavior. Every culture provides its members with cognitive maps which they use to organize their behavior — plans which are carried out in the achievement of goals. Individuals who are socialized into the culture of the tramps not only learn new identities, but also new patterns of behavior. One of these is to "make a jug," an activity learned as the value and importance of alcohol becomes significant in the lives of these men. They then learn systematic ways to achieve this goal along with the others that are important in this culture. They may appear "down and out on Skid Road" from the perspective of outsiders. In the experience of tramps there are many resources available — strategies which are especially appropriate to a nomadic style of life where drinking has enormous personal and social value.

Notes

The research for this paper was carried out from July 1967 to August 1968 in Seattle, Washington. This study was partially supported by the Departments of Psychiatry and Anthropology, University of Washington; U.S. Public Health Service Undergraduate Training in Human Behavior Grant, No. 5-T2-MH-7871-06 from the Institute of Mental Health; and the State of Washington Initiative 171 Funds for Research in Biology and Medicine.

The term "Skid Road" is used here in preference to "Skid Row" which appears in much literature. Skid Road is a term which originated in Seattle to describe the road down which logs were skidded to the sawmill and where bars, flophouses, and gambling houses were prevalent. The name often became Skid Row as it was adopted throughout the country, but in Seattle it remains Skid Road.

A more complete discussion of the methods used in this research as well as an analysis of other aspects of this culture appears in *You Owe Yourself a Drunk: An Ethnography of Urban Nomads* by the author (Little, Brown and Company, Boston, 1970).

Erving Goffman* has suggested that a common human trait is a desire for excitement. Adults can find their action fairly easily at the race track, Las Vegas, or some other legal enterprise that capitalizes on this desire for action. Most of these enterprises are closed to those under a certain age, but younger people too have a desire for excitement. One avenue left open to them is the commission of delinquent acts. Matza and Sykes question the divergence of values between delinquents and the public at large. Delinquent behavior may be an expression of an action orientation, and the values that delinquents hold and express may, in essence, be the values of society.

* Erving Goffman, *Interaction Ritual* (Garden City, N.Y.: Doubleday Anchor, 1967), pp. 144–270.

Juvenile Delinquency and Subterranean Values

David Matza and
Gresham M. Sykes

Current explanations of juvenile delinquency can be divided roughly into two major types. On the one hand, juvenile delinquency is seen as a product of personality disturbances or emotional conflicts within the individual; on the other hand, delinquency is viewed as a result of relatively normal personalities exposed to a "disturbed" social environment — particularly in the form of a deviant sub-culture in which the individual learns to be delinquent as others learn to conform to the law. The theoretical conflict between these two positions has been intensified, unfortunately, by the fact that professional pride sometimes leads psychologists and sociologists to define the issue as a conflict between disciplines and to rally behind their respective academic banners.

Despite many disagreements between these two points of view, one assumption is apt to elicit common support. The delinquent, it is asserted, is deviant; not only does his behavior run counter to the law but his underlying norms, attitudes, and values also stand opposed to those of the dominant social order. And the dominant social order, more often than not, turns out to be the world of the middle class.

We have suggested in a previous article that this image of delinquents and the larger society as antagonists

From *American Sociological Review*, vol. 26 (October, 1961), pp. 712–719. Reprinted by permission of the American Sociological Association and the authors.

can be misleading.[1] Many delinquents, we argued, are essentially in agreement with the larger society, at least with regard to the evaluation of delinquent behavior as "wrong." Rather than standing in opposition to conventional ideas of good conduct, the delinquent is likely to adhere to the dominant norms in belief but render them ineffective in practice by holding various attitudes and perceptions which serve to neutralize the norms as checks on behavior. "Techniques of neutralization," such as the denial of responsibility or the definition of injury as rightful revenge, free the individual from a large measure of social control.

This approach to delinquency centers its attention on how an impetus to engage in delinquent behavior is translated into action. But it leaves unanswered a serious question: What makes delinquency attractive in the first place? Even if it is granted that techniques of neutralization or some similar evasions of social controls pave the way for overt delinquency, there remains the problem of the values or ends underlying delinquency and the relationship of these values to those of the larger society. Briefly stated, this paper argues that (a) the values behind much juvenile delinquency are far less deviant than they are commonly portrayed; and (b) the faulty picture is due to a gross oversimplification of the middle-class value system.

[1] Gresham M. Sykes and David Matza, "Techniques of Neutralization," *American Sociological Review,* 22 (December, 1957), pp. 664–670.

THE VALUES OF DELINQUENCY

There are many perceptive accounts describing the behavior of juvenile delinquents and their underlying values, using methods ranging from participant observation to projective tests.[2] Although there are some important differences of opinion in the interpretation of this material, there exists a

[2] Frederick M. Thrasher, *The Gang* (Chicago: University of Chicago Press, 1936); Clifford R. Shaw and Maurice E. Moore, *The Natural History of a Delinquent Career* (Chicago: University of Chicago Press, 1931); Albert K. Cohen, *Delinquent Boys: The Culture of the Gang* (Glencoe, Ill.: The Free Press, 1955); Albert K. Cohen and James F. Short, "Research in Delinquent Subcultures," *Journal of Social Issues,* 14 (1958), pp. 20–37; Walter B. Miller, "Lower Class Culture as a Generating Milieu of Gang Delinquents," *Journal of Social Issues,* 14 (1958), pp. 5–19; Harold Finestone, "Cats, Kicks, and Color," *Social Problems,* 5 (July, 1957), pp. 3–13; Solomon Kobrin, "The Conflict of Values in Delinquent Areas," *American Sociological Review,* 16 (October, 1951), pp. 653–661; Richard Cloward and Lloyd Ohlin, "New Perspectives on Juvenile Delinquency" (unpublished manuscript); Dale Kramer and Madeline Karr, *Teen-Age Gangs* (New York: Henry Holt, 1953); Stacey V. Jones, "The Cougars — Life with a Delinquent Gang," *Harper Magazine* (November, 1954); Harrison E. Salisbury, *The Shook-Up Generation* (New York: Harper and Brothers, 1958); William C. Kvaraceus and Walter M. Miller (eds.), *Delinquent Behavior: Culture and the Individual,* National Education Association of the United States, 1959; Herbert A. Bloch and Arthur Neiderhoffer, *The Gang* (New York: Philosophical Library, 1958); Beatrice Griffith, *American Men* (Boston: Houghton Mifflin, 1948); Sheldon Glueck and Eleanor Glueck, *Unraveling Juvenile Delinquency* (New York: Commonwealth Fund, 1950).

striking consensus on actual substance. Many divisions and sub-divisions are possible, of course, in classifying these behavior patterns and the values on which they are based, but three major themes emerge with marked regularity.

First, many observers have noted that delinquents are deeply immersed in a restless search for excitement, "thrills," or "kicks." The approved style of life, for many delinquents, is an adventurous one. Activities pervaded by displays of daring and charged with danger are highly valued in comparison with more mundane and routine patterns of behavior. This search for excitement is not easily satisfied in legitimate outlets such as organized recreation, as Tappan has indicated. The fact that an activity involves breaking the law is precisely the fact that often infuses it with an air of excitement.[3] In fact, excitement or "kicks" may come to be defined with clear awareness as "any act tabooed by 'squares' that heightens and intensifies the present moment of experience and differentiates it as much as possible from the humdrum routines of daily life."[4] But, in any event, the delinquent way of life is frequently a way of life shot through with adventurous exploits that are valued for the stimulation they provide.

It should be noted that in courting physical danger, experimenting with the forbidden, provoking the authori-

ties, and so on, the delinquent is not simply enduring hazards; he is also creating hazards in a deliberate attempt to manufacture excitement. As Miller has noted, for example, in his study of Roxbury, for many delinquents "the rhythm of life fluctuates between periods of relatively routine and repetitive activities and sought situations of greater emotional stimulation."[5] The excitement, then, that flows from gang rumbles, games of "chicken" played with cars, or the use of drugs is not merely an incidental by-product but may instead serve as a major motivating force.

Second, juvenile delinquents commonly exhibit a disdain for "getting on" in the realm of work. Occupational goals involving a steady job or careful advancement are apt to be lacking, and in their place we find a sort of aimless drifting or grandiose dreams of quick success. Now it takes a very deep faith in the maxims of Benjamin Franklin — or a certain naiveté, perhaps — to believe that hard work at the lower ranges of the occupational hierarchy is a sure path to worldly achievement. The delinquent is typically described as choosing another course, rationally or irrationally. Chicanery or manipulation, which may take the form of borrowing from social workers or more elaborate modes of "hustling"; an emphasis on "pull," frequently with reference to obtaining a soft job which is assumed to be available only to those with influential connections: all are seen as methods of exploiting the social environment without drudgery, and are accorded a

[3] Paul Tappan, *Juvenile Delinquency* (New York: McGraw-Hill, 1949), pp. 148-154.

[4] Finestone, op. cit.

[5] Miller, op. cit.

high value. Simple expropriation should be included, of course, in the form of theft, robbery, and the rest; but it is only one of a variety of ways of "scoring" and does not necessarily carry great prestige in the eyes of the delinquent. In fact, there is some evidence that, among certain delinquents, theft and robbery may actually be looked down upon as pointing to a lack of wit or skill. A life of ease based on pimping or the numbers game may be held out as a far more admirable goal.[6] In any event, the delinquent is frequently convinced that only suckers work and he avoids, if he can, the regimen of the factory, store, and office.

Some writers have coupled the delinquent's disdain of work with a disdain of money. Much delinquent activity, it is said, is non-utilitarian in character and the delinquent disavows the material aspirations of the larger society, thus protecting himself against inevitable frustration. Now it is true that the delinquent's attacks against property are often a form of play, as Cohen has pointed out, rather than a means to a material end.[7] It is also true that the delinquent often shows little liking for the slow accumulation of financial resources. Yet rather than saying that the delinquent disdains money, it would seem more accurate to say that the delinquent is deeply and constantly concerned with the problem of money in his own way. The delinquent wants money, probably no less than the lawabiding, but not for the purposes of a careful series of expenditures or some long-range objective. Rather, money is frequently desired as something to be squandered in gestures of largesse, in patterns of conspicuous consumption. The sudden acquisition of large sums of money is his goal — the "big score" — and he will employ legal means if possible and illegal means if necessary. Since legal means are likely to be thought of as ineffective, it is far from accidental that "smartness" is such an important feature of the delinquent's view of life: "Smartness involves the capacity to outsmart, outfox, outwit, dupe . . ." [8]

A third theme running through accounts of juvenile delinquency centers on aggression. This theme is most likely to be selected as pointing to the delinquent's alienation from the larger society. Verbal and physical assaults are a commonplace, and frequent reference is made to the delinquent's basic hostility, his hatred, and his urge to injure and destroy.

The delinquent's readiness for aggression is particularly emphasized in the analysis of juvenile gangs found in the slum areas of large cities. In such gangs we find the struggles for "turf," the beatings, and the violent feuds which form such distinctive elements in the portrayal of delinquency. As Cloward and Ohlin have pointed out, we can be led into error by viewing these gang delinquents as typical of all delinquents.[9] And Bloch and Niederhoffer have indicated that many current notions of the delinquent gang are quite worn out and require reap-

[6] Finestone, op. cit.
[7] Cohen, op. cit.

[8] Miller, op. cit.
[9] Cloward and Ohlin, op. cit.

praisal.[10] Yet the gang delinquent's use of violence for the maintenance of "rep," the proof of "heart," and so on, seems to express in extreme form the idea that aggression is a demonstration of toughness and thus of masculinity. This idea runs through much delinquent activity. The concept of machismo, of the path to manhood through the ability to take it and hand it out, is foreign to the average delinquent only in name.

In short, juvenile delinquency appears to be permeated by a cluster of values that can be characterized as the search for kicks, the disdain of work and a desire for the big score, and the acceptance of aggressive toughness as proof of masculinity. Whether these values are seen as pathological expressions of a distorted personality or as the traits of a delinquent sub-culture, they are taken as indicative of the delinquent's deviation from the dominant society. The delinquent, it is said, stands apart from the dominant society not only in terms of his illegal behavior but in terms of his basic values as well.

DELINQUENCY AND LEISURE

The deviant nature of the delinquent's values might pass unquestioned at first glance. Yet when we examine these values a bit more closely, we must be struck by their similarity to the components of the code of the "gentleman of leisure" depicted by Thorstein Veblen. The emphasis on daring and adventure; the rejection of the prosaic discipline of

[10] Bloch and Niederhoffer, op. cit.

work; the taste for luxury and conspicuous consumption; and the respect paid to manhood demonstrated through force — all find a prototype in that sardonic picture of a leisured elite. What is *not* familiar is the mode of expression of these values, namely, delinquency. The quality of the values is obscured by their context. When "daring" turns out to be acts of daring by adolescents directed against adult figures of accepted authority, for example, we are apt to see only the flaunting of authority and not the courage that may be involved. We suspect that if juvenile delinquency were highly valued by the dominant society — as is the case, let us say, in the deviance of prisoners of war or resistance fighters rebelling against the rules of their oppressors — the interpretation of the nature of delinquency and the delinquent might be far different.[11]

In any event, the values of a leisure class seem to lie behind much delinquent activity, however brutalized or perverted their expression may be accounted by the dominant social order. Interestingly enough, Veblen himself saw a similarity between the pecuniary man, the embodiment of the leisure class, and the delinquent. "The ideal pecuniary man is like the ideal de-

[11] Merton's comments on in-group virtues and out-group vices are particularly germane. The moral alchemy cited by Merton might be paraphrased to read:

> I am daring
> You are reckless
> He is delinquent

Cf. Robert K. Merton, *Social Theory and Social Structure* (Glencoe, Ill.: The Free Press, 1957), pp. 426–430.

linquent," said Veblen, "in his un-scrupulous conversion of goods and services to his own ends, and in a callous disregard for the feelings and wishes of others and of the remoter effects of his actions." [12] For Veblen this comparison was probably no more than an aside, a part of polemical attack on the irresponsibility and pretensions of an industrial society's rulers. And it is far from clear what Veblen meant by delinquency. Nonetheless, his barbed comparison points to an important idea. We have too easily assumed that the delinquent is deviant in his values, opposed to the larger society. This is due, in part, to the fact that we have taken an overly simple view of the value system of the supposedly law-abiding. In our haste to create a standard from which deviance can be measured, we have reduced the value system of the whole society to that of the middle class. We have ignored both the fact that society is not composed exclusively of the middle class and that the middle class itself is far from homogeneous. [13]

In reality, of course, the value system of any society is exceedingly complex and we cannot solve our problems in the analysis of deviance by taking as a baseline a simplicity which does not exist in fact. Not only do different social classes differ in their values, but there are also significant variations within a class based on ethnic origins, upward and downward mobility, region, age, etc. Perhaps even more important, however, is the existence of subterranean values — values, that is to say, which are in conflict or in competition with other deeply held values but which are still recognized and accepted by many. [14] It is crucial to note that these contradictions in values are not necessarily the opposing viewpoints of two different groups. They may also exist within a single individual and give rise to profound feelings of ambivalence in many areas of life. In this sense, subterranean values are akin to private as opposed to public morality. They are values that the individual holds to and believes in but that are also recognized as being not quite *comme il faut*. The easier task of analysis is to call such values deviant and to charge the

[12] Thorstein Veblen, *The Theory of the Leisure Class* (Modern Library, 1934), pp. 237–238.

[13] Much of the current sociological analysis of the value systems of the different social classes would seem to be based on a model which is closely akin to an outmoded portrayal of race. Just as racial groups were once viewed as a clustering of physical traits with no overlapping of traits from one group to the next (e.g., Caucasions are straight-haired, light-skinned, etc., whereas Negroes are kinky-haired, dark-skinned, etc.), so now are the value systems of social classes apt to be seen as a distinct grouping of specific values which are unique to the so-

cial class in which they are found. The model of the value systems of the different social classes we are using in this paper is more closely allied to the treatment of race presently used in anthropology, i.e., a distribution of frequencies. Most values, we argue, appear in most social classes; the social classes differ, however, in the frequency with which the values appear.

[14] Robert S. Lynd, *Knowledge for What?* (Princeton: Princeton University Press, 1948).

individual with hypocrisy when he acts on them. Social reality, however, is somewhat more intricate than that and we cannot take the black and white world of McGuffey's Readers as an accurate model of the values by which men live.

Now the value of adventure certainly does not provide the major organizing principle of the dominant social order in modern, industrial society. This is especially true in the workaday world where so much activity is founded on bureaucratization and all that it implies with regard to routinization, standardization, and so on. But this is not to say that the element of adventure is completely rejected by the society at large or never appears in the motivational structure of the law-abiding. Instead, it would appear that adventure, i.e., displays of daring and the search for excitement, are acceptable and desirable but only when confined to certain circumstances such as sports, recreation, and holidays. The last has been frequently noted in the observation that conventions are often viewed as social events in which conventional canons of conduct are interpreted rather loosely. In fact, most societies seem to provide room for Saturnalias in one form or another, a sort of periodic anomie in which thrill-seeking is allowed to emerge.

In other words, the middle class citizen may seem like a far cry from the delinquent on the prowl for "thrills," but they both recognize and share the idea that "thrills" are worth pursing and often with the same connotation of throwing over the traces, of opposing "fun" to the routine. As members of the middle class — and other classes — seek their "kicks" in gambling, night-clubbing, the big night on the town, etc., we can neither ignore their use of leisure nor claim that it is based on a markedly deviant value. Leisure-class values have come increasingly to color the activities of many individuals in the dominant society, although they may limit their expression more sharply than does the delinquent. The search for adventure, excitement, and thrills, then, is a subterranean value that now often exists side by side with the values of security, routinization, and the rest. It is not a deviant value, in any full sense, but it must be held in abeyance until the proper moment and circumstances for its expression arrive. It is obvious that something more than the delinquent's sense of appropriateness is involved, but it is also clear that in many cases the delinquent suffers from bad timing.

Similarly, to characterize the dominant society as being fully and unquestioningly attached to the virtue of hard work and careful saving is to distort reality. Notions of "pull" and the soft job are far from uncommon and the individual who entertains such notions cannot be thrust beyond the pale merely because some sociologists have found it convenient to erect a simplified conception of *the* work values of society. As Chinoy and Bell, and a host of other writers, have pointed out, the conditions of work in modern society have broken down earlier conceptions of work as a calling and there are strong pressures to define the job as a place where one earns money as quickly and painlessly as possible.[15] If the delinquent carries this idea further than many of society's members might be willing to do, he has not necessarily moved into a new realm of values. In the same vein it can be argued that the delinquent's attachment to conspicuous consumption hardly makes him a stranger to the dominant society. Just as Riesman's "inside dopester," Whyte's "organization man," and Mills' "fixer" have a more authentic ring than an obsolete Weberian image in many instances, the picture of the delinquent as a spender seems more valid than a picture of him as an adolescent who has renounced material aspirations. The delinquent, we suggest, is much more in step with his times. Perhaps it is too extreme to say with Lowenthal[16] that "the idols of work have been replaced by the idols of leisure," but it appears unquestionable that we are witnessing a compromise between the Protestant Ethic and a Leisure Ethic. The delinquent conforms to society, rather than deviates from it, when he incorporates "big money" into his value system.[17]

Finally, we would do well to question prevalent views about society's attitudes toward violence and aggression. It could be argued, for one thing, that the dominant society exhibits a widespread taste for violence, since fantasies of violence in books, magazines, movies, and television are everywhere at hand. The delinquent simply translates into behavior those values that the majority are usually too timid to express. Furthermore, disclaimers of violence are suspect not simply because fantasies of violence are widely consumed, but also because of the actual use of aggression and violence in war, race riots, industrial conflicts, and the treatment of delinquents themselves by police. There are numerous examples of the acceptance of aggression and violence on the part of the dominant social order.

Perhaps it is more important, however, to recognize that the crucial idea of aggression as a proof of toughness and masculinity is widely accepted at many points in the social system. The ability to take it and hand it out, to defend one's rights and one's reputation with force, to prove one's manhood by hardness and physical courage — all are widespread in American culture. They cannot be dismissed by noting the equally valid observation that many people will declare that "nice children do not fight." The use of aggression to demonstrate masculinity is, of course, restricted by numerous prohibitions against instigating violence, "dirty" fighting, bullying, blustering, and so on. Yet even if the show of violence is carefully hedged in by both children and adults through-

[15] Daniel Bell, *Work and Its Discontents* (Boston: Beacon Press, 1956); Ely Chinoy, *Automobile Workers and the American Dream* (Garden City, N.Y.: Doubleday and Company, 1955).
[16] Leo Lowenthal "Historical Perspectives of Popular Culture," in Bernard Rosenberg and David M. White (eds.), *Mass Culture: The Popular Arts in America* (Glencoe, Ill.: The Free Press, 1957).
[17] Arthur K. Davis, "Veblen on the Decline of the Protestant Ethic," *Social Forces,* 22 (March, 1944), pp. 282–286.

out our society, there is a persistent support for aggression which manifests itself in the derogatory connotations of labels such as "sissy" or "fag." [18]

In short, we are arguing that the delinquent may not stand as an alien in the body of society but may represent instead a disturbing reflection or a caricature. His vocabulary is different, to be sure, but kicks, big-time spending, and rep have immediate counterparts in the value system of the law-abiding. The delinquent has picked up and emphasized one part of the dominant value system, namely, the subterranean values that coexist with other, publicly proclaimed values possessing a more respectable air. These subterranean values, similar in many ways to the values Veblen ascribed to a leisure class, bind the delinquent to the society whose laws he violates. And we suspect that this sharing of values, this bond with the larger social order, facilitates the frequently observed "reformation" of delinquents with the coming of adult status.[19] To the objection that much juvenile behavior other than simply delinquent behavior would then be analyzed as an extension of the adult world rather than as a product of a distinct adolescent subculture we can only answer that this is precisely our thesis.

[18] Albert Bandura and Richard Haig Walters, *Adolescent Aggression* (New York: Ronald Press, 1959), ch. 3.

[19] See, for example, William McCord, Joan McCord, and Irving K. Zola, *Origins of Crime* (New York: Columbia University Press, 1959), p. 21.

DELINQUENCY AND SOCIAL CLASS

The persistence of the assumption that the juvenile delinquent must deviate from the law-abiding in his values as well as in his behavior can be traced in part, we suspect, to the large number of studies that have indicated that delinquents are disproportionately represented in the lower classes. In earlier years it was not too difficult to believe that the lower classes were set off from their social superiors in most attributes, including "immorality," and that this taint produced delinquent behavior. Writers of more recent vintage have avoided this reassuring error, but, still holding to the belief that delinquency is predominantly a lower-class phenomenon, have continued to look for features peculiar to certain segments of the lower class that would create values at variance with those of the rest of society and which would foster delinquency.

Some criminologists, however, have long expressed doubts about the validity of the statistics on delinquency and have suggested that if all the facts were at hand the delinquency rate of the lower classes and the classes above them would be found to be far less divergent than they now appear.[20] Preferential treatment by the police and the courts and better and more varied means for handling the offender may have led us to underestimate seri-

[20] Milton L. Barron, *The Juvenile in Delinquent Society* (New York: Alfred A. Knopf, 1954).

ously the extent to which juvenile delinquency crops up in what are euphemistically termed "relatively privileged homes."

Given the present state of data in this field, it is probably impossible to come to any firm conclusion on this issue. One thing, however, seems fairly clear: juvenile delinquency does occur frequently in the middle and upper classes, and recent studies show more delinquency in these groups than have studies in the past. We might interpret this as showing that our research methods have improved or that "white-collar" delinquency is increasing — or possibly both. But in any event, the existence of juvenile delinquency in the middle and upper classes poses a serious problem for theories which depend on status deprivation, social disorganization, and similar explanatory variables. One solution has been to change horses in the middle of the stratification system, as it were, shifting from social environment to personality disturbances as the causative factor as one moves up the social ladder. Future research may prove that this shift is necessary. Since juvenile delinquency does not appear to be a unitary phenomenon, we might expect that no one theoretical approach will be adequate. To speak of juvenile delinquency in general, as we have done in this paper, should not obscure the fact that there are different types of delinquency and the differences among them cannot be ignored. Yet it seems worthwhile to pursue the idea that some forms of juvenile delinquency — and possibly the most frequent — have a common sociological basis, regardless of the class level at which they appear.

One such basis is offered, we believe, by our argument that the values lying behind much delinquent behavior are the values of a leisure class. All adolescents at all class levels are to some extent members of a leisure class, for they move in a limbo between earlier parental domination and future integration with the social structure through the bonds of work and marriage.[21] Theirs is an anticipatory leisure, it is true, a period of freedom from the demands for self-support which allows room for the schooling enabling them to enter the world of work. They thus enjoy a temporary leisure by sufferance rather than by virtue of a permanent aristocratic right. Yet the leisure status of adolescents, modified though it may be by the discipline of school and the lack of wealth, places them in relationship to the social structure in a manner similar to that of an elite which consumes without producing. In this situation, disdain of work, an emphasis on personal qualities rather than technical skills, and a stress on the manner and extent of consumption all can flourish. Insofar, then, as these values do lie behind delinquency, we could expect delinquent behavior to be prevalent among all adolescents rather than confined to the lower class.

[21] Reuel Denney, *The Astonished Muse* (Chicago: University of Chicago Press, 1957). See also Barbara Wooton, *Social Science and Social Pathology* (New York: Macmillan, 1959); Arthur L. Porterfield, *Youth in Trouble* (Austin, Tex.: Leo Potishman Foundation, 1946).

CONCLUSION

This theory concerning the role of leisure in juvenile delinquency leaves unsolved, of course, a number of problems. First, there is the question why some adolescents convert subterranean values into seriously deviant behavior while others do not. Even if it is granted that many adolescent are far more deviant in their behavior than official records would indicate, it is clear that there are degrees of delinquency and types of delinquency. This variation cannot be explained simply on the basis of exposure to leisure. It is possible that leisure values are typically converted into delinquent behavior when such values are coupled with frustrations and resentments. (This is more than a matter of being deprived in socioeconomic terms.) If this is so, if the delinquent is a sort of soured sportsman, neither leisure nor deprivation will be sufficient by itself as an explanatory variable. This would appear to be in accordance with the present empirical observations in the field. Second, we need to know a good deal more about the distribution of leisure among adolescents and its impact on their value systems. We have assumed that adolescents are in general leisured, i.e., free from the demands for self-support, but school drop-outs, the conversion of school into a tightly disciplined and time-consuming preparation for a career, the facilities for leisure as opposed to mere idleness will all probably have their effect. We suspect that two variables are of vital importance in this area: (a) the extent of identification with adult symbols of work, such as the father; and (b) the extent to which the school is seen as providing roles to enhance the ego, both now and in the future, rather than as an oppressive and dreary marking of time.

We conclude that the explanation of juvenile delinquency may be clarified by exploring the delinquent's similarity to the society that produced him rather than his dissimilarity. If his values are the subterranean values of a society that is placing increasing emphasis on leisure, we may throw new light on Taft's comment that the basic values in our culture are accepted by both the delinquent and the larger society of which he is a part.[22]

[22] Donald R. Taft, *Criminology* (New York: Macmillan, 1950).